THE
State
OF THE
Animals II
2 0 0 3

edited by **Deborah J. Salem**
and **Andrew N. Rowan**

Humane Society Press
an affiliate of

D1299690

Deborah J. Salem is director and editor in chief
of Humane Society Press.

Andrew N. Rowan is senior vice president for research,
education, and international issues and chief of staff
of The Humane Society of the United States.

First edition
ISBN 0-9658942-7-4

Library of Congress Cataloging-in-Publication Data

Salem, Deborah J.
  The state of the animals, 2001 / edited by Deborah J. Salem and Andrew N. Rowan—1st ed.
(public policy series)
Includes bibliographical references.

ISBN 0965894231

1. Animal welfare—History. 2. Animal welfare—Societies, etc.
3. Animal rights. 4. Human-animal relationships. 5. Animal experimentation.

I. Salem, Deborah J. II. Rowan, Andrew N. III. Humane Society of the United States.
IV. Title. V. Public policy series.
(Humane Society Press)

HV4708.S16 2001
179.3—dc21   2001131096

Printed in the United States of America

Humane Society Press
An affiliate of The Humane Society of the United States
2100 L Street, NW
Washington, D.C. 20037

Contents

Preface vii

1. **A Strategic Review of International Animal Protection**

   Paul G. Irwin 1

2. **Companion Animal Demographics in the United States: A Historical Perspective**

   Elizabeth A. Clancy and Andrew N. Rowan 9

3. **Humane Education Past, Present, and Future**

   Bernard Unti and Bill DeRosa 27

4. **Toward Biophilia: The Role of Children's Literature in the Development of Empathy and Compassion**

   Marion W. Copeland and Heidi O'Brien 51

5. **The No-Kill Controversy: Manifest and Latent Sources of Tension**

   Arnold Arluke 67

6. **Religion and Animals: A Changing Scene**

   Paul Waldau 85

7. **The Evolution of Animal Law since 1950**

   Steven M. Wise 99

8. **The Science and Sociology of Hunting: Shifting Practices and Perceptions in the United States and Great Britain**

   John W. Grandy, Elizabeth Stallman, and David W. Macdonald 107

9. **The Impact of Highways on Wildlife and the Environment: A Review of Recent Progress in Reducing Roadkill**
   Susan Hagood and Marguerite Trocmé 131

10. **Farm Disease Crises in the United Kingdom: Lessons to be Learned**
    Michael C. Appleby 149

11. **The EU Ban on Battery Cages: History and Prospects**
    Michael C. Appleby 159

12. **The State of Meat Production in Developing Countries: 2002**
    Neil Trent, Peter Ormel, Jose Luis Garcia de Siles, Gunter Heinz, and Morgane James 175

13. **The State of Wild Animals in the Minds and Households of a Neotropical Society: The Costa Rican Case Study**
    Carlos Drews 193

14. **Horse Welfare Since 1950**
    Katherine A. Houpt and Natalie Waran 207

15. **Wild Horses and Burros in the United States**
    Allen Rutberg 217

Contributors 223

Index 227

Preface

This volume is the second in a series reviewing the state of animal protection in North America and worldwide. The series is envisioned as the cornerstone of the Public Policy Series of Humane Society Press (HSP), founded in 2000 as an affiliate of The Humane Society of the United States (HSUS). HSP's Public Policy Series is planned as a source of information and informed opinion for policymakers, the academic community, animal advocates, and the media.

The introductory volume in the series, *The State of the Animals: 2001*, has enjoyed a most gratifying reception: it has been adopted for course work by instructors at a number of universities, purchased by libraries throughout the country, and favorably reviewed by media as diverse as *amazon.com*, *Choice: Current Reviews for Academic Libraries*, and *Animal People*.

This second volume is more international in focus, as evidenced by Paul G. Irwin's introductory chapter, "A Strategic Review of International Animal Protection," and by the wide-ranging backgrounds of the contributors. Although not a conscious change of direction, this international focus does reflect the current and changing climate for animal protection worldwide.

The editors wish to thank Lester Brown and the World-watch Institute for providing an excellent model for this volume in their State of the World series. We especially wish to express our appreciation to all of the contributors for their commitment to this project. We also thank HSUS President Paul G. Irwin for his encouragement and support and the HSUS staff members who helped guide the volume through the production process, most notably Creative Director Paula Jaworski, and copyeditor Wendy A. Jordan.

Our hope is that this volume will serve as an enlightening introduction to the issues of animal protection for those new to the field and as a welcome addition to the bookshelves of seasoned observers.

A Strategic Review of International Animal Protection

Paul G. Irwin

Introduction

The level of animal protection activity varies substantially around the world. To some extent, the variation parallels the level of economic development, as countries with high per capita incomes and democratic political structures have better financed and better developed animal protection organizations. However there is not a one-to-one correlation between economic development and animal protection activity. Japan and Saudi Arabia, for example, have high per capita incomes but low or nonexistent levels of animal protection activity, while India has a relatively low per capita income but a fairly large number of animal protection groups.

The level of animal protection activity appears to be influenced not only by the wealth of a country but also by its sociopolitical background and its dominant religious traditions. Wildlife and food animal issues predominate in developing nations, whereas companion animal issues have been the driving force behind the development of animal protection in most of the developed nations.

Early Activities in International Animal Protection

Organized animal protection began in England in the early 1800s and spread from there to the rest of the world. Henry Bergh (who founded the American Society for the Prevention of Cruelty to Animals, or ASPCA, in 1865) and George Angell (who founded the Massachusetts Society for the Prevention of Cruelty to Animals, or MSPCA, in 1868) both looked to England and the Royal Society for the Prevention of Cruelty to Animals (RSPCA) as a role model for their own efforts, as did the founders of many other societies for the prevention of cruelty to animals (SPCAs) in the British Empire and elsewhere. In 1877 a group of American organizations established the International Humane Society—the first to carry the adjective "international"—although the name later changed to the American Humane Association (AHA).

Prior to the modern period of animal protection (starting after World War II), international animal protection involved mostly uncoordinated support from the larger societies and certain wealthy individuals and a variety of international meetings where animal protection advocates gathered together to exchange news and ideas. One of the earliest such meetings occurred in Paris in June 1900 although, by this time, there was already a steady exchange of information among animal protection organizations around the world. These exchanges were encouraged further by the organization of a number of international animal protection congresses, including one in Philadelphia, Pennsylvania, in 1908, followed by another in London in 1909.

In 1910 an International Humane Congress covering both child and animal protection was organized in Washington, D.C., under the auspices of AHA. The report of this meeting (American Humane Association 1910) is 228 pages long and includes a list of SPCAs outside the United

Table 1
Animal Protection Organizations Represented at the 1910 International Congress in Washington, D.C.

Country		Country		Country	
United Kingdom*	200	Austria-Hungary	110	Argentina	3
		Belgium	20	Brazil	2
Australia	8	Crete	1	Mexico	5
Burma	2	Denmark	140	Nicaragua	1
Canada	40	France	16	Panama	1
Caribbean	9	Germany	500	Surinam	1
Ceylon	1	Italy	20	Uruguay	1
Cyprus	5	Monaco	1	Venezuela	1
Egypt	8	Netherlands	35		
India	23	Norway	12	Algiers	5
New Zealand	3	Portugal	2		
Singapore	3	Roumania	2	China	2
South Africa	12	Russia	180	Japan	3
		Spain	4		
		Sweden	120	United States	300
		Switzerland	40		

* RSPCA branches
Source: American Humane Association 1910

States as an appendix. Table 1 identifies the approximate number of societies (or organizations with either a president or secretary) identified in the printed report of the meeting as being active in particular countries.

Other international congresses were organized in 1911 and 1927 (London), and five more were held in Helsingborg, Copenhagen, Philadelphia, Brussels, and Vienna between 1911 and 1947 (Anonymous ca. 1947). The Animal Defense and Anti-Vivisection Society's International Humanitarian Bureau was established in Geneva (the home of the League of Nations) in September of 1928 (Anonymous ca. 1947). The bureau organized a deputation, supported by more than 1,400 animal protection societies throughout the world, to the president of the Conference for the Reduction and Limitation of Armaments in 1932.

The records of the 1910 Washington meeting indicate that many of the societies outside Europe, the United States, and the British Commonwealth were represented by expatriates (American Humane Association 1910). One example of a foreigner setting up an organization is the American Fondouk. This entity was established in 1920 in Morocco by American traveler Amy Bend Bishop to take care of the needs of animals. She asked the MSPCA to oversee the program, and today the Fondouk treats 15,000 animals annually.

Modern International Animal Protection

After World War II the level of organized international animal protection expanded as national movements grew and flourished. Today there are four major international entities and a number of international activities sponsored by a variety of organizations. The four major entities (listed in descending size) are the International Fund for Animal Welfare (IFAW), the World Society for the Protection of Animals (WSPA), the international program of the

RSPCA, and Humane Society International (HSI), the international affiliate of The Humane Society of the United States.

IFAW

IFAW was founded by Brian Davies. (The actual incorporation of IFAW in Massachusetts was in 1975.) Davies's initial focus was the Canadian seal pup cull and, as a result of his campaigns, the Canadian seal issue is now well known around the world. Davies slowly built IFAW into the largest international animal protection organization, with an annual budget of more than $60 million per annum (the largest amount being raised in the United Kingdom) contributed by more than 2 million donors around the world. Its expansion in the 1990s was particularly impressive, as its budget increased from $30 million in 1994 to $62 million in 1998; the number of donors grew from 750,000 to 1.8 million over the same period. IFAW employs more than two hundred staff persons in its Massachusetts headquarters and in offices in another thirteen areas around the world (Asia/Pacific, Canada, China, East Africa, the European Union, France, Germany, India, Latin America, the Netherlands, Russia, Southern Africa, and the United Kingdom).

A few years ago, IFAW divided its programs into three broad areas—reducing commercial exploitation and trade, saving animals in distress, and preserving habitat for animals. These programs include working on trade through the Convention on International Trade in Endangered Species of Wild Fauna and Flora (known as CITES), elephant protection, seal protection, opposition to bushmeat (usually understood to refer to the meat of terrestrial wild animals consumed for food), providing emergency relief, and working to establish marine reserves.

WSPA

The World Federation for the Protection of Animals (WFPA) was founded in 1953 by Dutch animal protection interests and was headquartered for most of its existence in Geneva. It tended to draw most of its support from animal groups in Europe, although The HSUS became involved in WFPA's governing body in the 1970s. Another organization, the International Society for the Protection of Animals (ISPA), was established in 1959 with the support of the RSPCA and the MSPCA. It had its headquarters in London but it had an office in Boston as well. ISPA became known for its disaster and emergency relief work—John C. Walsh, currently WSPA International Projects director, in particular, was involved in a number of dramatic rescue operations—while WFPA was recognized for its work on the development and eventual passage of several animal protection conventions at the Council of Europe.

The 1960s was marked by significant competition between WFPA and ISPA. During the 1970s, however, the leaders of both organizations recognized that there would be considerable benefits from a merger, and they began to work toward this end. In 1981 the two organizations formally merged to become the World Society for the Protection of Animals (WSPA), with offices in the United States, the United Kingdom, and Switzerland. In the 1980s the Swiss office was closed, but WSPA established new field offices in Costa Rica, Colombia, and Canada. Today the organization has offices in thirteen countries; 400 animal protection organizations from 91 countries as members; more than 400,000 individual supporters; and an annual budget of approximately $15 million.

RSPCA

The RSPCA has been the model that organizations have followed when establishing animal protection groups in countries outside the United Kingdom. It also has supported animal protection overseas for much of its more than 175-year existence. Currently its international programs are overseen by an internal division.

The International Department can call on any of the professional staff in the RSPCA's U.K. headquarters to assist with international projects.

The RSPCA was a key supporter of the establishment of ISPA and, more recently, was the initiator of Eurogroup for Animal Welfare (see below). The RSPCA works proactively in East Asia and in Southern, Central, and Eastern Europe. It uses a variety of tools to improve animal welfare, including training courses for government officials, nonprofit groups, and others. It gives out grants and has an association scheme to link with groups worldwide. It has run more than a hundred training courses in the past few years and in 2002 funded projects in more than forty countries.

HSI

HSI was established in 1991 to provide coordination for the international efforts of The HSUS. It has some similarities to the RSPCA international program in that it is able to draw on the program experts of The HSUS to provide expertise as needed. However, unlike the RSPCA, HSI has offices overseas. As of 2003 it had major programs in Costa Rica, Australia, and Europe, and new offices had been established in Asia, the United Kingdom, France, and Germany. Other affiliates of The HSUS, including EarthVoice and the Center for the Respect of Life and the Environment, also support international activities on the environment and animals.

Other Groups

The RSPCA and various groups in Europe formed Eurogroup for Animal Welfare in 1980. Eurogroup now is supported by leading animal welfare organizations in all fifteen member states of the European Union. Headquartered in Brussels, Eurogroup's role is to present a united animal welfare voice and to lobby for new or improved European legislation to provide greater protection of animals. It is recognized as an influential and powerful lobby with many achievements to its credit.

For many decades the MSPCA has overseen animal protection programs in North Africa and Turkey. Various organizations in the United Kingdom have raised money to support animal protection activities in Japan, Greece, and North Africa—the Society for the Protection of Animals in North Africa (SPANA) is a particularly successful example—also for decades. The North Shore Animal League (Long Island, New York) and the National Canine Defense League (United Kingdom) teamed up in the mid-1990s to organize a series of capacity-building conferences in Eastern Europe focused around the idea of no- or limited-euthanasia programs. The U.S.-based People for the Ethical Treatment of Animals (PETA) recently has established offices overseas and is becoming more engaged in international activities. A consortium of animal protection groups has come together to represent animal protection interests on alternatives to animal testing at meetings of the OECD Chemicals Directorate. As of 2003 the Hong Kong SPCA was organizing a capacity-development and training conference for Asian and other groups to follow up on an earlier conference in the Philippines.

Current State of Animal Protection

International animal protection is healthy and expanding in both influence and sophistication. Table 2 provides some indication of the level of animal protection activity in different regions around the world. This table is compiled from a variety of sources. The number of animal protection organizations in each country was obtained from the International Directory of World Animal Protection; wildlife conservation groups were not included in the tally. (The directory does not include a complete tally of organizations, but the numbers probably are accurate enough for the rough analysis provided in the table.)

The country populations were obtained from the U.S. Central Intelligence Agency's World Factbook on the Worldwide Web (*www.cia.gov/ cia.publications/factbook*). The approximate per capita income in Purchasing Power Parity (PPP) also was obtained from the Worldwide Web. (PPP incorporates differences in cultural demand to provide a picture of comparative standards of living that is more accurate than a simple comparison of annual per capita incomes in local currencies.) The analysis could have been refined further to attempt to incorporate broad cultural factors (e.g., dominant religions) but that would have produced a level of detail and fragmentation not necessarily helpful for the level of analysis discussed here.

Briefly, there are three regions in the world (North America, Northern Europe, and Australia/New Zealand, or Group A) where support for animal welfare is very strong and where there is a robust and well-funded animal protection presence. All three regions tend to be characterized by high standards of living and Protestant religious traditions.

In four regions of the world (Southern Africa, the Caribbean Islands, Southern Europe, and Eastern Europe, or Group B) animal protection activity is reasonably healthy, although all four regions could use help to bolster their programs and the level of animal protection expertise available to them. The activity in Southern Africa and the Caribbean is almost certainly a legacy of British colonial traditions and/or proximity to the United States (producing a supply of expatriates to staff animal protection programs and some funds to support projects and organizations). Southern and Eastern Europe are upgrading their animal protection activities because of parity demands within the EU (in the case of countries in the EU) or in hopes of being able to join the EU sometime in the future. However, none of the organizations in these countries is well-funded.

Of the other regions, Central and South America (in Group C) have weak animal protection activities but exhibit signs of a growing interest and some hope for the future. These regions have reasonably high standards of living, but cultural factors (including possibly their strong Roman Catholic religious traditions) seem to work against the development of a healthy animal protection capacity. Some attitude surveys in Central America (see Drews, in this volume) show that the public appears to have the same strength of humane sentiment as that seen in the United States. However without the tradition of animal protection activity, those attitudes are not yet being translated into behaviors that support animal protection.

Group D includes most of Asia, most of Africa, and most of the former Soviet countries. In Asia animal protection is mostly weak to nonexistent. Japan has a very high standard of living, which usually is equated with concern for animals, but perhaps the religious and cultural traditions discount moral concern for animals (e.g., see Kellert 1993). Nonetheless there are some signs of an interest in developing an effective animal protection capacity in Japan, and recently a group of Japanese animal groups came together to try to develop a more robust political presence.

In India the standard of living is relatively low but the religious traditions tend to support moral concern for animals. India has a relatively large number of animal protection organizations, but they tend to be financially weak. Maneka Gandhi has provided strong leadership to help develop improved animal welfare standards, but economic barriers and the sheer size of the country make her task formidable indeed. She was removed from her position as a minister in the Indian government in 2002 and, therefore, no longer has the political power that she used quite effectively to challenge such activities as animal research oversight.

In the rest of Asia (including Indonesia, the Philippines, China, and the Koreas) animal protection is con-

Table 2
Animal Protection Activity Around the World

Region	Exemplar Countries	Total Population	# of Animal Protection Orgs. (APOs)[1]	# APOs/m people	Approx. per Capita Income (000s) (PPP$)[2]	Group
Europe— Western and Northern	United Kingdom, Germany, Scandinavia	211 million	1,865	8.840	22.5	A
Europe— Southern	Spain, France, Greece	178 million	348	1.960	18.0	B
Europe— Eastern	Poland, Hungary, Ukraine	194 million	158	0.820	4.5	B
Middle East	Turkey, Iran, Israel	239 million	46	0.190	5.4	C
Russia and Central Asia	Russia, Kazakhstan, Georgia	219 million	22	0.100	3.6	D
Asia— India and neighbors	Afghanistan, Bangladesh	1,367 million	128	0.094	1.5	D
Asia— Southeast	Thailand, Malaysia, Laos	229 million	16	0.070	3.5	D
Asia— Indonesia and Islands	New Caledonia	217 million	3	0.014	3.3	D
Australasia	Australia and New Zealand	23 million	220	9.690	19.0	A
Asia— Philippines and Islands	Philippines, Tonga, Guam	78 million	5	0.060	3.6	D
Asia— China and Korea	China, North and South Korea	1,358 million	8	0.006	3.3	D
Asia— Japan	Japan	127 million	30	0.240	23.4	C

(continued on next page)

(continued from previous page)

Table 2
Animal Protection Activity Around the World

Region	Exemplar Countries	Total Population	# of Animal Protection Orgs. (APOs)[1]	# APOs/m people	Approx. per Capita Income (000s) (PPP$)[2]	Group
America— North	U.S.A. and Canada	310 million	6,400	20.675	27.0	A
America— Central	Mexico, Panama	135 million	27	0.200	5.5	C
America— Caribbean	Bahamas, Cuba	38 million	44	1.157	3.5	B
America— South	Chile, Brazil, Columbia	346 million	112	0.324	6.3	C
Africa— North	Morocco, Egypt, Ethiopia	292 million	7	0.024	1.0	D
Africa— West	Guinea, Nigeria, Ghana	186 million	5	0.027	1.5	D
Africa— Western/ Central	Congo, Cameroon	74 million	0	0.000	1.2	D
Africa— Eastern/Central	Uganda, Burundi, Tanzania	102 million	10	0.098	1.0	D
Africa— Southern	Angola, South Africa, Mozambique	126 million	115	0.913	3.0	B
Total		**6,049 million**	**9,569**	**1.580**	**6.0**	

[1]Taken from World Animal Protection Directory
[2]PPP stands for Purchasing Power Parity and is used by the World Bank to compare countries.

fined to a few pockets of effective activism or to leftovers from colonial times (e.g., the Hong Kong and Singapore SPCAs). Africa north of the Zambesi River is mostly lacking in any significant animal protection activity (with a few noteworthy exceptions in East and North Africa), as is the Middle East, where only Israel has any active groups. There are signs of a stirring of animal protection interest in Russia and some of the other Soviet republics, but the movement is still very new and weak.

Types of International Activities

International animal protection activities can be segmented into several areas. One obvious activity is the pressuring of international organizations—e.g., the World Trade Organization (WTO), Food and Agriculture Organization (FAO) (see Trent et al. in this volume), International Whaling Commission (IWC), and CITES—

to adopt more animal-friendly policies. In terms of hands-on animal protection activities, the programs can be divided into those that address dog and cat issues, those that address farm and draft animal issues, and those that address wildlife issues. Some organizations are engaged in programs to set aside land for wildlife and to promote humane, sustainable development activities.

Advocacy

All four of the major international organizations are active in advocating for animals on a wide range of international issues. The WTO is currently a particular concern, because countries with strong animal protection laws are being threatened with trade sanctions if they use those laws to restrict the import of animal products from countries with weaker or nonexistent animal protection legislation or enforcement. However animal protection has had a major presence at CITES since its establishment in 1973 and at the IWC for the past thirty years. Indeed the current restrictions on whaling are largely a result of the effectiveness of animal advocates over this period. Some of the other international treaties that intersect with animal protection concerns are:

IATTC/IDCPA: Inter-American Tropical Tuna Commission and dolphins (dolphin protection);
WSSD: sustainable development, animal agriculture, fisheries, driftnets;
ISO: international standards involving humane farming and trapping;
FAO: trade, fisheries, whaling, farm animal husbandry, slaughter and transport;
SPAW: specially protected areas and wildlife in the Caribbean;
CMS: Bonn Convention on migratory species;
CBD: convention on biological diversity.

Several organizations (including HSI and WSPA) now have consultative status at the United Nations and are using that status to campaign for animals at the level of these international organizations.

Dogs and Cats

Although companion animals are a driving force behind the development and growth of animal protection organizations in Group A countries, they have not carried the same weight in countries in Groups B, C, and D. Most of the organizations established in developing countries were set up to address domestic dog and cat issues, however, often by expatriates from Group A countries. Currently most of the companion animal activities are focused on attempts to gain some control of community and stray dog populations. In developing countries the "pet" dog makes up a relatively small proportion (perhaps 5 percent or less) of the total dog population. Most of the dogs are either community dogs, with some tenuous connection to a household or group of households, or true strays who survive exclusively by scavenging. These populations can be very significant; for example, 85 percent of households in Miacatlan, a Mexican village, have stray/community dogs who use the house as home base for their territory (Orihuela and Solano 1995).

Because community and stray dogs are an important conduit through which humans contract rabies (and a range of other diseases, such as hydatidosis), the World Health Organization has worked with WSPA to develop approaches to control populations of stray and community dogs. For the most part, developing countries have tried to deal with stray dog issues by periodically killing as many dogs as they can (often by poisoning). However canids respond to such programs by having larger litters and breeding more frequently, therefore 70 percent or more of a dog population must be killed before a significant drop in the population may be noticed. Such dog control programs rarely have the resources to take the first essential step—to conduct dog population studies.

Over the past ten years, it has been suggested that a variation of the "trap, neuter, vaccinate, and release" approach currently used to control stray cats in developed countries might be used for control of community and stray dog populations. Only a few of such dog trap, neuter, vaccinate, and release programs have included the collection of dog population data, so it is not yet possible to conclude that this approach can work. However a program in Jaipur, India, has recorded a decline in street dog populations (C. Townend, personal communication, n.d. 2003), and HSI (2001) reports that a Bahamian program reduced the number of strays on the streets, left the sterilized strays in a healthier state, and began to change the attitudes of local human populations toward the street dogs.

It is clear that dog and cat welfare projects in the developing world cannot involve simply the direct application of approaches that have been used in Europe and North America. New, appropriate technology programs need to be developed that recognize that, although the nurture of animals is a universal phenomenon of human nature, appropriate nurturing behavior does not simply appear without role models acceptable to the local community and adequate opportunity to engage in such behavior. It must also be recognized that animal nurturance, and animal protection, cannot thrive where human communities do not have adequate security or opportunities to provide food and shelter for themselves.

Farm and Draft Animals

Farm and draft animals are vital in providing families with food security (in the context of availability, not of safety) and the means to support themselves in much of the developing world. In parts of Africa, cattle and other livestock are a family's social security system and "bank." Thus the welfare of these animals is tied closely to the welfare of families and communities. The FAO is working with HSI on a range of humane slaughter initiatives that not only address animal welfare but also include such elements as food security and hygiene for local communities and the relevant state. Draft animals (e.g., working equines) also are important for local communities, and it is important to help support their health and welfare with appropriate initiatives.

Wildlife

For most of the developing world, wildlife represents either a competitor for resources or a resource in itself. Therefore wildlife protection issues in developing countries involve:

(1) attempting to establish appropriate protected areas where wildlife can thrive;

(2) attempting to enforce protections for populations of threatened and endangered species; and

(3) dealing with the many associated cruelties of the trade in wildlife and bushmeat and attempting to address human-animal conflicts.

These issues frequently interest both wildlife conservation and wildlife protection groups and provide opportunities for such groups to work together to support land protection, conservation initiatives, and wildlife protection. The work of many conservation organizations already involves significant overlap with the programs put in place by the international animal protection groups. For example, HSI ran a three-year project to support wildlife rehabilitation around the world. Many zoos and conservation groups, most notably the Wildlife Conservation Society, which is based in the United States, support similar veterinary programs. Animal protection groups campaign against various aspects of wildlife trade. The U.K.-based WildAid runs active programs to educate people in source countries about the harmful impact of wildlife trade and provides training to rangers and customs officials in source countries to enable them to be more effective. WSPA has developed a very successful bear protection initiative ("Libearty") to address the cruelties involved in harvesting bear products for the traditional medicines market and in performing-bear activities throughout Asia.

While the U.S.-based Nature Conservancy is the giant of land preservation activities, other organizations also do their part. For example, Earth-Voice has been working with U.K.-based Fauna and Flora International to set aside land in Africa and the Americas that secures important habitats for wild species. HSI has been engaged in a project to explore the potential of developing an immunocontraceptive vaccine to manage elephant populations in Southern Africa without resorting to culling.

Conclusions

International animal protection has been growing in its sophistication, reach, and impact for the past quarter century. The Internet provides a valuable new tool to support the activities of the major international groups as well as assist local individuals to be more effective in their advocacy. In ten years animal protection will have a foothold in those countries where it is now mostly a curiosity and will be much stronger around the globe. The message of kindness to animals is developing sophisticated new clothing. As the habit of helping and protecting animals spreads around the world, not only will the animals will be better off, but humans, and the communities, societies, and nations they people, also will grow less violent and more civil. The dream of a safer and more nurturing world gradually will emerge into reality.

Literature Cited

American Humane Association. 1910. The First International Humane Congress. Washington, D.C. October 10–15.

Anonymous. (undated but circa 1947). *You and the animals in peace and war*. London: The Animal Defence and Anti-Vivisection Society.

Humane Society International (HSI). 2001. *Dogs on Abaco Island, The Bahamas: A case study*. Washington, D.C.: HSI. July.

Kellert, S.R. 1993. Attitudes, knowledge, and behavior toward wildlife among the industrial superpowers: United States, Japan, and Germany. *Journal of Social Issues* 49: 53–70.

Orihuela, T.A., and V.J.Solano. 1995. Demographics of the owned dog population in Miacatlan, Morelos, Mexico. *Anthrozoös* 8: 171–175.

Companion Animal Demographics in the United States: A Historical Perspective

CHAPTER 2

Elizabeth A. Clancy and Andrew N. Rowan

Introduction

There are a variety of welfare concerns relating to companion dogs and cats in the United States but one of the more pervasive is the "pet homelessness," "pet overpopulation," or "pet surplus" problem. These widely used terms may discomfit some in the animal shelter community. Some of the terms can be misleading in that their use implies that the problem—however it is couched—could be solved simply by reducing the number of available dogs and cats. In addition the term *surplus* specifically implies a property function—that companion dogs and cats are inherently expendable whenever they fall outside of a stable human-animal relationship. A detailed examination of the population issue will reveal that it is not merely a case of the indiscriminate breeding of dogs and cats, but also a complex problem with both sociological and biological elements that has no simple solution.

Modern American society recognizes the crucial role of data and information in evaluating and effectively addressing societal problems.

Americans are bombarded with information on the economy, public health, social and psychological attitude trends, and other matters that are considered important. For example, no self-respecting politician would think of launching a political campaign or initiative without some sense of what the public might be worrying about. Addressing pet population issues should be no different. Data are needed in order to define the nature and scope of the dog and cat demographic challenge. Data can help people to understand the impact of "pet homelessness" on companion animals; to identify some of the characteristics of both successful and failed human-animal relationships; and to develop sound, effective, and long-lasting solutions that will strengthen humans' relationships with companion animals and enhance companion animals' welfare.

Given the need for reliable data, what is known now about trends concerning the companion animal population and the shelters that help address the "homelessness" problem?

National Dog and Cat Demographic Data

Base-line Population Data

The United States has never had a national system in place to collect, store and analyze data relating to pet care-giving. Although detailed demographic data on the human population are gathered by the U.S. Census Bureau, no similar database exists for companion dogs and cats. Our society routinely refers to household pets as "members of the family" but the census process does not accept that data on pets should be collected. Several attempts by animal industries and interest groups to gain approval for the inclusion of questions on pets on the U.S. Census have thus far been unsuccessful. One of us (A.N.R.) attempted to do this in the mid-1980s but, despite the support of numerous

Table 1
Pet Population Estimates

Total U.S. Household Dog and Cat Populations (millions)

	1987	1991	1996	2001
Dogs	52.4	52.5	52.9	61.6
Cats	54.6	57.0	59.1	68.9

Percent of Households with Dogs and Cats (mean number/household)

	1987	1991	1996	2001
Dogs	38.2(1.51)	36.5(1.52)	31.6(1.69)	36.1(1.6)
Cats	30.5(2.04)	30.9(1.95)	27.3(2.19)	31.6(2.1)

Source: AVMA Survey 1997, 2002

academics, animal industries, and animal advocates, did not succeed.

Nonetheless relatively accurate data are available on the number of household dogs and cats in the United States now and historically. These data are collected primarily by veterinary organizations (e.g., the American Veterinary Medical Association, or AVMA, and the American Animal Hospital Association) and pet industry organizations (e.g., the American Pet Products Manufacturers Association, or APPMA, and the Pet Food Institute)—groups whose work depends on having reliable and current data on dog and cat populations. The APPMA has conducted national surveys on pet populations every other year since 1988. The AVMA has published data from national surveys in 1983, 1988, 1992, 1997, and 2002.

Two basic approaches have been used to gather data on dog and cat populations. The first uses surveys of sample populations drawn from an already established panel of U.S. households. Both the APPMA and the AVMA use this method. The panels are recruited on the understanding that the participants will complete periodic mail surveys. (Response rates typically are high—around 70 percent.) A sample of households is drawn from the panels so as to make them representative of the U.S. population. To be included in such a panel, a person must have resided at the current address for a year or more. Therefore these panels cannot represent the more transient elements of the United States.

The second approach uses telephones and random digit dial technology to sample the population. This method under-samples households at the lower end of the economic pyramid because they are less likely to have telephones.

Thus both approaches have limitations and appear to produce differences in estimates of the national dog and cat population. As demonstrated by Patronek and Rowan (1995), the household panel approach produces estimates that are approximately twenty percent higher than those obtained from telephone surveys. In Massachusetts telephone surveys conducted by both the Massachusetts Society for the Prevention of Cruelty to Animals (MSPCA) (C. Luke, personal communication with A.N.R., n.d. 1991) and Manning and Rowan (1992) in the same time frame produced estimates of state pet populations that were substantially lower than those obtained using data collected by the AVMA in 1991. In Indiana Patronek found similar disparities between data he collected using telephone sampling and the AVMA esti-

mates of Indiana pet populations.

The latest data published by the AVMA indicate that in 2001 Americans shared their households with 61.6 million dogs and 68.9 million cats. An examination of Table 1 illustrates that, on a national level, the owned dog population remained relatively stable between 1987 and 1996 (although the rate of care-giving fluctuated quite widely), while the owned cat population increased from 54.6 to 59.1 million (AVMA 1997, 2002).

While the AVMA population estimates may be on the high side, the fact that the same technique has been used for all four AVMA surveys should mean that the trends are accurate. Thus between 1996 and 2001 the total population numbers increased substantially for both dogs (8.7 million increase) and cats (9.8 million increase) (AVMA 2002). The substantial jump in population estimate in 2001 is the result of a jump in the percentage of households with either dogs or cats. It is not clear why the AVMA surveys show a downward trend in 1996. The APPMA surveys show no such dip (APPMA 2002).

Another factor to keep in mind is that the number of households in the United States increases steadily. Thus the dog population remained stable between 1987 and 1996 even though the rate of care-giving (household

Table 2
Percent of Households with Animals

Year	Dogs	Cats
1988	37	30
1990	38	33
1992	38	32
1994	36	30
1996	37	32
1998	39	32
2000	39	34

Source: APPMA Survey 2002

percentage) dropped from 38.2 to 31.6 percent. See Table 2 for changes recorded by the APPMA in rates of dog and cat households in the United States. The fluctuations from one year to the next may be due mostly to random statistical variation in the survey.

The estimated 130.5 million dogs and cats in American households drawn from the AVMA 2001 survey reside in approximately 53 percent of the approximately 100 million households (58.3 percent of households contain a pet of any sort) (AVMA 2002). Thus more than half the households in this country include an animal companion. The average household with pets has the characteristics indicated in Table 3. In general dog sterilization rates are lower than those of cats because of the reluctance of dog care-givers (used in place of "owner") to have their male dogs neutered. The same reluctance is not observed among care-givers who have male cats. The fact that fewer cat care-givers report taking their animals to the veterinarian in the previous year is consistent with the observation that cats tend to require lower levels of involvement and cat care-givers generally are somewhat less attached to their cats

than dog care-givers are to their dogs.

Attachment levels were measured by a research group in Kentucky using the Lexington Attachment to Pets Scale, or LAPS (Johnson, Garrity, and Stallones 1992). The researchers used a twenty-three-item scale (e.g., My pet understands me, I enjoy showing other people pictures of my pet) to obtain relative scores of attachment. The scores indicating level of attachment were based on the interviewer's rating. The proportions of the population identified as being very or somewhat attached are what one might intuitively expect (Table 4). This scale has not been put into practical use, but there is no apparent reason it could not be explored as part of a questionnaire used by shelters to assess the suitability of a prospective animal adopter. The candidates could be administered the LAPS assessment regarding their previous or a current favorite pet and then scored to see how attached they were (or are).

It should be noted that, in studying the Miller-Rada "commitment to pets" scale, Staats et al. (1996) demonstrated that "attachment" is different from "commitment." It is possible that the Miller-Rada instrument for measuring commitment might prove to be a better approach

to assessing the suitability of potential adopters. However the characteristics of the Miller-Rada "commitment instrument" have not been established for a national probability sample. At present any suggestions regarding potential connections between attachment, commitment, and animal relinquishment are pure speculation.

Regional and Life Stage Differences in Pet Care-giving

The national pet population surveys also indicate that there are regional differences in pet care-giving. This is an important factor when addressing welfare concerns relating to pet care-giving. The 2001 AVMA survey revealed significant differences in the percentage of households providing for pets around the country. Table 5a shows the highest rates of pet care-giving in the Mountain Pacific and West South Central regions of the United States, and the lowest rates in the Middle Atlantic, South Atlantic, and New England regions (AVMA 2002).

In fact, as seen in Table 5b, state to state differences in dog and cat care-giving rates can vary by a factor of two from highest to lowest (AVMA 2002).

Table 3
Characteristics of Animal Care-giving Households and Their Pets in the United States

	Dogs	Cats
Time household has included pets	18 yrs.	18 yrs.
Average age of "main" pet	6.6 yrs	6.4 yrs
Animal(s) kept indoors during the day	43%	54%
Households did not visit vet in past year	9%	27%
Pets sterilized	70%	82%
Average annual veterinary expenses	$196	$104

Source: APPMA 2002

Table 4
Levels of Attachment to Companion Animals in the Household

	Percent of Care-givers	Average LAPS Score
Very attached	50.0	54.9
Somewhat attached	35.7	44.8
Not very attached	12.4	32.6
Not at all attached	1.9	26.2

Average LAPS Score for Demographic Categories

Category	Average LAPS Score
Household size = 1	52.8
Household size = 5+	43.5
Never married/sep./div.	52.0
Married	45.7
Female	50.0
Male	45.1
White	47.6
African American	53.8
Household income under $30k	51.5
Household income over $50k	43.2
Household education: less than high school	53.0
Household education: college graduate	44.2
Favorite pet is dog	49.2
Favorite pet is cat	45.1

Source: Johnson, Garrity, and Stallones 1992

Table 5a
Pet Care-Giving by Region

Region	Pet Care-giving Households (percent)
Mountain	61.9
Pacific	60.6
West South Central	60.5
East South Central	56.7
East North Central	55.2
New England	54.1
South Atlantic	53.8
Middle Atlantic	50.2

Source: AVMA Survey 2002

Thus use of national survey data to assess care-giving of regional or state pet populations can lead to significant over-estimates or under-estimates. Local studies of pet care-giving also indicate significant urban to suburban differences. Unpublished data from Massachusetts revealed differences in pet care-giving rates between Boston, an urban center, and Wellesley, an affluent suburb within commuting distance of Boston. The rate of dog care-giving was 25.4 percent in Boston compared with 37 percent in Wellesley; the rate of cat care-giving was 37.8 percent in Boston compared with 26 percent in Wellesley (Rowan and Williams 1987). Pet care-giving rates generally are significantly lower in dense urban complexes than they are in suburban communities. National surveys of pet populations usually do not focus on differences among urban, suburban, and rural communities; thus they overlook significant causes of error in estimates of pet populations.

These differences in pet care-giving around the country mean that a "one size fits all" approach will not be sufficient to resolve the pet population crisis, and that it is crucial for regions and communities to initiate and maintain their own data collection efforts in order to have reliable and accurate information with which to serve the pet care-givers in their jurisdictions. Communities can use the available national data as a guide to direct their own data collection efforts. They should be cautious, however, about relying on rote formulae derived from national data to estimate their own dog and cat populations. Using the APPMA (2002) survey data, it has been suggested that one can calculate the number of dogs in a community. The technique is to multiply the number of occupied households (derived from the census data) by 0.39 (the percentage of households nationally containing dogs) and then multiplying by 1.7 (the average number of dogs in each household). However this will overestimate dog populations in a Northeastern urban community and underestimate dog populations in a

Table 5b
Pet Care-giving by Species in
Selected States (percent of households)

State	Dog Care-giving	State	Cat Care-giving
MA	21.4	LA	26.1
NY	26.1	MI	26.1
NJ	26.2	MD	26.5
CT	28.4	IL	28.0
MT	46.6	MT	44.6
ID	48.1	WY	44.6
OK	48.5	OR	45.2
WV	50.3	ME	46.3

Source: AVMA Survey 2002

Table 6
Varying Rates of
Pet Care-Giving
by Life Stage

Life Stage Category	Percent with Pets
Young singles	50.2
Young couples	72.5
Young parents	64.1
Middle singles	44.4
Middle parents	74.8
Older parents	69.0
Working older couple	58.9
Retired older couple	39.8
Older singles	29.7

Source: AVMA 2002

rural part of the Southeast or Southwest. Nonetheless such formulae are useful first approximations of the number of dogs and cats in a particular community.

Animal care-giving rates also vary dramatically according to the "life stage" of the household (see Table 6). It is generally known that families with children between the ages of five and seventeen have the highest rates of pet care-giving (almost four out of five have pets). However, as indicated by Table 4, these families are less attached to their pets (just as there is less time to devote to each family member the more there are). As can be seen from Table 6, singles households are less likely to have pets (about 20 percent lower rate than that of families), and pet care-giving declines with age. No known studies assess relinquishment rates by life stage of the care-giver.

Acquisition of Pets

Pet care-givers acquire dogs and cats from a variety of sources. These sources are believed to play an integral role in pet population problems. According to the APPMA National Pet Owners Survey, pets in 1998 were acquired as indicated in Table 7 (APPMA 2000, 2002). Use of those sources marked with an asterisk indicates that some forethought and planning usually went into the acquisition of the pet. The total percentage of dogs acquired from such sources is 74 (or about 48 percent of the identified

sources); the total percentage of cats acquired from these sources is 38 (or about 29 percent of the identified sources). This indicates that cats are more likely to be acquired on a whim.

Other surveys have shown similar differences between the sources of dogs and cats. Nassar, Mosier, and Williams (1984) found that in Las Vegas cats (24.5 percent) were much more likely to be acquired from the stray population than dogs (8 percent), but only 9 percent of cats were purchased compared with 26 percent of dogs. In Massachusetts 71 percent of pet care-givers had planned to acquire their dogs, going to such sources as breeders (33 percent), shelters (16 percent), and pet stores (7 percent) (MSPCA 1996).

Feral/Stray Dogs and Cats

No discussion of the nation's dog and cat populations is complete without an estimate of the feral/stray population. In the past two decades, it appears that the number of stray and feral dogs has fallen to a very low level (with the possible exception of some communities in dense urban, very rural, and Native American areas). The same is not true of cats. This population is not easy to define because household cats may join and leave the perceived "stray" population. The Humane Society of the United States (HSUS) 1999 "Statement on Free-Roaming Cats" notes,

> Cats elude simple categorizations. Free-roaming cats are often referred to as either stray or feral, but these designations do not reflect the many types of outdoor cats. Free-roaming cats can be owned cats who are allowed to roam; owned cats who have become lost; previously owned cats who have been abandoned and no longer *have* a home; quasi-owned cats who roam freely and are fed by several residents in an area but "owned" by none of them; and so-called working cats who serve as "mousers." Almost every community also has feral,

Table 7
Sources from Which Dogs and Cats Were Acquired

Source (percent)	Dogs	Cats
Friend/relative	34	40
Breeder*	29	4
Newspaper/private party*	20	11
Stray	18	32
Animal shelter*	17	18
Puppy/kitten from own pet	16	12
Pet store*	8	5
Gift	7	2
"Other"	5	5
Veterinarian	1	4
TOTAL	**155**	**133**

Respondents could name more than one source.
Therefore the percentage totals amount to more than 100.

*Some forethought and planning usually went into the acquisition of the pet.

Source: APPMA 2002

unsocialized cats who may be one or more generations removed from a home environment and who may subsist in a colony of similar cats living on the fringes of human existence. Because cats exhibit varying degrees of sociability, even an animal care and control professional may not immediately be able to tell the difference between a feral cat and a frightened indoor-only cat who has escaped and become lost.

In a national survey of pet caregivers commissioned by The HSUS, respondents were asked if they fed stray cats and, if so, how many they fed (Anonymous 1993). It was possible to extrapolate that pet care-givers fed about 32.7 million cats (assuming no cats were fed by more than one household). However The HSUS questioned these "cat-feeder" results and exhorted caution in using the data to establish a national estimate of stray and feral cats (G. Handy, personal communication, n.d. 2003). Nonetheless one of the authors (A.N.R) has used the survey to estimate the American feral/stray cat population at roughly 30–40 million (or about 60–70 percent less than the number of cats being cared for in households). Some support for this estimate comes from two regional surveys in California that have produced similar percentages for the stray/feral cat population (Anonymous 1995, 1996).

Animal Shelter Demographics: A Historical Perspective

In the United States a network of animal shelters exists to address and manage pet population control. One of the primary functions of U.S. animal shelters is to attempt to find new homes for dogs and cats who, for a variety of reasons, have made the transition from owned animal to homeless animal. Because the number of animals entering shelters currently exceeds available home placements, many pet population management policies allow euthanasia of animals who cannot be placed in an acceptable home. Animals who are killed include healthy, adoptable animals, as well as animals deemed unadoptable due to illness, age, aberrant behavior, or some other characteristic. Recent attention has focused on collecting data on "animal shelter demographics," including data that describes the animals populating shelters and that tracks trends in the movement of animals into and out of shelters.

The 1960s and 1970s: Experiential Policy

The early 1970s is considered by many to be a defining period for changes in the American approach to pet population issues. In 1974 a survey of U.S. mayors ranked animal-related issues as the number one complaint received by their offices (Bancroft 1974). During the 1970s attention to and awareness of what were perceived as growing pet population concerns led to development of a new approach that was to shape the course of pet population policy well into the 1990s. Called LES (Legislation, Education, and Sterilization), it was a three-pronged approach designed to reduce the numbers of animals that shelters were handling and subsequently to reduce the need for euthanasia as a population control method. LES was launched by Phyllis Wright of The HSUS with the catchy tag phrase "less born, less killed, and less cruelty." LES's major projects included establishment of sterilization programs, mandating adequate licensing fees, and educating the community via humane education programs, the media, and veterinarians. The HSUS also called for and helped organize two national conferences of interested parties (e.g., the

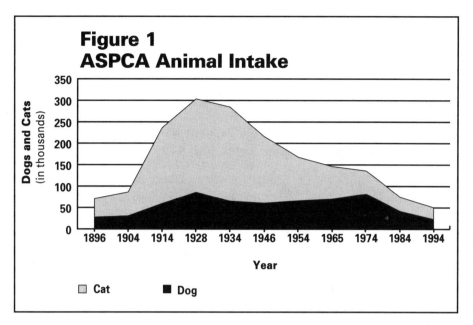

Figure 1
ASPCA Animal Intake

Dogs and Cats (in thousands)

Year

☐ Cat   ■ Dog

AVMA, the American Kennel Club, and other animal-related groups) in 1974 and 1976 to address the pet population crisis (Rowan and Williams 1987).

The rationale for the LES approach was based largely on anecdotal reports from animal shelters around the country. Few shelters were keeping any data on the numbers of animals handled, on those returned-to-care-givers (RTC), or on those adopted and euthanized. No regional or national organizations focused on data collection for homeless pets. From the limited data available, it was estimated that in 1973 approximately 20 percent of the dog and cat population in households was being euthanized in shelters (Rowan and Williams 1987). Since then some data has been published on the experiences of the ASPCA in New York City from 1896 to 1994, when it gave up animal control for New York City (Zawistowski et al. 1998). Figure 1 shows the trends in animal intake over this 98-year period. What is readily apparent is that, even in 1973 when the alarm was raised about too many dogs and cats and not enough homes, the situation was much improved over the 1920s and 1930s. Up until 1950 the ASPCA was euthanizing 95 percent or more of the animals brought into the

shelter. It should also be noted that the shelter intake numbers were falling at a time when the population of New York City was growing (from 5.63 million in 1928 to 8 million in 1954, where it has remained).

It is not clear why alarms were raised about unwanted and stray dogs and cats in the early 1970s (cf. Djerassi, Israel, and Jochle 1973), although it may be that Djerassi, known as the inventor of the birth control pill, was looking for possible new markets for his invention. However, his article led to others in which the focus was not on cats (the ASPCA data indicates that cats formed the bulk of the animal intake) but on the stray dog population. The stray dogs were portrayed as presenting a public health and safety risk as well as welfare issues for the dogs themselves (Marx and Furculow 1969; Beck 1973; Feldman 1974). Schneider and Vaida (1975), in their surveys of dog and cat populations in California, argued that cats should not be overlooked.

Animal protection groups began pushing the concept of companion animal surgical sterilization as a pet population control method. Initially the veterinary community was resistant and suggested that the development of contraceptive drugs might be

a more viable solution (Anonymous 1978; Rowan and Williams 1987). Despite the lack of support from organized veterinary medicine, the Department of Animal Regulation in the City of Los Angeles set up a municipal spay-neuter clinic and a differential licensing system—in which it cost more to license intact dogs than neutered ones—in 1970. This clinic evoked a storm of protest from the veterinary community, but within ten years the proportion of licensed dogs in Los Angeles who were sterilized rose from 10 percent to 51 percent. The municipal clinic was doing far too few sterilizations to account for such a large change. There had to have been a change of behavior among the private veterinary practices. Over this same period, the number of animals taken in by the city's Department of Animal Regulation fell from about 140,000 a year, to about 85,000 a year (Rowan and Williams 1987).

Reliable and consistent data are crucial for an evaluation of the success of any proposed pet population program. Early data collection focused solely on determining how many animals were being killed as part of pet population control, without considering other aspects of shelter demographics, such as number of animals handled, the number returned to the caregiver, and the number adopted. In 1973 The HSUS commissioned a national survey of animal shelters. Although the response rate was low, the survey provided a baseline estimate of 13.5 million dogs and cats euthanized annually. A follow-up survey in 1982 suggested that the total number of euthanasias had declined to an estimated range of 7.6 million to 10 million, despite an overall increase in the owned pet population from an estimated 60 million in 1973 to an estimated 90 million in 1983 (Rowan and Williams 1987). Thus there had been not only a fall in absolute shelter euthanasia numbers but also an even greater fall in the relative numbers.

Table 8 provides additional evidence that shelter animal intakes declined substantially in the 1970s. These data come from a large county-wide program run by a humane society under a county contract in California (Savesky 2001). Basically the data show that animal intakes plunged in the 1970s, stayed more or less the same from 1980 to 1990, and then began falling again.

While the evidence cited above demonstrates that shelter intakes and euthanasias moved in the right direction (i.e., down) from World War II to the present, the prevailing view in the shelter community through the 1980s and even into part of the 1990s was that of wrestling with an intractable problem. Part of the problem was again a lack of solid data and the generation of inaccurate estimates of shelter intakes and euthanasias. In the 1980s some surveys estimated that as many as 20 million animals were being euthanized in shelters annually (Rowan and Williams 1987). These surveys continued to be quoted well into the 1990s. The result was that both humane society workers and the public continued to assess progress on pet population issues based on these old statistics, giving a "doom and gloom" outlook to the situation, when in fact a retrospective examination of euthanasia trends indicates that euthanasias appeared to be decreasing over time.

Reliable Estimates from Regional Data

Djerassi, Israel, and Jochle (1973) noted that the lack of comprehensive, high quality data was the biggest roadblock to efficient and effective program development and commented that this deficiency was a universal weakness, common even among those countries that had long established a sophisticated human census. The lack of a standardized list of animal shelters contributes significantly to the challenges that continue to be faced by researchers doing shelter surveys (Rowan 1992a). There have been two significant problems in developing reliable estimates of shelter animal numbers. First, there was and still is no reliable public list of shelters in the United States. Second, many shelters either do not keep appropriate program data or are very reluctant to release them for fear that the data will be used to criticize their organizations. An additional challenge is posed by the fact that the term *shelter* encompasses a wide range of entities, from an animal control facility that serves several towns and handles thousands of animals per year to the private citizen who rescues a few strays a year.

With the increasing utilitization of computers and the growing awareness of the value of shelter demographic data, more individual shelters had begun collecting and storing data by the 1990s. A recognition that euthanasia data alone was of limited value led to the collection of statistics on the number of animals entering shelters, as well as the disposition of the animals (e.g., adoption, RTC, euthanasia, death). The availability of some regional data enabled an analysis of regional shelter trends and estimates of the national picture. This analysis revealed that, just as there were regional differences in pet care-giving trends, there were regional differences in shelter animal populations.

Rowan examined regional data from New Jersey, Washington State, and Massachusetts and, by extrapolation, determined that, of approximately 110 million owned dogs and cats in the United States, an estimated 5 million–6 million, or 5 percent of the owned population, were euthanized. This was a much more conservative estimate than the range of 11.75 million–19.54 million found in AHA's 1990 survey (Rowan 1992a). Others then produced numbers similar to Rowan's extrapolation, based on a broader range of state data (e.g., Arkow 1994).

More recently The HSUS has been developing a list of shelters in which, to be identified as a shelter, the organization must possess a building that houses animals and has its own postal address. Beginning with a list of about 6,000 organizations, The HSUS removed duplicates and non-sheltered organizations, leaving approximately 3,500 entities. An unpublished 1999 HSUS survey of this group produced a 20 percent response rate and the following data. The duplicate and "address unknown" returns indicated that the accurate total of shelters was about 2,800–2,900. Of the respondents that identified their status, 38.2 percent were municipal entities, 43.6 percent were private entities with some form of municipal contract, and 18.2 percent were private entities with no municipal contract. In terms of size, 45.2 percent had annual budgets of $250,000 or less, 22.9 percent had budgets between $250,001 and $500,000, 16.6 percent had budgets between $500,001 and $1,000,000, and 15.4 percent had budgets exceeding $1 million. These data agree closely with those reported by Wenstrup and Dowidchuk (1999) in their smaller sample of shelters. Finally the shelters in The HSUS survey reported a mean of fourteen full-time (median: six) and five part-time (median: three) employees.

As Rowan (1992a) noted, the larger shelters handle a disproportionately large percentage of the animals. Thus in New Jersey, where the average shelter is small and town-based, 30 percent of the shelters handled 82 percent of the shelter animals. In Washington State, where the shelters are typically larger and county-based, 30 percent of the shelters handled 63 percent of the animals. Therefore if data were collected from the largest 50–60 percent of shelters (or approximately 1,500 entities), it is reasonably certain that these shelters would account for at least 90 percent of the animals handled annually.

Table 8
The Animal Intake/Disposition Experience of One Large California Shelter

Year	Dogs	Cats	Total	RTC/ADOP	Euth.
1970	23,500	22,600	49,100	9,130	37,025
1971	26,425	20,785	46,210	7,095	39,935
1972	18,265	14,212	32,477	7,650	24,917
1973	20,034	14,920	34,954	9,278	25,676
1974	17,131	10,890	28,021	9,989	18,032
1975	15,019	10,052	25,071	9,552	15,519
1976	12,530	8,528	21,058	7,250	13,808
1977	11,199	8,001	19,200	6,770	12,430
1978	9,949	6,899	16,148	5,073	11,775
1979	8,969	6,055	15,054	5,870	9,154
1980	7,603	6,628	14,231	5,580	8,651
1981	8,235	6,888	15,123	5,634	9,489
1982	8,301	7,833	16,144	5,789	10,345
1983	8,199	6,729	14,928	4,922	10,006
1984	8,360	6,639	14,999	5,041	9,958
1985	8,477	7,014	15,491	5,522	9,969
1986	8,141	8,010	16,151	6,099	10,052
1987	7,165	8,710	15,875	5,962	9,913
1988	7,171	8,916	16,087	6,199	9,888
1989	6,843	9,021	15,864	6,274	9,590
1990	5,866	9,211	15,077	6,088	9,009
1991	5,224	9,442	14,666	6,042	8,624
1992	5,226	9,702	14,928	6,176	8,752
1993	5,116	8,257	13,373	5,902	7,471
1994	4,723	7,312	12,035	5,797	6,238
1995	4,894	6,963	11,857	5,544	6,313
1996	4,925	6,499	11,424	5,624	5,800
1997	4,934	5,866	10,800	5,470	5,330

Source: Savesky 2001

Table 9a
Trends in New Jersey Dog Shelter Intakes and Euthanasia

Year	Impounded	Returned to Care-giver	Adopted	Euth.	Dead on Arrival	Euth. Rate (percent)
1984	95,813	14,372	19,360	47,703	7,000	53.7
1985	80,071	13,067	17,605	40,757	7,455	56.1
1986	75,784	12,604	20,365	37,115	7,669	54.5
1987	81,876	13,717	22,597	40,400	7,051	54.0
1988	72,887	12,560	21,917	34,175	6,110	51.2
1989	73,974	12,422	21,350	33,408	5,552	48.8
1990	66,870	12,426	21,273	28,937	5,126	46.9
1991	60,901	11,914	21,210	22,379	4,940	40.0
1992	56,760	13,290	20,030	20,131	3,641	37.9
1993	55,480	12,765	18,924	18,502	3,739	35.8
1994	52,092	13,375	19,372	15,188	3,426	31.2
1995	48,954	12,565	17,951	14,880	3,021	32.4
1996	52,791	13,178	17,489	17,429	2,993	35.0
1997	50,779	13,991	19,328	15,294	2,902	31.9

Note: The euthanasia rate is calculated by dividing the total euthanized by the total impounded less those who are dead on arrival.

Source: Data collated and provided by G. Patronek, from annual reports from C. Campbell (New Jersey Health Department) in 1998.

Tables 9a, 9b, and 9c provide data from New Jersey on dog and cat entries into the state shelters, and on outcomes. (These data were compiled by Dr. Gary Patronek of Tufts University from materials provided in 1998 by Colin Campbell of New Jersey.) New Jersey had established a program in 1984 to support low-cost sterilization of pets in needy households, but the program also required all shelters to register with the state health department and provide baseline data on animal acquisition and disposition. As the tables indicate, euthanasia rates declined from 1984 to 1997, although rates for cats remained higher than those for dogs (primarily because the RTC rate is so much lower for cats than for dogs). There are approximately 7.8 million people living in about 3 million households in New Jersey. Pet surveys indicate that these households probably include more than one million dogs and cats. Thus New Jersey shelters impound less than 2.5 percent of the dog population per annum (euthanizing less than 0.75 percent) and 3 percent of the cat population (euthanizing less than 1.5 percent). A comparison of these rates with the national shelter euthanasia rates of 20 percent or more in the early 1970s makes apparent how much progress has been made in dealing with pet homelessness!

Population Dynamics

The next advance during the 1970s in utilizing data to define and address the pet population crisis involved treating the transfer of owned animals to animal shelters not as an isolated event but as one piece of a dynamic process that is composed of many elements. The concept of a pet population model began as an estimate of animal populations from the readily available human population data (Schneider and Vaida 1975, Nassar and Mosier 1980), and subsequently was developed into a population model that could be utilized to estimate pet (or dog) populations in any community (Nassar, Mosier, and Williams 1984; Patronek and Rowan 1995). The models essentially track the source and number of animals entering the owned pet population in a defined area; what percentage of them enter the shelter system; and the population's final disposition. The population dynamics model is an important development in our under-

Table 9b
Trends in New Jersey Cat Shelter Intakes and Euthanasia

Year	Impounded	Returned to Care-giver	Adopted	Euth.	Dead on Arrival	Euth. Rate (percent)
1984	62,747	2,042	11,951	34,863	7,000	62.5
1985	53,788	765	13,292	32,365	7,044	69.2
1986	57,998	1,021	15,728	35,198	7,813	70.1
1987	72,243	1,153	17,690	45,506	8,509	71.4
1988	72,887	993	18,668	42,820	7,347	65.3
1989	75,380	1,190	18,658	45,432	7,542	67.0
1990	74,491	1,117	28,826	44,225	8,524	67.0
1991	70,515	1,446	18,582	39,102	7,462	62.0
1992	67,891	1,524	18,064	41,569	6,392	67.6
1993	63,424	1,517	18,087	34,756	7,381	62.0
1994	66,802	2,133	21,005	36,419	7,256	61.2
1995	64,974	1,202	20,361	33,359	5,831	56.4
1996	66,181	1,411	20,529	35,873	2,993	56.8
1997	60,172	1,394	20,990	31,597	5,389	57.7

Note: The euthanasia rate is calculated by dividing the total euthanized by the total impounded less those who are dead on arrival.

Source: Data collated and provided by G. Patronek, from annual reports from C. Campbell (New Jersey Health Department) in 1998.

standing of the pet population. Challenges to implementing the model include continued lack of standardized data in most communities and a lack of data on stray populations, especially in regard to cats.

The National Council on Pet Population Study and Policy

In 1993 the National Council on Pet Population Study and Policy (NCPPSP) was established as a coalition of interest groups with the goal of gathering and analyzing reliable data in order to characterize the number, origin, and disposition of owned dogs and cats in the United States and to make recommendations on program and policy development to address the pet population crisis (Zawistowski et al. 1998). NCPPSP's main mission was to be a driving force in centralizing and standardizing data collection for animal shelters.

The group initiated its shelter survey in 1994. It sent surveys to the 4,700 known sheltering agencies and requested a variety of data, including the number of dogs and cats handled, returned to their caregiver, adopted, and euthanized. The survey was repeated three more times. Unfortunately it experienced a relatively low response rate (approximately 23 percent, or 1,100 shelters and other organizations) and a limited overlap of respondents (Zawistowski et al. 1998). (Reportedly only 396 shelters responded in all four surveys, M. Armstrong, personal communication, n.d. 2003.) The authors of this chapter believe that municipal shelters were over-represented: in two of the surveys, these shelters accounted for 53 and 46 percent of the sample respectively.

Overall the surveys reported that 63 percent of animals being handled by the participating shelters were euthanized (71 percent of cats and 56 percent of dogs). Moreover dogs were returned to their caregivers at significantly higher rates than cats (16 percent versus 2 percent), while adoption rates were approximately 25 percent for both species (Zawistowski et al. 1998). These findings were similar to those of other studies.

After the 1996 shelter survey, the NCPPSP focused its efforts on implementing a regional shelter relinquishment study, a research project designed to explore pet and householder characteristics of cases where

Table 9c
Trends in New Jersey Euthanasia Rates

Year	Impounded	Euth. Rate (%)
1984	158,560	57.1
1985	133,859	61.3
1986	133,782	61.1
1987	154,119	62.0
1988	145,774	58.2
1989	149,354	57.9
1990	141,361	57.3
1991	131,416	51.7
1992	124,651	53.8
1993	118,904	49.4
1994	118,894	47.7
1995	113,928	45.9
1996	118,972	47.2
1997	110,951	45.7

Source: Data collated and provided by G. Patronek, from annual reports from C. Campbell (New Jersey Health Department) in 1998.

animals are relinquished. The survey, which involved four regions of the United States and twelve shelters, resulted in a database of thousands of animals (Salman et al. 1998). It is the most ambitious and extensive survey of the pet population crisis to date. This research effort reflected an increasing shift away from focusing on collecting shelter population data to a concentration on determining the characteristics of animals in shelters; the characteristics of their previous households; and the circumstances leading to their transition to the shelter.

Several studies have characterized the shelter animal population in terms of age, breed, and sterilization status. In a study conducted at a Pennsylvania shelter, 72.5 percent of dogs were one year of age or older and 59 percent of incoming dogs were mixed breed (Patronek, Glickman, and Moyer 1995). Results from the NCPPSP's regional shelter study showed that most dogs and cats surrendered to shelters were between five months and three years of age. Sixty-eight percent of dogs and 93 percent of cats were mixed breed (Salman et al. 1998). In the same study, animals relinquished by their care-givers were more likely to be intact, younger, and mixed breed (New et al. 2000). Another study of 186 shelters found that only 13 percent of animals entering shelters were puppies and kittens, apparently confirming the anecdotes that puppies are become rarer in the shelter population (Wenstrup and Dowidchuk 1999). However few shelters from the Southeast, the Southwest, and the Midwest, where puppies are still common, participated in this survey.

Numerous studies have defined shelter populations in terms of animals surrendered by their care-givers versus animals arriving at the shelters as strays and have identified variations in these populations by region as well as species. One survey found that approximately 54 percent of the shelter population was stray and approximately 42 percent was surrendered, with no significant differences between cats and dogs (Wenstrup and Dowidchuk 1999). In contrast unpublished data from Massachusetts indicated that 73 percent of dogs were surrendered and 27 percent were stray, while 42 percent of cats were surrendered and 58 percent were stray (Clancy, Birkholz, and Luke 1996). Such differences from one region to another reflect the changing ecology of stray animals. Many communities, particularly in the Northeast, report a minimal or nonexistent stray dog population, while the majority of the country is grappling with the remaining stray and feral cat population (Patronek 1998).

Clancy, Birkholz, and Luke found that, of 143,456 dogs and cats admitted to Massachusetts shelters in 1995, 36 percent were adopted, 34 percent were euthanized, and 20 percent were returned to their care-givers (1996). In addition a recent review of shelter demographic data reportedly collected from every "major" (major not defined) shelter in the country calculated a national euthanasia estimate of 4.4 million, the lowest estimate ever recorded. According to this review, which included an examination of trends over time, the euthanasia or disposal of animals in shelters likely peaked at approximately 23.4 million in 1970; by 1992 the number had dropped to an estimated 5.7 million. (The ASPCA data provided in Figure 1 indicate that shelter euthanasia may have peaked fifty years earlier. However there were far fewer shelters in the 1930s–1950s, so each shelter may have had to handle a larger number of stray and homeless animals.) Estimates for 1999 and 2000 were 4.5 million and 4.6 million, respectively. The 2001 evaluation concluded that the lowest rate of shelter euthanasia was in the Northeast and the highest in the South, with significant decreases in euthanasia rates occurring in the Midwest and the Sunbelt (Clifton 2002).

Two studies have confirmed that a sizable proportion of pet care-givers bring their pets to animal shelters to be euthanized. Data from a Pennsylvania shelter indicate that 17.2 percent of care-giver-relinquished animals were brought to the shelter for immediate euthanasia (Patronek, Glickman, and Moyer 1995). The regional shelter survey (Kass et al. 2001) found similar results: of 4,000 animals surrendered, 24 percent of dogs and 17 percent of cats were surrendered for immediate euthanasia. The primary reasons care-givers gave for requesting this service included old age, serious illness, and serious behavior problems. The median length of care-giving of these animals was ten years (Kass et al. 2001). This illustrates a function of the animal

Table 10a
Risk factors for Dog Relinquishment: Indiana (odds ratios)

Characteristic	OR	Characteristic	OR
Purchased or adopted	1	Two or more visits per year	1
Received as gift	0.6	One visit per year	2.6
Free from previous care-giver	3.0	Less than one visit per year	6.2
		No veterinary visits	40.4
Source: private (cost > $100)	1	Relinquishment age > 5 years	1
Source: private (cost: $31–$100)	3.6	Relinquishment age 3–5 years	4.1
Source: private (cost < $31)	5.0	Relinquishment age 0.5–3 years	9.7
Source: unknown	1.0	Relinquishment age < 0.5 years	18.3
Source: pet store	0.75	Acquisition age < 0.5 years	1
Source: born in home	4.0	Acquisition age 0.5–1 year	1.5
Source: stray	3	Acquisition age: 1–2 years	2.8
Source: shelter	6.1	Acquisition age > 4 years	2.1

Source: Patronek et al. 1996a

shelter that has been overlooked—that of potentially providing a euthanasia outlet and support for grieving pet care-givers. It also demonstrates that not all animals handled by shelters are potential candidates for adoption and adds another dimension to our understanding of the pet population situation.

Risk Factors for Relinquishment

Several studies have increased our understanding of some of the characteristics of care-giver relinquishment and have identified potential risk factors for relinquishment of pets to animal shelters. It is no surprise that there are differences for dogs and cats. The first good study of this issue—a case-control study in a community in Indiana—compared two groups of pet care-givers: those who had surrendered a pet to an animal shelter and those representing a random sample of pet care-givers in the community who had not surrendered an animal. Tables 10a and 10b outline the major risk factors for cats and dogs that were identified in this study (Patronek et al. 1996a, 1996b).

The study authors used a measurement called an Odds Ratio (OR) to assess what factors might make a dog or cat more likely to be relinquished by a care-giver. In developing an OR, a researcher identifies a factor (such as not visiting a veterinarian in the previous year) and then compares the group of animals who have that characteristic with a group who have a related but different characteristic (e.g., visiting a veterinarian once a year). Usually an odds ratio of greater than 2 is considered a significant difference. As Table 10a shows, the data collected by Patronek et al (1996a) refute at least one cherished belief (that dogs received as gifts or from pet stores are more likely to be given up) and confirm a number of others (that age is an important factor in relinquishment of dogs). The shelter community needs to be concerned that dogs acquired from their facilities are more likely to be relinquished and should emphasize the importance of pet care-givers establishing strong relationships with a veterinarian (their "other family doctor").

The OR data for cats is less interesting. Having a veterinarian is important but not so major a factor as it is for dogs, and shelter cats are not more likely to be relinquished than cats obtained from other sources. The relinquishment age data are very similar for dogs and cats.

These data are consistent with both previous and later studies that found that surrendered dogs were obtained most frequently from family or friends at no charge (Arkow and Dow 1984; Salman et al. 1998).

The NCPPSP's Regional Shelter Survey identified the top ten reasons for relinquishment based on 3,772 interviews of care-givers who surrendered a pet to the participating shelters. While these studies found many

Table 10b
Risk Factors for Cat Relinquishment: Indiana (odds ratios)

Characteristic	OR	Characteristic	OR
Purchased or adopted	1	Two or more veterinary visits per year	1
Received as gift	0.7	One veterinary visit per year	0.6
Free from previous care-giver	2.0	Less than one veterinary visit per year	0.9
		No veterinary visits	3.1
Source: private breeder or care-giver	1	Relinquishment age > 5 yrs	1
Source: pet store	1.2	Relinquishment age 3–5 years	4.3
Source: born in home	0.9	Relinquishment age 0.5–3 years	7.3
Source: stray	0.6	Relinquishment age < 0.5 years	14.2
Source: shelter	0.7		

Source: Patronek et al. 1996b

similarities between dogs and cats, there are a few differences (Table 11). The most common reasons for relinquishment include animal-centered issues, such as behavior and pet illness, as well as care-giver-centered issues, such as landlord issues and personal problems (Salman et al. 1998).

In the regional shelter survey, moving was the primary reason for surrender of dogs and the number three reason for surrender of cats. Most care-givers in this category were in the 25–39 age range and had lived with their pets for less than two years, perhaps suggesting that attachment or bonding factors may play a role in these surrenders. Additionally 40.8 percent of care-givers in this category noted that they were unable to find suitable new housing that would accommodate their pets, suggesting that working with landlords and housing authorities may be a helpful long-term strategy for care-givers in this group. Some relinquishers acknowledged that other factors may have played a role in their decision to surrender their pets when moving, such as behavior issues (New et al. 1999).

The study also grouped the 71 distinct reasons for relinquishment into three classes: health/personal issues (relating to the care-giver), behavioral (relating to the pet), and housing. Health/personal issues represented the leading class of surrender for cats and the third most significant class for dogs (after behavioral and housing, respectively). The top three reasons for surrender in the health/personal issues category for cats were a family member's allergy to cats, care-giver personal problems, and a new baby in the house. An examination of the same category for dogs revealed that lack of time, care-giver personal problems, and allergies were the most common (Scarlett et al. 1999).

The regional shelter survey revealed that many care-givers surveyed gave several different reasons for surrender, indicating that deciding to surrender a pet is a complex, multifaceted process. Indeed an ethnographic study of care-givers who had relinquished their pets found that a combination of challenges in the pet care-giver relationship combined with lifestyle pressures ultimately led to the relinquishment of the pet. In most cases the care-giver had accepted responsibility for the animal because otherwise he or she would have been taken to the shelter or abandoned. In other words the people started off as reluctant care-givers. These care-givers then tolerated the situation with the new animal for a varying period of time (up to a year) and put off relinquishment of the pet because such an action was perceived as a negative one that was likely to result in euthanasia. One other important finding of this study was that most of the relinquishers had other animals that were not being surrendered! This speaks to the importance of developing early intervention strategies that identify and support "at-risk" pet relationships (DiGiacomo, Arluke, and Patronek 1998).

Shelters and Data Collection and Analysis

Clearly there was a call for more attention to pet population and animal shelter demographics in the 1990s, but it is unclear what impact this has had in terms of changing policies and procedures of animal shelters. The focus of animal shelters has always been, and continues to be, direct animal care, and accomplishments relating to saving animals' lives and promoting adoption continue to be the emphasis of direct mail campaigns and other fundraising efforts. Most shelters are short-staffed and operate under stressful conditions and with limited budgets. Under such circumstances it is understandable that they may have difficulty recognizing the value of numbers and statistics, especially when immediate problems are clamoring (literally) for attention.

A relatively small proportion of the animal sheltering community attends organized educational events regularly. Few subscribe to the academic journals in which much of this data is published. However *Animal People* regularly reports on shelter animal handling (Clifton 2002), *Animal Sheltering* Magazine now includes more data in its pages, and the NCPPSP website (which includes copies of NCPPSP studies) enjoys a healthy traffic. Therefore it is likely that the latest data is reaching a greater, but still small, proportion of the animal sheltering community. A decreasing number of facilities lack basic computer technology that would facilitate the collection of data. Recent attempts at increasing organization awareness of the importance of data collection have focused on identifying what data shelters need to collect. Future efforts need to provide guidance regarding data analysis (Wenstrup and Dowidchuk 1999). Shelters that do perform analysis should be encouraged to publish their data, so that the information is available to other shelters and can serve as a model (Patronek and Zawistowski 2002).

To make it easier for shelters to develop data management protocols, several software packages for animal shelters have come on the market, including Chameleon and PetWhere. Some packages are offered free of charge to shelters. Generally such software allows for the collection of basic admission and disposition data and also allows the databases to be

---

Table 11
Top Ten Reasons Nationally for Pet Relinquishment

Dogs	Cats
Moving	Too many in house
Landlord issues	Allergies
Cost of pet maintenance	Moving
No time for pet	Cost of pet maintenance
Inadequate facilities	Landlord issues
Too many pets at home	No homes for littermates
Pet illness	House soiling
Personal problems	Personal problems
Biting	Inadequate facilities
No homes for littermates	Doesn't get along with other pets

Source: Kass et al. 2001

---

adapted to meet a shelter's specific needs. (The ASPCA has taken over responsibility for PetWhere and will continue to distribute it free of charge.)

In addition a trend toward collaboration in the sheltering community began to develop in the 1980s. This trend has increased awareness of the relevance of data collection and the issue of facilitating data sharing. Collaboration is occurring among shelters within a community area (e.g., the Washington, D.C., Denver, and San Francisco regions), and between shelters and other animal protection organizations, educational institutions, corporations, and the business sector. An increasing number of foundations and grant programs are funding companion animal welfare projects. Many of these foundations are requiring relevant, reliable, and consistent data in order to evaluate grant applicants and assess the success of funded projects (personal communication, N. DiGiacomo, n.d. 2002). Maddie's Fund, a well-endowed foundation, was founded in 1999 specifically to fund collaborative projects that seek to "guarantee loving homes

for healthy shelter dogs and cats across the country," and to "save the sick and injured pets in animal shelters" (Maddie's Fund 2002). Lastly donors are increasingly asking for statistical data, in addition to information regarding an organization's mission and programs, in order to make donation decisions.

While sterilization programs have remained a priority for many shelter organizations, the late 1990s saw a shift in organizational approach and program development. Due in part to the new data on care-giver relinquishment and behavior issues (and probably in part to the declining number of animals entering shelters, which potentially frees up resources for new initiatives), more shelters have devoted time and money to developing behavior programs. These programs range from largely informal approaches, in which potential adopters are educated about behavior issues and receive some training on site, to ambitious, structured programs targeted to current pet care-givers as well as the shelter dog population. Structured programs include behavior help lines, formal classes, and the work of on-staff trainers and behaviorists. The HSUS established the Pets for Life National Training Center in collaboration with Denver Dumb Friends League in 1999 to provide education and training for shelter personnel in companion animal behavior. This project is part of a broader HSUS campaign focusing on developing new ways to strengthen pet care-giver relationships.

Future Directions

New data on pet populations are beginning to move U.S. pet population policies in new directions. Nonetheless some significant deficits continue to slow progress. These include the failure to standardize and broaden data collection on such basic questions as how many animal shelters there are in the United States and how many animals are euthanized each year.

Brestrup (1997) and Fennell (1999) have challenged some of the prevailing views about pet population policies. Fennell, for example, approaches the issue from the perspective of a free market and suggests that discounting the consumer aspects of pet care-giving may be shortsighted. She observes that new perspective may be gained by examining the application of the laws of supply and demand, and the economic and cultural forces that govern the "production" and destruction of owned dogs and cats. Fennell argues a market model would shift the focus from placing blame on prodigal pet care-givers to a focus on the characteristics and roots of consumer choice regarding pets. Moreover research into what pet care-givers want may ultimately give animal shelters the tools they need to shift consumer demand in their direction. Fennell notes that the market for puppies and kittens, as represented by the pet store and breeding industries, is relatively orderly, well developed, easily accessible, and well understood by the public, despite the significant companion animal welfare concerns sometimes associated with these businesses. In contrast she argues that, from the public's perspective, the business of "re-homing" animals has been poorly organized, often inaccessible, and not well understood.

Many shelters are beginning to acknowledge the importance of marketing techniques by redesigning their facilities—both the physical plant and their policies and procedures—to make their organizations more "user-friendly" and appealing to the public. There is growing recognition that shelter animals must be presented in the best possible light in order to attract a greater pool of potential adopters. A recent study that examined predictors of adoption versus euthanasia outcomes reinforces this view: age, sex, coat color, and reason for surrender were important predictors for adoption. Dogs with brindle or black coats were least likely to be adopted, while cats with white, color point, or gray coats were more likely to be adopted than their brown or black counterparts (Lepper, Kass, and Hart 2002). One policy application of these data would be the development of creative means to bring positive attention to animals such as the brown and black cats who otherwise may be passed over.

New Research Directions

A largely overlooked area of investigation in pet population and shelter demographics is post-adoption follow-up. This investigation would be the logical next phase in long-term resolution of the pet population crisis. Little published data exists on failed adoption rates, including animals who are returned to the shelter as well as those who end up in other homes or shelters; on the duration of the adoptive relationship; on the short-term and long-term challenges for the adopter; and on the evaluation of effective support services. In addition there is very little information on the effectiveness of adoption prescreening systems. Do some adopter prescreens produce better outcomes (fewer failed adoptions) than others? As shelters continue to debate the practicality, usefulness, and ethics of various adoption protocols, it would appear that only sound data will serve to provide solid answers (Patronek and Zawistowski 2002).

Adoptions now take place in a variety of venues. "Virtual shelters," in which potential adopters can learn about available animals, are commonplace, and *Petfinder.com* is one of the 2,000 most-visited websites in the world. A recent study evaluated adoption success at three locations: a traditional animal shelter setting, an off-site adoption site at a pet store (PETsMART), and a special event "adoptathon." Satisfaction and retention were found to be associated with the pet's personality, behavior, and compatibility with the new household. The level of satisfaction with the adoption experience was not related to adoption setting. The survey identified some significant and troubling potential challenges to adoption follow-up: a full 58 percent of adopters could not be reached two weeks after adoption, and 6 percent of adopters declined to provide any information (Neidhart and Boyd 2002). The low success of the follow-up may have been related to the fact that the adoption centers were not traditional, well-established shelters. Anecdotal reports claim that well-established shelters (e.g., those in Marin County, California) have a much better rate of reaching and gaining the cooperation of adopters in post-adoption surveys.

A deeper understanding is needed concerning the decisions leading to adoption and euthanasia in the shelter, and the potential effect these decisions have on both shelter operations and shelter employees. As euthanasia rates continue to fall, a paradoxical result may be that the stressful effect of euthanasia on the employee and the organization (cf. Arluke and Sanders 1996, Arluke, in this volume) increases. It might seem likely that, as the number of euthanasias in a shelter falls (see Tables 9a, 9b, and 9c), the related stress might also decline. However as euthanasia becomes less routine, it is also possible that the opposite might happen. Arluke (this volume) provides hints that this might be the case. The HSUS as of 2003 was supporting a euthanasia study through Bowling Green University and providing "Compassion Fatigue" workshops that included the use of a survey instrument to measure both burnout and compassion fatigue. Initial results indicated that both compassion fatigue and burnout rates are very high among shelter employees (R. Roop, personal communication, n.d. 2002). As debate about euthanasia in shelters, and about the meaning of the terms *adoptable* and *nonadoptable*, continues, Americans desperately need some actual data to determine how best to proceed.

It also is necessary to go one step further in exploring regional and species differences. While regional differences have been identified and acknowledged, these data have not been utilized to discover the general criteria or patterns underlying the differences (Wenstrup and Dowidchuk 2001). Such information would enable researchers to get at the root causes of the pet population crisis. The questions to ask are: Why do these differences exist? What do they mean? What societal, cultural, and educational forces drive pet caregiver choices? In order to discover the answers to these questions, humane societies will need to broaden their point of reference. Past research has demonstrated consistently that animal shelters are not the most common source of pet dogs and cats—and are not the only care-giver option for pet relinquishment (Patronek and Zawistowski 2002). Prospective, long-term studies of representative pet care-giving populations, as well as a more visible role for animal shelters in the community, will enable shelters to become more common choices of potential care-givers and to provide increasingly professional advice and support for pet care-givers in the community.

Acknowledgements

Research for this paper was supported by the Bide-A-Wee Home Association and funded by the Edith Goode Trust.

Literature Cited

American Pet Products Manufacturers Association, Inc (APPMA). 2000. *1999–2000 APPMA national pet owners survey*. Greenwich, Conn.: APPMA.

———. 2002. *2001–2002 APPMA national pet owners survey*. Greenwich, Conn.: APPMA.

American Veterinary Medical Association (AVMA). 1997. *U.S. pet ownership and demographics sourcebook*. Schaumburg, Ill.: Center for Information Management, AVMA.

———. 2002. *U.S. pet ownership and demographics sourcebook*. Schaumburg, Ill.: Center for Information Management, AVMA.

Anonymous. 1978. Pet population control and ovariohysterectomy clinics: Reaffirmation of 1973 statement. *Journal of the American Veterinary Medical Association* 173(11): 1408.

———. 1993. Pet owner survey. *Anthrozoös* 6(3): 203–204.

———. 1995. Animal demographics of Santa Clara County (California). *Anthrozoös* 8(3): 178–179.

———. 1996. Stray and feral cats. *Anthrozoös* 9(2/3): 117–119.

Arkow, P.S. 1994. A new look at pet overpopulation. *Anthrozoös* 7(4): 202–205.

Arkow, P.S., and S.J. Dow. 1984. The ties that do not bind: A study of the human-animal bonds that fail. In *The pet connection*, ed. R.K. Anderson, B.L. Hart, and L.A. Hart, 348–354. Minneapolis: CENSHARE, University of Minnesota.

Arluke, A. 2003. The no-kill controversy: Manifest and latent sources of tension. In *The state of the animals II: 2003*, ed. D.J. Salem and A.N. Rowan, 67–83. Washington, D.C.: Humane Society Press.

Arluke, A., and C. Sanders. 1996. *Regarding animals*. Philadelphia: Temple University Press.

Bancroft, R.L. 1974. America's mayors and councilmen: Their problems and frustrations. *Nations Cities* 12(Apr): 14–16.

Beck, A.M. 1973. *The ecology of stray dogs: A study of free-ranging urban animals*. Baltimore: York Press.

Brestrup, C. 1997. *Disposable animals: Ending the tragedy of throwaway pets*. Leander, Tex.: Camino Bay Books.

Clancy, E.A., E. Birkholz, and C.J. Luke. 1996. Comprehensive models of dog and cat population flows in Massachusetts. Unpublished master's thesis. Tufts University School of Veterinary Medicine.

Clifton, M. 2002. Latest U.S. data shows shelter killing down to 4.4 million a year. *Animal People* (Sept.) 14.

DiGiacomo, N., A. Arluke, and G. Patronek. 1998. Surrendering pets to shelters: The relinquisher's perspective. *Anthrozoös* 11(1): 41–51.

Djerassi, C., A. Israel, and W. Jochle. 1973. Planned parenthood for pets? *Bulletin of the Atomic Scientists* (Jan): 10–19.

Feldman, B.M. 1974. The problem of urban dogs. *Science* 185: 931.

Fennell, L.A. 1999. Beyond overpopulation: A comment on Zawistowski et al. and Salman et al. *Journal of Applied Animal Welfare Science* 2(3): 217–228.

Humane Society of the United States (HSUS). 1999. Statement on free-roaming cats. Washington, D.C.: HSUS.

Johnson, T.P., T.F. Garrity, and L. Stallones. 1992. Psychometric evaluation of the Lexington Attachment to Pets Scale (LAPS). *Anthrozoös* 5(3): 160–175.

Kass, P.H., J.C. New Jr., J.M. Scarlett, and M.D. Salman. 2001. Understanding animal companion surplus in the U.S.: Relinquishment of nonadoptables to animal shelters for euthanasia. *Journal of Applied*

Animal Welfare Science 4(4): 237–248.

Lepper, M., P.H. Kass, and L.A. Hart. 2002. Prediction of adoption vs. euthanasia among dogs and cats in a California animal shelter. *Journal of Applied Animal Welfare Science* 5(1): 29–42.

Maddie's Fund. 2002. *http://www. maddies.org.*

Manning, A.M., and A.N. Rowan. 1992. Companion animal demographics and sterilization status: Results from a survey in four Massachusetts towns. *Anthrozoös* 5: 192–201.

Marx, M.B., and M.L. Furculow. 1969. What is the dog population? A review of surveys in the U.S. *Archives of Environmental Health* 19: 217–219.

Massachusetts Society for the Prevention of Cruelty to Animals (MSPCA). 1996. *Companion animal populations in Massachusetts.* A survey conducted for the MSPCA by Dorr Research Corporation. October.

Nassar, R., and J.E. Mosier. 1980. Canine population dynamics: A study of the Manhattan, Kansas, canine population. *American Journal of Veterinary Research* 41: 1798–1803.

Nassar, R., J.E. Mosier, and L.W. Williams. 1984. Study of the feline and canine populations in the greater Las Vegas area. *American Journal of Veterinary Research* 45: 282–287.

Neidhart, L., and R. Boyd. 2002. Companion animal adoption study. *Journal of Applied Animal Welfare Science* 5(3): 175–192.

New, Jr., J.C., M.D. Salman, J.M. Scarlett, P.H. Kass, J.A. Vaughn, S. Scherr, and W.J. Kelch. 1999. Moving: Characteristics of dogs and cats and those relinquishing them to 12 U.S. animal shelters. *Journal of Applied Animal Welfare Science* 2(2): 83–96.

New Jr., J.C., M.D. Salman, M. King, J.M. Scarlett, P.H. Kass, and J.M. Hutchison. 2000. Shelter relinquishment: Characteristics of shelter-relinquished animals and their owners compared with animals and their owners in U.S. pet-owning households. *Journal of Applied Animal Welfare Science* 3(3): 179–201.

Patronek, G.J. 1998. Free-roaming and feral cats—Their impact on wildlife and human beings. *Journal of the American Veterinary Medical Association* 212(2): 218–226.

Patronek, G.J., and A.N. Rowan. 1995. Determining dog and cat numbers and population dynamics. *Anthrozoös* 8(4): 199–205.

Patronek, G.J., and S. Zawistowski. 2002. The value of data. *Journal of Applied Animal Welfare Science* 5(3): 171–174.

Patronek, G.J., L.T. Glickman, and M.R. Moyer. 1995. Population dynamics and the risk of euthanasia for dogs in an animal shelter. *Anthrozoös* 8(1): 31–43.

Patronek, G.J., L.T. Glickman, A.M. Beck, G.P. McCabe, and C. Ecker. 1996a. Risk factors for relinquishment of dogs to an animal shelter. *Journal of the American Veterinary Medical Association* 209(3): 572–581.

———. 1996b. Risk factors for relinquishment of cats to an animal shelter. *Journal of the American Veterinary Medical Association* 209(3): 582–588.

Rowan, A.N. 1992a. Shelters and pet overpopulation: A statistical black hole. *Anthrozoös* 5(3): 140–143.

———. 1992b. Companion animal demographics and unwanted animals in the U.S. *Anthrozoös* 5(4): 222–225.

Rowan, A.N., and J. Williams. 1987. The success of companion animal management programs: A review. *Anthrozoös* 1(2): 110–122.

Salman, M.D., J.G. New, Jr., J.M. Scarlett, P.H. Kass, R. Ruch-Gallie, and S. Hetts. 1998. Human and animal factors related to the relinquishment of dogs and cats in 12 selected animal shelters in the U.S. *Journal of Applied Animal Welfare Science* 1(3): 207–226.

Salman, M.D., J. Hutchison, R. Ruch-Gallie, L. Kogan, J.C. New, Jr., P.H. Kass, and J.M. Scarlett. 2000. Behavioral reasons for relinquishment of dogs and cats to 12 shelters. *Journal of Applied Animal Welfare Science* 3(2): 93–106.

Savesky, K. 2001. *HSU case study: The Coastal SPCA.* Washington, D.C.: HSUS.

Scarlett, J.M., M.D. Salman, J.G. New, Jr., and P.H. Kass. 1999. Reasons for relinquishment of companion animals in U.S. animal shelters: Selected health and personal issues. *Journal of Applied Animal Welfare Science* 2(1): 41–57.

Schneider, R., and M.L. Vaida. 1975. Survey of canine and feline populations: Alameda and Contra Costa counties, California, 1970. *Journal of the American Veterinary Medical Association* 166: 481–486.

Staats, S., D. Miller, M.J. Carnot, K. Rada, and J. Turnes. 1996. The Miller-Rada commitment to pets scale. *Anthrozoös* 9(2/3): 88–94.

Wenstrup, J., and A. Dowidchuk. 1999. Pet overpopulation: Data and measurement issues in shelters. *Journal of Applied Animal Welfare Science* 2(4): 303–319.

Zawistowski, S., J. Morris, M.D. Salman, and R. Ruch-Gallie. 1998. Population dynamics, overpopulation, and the welfare of companion animals: New insights on old and new data. *Journal of Applied Animal Welfare Science* 1(3): 193–206.

Humane Education Past, Present, and Future

3

CHAPTER

Bernard Unti and Bill DeRosa

Introduction

From the earliest years of organized animal protection in North America, humane education—the attempt to inculcate the kindness-to-animals ethic through formal or informal instruction of children—has been cast as a fruitful response to the challenge of reducing the abuse and neglect of animals. Yet, almost 140 years after the movement's formation, humane education remains largely the province of local societies for the prevention of cruelty and their educational divisions—if they have such divisions. Efforts to institutionalize the teaching of humane treatment of animals within the larger framework of the American educational establishment have had only limited success. Moreover, knowledge, understanding, and empirical measures of the impact of humane education remain limited. In many respects humane education is best seen as an arena of untapped potential rather than one of unfulfilled promise.

The Origins of the Kindness-to-Animals Ethic

Appreciation for the value of cultivating kindness to animals in children flowed directly from John Locke's observations on the subject. Although others had made the point previously, in 1693 Locke offered the most prominent early statement of the need to correct children's cruelty. "This tendency should be watched in them, and, if they incline to any such cruelty, they should be taught the contrary usage," Locke wrote. "For the custom of tormenting and killing other animals will, by degrees, harden their hearts even toward men; and they who delight in the suffering and destruction of inferior creatures, will not be apt to be very compassionate or benign to those of their own kind" (Locke 1989).

Over time Locke's insight raised interest in the beneficial moral effect of childhood instruction favoring the kindly treatment of animals. Growing comprehension of the importance of childhood experience and its impact on youthful character sustained a robust transatlantic publishing industry devoted to the production of literature for children. In North America the first juvenile works infused with the humane didactic began to appear in the late 1790s and early 1800s. The earliest were reprints or excerpts of English titles, but the genre quickly gained important American enthusiasts, including Lydia Maria Child and Harriet Beecher Stowe (Pickering 1981; Unti 2002).

One explanation for the spread of the kindness-to-animals ethic lies in its consonance with the republican gender ideology of the post-revolutionary United States. Early American society assumed a set of paternalistic relationships both within and outside the family, emphasizing the importance of a virtuous citizenry devoted to republican principles of governance. This made education of the boy especially critical, since as a man he would assume authority over family, chattel, property, and social institutions. Responsibility for educating the child for his leadership role rested with women, who were assumed to be the repositories of gentle virtue, compassionate feeling, and devotion—buffers against the heartless struggle of the masculine public sphere. Humane education provided one means of insulating boys against the tyrannical tendencies that might undermine civic life were they to go unchecked. Animals were nicely suited for instruction that impressed upon the child their helplessness and dependence upon him and his considerable power over them (Kerber 1980; Grier 1999; Unti 2002).

The presence of the kindness-to-animals ethic in antebellum childhood experience had still broader implications for the process of class formation in North America. From the 1820s onward, sympathy with domestic animals, gradually encoded in education lessons for children, became an important means of inculcating such standards of bourgeois gentility as self-discipline, Christian sentiment, empathy, and moral sensitivity. Moreover, as a household companion, a domestic animal could serve as a convenient real life medium for the practice and expression of compassionate feelings. Merciful regard for animals became one hallmark of a developing middle-class culture rooted in Protestant evangelical piety (Grier 1999).

In addition to their sociocultural utility for instilling and enacting the principles of kindness and compassion, the presence of animals in children's literature fulfilled other didactic functions in nineteenth-century domestic ideology. Narratives of animal life offered idealized conceptions of middle-class family relationships and served as morality tales for human domestic relations. By their example the animal heroes of these narratives served to reinforce cherished norms of conduct and behavior (Grier 1999).

Over time such functions helped to consolidate the place of animals in the emotional framework of middle-class domestic life. By the 1850s the kindness-to-animals ethic was a staple of juvenile literature as well as a fixture of many middle-class homes. A generation before the advent of organized animal protection in America, the humane didactic was an established instrument of childhood socialization (Grier 1999; Unti 2002).

The Era of Organized Animal Protection

After the anti-cruelty societies formed in the late 1860s, humane education became a vital objective of a burgeoning social movement specifically devoted to the welfare of animals. In the earliest stages of anti-cruelty work, humane education referred broadly to the instruction of both adults and children. As the limits of law enforcement-centered approaches became clear, animal protectionists embraced early instruction in kindliness as a means of reducing adult crimes and prosecutions. Accordingly they shifted their emphasis to the education of children as a long-term response to the spread of

cruelty. Although many advocates adopted this approach, George T. Angell of the Massachusetts Society for the Prevention of Cruelty to Animals (MSPCA) stood at its forefront. Under Angell's leadership, the MSPCA and its sister organization, the American Humane Education Society (AHES), provided both the inspiration and the resources for humane education, which became central to the coalescence of a national animal protection movement during the last quarter of the nineteenth century (Angell n.d.).

Like the kindness-to-animals ethic itself, enthusiasm for humane education of children within organized systems of education predated the anti-cruelty societies, coinciding with the emergence of the common school movement. The massive influx of immigrants in the 1830s and 1840s led some educators to envision the school as a central instrument of assimilation, guiding immigrant children away from the "backward" cultures of their parents. Horace Mann (1796–1859), universal schooling's best-known proponent, based his educational philosophy on unlimited faith in the perfectibility of human beings and their institutions. His conviction that the public school could be the answer to all of the Republic's problems had roots in the deepest of American traditions, including Jeffersonian republicanism, Christian moralism, and Emersonian idealism. As Mann conceived the common school, it would be a guarantor of social order that reduced the destructive potential of class, political, or sectarian difference. This was not an unproblematic or unchallenged view, of course, and popular education was a subject of intense debate (Cremin 1969; Button and Provenzo 1983).

By 1860 Mann's ideals had reached fruition, with public schools operating in a majority of the states. Although their philosophies varied, supporters of the common schools hoped to improve children's character by inculcating morality and citizenship and to facilitate social mobility by promoting talent and hard effort. Through edu-

cation they would push young citizens toward what one reformer called the "civilized life" of order, self-discipline, civic loyalty, and respect for private property. Between 1860 and 1920, the common school movement, expanding its reach to include kindergarten, elementary, and secondary levels, became the dominant tradition in American education. During the same period, compulsory attendance requirements—rare before the Civil War—became universal, with Mississippi the one exception (Butts and Cremin 1953; Cremin 1969).

Mann recognized the value of humane instruction, noting that

> the good man grows in virtue, and the bad man grows in sin....From the youthful benevolence that rejoices to see an animal happy, one grows up into a world-wide benefactor, into the healer of diseases, the restorer of sight to the blind, the giver of a tongue to the dumb, the founder of hospitals....Another grows from cruelty to animals, to being a kidnapper, and enslaver, and seller of men, women, and children. (Mann 1861)

Over time, humane values were incorporated into formal systems of education, including those inspired by the object-teaching method associated with the State Normal School at Oswego, New York, and its president, Edward A. Sheldon (1823–1897) (Sheldon 1862).

Angell, influenced by Mann, stressed humane education's utility for ensuring public order, suppressing anarchy and radicalism, smoothing relations between the classes, and reducing crime. Humane education would be the solution to social unrest and revolutionary politics, he believed, and a valuable means for socializing the young, especially the offspring of the lower classes. Angell also appreciated the significance of the public school system as a forum for socialization in an increasingly secular society. He told the annual meeting of the American Humane Association (AHA) in 1885 that "the public school teachers have in the first fortnight of each school year, about four times as many children, and have them more hours, than the Sunday school teachers do during the whole year." Humane education provided a means of spreading the word that could be adapted easily by other advocates, especially women, in whatever region or situation they might be active. It did not require substantial funds, and anyone able and willing to work with children in the schools or elsewhere could participate (Unti 2002).

Angell's enthusiasm for humane education helped to make it one of the most important elements of animal protection work in the Gilded Age and the Progressive Era. The MSPCA directed tens of thousands of dollars toward the production and distribution of humane education literature, making it the preeminent source of such materials in the nation. It also invested time, effort, and funds toward the formation of Bands of Mercy. The English temperance movement's Bands of Hope, which rallied children against alcohol consumption and related evils, provided the model. Band of Mercy members pledged to "be kind to all harmless living creatures and try to protect them from cruel usage." Angell and Thomas Timmins, a minister who had assisted with the development of Bands of Mercy in his native England, introduced the concept to the United States in 1882. Timmins worked to form bands, while Angell strove to raise money and awareness (Timmins 1883). In 1889 this initiative coalesced as AHES.

From the 1870s onward, Angell had been on the lookout for suitable literature to guide the young toward the values of kindness. He found his ideal vehicle in *Black Beauty*, the novel dictated by a dying British invalid, Anna Sewell, and first published in 1878. In 1890 Angell circumvented copyright laws and brought out the first American edition under the auspices of AHES. In just two years, more than one million copies were in circulation. *Black Beauty* cast a long shadow over the field, and Angell, wishing to

inspire a canine analogue, advertised a contest for the purpose. The winning entry was *Beautiful Joe*, by Margaret Marshall Saunders of Nova Scotia. Later, a spate of autobiographical works—written by a host of maltreated animals—appeared, and the animal autobiography became a staple of humane literature. The other books in the AHES series anchored by *Black Beauty*—*Our Goldmine at Hollyhurst* (1893), *The Strike at Shane's* (1893), *Four Months in New Hampshire* (1894), and *For Pity's Sake* (1897)—were mainstays of the field well into the twentieth century. The books, along with cash awards, medallions, badges, and rewards of merit, were distributed in schools in recognition of good behavior, recitations, essays, acts of kindness, and other attainments (Sewell 1890; Anonymous 1893; Bray 1893; Saunders 1893; Barrows 1894; Carter 1897; Unti 2002).

In the post-Civil War period, the formation of character became "a new social religion and the dynamic for social change," especially for feminists and moral reformers. It was believed that the properly instructed child could resist temptation and internalize a morality consistent with middle-class ideals of social purity (Pivar 1973). Such preoccupation with youthful virtue provided humane advocates with both rationale and wider opportunities. The promotion of humane education as an antidote to depraved character and a panacea for numerous social ills brought animal protection into close alignment with other reform movements of the era. The movements for temperance, child protection, and humane treatment of animals, in particular, all reflected deep concerns about the ramifications of cruelty and violence for individuals, the family, and the social order. Each cause addressed issues that straddled the line between private and public spheres. Humane education work received an especially significant boost in the 1890s from the creation of the Department of Mercy as a division of the Women's Christian Temperance Union during

its "Do Everything" phase under Frances Willard (Unti 2002).

The Compulsory Humane Education Movement

The first discussion of compulsory humane education occurred in Massachusetts in the 1880s, and by 1886 George Angell had helped to secure a humane instruction mandate as part of compliance with an extant statute requiring "the teaching of humanity, universal benevolence, etc." By the early 1900s, the notion of a national campaign for compulsory humane education began to gather momentum. In 1905 William O. Stillman of AHA and professional educator Stella H. Preston formed the New York Humane Education Committee to advance a state requirement. In that same year, both Oklahoma and Pennsylvania passed state laws providing for moral and humane education. The Oklahoma legislation required humane instruction as part of the moral education of future citizens. Sponsors wanted educators

> to teach morality in the broadest meaning of the word, for the purpose of elevating and refining the character of school children... that they may know how to conduct themselves as social beings in relation to each other...and thereby lessen wrong-doing and crime.

The law mandated that one half hour each week be devoted to teaching "kindness to and humane treatment and protection of dumb animals and birds; their lives, habits and usefulness, and the important part they are intended to fulfil in the economy of nature" (Unti 2002).

In 1909 the compulsory humane education movement achieved its most important benchmark—the passage of legislation in Illinois that included sanctions for noncompliance and provisions for instruction in teacher-training schools. In November 1915 AHA adopted a resolution favoring establishment of compulsory humane education in every state, selecting the 1909 Illinois law as its model. However, of the twenty states that had humane education requirements in place by 1920, only two others—New York and Oklahoma—followed the Illinois model in providing sanctions for non-compliance. In New York compliance was tied to public funds, and the commissioner of education was directed to publicize the requirement (Unti 2002).

The emergence of the professional humane educator was a natural outgrowth of the compulsory humane education movement. The American Society for the Prevention of Cruelty to Animals (ASPCA) created a humane education department in 1916. The stated goal of the division was "not to do the humane education work in our schools, so much as to stimulate the work of the schools themselves." By the beginning of the academic year in autumn 1921, the ASPCA was promoting essay contests within the school system. That summer, the humane education department cooperated with four Lower East Side school districts in New York City to measure the effectiveness of humane propaganda with the children of the foreign-born. The activity the ASPCA chose to encourage was the rounding up of unwanted strays. During 1922 the department estimated that it had reached 300 New York City schools in the course of its work. Preston estimated that, in the summer of 1923, New York schoolchildren brought in more than 28,000 small animals from the streets. As an instrument of character development, the kindness ethic nicely served the goal of assimilation by exposing immigrant children to normative values and expectations (Shultz 1924; Unti 2002).

Throughout most of the nineteenth century, humane educators relied on eclectic anthologies and an array of didactic stories and novels devoted to kindness to animals. Many humane periodicals included selections for children, and some of these found their way into published works marked for use by Bands of Mercy (Firth 1883; Timmins 1883). In the 1890s, however, the first manuals and textbooks with systematic humane lesson plans, question and answer sets, and related offerings began to appear. In 1902 AHA formed a committee to promote the publication of textbooks that inculcated humane ideals and to draw up guidelines for publishers of children's textbooks. By 1930 about a dozen humane education titles had appeared (Unti 2002).

Here and there, progress in institutionalizing humane education ensued. In Colorado the State Teachers College adopted a course of study in ethical and humane education that was directed by the state's Bureau of Child and Animal Protection. For a time, humane advocates made efforts to canvass the meetings of the National Education Association (NEA), and it seems that animal protectionists were successful in their outreach to national and regional teaching organizations, as well as to school system administrators. In 1924 the NEA president endorsed humane education at the annual meeting of AHA (Unti 2002).

Despite such progress, the push for compulsory humane instruction was not necessarily instrumental in ensuring access or influence within the schools. The law was frequently a dead letter in those states where it was approved. Hostile and indifferent superintendents and teachers could ignore the statutes with little fear of recrimination, and effective texts and materials were not always readily available. Chicago, with its tradition of progressive experimentation in education, promised to be one place in which humane education might gain a significant foothold. But by 1923 advocates were casting doubt on the success of the movement for humane education even in Illinois. On the basis of her own experience in a small town outside New York City, a New York reformer concluded in the late 1930s that the law in her state was "unevenly observed," its enforcement usually contingent on "some superintendent, principal, or teacher with a kind heart, who personally has compelled action" (Shultz 1924; Krows 1938).

The Longevity and Impact of the Bands of Mercy

For years, *Our Dumb Animals* (the MSPCA's monthly magazine) reported extensively on the formation of Bands of Mercy. However, such reports were better reflections of speaking engagements than of actual clubs or groups that went on to continuous activity. Referring to the "sixty thousand branches of our American Bands of Mercy" in 1905, George Angell wrote, "What does this mean? It means that over sixty thousand audiences have been addressed on kindness both to human beings and the lower animals" (in Unti 2002, 588). Some years later AHES claimed that more than 103,000 bands had formed between 1882 and 1916. In 1922 Angell's successor, Francis Rowley, estimated that in forty years of activity, the Bands of Mercy had enrolled more than 4 million children (Unti 2002).

While admitting their positive influence, social scientist William Shultz underscored the "transitory character" of the bands. Where "no attempt is made to encourage them, they soon dissolve, leaving little or no effect upon the children's characters." AHA's William Stillman conceded that the bands "were not as carefully looked after or as rigorously followed up as they might be." Rowley believed that, in many cases, interest was sustained through the course of one school year, and that in successive years new bands would form at the instigation of teachers or humane educators who visited the schools again. In some cases, the bands enjoyed great longevity (Shultz 1924; Unti 2002).

In fact under Rowley's leadership AHES launched an ambitious effort to hold the bands together by maintaining humane educators in the field. None of the organizational initiatives of the early twentieth century matched the accomplishments of AHES in building and sustaining a cadre of humane missionaries during the period from 1910 to 1925. Educational outreach to the schools was especially robust in the pre-World War I years.

The success of the AHES initiatives depended heavily on its field representatives, at least some of whom were paid (Unti 2002). The field representatives were armed with a broad selection of humane education materials, including novels such as *Black Beauty*. By 1913 AHES was the world's largest publisher and distributor of humane literature by far. *Our Dumb Animals* enjoyed a monthly circulation of 60,000. In December 1916 931 new bands were reported, the largest figure ever for a one-month period, although one third of these formed in Massachusetts. That same year AHES estimated that it had spent more than $100,000 on literature and its distribution since 1882 (Unti 2002).

Once World War I began, the focus of many animal protection organizations shifted to war concerns. Not simply a distraction, however, the war threatened humane ideals more fundamentally as the United States prepared for battle. In the years before America joined the war, humanitarians could point to humane education as a powerful solution to the world's ills. With the war tearing Europe apart, American advocates cast it as an inoculant against the animosities and prejudices bred by conflict, and the guarantor of peace. But the wartime focus on preparedness also placed on the defensive humanitarians who had so closely identified themselves with anti-militarism. Humanitarians felt vulnerable to the charge that their own educational program would lead to the "softening" of American youth. Rowley met the matter straight on in an editorial, writing:

> Should anyone imagine that humane education means a generation of boys and girls with all iron sapped from their blood, a generation of cowards and cravens, he only reveals his total ignorance of what humane education is. The spirit of chivalry toward all the weak and defenseless, the hatred of injustice and cruelty. . . will make of the citizen, should the time demand it, a far better patriot and soldier than the selfish, bullying pugnacious spirit that often proclaims not a possible hero, but only an arrant coward. (in Unti 2002, 590)

In any case, once America entered the conflict, war animal relief filtered straight into Band of Mercy work and such other humane initiatives as Be Kind to Animals Week. The message of universal peace through humane education was subordinated to patriotic imperatives. The movement's most vital activity—its outreach to children—was reconfigured dramatically to serve the interests of American nationalism (Unti 2002).

The Failure of Institutionalization

It was not the war but the lack of success in institutionalizing humane education that led to its decline during the middle decades of the twentieth century. Very few of the initiatives launched by humane organizations gained the lasting attention of teacher-training institutions, and humane education certainly did not become a regular element of teacher preparation. The fate of a $100,000 donation to Columbia University in 1907, specifically earmarked for promoting humane education, was perhaps the most conspicuous setback on this front. Rather than direct the money toward Teachers College for studies and training in humane education, university president Nicholas Murray Butler used it to support a faculty position in social legislation. The funds disappeared into Columbia's general accounts and, with the exception of several historical studies, no progress toward the goal of the donor was realized (Unti 2002).

The Columbia initiative was the most significant missed opportunity in the history of humane education. Had the gift been allocated differently, it might have supported the review and validation of teaching methods and content; the resolution of differences between humane education, nature study, and science education; the development of a training program for humane education specialists; or the institutionalization of the kindness-to-animals ethic in the curriculum. However, the bias of Butler and the professors he consulted made it hard for them to take seriously such academic investigations of humane education (Unti 2002).

At least a few researchers in the pre-World War II era believed that humane education was a proper subject for scholarly inquiry. In 1931 concern for animals found its way onto the agenda of the Conference of Educational Associations, whose members came together annually to discuss educational theory and practice in Great Britain. That year Susan Isaacs, chair of the British Psychological Society's Education Section, spoke about her research concerning childhood socialization and attitudes concerning animals. Her method, applied in a small Cambridge school during the years 1924–1927, permitted children the greatest possible freedom to pursue their own interests. In her research Isaacs paid special attention to the conflicting tendencies toward cruelty and kindness to animals that she observed in children. She had proposed that educators should strive "to make a positive educational use of the child's impulses" so that children could be helped to reach "a more satisfactory psychological solution for their own internal conflicts." This method of instruction, she asserted, would become "an active influence in the building up of a positive morality of behavior towards animals, going beyond the mere negative standard of not being unkind to them, and expressed in an eager and intelligent interest in their life-histories, and a lively sympathy with their doings and happenings" (Isaacs 1930, 166).

Isaacs's special focus was on children's exposure to the death of animals and on dissection. The children she observed "showed greater sympathy with the living animals, and more consistent care, after they had 'looked inside' the dead ones, and fewer lapses into experimental cruelty," Isaacs reported. "In other words, the impulse to master and destroy was taken up into the aim of understanding. The living animal became much less of an object of power and possession, and much more an independent creature to be learnt about, watched and known for its own sake." Isaacs found that the children moved steadily toward the non-interfering, observational attitude of many modern naturalists, and developed a humane outlook and sense of responsibility toward their pets and toward animals in general (Isaacs 1930, 165–166).

Obviously, these findings, gathered in one school, could not be considered broadly representative or conclusive. Nevertheless, the very singularity of the approach taken by Isaacs and her colleagues makes one thing clear: fruitful research on children's psychological development and on the methods by which an attitude of respect and interest in animals could be inculcated was a neglected pursuit for much of the twentieth century.

The Mid-Twentieth Century

In the early twentieth century, arguments in favor of increased emphasis on education as distinct from practical relief work for animals surfaced regularly. If actively pursued, the emphasis on humane education promised to shift the balance of humane work. As an *Our Dumb Animals* editorialist, probably Rowley, optimistically predicted,

> More and more societies organized for the prevention of cruelty to animals will turn to the work of humane education. . .as their widest and most important field of service. Train the heart of the child aright, and the cruelty from which animals suffer will end far more quickly than by punishing the ignorant and cruel man. (Unti 2002, 610)

As it happened humane education did not become more central to the work of SPCAs in the years that followed. By the era of the Depression it had diminished greatly, as the practical and financial burdens of shelter and hospital work, animal control obligations, and law enforcement cast other initiatives, including humane education, to the margins of activity. What survived was the simple lesson of kindness to pets, carried into the schools by SPCA staff members and volunteers who continued to enjoy access to the earliest grades of elementary school. Changes (such as the advent of motor vehicles) that eliminated from Americans' daily experience the abuse of horses and other working animals rendered obsolete much of the earlier practical education concerning animal welfare. At the same time, the movement's educational focus, normally centered on acts of individual cruelty, failed to touch upon newer and socially sanctioned forms of animal use. Both self-censorship and the constraints imposed by educational institutions prevented humane education from reaching into the realm of the new cruelties—institutionalized uses of animals such as animal experimentation and the mass production of animals for food and fur that were well beyond the experience and influence of most individuals. Undoubtedly, too, the disillusionment wrought by war, depression, and other events deflated the grand claims and expectations expressed by Gilded Age and Progressive Era animal protectionists.

These considerations render the success of the campaign for compulsory humane education legislation highly ironic. Its clear relationship to moral instruction and the inculcation of good citizenship was endorsed in state houses all across America. Paradoxically, however, the determination to see such laws passed was not matched by commensurate effort to see them honored. In general, the cadre of SPCA activists committed to humane education dwindled, and efforts to see its principles enshrined in the curriculum of teachers' institutes and colleges failed (Unti 2002).

Ultimately, the difficulty of penetrating local and regional school system bureaucracies proved insurmountable for a movement with limited resources and more urgent concerns and responsibilities. Yet the blame for such failures should not be laid simply upon organized animal protection itself; the impact of countervailing forces was decisive. The classroom and the educational system were the subject of increasing struggles during the twentieth century, and the question of how humans ought to encounter and treat animals was implicated in several of these. Humanitarians were not the only ones with an interest in animals. Agricultural societies, industry associations, religionists, and science education groups also fought for a stake in shaping modern American education. Many of these interests promoted consumptive uses of animals that were at odds with humane imperatives (Unti 2002).

The fortunes of "nature-study," a contemporaneous education movement, were very similar to those of humane education, as both declined in the face of a professionalizing field of science instruction. The rise of a professional science education cadre, committed to the unification, rationalization, and standardization of American science curricula, crowded out both nature-study and humane education, incorporating some of their elements but ridding those elements of their romantic notions of affinity with nature and non-human animals. By the 1930s the term *elementary science* had subsumed nature-study, and humane education as a discrete subject of instruction was on the wane. As one scholar suggests, the "abstract rationalism" of biology instruction in the higher grades and in university courses also left little room for the empathy-building emphasis of nature-study and humane education approaches (Pauly 2002).

The anti-cruelty movement's overall loss of influence and lack of vitality in the interwar period also had its effect. Humane education suffered as much as any area of organized animal protection from the absence of enlightened and energetic leadership, and the loss of a receptive public. By World War II, organizations were using badly dated humane education materials, if any.

In some regions viable outreach programs undertaken by regional humane societies survived and enjoyed good access to public schools even during the mid-twentieth century decades (Matthewson 1942; Whyte 1948; Walter 1950; American Humane Association 1952). While humane education outreach now tended to focus on the treatment of companion animals and the benefits of keeping pets, it nevertheless reinforced the simple message of kindness to animals as an important standard of individual conduct. In addition, the kindness-to-animals ethic continued to resonate through children's literature (Oswald 1994) and other cultural media (Cartmill 1993). These influences certainly strengthened decades of effort aimed at promoting personal rectitude in dealings with animals.

After the post-World War II revival of organized animal protection (Unti and Rowan 2001), humane education gradually resurfaced as a priority of both national and local groups. In the mid-1960s, The HSUS began to invest serious attention and resources in humane education, collaborating with university researchers to formulate and test methods and techniques

of humane education. By the 1970s such efforts sparked the formation of a separate division of The HSUS, predecessor of the National Association for Humane and Environmental Education (NAHEE). Founded in 1973 NAHEE has become a preeminent source for information, research, and analysis in the field of humane education.

The Status Quo

Today the locus of humane education activity in the United States continues to be the animal care and control community, as elementary and secondary schools and colleges of education have yet to accept and integrate the teaching of most humane concepts into their curricula. Many animal care and control agencies (SPCAs, humane societies, animal rescue leagues, and the like) offer education programs in some form, working primarily at the municipal or county level. Such programs frequently involve partnerships with schools or other youth-oriented institutions.

What methodologies does humane education employ? What is being taught and how effectively? How significant is the role of youth education within the animal welfare movement?

A study conducted by Jaime Olin (2002), a graduate student at the Tufts University Center for Animals and Public Policy, provides some answers. Olin surveyed 600 animal shelters, selected at random from approximately 2,800 in existence nationwide, about the scope and nature of their efforts to teach children humane values. The results of her investigation paint a picture of humane education as a relatively widespread enterprise, yet one that typically is relegated to side issue status, addressed perfunctorily by most animal care and control organizations and simply ignored by others.

Of the 203 animal care and control agencies that responded to Olin's 32-item questionnaire, 144—71 percent—were classified as having a humane education program. Those respondents reported being involved in humane education for a median of ten years, and 42 percent reported relevant activity for between eleven and fifty years (Figure 1). The majority of shelters with humane education programs claimed reaching between 100 and 500 children per year, most of whom were of elementary school age (Figure 2). The vast majority of respondents—94 percent—indicated that they regard humane education as either "essential" or "very impor-

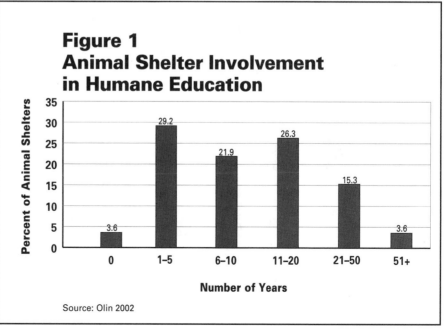

Figure 1
Animal Shelter Involvement in Humane Education

Source: Olin 2002

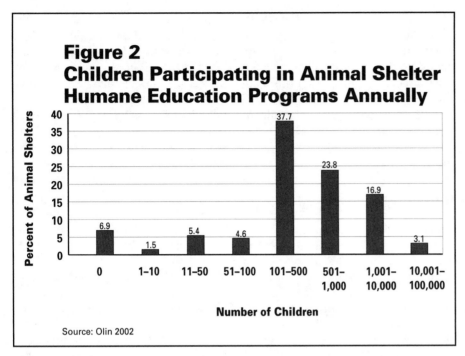

Figure 2
Children Participating in Animal Shelter Humane Education Programs Annually

Source: Olin 2002

tant" to their overall mission.

If classroom visits and shelter tours traditionally have been the educational methods of choice employed by animal shelters since the mid-twentieth century, then it appears from Olin's investigation that little has changed (Figure 3). Eighty-eight percent of respondents reported conducting classroom visits, and 77 percent included tours of their facilities in their programs. Fewer organizations reported offering youth community service programs (44 percent), junior volunteer programs (30 percent), after-school activities (23 percent), and summer camps (15 percent). Thirty-six percent reported serving as a source of curriculum-blended materials for classroom teachers. Children saw live animals in 86 percent of humane education programs and were allowed to touch an animal in 73 percent.

The content of humane education programs at the local level is dominated by companion animal issues (Figure 4). Olin's respondents indicated that responsible pet ownership accounted for an average of 49 percent of their programs' subject matter, safety around animals for 26 percent, and the role of animal shelters for 20 percent. On average, 8 percent of programming was devoted to wildlife issues, and 2 percent to topics related to farm animals. Obviously, this distribution of priority reflects the primacy of direct care and protection of companion animals in the missions and day-to-day activities of animal shelters. In addition, omission from youth education programs of such topics as intensive farming, the use of animals in research, and consumptive uses of wildlife may stem from other factors. These include the philosophical orientation of shelter administrators and boards of directors; sensitivity to local politics; the influence of competing and sometimes hostile interest groups; the view that such issues do not fall under the purview of animal care and control agencies; and the reluctance of school officials to accept special interest topics into the curriculum—especially those that may be considered age-inappropriate, inflammatory, or inimical to a community's values, traditions, or economic base.

Olin's investigation also reveals that 88 percent of local animal care and control agencies obtain at least a portion of their youth education materials from outside organizations. Materials were procured most often from national animal protection groups with a history of providing shelter-related services and disseminating youth education resources with a strong emphasis on companion-animal issues: The HSUS, the ASPCA, and AHA. Thirty-five percent of the respondents reported using *KIND News*, a classroom newspaper published by NAHEE. Sixty-four percent said they included their own materials in their programs.

If, prima facie, the above data shows humane education to be a vibrant enterprise, the deeper reality is that it remains a peripheral compo-

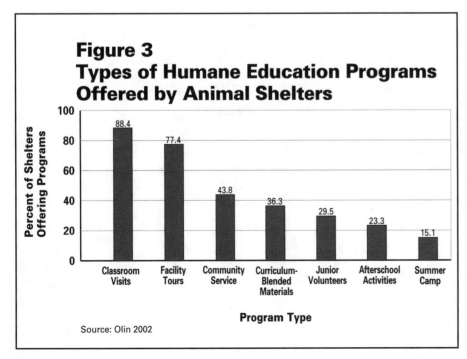

Figure 3
Types of Humane Education Programs Offered by Animal Shelters

Source: Olin 2002

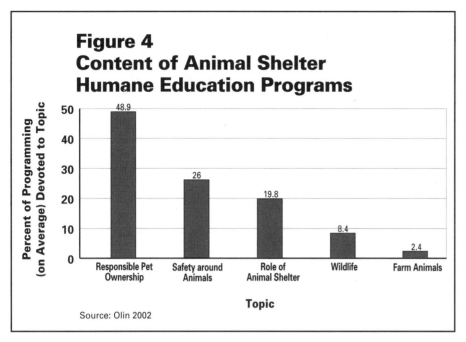

Figure 4
Content of Animal Shelter Humane Education Programs

Source: Olin 2002

57 percent of respondents said "media relations"; 51 percent said "adult education"; 33 percent said "animal behavior counseling"; 25 percent said "violence prevention"; and 23 percent said "pet therapy." Although some of those job duties are not unrelated to children, it is clear that youth education, per se, rarely is given the undivided attention of one or more staff members. That education personnel are spread thin is also reflected in the fact that an average of only 21 percent of children reached by Olin's respondents received more than one humane education intervention, e.g., more than one classroom visit or shelter tour, per year.

If youth education were a high priority in the animal care and control community, one might expect that formal education credentials would be a criterion in the hiring of staff assigned to teach children. Olin found, however, that only 15 percent of respondents reported that the staff member most directly involved with humane education had classroom teaching certification, while 50 percent cited "on-the-job-training" in lieu of such credentials. Twenty-four percent indicated that their education staff had informal teaching or youth leadership experience (Figure 9).

One of the most telling signs of generally tepid support for humane

nent of animal welfare activity, as it was throughout most of the last century. Despite the fact that a majority of local animal care and control agencies report offering humane education programs, have been doing so for quite some time, and regard humane education as mission-critical, commitment to youth education as measured by funding—perhaps the most salient measure—is anemic. Although the median annual budget reported by Olin's respondents was $200,000 (Figure 5), 63 percent of organizations with humane education programs reported allocating less than $1,000 to those programs, and only 21 percent reported having an annual humane education budget of $5,000 or more (Figure 6). Most respondents (74 percent) admitted that the amount of money budgeted for education was "not enough," while 26 percent said the amount their organizations had allocated was "just about right."

The animal care and control community's reluctance fully to embrace youth education also can be inferred from staffing-related data. Organizations responding to Olin's study reported a median of one paid education staff member (a significant number given that the median number of full-time, paid staff overall was four) and one education volunteer (Figure

7). But personnel responsible for youth education often are spread thin, charged with handling a wide variety of disparate job duties. For example, when asked to give the title of the person involved most directly with humane education, 26 percent of respondents indicated "shelter director," while only 12 percent cited "humane education director." Thirty-eight percent indicated "other," and in most cases, Olin found, that meant "animal control officer" (Figure 8).

When asked by Olin about other services performed by education staff,

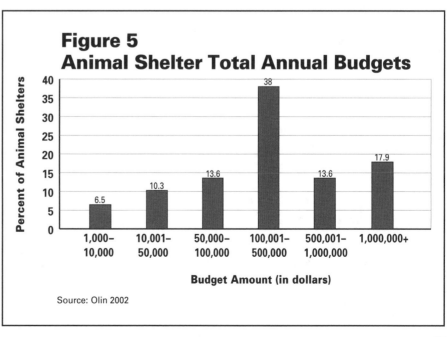

Figure 5
Animal Shelter Total Annual Budgets

Source: Olin 2002

education is that 29 percent of the organizations answering Olin's questionnaire did not respond to the item asking about the size of their education budget. Olin classified those organizations as not having a humane education program. While the assumption behind that classification (i.e., no education budget means no education program) may not be entirely valid, the fact remains that a significant number of animal care and control organizations make no effort to teach humane values to children, while most make a weak attempt at best. Why? Why would an undertaking that, at least intuitively, holds such promise for advancing the cause of animal protection and that was so energetically pursued during the early decades of the animal welfare movement be given such minimal attention nowadays by those most directly engaged in solving their communities' animal-related problems?

Answers from animal shelter professionals typically hinge on points about lack of time and/or funding—points raised, in fact, by some respondents to Olin's survey. Such rationales, however, beg the underlying question, since if youth education were seen as crucial to achieving animal protection objectives, time and funds to support it would be allocated

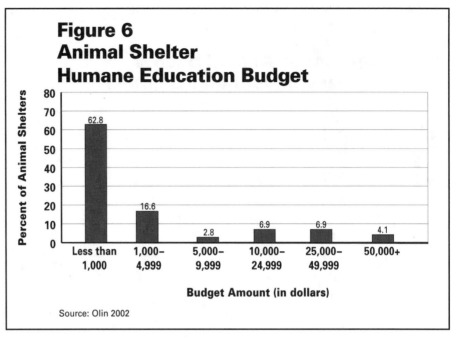

Figure 6
Animal Shelter
Humane Education Budget

Source: Olin 2002

or funds would be raised to augment existing budgets. Perhaps a more fundamental answer lies in the dilemma faced by animal care and control personnel: how can they meet basic, short-term needs—such as a community's need for adequate animal control and sheltering—and also reach broader, long-term goals, such as eliminating or significantly reducing animal abuse, neglect, and the overpopulation of companion animals? Although youth education is seen as an important means of permanently solving or preventing the problems animals face, it typically does not render the same immediate, tangible outcomes or level of emotional fulfillment as, for example, uniting a family with a homeless pet or rescuing a stray dog from the hardships of the street. In contrast its potential rewards may seem distant and abstract. So, while animal care and control professionals may view youth education as mission-critical in a long-range sense, it often is treated in the short term as a drain on resources that might otherwise be applied to more pressing, day-to-day concerns.

That seems to have been the prevailing reasoning for many years. In 1922 Francis Rowley speculated that the promise of immediate results was what kept so many humane advocates involved in direct relief of animals rather than humane education of subsequent generations (Unti 2002). It appears that similar forces are at work now. As a result, youth education continues to be a marginal if not entirely dispensable facet of animal welfare work in the United States.

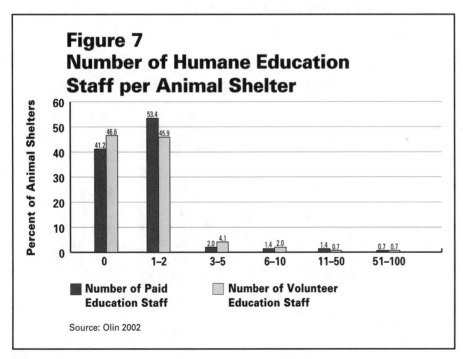

Figure 7
Number of Humane Education
Staff per Animal Shelter

■ Number of Paid
Education Staff

□ Number of Volunteer
Education Staff

Source: Olin 2002

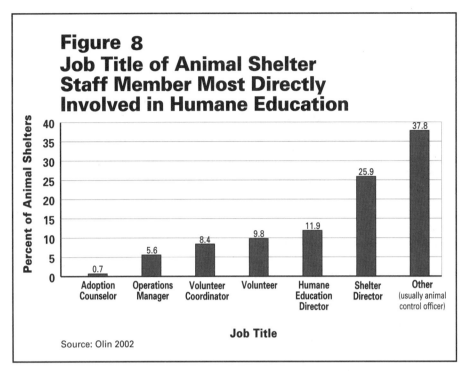

Figure 8
Job Title of Animal Shelter Staff Member Most Directly Involved in Humane Education

Percent of Animal Shelters

Adoption Counselor	Operations Manager	Volunteer Coordinator	Volunteer	Humane Education Director	Shelter Director	Other (usually animal control officer)
0.7	5.6	8.4	9.8	11.9	25.9	37.8

Job Title

Source: Olin 2002

Can Humane Values Be Taught?

If, as suggested, a lack of immediate—or at least immediately visible—results is a disincentive for humane organizations to expend resources on youth education, it would seem that definitive empirical evidence demonstrating the effectiveness of humane education programs would provide an important incentive. That is, if the intended benefits of teaching humane values to children (e.g., gains in general knowledge about animal protection issues and the development of positive attitudes and behavior toward animals) were consistently brought to light through program evaluation, perhaps humane education would come to be seen as more of an urgent imperative than an abstract panacea. But there is an obvious Catch-22 here: an interest in spending time and money to assess the effects of a humane education initiative presupposes a relatively high level of interest in committing resources to humane education in general, and such willingness has been in short supply.

Consequently, relatively little empirical evidence exists showing that humane education programs increase children's knowledge about or improve their attitudes and behavior toward animals. None exists showing that such gains are carried into adulthood. The issue is not that there is proof to the contrary—indeed, intuition, anecdotal evidence, and a handful of formal studies suggest that humane education *can* work. Rather,

it is simply that humane education initiatives typically are not subjected to formal evaluation to test their efficacy. Of the organizations responding to Olin's survey, for example, only 7 percent reported formally evaluating their programs. Given the relatively low level of support for humane education, this assessment gap is not surprising. But it is significant, for two reasons: first, a lack of formal evaluation limits understanding of what methodologies are most and least effective and how humane education programs can be improved; and, second, it deprives animal protection advocates of an important tool for convincing school officials, colleges of education, and the public that humane education is a worthwhile pursuit that deserves funding and representation in standard curricula.

Empirical studies conducted over the last twenty-five years have tended to show that education programs can indeed generate gains in knowledge of animal protection issues, improvement in attitudes toward animals, and improvements in *projected* behavior toward them. Positive results have been inconsistent, however, and investigations have not been undertaken to determine whether humane education results in positive changes in *actual* behavior related to animals.

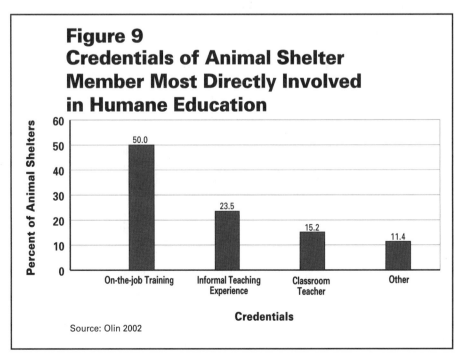

Figure 9
Credentials of Animal Shelter Member Most Directly Involved in Humane Education

Percent of Animal Shelters

On-the-job Training	Informal Teaching Experience	Classroom Teacher	Other
50.0	23.5	15.2	11.4

Credentials

Source: Olin 2002

The special challenges associated with assessing actual behavior toward animals—such as cost, difficulty of observation, and potential harm to animals and children—have, no doubt, hindered such inquiries.

Systematic research to test the effects of general approaches to humane education and specific programs peaked during the 1980s. Several studies conducted early in that decade relied on the Fireman Tests, assessment tools that presented children with a story about a boy whose house is burning down and who is given the opportunity to ask a firefighter to save certain household items (Vockell and Hodal 1980). A list of ten items is given, consisting of seven inanimate objects, such as a television and a checkbook, and three animals: a dog, a cat, and a canary. The tests asked children to select three items from the list which they think the boy in the story should tell the firefighter to save, the rationale being that the more positive an individual's attitudes toward animals, the more likely it is that he or she will choose the dog, cat, and canary for rescue. The first investigation employing the Fireman Tests sought to evaluate the effects that a single classroom presentation conducted by a visiting humane educator had on attitudes of third through sixth-grade students, compared with simply giving the children reading material (Vockell and Hodal 1980). The researchers found that the one-time presentation had no more impact on attitudes than did distributing the literature. The omission of a pretest from the study design, however, made interpreting those results problematic (Ascione 1992).

A year later another Fireman Tests study analyzed the impact of three different humane education treatments on the attitudes of fifth and sixth-grade students in Jefferson County, Colorado (Fitzgerald 1981). The three approaches tested were: light-treatment—reading material with no instruction; intensive treatment—reading material with one instruction session; and repeated treatment—reading material with four instruction sessions over a two-month period. (A control group received no instruction or materials.) The lessons and reading material focused on responsible pet ownership and related topics. In contrast to the earlier study, results showed that, although all three interventions led to an increase in positive attitudes toward animals, the intensive, one-lesson treatment had a greater positive impact on attitudes than did the reading material alone. Somewhat unexpectedly, however, the repeated treatment was not found to be more effective than the one-time presentation. The researcher suggested that the more focused nature of the intensive treatment contributed to its success compared with the repeated intervention, the content of which was only loosely connected. No differences in test scores were found between boys and girls or between fifth and sixth-graders.

Contradicting the results of that investigation was a similar one designed by the Animal Rescue League of Boston. Relying on the Fireman Tests as the assessment tool, the Boston evaluation found that a repeated humane education treatment consisting of lessons and materials presented over a period of several days had a greater positive effect on the attitudes of fourth and fifth-graders toward animals than either a one-time presentation or reading materials without instruction (Malcarne 1983). The fact that the repeated intervention in this case took place over a fairly concentrated period of time may have contributed to its success compared with the more diluted, two-month repeated treatment employed in the Jefferson County study.

An innovative study during the same period analyzed the effects of role-play as an empathy-building technique. Malcarne (1981) found that playing the role of animals is an effective means for children to increase their empathy with animals and that playing the role of children helps to increase empathy with other chil-

dren. Children who had been induced to empathize with animals, however, showed little tendency to extend that increased empathy to other children. That finding calls into question the validity of the transference theory, which holds that positive attitudes toward animals are transferable, or will generalize, to humans—a tacit assumption in much humane literature. Findings casting doubt on the transference theory also have been reported by Ray (1982) and Paul (2000), while Poresky (1990), Ascione (1992), and O'Hare and Montminy-Danna (2001) have found evidence to support it.

In one of the few efforts during the early 1980s to assess the impact of humane education on older children, Cameron (1983) compared the effects of two intensive, classroom-based interventions on the attitudes of eighth-graders. One relied on print material and media-based instruction (films and filmstrips), the other on print material and lecture-method instruction. A control group received no materials or instruction. Students receiving media-based treatment showed the greatest improvement in attitudes. The lecture treatment group also improved but to a lesser extent, while the control group showed no positive change in attitudes.

The Humane Education Evaluation Project

Perhaps the most ambitious attempt at program assessment was NAHEE's Humane Education Evaluation Project. In that investigation, Ascione, Latham, and Worthen (1985) sought to measure the impact of a curriculum-blended approach to teaching humane values, using as the prototype NAHEE's *People and Animals: A Humane Education Curriculum Guide*. The guide consisted of more than 400 classroom activities, each designed to teach a humane concept along with a skill or concept in language arts, social studies, math, or science. The study involved more than 1,800 children in kindergarten through sixth grade and 77 teachers from various urban, suburban, and rural school districts in Connecticut and California. Using a battery of instruments developed by the Western (formerly Wasatch) Institute for Research and Evaluation, the investigation was designed to test the effects of a relatively weak treatment: teachers were required to lead only twenty activities (the equivalent of about ten hours of instruction) from the curriculum guide over the course of an entire school year. The objective was to evaluate the materials as they realistically might be applied during a typical school year by teachers with many other curriculum requirements to meet. The instruments were designed to measure the curriculum guide's effect on (1) children's knowledge of animals; (2) their attitudes toward animals; (3) their projected behavior toward animals, i.e., their perceptions of how they *would* behave in situations that allowed humane or inhumane behavior; and (4) whether children's attitudes toward animals transferred, or generalized, to people. The assessment tools were administered as pretests and posttests to the study sample, which was divided into an experimental and control group, the latter receiving no instruction from the NAHEE curriculum guide at any point in the school year.

Results showed statistically significant gains in knowledge as a result of the curriculum guide intervention at the kindergarten and first-grade levels. Knowledge scores of second through sixth-grade children in the experimental group also improved, though not to a statistically significant degree. Attitudes toward animals improved along similar lines: kindergarten and first-grade children in the experimental group showed significantly more humane attitudes than their counterparts in the control group. Although experimental-group children at the higher grades also

showed improvement, generally their attitude gains were not pronounced enough to be statistically significant. The researchers suggested that the disparity in the treatment effects between the younger and older children may have been due to the possibility that conceptual knowledge and attitudes are more malleable at the earlier grades, or that baseline levels of knowledge and attitudes are lower at the earlier grades, leaving more room for improvement. They also cited the weak treatment as a possible factor in the inconsistency of experimental-group gains.

The NAHEE study's examination of projected behavior produced results that were somewhat the reverse of the knowledge and attitude findings in terms of age-group comparisons. At the kindergarten through third-grade level, the projected behavior scores of experimental-group children did not differ significantly from control group scores. In contrast, at the fourth through sixth-grade levels, the experimental group showed significantly more humane attitudes than did the control group. Why did older children respond more humanely on this measure, while younger students showed greater gains on the knowledge and attitude tests? According to the researchers, test format could have had an influence. The knowledge and attitude scales were composed of multiple-choice or yes/no items, which gave children a choice from which to select an answer. The instrument used to test projected behavior, on the other hand, required children to describe verbally the scenario depicted in a drawing, formulate a response to the situation, and explain why they responded as they did—tasks that the older children may have been developmentally more prepared to handle than were the younger students. In addition the researchers surmised that teachers at the higher grades may have been more likely than those at the lower grades to focus their instruction on the intentions and rationale behind humane behavior.

To determine if humane attitudes

toward animals would extend to people, the NAHEE project researchers developed two instruments: the Attitude Transfer Scale (ATS), which used photos depicting situations involving other children to which students could respond with varying degrees of kindness and compassion; and the Revised Aggression Scale (AG), a multiple-choice instrument that presented school and home situations to which children might react with varying degrees of aggression. (The AG was administered only to children in grade three and above.) Results of the ATS and AG showed no statistically significant differences between experimental and control group children at any grade except fourth. Surprisingly, fourth-grade boys in the experimental group had lower interpersonal kindness scores on the ATS than did their counterparts in the control group. Fourth-grade experimental-group children (girls and boys) also scored more aggressively on the AG than did fourth graders in the control group. The researchers noted, however, that the fourth-grade experimental-group scores were on the kind and non-aggressive ends of the continuum of scores for the attitude transfer measures.

Despite its somewhat ambiguous findings, the Humane Education Evaluation Project produced some encouraging—and intriguing—results overall. The instruments that were created, the conclusions reached, and the insights gained were valuable in providing direction for subsequent research and can aid in development and refinement of humane education methodologies.

Recent Research

Humane education program evaluation continued sporadically in the years following NAHEE's landmark study. In 1988 the MSPCA completed an extensive investigation to examine the impact of its statewide humane education program on the animal-welfare-related knowledge and attitudes of second through fifth-graders. Third, fourth, and fifth-grade children received three instruction sessions, and the investigation found gains in their knowledge and attitudes. This was not the case, however, among second-graders, who were exposed to a single classroom presentation. The researchers concluded that results were positive but limited, and suggested that a more marked impact might be achieved by consolidating the program, i.e., delivering a more intense intervention (Davis et al. 1988).

In a follow-up to the Humane Education Evaluation Project, Ascione (1992) assessed a treatment employing NAHEE's *People and Animals* curriculum guide and other materials in thirty-two first, second, fourth, and fifth-grade classrooms. Pretests and posttests were administered to assess changes in children's attitudes toward animals and human-directed empathy. (The attitude measure was the same as that used in the 1985 study.) Results showed that the intervention enhanced fourth-graders' humane attitudes to a statistically significant degree. In addition fourth-grade scores revealed a significant generalization, or transfer, effect from animal-related attitudes to human-directed empathy. Fifth-grade children in the experimental group also showed more humane attitudes than did the control group, though the difference was not statistically significant. Ascione suggested the more modest gains among fifth-graders were due to the fact that fifth grade control group teachers reported substantially more instruction related to humane education than their experimental group counterparts. (Ascione noted that restricting the content of control group teachers' instruction for purposes of the study would have been unacceptable.) No statistically significant effects on attitudes or human-directed empathy were found at the first and second-grade levels, although the first-grade experimental group children did show some gain in humane attitudes over first-grade children in the control group. In comparing those results to the more pronounced gains from the 1985 study, Ascione noted that the

mean attitude scores of the first and second-grade control and experimental groups were higher (more humane) than the mean attitude scores from the 1985 investigation. One reason, the researcher suggested, was the possibility that the children participating in the 1992 study were more aware of and better educated on humane and environmental issues than were their 1985 counterparts. If that was the case, by 1992 scores on the instrument used to measure the younger children's attitudes may have been reaching a "ceiling," which would make detecting differences between control and experimental groups more difficult. Ascione noted that the scale used to measure the older children's attitudes was less susceptible to such ceiling effects.

As a follow-up to the 1992 investigation, Ascione and Weber (1996) tested fifth-grade students who had participated a year earlier in the above study to determine if the effects found when they were fourth-graders were maintained. Results showed that fourth-graders who had received the *People and Animals* intervention the previous year scored higher on humane attitudes scales than did those who had not. Once again a generalization effect from attitudes toward animals to human-directed empathy was found. The researchers interpreted their findings as evidence that classroom-based, curriculum-blended humane education can be an effective means of developing sensitivity in children toward animals and people.

Positive results also were found by O'Hare and Montminy-Danna (2001) in a comprehensive evaluation of a humane education program for third and seventh-grade students. The program was offered by the Potter League for Animals, an animal care and control organization serving southeastern Rhode Island. The Potter League study was unique in that it employed qualitative research methods as well as more typical, quantitative techniques. It included the following components: (1) the administration of a true/false pretest

and posttest to determine the Potter League program's effect on animal-welfare-related knowledge, attitudes, and projected behavior; (2) a measure of attitude transference obtained by comparing pretest results with scores from instruments designed to gauge children's human-directed empathy and quality of peer relations; and (3) an examination of the intellectual, affective, and behavioral responses of children to the program through the use of student and teacher focus groups and classroom observation. The study sample consisted of 181 third-graders, who took part in eight weekly forty-five-minute classroom lessons, and 152 seventh graders, who participated in five weekly forty-five-minute lessons. The third-grade lessons covered such areas as basic pet care, the role of animal shelters, and safety around animals; the seventh-grade lessons covered animals in entertainment, endangered species, pet overpopulation, and animal-related moral dilemmas.

The Potter League investigation revealed statistically significant gains in knowledge, attitudes, and intended behavior at both the third and seventh-grade levels. In addition the examination of attitude transference indicated that children who were more knowledgeable about and favorably disposed toward animals also were more likely to respond with greater empathy to people and have better relationships with peers. Qualitative analysis yielded a wide range of information, most of which reflected positively on the Potter League program. Conclusions regarding the third-grade intervention included that the children enjoy the program (especially the opportunity to relate stories about their pets), that concepts are presented in a clear, age-appropriate manner, and that positive behavior toward animals is constantly reinforced throughout the program. During focus groups third-graders related evidence of behavior change, some stating that they had begun to spend more time with their pets, had stopped hitting or teasing them, or had shared their new knowledge with friends and family members.

At the seventh-grade level, classroom observations revealed that the Potter League material was presented in a way that allowed students to see both sides of controversial issues, that the program stressed the positive impact a single individual can have, and that it appeared to have an immediate effect on some students. (One boy, for example, said he would no longer shoot birds.) The researchers also noted that some seventh-grade students appeared somber after discussions of particularly hard-hitting issues. During focus groups several seventh graders, like their third-grade counterparts, suggested that their behavior had changed or would change as a result of the Potter League program. Some, for example, indicated that they had become kinder toward their pets and would be more willing to speak up about mistreatment of companion animals. Most seventh-grade students expressed concern about the uses of animals in entertainment and stated that they would curtail participation in activities that involved the mistreatment of animals. A few, however, thought the program's emphasis on the cruelty of circuses and other forms of entertainment was overstated. The findings of the Potter League evaluation were overwhelmingly positive, though the investigators noted several limitations of the study (i.e., that it lacked a control group; it did not measure the retention of cognitive or attitudinal gains over time; and its outcomes were based on the presentation of a program by only one instructor), and thus advised caution in interpreting its results. Nevertheless, the project generated a host of recommendations useful to the Potter League's education personnel—and potentially to others in the field—and represents an important contribution to the body of knowledge concerning the effectiveness of school-focused humane education programs.

Although the above survey of humane education program evaluation is not exhaustive, existing research still is too limited to tell us definitively whether children can be taught to think and behave kindly toward animals or what the best instructional methods might be. The empirical evidence compiled thus far, however, suggests that humane education has promise. Moreover, investigations such as those reviewed here are significant not just for what they may prove or disprove, but also for the questions they raise and the directions they provide for future inquiry. Do gains resulting from elementary-level humane education initiatives extend into the teen years and beyond? Do improvements in projected behavior translate into more humane behavior in fact? At what ages is humane education most effective? What impact, if any, do instructor enthusiasm and teaching style have on the efficacy of humane education interventions? Such are just a few of the questions waiting to be addressed in a field that is ripe for study, not only because of the paucity of existing research, but also because humane education seems especially relevant at a time when the connection between childhood cruelty to animals and interpersonal violence in adulthood is widely known, and the perceived moral decline of our nation's youth is a common and increasingly fervent lament.

The Road Ahead

Vitalizing humane education research would create a solid foundation on which to build a more prominent, influential humane education movement. A substantial body of empirical evidence not only would provide humane educators with the knowledge necessary to develop effective pedagogical strategies, it also would lend much-needed credibility and recognition to humane education as a serious discipline. Animal care and control organizations can become involved in humane education program evaluation in a variety of ways that need not be prohibitively elaborate, expensive, or time-consuming. Assessment can be as basic as interviewing teachers to ascertain whether and how they are using humane education materials provided to them. It can entail simply identifying program objectives, and administering brief surveys to students or teachers to determine whether those objectives, e.g., positive changes in attitudes toward animals, are being met. Even evaluation efforts as limited as these can provide valuable information that ultimately can help an agency make the most effective, efficient use of its humane education resources. Several national organizations, such as NAHEE and the Character Education Partnership, offer guides to basic program assessment. In addition, copies of the instruments used to assess the impact of the *People and Animals* curriculum guide in the 1985 Humane Education Evaluation Project are available from NAHEE and can be adapted for use in assessing other humane education initiatives.

Certainly, conducting rigorous experimental investigations of the impact of humane education programs requires expertise and resources beyond the reach of most animal shelters. But providing the impetus for such investigations and facilitating them does not. By partnering with college and university academic departments (including education, child development, social work, and psychology), animal protection organizations engaged in youth education can provide the subject matter for study and access to teachers, children, and classrooms. In return, academic institutions can offer expertise in instrument development, study design, and data analysis, as well as a pool of graduate and undergraduate students in search of topics for senior projects, master's theses, and doctoral internships and dissertations. In addition, since both universities and animal-protection agencies typically are skilled in the art of fundraising—and often have established relationships with philanthropic institutions—partnerships between the two can be mutually beneficial when it comes to obtaining grants to fund humane education research.

Back-to-Basics Revisited

Closing the assessment gap will not, by itself, ensure the advancement of humane education. Insofar as giving the teaching of humane values a more prominent, permanent place in American schools remains a goal, the chief obstacle continues to be humane education's identity as a special interest. Traditionally, special interests have been objectionable to school administrators, and low priorities for teachers (Underhill 1941; Westerlund 1982). The back-to-basics movement of the 1970s and 1980s rendered humane education and other special interests all the more superfluous to educators facing declining test scores and general complaints that children were advancing to higher grades with substandard reading, writing, and math skills. Today, back-to-basics thinking is reflected in the adoption of state curriculum standards by all states except Iowa, where directives regarding curriculum content are generated at the district level (Topics Education Group 2001). Curriculum standards enforced by state departments of education or school districts, combined with a growing emphasis on standardized testing (teacher career advancement is often directly tied to test scores now) has made schools and teachers more accountable—and more pressed for time. Consequently, winning representation in the classroom for the issues of special interest groups, including animal protection organizations, has become an increasingly formidable challenge.

Meeting that challenge will require that animal protection professionals keep the needs of teachers and schools paramount—a simple but sometimes overlooked precept. Failure to convince school officials of the importance of teaching humane values often has resulted from an inability or unwillingness on the part of humane education advocates to articulate the benefits of their programs within the framework of teachers' and administrators' priorities (Wester-lund 1982). For humane educators, recognizing school priorities typically has meant creating lessons and materials that are "curriculum-blended," i.e., provide instruction in core subject areas—math, English, science, and social studies—as well as convey a humane message. A prerequisite for the success of school-focused humane education initiatives in the future will be the addition of another dimension to curriculum blending: the alignment of humane education programs with state curriculum standards. Indeed, in their report to the Potter League, O'Hare and Montminy-Danna (2001) recommend that the league collaborate with school officials to tie its programs to curriculum standards. Teachers and administrators are likely to be more receptive to the teaching of humane values if they know specifically which curriculum standards a particular humane education program or lesson plan will help them meet. The task of linking lessons to curriculum standards need not be burdensome for humane educators. On the contrary, various Web resources, e.g., *www.explorasource.com*, provide ready access to all state curriculum standards, and the standards themselves can serve as valuable guideposts in developing pedagogical objectives and humane education program content.

The Character Connection

An obvious but not yet thoroughly exploited strategy for ensuring future representation for humane content in school curricula—and for invigorating humane education in general—is alignment with character education, an incarnation of the back-to-basics trend in the moral education realm. Today character education typically refers to the teaching of "core" or "consensus" values, basic principles of right and wrong, which, proponents argue, transcend political, cultural, and religious differences. In a return to a more traditional, virtues-centered moral education model, and in response to the widespread public perception that our youth have fallen into a state of moral decline, the modern character education movement departs sharply from the values-clarification trend of the 1960s and 1970s. While recognizing that debate about moral issues has an important place in the classroom, character education seeks not to assist children in clarifying their own personal values but to train them to develop certain fundamental character traits. Typically those traits include respect, responsibility, caring, fairness, and citizenship—principles that have formed the conceptual underpinnings of humane education since its inception. Over the last twenty years, the character education movement has benefited from growing public and legislative support and significant government funding (DeRosa 2001). In 2002 $25 million in federal grants was made available to state departments of education for the development and implementation of character education programs (Grenadier 2002). Such programs already have been incorporated into the curricula of thousands of schools nationwide, and the movement shows no signs of weakening.

The rise of character education and its conceptual symmetry with humane education present animal protection organizations with a clear opportunity for blending the teaching of humane values into school curricula. Relying on the widely recognized effectiveness of animal-related content for capturing children's attention and imagination, humane education has great potential for enriching and enlivening lessons in core values, making abstract concepts such as respect and responsibility more accessible and engaging for children. By providing programs that focus on the ways in which treating animals humanely is an essential part of good character, humane educators can serve as valuable resources to classroom teachers who increasingly are being required to incorporate formal character education lessons into their classroom activities (DeRosa 2001).

Alternative Methodologies

Aligning humane education program content with state standards and character education curricula will help ensure that proposals to introduce the teaching of humane values in schools will be well received by teachers and administrators. Actually institutionalizing humane education in schools—i.e., making the schools themselves a primary source of instruction in humane values—and providing teachers with the necessary training, tools, and motivation will require a reexamination of traditional humane education methodology. Standard practices such as classroom visits and shelter tours typically relegate the classroom teacher to the role of bystander, involved marginally at most in the presentation of humane concepts and lessons. Such approaches can reinforce the notion of humane education as a novelty or special interest, exclusively the purview of the animal protection organization, and both separate from and subordinate to core curricula. Making schools partners in the propagation of a humane ethic will involve, at the very least, cultivating ongoing working relationships with teachers and administrators. Creating humane education committees, composed of teachers representing target schools, to assist in the development of curriculum-blended interventions may be an effective first step in fostering such collaboration. Inevitably, however, integrating humane education in school curricula will require that animal protection professionals divert at least some of their attention from instructing children directly. Conducting professional-development workshops for teachers and providing them with instructional materials (aligned, ideally, with state standards and character education curricula), for example, will help transfer the locus of humane education from the animal protection organization to the schools themselves. Such an approach will enable humane educa-

tors to reach, albeit indirectly, more children more consistently than would be possible through classroom visits or shelter tours.

In addition to teacher training and support, other school-focused strategies may provide animal protection organizations with opportunities to maximize their impact while limiting the expenditure of time and money. These include the use of technology-based methodologies, such as chat rooms and videoconferencing, to link elementary and secondary teachers and their students to animal care and control professionals and to provide virtual field trips (Finch 2001). By positioning themselves as service learning sites, organizations with a particular interest in reaching teens— an audience traditionally neglected by humane education— also will benefit from the growth of service learning as an educational model in American high schools (Winiarskyj 2002). Working with education departments in colleges and universities to introduce the teaching of humane values in relevant courses will ensure that new teachers are familiar with humane education and that they understand its connection to character education and other curriculum areas. In shifting their primary role from practitioner to trainer and facilitator, humane education professionals can benefit from assistance offered by various national animal protection organizations—some of which offer supplementary classroom materials for the elementary and secondary levels—as well as training in such areas as the creation and implementation of teacher in-service workshops and strategies for reaching teens.

Exploring potentially more effective, efficient alternatives to traditional humane education practices may also take animal protection organizations away from the schoolhouse entirely. Savesky (2002) has argued that obstacles to classroom access, such as increased emphasis on standards and testing, have made school-focused approaches inefficient or unfeasible for many organizations. While access to classrooms and gen-

eral receptiveness to humane education will vary among school districts, animal care and control agencies may indeed find that non-school options provide an expedient use of limited resources. Such options may also provide a means of broadening programming beyond companion animal issues in cases where school officials are resistant to accepting potentially controversial subject matter into the curriculum. Strategies employed by organizations either as supplements to or replacements for school programs have included summer youth camps; family humane education programs; interactive shelter-based exhibits; programs designed to instill empathy in youth at risk for violent or antisocial behavior; Web-based instructional material on a broad range of animal issues; and the creation of partnerships with social service agencies, law enforcement, and pet product retailers. Other potentially productive non-school strategies include reaching out to faith-based youth organizations, home-schooled children, and after-school programs, especially those serving communities where children and families and their animals may be at high risk for abuse or neglect (D. McCauley, personal communication with B.U., July 3, 2002).

Ultimately, the success of any methodology, whether school-based, shelter-based, or dependent on collaboration with some other agency, will be measured primarily by a single standard: its effectiveness in improving children's attitudes and, most important, behavior toward animals. As a result commitment to a particular strategy must be accompanied by the resolve continually to evaluate it and, if necessary, improve or abandon it.

Conclusions

Virtually unlimited faith in the influence of humane education has long been a hallmark of organized animal protection in the United States. From an early stage, the humane movement pinned its hopes on education as the remedy to cruel treatment of animals by future generations. However, the movement has not supported humane education with practical and financial resources commensurate with this expressed interest. Moreover, the effects of humane education outreach remain unclear, and, for a variety of reasons, the work of promoting kindness to animals through school programs proceeds with limited prospect for measuring results and outcome. The movement's inability to institutionalize the teaching of humane education in teacher-training schools and related institutions has restricted its influence, and the penetration of humane education programs run by humane societies has proceeded unevenly where it has proceeded at all.

Nevertheless, there is no question that the diffusion of humane values throughout American culture has advanced in the years since the advent of organized animal protection in 1866. Whatever the level of success on other fronts of humane work, wanton acts of individual cruelty against animal pets are now usually seen as the signs of a maladjusted and sick personality. Conversely a kind disposition toward such animals is considered an important attribute of the well-adjusted individual (Lockwood and Ascione 1998). Humane education undoubtedly has reinforced such ideas about healthy social and psychological development. Indeed, it is unlikely that such awareness could have coalesced in the absence of a movement that accepted this perspective as a commonplace and pursued extensive measures to carry the lessons of kindness to generations of American youth.

Now, as at other times in the past, heightened interest in character education promises to increase opportunities for promoting humane education programs. Teaching kindness-to-animals is highly compatible with the focus of contemporary character education, concerned as it is with the inculcation of compassion, caring, responsibility, respect, and sociality. Animal welfare organizations may be able to take advantage of the growing

consensus about the importance of character education, by offering their services to schools and school systems, and by asserting the value of humane education to the objectives of the character education movement (DeRosa 2001). They may further enlarge their opportunities by providing humane education lessons that can be correlated with conventional subject matter.

For the most part, organized animal protection has been unable to secure the introduction and perpetuation of humane education programs and philosophy within institutions of higher learning and teacher training. This remains the great unrealized goal, and perhaps the most promising objective, in the field. Yet it presupposes an increased commitment to humane education strategies on the part of humane societies. Expanded levels of activity on this front can broaden possibilities for collaboration with institutions of higher learning and teacher training and generate opportunities for program evaluation and ongoing curriculum development.

One limiting factor undoubtedly will be the tenuousness of programs tied to humane societies and their budgets. American animal protection is highly decentralized, and the responsibilities of municipal animal control; fluctuations in donor support; and the press of other priorities have all had an impact on commitment to humane education by local societies. Without a steady investment of resources in this arena, the spread and impact of humane education efforts are likely to remain uneven and uncertain.

Humane education would seem to be an especially fruitful channel for foundation support. Historically, philanthropic foundations have played a crucial role in helping to shape the course of social change through strategic investments and subsidies. During the civil rights era, for example, foundations underwrote voting rights campaigns in an effort to direct the freedom movement's energies toward the creation of viable and last-

ing structures to enhance representative democracy. A similar approach might be taken for subsidizing the hiring and placement of humane education specialists within humane societies, or for the endowment of relevant positions and proper training programs within institutions of higher learning. Such an investment might serve to free humane education from subordinate status within organizations that otherwise are well equipped to promote the lessons of kindness to animals. Higher levels of activity, expanded levels of research, and more rigorous evaluation programs all will help to bring greater credibility to humane education and validate the hopes that advocates have attached to it in the several centuries since appreciation for the value of kindness to animals as a didactic instrument first surfaced.

Literature Cited

American Humane Association (AHA). 1952. National survey reveals vast humane education program. *National Humane Review*. March.

Angell, G.T. n.d. *Autobiographical sketches and personal recollections*. Boston: American Humane Education Society.

Anonymous [G.S. Porter]. 1893. *The strike at Shane's: A prize story of Indiana*. Boston: American Humane Education Society.

Ascione, F.R. 1992. Enhancing children's attitudes about the humane treatment of animals: Generalization to human-directed empathy. *Anthrozoös* 5(3): 176—191.

Ascione, F.R., and C.V. Weber. 1996. Children's attitudes about the humane treatment of animals and empathy: One-year follow-up of a school-based intervention. *Anthrozoös* 9(4): 188—195.

Ascione, F.R., G.I. Latham, and B.R. Worthen. 1985. *Final report, year 2: An experimental study. Evaluation of the humane education curriculum guides*. Report to the National Association for Humane and Environmental Education.

Barrows, E.A. 1894. *Four months in New Hampshire*. Boston: American Humane Education Society.

Bray, M.M. 1893. *Our gold mine at Hollyhurst*. Boston: American Humane Education Society.

Button, H.W., and E.F. Provenzo, Jr. 1983. *History of education and culture in America*. Englewood: Prentice-Hall.

Butts, R.F., and L. Cremin. 1953. *A history of education in American culture*. New York: Holt, Rinehart and Winston.

Cameron, L. 1983. The effects of two instructional treatments on eighth-grade students' attitudes toward animal life. Ph.D. diss., Purdue University.

Carter, S.N. 1897. *For pity's sake: A story for the times, being reminiscences of a guest at a country inn*. Boston: American Humane Education Society.

Cartmill, M. 1993. *A view to a death in the morning: Hunting and nature through history*. Cambridge: Harvard University Press.

Cremin, L. 1969. *The transformation of the school: Progressivism in American education, 1876–1957*. New York: Alfred A. Knopf.

Davis, F.A., G.E. Hein, B. Starnes, and S. Price. 1988. *Evaluation report: Massachusetts Society for the Prevention of Cruelty to Animals school outreach program, grades 2–5*. Unpublished.

DeRosa, B. 2001. The character connection. *Animal Sheltering* 24(4): 12–21.

Finch, P. 2001. Humane education's radical new era. *The Latham Letter* 22(4): 6–9.

Firth, A., comp. 1883. *Voices for the speechless: Selections for schools and private reading*. Boston: Houghton-Mifflin.

Fitzgerald, T.A. 1981. Evaluating humane education: The Jefferson County study. *Humane Education* 5(3): 21–22.

Grenadier, A., ed. 2002. Character education program grant announcement from U.S. Department of Education. *Essential Char-acter* (e-mail newsletter of the Character Education Partnership). April.

Grier, K.C. 1999. Childhood socialization and companion animals: United States, 1820–1920. *Society and Animals* 7(2): 95–120.

Isaacs, S. 1930. *Intellectual growth in young children*. London: George Routledge and Sons.

Kerber, L. 1980. *Women of the republic: Intellect and ideology in Revolutionary America*. Chapel Hill: University of North Carolina Press.

Krows, M. 1938. *The hounds of Hastings*. New York: Columbia University Press.

Locke, J. 1989. *Some thoughts on education*. eds. J.W. and J.S. Yolton. Oxford: Clarendon Press.

Lockwood, R., and F. Ascione, eds. 1998. *Cruelty to animals and interpersonal violence*. West Lafayette, Ind.: Purdue University Press.

Malcarne, V. 1981. What can humane education research do for you? *Humane Education* 5(4): 18–19.

———. 1983. Evaluating humane education: The Boston study. *Humane Education* 7(1): 12–13.

Mann, H. 1861. *Twelve sermons delivered at Antioch College*. Boston: Ticknor and Fields.

Mathewson, L.M. 1942. Humane education. Master's thesis, Brown University.

O'Hare, T., and M. Montminy-Danna. 2001. Evaluation report: Effectiveness of the Potter League humane education program.

Olin, J. 2002. Humane education in the 21st century: A survey of animal shelters in the United States. Master's thesis, Tufts University.

Oswald, L.J. 1994. Environmental and animal rights ethics in children's realistic animal novels of twentieth century North America. Ph.D. diss., University of Oregon.

Paul, E.S. 2000. Empathy with animals and with humans: Are they linked? *Anthrozoös* 13(4): 194–200.

Pauly, P.J. 2000. *Biologists and the promise of American life: From Meriwether Lewis to Alfred Kinsey*. Princeton: Princeton University Press.

Pickering, S.F. 1981. *John Locke and children's books in eighteenth-century England*. Knoxville: University of Tennessee Press.

Pivar, D. 1973. *Purity crusade: Sexual morality and social control 1868–1900*. Westport, Conn.: Greenwood Press.

Poresky, R.H. 1990. The young children's empathy measure: Reliability, validity, and effects of companion animal bonding. *Psychological Reports* 66: 931–936.

Ray, J.J. 1982. Love of animals and love of people. *The Journal of Social Psychology* 116: 229–300.

Rowley, F.H. 1916. Preparedness and humane education. *Our Dumb Animals* 48: 152.

Saunders, M.M. 1893. *Beautiful Joe*. Philadelphia: American Baptist Publication Society.

Savesky, K. 2002. Presentation delivered at The HSUS Animal Care Expo. Miami, Florida, April 3.

Sewell, A. 1890. *Black Beauty*. Boston: American Humane Education Society.

Sheldon, E.A. 1862. *Manual of elementary instruction for the use of public and private schools and normal classes*. New York: Charles Scribner.

Shultz, W.J. 1924. *The humane movement in the United States*. New York: Columbia University Press.

Timmins, T. 1883. *The History of the founding, aims, and growth of the American Bands of Mercy*. Boston: P. H. Foster.

Topics Education Group. 2001. Curriculum standards: The new K–12 mandate. *www.topicseducation. com/download/Topics_Research_B rief_v1n2.pdf*.

Underhill, O.E. 1941. *The origins and development of elementary-school science*. Chicago: Scott, Foresman, and Co.

Unti, B. 2002. The quality of mercy: Organized animal protection in the United States, 1866–1930. Ph.D. diss., American University.

Unti, B., and A. Rowan. 2001. A social

history of animal protection in the post-World War II period. In *The state of the animals: 2001*, ed. D. Salem and A. Rowan, 21–37. Washington: Humane Society Press.

Vockell, E., and E.F. Hodal. 1980. Developing humane attitudes: What does research tell us?, *Humane Education* 4(2): 19–21.

Walter, M.R. 1950. The humane education program in the public schools of Ohio and Wisconsin. Master's thesis, Kent State University.

Westerlund, S.R. 1982. Spreading the word: Promoting humane education with administrators and fellow educators. *Humane Education* 6(1): 7–8.

Whyte, M.L. 1948. A study in humane education. Master's thesis, University of Dayton.

Winiarskyj, L. 2002. Why generation Y? How service learning programs for teens can work for you. *Animal Sheltering* 26(2): 11–17.

Appendix
Milestones in Humane Education: A Pre-World War II Chronology

	Publications Released	Organizations Founded	Legislation Passed	Other
1693	John Locke, *Some Thoughts on Education* published			
1765	*Goody Two-Shoes* published			
1780	Jeremy Bentham, *Principles of Morals and Legislation* published			
1783	Dorothy Kilner, *The Life and Perambulations of a Mouse* published			
1785	Sarah Trimmer, *Fabulous Histories* published			
1792	Herman Daggett, *The Rights of Animals* published			
1794	American edition of *Fabulous Histories* published			
1794	American edition of Arnaud Berquin *Looking Glass for the Mind* published			
1802	American edition of *The Hare*, or *Hunting Incompatible with Humanity* published			
1824		Royal Society for the Prevention of Cruelty to Animals (RSPCA) founded		
1828	American Tract Society edition of *Louisa's Tenderness to the Little Birds* published			
1829			New York State anti-cruelty statute passed	
1835	*The Spirit of Humanity* published			
1845	American Sunday School Union edition of Charlotte Elizabeth's *Kindness to Animals; or The Sin of Cruelty Exposed and Rebuked* published			
1850		American Vegetarian Society founded	Fugitive Slave Act passed	Flogging in the U.S. in the U.S. Navy abolished
1851	Grace Greenwood, *History of My Pets* published			
1852	Harriet Beecher Stowe, *Uncle Tom's Cabin* published		Massachusetts compulsory school attendance legislation passed	

(continued from previous page)

Appendix
Milestones in Humane Education: A Pre-World War II Chronology

	Publications Released	Organizations Founded	Legislation Passed	Other
1866	Anson Randolph, *Autobiography of a Canary Bird* published	American Society for the Prevention of Cruelty to Animals (ASPCA) founded		
1867		Pennsylvania Society for the Prevention of Cruelty to Animals (PSPCA) founded		
1868		Massachusetts Society for the Prevention of Cruelty to Animals (MSPCA) founded		
1874		Women's Christian Temperance Union (WCTU) founded		
1875		New York Society for the Prevention of Cruelty to Children launched by Henry Bergh and Elbridge T. Gerry		
1877	Anna Sewell, *Black Beauty* published	American Humane Association (AHA) founded		
1882				Band of Mercy concept introduced to United States
1883	Abraham Firth, *Voices of the Speechless* published Thomas Timmins, *The History of the Founding, Aims, and Growth of the American Bands of Mercy* published	American Anti-Vivisection Society founded		
1886			Humane education mandate in Massachusetts spurred by MSPCA	
1889		American Humane Education Society (AHES) founded		
1890	AHES edition of *Black Beauty* published			
1891		WCTU Department of Mercy formed by Mary F. Lovell		
1892				AHA campaign against classroom vivisection spurred by Albert Leffingwell
1893	Marshall Saunders, *Beautiful Joe* published			

(continued from previous page)

Appendix
Milestones in Humane Education: A Pre-World War II Chronology

Publications Released	Organizations Founded	Legislation Passed	Other
1893 ASPCA, *Kindness to Animals: A Manual for Use in Schools and Families* published			
1894 American edition of Henry Salt's *Animals' Rights Considered in Relation to Social Progress* published		Ban on classroom vivisection in Massachusetts secured by MSPCA	
1895	New England Anti-Vivisection Society founded		
1897 Sarah J. Eddy, *Songs of Happy Life* published Emma Page, *Heart Culture* published			
1899 Ralph Waldo Trine, *Every Living Creature* published			
1902			AHA Textbook Committee formed
1904 Nora Finch, *Colliery Jim: Autobiography of a Mine Mule* published			William O. Stillman assumes presidency of AHA
1905	Humane Education Committee in New York State formed by Stillman and Stella Preston	Oklahoma and Pennsylvania pass compulsory humane education laws	
1906 J. Howard Moore, *The Universal Kinship* published Richard von Krafft-Ebing, *Psychopathia Sexualis* discusses sadistic behavior toward non-human animals			
1907	Henry Bergh Foundation for the Promotion of Humane Education established at Columbia University		
1909		Compulsory humane education legislation passed in Illinois	
1910 Flora Helm Krause, *Manual of Moral and Humane Education* published			
1911	Millennium Guild founded		
1913 S. Louise Patteson, *Pussy Meow* published			

(continued from previous page)

Appendix
Milestones in Humane Education: A Pre-World War II Chronology

	Publications Released	Organizations Founded	Legislation Passed	Other
1915				Be Kind to Animals Week launched AHA votes to seek compulsory humane education in every state
1916	Sandor Ferenczi, "A Little Chanticleer" (case study of a boy's cruelty toward humans and non-human animals) published			AHES produces the first humane education film, "The Bell of Atri" ASPCA creates humane education department
1917			Compulsory humane education laws passed in Maine, Wisconsin, and New York	
1919	Harriet C.C. Reynolds, *Thoughts on Human Education: Suggestions on Kindness to Animals* published			
1920			Kentucky approves compulsory humane education law	
1923			Florida approves compulsory humane education law	
1924	William J. Schultz, *The Humane Movement in the United States*, judges humane education the most important development of the previous decade Frances E. Clarke, *Lessons for Teaching Humane Education in the Schools* published			
1925	Alexander Ernest Frederick, *The Humane Guide: A Manual for Teachers and Humane Workers* published			
1931	Susan Isaacs, *Intellectual Growth in Young Children* published			

Toward Biophilia: The Role of Children's Literature in the Development of Empathy and Compassion

Marion W. Copeland and Heidi O'Brien

Introduction

The goal of humane education is to change the way society thinks about animals, the natural world, and/or other people—all with the hope that this change in attitude will influence people's behavior and lead to the improved treatment of animals, the environment, and one another. This chapter discusses the role of children's literature in the development of empathy and compassion, and the role of empathy and compassion in encouraging progression to a state of biophilia, or an affinity for all forms of life and the living earth. It gives a history of children's literature with humane themes and discusses narrative, or story, as an especially powerful tool in creating a world in which people and animals live in harmony.

Narrative as a Teacher of Values

Although strategies for moral education often have focused on formal discussion of rules, ethical principles, or abstract moral dilemmas, research suggests that a traditional approach to moral education—one centered on stories—may be much more effective. New York University Professor of Psychology Paul Vitz (1990) points out that, while people need abstract rules and maxims to guide them, they think more readily in images. According to Vitz, morality is best understood and most readily internalized in context—that is, in terms of actual human behaviors and interpersonal experiences, not abstract rules or generalizations. Studies indicate that moral development is deeply rooted in right-brained, or narrative, thought—a mode of thinking that relies on the kind of imagery, emotion, subjectivity, and detail that context provides.

Mirroring real-life situations, stories clearly illustrate a rule or a virtue by endowing it with context, a cast of characters, a setting, and concrete conflicts and consequences. Stories allow children to interpret ethical principles by giving them life and emotion. "A good story shows what it wants to tell," notes Susan Strauss (1996). In its most polished, masterful form, a story snares readers, pulling them into the lives and actions of the characters in what can only be described as a vicarious experience. This changes the readers and shapes the way they live. Jennifer Sahn (1995) asks adults to think back to their own childhood and remember the youthful perspective in which the world is a story where all beings have a potentially leading role. Stories, she writes, "speak in a language that is accessible and present scenarios that are resonant with a child's view of the world." They also "legitimize emotional responses to nature . . . nurturing in our children . . . affections for nature" which later will allow them to approach the "hard facts about ecology and environmental problems" with heart as well as mind (1995, 4–5).

A story can evoke strong emotions in the reader that help convey the lessons and values central to humane education, such as knowledge, respect, empathy, and compassion. Empathy is the ability to see and feel things as others experience them. According to Strauss, the relationship that a story creates gives a child the opportunity to develop an empathic understanding of others and to evaluate actions based on their potential to do harm or good. This narrative reasoning, in turn, guides children in assessing their own behavior: children begin mentally to construct their own moral scenarios, or stories, which guide them in thinking about the consequences of their actions. A story can create empathy for an animal by encouraging readers to care about animal characters. A good story—especially one that has a strong moral theme—can engender a sudden intuitive realization that makes the essence of an abstract rule or maxim crystal-clear. Empathy not only leads people to recognize what is morally good, it also leads them to embrace it and act on it. The dramatic nature of stories helps readers develop an emotional attachment to goodness and a desire to do the right thing, because they want to follow the good examples set by characters. Stories allow them to "rehearse" moral decisions, strengthening their solidarity with the good (Kilpatrick, Wolfe, and Wolfe 1994).[1]

Stories can also help people gain the perspective of other animals. Strauss, who is herself a storyteller, argues that story "creates relationship, translates information into image and excites our imagination—our sense of wonder," allowing the audience to learn to see freshly and regain the experience of sharing the world with other living, experiencing beings (1996, 4). To awaken compassion, it is not enough to provide information about other animals. Stories can help transport the audience beyond the boundaries imposed by the human culture story, bringing alive the natural world and its inhabitants for humans too frequently deprived of the immediacy of their presence.[2]

Judith and Herbert Kohl comment that "when observing animals we must try to give ourselves over to their experience and imagine worlds as foreign as any that can be found in novels or science fiction" (1977, 19). Their views of the oak extend Western human perception with the views of the fox, the owl, the bark-boring beetle, and the ichneumon fly, as well as with a spectrum of human views including those of the conservationist and logger, the Native American and Druid, the aerial geographer, and, last but not least, the child. The result is a convincing argument for how narrow and shallow most human perceptions are until the views of those considered "other" are added. Once people accept that "the human view of the world is only one of many," they are in a position to respect the views of other forms of life and, through those views, to enrich "our understanding of ourselves...and attempt to understand the experience of other animals" (109).

The Kohls are talking about observing animals in nature rather than in the pages of storybooks, but the characteristics they describe are those needed by adults engaged in translating the images of animals found in any literature for any age reader. Finally, stories are something that humans, by their very nature, crave (Vitz 1990). Note the popularity of television, most of which, as Vitz explains, "consists of stories of one sort or another," whether they take the form of sitcoms, soaps, or sports.

A History of Children's Books with Humane Themes

Literature from all ages and cultures and for children of all ages is replete with animal characters and their stories (sometimes as told by the animals themselves) and with humane themes or concerns. So are fairy tales, fables, and folktales, which are not specifically intended for children but often are treated as though they were.[3]

Folktales, Parables, and Fables

Anthropologists long have attested to the influence of stories, which are as ancient and universal as language itself. Stories have been used to communicate, indoctrinate, and hand down family traditions. Folktales, parables, and fables emerged as common and popular forms of moral instruction. Most of the great world religions, for example, have employed parables as teaching tools. Early Biblical, Hindu, and Buddhist scripture used the mysteries of parables and the curiosity they spawned to teach important moral lessons. Buddha, who is believed to have been born around 600 B.C., clearly understood the teaching power of a well-constructed parable in teaching moral lessons.[4] Wherever a human society has passed on its moral and cultural heritage, stories have had "substantial educational utility"—particularly in teaching children values and building character (Vitz 1990).

Roger Sale observes that animal characters in children's literature are "the strongest link between fairy tales and modern written children's literature" in which animals "talk or in other ways act like human beings." He notes that such anthropomorphized animals "are present in most children's literature, ancient and modern," and sees them as "the major source of the power of the best children's literature, a power that other kinds of literature had abandoned and forgotten before the nineteenth century" (1978, 77). That power is exactly what makes animal stories important in any effort to bring humans back into touch with the natural world and its nonhuman and human inhabitants.

Aesop's fables are early examples of such powerful animal stories. "The Ant and the Grasshopper," for example, teaches that it's best to prepare for days of necessity. "The Wolf in Sheep's Clothing" illustrates that appearances can be deceiving. Narratives such as Aesop's fables clearly were respected early as effective teaching tools worthy of being recorded in writing and safeguarded for posterity. Those stories relied heavily on animal characters to convey their messages, yet, like their predecessors in the oral tradition, few contained messages about kindness to animals. For the most part, animals in stories reflected human behavior more than their own. That was true whether the behavior of the animals was naturalistic, meaning some of their natural behaviors may have been employed to advance the plot, or anthropomorphized, meaning the animals were given what normally are regarded as human characteristics. The morals of the stories that employed animals rarely had anything to do with the animals' well-being.

Melson observes that "belief in the shape-shifting of humans into animals and animals into humans, visible in Paleolithic drawings and sculptures and universal among early hunter-gatherers, took root in ancient Egypt, spread into Greece, and by the sixth century B.C.E. entered the teachings of Buddha and the fables of Aesop" (2001, 145). Yet, over time, society has strayed from the original themes of art and story, in which other animals are central, because humans came to see themselves as not only different from but also better than other beings. Only children's stories (and a few stubborn genres of adult fiction, such as fantasy, science fiction, and regional literature) retain the unity of animal and human life reflected in the oldest art and stories.

Melson maintains that human development is biocentric rather than humanocentric and, therefore, that until "the pervasiveness of animals, real and symbolic in children's lives" is recognized and the human-animal bond considered, what we have is "a seriously incomplete portrait of the ecology of children." In "the biocentric view… animal presence in all forms merits neither facile sentimentalizing nor quick dismissal but serious investigation," adds Melson (2001, 4–5). Animal stories, then, are at the heart not only of humane education but also of our development as human beings. This view is sanctioned by other writers as well, including Paul Sheperd and James Hillman. By extension, concludes Melson, if the biophilia hypothesis is correct, humans have an "evolutionary heritage of attunement to animals," and the old ways of our hunter-gatherer ancestors "are engraved in [our] genes" (131).

It is also in children's literature that word and picture have remained united as they were—and are still—in the ritual of indigenous peoples. As a result, children's books more fully involve the senses in the world of the story than does much adult literature. That sensory involvement—including the sound of a loved and respected voice telling or reading the story—leads most successfully to the development of empathy for humans and other animals. Anthropomorphism in ritual, dance, and story was and remains the catalytic artistic device for leading an audience to enter the life of the Other, that character not themselves yet experienced as they experience self—indeed, often experienced more vividly than we experience self. This "willing suspension of disbelief," as poet Samuel Taylor Coleridge called it, is the key to opening doors to humane education for any audience, young or old.

The Seventeenth and Eighteenth Centuries

In Western culture children's literature had its beginnings in the educational theory of seventeenth-century British philosopher John Locke, who believed that children should enjoy reading and that children like animal stories with pictures, and in the response of eighteenth-century British publisher and entrepreneur John Newbery to Locke's ideas. Newbery opened a bookstore for children in London in 1744, making way for the proliferation of original, colorfully illustrated animal stories intended for young readers.

Newbery books were small like their readers' hands, profusely illustrated, and "filled with amusingly named [human] characters like Tommy Trip, Zig Zag, and Giles Gingerbread; and with friendly animals like Tippy the lark, Jouler the goat, and Willy the lamb" (Cott 1981, 50). Modern readers associate these book characteristics with the animal stories of Beatrix Potter and with many other picture books, as well as with cartoons and comic strips. One of the first Newbery books, *Valentine's Gift* (1765), introduces talking animal characters who tell their stories to a boy named Zig Zag. Thanks to a magic horn, Zig Zag is able to understand the languages of birds and beasts. The horn is the story's connection to the power of fairy tales; it appears in various guises in so many children's animal stories (and adult animal fantasies) that it might well be seen as a characteristic of the genre.

The majority of Newbery books—Newbery's eighteenth-century publications as well as contemporary Newbery Medal winners—focus on domestic animals. Some, such as the dog and cat, are very familiar. Many, such as the horse, once were familiar but have come to be strangers in the flesh to most contemporary children. The stories emphasize the sufferings inflicted on these animals by human beings, establishing what became by the end of the eighteenth century a familiar link between animal stories and moral lessons usually intended to teach kindness and compassion for animals (see Townsend 1967, 29–35).

British author Anna Sewell probably would not have written *Black Beauty* (1877) had she not grown up on the high-minded examples of such moralistic writers and educators as Dorothy Kilner, Sarah Trimmer, Anna Letitia Barbauld, Catharine Parr Traill, Mary Wollstonecraft, and her own mother. And with *Black Beauty*, Sewell went a step further; the book deserves to be recognized as one of the first animal stories for children with direct humane implications. We will return to it after looking at some of its influential predecessors.

Kilner's *The Life and Perambulations of a Mouse* (1783) was "a new type of animal tale... which used the natural behaviour of animals to point to a moral for human behaviour. The animals were not used as symbolic personifications of human characteristics [as some critics feel they are in Aesop's fables]; they were intended to be seen as their natural animal selves" (Swinfen 1984, 25). Cott comments that Kilner's "simple depiction of scurrying little mice"—Nimble, LongTail, Softdown, and Brighteyes— not only liberates the reader's imagination but also subverts "the restricting moral order," allowing a child "to envision a reality more open and connected to the instinctual forces of childhood" than earlier books had dared approach (1981, xvii). Traill's *Little Downy* (1822) also is the story of a mouse, a field mouse. And, as with the baby robins in Sarah Trimmer's *The History of Robins* (1786), Traill's tiny protagonists were "intended to be seen as their natural animal selves" (Swinfen 1984, 16).

Trimmer wants her young readers to be taught that the stories about the baby robins—Robin, Dicksy, Pecksy, and Flapsy—and their loyal parents are not meant to record the

> real conversations of birds (for that it is impossible we should ever understand) but [to be taken] as a series of fables intended to convey moral instruction applicable to themselves, at the same time that they excite compassion and tenderness for those interesting and delightful creatures on which such wanton cruelties are frequently inflicted, and recommend universal benevolence. (quoted in Townsend 1967, 121–122)

Mary Wollstonecraft's *Original Stories* (1788) belongs without question to the genre Newbery established. However, it introduces an important departure, with three stories that deal directly with the treatment of animals. It assumes that kindness to animals is the foundation for kindness to fellow humans and, as still is too often the case, justifies such kindness in those terms rather than seeing it as valuable in and of itself. Caring for

"the dumb family," says Wollstonecraft's Mrs. Mason to her two students, Caroline and Mary, in the book's preface, "has humanized my heart," preparing her as an adult to be "useful to my fellow creatures. I, who never wantonly trod on an insect, or disregarded the plaint of the speechless beast, can now give bread to the hungry, physic to the sick, comfort to the afflicted, and, above all... be fit for the society of angels" (15–16).

This is behavior Wollstonecraft believes essential to all young women, although she seems to share the assumption of the time that boys are hopeless candidates for either nurturing or kind behavior. In *The Rational Brutes: or, Talking Animals* (1799), Kilner seems to agree: her ass "is made to remark, 'Well, I think it would be the happiest thing for this nation that ever yet was thought of, if some plan could be contrived to destroy every boy upon this island'" (Egoff 1981, 107).

Along the way, Wollstonecraft's Mrs. Mason dispels the girls' squeamish dislike for "nasty creatures that crawl on the ground" (1788, 2). God, after all, made "those snails you despise, and caterpillars, and spiders" (3–4). In fact, Mrs. Mason's definition of goodness is, "first, to avoid hurting any thing; and then, to contrive to give as much pleasure as you can" (5). Farmers, if forced to destroy insects to save crops, ought do it "in the quickest way." Domestic animals must be afforded the best care and be made happy, for when "other creatures think only of themselves... man... feels disinterested love" toward the "poor dumb beasts" (10). Although none of Wollstonecraft's animal characters uses human language, Mrs. Mason cautions her charges that animals only appear dumb "to those who do not observe; but God, who takes care of everything, understands their language." She praises Caroline for understanding as well when she replaces a nest stolen by a thoughtless boy who seems "heedless of the mother's agonizing cries" (11).

Sarah Trimmer's *The History of*

Robins (1786), like Robert Mc-Closkey's *Blueberries for Sal* (1948), parallels human and animal families, suggesting that both provide useful models for the rearing of young. But her basic concern is to impress young readers with the importance of listening to and obeying their parents while McCloskey's is with recognizing the kinship between species. Trimmer's greater contribution was to produce *The Guardian of Education*, 1802–1806, in which she reviewed and offered editorial comment on children's books. Trimmer approved only those books that supported Christianity and the status quo, but she did create a link in the minds of educators among books for children, humane themes, and education.

The Nineteenth Century

There are numerous examples of narratives from the eighteenth and nineteenth centuries that promote teaching the humane ethic to young children. More and more, stories focused on animals and their daily travails at the hands of man. Baym (1994) points out that Anna Letitia Barbauld's (1743–1825) novels of manners were an important influence on other women writers in America as well as in her native England, especially on those, like Anna Sewell and Harriet Beecher Stowe, drawn to her stand against slavery and cruelty to animals. Baym might also have mentioned the influence of the British poet and editor's children's books *Hymn in Prose* and *Early Lessons* (both 1781). Widely read and translated, they were staples in the education of young people at the Barbauld's boarding school as well as at comparable schools in America and England: undoubtedly both Sewell and Stowe encountered them as part of their childhood reading.

Sewell, of course, would later write *Black Beauty*. Harriet Beecher Stowe, best known for *Uncle Tom's Cabin* (1852), wrote a number of animal stories concerned with the welfare of nonhumans, like "A Dog's Mission"

(1880). This made it particularly appropriate that George Angell, publishing the American edition of *Black Beauty* to spread the message of the Massachusetts Society for the Prevention of Cruelty to Animals (MSPCA), referred to Sewell's novel as "the equine *Uncle Tom's Cabin*."

Stowe was the first writer to use the sentimental novel in the cause of reform. As Hanne points out, "The key device employed by Stowe to persuade her readers of the wickedness of slavery is her presentation of the distress of slave characters in a way that invites the direct empathy of white readers, who are invited to imagine how they would feel if placed in the same situation" (1994, 89). Both in choosing the sentimental novel as a vehicle and in using empathy as a key device to encourage change of heart and mind, Sewell was indebted to Stowe as well as to Barbauld.

The extent of the effect of both *Black Beauty* and *Uncle Tom's Cabin* on reform has been "insufficiently recognized," observes Hanne. In both cases "[i]t was by tapping...almost universally shared emotional reservoirs that [they] achieved overnight a degree of moral reframing, or reconceptualizing...in the minds of vast numbers of readers" (1994, 89–90). Coleridge, who pointed to Barbauld as one of the writers who had "done most to make compassion toward animals 'universally fashionable,'" would certainly have added Stowe and Sewell to his list had he known their work (Thomas 1983, 182n).

Works that actually questioned the status of animals and expanded the perspective of their readers found both publishers and audience. Influential examples include Arabella Argus's *The Adventures of a Donkey* (1815), and its sequel, *Further Adventures of Jemmy Donkey* (1821), in which the animal narrator, the donkey, Jemmy, is not merely an observer of human vices and virtues—as is his classical progenitor, Apuleius's *Golden Ass*—but is also telling his own story. Without question, however, the most influential novel in the genre, and one Blount believes was directly

influenced by *The Adventures of a Donkey* (1975, 51), was *Black Beauty*. Presenting an abused cart horse's own account of his suffering, *Black Beauty* evokes sympathy for the animal, a quality that "has become a standard feature of juvenile fiction" (Allen 1983, 5). Because of *Black Beauty*, Sewell generally is recognized as one of the most important catalytic influences in the burgeoning animal protection movement. The story engendered heartfelt public sympathy, which spilled over into support for newly formed charitable organizations—including the MSPCA (founded in 1868), American Society for the Prevention of Cruelty to Animals (founded in 1866), and American Humane Association (founded in 1877)—all of which were chartered to prevent cruelty to animals. From their inception, these organizations viewed humane education as a critical factor in meeting their mission.

Recognizing *Black Beauty*'s potential as a humane education tool, Angell sent out more than a million copies of the book over a two-year period, a distribution effort unprecedented at the time. Although Angell is known for many humane education initiatives (he founded the American Humane Education Society and the famous Bands of Mercy children's clubs), he quickly realized that poignant books and stories about animals were the most powerful and effective teaching tools and means of gaining public support for animal welfare. With that in mind, he continued to publish books under the AHES banner, many of which remained staples in humane literature for years to come. One of the best known, *Beautiful Joe* (1893), is still popular. That story was written because Angell wished to produce a story that would engender sympathy for dogs in the same way that *Black Beauty* had for horses. He ran a contest for that purpose and the winning entry was *Beautiful Joe*, by Margaret Marshall Saunders. By the time Saunders's book was published, such realistic and sympathetic accounts of animals had become a standard feature of chil-

dren's literature. That legacy continues today.

It is useful, when working with older readers, to link Charles Darwin's *On the Origin of Species by Means of Natural Selection* (1859) with Sewell's *Black Beauty*. "Stanley Edgar Hyman describes [Darwin's] *Origin* as a scientific argument that reads like a dramatic poem in which animals are the actors" (1983, 8). Darwin and Sewell's books did the most to intervene in anthropocentric Western thinking and help forward the idea that man is no longer the supreme animal. Part of Sewell's biocentrism may well be an inheritance from the Society of Friends to which she and her family (and Stowe, for that matter) belonged. Certainly the use of story to teach empathy and compassion has roots in Quaker ideology, and Melson points out that "the Society of Friends established what most consider the first therapeutic environment utilizing animal and nature contact" at their York Retreat. The Quakers believed that "[c]aring for animals and tending gardens would draw patients' attention outwards, away from their own inward distress, toward engagement in the world" (2001, 107). A current manifestation of this theory, equine therapy, is now commonplace, yet its human practitioners may overlook its real source of power, the horses themselves. Each, like Beauty, is an individual with a life story to "tell," and not simply a tool to be used to a human end.

It is that consciousness of the animal with a life story to tell that marks Sewell's work as distinctly different from the work of her predecessors. It may explain why, when Angell decided that the dissemination of animal stories could aid his effort to create a compassionate America, *Black Beauty* was the first novel he distributed. As it had in Great Britain, *Black Beauty* had become a bestseller in the United States.

Those that followed, Saunders's *Beautiful Joe* and Gene Stratton Porter's *The Strike at Shane's*, continue to educate toward that enlightened end, as must any work if it is to make a difference in the welfare of nonhumans as well as humans. (It should be noted that Saunders includes boys in her League of Kindness, something that should be encouraged today. Unfortunately, the association between women, movements supporting the welfare and rights of animals, humane education, and animal stories has been used to detract from the importance of all four over the years.)

Although it is clear that *Black Beauty* originally was published for an adult audience, it almost always is treated as a child's novel. The movie and TV versions have been treated as works for children as well and actually are useful in demonstrating how animal stories are transformed into human stories, thereby losing their power to bring humans back into touch with their nonhuman kin. It was not until Caroline Thompson's 1994 film *Black Beauty* (Warner Bros.) that modern revisions abandoned the anthropocentric, or human-centered, vision that turned the story into a formulaic "boy or girl and a horse" saga and instead told the horse's story from the horse's point of view, in the horse's own voice, as Sewell did. While the horse's autobiography can be used with children, it is perhaps best presented in revised editions like the one retold by Quinn Currie and illustrated by Donna Ryan (1990) for Operation Outreach USA until children gain enough reading skill to handle the sophistication of Sewell's prose.

As Magee points out:

[T]he successful representation of animals in modern fiction, developing rapidly since the beginnings in *Black Beauty*, *Beautiful Joe*, and *The Jungle Books*, has added to literature a huge range of possible characters long ago exploited by sculptors and painters. In the careful inner studies as prompted by zoology and psychology, writers have found the means to a success denied to ancient, medieval, and Renaissance writers alike. Ani-

mals, who live in nature and even in the house for themselves and not for man, are credible in fiction only so long as they care about themselves first. The early modern stories, in which animals plead for human kindness or support romances of men raised by beasts, ventured on the new animal hero though special, nontypical applications of this care. (1969, 231)

Although women were the major contributors to the British and North American traditions, men made early and significant contributions to the development of the animal story.

One nineteenth-century writer whose sympathetic and delicate touch combined the natural behaviour of animals with just enough of human consciousness to make them moving... [was] Hans Christian Andersen. *The Ugly Duckling* (first English translation, 1846) is the classic example of this kind, in which the normal behaviour of farmyard animals and the lonely suffering of the duckling illuminate the theme of illusion and reality, of misleading outward appearances and inner worth. There is no magic in this story beyond the magic of nature itself. The duckling was always a swan. Nor do the animals personify human characteristics; they are simply themselves. The duckling suffers and endures with a human consciousness, but—as Andersen himself would have argued—how are we to know that animals, birds... do not suffer as we do? (Swinfen 1984, 16–17)

Another important work was Charles Kingsley's *The Water-Babies*, subtitled *A Fairy Tale for a Land-Baby* (1863). Its "waterscape lies beneath a real English river... peopled with fairies and water-babies, talking fish and fairy godmother figures, while Tom, the chimney sweep, becomes an eft [or baby eel]—3.879002 inches long" (Egoff 1988, 42). Such stories were reinforced by the work of Lewis Carroll and George MacDonald and

the lesser known Mark Lemon. The latter's *Tinykin's Transformations* (1869) features a forester's son who, like T. H. White's Wart in *The Sword in the Stone* (1938, rev. 1957), "becomes a fish, a bird, and a deer through the magic of the fairy queen and is finally transformed into a prince" (Egoff 1988, 66–67). A more realistic natural world is depicted in Richard Jeffries's *Wood Magic* (1881), which nonetheless is recognized as "the first genuine animal fantasy in children's literature" and still is quite accessible for young readers and useful to humane educators (Egoff 1988, 93).

The Twentieth Century

With the exception of Beatrix Potter's books, no twentieth century British animal story had—and still has—a greater influence than Hugh Lofting's Doctor Dolittle series, which began in 1920. It is a particularly useful humane education tool because of the variety of animal characters included, and the insistence of Polynesia, the Parrot, that the doctor learn animal languages in order to best treat and see to the general welfare of his animal patients rather than requires that the nonhuman do the learning. Jane Goodall recalls first dreaming of going to Africa "'after reading *Tarzan* and *Doctor Dolittle*'" (Cruickshank 1999).[5]

It is important to emphasize Lofting's concern that the animals serve as consultants when their futures are to be decided in a world where it is increasingly difficult for nonhumans to achieve the good life without human intervention. The popularity of the 2001 Eddie Murphy film, *Doctor Dolittle*, and of the song "Talk to the Animals," from the 1967 film version starring Rex Harrison, can be enormously useful to the humane educator striving to facilitate the human desire to communicate with other species, improve the lives of nonhumans, and provide audiences with pleasurable experiences.

By the turn of the twentieth century, North American writers had added their talents to the developing field of animal fiction for children. Albert Bigelow Paine's *The Arkansaw Bear* (1898) offers twin protagonists, the human boy Bosephus, a runaway orphan, and a talking, fiddling bear. Like Mowgli in Kipling's *Jungle Books*, though, Paine's maturing human Ratio decides to leave the animal world and seek education and advancement among humans. Kipling's skill in "convincing mingling of the animal world and that of humans" (Egoff 1988, 94) is paralleled by Paine's. But perhaps no one mingles those worlds as skillfully as British Beatrix Potter, the British writer whose animal characters, even when they wear human clothes and live in human houses, retain "their animal natures" (Egoff 1988, 96) and are the true central characters in their tiny Newbery-size books. American illustrator Maurice Sendak (1988) writes appreciatively about Potter's status as both natural historian and artist, recognizing her work as an important influence on his own.

Naturalism is the core of Potter's work, as it is of the naturalistic romances of Canadian Charles G.D. Roberts and American Ernest Thompson Seton.

> Roberts developed the wider exploitation of animal heroes for general stories in which conflicts outside the repertoire of human fiction are centered on animals. No matter whether they were emphasizing science or adventure, Roberts and his followers depended for their artistic appeal on the universality of the earthly challenges facing man and animal alike. They ask their readers to feel at one with their heroes in contrast to the myriad enemies to both. They also expose the limits as well as the vastness of the expanded range of characters and topics for fiction. (Magee 1969, 231–232)

Understandably perhaps, the often violent worlds of the animal characters of Seton and Roberts seem to have had less appeal to the parents and teachers of small children than have the worlds of Potter, Robert Lawson, and E.B. White. In *Rabbit Hill* (1944), Lawson creates a world in which humans and the animals of their rural area become partners in the business of survival, rather than enemies, as they frequently are seen to be in Seton and Roberts. Recently Brian Jacques's *Redwall* series (1986 to present) has provided an interesting meshing of violence and the small, appealing animal characters who are its victims in real life. The books are "animal fantasies about an abbey of woodland creatures who [together] fight off villains [mostly predators].... Several [Redwall books] have appeared on children's bestseller lists over the past several years." The popularity of the series is particularly encouraging because, unlike other, even more popular series (Odean singles out R.L. Stine's *Goosebumps*, Scholastic 1992–1997), "the Redwall books challenge readers with dozens of characters, difficult vocabulary and an occasional dose of broad British dialects" (Odean 1999, 88). The equally challenging, if not equally optimistic, novels of Richard Adams, such as *Watership Down*, feature these assets as well.

The meshing of violence in the world with appealing nonhuman characters also is found in fairy tales—especially the Grimms' versions—and in the work of Maurice Sendak. It helps educators introduce children to the realities of the world experienced by human and nonhuman animals alike. These literary elements also are useful in convincing readers of the value of compassion, community, nurturing, and appreciation of diversity in achieving the balance nature needs if any of us is to survive (see Acocella 1998).

E.B. White's *Charlotte's Web* remains a most valuable text because White does not avoid the hard realities of life for animals. As Egoff points out, "White's Charlotte, Wilbur, the hero pig, Templeton the Rat, and the goose who says everything twice are essentially what they are—barnyard animals." White neither used animals as personifications of human beings nor wrote for children on one level and adults on another. He believed, as did his contemporary, the British P.L. Travers, creator of Mary Poppins, that it is impossible not to write simultaneously for adults and children. White wrote, "'You do not chop off a section of your imaginative substance and make a book specifically for children for—if you are honest—you have, in fact, no idea where childhood ends and maturity begins. It is all endless and one'" (quoted in Cott 1981, 204). And it is always the case that educators who use animal stories address an extended audience—not only those seated around them but also members of families and communities, who hear of animal characters and stories secondhand. White himself referred to *Charlotte's Web* not as a moral tale teaching kind behavior—although it does that too—but as "'an appreciative story'" that "'celebrates life, the seasons, the goodness of the barn, the beauty of the world, the glory of everything'" and, of course, provides occasion for developing the imagination and empathy inherent in childhood's games of "Let's pretend" (Egoff 1988, 167).[6]

In recent years, especially with the advent of movies, many classic animal adventure stories with humane themes have become a part of popular culture. The film *Babe* (Universal Studios Inc. 1995), based on the book *Babe the Gallant Pig* (1983), by Dick King-Smith, was tremendously popular. Determined not to be another pig destined for the dinner table, Babe decides to prove he's more useful alive than dead. Putting his polite manners and sweet personality to work, he becomes Farmer Hoggett's best sheepherder. *Babe* fosters empathy by showing the animal characters' emotions: Fly the sheepdog is heartbroken over the sale of her pups; Ferdinand the duck is distraught over the possibility of being killed for dinner; and Babe is depressed when he learns of a typical pig's fate on a farm. The movie depicts farm animals as intelligent, sensitive, and worthy of a comfortable, happy life. While the movie shows the reality that farm animals are slaughtered, like *Charlotte's Web* it also depicts animals in a rural farmyard, where animals are, for the most part, allowed to move freely. If the humane educator's goal is to alert the audience to the realities of factory farming, children will have to be informed that, for most farm animals, such a life is a thing of the past. Possibly the mechanized manufacture of chicken pies in the film *Chicken Run* (Universal Studios Inc. 2000). could be discussed to contrast the ideal and the real. *Chicken Run* did create empathy for chickens, prompting people to rethink their diets and fast food chains to rethink what they wanted the public to conclude about their food sources.

Today

Melson offers an excellent discussion of the prevalence of animal characters in children's literature and in popular culture aimed at children (2001, 139–142). While most books for young children today have animal characters, not all have humane themes. The ASPCA's *Kids, Animals & Literature: Annotated Bibliography of Children's Books with a Positive, Humane Theme* (1997) and the National Association for Humane and Environmental Education (NAHEE) book award picks and recommended books are reliable sources of children's books with humane themes. While the majority of these recommended books center on wild animals, many focus on companion animal issues. Very few focus on farm animals.

NAHEE's 2001 KIND Children's Book Award went to *Hurry!*, a book illustrated by Caldecott winner Emily Arnold McCully. *Hurry!* (2000) is the story of ten-year-old Tom Elston and the legendary animal that eludes him. Peering into a crate at the back of a strange man's wagon, young Tom finds himself gazing into the smiling, softly burning eyes of a mysterious creature. "It talks," the wagon owner confides, adding that this animal is the last of its kind. Determined to buy the creature, called a farivox, Tom

races off to get the ten dollars he needs. "Hurry!" urges a voice in the crate. It will be the last that Tom sees or hears of the farivox. He and the readers are left wondering whether the face and voice were pure fantasy or those of an extinct species once as real and full of life as the Iowa prairie. *Hurry!* effectively introduces the reader to the issue of endangered species.

The 2002 NAHEE award winner, *"Let's Get a Pup!" Said Kate* (2001) by Bob Graham, has an important message about adopting older pets. In this touching and humorous tale, young Kate and her parents go to the animal shelter to adopt a puppy. After falling in love with Dave, a wee and bouncy pup, they encounter Rosy, who is "old and gray and broad as a table" and "radiated Good Intention." The family cannot resist Rosy and, in the end, gains the companionship of two wonderful dogs while giving them a much-needed home.

The fact that few children's books with humane themes cover farm animal welfare issues may reflect the difficulty in presenting the realities of modern-day farms to children. One notable book on the issue (and a Caldecott award winner) is *Click, Clack, Moo: Cows That Type* (2000), written by Doreen Cronin and illustrated by Betsy Lewin. In the book, cows acquire a typewriter and use it to give the farmer an ultimatum: they won't give milk unless they get electric blankets to make them more comfortable. Other animals on the farm follow suit. Kids are likely to enjoy the funny, even wacky, nature of the book, and learn that, like us, farm animals want to be comfortable. Another good book for young readers on farm animal welfare is *Hope* (1995) by Randy Houk, the true story of a downed pig (one no longer able to stand due to injury or debilitation) who is rescued and brought to a farm animal shelter operated by the group Farm Sanctuary.

Anthropo-morphism and Fantasy

Leonard Marcus (1983–84) suggests that few picture books "represent animals-in-themselves," animal characters who "live and act as they do in nature." One that does is *Blueberries for Sal*, in which "bears remain bears and people remain people" (1948, 135). In fact, McCloskey's lesson goes further, since his story depicts a bear mother and her cub on one side of a Maine hillside and a human mother and daughter on the other side of the hill, each family unaware of the other's presence as it harvests berries yet engaging in similar activities and experiencing similar emotions. Marcus comments that "the narrative is handled with such understatement, simplicity, and matter-of-factness that the very uneventfulness of the tale assumes tremendous dignity, a dignity behind which lies a deep respect for the natural world" (1983–84, 136). Such respect is, without question, another "source of the magical power" that Roger Sale (1978) recognized as the link between animal stories and the rich natural world of the fairy tale.

Biophilia may also explain why, although human beings claim language as a unique human achievement, they constantly, in art as in life, attribute language to other animals. "Our evolutionary heritage of attunement to animals led early humans to place themselves imaginatively within animal skins and animal minds"; consequently humans are predisposed to animal talk (Melson 2001, 130–131; see also Morton and Page 1992). It is not surprising, then, that anthropomorphism has an important place in children's literature with humane themes. Robert Michael Pyle notes:

Children's stories about animals are often faulted for being "anthropomorphic," or mere human projections. The danger of this lies in reducing animals to our own amplitude of motive by giving them human traits—"big bad" wolves, "wise" owls. But I believe that children relate to these fabulous animal characters more than to plain descriptive accounts. Because they're more accessible, these compelling stories can teach more of how real animals might behave. In Grahame's *Wind in the Willows*, Rat and Mole have human speech, but behave like their animal namesakes. Thornton Burgess's Grandfather Frog may have worn a waistcoat, but also did what frogs do. After all, emotion, play, and intelligence did not arise wholecloth with us. Jane [Goodall]'s work with the chimps demonstrated this conclusively. In giving them names and viewing them as personalities, which they patently possess, she mortally punctured the self-serving view of the world as a human-centered place. Maybe imagination is as good a way as science for individuals to discover this for themselves. (1998, 43)

Children can learn these lessons more quickly from reading Wilson Rawls's novel, *Summer of the Monkeys* (1999), originally published in 1976, than from studying any scientific information about the behavior of the chimpanzee and its kinship to humankind.

Similarly, what has been labeled as fantasy in literature may be rejected because its picture of animal characters and their relations to one another and to human characters is not what people have learned to value as realistic. But according to Egoff, fantasy, like the fairy tale,

[R]eturns to us what once belonged to us: a consciousness of the unity of natural and supernatural worlds, a view of our world that was wrenched apart with the coming of the "Age of Reason." Whatever strange figures we meet in fantasy...are reminders of continuity, solace

against the void, and redemption from despair. (1988, 18)

Egoff believes the real magic worked by animal characters in fantasy consists of how their stories and actions involve readers in worlds which too often remain invisible to humans. As a result humans have often distanced themselves "from egocentricity," which is her term for the dominant perspective of anthropocentrism, always seeing humans "at the center of things" (18).

Books that feature this magic include poet Randall Jarrell's *Fly By Night* (1976), illustrated by Maurice Sendak, which has as its protagonist David, a human child who, though "normal" by day, wakes at night able to float out of his house to encounter the creatures that inhabit the night. Meeting a mother owl who takes him to visit her two owlets, David shares an owl's "bedtime story... (about owls, of course)" (Apseloff 1989, 100). The special power carries limitations, since David cannot remember his adventure when he awakens (although, of course, the reader can). Jarrell's *Animal Family* (1965), also illustrated by Maurice Sendak, is a fantasy about "a solitary man in a timeless, nameless place beside the sea" who finds his life incomplete until he fills it with a mermaid, a bear cub, a lynx, and a little boy. "As is true of all the best children's stories, this one can be read on many levels—by a child as young as eight or nine and up to any age" (McNulty 1985, 142).

A magical power like David's is offered for slightly older readers in Selma Lagerlof's *The Wonderful Adventures of Nils* (1906) and *The Further Adventures of Nils* (1907). More recent examples include Mary James's *Shoebag* (1990) and *Shoebag Returns* (1996)—both of which have a cockroach narrator!—and a less fanciful but no less magical story for young adult readers, *Song of the Wild* (1980), by Allan W. Eckert. In the currently popular and useful Animorph series, the teenage heroes' magical ability to inhabit the bodies of nonhu-

mans is a gift from an alien being. The various versions of David's gift resemble in many ways Jarrell's explanation of his own poetic gifts and powers.[7] These are exactly the powers that the Kohls and Susan Strauss claim can help humans see the world from the animals' perspective.

Maligned Animals

Undoubtedly moved by the current emphasis on appreciation of diversity and difference, children's authors and illustrators such as Jarrell, Janelle Cannon, and Mary James tend to champion the least-loved—bats and snakes, cockroaches and worms. The subject deserves a study of its own, since these books would naturally prove of special use to humane educators. Jarrell's *The Bat Poet* (1971) "gives the reader a bat-eye view of bat activities rather than the usual frightened negative attitude toward them" (Apseloff 1989, 124). It surely influenced Cannon's wonderful children's book *Stellaluna* (1993), and its sequels, *Verdi* (1997), about a very individualistic young python, and *Crickwing* (2000), about a disabled tropical cockroach.

Humane educators can tailor a curriculum to one animal or type of animal using both natural history and books such as these (see sidebar on page 60).

Effect of Picture in Children's Literature

Illustrated by Maurice Sendak, Jarrell's animal stories are compelling examples of the profound effect of picture in children's literature. Lanes comments that Sendak's landscapes "move beyond illustration into the realm of visionary art akin to William Blake's" (1971, 75). Marcus (1983—84) suggests that to really "teach" a

Children's Books that Inspire Benevolence Toward the Coyote

Coyotes are an example of species that may be feared or disliked (for example, in communities where the animals are prevalent and may have attacked pets or other wild animals). Reading and discussing the following books makes an effective humane education program on learning about coyotes and living peacefully with them.

The Wild Pups: The True Story of a Coyote Family
(1975) by Hope Ryden

Hope Ryden is a wildlife biologist who followed a coyote pack in a national refuge. Through her real-life accounts of coyote life, she develops appreciation and empathy for the animal. The reader can observe firsthand the coyote's intelligence as well as the struggles the animal faces. Ryden uses anthropomorphism to show that coyotes experience feelings similar to those of humans. For example, the mother of the coyote family greets her mate "with kisses and playful taps of her paw." Ryden describes the coyotes as proud and capable of forming friendships. She refers to the coyote puppies as babies and compares them to domestic dog puppies.

Ryden shows the struggles of living in the wild; she describes hunting as a "hard way to make a living." Ryden writes that "the ice made their feet sore" and sometimes the coyotes had to "struggle across the blinding snow all day without finding anything to eat."

The author also touches on welfare issues concerning traps. Accompanying a photograph of a coyote in a trap is text explaining that a coyote may bite off his or her paw to escape. "Those who can-not free themselves must lie in the same position for days until the trapper returns to kill them. Many freeze or slowly starve." Ryden concludes that traps are cruel devices that many people want to see banned in this country.

Cleo and the Coyote
(1996) by Elizabeth Levy

The fictional Cleo and the Coyote shows the troubles a desert coyote must face through his relationship with the narrator, a domestic dog named Cleopatra. Cleopatra is a stray at Shea Stadium, the famous baseball stadium in Queens, New York, until a family brings her home. When the family moves to a relative's sheep ranch in Moab, Utah, Cleo meets Tricky the coyote. At first, the coyote is portrayed in a negative way, his howl an "awful noise" (1996, n.p.). Cleo sees a pair of yellow eyes eerily staring at her in the darkness, and the creature "strolled out from behind a rock like he owned the place" (n.p.). The coyote smiles and looks as if he thinks Cleo would make a tasty snack.

But Tricky befriends Cleo, bringing her chewed-up grasshoppers as his parents used to do when he was a pup. Cleo soon learns that Tricky's one short leg is the result of a trap that almost killed him, Levy's way of making the point about traps that Ryden makes. Tricky blames Cleo's guardians for this, as well as for his parents' death. Cleo denies this contention, saying her guardians are good people. When Cleo is surprised to see that it rains in the desert, Tricky smiles, "like the desert was one big practical joke" (n.p.). Cleo realizes that she has a lot of misunderstandings about the desert and its most cunning inhabitant.

Tricky saves Cleo from a natural disaster and brings her to shelter in a cave where Native Americans ("who thought coyotes were gods") used to live (n.p.). The two canines' life histories are blended together when they tell each other special stories from their past. Cleo tells a story about a baseball game when pretzels rained down from the sky, and Tricky tells a story in which the coyote god puts stars in the sky and makes all coyote and dog noses black. A two-page illustration accompanies this part of the story, one page with stars filling a night sky above the desert, the other with pretzels falling from a sunny sky above Shea Stadium. The two drawings meet and stars and pretzels mix in the middle, showing the coming together of the two canines' worlds, domestic and wild.

It is easy to empathize with Tricky, who had been victimized by humans. When Cleo asks why he was howling the night before, he says, "I was lonely after my mom and dad were killed" (n.p.). Cleo's family is looking for her, and Tricky accompanied her back to the ranch, only to meet a shotgun. Cleo saves Tricky from her owner's uncle's gun by knocking the man to the ground. Tricky asks Cleo to come with him but returns to his wild life alone when Cleo is called by her human owners. Separated by a canyon, Cleo and Tricky howl for each other at night.

Little Coyote Runs Away
(1997) by Craig Kee Strete

In this fictional story, the coyote is the protagonist, and that alone creates empathy for him. The story is likely to evoke emotion and encourage people to relate to coyotes. The illustrations in the book, which look like watercolor paintings, appeal to the reader with their beauty and artistic quality; this is important because even without the words they evoke emotion. One illustration, for example, shows the cute Little Coyote lying peacefully with his beautiful mother.

The story also can teach children a lesson about the need for family and the place of discipline in a young animal's life. Little Coyote becomes fed up with his mother's strictness and runs away. In his travels he comes upon a buzzard, a goat, and a bear, all of whom look big, hungry, or mean enough to eat a small coyote. Little Coyote uses the magic in his special medicine bag to distract these enemies or to hide himself from them. Eventually Little Coyote comes to a highway, and neither he nor his magic is any match for the speeding cars and trucks. He is illustrated here as lonely, desperate, and small compared to the relentless vehicles. Missing his cozy den and nice mother, the hungry little coyote runs home. "He yipped with coyote joy when he saw the entrance to his den" (1997, n.p.). He happily cleans his fur, as his mother has taught him to do, and eats his supper. If this story is to teach children about the importance of having a home in a scary world, the children must first relate to the coyote and recognize the animal's need for family. Thus, the lesson of running away is dependent on the lesson that coyotes have families and emotions, too.

Pecos Bill
(1983) by Ariane Dewey

This is the fictional story of a boy who is raised by coyotes after being rescued by one from a river. The coyotes raise him "like a pup" (1983, n.p.). Bill thinks he is a coyote. He learns to "run with the pack" and "howl at the moon." The book presents Bill as free; "he could do anything" living wild with the coyote pack (n.p.). When Bill is taken back to a life with humans, he is extraordinarily resourceful and ends up inventing the lasso. Showing a human in a close relationship with coyotes, the story conveys the message not only that humans can live with coyotes, but also that humans can learn from them.

Adult novels that encourage empathy and compassion for the coyote include, among others, Ursula Le Guin's *Buffalo Gals and Other Animal Presences* (1987), Ted Perry's *Rimshot* (1982), Melinda Worth Popham's *Skywater* (1990), and Barbara Kingsolver's *Prodigal Summer* (2001).

text with pictures, educators must understand the history of the animal in art as well as in literature. As Kennedy writes:

> Absorbing complex ideas through the combination of pictures and words is a new skill for most [adults], and one that takes a particular kind of intellectual effort in ways that neither words nor pictures alone can do. When we simultaneously experience both the visceral effect of pictures and the intellectual engagement of words, our brains connect with the material in a richer and more interactive way. Because we have to put the words and pictures together, we're more actively involved in constructing meaning and the effort wakes us up. (2002, L1–7)

Children can help adults with this difficult task. Even before they can read, children respond more independently to pictures than to words. That response, acknowledged, can be used to expand the themes of the text.

Sendak points out that illustrations can be vital to the development of empathy and compassion. One of his most convincing examples concerns Randolph Caldecott's drawings for the Mother Goose rhyme "Bye, Baby Bunting." His illustrations show father failing to kill a rabbit, going into town and buying a rabbit skin, and returning home to wrap the baby in it. When the page is turned

> [Y]ou see Baby and Mother strolling—Baby dressed in that idiotic costume with the ears poking out of her head—and up on the little hillside a group of rabbits playing. And...the Baby is staring with the most perplexed look at those rabbits, as though with the dawning knowledge that the...costume she's wrapped in has come from those creatures...Is this where rabbit skins come from? Does something have to die to dress me? (1988, 23–24)

Clearly Caldecott's illustrations suggest an interpretation. Without Caldecott's pictures, the rhyme itself would not readily serve a humane education goal.

Interpretation

The humane educator must recognize and grapple with children's confusion about the status of other animals and "the often contradictory mix of social codes governing animals and their treatment." That there are creatures accepted "as family members, stamped out as pests, saved from extinction, and ground into Big Macs" does not make much sense. Children's confusion "mirrors societal unease with culturally sanctioned uses of animals. If we wish to redefine those uses, children's relationships to animals may be the place to begin" (Melson 2001, 20–21).

Children may also be confused about how different "readers" can draw completely different themes from the same pictures (and words). In Anno's *Anno's Aesop* (1987), for instance, Mr. Fox, who doesn't read, interprets for his son the pictures that illustrate the fables. His interpretation will surprise adult human readers and suggest how a fox might really focus fables for a fox world. Human readers can then compare Mr. Fox's version with their own versions of Aesop's fables. This example shows that selection and interpretation of stories always are key to reaching the goals of knowledge, awareness, empathy, and compassion. The full impact comes from simultaneously experiencing the story, pictures, and a reinforcing discussion of theme and goal carefully designed not to take away from the audience's delight in hearing and seeing the story.

Interpretation in humane education is less a matter of explicating the text, as one might do in a literature classroom, than of listening to the voices the author creates and calling attention to details of the pictures. The adult reader/interpreter must also be careful to point out accuracies and inaccuracies in the storyteller's and illustrator's depictions of animals without belaboring the exposition, and consequently limiting the child's enjoyment of the book. The ideal is to develop readers capable of both delight and discrimination. For humane education purposes, depictions of animals, no matter how fanciful, must have their basis in accurate detail about the animals' lives and behaviors, and their relationships to one another and to humans. For example, when reading *Babe the Gallant Pig* and *Charlotte's Web*, the educator will want to explain that, while some small farms resembling those in the books still exist, most farm animals today live lives much different from those of Babe and Wilbur. In *Valentine's Gift* educators will want to help young readers see that, without the gift of a magic horn that lets the boy understand the language of animals, the otherwise anthropomorphized characters would be as seemingly silent as the animals they know in real life. Discussion of how humans can listen to animals without "magic" can lead to a new appreciation of the varied "languages" nonhumans use all the time, rather than to disappointment with what seems to be the inability of real animals to talk to us. Other factors that can enhance a story are sound and voice control (Storyteller Susan Strauss has run workshops at the National Association for Interpretation conferences, teaching educators these techniques.)

Part of Lifelong Humane Education

Children's literature is a wonderful and powerful humane education tool, one capable of sending messages that stay with a child for life and have significant influence. Many children are nurturing by nature and are likely to retain the values learned from one story and act on them. Most children, however, will need constant reinforcement of humane lessons long after their days of enjoying children's books are over. This reinforcement, to be effective, must be lifelong. As Melson points out, at present "[r]esources

thin out as reading levels rise, so that by high school, except for biology classes [and perhaps not even there], living [and fictional] animals have largely disappeared. Animals almost never figure as topics of study in their own right. Even rarer is the use of animals to structure teaching of other subjects" (2001, 78). The challenge, therefore, is for humane educators to develop more sophisticated programs for young adults and adults.

Literature is, of course, only one of many powerful tools. The possibilities are legion. Adults, like children, are influenced by the media, by outreach from humane societies, and by formal education (e.g., integration of humane lessons into traditional elementary school curricula, or inclusion of novels with humane themes in a college literature course).[8] Every effort is important, no matter how big or small. All successful humane education efforts are likely to open one's mind to future education, and people spread the messages learned to others (children, for example, often bring home to their parents the humane messages they learn in school).

Conclusion

Today, with so many strong and often negative influences competing for children's hearts and minds, teaching children values and building character is more important than ever. Humane educators have an excellent opportunity to use the magic of stories to create powerful humane education lessons. A humane education program that teaches children to celebrate life, "the beauty of the world . . . the glory of everything," as *Charlotte's Web* does, provides the occasion for developing imagination and empathy, and returning humans to the presence of animals. With continued care, these roots will flourish into responsible and mature compassion, and an empathy and concern for the welfare of the natural world.

Notes
[1]An example of this can be found in the first passage of Kilpatrick, Wolfe, and Wolfe (1994). It begins with the story of a four-year-old girl named Crystal whose younger sister begins to cry over a stuffed animal she has lost. Crystal gives her sister one of her own stuffed animals, saying, "She wants her Dogger." The night before Crystal had heard a story, called "Dogger," about a boy who loses his worn, stuffed dog, and his big sister, Bella, who trades a big, beautiful stuffed bear to get her little brother's worn, stuffed dog, Dogger, back for him.

In many ways Crystal's reaction to her sister's distress is a great example of how moral reasoning and empathy generated by a story can translate into real-life moral behavior. In fact, Kilpatricke, Wolfe, and Wolfe go on to state, "Crystal was putting into practice the good examples set by Bella. . . . " "[She] is beginning to develop a picture in her mind of the way things should be, of how people can act when they are at their best" (17).

[2]For each animal and habitat educators wish to make habitable for their students, Strauss recommends: "Do your research. Know your subject: Know its scientific or historic story and knowledge. Then speak out of your love for the subject and its story. Don't lose sight of your passion for the story. . . . Think of yourself as an artist more than an interpreter or educator. Remember Coyote—hero, creator and fool of Native American mythology. In the image of creator, Coyote was never satisfied within the bounds of accepted practices—curious, questioning, sniffing around in unknown territory—vulnerable, falls to his death and is reborn. "So, as Coyote imagined it," they say, "so, it was created! Sometimes Coyote brought back good things and changed the way society thought and did things" (1996, 141).

[3]Roger L. Welsch cautions that

An unfortunate tendency exists today to treat folktales of other cultures as the stuff of children's stories. While children enjoy traditional materials and learn from them, it is important for us to remember that folk narratives are almost always the subject of adult conversation and performance. . . . Folktales are, after all, a delicate and intricate kind of literature, maintained and refined by generations and generations of performance.

. . . The broader and longer experience of adults increases the chance that they will understand or at least sense the lessons and messages embedded within these tales. (1988, 487)

Melson adds:

Animal fables and fairy tales, originally serious entertainment for grownups—Socrates spent his days in prison putting Aesop's fables into verse form—are now part of the juvenile cannon. As one writer put it, "Once we stopped knowing animals as a direct matter of survival—as partners in work, as quarry to hunt, as predators to evade—fables could be read as stories about cute animals that could safely be given to children." (2001, 143)

[4]In a collection of parables compiled from ancient records originally published in 1894, Paul Carus (1999) includes this quote from Buddha:

I have taught the truth which is excellent in the beginning, excellent in the middle, and excellent in the end; it is glorious in its spirit and glorious in its letter.

But simple as it is, the people cannot understand it.

I must speak to them in their own language. I must adapt my thought to their thoughts. They are like unto children, and love to hear tales.

Therefore, I will tell them stories to explain the glory of the Dharma.

If they cannot grasp the truth in the abstract arguments by which I have reached it, they may nevertheless come to understand it, if it is illustrated in parables.

[5]University of Colorado biologist Marc Bekoff uses what has been referred to as a Dr. Doolittle approach to the study of animal behavior, something he may have learned from Jane Goodall when he studied with her in Africa. It would be interesting to document how many of those who spend their life in the company of animals would trace that passion as Goodall does to childhood reading. In *The New Yorker's* 1985 "Children's Books for Christmas," naturalist and writer Faith McNulty "began to ponder the hold animal books have on young imaginations" and, in the process, recalled that

[T]he animal books I read between the ages of six and twelve...held the greatest enchantment for me, and especially those...in which the animals talked. Eavesdropping...I felt I had the power given King Solomon by the magic ring, which allowed him to converse with animals in a language hidden from everyone else. (137)

[6]A grown-up version, championed by the Council of All Beings and certainly of use to the humane educator, is described in Seed et al. (1991). It makes clear that, with the right choice of story empathy and compassion can extend to all beings—animal, plant, environment, mountain, volcano, ocean, planet—an important expansion of humane education for humans of all ages.

[7]This ties in with findings, described by Chawla (1994), of her recent study of the influence of early childhood experiences with nature and animals. Chawla relies on the pioneering work of Cobb (1977), who claims that, in terms of attitudes toward nature and animals, the child is truly father to the man. If true or even partially true, one cannot overemphasize the importance of young children being introduced to the natural world by parents and educators concerned for its well-being and convinced of its intrinsic value. Chawla's study also convinced her of the need to integrate the sciences (including the social sciences, since she is a psychologist) and humanities if children are to develop and retain the synthesis of heart and mind requisite to a mature as well as a childish concern for nature and its creatures.

Similar positive childhood experiences by artists contribute to the role of nature and animals in artwork that is useful in extending humane education. Painter and sculptor Edwin Bogucki, for instance, recalls a childhood of unsupervised wandering in the woods and fields around his home. He remembers significant contact with animals, in particular horses, his major subject, from the age of two. He comments: "This spiritual connection with an animal is crucial to my work. I feel that I am what I create....I imagine that I am the horse, the rider, the hounds"

(Bogucki 1998, 34).

[8]Examples of good books for such a curriculum are Richard Adams's *Watership Down*, Akif Pirincci's *Felidae*, Renaldo Arenas's *The Doorman*, David Clement-Davies's *Fire Bringer* and *The Sight*, William Horwood's *Duncton Woods* and *The Wolves of Time* series, Barbara Kingsolver's *Prodigal Summer*, Robert Siegel's *Whalesong*, *White Whale*, and *The Ice at the End of the World*, Beat Sterchi's *Cow*, and Daniel Quinn's *Ishmael*. Contemporary horse autobiographies to update *Black Beauty* include John Hawkes's *Sweet William* and Jane Smiley's *Horse Heaven*.

Selected Animal Stories with Humane Themes for Children

Adams, R. 1975. *Watership down.* New York: William Morrow and Co.

Anderson, H.C., J. Pinkney, illus. 1999. *The ugly duckling.* New York: William Morrow and Co. (Originally published in 1846.)

Anonymous. 1765. *Valentine's gift.* Newbery.

Applegate, K.A. 1996—present. Animorphs series. New York: Scholastic. An active web site exists (*http://scholastic.com/animorphs/*) and a TV series began on Nickelodeon in September 1998.

Arenas, R., Koch, D.M., trans. 1994. *The doorman.* New York: Grove/Atlantic.

Argus, A. 1815. *The adventure of a donkey.*

———. 1821. *Further adventures of Jemmy Donkey.*

Cannon, J. 2000. *Crickwing.* New York: Harcourt Brace and Co.

———. 1993. *Stellaluna.* New York: Harcourt Brace and Co.

———. 1997. *Verdi.* New York: Harcourt Brace and Co.

Clement-Davies, D. 2000. *Fire bringer.* New York: Dutton Books.

———. 2002. *The sight.* New York: Dutton Books.

Eckert, A.W. 1980. *Song of the wild.* Boston: Little, Brown.

Hawkes, J. 1994. *Sweet William: A memoir of an old horse.* New York: Penguin USA.

Horwood, W. 1992. *Duncton Woods.* New York: HarperCollins.

———. 1996. *The wolves of time—Vol. 1: Journeys to the heartland.* Montague, Mass.: Acacia Press, Inc.

Jacques, B. 1986–present. *Redwall* series. New York: Philomel.

James, M. 1990. *Shoebag.* New York: Scholastic.

———. 1996. *Shoebag returns.* New York: Scholastic.

Jarrell, R., M. Sendak, illus. 1965, 1985. *The animal family.* New York: Pantheon.

———. 1964. *The bat poet.* New York: Macmillan.

———. 1976. *Fly by night.* New York: Farrar, Strauss and Giroux.

Jeffries, R. 1974. *Wood magic.* Okpaku Communications Corp. (Originally published in 1881.)

Kilner, D. 1783. *The life and perambulations of a mouse.*

———. 1799. *The rational brutes: or, talking animals.*

Kindall, E.A. 1798. *Keeper's travels in search of his master.*

Kingsley, C. 1995. *The water babies: A fairy tale for a land baby.* Minneapolis: Econo-Clad Books. (Originally published in 1863.)

King-Smith, D. 1983. *Babe the gallant pig.* New York: Random House.

Kingsolver, B. 2000. *Prodigal summer.* New York: HarperCollins.

Kipling, R. 1894. *The jungle book.*

Lagerlof, S., L. Klinting, illus. 1992. *The wonderful adventures of Nils.* Floris Books. (Originally published in 1906.)

Lagerlof, S.O., N. Johnson, Pantheon Books Staff, illus., V.S. Howard, trans. 1992. *The further adventures of Nils.* Skandisk, Inc. (Originally published in 1907.)

Larson, G. 1998. *There's a hair in my dirt: A worm's story.* New York: HarperCollins.

Lawson, R. 1944. *Rabbit Hill.* New York and London: Puffin Books.

Le Guin, U. 1987. *Buffalo gals and other animal presences.* Santa Barbara: Capra Press.

Lemon, M. 1869. *Tinykin's transformation.*

Lofting, H. 1997. *The story of Doctor Dolittle.* New York: William Morrow Books of Wonder. (Originally published in 1920.)

London, J., M. Gascoigne, illus. 1983. *The call of the wild.* New York: Penguin Putnam Books for Young Readers. (Originally published in 1903.)

McDonald, G. 1963. *At the back of the North Wind.* New York: Schocken. (Originally published in 1871.)

Paine, A.B. 1925. *The Arkansaw bear.* New York: Harper. (Originally published in 1898.)

Perry, T., J. Svendsen, illus. 1982. *Rimshot.* Broomall, Pa.: Chelsea House Publishers.

Pirincci, A. 1996. *Felidae.* New York: Random House Value Publishers.

Popham, M.W. 1990. *Skywater.* St. Paul: Graywolf Press.

Porter, G.S. 1999. *The strike at Shane's: A prize story of India.* Bedford, Mass.: Applewood Books.

Potter, B. 1988. *The tale of Peter Rabbit.* New York: Random House Value Publishers, Inc. There's a wonderful Web site: *http://www.peterrabbit.co.uk/.*

Quinn, D. 1995. *Ishmael.* New York: Bantam Books. Originally published in 1992.

Roberts, C.G. 1977. *The kindred of the wild: A book of animal life.* Ayer Company Publishers, Inc. (Originally published in 1896.)

Saunders, M. 1994. *Beautiful Joe: An autobiography.* St. Paul: Consortium Book Sales and Distribution. (Originally published in 1893.)

Seton, E.T. 1998. *Wild animals I have known.* Cutchogue, N.Y.: Buccaneer Books, Inc. (Originally published in 1898.)

Sewell, A., I. Andrew, illus., N. Lewis, foreword. 2001. *Black Beauty: His grooms and companions: The autobiography of a horse.* London: Kingfisher Press. (Originally published in 1877.)

Siegel, R. 1981. *Whalesong.* Crossways–Westchester, Ill.: Scott Foresman.

———. 1994. *The ice at the end of the world.* San Francisco: Harper San Francisco.

———. 1994. *White whale: A novel about friendship and courage in the deep.* San Francisco: Harper San Francisco.

Smiley, J. 2001. *Horse heaven.* New York: Ballantine Books.

Sterchi, B., M. Hofmann, trans. 1990. *Cow.* New York: Pantheon Books.

Travers, P.L. 1986. *Friend monkey.* New York: Dell Publishing Company, Inc.

Trimmer, S. 1786. *The history of robins.*

Universal City Studios, Inc. 1995. *Babe.* J. Cromwell and M. Szubanski. (Based on *Babe the gallant pig,* by Dick King-Smith.)

White, E.B. 1952. *Charlotte's web.* New York: Harper and Row.

White, T.H. 1985. The sword in the stone. In *The once and future king.* New York: Berkley. (Originally published in 1938, revised in 1957.)

The excerpts on pp. 53, 55, 61, 62, and 63 are reprinted by permission of the publisher from *Why the Wild Things Are: Animals in the Lives of Children* by Gail F. Melson, pp. 5, 20–21, 78, 107, 130–131, 145, Cambridge, Mass.: Harvard University Press, Copyright © 2001 by Gail F. Melson.

The excerpts on p. 52 are reprinted by permission of the publisher from *Fairy Tales and After From Snow White to E.B. White* by Roger Sale, p. 77, Cambridge, Mass.: Harvard University Press, Copyright © 1978 by the President and Fellows of Harvard College.

The excerpts on p. 62 are reprinted by permission of Fulcrum Publishing, Golden, Colorado, from *The Passionate Fact: Storytelling in Natural History and Cultural Interpretation* (1996) by Susan Strauss.

The excerpts on pp. 53, 54, and 57 are reprinted by permission of the author from *Pipers at the Gates of Dawn: The Wisdom of Children's Literature* (Random House, 1981) by Jonathan Cott.

The excerpts on pp. 58–59 from "In the Shadow of Jane Goodall" by Robert Michael Pyle and on p. 51 from *Bringing the World Alive: A Bibliography of Nature Stories for Children* by Jennifer Sahn are reprinted by permission of The Orion Society, 187 Main Street, Great Barrington, MA 01230.

The excerpt on p. 57 from "Endless Summer Reading," by Kathleen Odean (July/August 1999), is reprinted by permission of *Book* magazine, New York, N.Y.

The excerpts on pp. 54, 56, 57, and 59 from *Worlds Within: Children's Fantasy from the Middle Ages to Today* © 1988 by Sheila Egoff are reproduced by permission of the American Library Association.

The excerpt on p. 63 from *Truth Never Sleeps: Myths of the Omaha* by R.L. Welsh (1988) is reprinted by permission from *The World and I* magazine.

Literature Cited

Acocella, J. 1998. The big bad wolf is back. *The New Yorker*, November 30: 112–119.

Allen, M. 1983. *Animals in American literature.* Champaign: University of Illinois Press.

Anno, M. 1987. *Anno's Aesop: A book of fables by Aesop and Mr. Fox, retold and illustrated.* New York: Orchard Books.

Apseloff, M.F., compiler. 1989. *They wrote for children too: An annotated bibliography of children's literature by famous writers for adults.* Westport, Conn.: Greenwood Press.

American Society for the Prevention of Cruelty to Animals (ASPCA). 1997. *Kids, animals and literature: Annotated bibliography of children's books with a positive, humane theme.* New York: ASPCA.

Baym, N. 1994. *Women's fiction: A guide to novels by and about women in America, 1820–1870.* Champaign: University of Illinois Press.

Blount, M. 1975. *Animal land: The creatures of children's fiction.* New York: William Morrow.

Bogucki, K. 1998. Divine discontent. *The Equine Image* Aug/Sept: 30–34.

Carus, P., D. St. Ruth, eds. 1999. *Teachings of Buddha* (abridged), (originally published in 1894 as *Gospel of Buddha*). New York: St. Martin's Press.

Chawla, L. 1994. *In the country of first places: Nature, poetry, and childhood memory.* Albany: State University of New York Press.

Cobb, E. 1977. *The ecology of imagination in childhood.* New York: Columbia University Press.

Cott, J. 1981. *Pipers at the gates of dawn: The wisdom of children's literature.* New York: Random House.

Cronin, D. 2000. *Click, clack, moo: Cows that type.* New York: Simon and Schuster Books for Young Readers.

Cruickshank, D. 1999. If she could talk to the animals. *www.salon-magazine.com/bc/1999/03/23bc.html*.

Currie, Q. 1990. *Black Beauty*. Seattle: Storyteller's Ink.

Dewey, A. 1983. *Pecos Bill*. New York: Greenwillow Books.

Egoff, S. 1981. Beast tales and animal fantasy. In *Thursday's child: Trends and patterns in contemporary children's literature*, ed. S. Egoff, 105–119. Chicago and London: American Library Association.

———. 1988. *Worlds within: Children's fantasy from the Middle Ages to today*. Chicago and London: American Library Association.

Graham, B. 2001. *"Let's get a pup!" said Kate*. Cambridge: Candlewick Press.

Hanne, M. 1994. *The power of story: Fiction and political change*. Providence and Oxford: Berghahn Books.

Houk, R. 1995. *Hope*. Wheeling, Ill.: The Benefactory, Inc.

Kennedy, L. 2002. Pulp fiction. *The New York Times*, 26 May. Arts: L1, 7.

Kilpatrick, W., G. Wolfe, and S. Wolfe. 1994. *Books that build character: A guide to teaching your child moral values through stories*. New York: Simon and Schuster.

Kohl, J., and H. Kohl. 1977. *The view from the oak: The private world of other creatures*. San Francisco and New York: Sierra Club/Charles Scribner's.

Lanes, S.G. 1971. *Down the rabbit hole: Adventures and misadventures in the realm of children's literature*. New York: Atheneum.

Levy E., D. Bryer, illus. 1996. *Cleo and the coyote*. New York: Harper Collins Children's Books.

McCloskey, R. 1948. *Blueberries for Sal*. New York: Viking Press.

McCully, E.A. 2000. *Hurry!* San Diego: Browndeer Press. (Original text © 1972; adapted from *Farewell to the Farivox*, by Harry Hartwick.)

Marcus, L.S. 1983–1984. Picture book animals: How natural a history? *The Lion and the Unicorn* 7/8: 127–139.

Magee, W.H. 1969. The animal story: A challenge in technique. In *Only connect: Readings in children's literature*, ed. S. Egoff, 221–232. London: Oxford University Press.

McNulty, F. 1985. Children's books for Christmas. *The New Yorker*, December 2: 137–147.

Melson, G.F. 2001. *Why the wild things are: Animals in the lives of children*. Cambridge and London: Harvard University Press.

Morton, E.S. and J. Page. 1992. *Animal talk: Science and the voices of nature*. New York: Random House.

Nowicki, K. 1998. Baa! Meow! Woof! Great opportunities in the game of let's pretend with Turner's "Let's be animals." *Northampton* (Mass.) *Daily Gazette*, September 19–20: W1–W2.

Odean, K. 1999. Endless summer reading. *Book* July/August: 88–89.

Pyle, R.M. 1998. In the shadow of Jane Goodall. *Orion Afield*, Autumn: 42–43.

Rawls, W. 1999. *Summer of the monkeys*. New York: Bantam/Doubleday/Dell Books for Young Readers.

Ryden H. 1975. *The wild pups: The true story of a coyote family*. New York: The Putnam Publishing Group.

Sale, R. 1978. Animals. *In Fairy tales and after from Snow White to E.B. White*, ed. R. Sale, 77–99. Cambridge: Harvard University Press.

Sahn, J., comp. 1995. *Bringing the world alive: A bibliography of nature stories for children*. New York: The Orion Society.

Seed, J.D., I. Pugh, and P.F. Leming. 1988. *Thinking like a mountain: Towards a council of all beings*. Gabriola Island, B.C.: New Society Press.

Sendak, M. 1988. *Caldecott & Co.: Notes on books and pictures*. New York: Farrar, Strauss and Giroux.

Strauss, S. 1996. *The passionate fact: Storytelling in natural history and cultural interpretation*. Golden, Colo.: North American Press.

Strete C.K., H. Stevenson, illus. 1997. *Little Coyote runs away*. New York: The Putnam Publishing Group.

Swinfen, A. 1984. Talking beasts. In *In defence of fantasy: A study of the genre in English and American literature since 1945*, ed. A. Swinfen, 12–43. London and Boston: Routledge and Kegan.

Thomas, K. 1983. *Man and the natural world: A history of the modern sensibility*. New York: Pantheon.

Townsend, J.R. 1967. Articulate animals. In *Written for children: An outline of English-language children's literature*, ed. J.R. Townsend. New York: Lippincott.

Vitz, P. 1990. The use of stories in moral development. *American Psychologist* 45(6): 709–720.

Welsch, R.L. 1988. Truth never sleeps: Myths of the Omaha. *The World & I* May: 484–492.

Wollstonecraft, M. 1788. *Original stories*. Url no longer available.

The No-Kill Controversy: Manifest and Latent Sources of Tension

5

Arnold Arluke

Introduction

Traditionally, most animal shelter workers have denied that the killing, or euthanasia, of animals in their facilities was cruel, even when euthanized animals were adoptable, young, attractive, and healthy.[1] Workers have sustained a core professional identity of being humane, good-hearted "animal people" who want the very best for their charges, despite—or even because of—their euthanasia of animals. Killing has been taken for granted, regarded as a "necessary evil" having no alternative in their eyes.

One reason shelter workers have been able to maintain this self image is that, until the last decade, little if any organized criticism has been leveled at them. When criticism occurred, it tended to be case-specific, focusing on which animals were euthanized, how it was done, and whether the shelter shared this information with the public. Although a few shelters offered an alternative to the standard paradigm by restricting admission of unadoptable animals and billing themselves as "no-kill" shelters, they did not represent a serious threat to the continuation of "open-admission" policies toward euthanasia.[2]

However, criticism of euthanasia has mounted steadily in frequency and fervor from within certain segments of the sheltering community. In 1994 the Duffield Family Foundation created the Maddie's Fund, which sought to revolutionize the status and well-being of companion animals by championing the no-kill movement. No longer possible to ignore or discount as an outrageous idea, this movement has spurred debate at the national level about the proper role of euthanasia in shelter practice. The resulting challenges have strained the ability of conventional shelters and humane organizations to protect workers psychologically from the charge that euthanasia is a form of cruelty. Instead of preventing cruelty, which their mission maintains, these organizations now are seen as causing it. In response, the no-kill movement has been attacked by those who defend the practice of euthanasia and open admission.

Although some argue that everyone in the debate shares a passionate concern for the welfare of animals, a rift over this issue divides the shelter community. Ultimately, the best interests of animals may not be best addressed in a climate of controversy and criticism. To understand and perhaps reduce this controversy, the tensions fueling the no-kill conflict need to be identified and the breadth of the gulf separating its two camps assessed.

Method

I investigated the shelter community's response to the no-kill movement in two communities that have taken different approaches to the issue. Though located on opposite coasts of the country, these metropolitan areas are similar in size and wealth. The makeup and nature of their humane organizations, however, are quite dissimilar. One community is home to many independent organizations that individually have received praise or criticism over the years; until recently they have been a widespread group of equals sharing a common media market. Even animal control programs have been large, countywide, and sometimes-progressive players in their own right. In the other community, two key players are so large that they have dwarfed the role and significance of others; the two players have been conservative, lagging somewhat behind the nationwide trends in sheltering. These two communities have dealt very differently with the pet overpopulation issue. In one case the SPCA (society for the prevention of cruelty to animals) has embraced the no-kill concept, while in the other it has not. There are differences in the relationships between the SPCAs and neighboring humane organizations, as well; in the former community these relationships are uneasy, while in the latter they are cordial.

In each community I conducted participant observation at the SPCA shelter, the city animal control office, and nearby (i.e., within sixty miles) smaller shelters that either competed with or complemented the work of the SPCAs. "Sanctuaries" and rescue groups also were studied. Gatekeepers in these settings introduced me to respondents as a sociologist interested in understanding how people thought and felt about the no-kill issue. I was allowed to observe almost every facet of shelter and sanctuary operation, including, but not limited to, kennel cleaning, intake, adoption work, behavior training, and euthanasia. Ultimately I carried out more than 200 hours of observation and 75 interviews that elicited the interviewees' perspective on the no-kill issue and the animal overpopulation problem. In addition I attended the national meetings of the major no-kill and open-admission organizations, examined press accounts and shelter publications relating to no-kill, and combed several Internet news groups that discussed shelter issues.

Details about each camp's perspective were subject to respondents' biases, distortions, and memory limitations. Information obtained was treated as an accurate reflection of what people thought and felt, whether or not it was objectively true, since the perception of truth motivated and justified people's behavior. From these data I constructed, rather than assessed, the perspectives of both camps toward the no-kill issue. Although this approach follows that of sociologists and social historians, who argue that collective behavior is best understood by examining participants' own understandings in relation to their social context, it may frustrate those who think I should be more critical. However a critical approach would be neither faithful to my ethnographic method nor helpful in creating dialogue and common ground.

I also tried to sample a wide variety of shelter organizations by size, orientation, location, and financial health, but it was impossible, and perhaps unnecessary, to study every nuance and variation. The wide diversity makes it very difficult to characterize the perspectives of these camps. Indeed, at one level, the only thing that makes each camp identifiable as a group is the fact that one supports the role of and need for euthanasia, while the other does not. Even here, though, the why, the how, and the circumstances of euthanasia vary considerably. For example, the players, policies, and realities of animal sheltering in any one community vary in terms of numbers, composition, strength, and orientation of shelter organizations. Arguments and perceptions of individuals on both sides are informed by and respond to the realities of their own communities. In some cases, these local realities lead members of the same camp, who work in different contexts, to make very different comments about the opposition. Knowing this may help readers understand contradictory statements made by respondents on the same side of this controversy.

Manifest and Latent Tensions

Groups experience tension in two ways. At a manifest or surface level, group members are aware of and speak about superficial differences in attitudes or behaviors thought to cause various problems. These surface tensions are acknowledged publicly at group meetings, written about in professional and popular publications, and debated and mulled over by those who experience them. Since these manifest tensions are thought to be the root cause of problems, solutions are aimed at altering, neutralizing, or eliminating them.

While important to understand and manage, these manifest tensions are symptomatic of deeper, rarely verbalized tensions. These latent tensions are sensed by group members but rarely articulated in a conscious or deliberate manner. The tensions lurk beneath the surface of everyday communication, perhaps appearing in innuendos that stop short of saying what actually is on the minds and in the hearts of speakers. For those hoping to reconcile tense intergroup relations, it is crucial to identify and correct sources of latent tension. Attempts to reduce conflict often stop short, staying at the manifest level of perceived differences or problems and offering solutions that cannot significantly reduce group tension because issues, images, and implications below the surface remain untouched.

Certainly, the American humane community is no exception to this pattern. Discussions about no-kill have been more cathartic than analytic, allowing people to vent their confusion or anger and identify allies and enemies. These discussions have stayed at the manifest level of intergroup tension, involving issues of dirty work and dishonesty.

Manifest Tensions

Dirty Work

Some jobs important to the everyday operation of society are avoided by people who choose not to engage in disrespected occupations. This dirty work is seen as distasteful or discrediting because it casts a moral pall over those who do it (Hughes 1964). Most people turn a blind eye to this work, preferring that others do it but viewing those who do so as modern untouchables—members of a caste thought to be symbolically contaminated and best avoided or pitied because they are associated with unpopular, unpleasant, or unclean tasks.

Many of the open-admissionists I interviewed felt that no-kill shelters delegated euthanasia to them. They believed that they were judged to be morally tainted because they killed animals. They sensed they were uncomfortably tolerated, at best, for carrying out such an unpleasant task, and challenged, at worst, for continuing to do it. As one respondent said,

"Why am I now an enemy? It used to be the humane societies versus the pounds, who were the baddies. Now we are the baddies." Another respondent concurred, saying, "It's no fun being the villains with the black hats." As the "baddies," open-admission workers thought that no-kill advocates cast them as wrong-doers who were "looked down upon" (Milani 1997), "discredited" (Bogue 1998b) or "guilty...because they are murderers" (Caras 1997a) "...sadists, or monsters" (Caras 1997b). Moreover some respondents felt that, with the growing popularity of the no-kill concept, the public had joined this critical bandwagon to castigate them as bad people for euthanizing animals. The result was that open admissionists, rather than the public, were blamed.

The casting of open admissionists as "baddies" stemmed from the language used by no-kill advocates. Many open-admissionists argued that the term *no-kill* was itself an "attack" on them, implying a "put-down" of open admissionists as killers (Bogue 1998a). "When they say, 'no-kill,' what they really mean is, 'you-kill,'" claimed one critic (Miller n.d.). Indeed, there was concern that the terminology itself positioned open admissionsts as "pro-kill" (Paris 1997), since the term *no-kill* implies its opposite. "Open admission shelters are not 'kill' shelters any more than 'pro-choicers' are 'pro-abortion,'" explained one open-admission advocate. Not surprisingly, some open-admissionists have called for abolishing the "no-kill" label and substituting the term *limited admission*.

Even more provocative was language that accused open-admission shelters of killing animals in ways reminiscent of Nazi cruelties to humans. One charge labeled the open-admission approach the "final solution," a term referring to the Holocaust. Another charge was even more specific: referring to euthanasia by open-admissionists, a no-kill conference panelist described it as the "holocaust of family members [i.e., shelter animals] being put to

death." And a number of shelter directors have been called "butcher," "Hitler," and "concentration-camp runner" (Foster 2000; Gilyard 2001, 6–7). Short of specific references to the Nazi Holocaust, some no-kill advocates suggested genocide-like actions by open-admissionists because they were conducting "mass slaughter of animals" or "legitimized mass slaughter."

Slightly less provocative were charges of criminal-like action toward animals. "To me it's *criminal* if a dog with poor manners or who is a little bit standoff-ish should be euthanized for behavior reasons," noted one no-kill advocate. Sometimes the "criminal" metaphor was created through the use of such penal language as "execute." For example, one no-kill trainer was trying to modify the behavior of a very aggressive dog who bit two staff members, required muzzling for walks, and was kept in the shelter for sixteen months. She said that the dog would have been "executed" had the dog been in an open-admission facility. This terminology suggests that, if open-admission workers euthanized this difficult-to-adopt, potentially dangerous dog, their act would be morally equivalent to putting a criminal to death. While open-admission shelters spoke of "euthanasia rooms" and "euthanasia technicians," no-kill staff claimed that their shelters did not have "*execution* chambers" and maintained that they did not "kill" as did their open-admission peers.

At the core of this provocative imagery was the idea that open admissionists were killers, an idea that reinforced the no-kill distinction between killing and euthanizing. Open admissionists patently rejected this distinction, claiming that they only euthanized. Of course, when working with peers, open-admission workers did speak of killing. Shelter workers sometimes used the term *kill* when speaking with colleagues but were careful to say "euthanize" when speaking to the public. Use of this language was not an implicit acceptance of the no-kill distinction, but

rather a combination of black humor and informal understanding that they were using *kill* as a linguistic short-hand to describe their acts. Other shelter workers deliberately used the term *kill*, at least before the rise of the no-kill movement, as an interesting way to demonstrate their continuing lack of acceptance of euthanasia as a solution. For them it served as a reminder that this was something they did not like to do and wanted to eliminate the need for. Thus, while some objected to the use of this term because they were concerned about it making them look or feel callous, others supported its use, saying that it helped remind them that they were taking lives—a symbolic way of keeping fresh the commitment to attack the source of the problem.

Open admissionists resented the perception of them as killers because they felt it was unfair or hypocritical. In their opinion, by being forced to euthanize many animals, they were made to shoulder all the moral, emotional, and aesthetic heartaches that went with the job. One editorial argued that the harm of no-kill is that

> It punishes shelters that are doing their very best but are stuck with the dirty work. It is demoralizing and disheartening for humane workers who would do almost anything to stop that heartbreaking selection process. Humane workers who are brave enough to accept that dirty work deserve better than that. (Caras 1997c, 17)

Instead open admissionists called for what one interviewee described as "...sharing the burden. As long as there is euthanasia to be done, the resentment on the part of us is that we shouldn't be doing it all. Any shelter in the same town should be sharing the burden. That's like saying we are all working on the same issue. We are all going to take the good stuff and the bad stuff."

However, no-kill proponents argued that if anyone was to blame it should be open admissionists. In their opinion blaming no-killers for delegating dirty work sidetracked shelter workers from a more important matter. Open admissionists, they said, needed to see that they were guilty of complicity in killing because they made it "easy" for the public to handle their animals like unwanted consumer goods disposed of without forethought. "They [open-admission shelters] are teaching the public they can throw away their animals at the shelter, and the shelter will euthanize their problem for them, and they aren't to blame because they took the pet to the shelter."

No-killers saw charges of dirty work delegation as "garbage talk," contending that open-admission shelters needed to rethink their mission and identity so they could become no-kill themselves. Open-admission shelters should "get out of the killing business," as one no-kill worker said, for the sake of those working in such settings. Carrying out euthanasia was thought to be an "endlessly demoralizing activity" that stopped workers from focusing on their "core purpose: bringing an end to the killing of these animals."[3] Having sympathy for their euthanizing peers, many no-kill employees wanted them to have the opportunity to work in an environment where the killing of animals was rare and, when done, was for apparently extreme veterinary or behavioral problems. "People are drawn to work here because it is less scary," observed one no-kill worker. The scariness refers to the loss, guilt, and grief experienced if workers kill animals with whom they have established some relationship, especially if these animals were potentially adoptable. Another worker explained, "I don't have to worry that I am going to bond with an animal and then have to put him down, which is my perception of what happens in kill shelters. So I feel lucky that those are the kinds of emotions I don't have to deal with." This thinking suggested that no-kill workers were not ducking responsibility for delegating dirty work or refusing to share the burden. Instead, they wondered why open admissionists continued their traditional approach to euthanasia, given its adverse emotional impact on them.

No-kill proponents pointed out that they too have been discredited or demonized for not killing enough animals as opposed to killing too many. This stigma was felt, according to many no-kill spokespersons, when they were ignored by open-admission leaders. Several speakers at a no-kill conference lamented the lack of support for no-kill at national animal welfare and animal rights conferences, where companion animal issues were "not well represented." They felt that open-admission authorities spurned their well-intentioned advances for support of no-kill conferences and other activities. One national spokeswoman for the no-kill movement claimed that prominent open-admission leaders and academics even refused to return her telephone calls. This lack of recognition by mainstream humane authorities was seen as hypocritical, given their presumed concern for promoting the welfare of animals. As one speaker at a no-kill conference pointed out, "The most fundamental right of animals is to be allowed to lead their own lives and not be killed, yet this right has not been strongly embraced by open-admission animal welfare and rights groups." This was seen as a deliberate repudiation of the no-kill perspective.

No-kill advocates also felt ignored, misunderstood, and criticized at the national conferences of open-admission organizations, because euthanasia proponents seemed unwilling to enter into a "dialogue." As one no-kill advocate put it,

I don't like being demonized. So many people there were very resentful of us. They know the wonderful things we do here and how wonderful we are. We were expecting people to be, like, "Wow, you are affiliated with that wonderful group," and instead we were, like, getting slammed, shielding ourselves from the rotten vegetables being thrown at us. That feeling was very pervasive there [at national meeting].

Another no-kill worker felt "dissed" at a national humane meeting, recalling,

I didn't appreciate sitting in a workshop and having an HSUS employee speaking, saying to me, "It is the responsibility of all of us in the shelter profession to euthanize animals." That's a value judgment. They are communicating that no-kill is bad and that we should all be euthanizing animals. She was basically dissing no-kill. I immediately raised my hand to defend [no-kill shelters] but I was not called on.

Dishonesty

A palpable distrust existed between open-admission and no-kill followers. Members of each camp insisted that they were woefully misunderstood and misrepresented by the opposition, which, in turn, was seen as portraying itself dishonestly to professional colleagues and the general public.

Open admissionists attacked the honesty of no-kill shelters and spokespersons on a number of counts. First, they said, no-kill advocates lied about not killing shelter animals when the term was taken literally. "I believe they are trained to lie and there is deception to the public...that animals are not euthanized," said one worker. One critic maintained that some no-killers euthanized animals "surreptitiously, behind closed doors," so supporters would not find out. To many respondents this "deception" was terminological: "What is a shelter's definition of *no-kill*? At our shelter it is that we do not kill for overcrowding or when a dog's 'time runs out,' but we do euthanize for behavioral and health reasons. Now to me that's *not* no-kill. It makes that terminology close to a lie. What do the press and the public and donors think it means? Probably they take the words literally—'We don't kill dogs, ever'—well, they do!" On the grounds that the term was false if taken literally, some critics proposed new terminology, calling no-kill shelters rarely-kills or *low kills*. Another problem that has less to do with terminology, but still was regarded as a matter of dishonesty, has to do with misrepresentation. Open-admissionists claimed that no-kill shelters misrepresented themselves by shifting responsibility for killing to other shelters; this made the no-kill shelters accomplices to death, argued the open-admissionists, although the shelters distanced themselves from it. One such critic maintained, "...The reality of a 'no-kill' approach to sheltering simply means 'let someone else kill'" (Savesky 1995a, 4).

Second, open-admissionists said no-killers were deceptive in claiming to adopt out all their animals, a tactic some critics called a "smart marketing strategy." This point was underscored by one critic who claimed that "their almost no-kill policy" resulted from only accepting "very adoptable animals," leaving the "burden" of euthanizing turned-away animals to open-admission shelters. It was alleged that no-kill shelters "take in the 'movie star' dogs and cats, the pretty ones they know they can place in new homes, and turn away the rest" (Caras 1997c, 17). The result of such policies, open-admissionists said, was that most animals wound up at open-admission shelters. "They are strays, 'too old,' unsocialized, injured, or diseased. They are considered unadoptable by no-kill shelters so they are brought to us" (Bogue 1998b). One person compared this self-serving policy to a school that always has impressive SAT scores because it accepts only bright students in the first place. No-kill shelters were seen as excessively "picky," rejecting some animals with extremely minor problems that could be used as excuses for turning them away. Expanding on this point, one respondent said, "If an animal has the tiniest patch of flea allergy, dermatitis, which is curable, they say no if they want to. Bad teeth, they say no if they want to. Any animal they can say no to, they are going to say no. They don't take many that need treatment." One respondent said that even "color" could be used as a reason to classify an animal as "unadoptable," if there

were too many similar looking animals together in a shelter, such as tiger-striped kittens. Some critics also charged that no-kill shelters used a "changeable" classification, whereby a placeable animal could be reclassified as unplaceable if the animal was not adopted, enabling the shelter to claim a "huge" percentage of their "placeable" animals were adopted. Some felt that this classification "game" was so capricious it made no-kill "a joke." All of these manipulations, some charged, enabled the "no-kill propagandists" through "deception" to produce statistics apparently documenting low rates for euthanasia and high "save rates."

Third, critics charged that no-kill shelters misrepresented the cause of behavior problems in dogs, not admitting that these difficulties were due to long-term confinement and/or the kind of training they received. For instance, "excuses" were made for the bad behavior of animals, as in the case of a dog showing "guarding behavior" around food whose actions were "explained away" by pointing to the lack of food the dog had experienced. One worker spoke about "the betrayal the public would feel if they were aware that the shelter they trusted has made them the subject of an experiment in placing rehabilitated biting dogs, an experiment with so many failures." Critics maintained that the aggressiveness of shelter dogs was not fully disclosed to adopters. Upset by this problem, a worker described a shelter that was being sued for adopting out a Rottweiler who was known to have killed one dog, only to have him knock down his new owner and kill her pet dog. The same worker also claimed that this shelter concealed from potential adopters that another dog had bitten seven volunteers. In response, she resigned from her organization, noting: "They adopted out any and all dogs, no matter their history and, worst of all, did not tell adopting families if the dog had bitten previously." Another no-kill worker, uncomfortable with her own shelter's policy, gave credence to this

open-admission critique when she reported "incredible feelings of guilt," making it "hard to sleep at night," because she felt "complicity" in adopting out dangerous animals to clients from whom information was hidden about these problems and who were blamed by staff when animals were returned.

Some critics claimed that, if not deliberately dishonest, no-kill shelters misrepresented themselves because they were unrealistic. One open-admissionist wrote, "The concept of the shelter where no animals must die is a fantasy that seems too good to be true" (Caras 1997c, 16). These "fantasies," argued open admissionists, made donors and the general public "feel good." As one worker said: "The truth is that it is impossible. They are encouraging an expectation that is unrealistic." These expectations

> ...raise false hopes and wishes for pet owners and our communities that animal abandonment is going to be prevented simply because the killing of adoptable animals is going to be prohibited. The complexities of the problem of killing so many animals in our shelters is not simply due to the perception that an unwanted pet is "better off alive on the streets than being killed at the pound." (Cubrda 1993)

Critics argued that, in addition to raising false hopes, these fantasies led people mistakenly to believe that euthanasia was unnecessary at their local humane society, a strategy that siphoned funds away from open-admission shelters.

No-kill advocates maintained that their aims were distorted, bemoaning the "warfare" and frequent "bashing" by open-admission spokespersons that resulted in "credibility hits" against them. One no-kill staff member spoke of her frustration with people who misconstrued the meaning of no-kill as a preference for animals to be kept alive in unpleasant or unhealthy circumstances. She noted, "I don't know if there is any sane person who would agree that a warehouse kind of life. . .is better than death. I don't think anybody is arguing that, except for an extremely small subset of people who are not in the mainstream of the no-kill movement." No-kill advocates also disagreed with those who criticized the concept of no-kill because it failed to be literally true, admitting that a few animals, albeit a tiny number when compared to open-admission shelters, were euthanized. Some even refused to label their shelters as no-kill or minimized use of this term because their euthanasia rates were not zero.

For their part no-kill shelters argued that open-admission organizations "kill healthy animals" (Foro 1997, 16) and misrepresent the real meaning of euthanasia. Seeking to undermine the semantic justification for killing so many animals, one no-kill spokesperson wrote: "The term *euthanasia*, as used by these practitioners [open admission and animal control staff] in the destruction of healthy animals, softens the reality and lessens its impact on the public. Sadly, to mislabel killing as euthanasia for controlling animal overpopulation does not allow society to deal with the tragedy or to accept responsibility for making this happen" (17). "True," "authentic," or "dictionary-defined" (17) euthanasia was spoken about to separate "killing" from other instances where extreme, untreatable, chronic suffering mandated euthanizing animals. No-kill advocates also reclaimed the concept of euthanasia by asserting that humane death be done only for the sake of suffering animals rather than for owners who had their own agenda for requesting euthanasia, suggesting that open admissionists wrongly blurred this distinction. Not surprisingly open-admission advocates rejected this distinction, claiming that it was mere "semantics."

No-kill proponents also refuted the charge that they were "picky" to ensure high adoption rates. They claimed to take many animals that were far from the "cream of the crop," as one worker pointed out. "We

get only the worst here; everybody thinks we take only the best dogs here. It's hard for me to find a family dog in our shelter because we are taking the ones no one else takes." In fact, in one no-kill shelter, there was strong internal pressure on intake workers to accept as many dogs as possible from the nearby animal control office, regardless of their bad or "spooky" behavior or poor condition; otherwise the dogs were likely to be euthanized. In one instance, after an intake worker refused an aggressive, six-month-old dog offered to her shelter, several coworkers chided her and called her a murderer. Challenging back, some no-kill shelters felt that their save rates might be even better were it not for having difficult and unadoptable animals dumped on them by animal control organizations. A respondent explained,

We could inflate our save rate even more if we had a bar that resembled anything like another shelter['s], where they see the hint of a curl of a lip and that animal is euthanized and it never goes to their staff as an adoptable animal, where we would not even flinch at that. So I would say our numbers are possibly even better in so far as we are taking some serious-behavior animals—dogs that bite you, dogs that are aggressive.

Latent Tensions

Identifying manifest tensions helps to detail the no-kill controversy but does little to diffuse it. Most proposals to allay the conflict come from the open-admission camp, which has called for no-kill advocates to modify their provocative language. However, those concerned about inflammatory speech in the no-kill controversy have tuned into only a small part of the bigger picture that informs this controversy. Provocative language is a symptom and not a cause of the problem; its social and psychological roots are concealed and complex. To explain the persistence and fervor of the strife, it is necessary to analyze

the unexpressed, complicated, and recalcitrant issues that underlie manifest tensions.

Vested Interests

Much like the abortion debate, the persistence of which stems from the vested interests of pro-life and pro-choice proponents, the no-kill controversy is stubborn and resistant to easy compromise. No-kill and open-admission followers cling to and defend their vested interests, including their collective identities, occupational lifestyles, and world views. These vested interests underlie any debate about the merits of different policies for controlling and managing pet overpopulation or dealing "humanely" with its victims.

Members of each camp in my research had a vested interest in protecting their humane identities. For no-kill followers this identity provided some cachet because it empowered them. They saw themselves as "rediscovering" who they were, as opposed to open-admission workers whom they felt "have forgotten our mission and are lost in the overwhelming job of euthanasia," according to one shelter worker whose organization was switching from open admission to no-kill. In the opinion of no-killer followers, open-admission work was simply not the work of a "'humane' society." Their new identity also was empowering because it had an outlaw quality; this made it an attractive and powerful label for no-kill workers who felt alienated, misunderstood, and excluded from the humane powers that be. Believing that they were disempowered framed their camp's stance as "anti-establishment" relative to open admissionists (Foro, n.d.a). Poorly endowed, small shelters especially were drawn to the identity tag of no-kill because it symbolically represented their perceived powerlessness in an animal community dominated by a few large and powerful national organizations. The charge made by some that the San Francisco SPCA (SF SPCA) had "sold out" to The HSUS (which is viewed as pro open admission in its orientation) by increasing the number of animals it euthanized from almost none to a few, speaks to the current importance of boundaries in conferring identity in the humane community.

Other features of the no-kill identity that offered some cachet came from its evangelical quality, calling for people to see the "right" way to approach this problem and convert to this "movement," leaving behind their former, ill-conceived approach. Several respondents commented on the "religious fervor" of no-kill followers; one said that there was a "kind of saintliness" about the movement. There even were rare attempts to include elements of Buddhism and vegetarianism as part of the "no-kill philosophy" (Foro, n.d.b).

Perhaps the most cachet came from unintentional piggybacking on the pro-life movement. Large and successful social movements provide an assembly of symbols and ideological trappings—a cultural resource—that other groups can use to fashion their own thinking and model their own actions, or from which they can draw emotional power and symbolic coherency. While there was little evidence that no-killers subscribed to pro-life beliefs, there were many parallels between the ideologies of these two groups that empowered the no-kill movement and emotionally charged the identity of its followers. Just as the pro-life movement campaigns to save the "helpless unborn" who should not be "killed," the no-kill movement questions the moral, as well as the practical, basis for killing unwanted or undesirable shelter animals. The "killing" of shelter animals signaled a moral assault on the fabric of human-animal relationships that was unimaginable to no-killers, much as abortion was to pro-lifers (Ginsburg 1986; Kaufmann 1999). Many no-kill proponents saw the open admissionists' version of euthanasia as murder committed by selfish owners and unimaginative shelter workers willing to accept the status quo, in the same way that pro-life advocates defined abortion as a crime approved by a legal system which protected murderers and left victims unprotected (Doyle 1982).[4] In the end this cachet was strong enough to make it virtually impossible to stop using some language, including the very term *no-kill*. Its advocates were unlikely to curtail use of this self-moniker because it so powerfully organized their identity.

Open admissionists have discovered little if any cachet in their humane identity, at least compared with no-killers. For the most part, they have refined their former identity in a reactive and defensive manner by digging in their psychological heels and reaffirming their long-standing image as the standard bearers for humane treatment of animals. Ironically their "new" identity has made them appear to be victims facing a more powerful enemy. For example some open admissionists spoke as though they were on the "wrong side of the street" because the "dirty work" of killing was delegated to them. They felt powerless to stop this flow of animals and the undesirable task of euthanizing so many. Some staff in open-admission shelters and animal control offices, especially in cities that had strong and financially stable no-kill programs, lamented having poorer facilities and less public attention. This difference was noted in a major magazine article about animal shelters, which referred to one city's animal control office as a "tenement" and its no-kill operation as a "palace" (Hess 1998).

Open-admissionists also failed to piggyback their identity on a cultural resource that could give it momentum, coherency, and cachet. In contrast, pro-choice advocates linked their cause to the feminist movement's protection of the rights of women. Support from animal rights groups, such as People for the Ethical Treatment of Animals (PETA), did not provide this cachet. One reason is that no-kill groups also claimed to be protecting the rights of animals by opposing traditional euthanasia policy, making the rights issue somewhat of a wash. It was true that open admissionists focused on the issue of easing the suffering of animals and providing options to owners who no longer could or wanted to care for their pets. However this symbolism paled in comparison with the no-kill movement's moral concern for what were seen as innocent, helpless, and desirable animals, a stance similar to the pro-life movement's symbolic construction of the fetus (Doyle 1982; Sheeran 1987). In American society anti-death icons trump almost any other image except that of freedom, and this appears true in the present case. Moreover, although some open admissionists wish to develop their own label conveying a new identity rivaling "no kill," this would perpetuate the tension rather than remedy it.

Workers also had vested interests in protecting lifestyles, whether personal or occupational, associated with either the open-admission or no-kill approach. They sought to defend what was familiar to them at work, while questioning others who threatened this routine. For instance, at one level, the open-admission approach to euthanasia was easier for established bureaucracies that had worked this way for years and had developed suitable defenses to cope with it. Mainstream open-admission shelters have had the resources to garner large-scale support for euthanasia as the best way to deal with pet overpopulation, and they have grown comfortable with their established methods of doing so. One respondent claimed,

> We are all vulnerable to the possibility that euthanasia just makes my day go a little bit easier. If you suddenly ended euthanasia for reasons of space, you've got a big problem, don't you? You are going to have 20 or 80 percent more population than before. Solve that problem. If there is euthanasia, it does make things a little bit easy, doesn't it, to have your shelter running very smoothly and efficiently?

No-kill workers also developed organizational routines that made their work easier for them. Those most outspoken in their criticism of euthanasia took the moral high ground by distancing themselves from it while on the job. In their shelters they regarded euthanasia as a clinical, veterinary act performed elsewhere by technicians in animal control agencies, or an infrequent, highly ritualized and emotionally upsetting treatment of a "good friend" done by in-house veterinarians. They provided a language and set of rationalizations to ensure that such rare, in-house killings would be seen as impossible to avoid, without any ambiguity about the wisdom of doing them. These steps made them comfortable and secure while on the job. Like their open-admission counterparts, they came to see their particular organizational way of life as the best one for animals and themselves.

Finally, these accustomed ways of working endured because workers accepted the presumptions that propped up, defended, and explained them. Usually the presumptions were expressed by people as "truths" that were rarely questioned and often thought to be self-evident. It was predictable that the workers could not see the tenuousness of such "truths," since ideologies make those who profess them shortsighted as to the implications of their beliefs. The beliefs function as "reality" anchors for people and, as such, are clutched tenaciously. Respondents in my research supported these anchors by use of key terms, such as *shelter*, *euthanasia*, *adoptable animal*, and *humane*, whose meanings were ambiguous and therefore modifiable to be consistent with each camp's truths. The terms became a linguistic code to define a camp's position relative to other groups.

For example, while both open-admission and no-kill advocates abhorred euthanasia, they had different takes on killing because they had different conceptions of the fundamental problem. Each group defined the problem somewhat differently, making for different solutions. Open-admission shelter workers saw the problem as an *animal* problem—one of managing pet overpopulation. They argued that no-kill approaches did

not solve this problem but merely shifted the responsibility for euthanasia to another shelter or agency. No-kill advocates, however, saw the fundamental problem as a *person* problem—one of changing the nature of shelter work so that workers could have a professional identity uncontaminated by the contradictions posed by conducting frequent euthanasia, especially if it involved animals thought to be adoptable. Evidence of this changing emphasis from animals to people came from the public justifications of shelters that have abandoned their prior open-admission/euthanasia policies for no-kill approaches. When a major SPCA did so, the *New York Times* headline proclaimed: "ASPCA Plans to Give Up Job Killing New York Strays." The text explained that

> Killing stray dogs and cats has obscured its mission—and its image . . . . The society has backed away from killing, which it calls animal control. "Philosophically, it's a nightmare to kill 30,000 to 40,000 animals a year. . . . That's not our mission.". . . Being perceived as an animal killer has. . . saddled it with an image far different from the one it wants—that of an animal care and adoption agency. (Hicks 1993, B14)

These divergent views were bolstered by the isolation of workers from the realities of shelters unlike their own. Most workers in each camp had little if any firsthand experience with the opposing group. As in the abortion controversy, where pro-life participants had little or no direct exposure to abortion (Luker 1984), most workers in no-kill facilities had scant exposure to euthanasia. Not having direct contact can exaggerate the emotional difficulty of doing something, making it seem even more wrenching than it might be in reality, and making it seem even more horrific or ghastly than it seems to those workers who have learned how to rationalize or cope with it. Similarly, many open-admissionists never worked in no-kill settings; this lack of experience certainly made any other

approach seem impractical or even outlandish.

Attacking the Problem

Differing approaches to dealing with animal overpopulation resulted in a second latent tension. No-kill workers "fought the good fight" for each animal who came their way, expending as much time, labor, and money as necessary to ensure that he or she was cared for, loved, and, they hoped, adopted. Workers could feel as though they championed individual animals. As one respondent said, "We dare to think that every individual life does matter. . . that that individual's life *actually* matters." This focus on the welfare and fate of individual animals, combined with the knowledge that euthanasia was very unlikely, allowed these workers to indulge their "rescue instinct" and their need to have emotionally deep and complex relationships with shelter animals, even though they knew that many animals would be adopted.

The major force behind fighting the good fight was the unabashed desire of no-killers to rescue or save animals, believing that it almost always was worth trying to find homes for all animals, even if others classified them as unadoptable. As one respondent said,

> There are a lot of self-proclaimed experts who will tell you that this or that dog is unadoptable, don't even bother trying. And we don't accept that. You can get terrifically good outcomes. . . . It's a question of when can you and when can't you. The jury is out on our animals until we have exhausted all reasonable attempts.

No-kill trainers believed they could rehabilitate most problem animals, including those exhibiting aggressiveness. One trainer compared this challenge with working with criminals, concluding that both animals and criminals can be rehabilitated if people try hard enough. "If you've gotten people who've committed certain levels of crime, can they be rehabilitated? If you give them the right counseling, can you turn them around, or is it always in them? I would submit that the right kind of effort hasn't been tried."

No-kill workers felt that open-admission shelters turned their backs on animals that were less than "perfect," euthanizing those that could be placed in homes if given behavioral or medical attention, along with time and careful placement. One no-kill worker elaborated on this view, saying,

> Where do you draw the line? Does everything have to be pristine and perfect, and you kill everything else? We want to give animals a chance that we think ought to be given a chance. It's kind of like a "quantity versus quality" type of thing. I mean, the Blackies and the Willies out there, they would be killed because they are not perfect, and I see this wonderful pet that would make a great companion for someone and I think they are worth investing the resources into.

This logic meant that no-kill facilities could "save" or "rescue" animals from open-admission shelters, and that those shelters denied the value of rehabilitating animals who could be improved and perhaps adopted.

Saved animals often faced a severely reduced pool of potential adopters, since it took a very special adopter to be the right match for an animal with behavioral or veterinary problems, let alone one that was old or unattractive. Despite this, no-kill workers convinced themselves that perfect adopters existed for virtually all of their charges. Having this view, however, justified keeping animals for a long time as staff searched for suitable adopters. This search could be particularly trying when dogs were highly aggressive and needed muzzling and constant monitoring. When a no-kill worker was asked who would be an appropriate adopter for such a challenging animal, she said a dog trainer would come to the shelter one day and adopt one. However, she acknowledged—without apparent irony—that no such adopter had come to her shelter since she had arrived there three years earlier.

Fighting the good fight for all animals made euthanizing any of them a difficult and labored decision. One facility had formal guidelines for deciding on all acts of euthanasia (except for extreme emergencies). The guidelines included obtaining signatures of approval from the president, vice president, and initiating department head, and requiring that the animals' names be posted so no staff would be shocked by inadvertently discovering that a "friend" had been euthanized. After completing this paperwork, cats slated to be euthanized were given special foods and treats; soft, comfortable, secure bedding; adequate scratching posts; and visits from the staff. Dogs were given similar bedding; a rawhide bone during the day; a beef bone at night; special food and "extra special goodies"; a cloth toy; and visits from staff members who would give them "quality time" through long walks, outdoor play "with their special buddies," or quiet time. This "spoiling period," an informal practice at many no-kill facilities, involved special consideration for animals after the decision was made to euthanize them. Spoiling periods "were awkward" for the staff because they knew that animals were to be "put down," but the special treatment also made the staff feel better about the euthanasia decision. One worker said,

> The last days are so difficult. I find it very hard to look at a dog carrying on its normal life, when I know that soon it will all be over. But I think it helps us to know that our dog's last day or so was really special. It seems to bring peace to the people around the dog who are suffering, knowing that the dog is going to get euthanized.

The individualization of shelter animals meant that no-kill workers were very disturbed when euthanasia took place, even though, or perhaps because, this was a rare event. "It is always such a big deal. I just cannot get used to it," observed one worker. Enormous internal resistance occurred at one no-kill shelter when a small number of overly aggressive dogs were slated for euthanasia. "We could not fix them. We were at the end of our ability," lamented one worker. Some dogs had become a danger to the staff and were a liability risk. Management held special meetings with different groups of workers and volunteers to deliver this news, calm those upset or in "shock," and reset the organization's "bar" for rehabilitating difficult dogs. During the meetings senior staff placed most of the blame on external forces, saying, "Our hand has been forced by elements in society." Those external forces included what the staff described as unreasonable expectations for the behavior of animals, and society's excessive litigiousness. Trying to ease distraught and confused listeners, senior staff claimed they "did not have choices" and "couldn't" do anything else with these dogs.

Nevertheless senior managers withdrew their initial list as pressure mounted to spare these animals; a few workers and volunteers demanded meetings with shelter officials to protest this list, and rumors circulated about a volunteer protest strike and leaks to the press. Workers feared that conducting euthanasia on this scale would subvert their identities as no-kill advocates. One uneasy worker spoke about the slippery slope created by doing even a small number of euthanasias: "We are in a position now of either becoming like every other shelter and we save only perfect dogs who need nothing or what...?" Considerable, continued pressure by workers resulted in several dogs being taken off the list and sent to sanctuaries.

Despite these efforts a few dogs from the list were euthanized. The most unsettling case involved a dog having a history of aggression, but with whom the animal's "fan club" had bonded intensely. Only this inner circle was permitted to attend Maria's euthanasia; lights were dimmed in the dog's quarters, and the mood was extremely solemn if not despondent. Many workers were tormented; a few chose not to attend the euthanasia because they were so distressed. One staff member was hospitalized because she was so disturbed by the event, and several others took "sick days" because of their grief. During the hours preceding the euthanasia, as well as the days following it, workers could be seen embracing each other, offering words of comfort, and shedding tears. "People are walking around like zombies," said one sad worker about her peers. A wake held the evening of the euthanasia again excluded those outside the inner circle of mourners; a poem in honor of Maria was available; stories were swapped about the animal along with photographs of her; flowers and wine were there for the occasion. As one worker said, the sentiment was: "We love you guys, you did good work but this one just didn't work." Contrary to shelter policy, one of the workers requested Maria's ashes; a few staff members thought this was going "overboard."

Open-admission workers, in contrast, related to shelter animals less with their hearts and more with their heads. Unquestionably they too wanted the best for animals that came their way, but their approach was colored by what they saw as a more important issue than the need to feel good about their relationships with individual animals—namely, the need to attack the overpopulation problem by increasing the number of adoptions through euthanasia of animals deemed unadoptable. They also used their heads because they felt it was important never to say no to surrenderers of animals; despite their frustration and anger with surrenderers, open admissionists feared what might happen to the animals if they were not left at the shelter. This thinking forestalled deeper emotional relationships with their charges, because all the animals stood some chance of being euthanized and usually were in the shelter for relatively short periods. One worker aptly summarized this type of thinking as follows: "There's a part of me that I don't give to the dogs—not to that dog—because that would inhibit what

I can do for so many others. I always have to come back to looking at numbers. I can't afford to get attached to a new dog. I have to think with my head. I have to keep part of me for the good of the whole. I won't sacrifice a few for the many."

According to open admissionists, relating to shelter animals with one's heart caused ethical and emotional problems. They claimed that no-kill shelters had such a narrow definition of suffering, they often could not "see" it; certain animals might not be euthanized even to end their suffering. Without clearly seeing suffering, workers as well as animals suffered, although the workers' suffering was emotional.

These problems were evident at Maria's euthanasia, according to shelter staff members who sympathized with the open-admission approach. The fact that this euthanasia was for behavioral rather than medical reasons made it especially difficult for workers to say that Maria's "suffering" justified her death. One exception was a staff member who had worked previously at an open-admission shelter. She commented,

Whenever I put an animal down, I always found it to be redeeming because the dog has been in torment—and any dog I have put down has either had an aggression issue or just not been happy, has had a bad life. For me it was the one thing I was able to do for that dog—give it some peace. I was able to end the suffering.

Indeed, a number of workers at this shelter felt that the strong emotional reaction to the death of Maria was "unfair" to some staff members and out of proportion with what should happen after the loss of an un-owned shelter dog with a history of biting. One such dissenter said that, if anything, members of Maria's fan club were "mourning their failure" to rehabilitate this highly aggressive dog. Moreover, his opinion was that, although he thought it might sound "cold," it was a better idea for emotional reasons to have a veterinarian and technician be alone when eutha-

nizing animals. Having
all the people who were involved in his [the dog's] life standing around him, pushing their emotions on the doctor.... it could be difficult for the doctor not to cry. That's not fair to do to the doctor or the tech holding the dog. Why should they be forced to have an emotion for an animal that they have no connection to? They are forced to feel sympathy.

These ethical and emotional drawbacks of bonding so closely to shelter animals were worrisome not just to the no-kill workers but also to open-admission proponents who pondered the fate of their no-kill peers.

By comparison, a nearby municipal animal-control office routinely and unceremoniously euthanized animals. While bemoaning euthanasia, workers there felt that it was the right thing to do given the large number of surrendered animals and the limited space and resources available. They, like other open-admission workers, rejected the notion that they were the "baddies" because no-kill workers needed to "rescue" their shelter animals. The implication of using this language was that these animals were salvageable as potential pets and therefore should not be killed. The problem, according to open admissionists, was that if no-kill workers "rescued" with their hearts, they would neglect the "bigger picture," which the former could see. This criticism was expressed even by some no-kill workers who bemoaned turning away so many animals for lack of sufficient resources to deal with them all. To open admissionists, this was a management problem—a combination of poor resource allocation and bad judgment—that allowed workers to be self-indulgent. Such shortsighted policies were seen as beneficial to workers, since they gained emotional gratification at the expense of animal welfare.

The above-mentioned animal-control office, like many open-admission shelters, had no formal protocol calling for signing off on euthanasia decisions or for in-house postings of the events. Nor was there a spoiling period for animals being euthanized, although the workers here, like their peers in open-admission shelters, maintained that they "spoiled [the animals] as much as possible" for as long as they were in their shelter "...not [just for] twenty-four hours." Spoiling periods per se were thought to be more for the psychological benefit of workers than for the animals and to place a "huge emotional burden" on the staff members doing the spoiling. While workers lamented having to euthanize animals, they handled it quite differently from their no-kill peers. Rather than expressing their emotions about preventing euthanasia or grieving when it occurred, these workers blocked their emotions when it came to euthanasia. As one worker recalled, "I was like a killing machine, a certified euthanasia tech that euthanized 60 to 100 plus animals every single day. Some days that's all I did—clean and kill. And go home. You put your feelings on the shelf. You just do your job. You have to deal with that sometime down the line."

Being Humane

Short of the most extreme manifestations of physical suffering in animals, no-kill and open-admission workers had very different perceptions of what constituted suffering, or at least enough discomfort to justify killing an animal for his or her own sake. Having conflicting ideas about the nature of suffering led to suggestions that members of the opposite camp were being cruel to shelter animals because they caused needless suffering, either for killing them or for keeping them alive. Alternative notions of suffering also allowed both open-admission and no-kill workers to see themselves as humane because they could say that they were acting in the best interests of animals compared to their peers in the other camp.

Some open-admission representatives argued that no-kill workers were cruel to turn their backs on so many needy or less desirable animals, and that open-admission shelters actually

were responsible for "saving" more animals. One open-admission defender wrote in an editorial, "The Door Remains Open," that "no-kill shelters seldom operate programs to rescue sick and injured animals off the streets," suggesting that animals in need are turned away (Savesky 1995b, 2), while open-admission shelters "rescue sick and injured animals every day...dogs hit by cars, cats tangled in debris, animals injured by other animals, victims of all sorts of accidents." In addition, no-kill shelters, according to Savesky, "often turn away older animals, those with minor health or behavioral problems, or those that they otherwise classify unadoptable." Moreover, this author added that "no-kill shelters seldom investigate and prosecute complaints of cruelty and neglect" (2). By contrast, she argues that many such animals have a greater chance of being adopted in open-admission shelters.

People working in open-admission shelters also thought it was cruel to "warehouse" animals past the point where they should be "humanely euthanized." Some claimed that warehousing was cruel because of the harmful psychological effects of keeping dogs and cats in long-term housing, especially if caged with multiple animals and given minimal stimulation and human contact. But in discussions less-than-ideal caging or animal care often fell short of being labeled as cruel. One animal control worker, for instance, was uncomfortable with the local no-kill shelter's practice of putting animals into boarding kennels when space ran out in the facility. "Who do they have to love them? They are going from one cage to another just to keep them alive. I don't know if it is cruel; it just seems...neglectful. The reason why it is hard to say it is cruel is that it is not for a bad reason. The intention is 'Hold on, hold on, you'll get your chance.'" Another respondent hesitated to use the word *suffer*, but spoke of the unintentional emotional "neglect" of dogs who are confined in cages and have to deal with many different handlers and visitors—all of

which takes a "toll." One respondent, however, did use the word *suffer*, claiming that some no-kill shelters kept animals so long that they developed "that nervous thing, like dogs spinning, or some of the barking [which] sounds like suffering to me. They are just unhappy and crying." Similarly, another critic of warehousing pointed out after visiting a no-kill shelter that "it was spotless.... They had air conditioning, climbing trees, toys, and good food. But when you walked in, they were all over you. I had cats attached to my legs and arms, on my shoulders and my head. I had scratch marks for a week after that but not from aggression. These cats were starved for human contact. That's what breaks my heart about these places" (Donald 1991, 4). Some critics suggested that workers compounded the detrimental psychological effects of long-term housing by using inappropriate behavior and training techniques. As evidence, one respondent cited a case of several dogs who were born in a no-kill shelter and stayed there for seven years. All displayed serious behavior problems that were attributed to the methods used in their training.

Open-admission spokespersons also argued that warehousing in no-kill shelters could cause physical harm. This critique was echoed in a popular magazine, which reported the following reaction of a 4-H group leader after taking the group to visit a no-kill shelter: "Dogs limping around with mange and open sores. Others gasping for air or dragging broken legs, struggling to fight off vicious packs in the large communal pen. 'I might as well have taken them to a horror show'" (Foster 2000). The reporter who wrote this article referred to the "atrocious conditions" at some no-kill facilities, and the "luckless inmates" who are "condemned" to "filth" and who "suffer" from long-term caging. Indeed, one respondent claimed that the "quality of care of animals is horrific. They [no-kill shelters] need to do it right and have some standard of care." For example, he pointed to a no-kill facility that called his shelter in hopes of transferring some of its 110 animals to reduce overcrowding. When the respondent visited the no-kill shelter, he found that the facility was very cold, merely a "semblance" of a building, and that some of the animals were dead. In addition, when the no-kill shelter was told it could transfer some animals, its manager declined because the open-admission director could not rule out their euthanasia.

Most no-kill respondents denied "warehousing." They felt that they addressed the "quality of life" issue and provided a better life for animals in shelters than some had in adoptive homes. Although one worker admitted that, "from the dogs' perspective, they are always prisoners," she felt that their quality of life was "as good if not better than the [homes where] many open admission shelters place their dogs. . . . I know a good many dogs in suburbia who don't get walked, have minimal veterinary care, don't get socialized. They don't get patted much by their owners. They're in the yard." Others defended extended stays; one respondent said they were "less than ideal, however it is fortunate that [the animals] get a chance to end up in a wonderful home where they are completely loved and adored."

Well-funded no-kills described "lavish" surroundings for shelter animals to counter charges of inhumane warehousing—though these surroundings were sometimes belittled by the press or open-admission shelters as excessive, and better than facilities provided for some homeless people. One no-kill "Q and A" included a question asking how it could justify such a "beautiful" and expensive shelter with "luxury suites for animals, replete with toys, TVs, and playrooms," when "most humans don't have quarters like these." The reply, in short, claimed these "amenities" were not excessive but "important for the animals" to reduce their stress and make them "healthier and happier. So the toys and playrooms are not frivolous. They're just what the doctor ordered."

Part of their defense also rested on the language used by no-kill advocates to describe physical and mental problems of animals housed for long periods of time in shelters. The advocates fought hard to describe these problems in ways that did not lead quickly to perceptions of hopelessness for the animals. For example, in one such facility, animals with behavior problems who would have been euthanized in open-admission shelters were described as having "issues." The word "issues" conjures up psychological problems in humans that can be lived with and managed, as opposed to more troubling behavior that is difficult to tolerate and control. In one case a shelter dog had a history of snapping at children, and was spoken about as "having an issue with children." The solution was to work on ridding the dog of that "issue," while seeking childless adopters who could keep the dog away from children.

Language modification also helped lessen the image of dangerous animals so they might appear as "nice, soft." One group of no-kill trainers was particularly concerned, for legal reasons, about written records that created an image of dogs as vicious, perhaps indiscriminate biters. They started a "language project team" not to "hide data," but

> [T]o be cautious. If somebody reports something, even if it's literally a puppy who puppy-bit, that would go down on the record. We are trying to clean up all that junk. . .trying to make a big distinction between when a dog play-bites versus really bites. We are giving people who do the reporting a multiple-choice form rather than letting them editorialize about it. [One choice is] "dog play-bit hard with bruising."

In any case keeping compromised animals alive or warehousing them was not as bad as killing them, according to no-kill respondents. They countered criticism with the charge that euthanasia itself was often cruel by definition, if not by practice, because most shelter animals could be kept alive and even adopted. Some methods of euthanasia were easier for critics to decry on the grounds that they caused animal suffering. For example critics of a shelter that used carbon monoxide deemed this gassing to be morally "wrong" and "cruel" because animals cried out in pain or fear and saw other animals dying (Gilyard 2001). The more common method used, injection of lethal drugs, still was attacked as cruel.

Moreover most no-kill workers felt that if adverse "warehousing" existed it was at a facility other than their own. Some no-kill proponents were very clear that shelters whose mission was to adopt animals should not keep unadoptable animals in too-small quarters for extended periods of time; to do so was considered inhumane. Other advocates acknowledged that these abuses probably occurred in at least some no-kill facilities, but they were marginalized and viewed as exceptions rather than as representing the vast majority of no-kill shelters. Indeed one common way to create this "bad egg" hierarchy was to refer to the abusing facility as a "sanctuary" (used here pejoratively) rather than a no-kill shelter, thereby distancing it from "better" organizations.

In fact no-kill proponents felt that keeping behaviorally or medically difficult animals was a sign of success and an opportunity to save more animals, rather than evidence of their insensitivity or cruelty. One hopeful no-killer said these animals were a challenge to rehabilitate, and her goal was to make ever sicker animals into adoptable ones: "We are raising the bar for what we can handle medically or behaviorally. We've got animals with chronic health conditions. We've got aggressive dogs. We are trying to rehabilitate them so they can be made adoptable." By "raising the bar," no-kill workers felt they were attempting to reduce suffering in animals rather than increase it through prolonged caging. For the most part, they denied the latter happened. For example, when discussing a highly aggressive dog who had been sheltered for eighteen months, a no-kill worker said the animal was not a candidate for euthanasia because that "means you are ending suffering, and he is quite enjoying his life."

Toward a Common Ground

Unearthing the manifest and latent tensions behind the open-admission and no-kill perspectives suggests that a large and perhaps insurmountable gulf exists between the camps. However it would be wrong to portray these differences as antithetical. Situations exist where each camp's defenses are down, vulnerable to concession or change. This offers hope of a common ground between camps that would improve dialogue, enhance cooperation, and mollify tensions. Four bases exist that auger well for such change, including internal dissent, shared values, mutual identification, and maturation and change.

Internal Dissent

Far from public posturing that yields rigid ideological distinctions, there was internal dissent within the open-admission and no-kill camps over the proper handling of specific shelter animals—a dissent that mirrors the same criticisms made between the camps.[5] It was common to find some workers within open-admission and no-kill shelters who were uneasy with their own shelter's ideology but remained on the job because they strongly believed in the importance of voicing an alternative view in their own shelter, even if this marginalized them from peers. In larger facilities, there were cliques devoted to such dissent, but they, too, felt alienated from their own shelter's dominant outlook on these issues. Whether individuals or cliques, the concerns of these workers came to a head over the handling of particular shelter cases.

For example workers within some no-kill shelters sometimes debated the appropriateness of their facility's stance on euthanasia when that issue was raised for certain animals. As they discussed the fate of these animals, workers mulled over the various arguments now associated with the no-kill or open-admission perspective. Workers at one no-kill facility were sharply divided over the proposed euthanasia of several dogs with threatening behavior who had been sheltered for several months. Most strongly opposed the death of these animals, believing that their quality of life was satisfactory and that their risky behavior was modifiable, while some supported it on the grounds that their lengthy caging adversely affected them and that they were dangerous to adopt out. Those in the dissenting minority espoused a view that at times was closer to the open-admission than the no-kill stance, since it saw euthanasia as an acceptable alternative to the deleterious effects of long confinement. The two factions within the shelter were engaging in a meta-discussion about the proper handling of all shelter animals who faced a similar quandary. At this general level, they were debating and considering the merits of both no-kill and open-admission stances; this process allowed for the possibility that features of these perspectives might be merged.

Open-admission shelters also had their share of internal dissent. Traditionally, workers who became attached to individual animals quietly resisted the euthanasia of their "favorites" or, over time, quit because of "burnout" from the routine of killing. Perhaps empowered by the no-kill movement and seepage of its ideas into the open-admission camp, these workers were more willing than in the past to express doubts about the rationale for euthanasia and to garner support for such resistance from fellow workers. At these times, workers and shelter managers, much like those in no-kill shelters, debated the appropriateness of euthanasia in ways that echoed sentiments from both camps.

This dissent can become a building block for establishing a common ground. Although twenty years ago individuals in shelters expressed doubts about their shelter's policies, these questions were unlikely to have credibility because they were coming from a single person having no larger voice. Instead of having their objections considered seriously, dissenters probably risked being seen as "problem children," "difficult employees," not "team members," or the like, with the expectation that they needed to adjust to the job, become silent, or leave. With the growth of the no-kill movement and crystallization of the open-admission identity, dissenters now can name, and thereby attach their individual doubts to, something larger and more legitimate. When they speak it is from a position of strength. Giving voice to both perspectives provides an opportunity for healthy, albeit critical, debate and discussion at the ground level. Such empowered discussions within shelters make it possible for previously defensive workers to hear the other camp's views.

Shared Values

While internal dissent over the management of specific cases permitted the expression of opposing views within each camp, there also was more general evidence of mutual subscription to fundamental sheltering goals. When their guards were down, many respondents spoke about their work in ways that were far less polarized than the sheltering oral culture and literature suggested. Linguistic flashpoints used for public consumption and for posturing by spokespersons were not necessarily accurate reflections of the feelings and actions of everyday workers. If workers were confronted about their use of these terms, stark and inflammatory distinctions started to blur or fade. In fact, there was some agreement as to the meaning of important language that typically divided the camps. In this regard people in both camps demonstrated common rather than conflicting values about basic issues and concerns faced by all.

To some degree both camps had similar views of what constituted "suffering" and what conditions justified euthanasia. Despite what open admissionists assumed about no-killers, many of the latter were willing, in principle, to euthanize animals when their "fates were worse than death," a position championed by open admissionists. As one no-kill advocate claimed: "I haven't heard one person [at the no-kill facility] saying, 'Yeah, I think it is much better if we let the animal go on the highway then euthanize them....Better the animal is free and roaming around with mange and starving to death than to be killed.' I think that's nutty. [Is that cruel?] Absolutely. Absolutely. I would pick euthanasia over that." Another no–kill proponent, agreeing with this view, likened the plight of some animals whose suffering merited death to that of humans facing dire situations. This no-kill worker criticized "sanctuaries" that kept animals alive to the point where they suffered, arguing that humans do not let that happen to each other. In her words,

If you are not being humane, and the animal is in mental or physical distress, that may be considered a 'sanctuary' [living out their lives until they end naturally]. Technically we don't even do that for humans anymore. If someone is in pain, they usually are put on a morphine drip with the dosage slowly increased to reduce their discomfort. The reality is morphine suppresses the respiration.

Other no-kill respondents also spoke of euthanasia as a humane option by comparing the plight of some shelter animals with that of humans isolated from society. As one said,

What happens when you confine humans? What happens when you put humans in mental institutions? You can make it acceptable for some time for some dogs. Some can handle kenneling. Oth-

ers need the bond. . .[of] something or someone, and sitting in that kennel is not the same for them. They just can't hack it.

Members of both camps also saw almost all shelter animals as potentially adoptable and not requiring euthanasia, despite their physical and emotional limitations. Sounding quite like a no-kill advocate, one open-admissionist explained: "Most of the animals we kill are to us adoptable. That's why we don't use the word adoptable in any of our literature. A kitten with two legs who is four weeks old is adoptable to a person who wants to adopt her. Adoptability is only about who wants this animal. We had a thirteen-year-old dog with no front legs. She gets around. She kisses everyone. And she was placed." Of course, some open-admission respondents did not work in shelters that had resources to treat or keep such compromised and difficult-to-adopt animals. But they clung just as strongly as their no-kill peers to the hope that almost every shelter animal, regardless of disability, age, or unattractiveness, could be placed if given sufficient time.

Most respondents from both camps saw shelters—even the "best" of them—as unhealthy, if not destructive, environments for animals. Everyone agreed that, in an ideal world, shelters would not exist or, if they did, would serve only as temporary way stations to rehabilitate and home needy animals. One no-kill worker admitted that even her own "nice" shelter was "still" a shelter, as she questioned the "quality of life" of one animal who had been in her shelter for more than five hundred days. "I don't care how wonderful we make it for them, they are still institutionalized. Caretakers are there for thirty minutes to an hour and then the dog is alone, not able to do any of the innate things that a dog is supposed to be doing." Another no-kill worker agreed with this sentiment, saying, "We've had dogs here for a year or two and you look at when they came in

versus when they went out or were put to sleep, and they get worse not better. Shelters aren't always great places for dogs. And the longer they are here, the more likely we are to make them worse."

Recognition of shared values is an important tool for building common ground. Most workers in both camps are not absolutists; they neither unthinkingly carry out every euthanasia nor rigidly oppose every possibility. Despite such overlap in values, however, most workers believed that members of the other camp did not share their own broad, if not ambiguous, perspective toward fundamental animal sheltering issues. This thinking served only to polarize further the no-kill controversy because it emphasized differences in values and exaggerated the ideological distance between the two camps. Discovering, noting, and acknowledging shared values would help proponents and workers "see" their common interests and change their current thinking and practice.

Mutual Identification

Although public posturing toward and stereotyping of the no-kill and open-admission approaches commonly occurred, when individuals aired their thoughts in private, they sometimes identified with those in the opposing camp. Research on pro-life and pro-choice supporters also has found their differences to be less pronounced than their public rhetoric (Dworkin 1993; Kaufman 1999). Among shelter workers, mutual identification was evident when respondents spoke informally with peers or with the author; at these times, political and rhetorical guards were lowered enough to reveal more overlap in humane identities than many might realize or admit.

For example, there were occasional expressions of empathy for workers in the other camp. No-killers, as seen earlier, reported pity for open-admission workers who had to euthanize animals, or even work in a shelter that did this, because of the emotional toll such actions were believed to take. One no-kill worker felt that open-admission shelter staff might resent the greater resources available to the few well-endowed no-kill shelters. She explained,

It's a horrible thing to have to euthanize animals every day. I feel fortunate that I am working in an organization where we don't have to do that. I can understand them [open-admission shelters] being resentful that we have the resources that we do and are able to run things the way we do. And that is where this [tension] is coming from. They have the same amount of compassion that we do have, but because they have fewer resources, they can't do what we do.

Open admissionists sometimes pitied no-kill workers who had to say "no" to people wanting to drop off their pets, only to tell them there was no room or a very long waiting list and that they either had to take their animals to some other shelter, go to a veterinarian for euthanasia, or find a neighbor or friend to adopt the animal. One respondent said that he thought it was at least as upsetting for no-killers to tell many people "no" as it was to euthanize animals "eight hours a day." How hard, he conjectured, it must be to turn away people who sometimes are pleading for their animals to be taken. He even computed the number of people who are told "no" at a prominent sanctuary, estimating many thousand each year, and finding the thought of doing this to be mind boggling.

Mutual identification was manifested in ways other than pity. There was recognition by some that, in the end, both camps resorted to a similar process for deciding the fate of animals when space became limited. At these times, said one respondent, "You go through your populations and you are going to try and euthanize the animals that are the least placeable...the ones with the worst health, or the oldest, or the ones not doing well in the shelter environment." Workers who shared this thinking felt that their peers in the other camp were forced to go through the same excruciating decision making to decide the fate of shelter animals. Because they did this too, they felt collegial and cohesive rather than confrontational and competitive.

Identifying and acknowledging mutual identification can help to lessen the present polarization that leads to overgeneralization and blanket assumptions about those in the opposite camp. In such a hostile environment, people are likely to feel unfairly and negatively judged by others, and certainly unappreciated for their emotional and ethical labors. Sympathy can be the starting point that opens lines of communication and support for different, but not necessarily antagonistic, ways of managing shelter animals.

Maturation and Change

New common ground will be discovered over time as the "no-kill issue" matures in the humane community. This is likely to happen as more people reject simplistic characterizations of the no-kill "debate" or "controversy" that pit one camp against the other, even though the present study could be faulted for doing so. Although many people consider the no-kill controversy to be highly polarized, it is more accurate to think of it as a range of views about the appropriateness of killing shelter animals. While some tension no doubt occurs as these differences are negotiated, a working order probably will be created that, despite occasional bumpiness, allows most shelters to draw on and be comfortable with different perspectives toward euthanasia. This diversity of views should be seen as a healthy form of organizational conflict that allows both perspectives to exist under the same roof. Such a plan means that the humane community will have to live with some residual uneasiness about the nature and role of euthanasia and to see that discomfort as a sign of correctly managing a complex and subtle issue.

As the no-kill issue matures, other organizational changes are likely to reduce the distance between camps. Some no-kill groups will become institutionalized over time, if they have not already, moving them closer to a humane centrist position. As this happens, they will reject, with the same conviction and vehemence as traditional humane groups, "fringe" or "lunatic" groups also claiming to be no-kill. Some no-kill leaders have acknowledged the existence of these marginal "shelters," and the need for them to be improved or eliminated. More centrist no-kill organizations will move to some degree toward the open-admission camp. To wit, there has been some response to the open-admission plea for less provocative language and to stop using the label "no kill" or inflammatory terms that compare open admissionsts to Nazis, criminals, or other killers. Aware that the no-kill language hurts or angers others, some in the movement sympathize with this concern and have curtailed use of such terms. In one instance the director of a major no-kill shelter publicly acknowledged that, because the term *no-kill* can offend others, he consciously tries to stop using it when speaking publicly. And several shelters whose policies were no-kill in practice and principal refused to label themselves as no-kill because they had various problems with the term's meaning and its effect on open-admission shelters and staff. In one case, the president of a no-kill shelter claimed that she did not "tout" her organization as no kill:

The only reason we are "no kill" is because, unlike animal shelters, we have the ability to turn people away.... Just because one organization is not killing does not mean that animals are not dying en masse. The animals we unfortunately must turn away very likely end up at the end of a needle in a shelter. (Stinson 1997)

Finally, the organizer of the national

no-kill conference decided to drop "no kill" from the name of this meeting, so as to include rather than exclude people from the open-admission perspective. The organizer renamed it the "Conference on Homeless Animal Management and Policy."

More progressive open-admission groups, in turn, are likely to rethink their mission and identity, moving somewhat closer to the no-kill camp by adopting more aggressive adoption policies; questioning long-standing definitions of what constitutes "acceptable" rates of euthanasia; and trying to lower these rates. Some open admissionists also have shown a willingness to embrace a no-kill identity in their speaking. For instance at one shelter that has had great success in controlling dog overpopulation, a senior staff member commented, "We are no-kill with puppies." Even if said tongue in cheek, his language suggests a recognition that no-kill is a worthy aim and a sign of success. A few open admissionists are even styling themselves as "no-kill advocates," although this is laughable to no-kill workers. Perhaps there is more substance to this claim; certainly, no shelter worker wants to euthanize animals. If these organizational changes take place, friction between camps will subside, leaving a small number of marginalized humane organizations outside the boundaries of mainstream shelter culture.

Conclusion

Maturation and change in the no-kill controversy is likely to lead to new language and ideology for speaking and thinking about issues facing all shelter workers. This will happen as the humane community chooses not to fan the fires of current tensions, or even focus on them, but rather to look upon them as an opportunity to redefine to shelter workers and the public its identity and mission. Some divergent ideas from both camps will become synthesized and appeal to most shelter workers, while others

will be dropped by the wayside because they lack this broad interest. The result will be a new humane ideology that can be embraced by no-kill and open-admission advocates alike.

This change will require refashioning the meaning of familiar concepts or creating entirely fresh ones that bridge tensions rather than create them. The very ambiguity of such terms as *shelter*, *humane*, and *euthanasia* frustrates people, but this vagueness can benefit those who want to give them new meanings that resonate for all shelter workers. To bridge the tensions, superordinate concepts must draw from common ground between camps—shared practices, values, and identities—so that most workers can agree with and extol them in professional and public arenas.

The notion of welfare could serve aptly as one superordinate concept to unite rather than divide the shelter community. Although somewhat tricky to reinvent because of its present political connotations in the general animal community, the term nevertheless has the potential to bridge tensions underlying the no-kill debate, just as others have suggested using the concept of welfare to quell the abortion controversy (Kaufmann 1999). Concern for the welfare of animals deeply motivates both no-kill and open-admission advocates. It is a major area of common ground, leading virtually all shelter workers, regardless of their camp, to preserve and improve the quality of life for animals. When threads of common ground surface in dialogue between members of the two camps, workers can understand how the same concern for animals triggers one person's decision to be no kill, the other's to be open admission. The lifework inspired by this motivation is different for the two camps, but it is work that both parties can admire. Focusing on this common ground can foster mutual respect, as the enemy image is replaced by the actual presence of another shelter worker strug-

gling to respond to the difficult situations of everyday life. Workers see for themselves that within their world views is a shared concern for animals.

Certainly there are many other notions, long familiar to shelter workers, that can be infused with new meaning to connect rather than separate open-admission and no-kill supporters. Indeed, entirely new concepts unfamiliar to the shelter world may be brought into this community to bridge its camps. Whether old ideas are being reinvented or new ones are being imported, to succeed they must be based on common ground between camps. The challenge facing the American sheltering community is to discover additional bases for this common ground and to articulate a new language to reaffirm it.

Acknowledgements

I wish to thank Kathy Savesky, Natalie DiGiacomo, and Anne Lindsay for providing advice and criticism. I am also grateful to the Edith Goode Trust and the San Francisco Society for the Prevention of Cruelty to Animals for their support of this research.

Notes

[1]My use of the term *kill*, except when specifically discussing its meaning to shelter workers or quoting them directly, is made without symbolic or political connotation.

[2]Throughout this report the terms *open admission* and *no kill* are used because most members of the respective camps accept these labels as self descriptions, while rejecting other terms for themselves. Open-admission advocates reject the label "kill shelter," and even the less sensitive language of "full service" or "traditional" are received ambivalently. Similarly no-kill proponents reject the term *limited admission* for their facilities.

[3]Open-admission advocates use the same argument against no-kill proponents when they contend, in so many words, that "all that money and effort on keeping animals alive keeps them from their mission of preventing births in the first place."

[4]While this piggybacking on the pro-life movement's symbolism offers cachet to the no-kill identity, it also escalates the controversy because it confuses two reasons for believing that euthanasia is often, if not always, wrong. Like the pro-life movement's ideological confusion over whether it is wrong to abort a fetus because the fetus has a right to live or because all life has intrinsic value (Dworkin 1993), the no-kill movement's confused ideology argues both that the unwanted or undesirable shelter animal has a

right to live and that euthanasia as commonly practiced shows disrespect for animal and human life.

[5]It is important to be cautious about the significance of such dissent, especially when it involves a new social movement. Rather than serving as a common ground, internal diversity and emotional fervor can divide and weaken camps. Hints of this can be seen in tensions between behavior/training staff and adoption staff in some no-kill shelters or, at a different level, between doctrinaire no-kill advocates and other no-kill proponents who occasionally resort to euthanizing their animals.

Literature Cited

Bogue, G. 1998a. Readers climbing on the no-kill bandwagon. *Contra Costa Times*, n.d.

———. 1998b. Shelters need to join forces to stop killing. *Contra Costa Times*, n.d.

Caras, R. 1997a. Letter to Richard Avanzino, July 9.

———. 1997b. Letter to Val Beatty and Bonney Brown, August 21.

———. 1997c. Viewpoints. *Animal Sheltering* Sept./Oct.: 16–17.

Cubrda, E. 1993. Letter to Mark Hamilton from the California Humane Society, Los Angeles SPCA, October 15.

Donald, R. 1991. "The No-Kill Controversy," *Shelter Sense* September: 3–6.

Doyle, M. 1982. In-house rhetoric of pro-life and pro-choice special interest groups in Minnesota: Motivation and alienation. *Dissertation Abstracts International* 43 (11): 3454. (University Microfilms No. AAC83-08038.)

Dworkin, R. 1993. *Life's dominion: An argument about abortion, euthanasia, and individual freedom.* New York: Alfred A. Knopf.

Foro, L. 1997. Viewpoints. *Animal Sheltering* Sept./Oct.: 16–17.

———. n.d.a. Know the thrill of no kill—Retreat, Hell! *Online Doing Things for Animals.*

———. n.d.b. Vegetarianism and no kill. *Online Doing Things for Animals.*

Foster, J.T. 2000. A fate worse than death: Are "no-kill" shelters truly humane? *Reader's Digest*, July 20.

Gilyard, B. 2001. Out of gas. *Showing Animals Respect and Kindness*, August: 6–7.

Ginsburg, F. 1986. *Contested lives: The abortion debate in the American community.* Los Angeles: University of California Press.

Hess, B. 1998. Shelter skelter. *New York Magazine,* October 19.

Hicks, J. 1993. A.S.P.C.A. plans to give up job killing New York strays. *New York Times*, March 26: B14.

Hughes, E. 1964. Good people and dirty work. In *The other side*, ed. H. Becker, 23–26. New York: Free Press.

Kaufmann, A. 1999. The pro-choice/pro-life conflict: An exploratory study to understand the nature of the conflict and to develop constructive conflict intervention designs. Ph.D. diss., George Mason University.

Luker, K. 1984. *Abortion and the politics of motherhood.* Berkeley: University of California Press.

Milani, M. 1997. The no-kill controversy. *Journal of the American Veterinary Association* 210: 26–27.

Miller, P. n.d. "Chain Reaction: 'No-Kill...' or 'You Kill?'" *California Humane Action and Information Network Letter* 4: Fall.

Paris, P. 1997. HSUS animal shelter no-kill article. Interoffice memo. New York: American Society for the Prevention of Cruelty to Animals, September 24.

Savesky, K. 1995a. Letter to James Chimera, May 25.

———. 1995b. The door remains open. *Paw Prints*, 2–3.

Sheeran, P. 1987. *Women, society, the state, and abortion: A structuralist analysis.* New York: Praeger.

Stinson, P. 1997. Letter to Roger Caras, June 25.

Religion and Animals: A Changing Scene

6

CHAPTER

Paul Waldau

In 1903 W.E.B. Du Bois predicted, "The problem of the twentieth century is the problem of the color line" (1969). One hundred years later, we can hope that the twentieth century achieved important advances for human liberation—not only racial but also sexual and political. Will that moral trajectory—the expansion of fundamental protections now easily seen as the hallmark of the last century—continue? Will the problem of the twenty-first century be the problem of the species line?

For protections to evolve to include nonhuman species, religions—through their leaders, their institutions, and above all their believers—must take seriously the important role that they have played, and certainly will continue to play, in humans' engagement with the lives beyond our species line. Religions have such a central role in the transmission of basic images and values regarding living beings that, without their help, the problem of the species line will not be solved in this century. A central question for this century is whether influential religious institutions will continue to convey images that radically and absolutely dismiss nonhumans, or will religions offer support for the broadening movement to include nonhuman animals in humans' moral scope.

If religions notice other species and take them seriously, ethical sensibilities regarding nonhuman animals may blossom as fully as did sensibili-

ties regarding the importance of the human individual. Various positive signs at the end of the twentieth century suggested that religions may yet play an important role in dispelling the dismissive caricatures of nonhumans animals that prevail in, for example, industrialized societies. One of these signs was that religions' role in the origin and persistence of both negative views and positive evaluations of other animals finally was well described. Another was that many believers began the difficult task of engaging their fellow believers in dialogue regarding religions' strengths and weaknesses in addressing the issue of the value of the nonhuman lives around them.

Where will this vital discussion go in the new century? Will it help people see the myriad ways in which religious traditions have been vitally involved in developing the often-dismissive views of nonhuman lives? Will the discussion bring to the foreground the animal-friendly features found in every code of religious ethics? Will religious leaders and scholars fully delineate the contributions of religion—both good and bad—to people's ability to take other animals seriously? Will many religious leaders continue to claim that it is *only* human lives that *really* matter? Will religious traditions be formed not solely by theologians but also by grassroots believers attempting to commit their religion's resources to the fullest possible recognition of ani-

mals as beings possessing integrity and value wholly independent of human needs?

However believers and their leaders answer these questions, religions will play a decisive role in humans' encounters with the nonhuman others in and near our communities. And whatever choices any particular religious tradition and its believers make, a central problem inside and outside religion will be, without doubt, the problem of the species line.

1900–1950: The Dismissal of Nonhuman Lives

The science establishment of the western industrialized countries began in the early twentieth century to recognize that nonhuman primates were subject to many of the same diseases as were humans. The remarkable physical (and, it was later recognized, psychological and social) similarities of nonhuman primates to humans, however, did not lead scientists, on the whole, to recommend similar ethical protections for these evolutionary cousins.

An irony in the thoroughgoing dismissal of all nonhuman lives so characteristic of the first half of the twentieth century was that turn-of-the-century scientists had inherited a resurgent interest in the importance and complexities of nonhuman animal lives. The 1859 publication of Darwin's pivotal *Origin of Species* had spurred much new interest in nonhuman lives. In some quarters at least, commitments to take other animals seriously flowered relative to the absolute dismissal and caricature of nonhuman lives that had prevailed in western scientific and religious circles before Darwin's groundbreaking achievement.

Curiosity about other animals' lives manifested itself in many ways, from increased observation to invasive studies such as those done in the 1870s by the British physician David Ferrier, who looked at the relationship of humans to other primates (Blum 1994). Ferrier's idea of a systematic study of primate-human relationships was to take apart the brains of nonhuman primates in order to say something about the similarity of humans to other primates. Whole lives in context, which of course must be part of any truly systematic study, also were engaged increasingly, as exemplified by R.L. Garner's study in the 1890s of free-living chimpanzees (Wrangham et al. 1994). The extensive works of George Romanes —*Mental Evolution in Animals* (1885) and *Animal Intelligence* (1886)—went through multiple editions. While often based on anecdote rather than the rigorous observation standards of late twentieth century ethology, Romanes's work and that of others reflected deep interest in the lives of the animals described and an openness to the possibility that some nonhumans were, like humans, possessed of social, cognitive, and individual complexities.

As Ferrier's work shows, by no means all of what was happening in the study of nonhuman animals at the end of the nineteenth century was of a moral or otherwise sensitive nature. Darwin's co-originator of the notion of natural selection, A.R. Wallace, shot orangutans in order to study them—and sadly this was typical of Victorian naturalists (Galdikas 1995). Such insensitivity was perhaps a harbinger of attitudes to come, for

in crucial ways and in important institutions, scientific attitudes toward other animals were about to go through a regressive narrowing in the twentieth century's first fifty years.

The Narrowing

John Watson (1913) published an essay that was to set the tone of scientific research into other animals' cognitive abilities for the next half-century. Watson's approach, which involved a denial of the mental life of other animals, was unusual in several senses. First, a denial of mental life begs obvious questions. As the Oxford historian Keith Thomas has noted, "That there are some footsteps of reason, some strictures and emissions of ratiocination in the actions of some brutes, is too vulgarly known and too commonly granted to be doubted" (1984, 124: n.8).

Second, from the scientific perspective, Watson's views, which were the foundation of behaviorism, left much to be desired. Behaviorism, which in its strictest form emphasizes the stimulus-response model and holds that all behavior is learned through either classical or operant conditioning, is very *ideological*, in the narrowest sense of that term. Many contemporary scientists hold that behaviorism involves an explanatory monism—that is, an unnecessarily narrow attempt to provide an exhaustive causal account of even the most complex living organism built arbitrarily upon stimulus-response generalizations drawn solely from an isolated part of that being's complexity. In this regard, behaviorism can in fact be unscientific, because the explanatory monism neglects a significant range of data.

Historically behaviorists drew their inspiration from the philosophical paradigm of positivism, which led it to be unnecessarily reductive. Behaviorism's explanatory monism violates both observation and such cherished methodological principles as that of parsimony. Sometimes it is simply more consistent with observation and considerations of parsimony to

explain actions of a living being by means of higher level functions than by behaviorism's simplified stimulus-response paradigm. In biology intelligence and other "higher level" cognitive functions often are far more economical as explanations than are explanations that rely on long chains of stimulus-response relations.

When the minds of other animals are ignored, it becomes easier to treat them as mere machines or inanimate things. The result of such a radical dismissal of the more complex features of other animals' lives is that humans use them as experimental tools or unfeeling resources. Such use, and in particular its problems from the standpoint of both informed, sensitive science and ethically integrated religion, is well symbolized by Tom Regan's film *We Are All Noah* (1986b), which refers to the use of thousands of nonhuman animals as experimental subjects on a boat dubbed "the Atomic Ark" in the U.S. military's 1946 Bikini Island nuclear test in the Pacific.

The Opening

Of course not every development in science in the first half of the twentieth century reflected a dismissal of other animals from humans' ethical horizon. R.M. Yerkes published *The Great Apes* in 1927, but, when doing his research, he was astonished to find only travelers' accounts (Galdikas 1995). Garner's attempt in the 1890s to study nonhuman great apes in the field was to be the only real attempt before Nissen's attempt in 1930—which lasted all of four months (Goodall, in Wrangham 1994). Thus for Yerkes the available sources of information were travelers' tales

[S]uch as those by T.S. Savage and J. Wyman in the Ivory Coast in 1842.... [These] provided almost everything that was known of chimpanzee behavior in the wild (although the African peoples who lived in or near the forests could have told us more) until the flurry of field studies began after the Second World War in the early sixties

(Goodall, in Wrangham, xv).
The first successful study of a wild ape took place in Asia in the 1930s when C.R. Carpenter studied white-handed gibbons in Thailand. His work was important because Carpenter identified such crucial features of gibbon adaptation as territoriality and monogamy. But afterwards all the gibbons were shot, and it was almost thirty years until another study (that of Goodall) was launched (see Galdikas 1995).

From the late 1930s to the late 1940s, a modern version of Darwin's views, sometimes referred to as "the evolutionary synthesis," became the consensus view among established biological scientists. This development "settled numerous old arguments once and for all, and thus opened the way for a discussion of entirely new problems" (Mayr 1982, 569).

A foreshadowing of much broader concerns appeared in 1946 when the International Whaling Commission, an association of more than two hundred members from forty nations, was formed under the International Convention for the Regulation of Whaling. Although committed not to the elimination of the killing of cetaceans but instead to the management of resources, this international effort paved the way for both conservation and abolitionist efforts that developed later in the century, such as the 1986 ban on commercial whaling.

In the 1950s and 1960s, there were significant developments in various life sciences regarding a fuller engagement with other animals on the basis of their realities. Some of these developments came at the prompting of various ethical traditions (though in virtually every case an ethical tradition *outside* religion). Many came from a reassertion of basic scientific values, such as the importance of humble, patient empirical observation. In the early 1960s, careful fieldwork was commenced (Kortlandt in eastern Zaire; Goodall in Gombe, Tanzania; Itani and others in Kabogo, Tanzania; and Nishida in what is now Mahale Mountains National Park, Tanzania). Undoubtedly the most important sci-

entific study for the subsequent tradition of careful observation was that of Jane Goodall on the chimpanzees of Gombe. Begun in 1960 this effort continues today (see van Lawick-Goodall 1971). Through a series of National Geographic television specials, Goodall's work, though initially controversial, stimulated a new generation to pursue careful, observation-based studies of animals of all kinds. Stephen Jay Gould of Harvard, referring to Goodall as "one of the intellectual heroes of this century" (1995, 23), described her study as "one of the Western world's great scientific achievements" (in Miller 1995).

The fundamental change from the first half of the century to the second half also is epitomized by the change in thinking known as the "Cognitive Revolution." In this recent revolution in psychology, information processing has been emphasized and the behaviorists' exclusive focus on conditioning through stimulus-response models has been de-emphasized (see Gardner 1985; Griffin 1992).

Because of this revolution, there is a much richer evaluation of the mechanisms of any animal, human or otherwise, that are involved in modification of behavior during growth and after experience, as well as the relationships among cognition, learning and development, information processing, representation, imitation, and problem solving generally.

This important change has not solved all problems. According to Griffin, there remains a reluctance to attribute subjective states to nonhuman animals: "This antipathy to consideration of consciousness threatens to become a sort of self-inflicted paralysis of inquiry, and obsolete hindrance to scientific investigation" (1992, viii).

Yet the bottom line is that science now has delivered evidence that *some* nonhuman animals' cognitive abilities are far richer than ever imagined in the western scientific establishment and, arguably, in the theological and philosophical establishments as well.

Religion and Other Animals

In neither 1900 nor 1950 would religious believers in North America, Europe, and other parts of the industrialized, "developed" world have been well described as "concerned" about the earth's nonhuman animals. Some believers were compassionate, no doubt, but institutions and religious rhetoric were, on the whole, insensitive to nonhuman animals' interests. Indeed, the vast majority of religious believers were not only unconcerned but also ignorant and blind insofar as nonhuman animals were concerned.[1]

In the succeeding half-century, however, developments within specific religious traditions have revealed that religious traditions offer many perspectives, ethical values, and other resources for engaging all animals, human and otherwise, far more sensitively than occurred in the first half of the twentieth century. In the world of academic study of religion, the "Caucus on Religion, Animals, and Ethics" first met in 1998 and has been formalized by the American Academy of Religion. In 1999 the Center for Respect of Life and Environment (affiliated with The Humane Society of the United States) sponsored a major conference of international scholars at Harvard University. This conference was part of the follow-up to the groundbreaking series of ten conferences organized by Mary Evelyn Tucker and John Grim that established the now flourishing field of religion and ecology.

These developments, along with the seminal theological work of Linzey (1987, 1994b), Cohn-Sherbok (1997, with Linzey), and Masri (1987, 1989), have led to the emergence of a group of scholars who now pursue the new field of religion and animals systematically for the first time in history.

Thus in the last fifty years the state of animals in religion has, at least in some respects, changed significantly. The radical change from the first half of the twentieth century to the second half, described more specifically below, stimulates many to speculate on what additional changes may be seen in both the new century and, indeed, in this new millennium.

Pre-1950 Religion and Animals

In 1888 the influential Catholic theologian Joseph Rickaby summed up a view that in many different ways has dominated the Christian tradition on the issue of the moral status of nonhuman animals:

> Brutes are as *things* in our regard: so far as they are useful for us, they exist for us, not for themselves; and we do right in using them unsparingly for our need and convenience, though not for our wantonness (1988, 250).

While neither Christianity nor the other Abrahamic traditions (Judaism and Islam) are exhaustively represented by such a bald assertion (as will be shown by what follows), the underlying mentality that nonhuman animals are on the earth for humans' use is representative in two respects of the ways in which most religious believers in these traditions viewed nonhuman animals before the mid-point of the twentieth century.

First and foremost such a claim is grounded in what often is referred to as an instrumentalist view, which holds that other animals can, unlike humans, be used in good conscience for an individual human's own benefit.[2] Second, as Rickaby's quote reflects, there was a limiting factor, namely the injunction not to act "cruelly" or "wantonly." Such a concern reflects, no doubt, the deep concern of some Jews, Muslims, and Christians for the welfare and lives of nonhuman animals. Interestingly, however, in the Christian tradition some very prominent official objections to acts of wanton cruelty did not argue that the problem was the ensuing harm to nonhuman animals. Rather,

cruel acts were wrong because they might lead weak-minded humans to harm other humans in some way.[3]

Religious traditions hold, of course, that humans are special because of their remarkable moral abilities. But from 1900 to 1950, religion in many places, including most circles in North America and Europe, actively advanced the view that humans, when using their considerable moral abilities, need focus only on members of the human species. Such a view is sometimes referred to as "ethical anthropocentrism," and it frequently is accompanied by an instrumentalist view of other animals as mere things rightfully excluded from the moral circle.

It is important to note, however, that the combination of anthropocentric ethics with instrumentalist views of other animals is not the only view of other animals found within religious traditions. Within Christianity, for example, more compassionate views such, as those espoused by St. Francis of Assisi, long have represented a significant, though often subordinated, sub-tradition regarding the value of other animals. In general, however, even if the list of Christians who have advocated compassion for nonhuman animals is long and distinguished, it is far shorter, and characterized by far fewer major figures, than is the list of those who have advocated an anthropocentric standard. On the longer list is, for example, Pope Pius IX, who led the Catholic tradition from 1846 to 1878. He is reported to have said to the anti-vivisectionist Anna Kingsford, "Madame, humankind has no duties to the animals," and then backed this up by opposing the establishment of a society for the protection of animals in Rome (see Gaffney 1986; Kalechofsky 1991).

Apart from its dominant position in the hierarchy of Christian institutions and in the mainline theology of the tradition, ethical anthropocentrism in one form or another can also be found in other religious traditions

(Waldau 2001a). Yet they, like Christianity, have moderating sub-traditions that allow adherents to be *both* "true believers" and respectful of nonhuman animals' interests. In such sub-traditions, considerable respect has been accorded to both other animals' place in the moral circle and their status as living beings with whom we share the earth.

Mid-Century Winds of Change

From the midpoint of the twentieth century onward, certain developments have pushed many religious traditions to become more sensitive to nonhuman animals as candidates for moral concern. These developments include increasing interfaith dialogue; greater historical awareness of the traditions' own pro-animal sub-traditions and the irrational prejudices against nonhumans within and across traditions; increasing interest in the relationship of human ethical abilities to environmental issues; and, above all, better information about nonhuman animals.

Such developments have enhanced the ability of religious believers to "see" other animals better. This, of course, is relevant to how those believers' ethical abilities might be engaged, for, as the English philosopher Stephen Clark has said, "One's ethical, as well as one's ontological framework is determined by what entities one is prepared to notice or take seriously. . . " (1977, 7).

An essay written by C.S. Lewis (1963) at mid-century can be used to highlight dormant possibilities within religious institutions, especially because it reveals that even those traditions thought not to be "animal friendly" have resources for a full engagement with nonhuman lives. This is so because each of the traditions is, in fact, an extraordinarily rich cumulative tradition within which many past believers have recognized the relevance of human ethical abilities to nonhuman lives. Apparent in the re-emergence of these oft-subordinated possibilities are the beginnings of an important series of changes that continue to this day in the established religious traditions in North America.

Lewis's essay first appeared in 1947 in the journal of the New England Anti-Vivisection Society. Later it appeared in other publications.[4] This seminal article appeals to core beliefs of Christians about the special qualities of humans' moral abilities. Thus even though the arguments are stated in terms of the dualism "humans and animals" that Lewis was trained to use by his own religious and cultural traditions, the article reveals that the Christian tradition has much to offer those who care enough to engage the realities of other animals' actual lives.

Lewis lures the reader into engaging the issue openly by observing that it is "the rarest thing" in the world to hear "a rational discussion of vivisection." He then argues that a rational discussion must begin with whether pain is an evil. If pain is not an evil, Lewis suggests, then the cases both for and against vivisection fail. He reasons that if pain is not an evil, its infliction on nonhuman animals need not be opposed, but, *also*, if pain is not an evil, there is no reason to look for ways to ameliorate it in humans. The discussion, then, must begin with recognition that pain is an evil.

Focusing on the standard Christian position "in the Latin countries. . .that we are entitled to do anything we please to animals because they 'have no souls'" (1963, 154), Lewis notes that if this is the case then infliction of pain on them is "harder to justify,"

> [f]or it means that animals cannot deserve pain, nor profit morally by the discipline of pain, nor be recompensed by happiness in another life for suffering in this. Thus all the factors which render pain more tolerable or make it less totally evil in the case

of human beings will be lacking in the beasts. "Soulessness," in so far as it is relevant to the question at all, is an argument against vivisection.[5]

Lewis then appeals to a fundamental claim at the very heart of the Christian and many other religious positions, namely, the belief that humans alone among the earth's creatures are moral beings. He uses this important claim to challenge facile Christian acceptance of instrumental uses of nonhuman animals:

> [W]e may feel that though objective superiority is rightly claimed for man, yet that very superiority ought partly to *consist in* not behaving like a vivisector—that we ought to prove ourselves better than the beasts precisely by the fact of acknowledging duties to them which they do not acknowledge to us. (1963, 154)[6]

Relying relentlessly on common sense, logic, and frank appraisals of the general nature of instrumental uses of other living beings, Lewis adds many other creative arguments. He suggests that it was *non*-Christian values that promoted the argument to allow vivisection, and he reminds us that, at least in England, Christian society in the eighteenth and nineteenth centuries had many resources for seeing the anti-vivisectionist as a religious person.[7] Lewis's principled and, most relevantly, *fully Christian* engagement with a facile acceptance of contemporary instrumental uses of living beings pushes him to repudiate completely any casual acceptance of instrumental uses of other animals:

> The victory of vivisection marks a great advance in the triumph of ruthless, non-moral utilitarianism over the old world of ethical law, a triumph in which we, as well as animals, are already the victims, and of which Dachau and Hiroshima are the more recent achievements. (1963, 155)

Traditional and Compassionate Views

Lewis's essay exemplifies both typical and unusual features of the religion and animals landscape at mid-century. His arguments are typical in that, despite his obvious compassion for pain in other animals, he reflects what amounts to a dismissal of other animals' complex lives as relevant to their moral standing. In the passages quoted above, he implies very negative images of nonhuman animals. In particular, his argument assumes that because humans understand that some nonhuman animals act in ways that humans see as cruel, *all* nonhuman animals are cruel. This involves not only the obvious fallacy of overgeneralization, but also the standard caricature of nonhuman animals that has dominated western cultures since the classical Greeks.

Thus because Lewis knew virtually nothing of the behaviors of the more complex nonhuman animals and existed at a time when his culture sanctioned such ignorance, in an important sense his arguments merely perpetuate the following culturally significant stereotypes: (1) of the earth's denizens, only humans are complicated beings; (2) nonhuman animals live without any kind of moral or social regard for each other; (3) for all intents and purposes, all other animals lack intelligence in any significant sense.

When seeking to understand either the history or the future possibilities of religion on the issue of nonhuman animals, it is crucial to recognize that not all religions have dismissed nonhuman animals in this way. Indeed, at certain times and places some religious believers have had significant, empirically based knowledge of other animals. Accordingly they could be called upon to point out the caricatures and ignorance that underlie the generalities used by Lewis. The fallacy is, of course, that the absence of evidence has been taken as evidence of absence. The prevailing ignorance is not dispelled because no one is looking for complexities, and hence none is found.

Lewis's own religious tradition, along with the other traditions that have had a significant influence in the industrialized world, has lost much of the experienced-based knowledge of the natural world and its nonhuman animals that is found, among other places, in certain religio-cultural traditions now classified among the "indigenous" traditions. Similarly, the Christian culture into which Lewis was born was not characterized by any ethically developed sense of humans' continuity with other animals, although examples of this can be found throughout the Hindu, Jain, and Buddhist traditions.[8] In fact the negative views and radical dismissal of other animals' lives that underlie Lewis's failure to engage any specifics of the nature and abilities of nonhuman animals relative to humans are characteristic of many of the most influential institutions and voices within those religious traditions that have the most influence in the industrialized world. In effect these institutions and loud voices, as it were, have drowned out the voices of the more compassionate sub-traditions from within their *own* circle that have been willing to promote the moral significance of nonhuman animals.

Nonetheless Lewis's essay has some features that begin to bring to light the additional Christian possibilities for seeing nonhuman animals. In this respect Lewis foreshadows some of the developments seen in other traditions' believers, engaging insights sometimes buried deep within the religion and animals landscape at mid-century. For example, it is worth noting that Lewis is arguing *as a Christian* and that he reaches his conclusions even though he adheres to, and in some ways promotes, aspects of Christianity's traditional, ignorance-based appraisal of other animals. Thus, in spite of his traditional views, his profound religious beliefs

connect him to life generally, and he thus finds a way to assert that other animals *should* matter to Christians as moral agents. It is as a *Christian* that Lewis speaks of the value of other animals' lives, and his concern clearly is to reach Christian colleagues as Christian, as well as the Christian establishment that had been quiet about humans' instrumentalist uses of other animals. This is precisely why Lewis emphasizes the cherished senses of (1) human uniqueness and (2) human moral abilities that lie at the center of Christianity and all other religious traditions. Through a focus on our important ability to care about others, be they human or not, Lewis questions the facile, absolute dismissal of all nonhuman animals that dominated his own religious traditions during his lifetime (he died in 1963). In making this challenge, Lewis reflects the internal resources established religion has available for the task of reexamining modern industrialized societies' radical marginalization of other animals.

In reflecting both the traditional and more compassionate sides of contemporary religious traditions, Lewis reflects well the dilemma regarding nonhuman animals faced by religion in the twentieth century. His essay, particularly as it highlights the very *un-Christian* (in Lewis's view) features of the modern practice of vivisection, sets the stage well for understanding the complex trajectory of developments within religious traditions since 1950 on the issue of "animals." During the last half of the twentieth century, informed religious believers had to come to terms with the consequences of the modern world's increasingly radical, virtually absolute dismissal of all nonhuman animals as valued individuals deserving protection as *individuals*. It is noteworthy, for example, that Lewis does not argue the Christian's duty is to *species*, and he never alludes to the issue of loss of species. His concern is with individuals who are harmed by a specific practice, not the qualitatively different concern for biodiversity. It is

this standard of sensitivity to other living things as individuals that Lewis names in this essay as the proper *Christian* standard. Even if such sensitivity is not altogether new, but rather a reaffirmation of a sub-tradition that has existed in Christian and other religious traditions all along, it provides a challenge to contemporary mainline Christianity. This is a formidable and identity-threatening challenge, for the mainline Christian tradition, not unlike mainline interpretations of other religious traditions, has in its ancient, medieval, and contemporary theology promoted anthropocentric, exclusivist views and practices among its believers and churches.

Competing Tensions

The tension in Lewis's article between elements of the traditional view that humans are superior to all other animals, on the one hand, and those morality-based implications so creatively argued by Lewis, on the other hand, can be used to frame not only the issues that faced religion at mid-century on the issue of the status and importance of nonhuman animals, but also the issues facing today's religious communities, churches, synagogues, mosques, and other places of worship or meditation.

First, tension is occasioned by the very questions Lewis and other believers ask concerning modern practices in an environment where religious communities and believers promote a status quo dominated by anthropocentrism in ethics as well as in politics, economics, law, and even academia. Lewis's modeling of possibilities of extending concern and compassion can easily be based on passages in the Qur'an, the Hebrew Bible, the Christian New and Old Testaments (in their original and translated forms), the Vedas from Hinduism, any of the Buddhist canons, or the astonishingly rich stories of indigenous religious traditions that support the extension of deep concern to nonhuman animals. These stories have remained a part of even the main line, anthropocentric interpretations of those religious traditions that predominate in the industrial world. Thus even if the dominant stories in Christianity and other religions take an instrumentalist approach to "humans and animals" and confine their believers' focus to humans alone, believers still can find elements of compassion that can be extended to nonhuman animals. If they do so, they are likely to find tension between that choice and the standard assumptions made in their own community or place of worship.

Second, merely naming the possibility of a more compassionate view as the truest Christian (or Jewish, Muslim, etc.) position creates tension. Lewis was extraordinarily popular in his native England, and he remains an icon in many conservative Christian circles in the United States. Yet despite the fact that Lewis is widely held by conservative Christians to be a person of vision, his conclusions in *this* essay remain unrealized. What's more, they are rarely, if ever, cited. The latter fact suggests that, although certain concerns for nonhuman animals that are grounded in the Christian tradition's most basic values have been and continue to be brought to the forefront by some major voices heard in contemporary circles, they have had but a limited effect. There are, without question, very strong competing values in the Christian tradition that negate concern for nonhuman animals. Still, Lewis's gambit remains a constant challenge on explicitly Christian grounds to the practice of vivisection. His arguments can be seen as a foreshadowing of the contemporary debates both within and without religious circles on the issue of nonhuman animals' moral significance.

Third, even greater tension now is evident on the issues Lewis addressed, for when he published this essay instrumental uses of nonhuman animals were just beginning to increase. The extraordinarily harsh features of intensive, or factory, farming; widespread use of nonhuman animals in experiments; and, of course, genetic engineering of animals to model human diseases were basically unknown to Lewis. These uses, some of which are described elsewhere in this volume, now dominate humans' relations with other animals.

Yet even if the Christian and other Abrahamic traditions have not yet given Lewis's reasoning any real standing in the debate over the propriety of the widespread contemporary practices that so obviously inflict pain and suffering on nonhuman living beings, Lewis's and other similar arguments continue to mark the possibilities of religious believers being open to the significance of other animals' lives. Since Lewis wrote this essay as a Christian argument for other Christians, his work continues to suggest that Christianity and other religions can use their own internal resources to provide insights into the importance of the lives of other animals.

The Image of God and Dominion

Ethical anthropocentrism characteristically is driven by the notion that humans are different from "animals." That humans are different in significant respects is, of course, both important and true, though this point often is overstated in the extreme. As Radner and Radner note:

> Obviously there are differences between humans and other species. Every species is different from every other species: this much is plain biology. The ideology lies not in the search for differences, but in the unwavering belief that humanity is defined by attributes that have absolutely no precedent in the rest of the biological world. (1989, 8)

In many contemporary forms of religious traditions, in particular the Abrahamic traditions, as well as in many secular traditions, the separation of humans from other animals is one of the forces that prevent humans from achieving a better understanding of their place in the ecological webs that link all lives. White, in a piece that has become one of the most notorious of modern essays, argued that the Christian doctrine of creation, particularly as it was elaborated in medieval times, forms "the historical roots of our ecological crisis," and that "orthodox Christian arrogance toward nature" thus "bears a huge burden of guilt" for present problems. White's thesis was based on the premise that our increasing ability to control and harness natural forces is flawed by the assumption that "we are superior to nature, contemptuous of it, willing to use it for our slightest whim" (1967, 1206). This led White to comment:

> Especially in its Western form, Christianity is the most anthropocentric religion the world has ever seen. . . . Christianity, in absolute contrast to ancient paganism and Asia's religions. . . not only established a dualism of man and nature but also insisted that it is God's will that man exploit nature for his proper ends. (1205)

White's analysis can be seen, upon even superficial consideration, to be in important respects a rhetorical and unfair overstatement, for a wide variety of factors other than religious ones, such as economic, social, political, and historical, underlie contemporary environmental practices (see also Merchant [1980] for the change from an organically oriented mentality to a mechanically oriented mentality between 1500 and 1700).

White's thesis has been very valuable, however, in raising awareness of how profoundly religious values have influenced the ways believers approach living beings. Jeremy Cohen (1989), among others, has argued persuasively that White's claims are wrong in some important specifics, since the dominion charge of Genesis 1:28 (relied on heavily by White) was not taken by ancient and medieval readers as any sort of license "selfishly to exploit the environment or to undermine its pristine integrity" (309). Cohen notes, however, that the language of Genesis 1:28 (which reads, in the Revised Standard Version, "Be fruitful and increase, fill the earth and subdue it; and have dominion over the fish in the sea, over the birds of the air, and over every other living thing that moves on the earth") was consistently taken as a divine call to rule over other animals. This analysis provides an interesting example of the how "environmental" issues and "animal" issues are by no means identical and do not overlap perfectly, even though they are obviously related. Conflating them under the rubric "environmental concerns" can, interestingly, make many nonhuman animals disappear from the moral landscape altogether. This happens, for example, when the exclusive focus is on species conservation and not on treatment of individuals from species that are not threatened. The upshot is that many morally relevant issues regarding nonhuman animals sometimes disappear in environmental discourse even if those who employ language that is eminently "environmental" have the best of intentions and are obviously in earnest about the relevance of the lives of nonhuman animals to us as moral agents.

The Realities of Change

Of great relevance to understanding the possibilities of change in religious views of nonhuman animals is the fact that religion at the start of the twenty-first century is, as it were, a different animal from what it was in the middle of the twentieth century. Negative factors pushed such a change, including astonishing ethnic, political, religious, and economic oppression, widespread ecological damage, and a proliferation of refugee crises brought on by countless wars. Positive factors pushing this change included increased communication, changing demographics, and interfaith dialogue.

The result of these and other factors prompting change has been that religious traditions and their believ-

ers often exhibit far more mutual understanding now and better awareness of each other. In general the leadership of religious institutions has become much more willing to tolerate, talk to, and even respect, believers of other religious traditions, though, of course, many well-known problems involving religious toleration remain unsolved.[9] Nonetheless pluralism has become an accepted phenomenon, grounded institutionally, politically, and philosophically by the open-minded work of the World Council of Churches and such pioneers as John Hick, Masao Abe, Ninian Smart, Sallie McFague, Rosemary Radford Ruether, Karl Rahner, John Cobb, Huston Smith, and Wilfred Cantwell Smith. Their work has been advanced by other philosophers, comparativists, theologians, and religious leaders, including Diana Eck, Arvind Sharma, Sulak Sivaraksa, Keith Ward, Jonathan Smith, Karen Armstrong, David Tracy, Langdon Gilkey, Mary Evelyn Tucker, Dan Cohn Sherbok, and Jay McDaniel. Such believers reflect well the openness that religious belief can stimulate when it notices and takes other perspectives seriously.

The Prevailing Context and Reality

The changes discussed here in the vast and diverse realm of religion took place in the late twentieth century, and continue in the new century, at the same time as an extraordinary ferment concerning perspectives on the diverse group of living beings referred to as "animals." One influential philosopher describes the changing values regarding nonhuman animals, especially as these values are enshrined in federal protections of laboratory animals, as a changing social ethic (Rollin 1999).

These important changes have been manifested in countless ways outside of religious traditions. In media and literature, discussions regarding the

status of nonhuman animals now abound, as they do in the ever-proliferating forest of biological sciences. Awareness of nonhuman animals in recent decades has not, however, been led by religious traditions. It has been led more by two forces: (1) primarily secular forces in industrialized countries, and (2) various life sciences such as primatology and marine mammalogy under the guidance of such recognized authorities as Goodall (chimpanzees), Roger and Katy Payne (whales), and Cynthia Moss, Joyce Poole, and Katy Payne (elephants). In philosophical circles a broad discussion has been taking place concerning ethical issues as a secular matter; this has been especially prominent since the 1975 publication of *Animal Liberation*, by Peter Singer.

The emergence of widespread interest in protecting nonhuman animals in some manner or another has led to a complex social movement, often misleadingly labeled "animal rights."[10] This broad movement is a particularly forceful manifestation of many humans' concern to include at least some animals as "others" whom their ethical values address. Environmental interests, though often exceedingly anthropocentric, also were part and parcel of the industrialized world's expansion of the moral circle in the late twentieth century and surely will continue to be relevant to the protection of nonhuman animals. Of particular significance is the development and popularization of science-based information regarding nonhuman animals. This has occurred in such fields as ethology, conservation biology, animal behavior, and cognitive science.

These developments are powerful supports for the burgeoning social concern for nonhuman animals. Of perhaps even greater importance, however, is the dramatic change in attitudes and values, described elsewhere in this volume, regarding companion animals. This phenomenon alone is pushing remarkable changes in awareness (see Rowan 1988; Manning and Serpell 1994), as evidenced in the changing landscape of veterinary medicine and values (see Rollin 1999; Tannenbaum 1995).

The changes in values and attitudes toward nonhuman animals have been so rapid and dramatic that even some of the most conservative realms of industrialized societies, including major religious institutions, now reflect such changes, though often in only small ways. In the United States, lawyers have been instrumental in pushing the legal system to consider whether moral standing for nonhuman animals should be enshrined by way of legal rights in legislative and litigation arenas.[11] Law is, of course, an area of society whose discourse is often "privileged," that is, legal discussions and terminology often are given a special level of respect by society at large and by media. Thus law has a profound effect on many other areas. Other privileged areas are politics, economics, academics, and, importantly, religious discussions. Debates, media, and other ongoing conversations in any one of these realms can affect many outside that realm. Ferment in these areas can, thus, be of extraordinary significance in fostering cultural changes.

Animals at the End of the Twentieth Century

The second half of the twentieth century and the beginning of the twenty-first have manifested an extraordinary increase in humans'—and thus religious believers'—interest in animals. This has been promoted by better observations, a phenomenon helped along by the fact that assessments of other animals no longer are dominated by (1) the ideology of narrow, dismissive views that, in large part, originated in religious traditions; (2) the equally narrow-minded ideology of early twentieth-century science (in the form of behaviorism and its dismissive, Cartesian premises); or (3) the longstanding tradition of anthro-

pocentric ethics that dominated Western daily and intellectual life, and which had roots in both the Abrahamic traditions and classical Greek presuppositions about the special nature of human minds.

A consensus is emerging in which many humans now understand that humans cannot continue to destroy the ecological niches they occupy; that the earth itself needs to be the beneficiary of human ethical sensitivities; and that at least some nonhuman living beings are complex beings worthy of ethical consideration in their own right. This consensus is the foundation for a change in perspective on nonhuman animals that is pushing religious traditions to revamp their conceptuality and discourse.

To be sure the changes in attitudes toward nonhuman animals that have taken place since 1950 have not all been positive. In some senses nonhuman animals are treated worse than ever before. This certainly is true in terms of numbers killed for human use and in terms of the environmental destruction that affects so much nonhuman life. Hence there remains tension of many kinds—over wildlife in backyards, the use of nonhuman animals for experiments, the destruction of so many unwanted companion animals by shelters, genetic engineering of nonhuman animals, captivity of animals in zoos, and experimentation. These tensions were, at the end of the twentieth century, being addressed by more than 10,000 organizations in more than 130 countries (de Kok 1999).[12]

The Complex Terrain at Century's Dawn

The ferment in the fields studying religion and in those engaging nonhuman animals will, no doubt, produce extraordinary challenges—and opportunities—for the emerging study of religion and animals. As conservative as many parts of the worlds

of religion and religious studies remain, these domains in some respects are advanced relative to the discussions now going on in the legal, political, and business worlds. The academic world reflects openness to the study of religions but remains quite conservative on the issue of moral value beyond humanity. Discussions in academic circles remain uneven and as yet without much impact on politics and business practices. But in some realms—including the academic study of religion and of law—concerns for other animals now surface in interesting ways. The 1999 conference "Religion and Animals" and the emergence of "animal law" classes at leading law schools are but two examples of the ways in which the world of education reflects an increased profile for the interests of nonhuman animals.

The upshot of such profound, complex, and widespread change is that many people perceive other animals differently now from how they did in 1950. This is particularly true not only of companion animals, who have become significantly more important in private lives, but also of wild animals and experimental animals. Noticeably absent, though, are food animals, who in the vast majority of cases remain without effective legal protections of even a minimal sort.

Such changes create additional pressure on religious traditions, for they remain the primary source of ethics and world view for the majority of the human race. As might be expected, in such a context of change noteworthy concern has emerged in religious communities. They, like so many other communities in contemporary society, reflect the profound changes at many different levels and in many different ways. This is apparent in the daily activities of believers as well as at the most learned levels, such as contemporary theological thinking on the environment (see, for example, the website of the Forum on Religion and Ecology).

In assessing how religious traditions have responded, it is good to recall that concern for nonhuman animals is a venerable tradition that reaches well back into all religious traditions (see Regan 1986; Masri 1987, 1989; Salisbury 1994; Linzey and Cohn-Sherbok 1997; Grant 1999; and Waldau 2001b). Some of the best-known concerns are those manifested in the religions that originated in India, such as the Hindu traditions, the Jain religion, and various forms of Buddhism. In addition many indigenous traditions, including those of the original inhabitants of North America, often are cited for their animal-friendly concerns. Such concerns also abound in the ancient strata of Judaism, Christianity, and Islam, and often are cited when the importance of other animals is discussed.

Despite the availability of these profound resources, the situation is, in many respects, one of continuing myopia. There is a certain irony in this, since White argued that even though

> [w]e shall continue to have a worsening ecological crisis until we reject the Christian axiom that nature has no reason for existence but to serve man... [b]oth our present science and our present technology are so tinctured with orthodox Christian arrogance towards nature that no solutions for our ecologic crisis can be expected from them alone. ... [S]ince the roots of our trouble are so largely religious, the remedy must be essentially religious, whether we call it that or not. (1967, 1207)

White's main hope was a refocused Christianity rather than a wholesale repudiation of it; he suggested a return to the alternative Christian views of humans' relation to the earth, especially as such alternatives are exemplified by St. Francis's respect for the living world.

Yet a contemporary example suggests how shallow and incomplete the changes within religious communities have been on essential issues. In 1993 the Parliament of the World's Religions held a meeting in Chicago, the end product of which was a short declaration (Küng and Kuschel 1993). The meeting took place a century after the original Parliament of World Religions, which did so much to promote interfaith dialogue throughout the twentieth century. A careful reading of the document signed at the 1993 meeting reveals that it perpetuates the traditional, harmful prejudice in favor of all humans to the exclusion of all other animals (Waldau 1995). This continuing shortsightedness causes a failure to see those other animals as the diverse and sometimes complex creatures they are.

To be sure, the 1993 document has some inclusive features. Addressing the important needs of all humans and giving prominence to environmental concerns, the introductory paragraphs are dominated by themes of inclusion, consideration, protection, and involvement. Within its opening sentences, the declaration acknowledges that global problems affect all life on earth. The introduction goes on to mention "life" several more times, the "ecosystems," "community of living beings," "animals," "plants," "preservation of Earth, the air, water and soil," and "nature-friendly ways of life" (Küng and Kuschel 1993, 13–16).

Despite this auspicious beginning, these seemingly inclusive references are bracketed by at least eleven explicit references to human interests alone. There is an irony in this, given that many nonhuman individuals possess considerable complexity and, in important ways, share identical, similar, or comparable interests as a matter of biology and/or personality (see, for example, Parker and Gibson 1990; Cavalieri and Singer 1994). But by and large, at the end of the twentieth century, religions had failed to engage such specifics. The declaration's preoccupation with the interests of the human species to the effective exclusion of the interests of all other species is an imbalance that threatens to perpetuate the traditional view that, of all the species on earth, the only one of real significance, because its individuals are distinctive and of value in their own right, is the human species. The declaration does not really engage the deeply meaningful proposition that there can be value and integrity in nonhumans completely independent of exclusively human interests.

Major figures in contemporary theology manifest this anthropocentrism. J. Moltmann, whose Gifford Lectures in 1984–1985 were published under the inspiring title *God In Creation: An Ecological Doctrine of Creation* (1985), spends a great deal of time on arguments about human arrogance, which he calls "anthropocentrism," and this naturally leads the reader to expect that his broadly titled text will engage the possibility of seeing other animals. Yet tellingly, nonhuman animals are ignored in the book, as there is no mention of any nonhuman animals that carries any significance. Similarly the highly respected theologian Wolfhart Pannenberg published *Toward a Theology of Nature: Essays on Science and Faith* (1993). This text is more of the same, as it in no way engages the extraordinarily rich perspectives developed in such biological sciences as primatology and marine mammal studies (Waldau 2001b).

Catholic documents from the end of the twentieth century continue to reflect the fact that anthropocentrism in ethics has important and still powerful strongholds in established religion. The 1995 encyclical *Evangelium Vitae* is not nearly as broad as its beautiful title (translated as "the gospel of life") suggests, for its language and arguments continue to promote an unabashed ethical anthropocentrism—the only "life" it focuses on is human life. None of the twenty references to nonhuman living beings gives any hint of, let alone makes serious reference to, the value of the lives of any living beings outside the human species. What makes for a certain irony in this approach is the extremely heavy concentration in the document on humans before they are born. As noted by the feminist whose work most fully engages the moral significance of nonhuman animals,

The speciesism of Homo sapiens is perhaps nowhere more pronounced than in the protestation about the fate of the human conceptus and zygote, while the sentiency of the other animals is declared morally irrelevant because they are not human beings. (Adams 1994, 60)

Noting this irony is not meant to suggest that "the fate of the human conceptus and zygote" should be unimportant, subordinate, or in any way treated as irrelevant. The lives of future humans are, by almost total consensus in contemporary societies, extremely important to all humans even if the right of a future human to be born conflicts dramatically with the obviously important issue of an individual woman's need to make her own moral decision about what is happening within her own body. But the absence of any meaningful reference to nonhuman animals in a major doctrinal statement that by its own title purports to deal with the importance of "life" suggests that nonhuman animals are not yet an important concern for the hierarchy of this large and influential religious tradition within Christianity.

Such lack of references to the realities and importance of nonhuman animals is ironic, given that some animals have the very traits that we value in ourselves as the basis of our own moral significance—such as family connections and loyalty, intelligence, communication, emotions, social structure, and even cultural transmission. The daily realities of nonhuman animals are addressed in ethology and related sciences; of particular interest in recent years has been the development of "cognitive ethology," which is providing much more information about the mental, emotional, and social dimension of nonhuman lives (see, for example, Allen and Bekoff 1997.) That the Catholic Church is likely to continue to ignore such realities and espouse what above has been called an instrumentalist view is confirmed by the following pronouncement in the 1994 revised Catholic Catechism: "Animals [mean-

ing, of course, 'all *non*human animals'], like plants and inanimate things, are by nature destined for the common good of past, present, and future humanity" (para. 2415).

As C.S. Lewis might have argued in 1950, approaches to *creation* (to use Moltmann's 1985 term), *nature* (Pannenberg's 1993 term), and *life* (the term so central in the 1995 encyclical *Evangelium Vitae*) that continue to ignore nonhuman animals completely are in some ways contrary to a core message and value found in religious traditions. Acting on this intuition or value is a central feature of a moral and/or religious life generally. And even if a specific religious tradition makes claims about human superiority, that message does not excuse, as Andrew Linzey (1987, 1994b) has so well shown, complete failure to take any nonhuman animals' lives into account.

Indeed it is virtually impossible to argue that any religious tradition's core message is that other life is unimportant, although this is admittedly a subtext or "meta-message" of the rhetoric of many well-respected religious leaders. Religious believers may be heirs to the claim that humans are theologically more significant than any other animals, but that claim has *nothing* to do with the logically distinguishable claim that the religion authorizes humans to ignore the realities of other animals.

The great value of Lewis's essay is its suggestion that it is part of the Christian view of humans' theologically superiority that religious believers be responsible for, and learn about, the consequences for nonhuman animals of humans' current manner of living. This same kind of reasoning, so reliant on the internal resources of each religious tradition, is available to any religious believer when the issue is the suffering, death, and other material effects—including environmental consequences—that a believer's consumer choices and political decisions have on nonhuman individuals.

Prospects in the Twenty-first Century

One could fairly conclude, then, that religions can rise above the obviously anthropocentric concerns that have dominated so many religious traditions in the twentieth century. The manifest lack of church, synagogue, mosque, and other religious community involvement in challenging the most egregious abuses of nonhuman animals remains a principal feature of the contemporary religious scene. That this is true in North America is suggested by respected sociologists when they comment, "The animal rights movement [is] a new social movement noted for its participants' lack of ties to traditional Judeo-Christian religion" (Peek, Konty, and Frazier 1997, 429). Changing this reality is, no doubt, the principal challenge facing religion in North America, dominated as it is by what is sometimes referred to as the Judeo-Christian tradition.[13] Traditions do not necessarily need to reach outside themselves to solve the current dilemma for, as Lewis's essay suggests, religious traditions can have "core" or fundamental values that are both relevant and buried and which, once "unearthed," as it were, can be brought to bear on the prevailing indifference toward nonhuman animals. There is evidence of this kind of movement, but it remains marginalized. Linzey and Cohn-Sherbok have written often and eloquently of the values manifest in both theological and historical parts of their traditions (respectively, Christian and Jewish) (see, for example, Linzey and Cohn-Sherbok 1997). Similar analyses exist for Islam (for example, Masri 1987, 1989), and of course for Hindu, Jain, Buddhist, and many indigenous traditions in Africa, Asia, South America, North America, Australia, and various island cultures (see Suzuki and Knudtson 1992; Grim 2001). Indeed plumbing the conservative views of the Catholic hierarchy reveals that there is some movement within that tradition. For the first time ever, the Catholic Catechism issued in 1994 included an official statement from the Catholic Church that believers have more than indirect obligation to nonhuman animals.[14] A required "religious respect for the integrity of creation" is explained in paragraph 2416, which states:

> Animals are God's creatures. He surrounds them with this providential care. By their mere existence they bless him and give him glory. Thus men owe them kindness. We recall the gentleness with which saints like St. Francis of Assisi or St. Philip of Neri treated animals.

Before celebrating this important movement, it is important to acknowledge that, while this first-ever Catholic Church admission indicates that humans owe duties directly to some nonhuman animals (thus implying that the lives of these nonhuman animals have a moral dimension), the concession is *extremely* limited. Paragraph 2415, in addition to the passage already quoted, includes various factors that override Paragraph 2416's historically new concern for direct duties to nonhuman animals. These factors include our duties to "neighbors" and "future generations," both of which, predictably, refer to humans alone even though the terms "neighbors" and "future generations" on their face apply to nonhuman animals. In other words, the primary concern of the revised Catholic Catechism is the traditional, exclusive focus on members of the *human* species alone.

It is fair to ask whether this really is much movement, and what will happen in the future given the new abilities of humans to use nonhuman animals under the power of such technologies as genetic engineering. On the whole such complex specific problems, including widespread and uncontrolled experimentation on nonhuman animals for humans' benefit or profit, and the cruel conditions of intensive rearing conditions (see Regan 1986a), remain unaddressed by the vast majority of the religious establishment and its leaders. This means that the "on the ground realities" in ordinary churches remain anthropocentric in the extreme.

One hope, of course, is the burgeoning concern in religious traditions for the "environment."[15] This reflects the increasingly inclusive nature of ethics today, as well as the implicit theological dimensions of any ethical discussion. Holistic, environmental themes increasingly are found in works by religious believers as *religious believers*, examples of which include Christian thinkers such as Thomas Berry, Dieter Hessel, and Jay McDaniel; Muslim thinkers such as Mawil Y. Izzi Deen and B. A. Masri; Buddhists such as Sulak Sivaraksa and the Dalai Lama; and numerous representatives from Judaism, Hinduism, and a wide range of indigenous traditions.

The state of current literature, however, is a signpost of how little has been done regarding other animals, even though other animals often are mentioned in studies of symbolism. These studies form, however, classic examples of what Adams (1994) calls the "absent referent"—in other words, the animals themselves are nowhere to be found. At the dawn of the new millennium, there still was no systematic work on the topic of religion and animals, although the papers from the "Religion and Animals" conference were close to publication.

A Continuing Role for Traditions

Any member of any of the major world religions, including Muslims, Jews, Christians, Buddhists, Hindus, as well as adherents of indigenous and other religious traditions, can fully embrace nonhuman animals and remain completely faithful to their own tradition. As with ecological insights, compassionate concerns for other animals are well grounded in the ethical insights of virtually all religious traditions. Thus humane reforms, as is the case with ecological reform, can find homes in the cosmologies, stories, and communities of contemporary religions.

But will religious traditions continue to promote anthropocentric ethics alone, or will they enlarge their moral circles? One important factor in the future trajectory of religious concerns for nonhuman animals will be the continuing revolution in values in developed world societies, for as the philosopher Bernard Rollin suggests (1999, 3), "Most now realize . . . that society is in the process of changing its view of animals, and of our obligation to animals."

Religious traditions can advance or retard such changes, or they can take a unique leadership role in this process because of their profound commitment to the ethical abilities of humans.

Today the fundamental questions for religions, as for all humans, are these: Who are the "others?" Will the "others" protected by human, religious, and ethical sensibilities be only humans? Will religions cross the species line in the twenty-first century? The verdict remains out on just what kind of force religious traditions will become in this important area of human existence.

Notes

[1] Religions were also, to be sure, blind to many *humans*, as evidenced by both widespread religious intolerance and the all too cozy relationship between established religious institutions and oppressive regimes, imperialist foreign powers, and capitalist corporations. The major theological movement known as "liberation theology" describes the latter; see, for example, Brown (1993).

[2] Because this attitude focuses on the usefulness of nonhuman animals for human purposes, such views sometimes are described as "utilitarian" (for example, by C.S. Lewis in a passage quoted below). If such a description is used, however, one must be careful not to confuse this attitude with the very distinctive, animal-friendly theory of ethics called "utilitarianism" historically associated with the eighteenth-century philosopher Jeremy Bentham and the nineteenth-century philosopher John Stuart Mill and exemplified today by the works of Peter Singer. See, for example, Singer (1990).

[3] This is the traditional Catholic position. See, for example, Thomas Aquinas, *Summa Theologiae*, 2a, 2ae, q. 64. art. 1, ad. 3; *Summa Contra*

Gentiles Bk. 3, Pt. 2, ch. 112, art. 13.

[4]The original title was simply "Vivisection." Clyde Kilby reports (1995) that the article was published in 1948 in London for the National Anti-Vivisection Society. As late as 1963 it appeared in *The Anti-Vivisectionist* (March/April, 154–5), where it has the longer title "Can Christians Support Vivisection?" The page numbers given here are from the 1963 version.

[5]As a technical matter, this is the position of only some Christians. The leading theologian of Catholicism, Thomas Aquinas, followed Aristotle in holding that all living beings have a soul. The practical consequences of this are not significant, however, in that Catholic theology, as noted below, has always asserted humans' complete superiority to nonhuman animals.

[6]Lewis also makes another argument as to why the standard Christian position is troubling: "We may find it difficult to formulate a human right of tormenting beasts in terms which would not equally imply an angelic right of tormenting men" (154).

[7]It is interesting to contrast this with today's general view that the animal rights movement is a *secular* phenomenon. See, in particular, the comment at the end of this chapter made by sociologists Peek, Konty, and Frazier (1997) regarding the non-involvement of the Judeo-Christian tradition.

[8]It would be misleading to infer from this comment that these other traditions have been without problems in the many ways in which they have seen and otherwise engaged nonhuman animals. On the limitations in the views and values regarding other animals in various other traditions, see Waldau (2000 a,b,c; 2001a).

[9]The term *interfaith dialogue* frequently is used to describe the many conversations now taking place. The journal *World Faiths Encounter*, in which Waldau (1995) was published, is a good example of the breadth and depth of this phenomenon.

[10]The term is misleading because not all proponents seek either moral or legal rights. For the history of the animal protection movement in the twentieth century, see Jasper and Nelkin (1992) and Finsen and Finsen (1994).

[11]There now are many courses on "animal law," the most publicized of which is the Harvard Law School class that began in 2000. The trend toward inclusion of this topic continues, with Yale Law School most recently offering an animal law study group in spring 2003. The best-known legislation is the Animal Welfare Act, first enacted in 1966 and regularly amended thereafter.

[12]In the United States alone, more than 10,000 animals per day are killed for want of a home. Details are available at the website of The Humane Society of the United States, *www.hsus.org*.

[13]Some scholars, such as Kimberley Patton of Harvard Divinity School, observe that this is a very misleading phrase, for it fails to signal that the Jewish and Christian traditions are much less alike than, say, the Islamic and Jewish traditions.

[14]Andrew Linzey (1994a) has noted that these 1994 statements of the Catholic Church go beyond the pre-1994 official position of the Catholic Church, which Linzey has described as "we [humans] do not have direct duties" (1987). Linzey also refers to some limitations on humans' "stewardship" in the 1987 encyclical *Sollicitudo Rei Socialis*.

[15]A Harvard series on "religion and ecology" (the individual titles can be found at *http://environment. harvard.edu/religion*, the website of the Forum on Religion and Ecology) includes many decidedly positive estimates of how local religious communities already are undertaking environmentally sensitive programs that affect many nonhuman animals in favorable ways.

Literature Cited

Adams, C.J. 1994. *The sexual politics of meat: A feminist-vegetarian critical theory*. New York: Continuum.

Allen, C., and M. Bekoff, 1997. *Species of mind: The philosophy and biology of cognitive ethology*. Cambridge: Bradford/MIT Press.

Aquinas, T. Latin text and English trans. by T. Gilby et al. 1964–1981. *Summa theologiae*. New York: McGraw-Hill.

———. Trans. and with an introduction and notes, by A.C. Pegis, J.F. Anderson, J.Bourke, C.J.O'Neil. *Summa contra gentiles*. 1975. Notre Dame. (Originally published as Saint Thomas Aquinas, *On the truth of Catholic Faith*, New York, 1955–57.)

Blum, D. 1994. *The monkey wars*. New York: Oxford University Press.

Brown, R.M. 1993. *Liberation theology: An introductory guide*. Louisville: Westminster/John Knox.

Cavalieri, P., and P. Singer, eds. 1994. *The Great Ape Project: Equality beyond humanity*. New York: St. Martin's Press.

Catechism of the Catholic Church. 1994. London: Geoffrey Chapman.

Clark, S.R.L. 1977. *The moral status of animals*. Oxford: Clarendon.

Cohen, J. 1989. *"Be fertile and increase, file the earth and master it": The ancient and medieval career of a Biblical text*. London and Ithaca, N.Y.: Cornell University Press.

Darwin, C. 1859. *On the origin of species by means of natural selection*. London: Murray.

de Kok, W., ed. 1999. *World animal net directory*, Edition 1.1. Boston: World Animal Net.

Du Bois, W.E.B. 1969. *The souls of black folk*. New York: Signet/New American Library.

Finsen, L., and S. Finsen. 1994. *The animal rights movement in America: From compassion to respect*. New York: Twayne.

Forum on Religion and Ecology. *http://environment.harvard.edu/religion* (accessed March 16, 2003).

Gaffney, J. 1988. The relevance of animal experimentation to Roman Catholic ethical methodology. In *Animal sacrifices: Religious perspectives on the use of animals in science*, ed. T. Regan, 149–170. Philadelphia: Temple University Press.

Galdikas, B.M.F. 1995. *Reflections of Eden: My life with the orangutans of Borneo*. London: Victor Gollancz.

Gardner, H. 1985. *The mind's new science: A history of the cognitive revolution*. New York: Basic.

Gould, S.J. 1995. Animals and us. *The New York Review of Books*, August 19.

Grant, R.M. 1999. *Early Christians and animals*. London and New York: Routledge.

Griffin, D. 1992. *Animal minds*. Chicago: University of Chicago Press.

———. 1998. From cognition to consciousness. *Animal Cognition* 1: 3–16.

Grim, J., ed. 2001. *Indigenous traditions and ecology: The interbeing of cosmology and community*. Cambridge: Harvard University Press.

Jasper, J.M., and D. Nelkin. 1992. *The animal rights crusade: The growth of a moral protest*. New York: The Free Press.

John Paul II. Sollicitudo Rei Socialis. 1987. Available at *http://www.vatican.va/holy_father/john_paul_ii/encyclicals*.

———. *Evangelium vitae*. 1995. London: Catholic Truth Society.

Kalechofsky, R. 1991. *Autobiography of a revolutionary: Essays on animal and human rights*. Marblehead, Mass.: Micah Publications.

Kilby, C. 1995. *The Christian world of C.S. Lewis*. Grand Rapids, Mich.: Wm. B. Eerdmans Publishing.

Küng, H., and K.J. Kuschel. 1993. *A global ethic: The declaration of the parliament of the world religions.* London: SCM Press. Preface and commentary translated by J. Bowden from *Erklärung zum Weltethos. Die Deklaration des Parlementes der Weltreligionen.* 1993. Münich: R. Piper GmbH and Co. KG.

Lewis, C.S. 1963. Can Christians support vivisection? *The Anti-Vivisectionist* (March/April) 154–155.

Linzey. A. 1987. *Christianity and the rights of animals.* New York: Crossroad.

———. 1994a. Why Catholic teaching perpetuates cruelty. *The AV Magazine* 102 (9): 8–11.

———. 1994b. *Animal theology.* London: SCM Press; and Chicago: University of Illinois.

Linzey, A., and D. Cohn-Sherbok. 1997. *After Noah: Animals and the liberation of theology.* London: Mowbray.

Manning, A., and J. Serpell, eds. 1994. *Animals and human society: Changing perspectives.* London and New York: Routledge.

Masri, B.A. 1987. *Islamic concern for animals.* Petersfield, England: The Athene Trust.

———. 1989. *Animals in Islam.* Petersfield, England: The Athene Trust.

Mayr, E. 1982. *The growth of biological thought: Diversity, evolution, and inheritance.* New York: Belknap Press.

Merchant, C. 1980. *The death of nature: Women, ecology and the scientific revolution.* San Francisco: Harper and Row.

Miller, P. 1995. Jane Goodall. *National Geographic* 188.6: 102–129.

Moltmann, J. 1985. *God in Creation: An ecological doctrine of Creation.* London: SCM.

Pannenberg, W., T. Peters, ed. 1993. *Toward a theology of nature: Essays on science and faith.* Louisville: Westminster/John Knox Press.

Parker, S.T., and K.R. Gibson, eds. 1990. *"Language" and intelligence in monkeys and apes: Comparative developmental perspectives.* Cambridge: Cambridge University Press.

Peek, C.W., M.A. Konty, and T.F. Frazier. 1997. Religion and ideological support for social movements: The case of animal rights. *Journal for the Scientific Study of Religion* 36(3): 429–439.

Radner, D., and M. Radner. 1989. *Animal consciousness.* Buffalo, N.Y.: Prometheus.

Regan, T., ed. 1986a. *Animal sacrifices: Religious perspectives on the use of animals in science.* Philadelphia: Temple University Press

———, director and narrator. 1986b. *We are all Noah.* Raleigh: Culture and Animals Foundation.

Rickaby, J. 1888. *Moral philosophy.* London: Longmans, Green.

Rollin, B.E. 1999. *An introduction to veterinary medical ethics: Theory and cases.* Ames: Iowa State University Press.

Tannenbaum, J. 1995. *Veterinary ethics: Animal welfare, client relations, competition, and collegiality.* St. Louis, Mo.: Mosby.

Romanes, G.J. 1885. *Mental evolution in animals.* London: Kegan Paul, Trench.

———. 1886. *Animal intelligence.* London: Kegan Paul, Trench.

Rowan, A., ed. 1988. *Animals and people sharing the world.* Hanover, N.H., and London: University Press of New England.

Salisbury, J.E. 1994. *The beast within: Animals in the middle ages.* New York and London: Routledge.

Singer, P. 1990. *Animal liberation.* Second edition. New York: Avon.

Suzuki, D., and P. Knudtson. 1992. *Wisdom of the elders: Honoring sacred native visions of nature.* New York: Bantam.

Thomas, K. 1984. *Man and the natural world: Changing attitudes in England 1500–1800.* London: Penguin.

van Lawick-Goodall, J. 1971. *In the shadow of man.* Boston: Houghton Mifflin.

Waldau, P. 1995. Interfaith dialogue needs an inclusive global ethic. *World Faiths Encounter* 11: 58–65.

———. 2000a. On breadth and exclusion in concepts of nonviolence. *Philosophy East and West* 50: 3 (July): 468–471.

———. 2000b. Buddhism and animals rights. In *Contemporary Buddhist Ethics,* ed. D. Keown, The Curzon Critical Studies in Buddhism Series, 81–112. Richmond, Surrey, England: Curzon Press.

———. 2000c. The question of nonviolence in Hinduism and other traditions. *International Journal of Hindu Studies* 4:1: 104–106 (review of *Subverting hatred: The challenge of nonviolence in religious traditions*).

———. 2001a. *The specter of speciesism: Buddhist and Christian views of animals.* New York: Oxford University Press.

———. 2001b. Religion and which sciences? Science and which community? *The Journal of Faith and Science* IV: 115–142.

Watson, J.B. 1913. Psychology as the behaviorist views it. *Psychological Review* 20: 158–177.

White, L., Jr. 1967. The historic roots of our ecologic crisis. *Science* 155: 1203–1207.

Wrangham, R.W., W.C. McGrew, F.B.M. de Waal, and P.G. Heltne, eds. 1994. *Chimpanzee cultures.* Cambridge: Harvard University Press.

The Evolution of Animal Law since 1950

7

Steven M. Wise

Over the last half century, the law has assumed an increasingly important place in animal protection even as it has begun to point in the direction of true legal rights for at least some nonhuman animals. In this chapter I briefly discuss five aspects of the law: anti-cruelty statutes; the necessity of obtaining standing to litigate on behalf of the interests of nonhuman animals; evolving protections for great apes; the movement toward legal rights for at least some nonhuman animals; and the state of legal education concerning animal protection.

Anti-cruelty Statutes

"Anti-cruelty" is not necessarily synonymous with "animal welfare." British law professor Mike Radford notes that to

> cause an animal to suffer unnecessarily, or to subject it to any other treatment which amounts to an offence of cruelty, is self-evidently detrimental to its welfare. To that extent, there is a degree of affinity between cruelty and welfare, but the two are far from being synonymous: prejudicing an animal's welfare does not of itself amount in law to cruelty.[1]

"Anti-cruelty" is also not synonymous with "animal rights." Speaking of the entire body of legislation in the area of nonhuman animal welfare in the nineteenth century, Radford explains that "while this legislation imposed restrictions on how animals could be treated, none of it—nor, indeed, any enacted subsequently—change [*sic*] the traditional legal status accorded to animals by the courts."[2] That status was as property[3], and property generally lacks rights.

There is no federal anti-cruelty statute in the United States. But, according to American law professor David Favre, the anti-cruelty statutes of the fifty states "are so similar in nature and the issues so fundamental that there is very little variation in judicial outlook around the country."[4] In 2002 these statutes strongly resembled not just each other, but also the anti-cruelty statutes that existed in 1950, in 1900, and, indeed, in 1850.[5] Radford says that, in both the United States and the United Kingdom, "(t)he gist of the offense" today is as it has been for nearly two hundred years, "the infliction of unnecessary abuse or unnecessary or unjustifiable pain and suffering upon an animal."[6] In neither country, explains the leading American legal encyclopedia, has it been "the purpose of such statutes to place unreasonable restrictions upon the use, enjoyment, or possession of animals or to interfere with the necessary discipline or government of animals."[7]

The last half-century has seen two significant changes in American anti-cruelty statutes, and they are rapidly trending in opposite directions. The penalties for violating state anti-cruelty statutes have gotten tougher and tougher, but the statutes themselves apply to fewer and fewer perpetrators of nonhuman animal pain and suffering.

First, there has been a stiffening of penalties for conviction. In 1950 the barest handful of state legislatures had enacted anti-cruelty statutes that were felonies or that even provided for a maximum penalty exceeding one year of imprisonment.[8] The problem of low penalties, Favre says, "is the ultimate weakness of most [anti]cruelty statutes, for no matter how expansive the language, if the punishment is not sufficient, then no real deterrent against the acts exists."[9] The maximum penalty that a criminal statute allows is an important benchmark. It signals to a judge how opposed legislators think a society actually is to a particular wrong, for it sets the stiffest penalty that a wrongdoer who commits a crime in the most unimaginably horrific way—or who commits it repeatedly—can suffer. Because a judge usually will not impose a penalty near the maximum for a first or "run-of-the-mill" offense, the typical penalty for cruelty will remain low so long as the maximum penalty remains low. This problem has begun to ease. While most anti-cruelty statutes continue to be misdemeanors, or lesser crimes, by 2002 thirty-four American states and the District of Columbia had enacted at least one felony anti-cruelty statute. Felonies generally are understood to be graver crimes that carry longer sentences of imprisonment.[10]

The second trend has been more ominous for nonhuman animals, because many of the humans who commit forms of institutionalized cruelty have been exempted from the reach of anti-cruelty statutes. The most notorious example is that of nonhuman animals raised and killed for food. According to the U.S. Department of Agriculture's National Agricultural Statistics Service, in 1998 approximately 9,443 million nonhuman animals were killed for food in the United States; these include cows, pigs, sheep, chickens, turkeys, and ducks.[11] Yet twenty-five American states exempt common farming practices entirely from cruelty prosecution. Five others exempt some of them.[12] As of 2002 eighteen of these thirty states had amended their anti-cruelty statutes to add these exemptions within the previous thirteen years, seven in the previous eight years.[13] More states are likely to follow.

In the famous English "McLibel" case, two plaintiffs—McDonald's Corporation and its English subsidiary—sued for defamation for, among other things, statements that they engaged in cruelty toward the nonhuman animals whom they served for food. The corporations urged the trial judge to rule that in England, as in most American states, customary farming practices should be deemed acceptable. He refused, observing that a farming practice could be both cruel and legal, and rejected the McDonald's request, saying that not "to do so would be to hand the decision as to what is cruel to the food industry completely."[14]

That is precisely what the majority of American states do. Professor David Wolfson has observed that the "effect of this trend of amendments cannot be overemphasized. The trend indicates a nationwide perception that it was necessary to amend anti-cruelty statutes to avoid their possible application to animals raised for food or food production. Amendments specif-

ically exempting customary husbandry practices indicate that, but for the exemption, such practices would be determined to be cruel."[15]

The same problem exists for the millions of nonhuman animals forced to be subjects of biomedical research. The only American biomedical researcher convicted under an anti-cruelty statute—perhaps the only one ever charged—was Edward Taub. Even his conviction for failing to provide necessary veterinary care to a monkey named Nero was reversed on appeal, on the ground that the Maryland anti-cruelty statute under which he was charged was addressed to "unnecessary" or "unjustifiable" pain or suffering, and pain or suffering inflicted pursuant to biomedical research was not that kind.[16] Thirty states, along with the District of Columbia, now exempt nonhuman animals used in biomedical research from the reach of their anti-cruelty statutes.[17] Many of these statutes, however, condition their exemptions upon compliance with the minimal dictates of the federal Animal Welfare Act, enacted in 1966. However the Animal Welfare Act itself exempts the great majority of nonhuman animals actually used in biomedical research.[18]

Standing

Lacking legal personhood and legal rights, nonhuman animals are essentially invisible to civil judges. This means that no one can file lawsuits directly on their behalf. Their interests can be protected only indirectly. This can happen when a legal person, who has legal rights (usually an adult human being) files a lawsuit either to stop an illegal act or to seek compensation for injuries already inflicted.

Not just any legal person can sue to protect animals. American courts generally prohibit a litigant from asserting the legal rights of another person.[19] Judges, federal and state, usually restrict those able to obtain a judicial decision to plaintiffs with a sufficient large stake in the outcome of a controversy.[20] This is the doctrine

of "standing." It allows persons to sue to redress an injury that they, and only they, have suffered as a result of an illegal act. Their remedy may indirectly protect nonhuman animals who are being injured at the same time. And that is all the protection that nonhuman animals ever get from the civil law.

I limit my discussion of standing to how it operates in America's federal courts and focus on common ways in which it has an impact on litigation that seeks to protect the interests of nonhuman animals. Bear in mind that the struggle of judges with what may appear to be a straightforward standard has led to a federal law of standing that has been rightly accused of "suffering from inconsistency, unreliability, and inordinate complexity."[21]

The source of federal judicial power is Article III, section 2 of the U.S. Constitution. Federal judges may only decide "cases" and "controversies." In order to surmount the constitutional obstacle of standing, a plaintiff in a federal court must allege and prove that he or she has suffered what has come to be called routinely an injury-in-fact. It was not until 1970 that the U.S. Supreme Court adopted this relatively lenient standard.[22] Before then, one could obtain standing only if one could show that one's legal right had been invaded.[23] An injury-in-fact must then be "fairly traceable to...allegedly unlawful conduct and likely to be redressed by the requested relief."[24]

But injury-in-fact, traceability, and redressability are just the constitutional requirements. There may be others. The most common of the so-called prudential requirements for standing is that a plaintiff's claim "must fall within the zone of interests protected by the law invoked."[25] This requirement arises when plaintiffs seek review of the decision of a federal agency under the federal Administrative Procedures Act.[26] It guides a court in deciding whether the particular plaintiff who has challenged an agency's decision should be heard.[27]

If the court decides that the plaintiff's interests are "so marginally related to or inconsistent with the purposes implicit in the statute or that it cannot be reasonably assumed that Congress intended to permit the suit," it will not hear the claim of the particular plaintiff.[28]

In the 1990s the Animal Legal Defense Fund (ALDF) brought a landmark trio of cases in the federal courts in Washington, D.C., to try to obtain standing to litigate in the interests of nonhuman animals. Three times ALDF won in the District Court and three times these victories were overturned by a three-judge panel of the Court of Appeals. On the appeal of the third decision to the full bench of that court, ALDF achieved a singular success.

In the first case, Animal Legal Defense Fund v. Espy (I),[29] an inactive researcher and a lawyer-member of an animal oversight committee, as well as two animal protection organizations, complained that the Secretary of Agriculture had excluded 90 percent of the nonhuman animals who were used in biomedical research—rats, mice, and birds—from the definition of "animal" in the regulations he was required to issue under the federal Animal Welfare Act.[30] A three-judge panel of the Court of Appeals for the District of Columbia found the researcher had not suffered the required injury-in-fact because it was not immediate, while the lawyer was said to be improperly trying to compel a general executive enforcement of the law. The organizations were dismissed from the suit, for although they met the three constitutional requirements for standing, they did not fall within the zone of interest of the Animal Welfare Act.

In a second case, Animal Legal Defense Fund v. Espy (II),[31] the same Court of Appeals turned aside for lack of standing a challenge to the sufficiency of the standards that the Secretary of Agriculture had issued for the exercise of dogs used in biomedical research and to promote a physical environment adequate to meet the psychological well-being of primates. This time an ape language researcher was said to lack standing because it was his university, and not he, who might have suffered an injury, while a business that sold primate housing that could be used if valid standards had been issued lacked standing because it fell outside of the zone of interests.

In 1996 the ALDF tried a third time, claiming once again that the Secretary of Agriculture had failed to issue the minimum standards required to promote the psychological well-being of primates. One plaintiff, Marc Jurnove, was alleged to have visited a zoo repeatedly and seen primates kept in inhumane conditions whom he intended to continue to visit regularly. For the third time, a panel of the Court of Appeals reversed a lower court victory for the Animal Legal Defense Fund. This time a further appeal was requested before all the judges of that Appeals Court, and they ruled, 7 to 4, that Jurnove had standing.[32] The majority said that people have a protected aesthetic interest in observing animals free from inhumane treatment. It turned back arguments that the dissent embraced that a plaintiff could obtain standing only if he alleged that animals whom he wished to observe faced extinction, not just suffering; that causation did not exist because the Department of Agriculture had not authorized the inhumane treatment, but had just not acted to prevent it; and that one could only speculate that any changes in the treatment of the primates would actually satisfy Jurnove's aesthetic sensibilities. In 2000 other plaintiffs used this victory to obtain standing in, and finally to win, another lawsuit that complained that the Secretary of Agriculture had illegally excluded rats, mice, and birds from the definition of "animals" to be protected by the Animal Welfare Act.[33] Unfortunately, in 2002 Congress enacted an exemption to the definition of *animals* that nullified this win. The standing victory remains, however.

Toward Protection for Great Apes

In *Rattling the Cage: Toward Legal Rights for Animals* (2000), I argued that, under the common law, entitlement to legal rights turns on the nature of an animal's mind; that numerous scientific investigations have demonstrated that at least two great apes, chimpanzees and bonobos, possess minds so extraordinary that they tower above the minimum sufficient for rights; and that the day has come to grant basic legal rights to these apes. In *Drawing the Line: Science and the Case for Animal Rights* (2002), I made the same argument on behalf of the other two great apes, gorillas and orangutans.

That day in which the great apes obtain legal rights will cap a long legal and political process. Among its first fruits were the 1985 amendments to the Animal Welfare Act. There the Secretary of Agriculture was directed to "promulgate standards to govern the humane handling, care, treatment, and transportation of animals by dealers, research facilities, and exhibitors... [and to] include minimum requirements... [for] a physical environment adequate to promote the psychological well-being of primates."[34] This amounted to a recognition by Congress that primates had a psychology that could be in good health or poor.

Britain was next to step in the direction of legal rights for great apes. In 1997, on its own initiative, the British government's Home Secretary banned the use of all four species of great apes, not just chimpanzees and bonobos but orangutans and gorillas, too, as biomedical research subjects.[35] This ban on the use of great apes, he wrote, "was a matter of morality. The cognitive and behavioural characteristics and qualities of these animals mean that it is unethical to treat them as expendable for research."[36] Under current British legislation, there must be a weighing of the cost to a nonhuman animal of a biomedical procedure with the benefit to human beings. Only when the human benefit outweighs the nonhuman cost may the procedure be licensed. Steve Wilkes, head of the Home Office's Animal Procedures Section, said that the benefit to a human being could never outweigh the cost to a great ape.[37]

In New Zealand a 1998 attempt led to formal Parliamentary hearings that were highly publicized around the world. Prominent New Zealand advocates of legal rights for great apes, including lawyers, professors, scientists, and philosophers, sought to build upon an idea that had been the focus of a powerful book, *The Great Ape Project: Equality Beyond Humanity.*[38] Animal Welfare Bill No. 2, which sought to streamline and modernize Kiwi animal protection law, was pending before the New Zealand Parliament. The submitters sought to have it amended as proposed by the group Great Ape Project (New Zealand) in order to grant great apes three basic legal rights. These were the rights not to be deprived of life, not to be subjected to torture or cruel treatment, and not to be subjected to medical or scientific experimentation. They also sought to provide for the appointment, when necessary, of human guardians to defend these great ape rights.[39]

In their Submission to Parliament, the submitters argued that

> [b]eing fellow hominids, the great apes are more closely related to humans than to any other animals. They share many of our characteristics including some that we thought were uniquely ours, such as self-awareness, the ability to reason and the ability to imagine what others are thinking and feeling. In humans, these traits are often cited as a basis for ascribing basic legal rights. We believe that a strong case now exists for giving basic legal rights to the other members of the Hominidae family.

The Animal Welfare Act of 1999 that eventually cleared the New

Zealand Parliament did not grant legal rights to the great apes. Instead it prohibited research, testing, and teaching involving the use of a great ape without approval of the director-general who, in granting approval, must be satisfied that use of the ape is in his or her best interests or in the best interests of his or her species, and that the benefits to be derived are not outweighed by the likely harm to the ape.[40]

In the United States, at least chimpanzees, but likely all the great apes, appear to be edging toward a de facto "right" to life. If not the most expensive nonhuman animals to maintain in biomedical research, chimpanzees certainly are among the most expensive. In 1995 it was estimated that it cost between $113,000 and $321,000 to maintain a captive chimpanzee used in biomedical research over his or her natural lifespan.[41] That it would doubtless be far cheaper to kill them the way mice and rats routinely are killed when their usefulness has ceased was forcefully etched in a minority statement appended to a report of the National Research Council, an arm of the National Academy of Sciences, in 1997. The statement firmly opposed the use of public money to support chimpanzees in retirement sanctuaries, "since there is no potential return on research dollars invested in chimpanzees permanently removed from the research pool," and urged that they be euthanized.[42] The majority, however, rejected euthanasia as a method of population control of captive chimpanzees on the grounds that

> the phylogenetic status and psychological complexity of chimpanzees indicate that they should be accorded a special status with regard to euthanasia that might not apply to other research animals, for example, rats, dogs, or some other nonhuman primates. Simply put, killing a chimpanzee currently requires more ethical and scientific justification than killing a dog, and it should continue to do so.[43]

In 2002 a move was afoot to have

all the countries of the world, but especially the so-called range countries, embrace an international Declaration for the Protection of Great Apes and a subsequent Convention for the Protection of Great Apes that name the great apes as "World Heritage Species." This is a new category roughly modeled on the existing treaty that allows for the designation of World Heritage Sites. If this declaration materializes, the new category of World Heritage Species would tighten the protection of great apes under international law and under the domestic law of range countries and provide special protections under international law.

Toward Legal Rights for Animals[44]

The ancient Greek and Roman worlds were dominated by the belief that the universe was designed for human beings. Small wonder that from these worlds emerged the jurisprudential idea that, in the words of the early Roman jurist Hermogenianus, "All law was established for men's sake."[45] Why should law not have been established just for the sake of men? According to the early Greeks and Romans, everything else was. In Roman law, "persons" had legal rights, while "things" were the objects of the rights of persons. And all those beings who were believed to lack free will—women, children, slaves, the insane, and nonhuman animals—were at some time classified as property.

Roman law has had a tremendous effect upon Western law as a whole, and especially upon property law. The law of nonhuman animals in the United States at the beginning of the second millennium is nearly identical to the Roman law of nonhuman animals as it existed when the first millennium turned. While all humans are legal persons, all legal persons are not human beings. Some are artificial persons, like corporations and ships.

However, all of the more than one million species of nonhuman animals—chimpanzees, cheetahs, cats, and cockroaches—are not legal persons but are legal things.

Some may confuse being the object of legal protection with having legal personhood. They may point to the criminal anti-cruelty statutes, which I briefly discussed, that have existed for well over a century in every American jurisdiction as evidence that nonhuman animals are legal persons with legal rights. But they would probably be wrong. Criminal statutes are prohibitions enacted by legislatures. Sometimes they protect persons, as when legislatures make it a crime to assault a fellow human being. But they may also commonly protect things. For example, in Massachusetts it is a felony, punishable by imprisonment for up to five years, to destroy a cemetery shrub. It also is a crime to smash the windshield of your neighbor's automobile or set his dog afire. Violate these prohibitions and you may be charged with a crime by the state, convicted, and punished. But neither the shrub nor the automobile nor the dog has thereby been given any legal rights.

What are legal rights? Potter Stewart, a twentieth century justice of the United States Supreme Court, famously observed about pornography, "I know it when I see it."[46] Similarly, people have an intuitive "feel" for what legal rights are, even if they can't quite define them. Some of the most important rights, such as bodily integrity and bodily liberty, act like a suit of legal armor, shielding the bodies and personalities of natural persons from invasion and injury. These rights are so important that they usually are enshrined in the bills of rights of state and federal constitutions.

For most of the last century, legal scholars, judges, and lawyers often classified legal rights in the way that Wesley Hohfeld, a professor at Yale Law School, proposed during World War I. Hohfeld said that a legal right was any theoretical advantage conferred by recognized legal rules. He broke legal rights into their lowest common denominators, using terms that judges commonly employ, such as *privilege*, *claim*, *duty*, *immunity*, *disability*, *power*, and *liability*, but he never formally defined them. Instead, he spelled out how the common denominators relate to each other. According to Hohfeld, legal relationships can exist only between two legal persons and one thing. One of the two persons always has a legal advantage (or right) over the other. The other person has the corresponding legal disadvantage. Just as a man can't be a husband without a wife and a woman can't be a wife without a husband, neither a legal advantage nor a disadvantage can exist all by itself.

The legal rights of nonhuman animals might first be achieved in any of three ways. Most agree that the least likely will be through the re-interpretation or amendment of state or federal constitutions, or through international treaties. For example, the Treaty of Amsterdam that came into force on May 1, 1999, formally acknowledged that nonhuman animals are "sentient beings" and not merely goods or agricultural products. The European Community and the member states signatory to the treaty are required "to pay full regard to the welfare requirements of animals." In 2002 the German Parliament amended Article 26 of the Basic Law to give nonhuman animals the right to be "respected as fellow creatures" and to be protected from "avoidable pain." Half of the sixteen German states already have some sort of animal rights provisions in their constitutions.[47]

In the United States, most believe that gaining personhood is much more probable through legislative enactment than through a constitutional change. But a change in the common law (which Germany does not have) may be the most likely of all. What is the common law? Lemuel Shaw, the nineteenth century chief justice of the Supreme Judicial Court of Massachusetts, provided this good definition: it "consists of a few broad and comprehensive principles, founded on reason, natural justice, and enlightened public policy, modified and adapted to all the circumstances of all the particular cases that fall within it."[48]

Why the common law over legislation? The common law is created by English-speaking judges while in the process of deciding cases. Unlike legislators, judges are at least formally bound to do justice. Properly interpreted, the common law is meant to be flexible, adaptable to changes in public morality, and sensitive to new scientific discoveries. Among its chief values are liberty and equality. These favor common law personhood, as a matter of liberty, at least for those nonhuman animals, such as chimpanzees, bonobos, gorillas, orangutans, dolphins, and whales, who possess such highly advanced cognitive abilities as consciousness, perhaps even self-consciousness; a sense of self; and the abilities to desire and act intentionally. In other words, they have what I call a "practical autonomy," which is, I argue, sufficient, though not necessary, for basic legal rights.[49] An animal's species is irrelevant to his or her entitlement to liberty rights; any who possesses practical autonomy has what is sufficient for basic rights as a matter of liberty.[50] And as long as society awards personhood to non-autonomous humans, such as the very young, the severely retarded, and the persistently vegetative, then it must also award basic rights, as a matter of equality as well, to nonhuman animals with practical autonomy.

Legal Education in Animal Law

I have written that an animal rights lawyer should not expect a judge to appreciate the merits of arguments in favor of the legal personhood of any nonhuman animal the first time, or the fifth time, he or she encounters them. While a sympathetic judge might be found here and there, no appellate bench will seize the lead until the issue has been thoroughly aired in law journals, books, and conferences. Law reviews discussing animal legal rights must be established around the country in order to provide an important scholarly forum in which the relevant legal issues can be explored. Legal conferences must be organized, law school courses devoted to educating students on animal law issues must be established, animal rights lawyers and law professors must reach out to acquaint the profession with the importance of their work and the power of their arguments.[51]

Legal education, in every sense of that term—law reviews, legal conferences, and law school courses—is critical to the legal changes that animal rights lawyers seek. As of 2002 much work remained. In 1950 it had not even begun. The wildlife legal scholar Michael Bean has written that, even in 1977, "the very term 'wildlife law' was novel, for few had seen fit to distinguish such a body of law from the broader categories of 'environmental law' or 'natural resources law.'"[52]

In 1950 no law reviews—those scholarly journals published by the students of every American law school—were devoted exclusively to even environmental (much less animal rights) law. That gap was not plugged until 1970, when *Environmental Law* began to be published by students of the Northwestern School of Law of Lewis and Clark College in Portland, Oregon. In the middle of the twentieth century no law school classes solely addressed environmental law, much less wildlife law. The more arcane subjects of animal protection law and animal rights law lay nearly forty years in the future.

There were no animal law conferences in 1950. In the 1980s the Animal Legal Defense Fund held sporadic conferences. By 2002 four state bar associations (in Washington, Texas, Michigan, and Washington, D.C.) had formed animal law sections, as had the New York City and San Diego County bar associations. Several states (Connecticut, Florida, Georgia, and Oregon) appeared to be in the process of forming animal law sections. Since 1995 the Committee on Legal Issues of the Association of the Bar of New York City has held a continuing series of educational seminars on animal issues, and annual full-blown legal conferences. This series of programs was capped by "The Legal Status of Non-Human Animals," a 1999 conference that attracted speakers from three continents and hundreds of participants.[53] The Center for the Expansion of Fundamental Rights has begun a program to take the issue of animal rights law directly to the judges who will be making the decisions, by offering to send speakers to judicial conferences throughout the United States.

Precisely a quarter century after *Environmental Law* was founded, *Animal Law* joined it as a sister publication. David Favre wrote in the premiere issue that,

> [i]n the tradition of the prior students at Lewis and Clark, a substantial number of present students have focused upon what will be a cutting area of scholarship for the next generation of law students—animal related legal issues. In the 1970s the new area of jurisprudence was environmental law. In the 1990s there is a growing interest in animal issues."[54]

Animal Law is important because it was, and remains, both a cause and an effect of the intensifying interest in animal law within the legal profession, an interest that must continue to build if animal rights lawyers are to succeed. (As of 2002 a second animal law review, this one a Northeast regional publication, was in the planning stages.) It is important that general law reviews have begun publishing animal law articles, including those written by such prominent legal academics as Cass Sunstein of the University of Chicago School of Law and Anthony D'Amato of the Northwestern University School of Law. Oxford University Press has just published a series of groundbreaking essays edited by Sunstein and Martha Nussbaum in *Animal Rights: Current Debates in New Directions*.

The first American law school class in animal law was offered by the Pace University School of Law in White Plains, New York, in the mid-1980s. The instructor was adjunct professor Jolene Marion, a pioneer in animal rights law. Though it lasted just a few years, it paved the way for every animal law class that followed. In 1990 I began teaching a law school class at the Vermont Law School, again as an adjunct. This course, entitled "Animal Rights Law," focused on whether nonhuman animals should be eligible for basic legal rights.

In 2002 animal law classes were being offered at nineteen American law schools, including Harvard, Georgetown, UCLA, Hastings, and George Washington universities. Courses were being offered in the United Kingdom, Holland, and Austria. Most of these courses were taught by practitioners acting as adjunct professors or lecturers on law. They offered such an intellectual smorgasbord that a student might attend several and encounter little repetition.

Most focused on "animal law" and surveyed either the statutes and case law in which the nature of nonhuman animals is important, or "animal protection law," which addresses how attorneys can protect the interests of nonhuman animals within a legal system that considers them to be legal things. Some courses, however, concentrated on "animal rights law," in which the arguments are explored for and against having judges recognize that at least some nonhuman animals possess at least some basic legal rights. All classes were given a boost by the publication in the year 2000 of *Animal Law*, the first casebook exclusively concerned with animal law issues.[55] As its authors noted, "There has been a reticence in many legal quarters to teach, learn, or practice in the area specifically because of the absence of meaningful assistance and coverage." The authors' hope that their casebook will "serve as a valuable guide to students and professors stepping onto this new frontier and provide more law schools with a template for animal law courses" has been fulfilled.[56]

The last fifty years—and especially the last ten—have seen tremendous strides in the evolution of animal protection law, both in its teaching and in the laying of the foundations for true animal rights law. The first serious attempts to gain legal rights for at least some nonhuman animals will likely be upon us in this decade.

Notes

[1]Radford, M. 2001. *Animal welfare law in Britain—Regulation and responsibility* 261. New York: Oxford University Press.

[2]*Id.* at 99.

[3]*Id.* at 99–100, 101.

[4]Favre, D., and V. Tsang. 1993. The development of anti-cruelty laws during the 1800s. *Detroit College of Law Review* 1, reprinted in D. Favre and P.L. Borschelt, 1999, *Animal Law and Dog Behavior* 251, 264 Tucson, Ariz.: Lawyers and Judges Publishing Co., Inc.

[5]*Id.* at 251.

[6]Radford, M. 1999. 'Unnecessary suffering': The cornerstone of animal protection legislation considered, *Criminal Law Review* 702; Annotation, "What constitutes statutory offense of cruelty to animals," 82 ALR 2d 794, 798.

[7]Annotation, note 6, *supra*, at 799.

[8]Leavitt, E.S. 1968. *Animals and their legal rights: A survey of American laws from 1641 to 1968.* Washington, D.C.: Animal Welfare Institute.

[9]Favre, D.S., and M. Loring. 1983. *Animal law* 127 Westport, Conn.: Quorum Books.

[10]Personal communication from Pamela Frasch, April 16, 2002; P.D. Frasch et al. 1999. State anti-cruelty statutes: An overview, 5 *Animal Law* 69: 69.

[11]USDA/NASS "Meat Animal Production, Disposition, & Income(1998); USDA/NASS "Broiler Hatchery" (October 1999); USDA/NASS "Chicken and Eggs (October 1999); USDA/NASS Turkey Hatchery (October 1999); USDA/NASS Livestock Slaughter 1998 Summary (March 1999); USDA/NASS Poultry Slaughter 1998 Summary (February 1999).

[12]Wolfson, D.L. 1999. *Beyond the law: Agriculture and the systemic abuse of animals raised for food or food production* 27 Watkins Glen, N.Y.: Farm Sanctuary, Inc.

[13]*Id.*

[14]*McDonald's Corporation v. Steel*, http://www.mcspotlight.org/case/trial/verdict/jud2c.html, at page 5 (High Court of Justice, Queen's Bench Division June 19, 1997), rev. in part on other grnds (Court of Appeals, March 31, 1999).

[15]Wolfson, D.L., note 12, *supra*, at 31.

[16]*Taub v. State*, 443 A. 2d 819, 821 (Md. 1983).

[17]P.D. Frasch et al., note 10, *supra*, at 76–77 and note 31.

[18]*Id.* at 76–77.

[19]*Allen v. Wright*, 468 U.S. 737, 751 (1984); Warth v. Selden, 422 U.S. 490, 499 (1975).

[20]*Sierra Club v. Morton*, 405 U.S. 727, 731 (1972).

[21]Davis, K.C., and R.J. Pierce, Jr. 1994. Administrative Law Treatise, (3rd. ed.) sec. 16.1. Boston: Little, Brown and Company.

[22]*Barlow v. Collins*, 397 U.S. 159 (1970); *Association of Data Processing Service Organizations v. Camp*, 397 U.S. 150 (1970). See Tribe, L.H. 1999. *American Constitutional law* (third edition) 393 New York: Foundation Press.

[23]*Tennessee Electric Power Co. v. Tennessee Valley Authority*, 306 U.S. 118, 137–139 (1939).

[24]Allen, note 19, *supra*, at 751.

[25]*Id.*

[26]5 U.S.C. 702.

[27]*Clarke v. Securities Decision Association*, 479 U.S. 388, 399 (1987).

[28]*Id.*

[29]23 F. 3d. 496 (D.C. Cir. 1994).

[30]Compare 7 U.S.C. 2132(h) with 36 Fed. Reg. 24, 917, 24, 919 (1971).

[31]29 F. 3d.

[32]*Animal Legal Defense Fund v. Glickman*, 154 F. 3d 426 (D.C. Cir. 1998)(en banc), cert. den. 119 S.Ct. 1454 (1999). For an excellent treatment of the case, *see* R.R. Smith, "Standing on their own four legs: The future of animal welfare litigation after *Animal Legal Defense Fund, Inc. v. Glickman.*" 1999. 29 *Environmental Law*: 989.

[33]*Alternatives Research & Development Foundation v. Glickman*, 101 F. Supp. 2d 7 (DDC 2000).

[34]7 U.S.C. sec. 2143(a)(2)(B)(1985).

[35]Personal communication from S. Wilkes, head of Animal Procedures Section, Home Office, Constitutional and Community Directorate to Steven M. Wise, March 26, 1998; Supplementary Note to the Home Secretary's response to the Animals Procedures Committee—Interim report on the review of the operation of the Animals (Scientific Procedures) Act 1986 para. 10 (November 6, 1997).

[36]Supplementary Note to the Home Secretary's response to the Animals Procedures Committee—Interim report on the review of the operation of the Animals (Scientific Procedures) Act 1986, note 35, *supra*, at para. 11.

[37]*PACE News*. 1998. at 8:1 (January–March).

[38]*The Great Ape Project: Equality beyond humanity.* 1993. Cavalieri, P., and P. Singer, eds. New York: St. Martin's Press/Griffin.

[39]Submission of David Penny and 37 others to the Parliamentary Select Committee on Primary Production concerning the Animal Welfare Bill No. 25, 14 (October 27, 1998).

[40]New Zealand Animal Welfare Act of 1999, sec. 76A.

[41]B. Dyke et al. 1995. "Future costs of chimpanzees in U.S. research institutions," 37 *American Journal of Primatology* 25.

[42]*Chimpanzees in research: Strategies for their ethical care, management, and use.* 1997. 66–67 Washington, D.C.: National Research Council.

[43]*Id.* at 28.

[44]This section has been adapted from S.M. Wise, *Rattling the cage: Toward legal rights for animals* (Perseus Books 2000); S.M. Wise, Hardly a revolution: The eligibility of nonhuman animals for dignity: Rights in a liberal democracy, 22 *Vermont Law Review* 793 (1998); S.M. Wise, Legal rights for nonhuman animals: The case for chimpanzees and bonobos, 2 *Animal Law* 179 (1996); S.M. Wise, The legal thinghood of nonhuman animals, 23(2) *Boston College Environmental Affairs Law Review* 471 (1996); and S.M. Wise, How nonhuman animals were trapped in a nonexistent universe, 1 *Animal Law* 15 (1995).

[45]Momsen, T., P. Krueger, and A. Watson, eds. 1985. Dig. 1.5.2 *Hermogenianus, Epitome of law, Book 1.* Philadelphia: University of Pennsylvania Press.

[46]*Jacobellis v. Ohio*, 378 U.S. 184, 197 (1964)(Stewart, J., concurring).

[47]Koenig, R. 2000. Animal rights amendment defeated. 288 *Science*: 412. April 21.

[48]*Norway Plains Company v. Boston and Maine Railroad*, 67 Mass. (1 Gray) 263, 267 (1854).

[49]S.M. Wise (*Rattling the cage*), note 44, *supra*, at 243–248.

[50]*Id.* at 63–87, 243–270.

[51]S.M. Wise. 1999. Animal thing to animal person: Thoughts on time, place, and theories. 5 *Animal Law* 61: 66–67.

[52]Bean, M. 1983. *The Evolution of National Wildlife Law.* Revised and expanded edition 1. New York: Praeger Publishers.

[53]The proceedings were published in 8 *Animal Law* (2002).

[54]Favre, D. 1995. Time for a sharper legal focus. 1 *Animal Law* 1: 1.

[55]Frasch, P. et al. 2000. *Animal law.* Durham, N.C.: Carolina Academic Press.

[56]*Id.* at xviii.

The Science and Sociology of Hunting: Shifting Practices and Perceptions in the United States and Great Britain

8

CHAPTER

John W. Grandy, Elizabeth Stallman, and David W. Macdonald

Introduction

Between the late nineteenth and early twenty-first centuries, both the rationale for and perception of hunting shifted in the United States, coinciding with demographic changes in the U.S. population (Duda 1993). Similar changes in attitude, though largely undocumented, probably occurred in the United Kingdom. (For example, foxhunting did not emerge as a substantial sport until the second half of the eighteenth century; before that, foxes were widely perceived as pests and killed whenever the opportunity arose [Marvin 2000]). Our purpose in this chapter is to compare these two countries in order to reveal some of the science and the sociology relevant to hunting (the latter just one of many interacting environmental issues about which human society faces complicated judgments

within rapidly shifting political and cultural areas).

While hunting was once necessary for the survival of European colonists and Native Americans, the number of people reliant upon subsistence hunting in the United States and Western Europe is now small. For the general public in both the United States and Europe—including non-hunters and hunters—the acceptability of hunting today hinges on ethical considerations such as "fair chase"; whether the hunt is conducted primarily for sport, recreation, trophy, or food; and perceived effects on conservation or animal welfare (e.g., Kellert 1996).

Paralleling changes in public attitudes, the discipline of wildlife management in the United States has shown evidence of a gradual evolution away from "game" management and

toward whole-ecosystem management (Dasmann 1964; Decker et al. 1992; Woolf and Roseberry 1998; Bolen 2000; Peyton 2000). Despite the shift in the focus of wildlife management, as well as a steady decline in the popularity and acceptance of hunting, the generally dwindling stakeholder group associated with sport hunting continues to exert a strong influence on wildlife management (Bissell 1993; Woolf and Roseberry 1998), often encouraging the production of "harvestable surpluses" of favored game species for the sake of providing recreational hunting opportunities (Holsman 2000; Peyton 2000). Consumptive users of wildlife (hunters, trappers, and anglers) have a financial—and perhaps, therefore, influential—impact on wildlife management via the purchase of hunting and fishing licenses and duck stamps, and payment of federal excise taxes on sporting arms, handguns, ammunition, and archery equipment (Schmidt 1996; Holsman 2000). This potential influence of hunters on management decisions has three potential effects: it may (1) promote the killing of wildlife as a form of public recreation; (2) reduce the emphasis by wildlife agencies on non-game species; and (3) affect the movement toward ecosystem management.

In contrast to the United States, mammalian wildlife populations in the United Kingdom exist almost entirely on privately owned land and are managed by individual landowners within the constraints of European and U.K. legislation regarding seasons, permitted methods of killing or hunting, use of firearms, and protected species (Macdonald et al. 2000). The organization of wildlife management is much less institutionalized in the United Kingdom than in the United States. For example, provided that permitted methods are used, strict firearms regulations are followed, and closed seasons recognized, the decision as to how many deer to cull lies almost entirely within the control of individual landowners. No hunting license is required (although individual landowners may charge a fee for the right to hunt on their land) and, except for deer in Scotland, there is no requirement for hunters to report the number of animals killed. There is no legally enforced regulation in the United Kingdom, although landownership and informal groupings (e.g., deer management groups, fox destruction clubs, and shooting syndicates) may achieve a similar effect. Very recently, and as a significant change, many organizations hunting with dogs have submitted themselves to voluntary regulation by the Independent Supervisory Authority for Hunting. However, the U.K. situation generally contrasts sharply with the situation elsewhere in Europe, where wildlife culling is subject to a statutory licensing system and/or cull plans approved by government authorities,

often covering a defined area of land (Gill 1990; Myrberget 1990; Stroud et al. 1999). Of course, management of mammalian wildlife in the United Kingdom is perhaps less complex than elsewhere in Europe or in the United States because there are no remaining populations of large predators and only a handful of larger herbivores.

In the United Kingdom, most available data on public attitudes toward wildlife management are collected through opinion polls for political purposes, and these generally are scientifically wanting (Macdonald et al. 2000). However, one particular aspect of hunting that certainly causes great public concern is the use of dogs to chase and kill wild mammals such as foxes, deer, and hares (Ministry of Agriculture, Fisheries, and Food 2000). A number of European countries, including Germany, Sweden, and Denmark, have banned or partially banned hunting with dogs (Burns et al. 2000). Although hunting with dogs is an ancient occupation in the United Kingdom (Macdonald 1987; Macdonald and Johnson 1996), the longstanding and fierce debate as to whether it should be allowed to continue recently culminated in a ban in Scotland; it is not yet resolved in England and Wales. The Scottish legislation abolished mounted fox-hunting and hare coursing and prevents the hunting of deer, boar, and mink with dogs. In 2002 ministers of Parliament voted overwhelmingly to ban hunting with dogs in England and Wales, but progress was blocked by the House of Lords. Following a period of consultation, new legislation proposed in late 2002 was again supported by the House of Commons but was also likely to face opposition from the Lords when it was to be voted on in late 2003 or 2004. The proposed bill, as amended in committee, bans hunting with dogs unless two tests are passed: first, that the hunting is necessary to prevent serious damage of some kind and, second, that the damage cannot be prevented using a method involving less suffering.

U.S. Wildlife Management and Hunting

Early European colonists considered wildlife on the North American continent to be essentially infinite in abundance (e.g., Mighetto 1991; Posewitz 1999). There was no need to justify hunting to the public. Hunting for subsistence was a way of life and was believed to be justified by the desire to conquer the wilderness of the New World. Thus, little need was seen for restraint in hunting and trapping those wildlife species whose meat could be used or whose hides or fur could be traded within the colonies or sold to financiers in Europe. European colonists saw many wildlife species, as well as the wilderness itself, as hostile and a deterrent to progress. In Connecticut, for example, the first restriction on hunting deer, in the form of a closed season, was not in place until 1698, by which time deer had been nearly wiped out in that area (Conover and Conover 1987). Bounties on wolves and cougars—placed only partly for the sake of protecting livestock—succeeded in extirpating large predators from the East and later from much of what was to become the forty-eight contiguous states (Leopold 1933; Conover and Conover 1987; Mighetto 1991; Paquet and Hackman 1995).

By the late 1800s, however, some hunters began to write about the need for conservation of declining populations of game species—most notably the bison and the passenger pigeon—and to increase public awareness of the loss of wildlife to market hunting (Mighetto 1991). Deer, beaver, wolves, bears, cougars, and other animals killed by hunters or trappers had been nearly extirpated from most of their range in North America, and many waterfowl species were in serious decline (Nichols, Johnson, and Williams 1995; Paquet and Hackman 1995; Woolf and Roseberry 1998). Massachusetts was the first state to close deer hunting for a number of years; by 1880 state game laws became widespread throughout the country, imposing bag limits, rest days, closed seasons, and buck laws, the latter of which prohibited the shooting of anterless deer (Leopold 1933; Conover and Conover 1987; Woolf and Roseberry 1998). Restrictions on waterfowl hunting were nonexistent until passage of the Migratory Bird Treaty Act (MBTA) in 1918 authorized the federal government to implement hunting regulations (e.g., Nichols, Johnson, and Williams 1995).

Hunters and anglers around the turn of the twentieth century frequently are credited with kick-starting the early conservation movement that eventually led to passage of the Lacey Act of 1900, the MBTA, and associated treaties, and an end to destructive market hunting (Leopold 1933; Mighetto 1991; Schmidt 1996). Critics point out that these sport hunters-turned-conservationists acted for the "selfish" purpose of providing "abundant sport for themselves" (Grinnell, in Mighetto 1991, 41). Regardless of the motives of the hunters of the past, their actions resulted in the initiation of early wildlife conservation.

While hunters of this era pushed for laws and regulations that would protect the game species they found valuable, they simultaneously refined the "sporting" aspects of hunting by emphasizing particular ethical standards, such as the concept of fair chase and self-imposed restrictions on the number of animals killed to allow wildlife populations to rebuild—and, ultimately, be used by future generations of hunters (e.g., Posewitz 1999). The need to hunt for subsistence was rapidly diminishing, and humanitarians concerned for the welfare of individual animals began to pay attention to the suffering of at least some hunted wildlife species. Mighetto (1991) suggests that the publication in 1859 of Darwin's theory of natural selection may have been a catalyst for the concern of humanitarians for animal welfare, because the theory clearly indicated that humans and other animals share a common origin.

During the early 1900s, increasing populations of some wildlife species allowed wildlife managers to move away from a strategy of simply restricting hunting to recover scarce wildlife populations, adopting instead a strategy in which the "cropping" of game species was emphasized. (Cropping, as a management technique, involves encouraging the reproduction and survival of animals so that many will be available to be killed by recreational hunters without decreasing the population beyond the capability of the next reproductive cycle to replenish the population.) This strategy was accomplished through attempts to limit the negative impact on wildlife of hunting, as well as to mitigate the effects of disease and habitat degradation. Refuges and parks were also established on which hunting was prohibited or restricted (Leopold 1933). Sport hunters in the early and mid-1900s were provided with hunting opportunities and in turn provided a means to limit now-increasing deer herds which, though still limited by food and disease, were no longer being held in check by large predators such as wolves and cougars (Woolf and Roseberry 1998). Sport hunters became a self-designated "tool" for wildlife management and began funding state and federal wildlife management agencies through a tax in the form of fees for the purchase of hunting licenses and duck stamps (Migratory Bird Hunting Stamp Act, 1934) and via excise taxes imposed on purchases of sporting arms and ammunition (through the Pittman-Robertson Federal Aid in Wildlife Restoration Act of 1937). The notion of hunters as the "clients" of U.S. state wildlife agencies has largely persisted to the present day, as has the wildlife management strategy of producing wildlife for hunters to kill, in spite of the fact that Leopold's (1933) embrace of cropping wildlife came at a time when production of wildlife seemed a responsible alternative to the exploitation of scarce wildlife populations. Some authors now suggest that continuation of the cropping strategy as a primary goal of wildlife management may hinder progress toward whole-ecosystem management (Peyton 2000). Even in those regions where some wildlife populations, such as white-tailed deer, are considered too abundant, state wildlife agencies often respond to pressure from sport hunters by continuing to manage habitat to provide increased food and cover for deer so that hunter satisfaction remains high (Woolf and Roseberry 1998). In areas where native predators have returned (e.g., cougars in the West) or have been replaced by others (e.g., coyotes replacing wolves in Maine), hunting and trapping seasons for these predators often are established or liberalized under the generally untested assumption that this will increase populations of popular game species.

The American public, including wildlife managers and some hunters, has begun to question more critically the emphasis of state wildlife agencies on satisfying the desires of hunters (e.g., Williams 1986). In response to this and other criticisms, hunters' organizations in several states have lobbied for passage of legislation establishing their "right" to hunt (Table 1). It is not yet clear what effect this will have on wildlife management strategies or hunting regulations.

Table 1
States that Currently Have a Constitutional Amendment Guaranteeing the Right to Hunt for All Citizens

State	Bill or Amendment	Highlights of Text
Alabama	Alabama Constitution, Amendment No. 597(2002)	"All persons shall have the right to hunt and fish in this state in accordance with law and regulations."
Florida	Section 8, Section 372.002, Florida Statutes (2002)	"The legislature recognizes that hunting, fishing, and the taking of game are a valued part of the cultural heritage of Florida and should be forever preserved for Floridians...."
Minnesota	Minnesota Constitution, Article XIII, Section 12 (2001)	"Hunting and fishing and the taking of game and fish are a valued part of our heritage that shall be forever preserved for the people...."
Missouri	Title XXXVIII. Crimes and Punishment; Peace Officers and Public Defenders Chapter 578.151	"It is the intent of the general assembly of the state of Missouri to recognize that all persons shall have the right to hunt, fish and trap in this state...."
New Hampshire	Title XVIII. Fish and Game Chapter 207 General Provisions as to Fish and Game Jurisdiction. 207:58 (2001)	"...The general court further finds that it is in the best of the state and its citizens that the fish and game recognize, preserve, and promote our special heritage of hunting, fishing, trapping, and wildlife viewing by providing opportunities to hunt, fish, trap, and view wildlife...."
North Dakota	North Dakota Constitution, Article 11, Section 27 (2002)	"Hunting, trapping, and fishing and the taking of game and fish are a valued part of our heritage and will be forever preserved for the people...."
Virginia	Virginia Constitution, Article XI, Section 4 (2002)	"The people have a right to hunt, fish, and harvest game...."

Hunters in the United States

Absolute numbers of hunters (paid license holders) in the United States have decreased over the past two decades, from approximately 16.3 million in 1980 to 15 million in 2000. The popularity of hunting, measured by the proportion of the U.S. population that purchases hunting licenses, has declined steadily, from an estimated 7.18 percent in 1980 to 5.35 percent in 2000 (Table 2a) (U.S. Fish and Wildlife Service 1981; U.S. Census Bureau 1996; U.S. Census Bureau 2001; U.S. Fish and Wildlife Service 2001). Trends in most states follow the national trend, though there is substantial variation in hunting

Table 2a
Percentage of the United States Population Holding a Hunting License

	1980	1990	2000
Number of Paid Hunting License Holders [1]	16,257,074	15,806,864	15,044,324
U.S. Population [2]	226,542,199	248,709,873	281,421,906
Percentage of Population Holding a Hunting License	7.18	6.36	5.35

[1]Source: U.S. Fish and Wildlife Service, based on data provided by state wildlife agencies. A paid license holder is one individual regardless of the number of licenses purchased. Some states do not require the purchase of a hunting license by senior citizens, youth, or disabled individuals; some unprotected species, such as prairie dogs or marmots, may be shot without a license in some states.

[2]Source: U.S. Census Bureau

participation among states (Table 2b). Between 1980 and 2000, nineteen states showed a decrease of 2 percent or more in the percentage of the population that purchased licenses; however, a few states (Montana and the two Dakotas) showed an increase of at least 2 percent in the percentage of paid license holders. (It is not clear the extent to which non-resident trophy hunters may affect state-by-state variation in these trends.) These recent trends contrast with the period 1955–1975, during which the number of paid license holders in the United States increased 46 percent, from 11.7 million to 14.0 million (U.S. Department of the Interior 1997).

Another measure of participation in hunting is the average number of days hunted per year. Between 1991 and 1996, hunters spent, on average, approximately 17 percent fewer days hunting annually than in 1975, 1980, and 1985 (U.S. Department of the Interior and U.S. Department of Commerce 1997). Enck, Decker, and Brown (2000) point out that most of this decrease can be accounted for by a decrease in time spent hunting small game (a 40 percent decrease in days spent hunting); days spent hunting big game and waterfowl actually increased by 28 percent and 5 percent, respectively, between 1980 and 1996 (see also U.S. Department of the Interior and U.S. Department of Commerce 2002). These authors suggest further that the reduced interest in small-game hunting may be indicative of reduced participation by younger hunters, for whom small-game hunting is often part of the introduction to hunting (Enck, Decker, and Brown 2000). Perhaps for this reason, hunter recruitment efforts by state wildlife agencies and non-governmental hunting associations often focus on encouraging young people to begin or continue hunting, though efforts to recruit minority groups and women are also becoming more common (e.g., Matthews 1993; Mangun, Hall, and O'Leary 1996).

Table 2b
States Showing an Increase or Decrease of 2 Percent or More in Hunting Popularity, 1980, 2000

| | Percent of State Population Holding a Hunting License | |
	1980	2000
Hunting Popularity Increases		
Montana	27.64	31.46
North Dakota	15.33	19.23
South Dakota	20.66	30.23
Hunting Popularity Decreases		
Alaska	17.96	15.55
Arizona	7.31	3.83
Colorado	10.81	7.85
Georgia	7.03	4.03
Idaho	25.21	19.26
Kansas	10.51	7.80
Louisiana	9.14	6.23
Maine	21.28	16.37
Mississippi	11.45	8.86
Nevada	6.53	3.02
New Hampshire	9.07	6.17
New Mexico	11.08	6.00
Oregon	14.98	9.09
Pennsylvania	10.73	8.37
Utah	19.68	7.69
Vermont	26.86	16.70
Virginia	8.78	4.45
Washington	8.73	3.65
Wyoming	41.21	29.90

Popularity of hunting is indexed as the number of paid hunting license holders divided by the total U.S. population.

Sources: U.S. Fish and Wildlife Service, based on data provided by state wildlife agencies and the U.S. Census Bureau. A paid license holder is one individual regardless of the number of licenses purchased. Some states do not require the purchase of a hunting license by senior citizens, youth hunters, or disabled individuals; some unprotected species of wildlife, such as prairie dogs or marmots, may be shot without a license in some states.

Several factors may be contributing to the apparent decline in the popularity of hunting in the United States, but urbanization is the factor most frequently cited. The trend toward an increasing concentration of the human population in urban areas was recognized and lamented by hunters and outdoors enthusiasts in the late 1800s. For example, Theodore Roosevelt in 1893 complained that American society was becoming too civilized and was in danger of losing the toughness—or "vigorous manliness"—that only dangerous and physically demanding experiences such as hunting could provide (Roosevelt 1900, 7–8). John Muir, on the other hand, observed that the trend toward urbanization and the "deadly apathy of luxury" had at last awakened in Americans an appreciation for nature (1901, 1). Wildlife management professionals today complain that an increasingly urbanized and suburbanized America is losing touch with nature and holds idealized notions of wildlife populations that can exist free of human intervention (e.g., Organ and Fritzell 2000), an idea supported by Kellert (1996). On the other hand, however, Kellert (1996) asserts that attitudes of rural residents are biased in another direction: these residents are more likely to value wildlife and the land primarily because of their usefulness to humans, rather than through an appreciation of their role in natural ecosystems.

Hunting is, in fact, more popular in rural populations, as indicated by the fact that rural residents are more likely to hold hunting licenses or to have hunted at least once (Duda 1993). In a regression analysis of factors associated with hunting participation, Heberlein and Thomson (1991) found that declining participation was associated with a decreasing percentage of individuals who spend their teens in rural communities, and, in general, an increasing number of people living in urban, as opposed to rural, settings. Other factors correlated with decreasing hunting participation included a declining percentage of the white population and increasing average education level (Heberlein and Thomson 1991). Related factors affecting declining hunting participation may include a lack of a family mentor who hunts and isolation from social systems that support hunting (e.g., Decker, Provencher, and Brown 1984; Brown et al. 1987; Applegate 1991; Organ and Fritzell 2000). Other wildlife-dependent activities, such as bird watching, appear not to be predominantly rural (McFarlane and Boxall 1996).

Public Acceptance of Hunting in the United States

Public acceptance of hunting in the United States hinges on ethical considerations such as fair chase, the perceived humaneness of the hunting method, whether hunting is conducted primarily for sport/recreation, the extent to which hunting is viewed as necessary (e.g., to resolve a human-wildlife conflict or to provide food), and whether hunters respect laws and regulations (Duda 1993; Posewitz 1994; Kellert 1996). For example, in a survey Kellert (1988) found that more than 80 percent of the general public approves of Native American subsistence hunting as well as any hunting done exclusively to obtain meat. Hunting for sport or recreation is acceptable to most Americans (64 percent) only if the meat is used. However, 60 percent of those surveyed indicated an opposition to hunting done solely for recreation or sport, and 80 percent were opposed to trophy hunting (Figure 1). Results of other surveys have mirrored these findings, indicating that public approval of hunting is stronger when the motivation for hunting is not solely for recreation or a trophy (Bissell, Duda, and Young 1998; Minnesota Department of Natural Resources 1992).

Urban vs. rural residency is correlated with public opinion on hunting in the United States (as elsewhere, see Macdonald and Johnson 2003) and with attitudes toward wildlife and other animals in general. In survey studies, Kellert (1996) found that people who own large amounts of land or reside in open country areas tend to hold a more utilitarian view toward

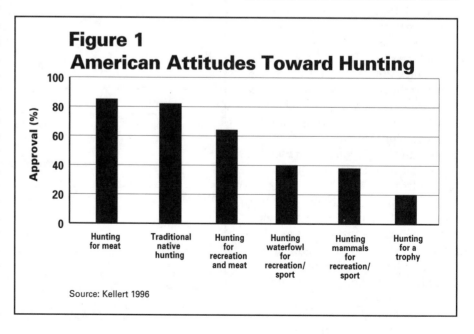

Figure 1
American Attitudes Toward Hunting

Source: Kellert 1996

nature and animals compared with those who live in large cities, own little or no land, or are college-educated, and compared with younger adults. Relatively "urban-oriented" people in the United States tend to express a greater concern for the protection of wildlife and wildlife habitat, and exhibit levels of knowledge about nature that are not significantly different from those of rural residents. Similarly, Manfredo and Zinn (1996) found that urban Coloradoans are more likely than rural residents to have positive value orientations toward wildlife rights or welfare, and are less likely to value wildlife use, including hunting (Figure 2).

Perhaps because of changing demographics, the prevalence of Kellert's (1988, 143) "utilitarian" attitude, defined as the "practical and material exploitation of nature" for the purpose of "physical sustenance/security," appears to have declined substantially between 1900 and 1976 (Figure 3). This analysis was based on the frequency of occurrence of the utilitarian attitude in newspaper articles from two rural and two urban newspapers. Interestingly, the decline in utilitarian attitudes depicted by Kellert (1988, 1996) would be more substantial if Kellert had accounted for the fact that the proportion of the human population living in rural areas had changed from 60 percent in 1900 to 25 percent in 1976.

In addition to the urban-rural split, several researchers have found opinions of hunting in the United States that vary with age. Kellert (1996) suggests that changing values of young children may reflect, at least in part, a developmental process similar to Kohlberg's (1984) stages of moral development in children. For example, very young children view animals in egocentric, exploitative ways. However, by age nine, children appear to "develop a conscience toward the nonhuman world, recognizing animals and nature as having the right not to be selfishly manipulated, a view

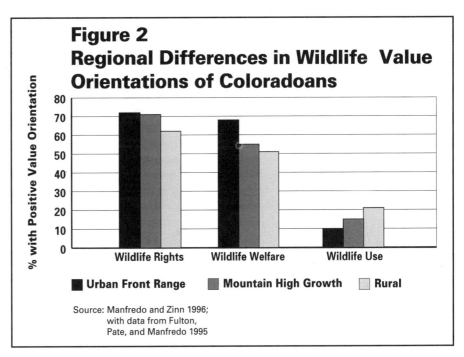

Figure 2
Regional Differences in Wildlife Value Orientations of Coloradoans

Source: Manfredo and Zinn 1996; with data from Fulton, Pate, and Manfredo 1995

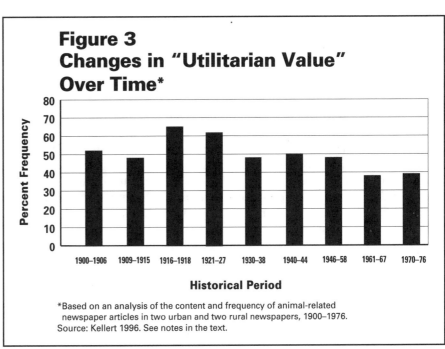

Figure 3
Changes in "Utilitarian Value" Over Time*

*Based on an analysis of the content and frequency of animal-related newspaper articles in two urban and two rural newspapers, 1900–1976.
Source: Kellert 1996. See notes in the text.

motivated by more than just the possibility of being punished for harming other creatures" (Kellert 1996, 49). Utilitarian aspects of children's attitudes toward animals decrease by their late teens, while attitudes reflecting support for conservation or an interest in animal welfare increase.

Kellert (1996) also found that views toward wildlife differ between young

adults and older individuals. In particular, elderly Americans tend to have less interest in and affection for animals and for nature in general. Manfredo and Zinn (1996) also found differences between young adults and older age groups in Colorado: younger adults (ages 18–30) tended to view wildlife rights or welfare more positively and wildlife use (e.g., hunt-

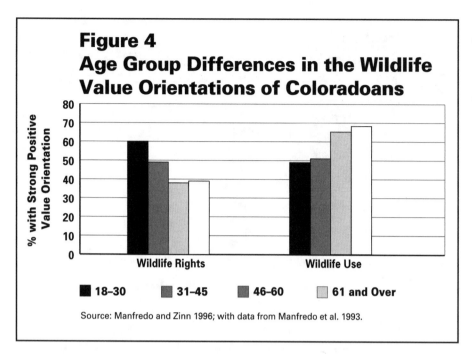

Figure 4
Age Group Differences in the Wildlife Value Orientations of Coloradoans

Legend: 18–30 | 31–45 | 46–60 | 61 and Over

Source: Manfredo and Zinn 1996; with data from Manfredo et al. 1993.

ing) more negatively compared with older adults (Figure 4). Manfredo and Zinn interpreted these age-related differences in values as a generational change. Kellert (1996), however, implies that these differences may also reflect continuing moral development in adulthood. Longitudinal studies, in which the same individuals are followed for several years, will be required to determine the extent to which age-related differences in opinions toward wildlife and acceptance of hunting indicate a developmental change within an individual versus a generational change reflective of the changing values of American society.

Clearly, not all non-hunters are "anti-hunter." However, even people who are not strictly opposed to hunting may be concerned with the suffering of individual animals that can occur as a result of hunting. Based on group interview sessions with individuals claiming to have a neutral opinion toward hunting, Rohlfing (1978) identified and ranked 115 problems associated with hunting and hunters. Of the top ten most bothersome problems, five were related to the suffering of wounded animals left to die a "slow," "painful," or "horrible" death. Two of the ten most bothersome problems, including the number one problem, involved hunting

accidents that kill or injure humans.

Many members of the American public are concerned with animal suffering and the unnecessary killing of wildlife, particularly if it occurs as part of a recreational activity. Some types of hunting may be viewed as more purely recreational, even if the animals killed are sometimes used for food or other purposes. Waterfowl hunting, dove hunting, varmint (or "pest") hunting, and traditional British fox hunting from horseback (see page 119) are examples of more purely recreational forms of hunting for which justification as a form of "management" frequently is weak. Predator hunting is another practice that is less likely to be defended for population management purposes or as a way to provide food. Public attitudes toward predator hunting indicate that this practice may be viewed as less justifiable, especially when hounds are used. For example, Teel, Krannich, and Schmidt (2002) found that Utah residents showed general opposition to bear and cougar hunting. Though rural residents were less opposed than urban residents to bear and cougar hunting in general, a majority of both rural and urban residents was opposed to the use of hounds to hunt cougars and black bears.

Attitudes of U.S. Wildlife Management Professionals

Changes in both attitudes and curriculum also are evident in the professional wildlife management community. Organ and Fritzell (2000) conducted a survey of university fisheries and wildlife programs in the United States to assess changes in student interests and attitudes and in the curriculum and course content. Senior faculty members from the twelve programs responding to the survey estimated that approximately 25 percent of fisheries and wildlife program undergraduates participate in hunting. Faculty estimated that as many as 24 percent of the undergraduate students in this discipline are likely have "anti-hunting" views, though this ideology was attributed more often to fewer than 10 percent of the students. Over the past twenty years, the numbers of students who hunt were estimated to have decreased by 10 to 60 percent, while the numbers of students opposed to hunting may have increased by 30 to 50 percent. Changes in course content at the universities surveyed by Organ and Fritzell (2000) include a greater emphasis on conservation biology and rare-species conservation and reduced time devoted to harvest management. These estimates and trends are based solely on the perceptions of senior faculty members at a small number of universities and should be interpreted with caution. However, this brief survey suggests that the ethical views of students going into the wildlife management field are changing along with those of the public as a whole.

Among members of professional associations of wildlife biologists and wildlife managers in the United States, Muth et al. (1998) found that 49.4 percent considered themselves to be hunters; as one would expect, this is a much higher percentage than is found in the public as a whole (see Table 2a). Surprisingly, however, only a bare majority—52.5 percent—of those surveyed agreed with the statement that "[w]ildlife and fish species are resources to be harvested in a sustainable way and used for human benefit." This suggests that one of the foundations of the wildlife management discipline (Leopold 1933) has not prevailed in the seventy years or so since its establishment. Organ and Fritzell (2000) cite unpublished data suggesting that wildlife managers who had been in the profession for five years or fewer are much less likely to support consumptive uses of wildlife (e.g., hunting, trapping, and fishing) compared with veterans of twenty years or more. Thus, individuals now entering the wildlife management discipline in the United States appear to represent a change in ethical views. This shift may be reflected in growing consideration for the humaneness of management actions and for management actions that benefit non-game species.

Divisions Among U.S. Hunters

In 1913 Theodore Roosevelt identified three groups of people concerned with wildlife conservation: "the true sportsman, the nature-lover," and "the humanitarian" (Roosevelt 1913, 161). Today these categories may still approximate, respectively, the subset of hunters concerned with conservation; non-hunting conservationists such as bird watchers; and animal protectionists. However, the distinctions among these categories often are blurred and each could be further subdivided. For example, only some hunters actively participate in conservation, beyond the now-involuntary contributions to wildlife conservation through the purchase of licenses or equipment (Holsman 2000). Bird watchers and other naturalists may be hunters or may lean more toward an animal welfare or animal rights

philosophy. Finally, there is a growing number of people who consider themselves to be both animal protectionists and conservationists.

Divisions among hunters in terms of their concern for conservation, animal welfare, or other ethical considerations have certainly existed since the late 1800s and early 1900s. Mighetto (1991) provides several illustrations of interpersonal differences among hunters. For example, one may contrast Roosevelt's writings, which focused on the excitement of pursuit and of the kill, with those of Ernest Thompson Seton. Roosevelt particularly relished hunting dangerous predators and, in general, revealed through his writings a "streak of bloodthirstiness" (Mighetto 1991). Seton was also a hunter, but in his writings, such as *Wild Animals I Have Known*, he portrayed animals as individuals and showed concern for their suffering, in part by using anthropomorphism as a literary device. Another contrast can be seen between Aldo Leopold and those hunters who vexed him through their increasing dependence on "gadgets" as a means of facilitating hunting (Leopold 1966, originally 1949). Interestingly, Leopold started off with a Rooseveltian disrespect for wolves and other predators; his attitude toward wolves later changed with his realization of the important role of predators in an ecosystem (Leopold 1966).

More recently, several authors have attempted to differentiate types or subgroups of hunters based on different motivations for hunting and/or the degree of specialization (Duda 1993). Kellert (1980, 1996) characterizes the attitudes and values of three main types of hunters. "Nature hunters" include those who emulate Aldo Leopold in their desire to be a part of nature, filling a role that they consider to be much like that of a nonhuman predator. Nature hunters include a greater proportion of women compared with other categories and are, on average, more likely to be college educated and to engage in nonconsumptive wildlife activities such as wildlife watching or hiking (Kellert

1980). Kellert (1996) estimates that nature hunters make up 10 to 20 percent of all hunters in the United States. Another category, "meat hunters," includes those whose primary motivation for hunting is obtaining food. These hunters are more likely than nature hunters to be older and male and to live in rural areas. Meat hunters, according to Kellert (1996), make up around 40 percent of all hunters. Of course, most of Kellert's meat hunters are not true subsistence hunters in that they do not depend upon meat obtained in this way to survive. It is conceivable that some meat hunters use the meat of the animals they kill as a source of protein in much the same way that they would use farm animals; however, it is likely that the use of wild meat as a substitute for farm animals is decreasing in the United States. Finally, "sport hunters," who account for around one-third of all hunters, hunt primarily for recreation rather than for food or to be close to nature. These hunters primarily cite reasons for hunting that are related to social companionship and a chance for competition. Sport hunters differ from nature hunters in that they tend not to have exceptional knowledge regarding wildlife. Moreover, unlike meat hunters, they are less concerned for the usefulness of the animals they kill (e.g., for meat). Hunting purely to obtain a trophy is included in this category (Kellert 1980; Kellert 1996). Other studies have generally supported these or similar categorizations (e.g., Brown et al. 1987; Allen 1988; but see Causey 1989). Some authors suggest that a temporal progression often occurs in a given individual's motives for hunting that essentially leads from a sport hunter perspective to one of a nature hunter (e.g., Decker et al. 1987). Others suggest that, when changes in attitude occur over a hunter's lifetime, this often can be characterized as an increase in specialization, in terms of either the species hunted or the hunting method employed (e.g., Bryan 1979; Ditton, Loomis, and Choi 1992). Some of the more specialized

Data and Observations on Duck Hunting in the United States

For nearly a century, wildlife managers have pointed to waterfowl conservation, an ambitious effort designed to preserve an abundance of ducks across the length and breadth of a continent, as the crown jewel of North American wildlife management.

It began in 1916 with the signing of the North American Migratory Bird Treaty between the United States and Canada. A second treaty with Mexico in 1936 extended these protections south of the Rio Grande. This allowed each North American nation to ban the commercial sale of wild waterfowl and restrict the sport kill to prevent over-shooting.

A second initiative began in the 1930s when severe drought seized the northern prairies, the major breeding ground of North America's continental flocks. Duck populations plummeted. This prompted a drive to protect breeding wetlands in both the northern United States and prairie Canada. Protection of breeding grounds was accompanied by the establishment of waterfowl refuges across the middle and southern United States to provide wintering habitat and give ducks a measure of protection from hunters. The protection was accomplished via both public and private efforts that continue to this day.

But it was not until the latter half of the twentieth century that the focus shifted to attempts to develop a scientific management approach, based on data collection and mathematical analysis.

The 1950s witnessed the first continental surveys of the breeding and wintering grounds. The breeding grounds extend from South Dakota northward across the Canadian Prairie provinces and boreal forest to the Beaufort Sea. The wintering grounds extend across the middle latitude and southern United States into Mexico.

These surveys were (and are still today) unprecedented in scope. Although they are still incomplete, they represent the longest-running continental wildlife surveys in the world. The breeding-ground survey tallies eleven species—mallards, northern pintails, gadwalls, shovelers, wigeon, green-winged teal, blue-winged teal, canvasbacks, redheads, and scaup (both lesser and greater). The survey data are the basis for the government analysis used to judge whether populations are

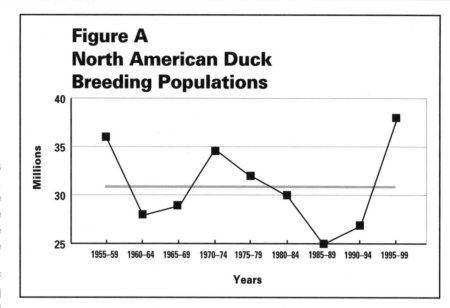

Figure A
North American Duck Breeding Populations

Figure A.

The number of ducks counted each spring across the North American waterfowl breeding grounds has remained essentially stable during the years 1955–2000, as shown by the solid trend line. The populations are five-year averages (Wilkins and Otto 2002).

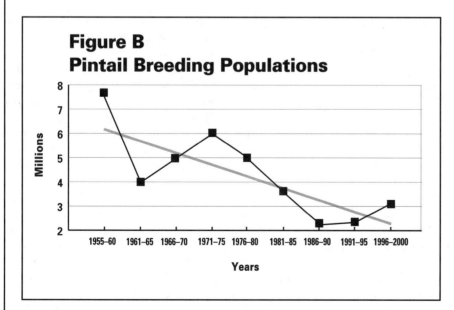

Figure B
Pintail Breeding Populations

Figure B.

The northern pintail, once the second most abundant North American duck, has dropped from an average population of 7.4 million in 1955–1960 to 3.0 million in 1996–2000, a 59 percent decline according to the plotted trend line (Wilkins and Otto 2002).

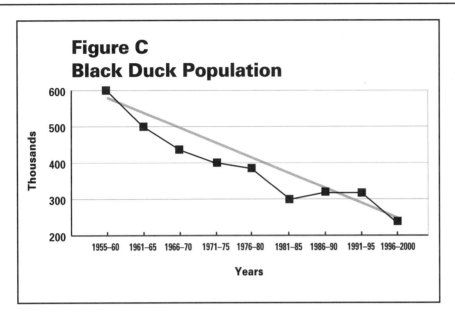

Figure C
Black Duck Population

Thousands (y-axis): 200, 300, 400, 500, 600

Years (x-axis): 1955–60, 1961–65, 1966–70, 1971–75, 1976–80, 1981–85, 1986–90, 1991–95, 1996–2000

Figure C.
Wintering-ground surveys disclose that the average number of black ducks has fallen from 603,000 in 1955–1960 to 274,000 in 1996–2000, a decline of 56 percent (Fronczak 2002).

breeding-ground survey suggests that, despite weather-related population fluctuations, the overall numbers of ducks have remained essentially stable in the past half-century.

Critics argue that the monolithic "total-duck" argument avoids the central issue of whether wildlife managers have really learned how to manipulate waterfowl populations. They point to declining numbers of those species most prized by hunters—northern pintails, black ducks, scaup, and mallards—as evidence that management is not achieving what it claims. Some indication of the trend line for duck populations from the late 1800s through the early 1900s might have helped support or refute management claims. Unfortunately, no data are available prior to the 1950s.

Two primary causes for the pintail's losses are given by wildlife managers—the loss of short-grass prairie nesting habitat on the western plains and overshooting, especially in recent years.

Unlike prairie-nesting species, the black duck has not suffered extensive loss of its eastern-forest nesting habitat. Its decline is attributed largely to

increasing or decreasing.

In 1961 biologists began gathering additional data designed to give them greater insight into the population dynamics of various species. These data include counts of nesting potholes on the northern-prairie breeding grounds; age-ratios of ducks taken by hunters (which index annual reproductive success); numbers of hunters; and the number of each species killed by hunters. In addition, a number of ducks each year are captured and fitted with leg bands. When hunters return these bands, the data are used for statistical estimates of annual mortality from natural causes (disease, predation, etc.) and sport hunting.

These data are designed to allow biologists to create a population model that will allow waterfowl managers to predict and control numbers of ducks. They permit wildfowl managers to make decisions, largely based on chang-

ing hunting regulations, that should lead to an increase in the breeding population of a species in decline or to a reduction in the numbers of an overabundant species.

However, the enormous amounts of data have not yet led to a general agreement on what determines spring breeding success and whether changing hunting regulations have any significant impact (see Grandy 1983).

Those who assert that waterfowl management has succeeded in maintaining an abundance of waterfowl cite as evidence the overall breeding-ground counts. A look at the average numbers of all species counted during the spring

Figure D.
Biologists remain baffled over the decline of scaup, medium-sized diving ducks whose populations have dropped from an average of 6.4 million in the period 1976–1980 to 4 million in the period 1995–2000, a decline of 38 percent (Wilkins and Otto 2002). The primary cause of their decline remains unknown, although some believe over-shooting in the 1970s and early 1980s played a significant role (Allen et al. 1999).

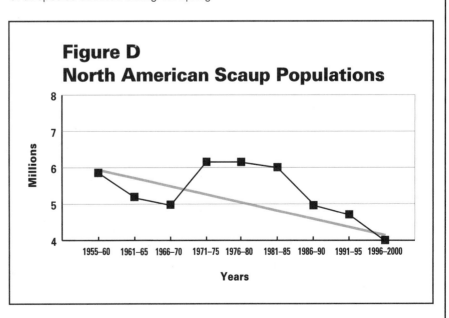

Figure D
North American Scaup Populations

Millions (y-axis): 4, 5, 6, 7, 8

Years (x-axis): 1955–60, 1961–65, 1966–70, 1971–75, 1976–80, 1981–85, 1986–90, 1991–95, 1996–2000

Continued from previous page

over-shooting, although some argue that mallards have displaced black ducks from portions of their range.

Restrictive hunting regulations have been imposed for nearly a quarter-century, but these restrictions have not allowed the species to rebuild its numbers. In recent years, in spite of the low population levels, hunting regulations have been liberalized, permitting an even greater kill of black ducks by hunters. A detailed analysis and critique are provided in Grandy (1983).

The remaining species—gadwall, shovelers, wigeon, green-winged teal, and blue-winged teal—make up approximately another 12 million wildfowl but have not been subjected to much analysis.

Half a century of data collection and associated scientific analysis does not appear to have brought the authorities much closer to their goal of understanding the factors affecting duck populations.

The debates continue unabated. Some blame the loss or degradation of northern-prairie breeding habitat. However, no study has shown that all available nesting habitat for any species is filled to capacity. Indeed, the evidence suggests—and several studies have found—that there is more habitat than ducks to occupy it, especially for mallards and pintails (Bethke and Nudds 1995). However, few studies have attempted to determine the carrying capacity of available nesting habitat in the northern prairies or whether carry-

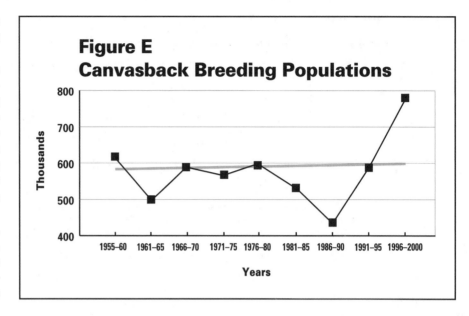

Figure E
Canvasback Breeding Populations

Figure E.

The beleaguered canvasback, once the most celebrated duck in North America, has so far not responded to a forty-year effort to increase its breeding numbers, although the last ten years have produced an upward trend. This increase may not continue because hunting of this species was closed in the 2002 season when breeding numbers dropped to 487,000 (Wilkins and Otto 2002).

hunters may include those who come to rely on those gadgets to which Leopold (1966) was so opposed (Peyton 2000), which would seem to disqualify them from the ranks of nature hunters.

Evidence of the divisions among general types of hunters also has been manifested in criticisms directed toward hunters by their peers, or by other writers who generally support hunting. For example, Williams (1986) sharply criticizes hunters who shoot the pheasants who are raised in captivity and released by state wildlife agencies to provide a put-and-take (i.e., release and kill) recreational hunting opportunity. Williams questions the ethic—on the part of both the pheasant shooters and the wildlife managers—in promoting this artificial type of hunting experience involving the killing of half-tame non-native

birds, sometimes within forty-eight hours of their release. Other authors have expressed concern over the ethics of some hunting activities, and what the activities mean for the future of what they consider legitimate forms of hunting. Peyton (2000, 777), for example, criticized some hunters' "overzealous attitudes toward wildlife as a crop," such as those individuals who frequent game farms that resemble a "barnyard" more than a hunting opportunity.

Similarly, Peyton states that landowners in Michigan (and elsewhere) who feed free-ranging deer have essentially created game farms without fences. Varmint hunters, who shoot ground squirrels, prairie dogs, and other rodents, often purely for sport, are sometimes viewed by other types of hunters as "wasteful" or otherwise unethical. Teel, Krannich, and

Schmidt (2002) found that, although a majority of Utah hunters approve of cougar and black bear hunting (66 percent and 57 percent approval, respectively), most hunters (64 percent) disapprove of the practice of bear baiting. This study also indicates that a surprising number of hunters in Utah have negative views toward the use of hounds to hunt predators: one-third of Utah hunters disapprove of the use of hounds to hunt cougars and nearly half oppose the use of hounds to hunt black bears.

In a similar vein, some authors assert that hunters often display opinions and behaviors that are not in the best interests of conservation or the environment, despite the prevailing claim to the contrary by modern-day hunters. In particular, Holsman (2000) reviews several studies from the 1990s indicating that hunters at

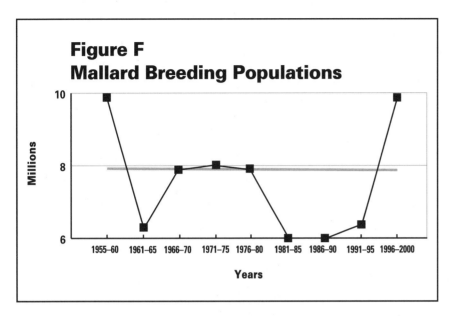

Figure F
Mallard Breeding Populations

Millions (y-axis): 6, 8, 10

Years (x-axis): 1955–60, 1961–65, 1966–70, 1971–75, 1976–80, 1981–85, 1986–90, 1991–95, 1996–2000

Figure F.
The population of the mallard, North America's most abundant and adaptable duck, has essentially been stable over the last fifty years (Wilkins and Otto 2002). The data indicate that mallards are holding their own in the face of heavy shooting pressures and agricultural degradation of the northern-prairie breeding grounds.

ing capacity in this region has been reached.

Some blame increasing predation on nests and nesting hens for the failure of some species to rebuild their numbers. But losses to natural predators generally affect only duck populations that are declining for other reasons, such as over-hunting or habitat loss (Côté and Sutherland 1997). These losses may be alleviated by reducing the kill of hens by human hunters but, to date, this has been attempted only for the mallard.

The data represent a continuing challenge for wildlife management and modern-day duck hunting in the United States. Regulators have long since concluded that duck hunters will not go "afield" (i.e., to shoot) if they are unable to shoot enough ducks to make it worth their while. Therefore, in most areas, hunters can kill a "basic bag" of six ducks. To that they can add up to five mergansers ("fish-eating" ducks) and fifteen coots. However, mergansers and coots are rarely if ever eaten (one of the justifications given for duck shooting).

The data gathered over the past fifty years continue to challenge the assumptions and premises upon which wildfowl management is based. For those who appreciate the beauty of ducks and the joy of watching them undisturbed, modern waterwildfowl management is, to date, more of a failure than a success.

—John W. Grandy

that time were among those *least* likely to support conservation of biodiversity or an emphasis on management of endangered species; according to these studies, hunters also were least likely to engage in environmentally responsible behaviors. Williams (1986) and Holsman (2000) both cite examples of hunters and hunters' associations opposing attempts to restore native wildlife to regions from which they have been extirpated, especially wolves and other predators. More recently the U.S. Sportsmen's Alliance has opposed efforts to end bear baiting and to restrict the release of pen-raised non-native pheasants.

Other outdoor recreation enthusiasts, such as bird watchers, may be more likely to support such goals, either by volunteering their time or through financial contributions

(Theodori, Luloff, and Willits 1998; see also McFarlane and Boxall 1996 for evidence of bird watchers' willingness to contribute to conservation). Wildlife protection advocates also are demonstrating their willingness to protect habitat. For example The Humane Society of the United States Wildlife Land Trust, an affiliate of The HSUS, has grown steadily since its inception in 1993 to encompass sixty thousand acres in twenty one U.S. states and four countries outside of the United States. The Wildlife Land Trust is one of a growing number of organizations that seek to protect wildlife, not only through habitat protection but also by prohibiting hunting and trapping in protected sanctuaries.

Hunting and Shooting in the United Kingdom

"Hunting" versus "Shooting"

In the United Kingdom, the term *hunting* generally refers to the use of dogs—hounds, fast coursing dogs, and sometimes terriers—in a hunt; it does not include the use of retrieving dogs or pointers, which neither pursue nor kill the quarry. Typically hounds chase the fox, deer, hare, or other animal and humans follow on horseback, on foot, or in vehicles. The term *shooting*, on the other hand, is used in the United Kingdom to describe the use of a rifle or shotgun to kill foxes, deer, or other animals and does not involve the use of dogs for pursuit.

In the case of fox hunting as defined above, despite wide variation, the average pursuit lasts half an hour (Macdonald and Johnson 1996; Masters of Foxhounds Association [MFHA] 2000), and about 75 percent of foxes found during a mounted hunt evade capture (n=149 hunts, data, 1990–1996). On average, 64 percent of fox kills are made by the hounds. In 30 to 40 percent of cases where a fox is killed (by any means) during a mounted hunt, a terrier is used either to kill the fox underground or to locate it or flush it out so it can be killed by hounds or shot. In the United Kingdom, packs of foxhounds, occupying largely non-overlapping territories, are registered with the Masters of Foxhounds Association. In common British usage, each of these is referred to as a *Hunt*. (The proper noun distinguishes these organizations from a *hunt*, the common noun referring to a particular chase. Internationally, this usage can be ambiguous, so here we refer to each "club"— a word that itself would have different connotations in this context in Great Britain—as a "pack of foxhounds.") However there is enormous variation among packs of foxhounds: some dig out no foxes, while in others up to 86 percent of fox kills are dug out by terriers, having gone underground after being pursued (Macdonald et al. 2000). Digging to reach the fox and/or fighting between fox and terrier underground may last from ten minutes to three hours (Phelps, Allen, and Harrop 1997). This activity is not considered to be part of hunting "proper." From an anthropological perspective, at "this point hunting has ceased and vermin control takes over" (Marvin 2000, 195). Indeed, MFHA rules stipulate that those out hunting may not participate in digging to reach a fox.

In a deer hunt, the average overall time for a deer to be successfully hunted, brought to bay, and killed is around three hours, though hunts can go on for up to six hours (Bateson 1997). More than 80 percent of hinds are pregnant during the hind hunting season (Langbein 1997); the extent of abortions among hinds that escape the hounds is not known. More than half of the deer roused and hunted escape without being brought to bay (Masters of Deerhounds Association 2000). Once the deer has been brought to bay or has stopped running and attempting to escape, it normally is killed by a shot at close quarters with a modified shotgun, pistol, or, under some circumstances, a humane killer (a captive bolt pistol used from extremely short range). Staghounds are trained to surround the deer and bark at the end of the hunt, and should not attack or savage the deer, although Bradshaw and Bateson (2000) report attacks by dogs in one out of four deer kills observed. Hunting deer to hounds is now restricted almost entirely to one small part of England lying within West Somerset and North Devon.

Hares are hunted with dogs either using packs of hounds, or by coursing in competitions or on an ad hoc basis. With packs of hounds, a hunt usually lasts for an hour to an hour and a half, and only an estimated 5 percent of hares sighted are killed (Association of Masters of Harriers and Beagles 2000). During organized competition coursing, dogs are not released until the hare is at least 80 meters away; the hare must be "in a fit condition"; nothing must hinder the hare's escape; and it must have "sufficient knowledge" of the ground (National Coursing Club 2000). An average greyhound course lasts 35 to 40 seconds, and an average of 13 percent of the hares chased are killed, either by the dogs or by human "pickers-up," the latter of whom have a duty to ensure that hares are killed quickly and humanely (National Coursing Club 2000). There are no data on the extent or nature of ad hoc coursing, which often is associated with illegal gambling and use of land without the owner's permission.

Although it has attracted a much lower level of public controversy than has hunting with dogs in the United Kingdom, and access to guns is regulated heavily, shooting is widespread and is probably the predominant means of wildlife culling (Macdonald et al. 2000). Shooting by stalking with a rifle or large bore shotgun is the most common method used to cull deer in England and Wales, as well as in Scotland and Northern Ireland (British Association for Shooting and Conservation 2000; British Deer Society 2000). Shooting, particularly as part of organized Deer Management Groups (groups of adjoining landholders coordinating their deer management), is the method of deer control recommended by government (MAFF 2000). From its 1996 survey, the British Association for Shooting and Conservation (BASC) estimated that 10,000 of its members were active deer stalkers. Of these, 87.6 percent (8,700) were "recreational" stalkers, and 12.4 percent (1,300) were "professional" deer stalkers who accounted for 40 percent of the total deer cull.

One part of the debate surrounding the hunting of foxes with dogs in the United Kingdom is whether it is more or less humane than shooting. Supporters of hunting argue that shooting leaves wounded foxes to die long, lingering deaths and that shooting would necessarily increase should hunting be banned. An alternative view is that foxes killed by shooting die quickly and painlessly, without the distress of the chase and capture. Foxes are shot mainly either at night with a spotlight and rifle (known as "lamping") or during the day by groups or individuals, sometimes at the cubbing den (or "earth"). Gun packs and shooting at earths may combine shooting with the use of dogs to find, bolt, or flush out foxes. Research commissioned by the All Party Parliamentary Middle Way Group (Fox et al. 2003) formed the first experimental attempt to address the humaneness of shooting foxes. The research used colored cut-out fox silhouettes as targets to assess the penetration, kill rate, and wounding rate of fifty-one different shooting

Table 3
Responses of Urban Dwellers and Farmers Regarding the Acceptance and Need for Fox Control

Questions	Urban Respondents (percent in agreement)	Rural Respondents (percent in agreement)
Where do foxes need to be controlled?		
In the country?	47.7	73.9
In towns?	61.9	70.7
Why do foxes need to be controlled?		
To control disease?	56.6	45.7
To protect livestock?	48.7	67.6
To protect game species?	14.4	44.5
Foxes too numerous	21.1	65.1
Do you approve of fox control for these reasons?		
To improve shooting?	6.7	42.0
For pelts?	3.3	16.8
For sport with hounds?	11.8	68.4
Do you approve of active conservation of foxes?	46.0	19.3

Source: Macdonald and Newdick (1978). Results are based on a questionnaire distributed to 14,000 households in Oxford, England, of which 3,468 (26 percent) were returned the following day. The differences between urban and rural respondents were statistically significant overall: $X^2_{(1)} > 23$, $P<0.0001$.

regimes, including different shot sizes and user competencies. Fox wounding rates increased significantly when No. 6 shot was used in shotguns, due to poor penetration, but the use of BB shot minimized wounding rates. Experienced shooters using correctly zeroed rifles achieved a high kill rate. While studies such as this can point to ways of making culling more humane, it remains extremely difficult to compare different types of suffering. Welfare science is advancing rapidly in this respect; for example, McLaren et al. (in press) have recently described a measure of stress based on leucocyte competency that can provide rapid results in the field.

Attitudes toward Hunting/Shooting in the United Kingdom

There have been few studies examining attitudes of either the general public or landowners toward hunting and shooting. Those that do exist have occurred largely in response to public concern over mounted fox-hunting, therefore this section focus-es largely on culling of foxes, the most abundant mammalian carnivore in the United Kingdom. Although both include a significant element of sport, hunting and shooting in the United Kingdom often are justified in terms of their contribution to pest control (Burns et al. 2000). When questioned, however, neither farmers nor members of the public necessarily consider either method—especially hunting with dogs—to be acceptable or effective for wildlife damage reduction or sport.

For example, in a public opinion poll of 801 adults throughout Great Britain regarding fox hunting, 63 percent of respondents either supported or strongly supported a ban on hunting foxes with dogs. Most people (69 percent) disagreed with the statement that fox hunting is a necessary means of preserving the balance of wildlife in the countryside; more rural (39 percent) than urban (20 percent) respondents considered fox hunting to be necessary (Macdonald et al. 2000). As in the United States, urban residents appear less likely than farmers to find culling of foxes by any method to be acceptable. In a questionnaire-based study, Macdonald and Newdick (1982) found that urban dwellers were much less likely to state that foxes needed to be controlled and were less likely to state that any of the listed motives for culling was acceptable (Table 3). Urban dwellers were also more likely to approve of the active conservation of foxes. Upbringing appears to play a role in attitudes toward fox hunting and other forms of fox control: respondents raised in the country were significantly more likely to favor fox control in the countryside (53 percent) than were those brought up in the city (46 percent).

Baker and Macdonald (2000) asked farmers in the county of Wiltshire to say which, among a list of non-exclusive options, were their principal motivations for hunting. All respondents opted for "recreation," while 55 percent said "to control foxes as a pest." Farmers' perceptions and practice of hunting and shooting are likely to be colored by the extent to which they consider target species to be a pest, the extent to which they

Table 4
Farmers' Attitudes toward Hunting on Their Land, according to Enterprise, "Pest" Status, whether Gameshooting Took Place, or the Farmer Himself Hunted[1]

	Encourage Hunting	Tolerate Hunting	Discourage Hunting	Disallow Hunting	
All Farms (n=97)	30.9	50.5	12.4	6.2	
Dairy (n=63) N.S.	23.8	55.6	14.3	6.4	
Non-Dairy Stock (n=13)	53.9	30.8	7.7	7.7	N.S.
Mixed (n=16)	31.3	50.0	12.5	6.3	
Arable (n=5)	60.0	40.0	0.0	0.0	
"Pest" Farms[2] (n=25)	40.0	56.0	4.0	0.0	X^2=4.68
"Non-Pest" Farms (n=52)	26.9	50.0	17.3	5.8	P=0.094
Game-shooting Farms (n=31)	41.9	48.4	9.7	0.0	X^2=3.76
Non-Game-shooting Farms (n=66)	25.8	51.5	13.6	9.1	P=0.052
Hunting Farmer (n=12)	66.7	33.3	0.0	0.0	Fisher's Exact, P=0.036
Non-Hunting Farmer (n=63)	23.8	55.5	15.9	4.8	

Numbers shown are percentages of farmers who encouraged, tolerated, discouraged, or disallowed hunting.

[1]Some farms comprised Council Farms on which the farmer surveyed was a tenant and may not have had control over whether or not hunting occurred on his land.

[2]Pest status indicates whether a given farmer considered the fox to be a pest.

Source: Baker and Macdonald (2000)

themselves hunt or shoot for sport, and the extent to which they believe a method to be humane and effective for pest control (Macdonald and Johnson 2002).

Mounted fox hunting occurs over about two-thirds of England and Wales (Macdonald et al. 2000), but a farmer allowing hunting on his land does not necessarily see it as part of a strategy for fox control. For example, in the English county of Wiltshire, only 31 percent of farmers encouraged the hunt; 6 percent did not allow it and 63 percent "tolerated" or "discouraged" it (Table 4) (Baker and Macdonald 2000). The high proportion of tenant farmers, and the retention of sporting rights (Parkes and Thornley 1994) by the local authority (Wiltshire County Farms Estate), may create this complex situation in Wilt-

shire. In 1995 the sporting rights on 88 (73 percent) of the local authority's 120 farms had been retained by the local authority, and fox hunting was automatically permitted regardless of the farmer's wishes. In a questionnaire survey of gamekeepers, slightly fewer than half (48 percent) of 203 respondents (persons employed on shooting estates) cited hunting with dogs as one of the methods they used to cull foxes (National Gamekeepers' Organisation 2000). Arable farmers (those who raise food crops but not livestock) are less likely than those with game birds or livestock, especially more vulnerable animals such as chickens, to consider the fox a pest on their farm, although most farmers consider the fox to be a pest in the wider sense (Baker and Macdonald 2000; Heydon and

Reynolds 2000a).

Two questionnaire surveys, one covering 859 farmers from ten regions in England in 1981 (Macdonald and Johnson 1996) and the other covering 72 farmers in Wiltshire in 1995 (Baker and Macdonald 2000), have assessed whether farmers believe different methods of fox control are "humane." In both surveys and all regions, shooting was consistently considered the most humane method of fox control (69 percent overall in 1981, 58 percent in 1995; Table 5); in 1995 49 percent considered it effective as well as humane. In 1981 a high proportion of farmers believed both hunting with hounds (55 percent overall), and gassing (49 percent) to be humane; in Wiltshire in 1995, however, only 29 percent believed gassing was humane, although more than half still thought hunting with hounds humane. Macdonald et al. (2000) investigated whether these farmers' judgments regarding the humaneness of different methods, and the justification of different motives, were influenced by damage they had sustained that they attributed to foxes, and by the field sports in which they participated. In Wiltshire the proportion of farmers who considered each method to be humane did not vary significantly from the proportion who had, and had not, designated the fox a pest on their farms (Baker and Macdonald 2000). However, more farmers reporting actual stock loss to foxes in the previous year said hunting was humane compared with those who did not. This contrasts with findings in 1981 (Macdonald and Johnson 1996), which suggested that farmers were more likely to think shooting, snaring, poisoning, or the use of terriers humane if they had suffered losses to foxes, but that their opinions of hunting and gassing were not affected. The differences between these studies could reflect regional variation,

changes since 1980, or the smaller sample size in the Wiltshire study.

According to 1981 data, farmers who reported that they had sustained damage by foxes were more likely to say that killing foxes to improve pheasant shooting or for fur were acceptable motives (Table 6). Damage had no effect on the likelihood of farmers approving the active conservation of foxes. Hunting farmers were less likely to say that shooting and gassing were humane and more likely to state that digging with terriers was humane. Paradoxically, farmers who considered hunting to be a form of pest control were also more likely to approve of the active conservation of foxes. This may be because hunting farmers are more likely both to cite pest control as a rationale for the sport and to want foxes to persist in the locality of a pack of foxhounds.

In the United Kingdom as a whole, 75 percent of farmers (including those who did not consider foxes a problem on their farms) said they would instruct their member of Parliament (M.P.) to vote for "no

change" in the legislation governing fox hunting (Produce Studies, Ltd. 1995; n = 831); 11 percent said they would instruct their M.P. to vote for a ban on foxhunting; while 14 percent held no strong view. Regionally, those in favor of no change varied between 86 percent (southwest England) and 56 percent (Scotland). Those in favor of a ban varied between 6 percent (southwest England) and 26 percent (Scotland).

Hunting/Shooting and Wildlife Damage Reduction

The motives for culling wildlife in the United Kingdom are not always clear-cut, and different groups of people take contrasting views on the desirability of certain motivations. For example, the only way to prevent local extinction of some populations of water voles, a species native to Britain, is to remove (de facto, to kill) American mink, an introduced species. Conservationists may see this as a regrettable necessity, whereas

Table 5
Percentage of English Farmers Replying "Yes" When Asked Whether They Believed a Method Was Effective or Humane in Controlling Foxes

Control Methods	Wiltshire County (1995 study) n=72, except hunting and snaring, n=71		10 Regions in England (1981 study) n=859	
	Effective	Humane	Effective	Humane
Shooting	62.5	58.3	68.8	68.8
Hunting	54.9	52.1	43.7	54.8
Gassing[1]	38.9	29.2	61.0	49.2
Poisoning[1]	22.2	8.3	41.2	8.3
Terriers/digging	19.4	9.7	34.2	23.0
Snaring	7.0	1.4	39.1	13.2

Adapted from Baker and Macdonald (2000); Macdonald and Johnson (2000, 2003).

[1]Gassing was made illegal in 1987, poisoning in 1963.

Table 6
The Effect of Fox Damage and Hunting Participation on the Perceived Humaneness of Different Control Methods

	Fox Damage?		Farmer Hunts?		Farmer Shoots?	
	No	Yes	No	Yes	No	Yes
Motive						
Protect pheasants	35.3	56.5	43.8	39.5	22.9	62.8
For fur	12.8	25.1	18.9	12.2	12.7	22.1
Humaneness						
Shooting	70.7	77.3	80.5	59.1	76.4	77.4
Gassing	48.8	62.0	59.9	38.7	56.6	64.1
Snaring	9.1	24.6	14.3	13.4	11.4	18.3
Hunting	59.0	59.3	41.4	91.2	44.0	44.0
Poisoning	17.4	32.6	24.2	36.5	24.2	28.9
Terriers	21.2	34.8	19.1	36.5	21.3	36.1

Percentage of respondents approving of the motive or stating that the control method is humane

welfarists may not. Another recent example in the United Kingdom is the proposed cull of introduced hedgehogs from Scottish islands where they threaten endangered seabirds. In general, however, the two major reasons people hunt or shoot in the United Kingdom are, first, to control wild mammal populations that are believed to damage livestock, game birds, or crops and, second, for sport (Macdonald et al. 2000). Conflicting management aims therefore arise, particularly for species such as hares and some deer, which are simultaneously considered pests, game species, and quarry, and are of conservation concern.

Although damage reduction is a frequently cited motive and justification for hunting and shooting in the United Kingdom, there are few comparative assessments of the effectiveness of different control methods in the literature for any mammalian species. Assessing effectiveness is complicated by a lack of data pertaining to cull levels (as there is no obligation to report numbers killed) and to population sizes (monitoring is largely absent or rudimentary); by the lack of coherent management goals and strategies over areas larger than individual estates or farms; and by the fundamental difficulty in assessing the extent of damage attributable to any one species. Nevertheless such studies as there are for foxes have generally found that the population impact of hunting and shooting is small (Phillips et al. 1972; Hewson and Kolb 1973; Storm et al. 1976; Harris 1977; Macdonald 1980; Hewson 1986; Voigt 1987; Wandeler 1988; Baker, Harris, and Webbon 2002), though, in some upland areas of the United Kingdom, hunting may contribute more substantially to fox mortality (Heydon and Reynolds 2000a,b). Macdonald et al. (2000) estimated that registered mounted foxhunts, together with upland foot and gun packs, probably take a cull in the region of 21,500 to 25,000; this represents perhaps 4 percent of annual fox mortality in the United Kingdom. There are no U.K.-wide data regarding numbers of any mammal shot. However in three regions of England, the proportion of the fox cull taken by methods involving shooting was 46 percent, 62 percent, and 68 percent, in mid-Wales, east Midlands, and west Norfolk, respectively, while that taken by methods involving dogs (some of which also involved shooting) was 73 percent, 18 percent, and 11 percent for the same three regions, respectively (Heydon and Reynolds 2000a,b; Heydon, Reynolds, and Short 2000). Attempts to model the effects of hunting with hounds further suggest that this method, by itself, has little impact on the abundance of foxes at a national or regional level. Shooting is more likely to effectively reduce populations regionally, provided that it takes place over a high proportion of the region (Macdonald et al. 2000). In addition to human-induced mortality, fox populations appear to be regulated by density-dependent effects on reproductive output, likely as a result of food availability and social (stress-mediated) suppression of reproduction (e.g., Macdonald et al. 2000; Heydon and Reynolds 2000b).

Stag hunting kills, on average, 228 red deer per year, roughly 13 to 17 percent of the total cull required to prevent further population increases within the stag hunting area. Shooting with a rifle kills at least 1,000 per year (Macdonald et al. 2000). Shooting is the most common method to control population numbers of all six of the deer species present in Britain, as well as in most other countries throughout Europe and in North America, though it is not clear the extent to which human-induced mortality may be compensatory with other sources of mortality. The total annual red and roe deer mortalities due to shooting during 1995–1996 in six countries of Western Europe were 110,000 and 1,750,000, respectively (Deutscher Jadgschutz Verband 1997). Macdonald et al. (2000) calculate that, as a percentage of the pre-breeding population (Harris et al. 1995), shooting kills approximately 14 to 20 percent of red deer, 29 to 40 percent of fallow deer, and 16 to 22.5 percent of roe deer. These estimated percentages fall within the range of human-induced mortality thought to be necessary to contain population increase, provided that population sizes are not greatly underestimated. There are no data on the extent to which population control is reflected in damage control.

Macdonald et al. (2000) concluded that, for deer, foxes, mink, and hares, hunting with dogs is generally less effective than alternative methods of population and damage control, with the possible exception of the use of terriers to control foxes in upland areas. The potential for non-lethal methods to mitigate the need for lethal control is at an early stage of exploration (Baker and Macdonald 1999).

Hunting and Shooting as Monitoring Tools

While there is no legal requirement for packs of hounds to record the number of foxes killed, MFHA packs record this information voluntarily and have proven willing to make it available for scientific scrutiny. In the context of monitoring in general in the United Kingdom, the use of voluntary contributions seems likely to continue to form an important component of the total endeavor. While the ecological importance of monitoring is reflected in national and international agreements, govern-

ment core-funding will not be adequate to supplant the need for voluntary involvement for the foreseeable future (Macdonald and Tattersall 2002). Some effort is now being applied to assessing the factors determining the efficiency of volunteers (e.g., Newman, Buesching, and Macdonald 2003).

Macdonald and Johnson (1996) analyzed a time series of approximately thirty years of cull data generated by MFHA packs, quantifying both regional differences and temporal trends; these were thought to reflect real patterns in fox abundance. The recent establishment (in 2000) in the United Kingdom of an Independent Supervisory Authority for Hunting (ISAH) has presented an opportunity to standardize and regulate the collection of these data and to ensure that all potentially useful data are recorded. Packs of hounds are now recording, where possible, the sex and age of culled foxes. Early returns suggest interesting and hitherto unrecognized patterns. For example of the approximately 6,000 foxes culled in the (at the time of writing, incomplete) 2002/2003 season, the sex ratio (male:female) as recorded for adults is approximately 2:1.

The commissioners of the ISAH (who include D.W.M.) have encouraged the MFHA to maximize their utility in monitoring a number of other species. These wildlife reports seem likely to yield some fascinating geographic patterns when subjected to close scrutiny. For example at a national level, we can already see that perceived trends in deer species differ markedly: the majority of respondents record that Roe and Muntjac deer are more abundant than they were ten years ago, while most record no change in fallow deer numbers.

The United Kingdom's Game Conservancy Trust has for some time made similar efforts to use shooting bags and gamekeeper records to study trends in pest and quarry species on large estates. Tapper (1992) gives an account of these data.

Hunting, Shooting and Habitat Preservation

In the United Kingdom, where much of the landscape is dominated by the effects of farming, the existence of hunting and shooting as sports activities may provide an incentive for the preservation and restoration of some habitat types. For example, mounted packs have traditionally managed woodland and copses as cover for foxes and maintained their hedgerows and dry stone walls to provide jumps for followers on horseback (where otherwise lower-maintenance wire fences, which are much less desirable from the biodiversity perspective, might have been substituted). Macdonald and Johnson (2000) used farmer questionnaire data to identify patterns in habitat management across different sporting interest groups in the 1970s and 1980s. They found that there was a tendency for hunting and shooting farmers to report having removed less hedgerow in the decade preceding the survey, particularly in the 1970s (rates of removal were everywhere much lower in the later period). There was also evidence that other non-productive habitats were better treated by these interest groups. Oldfield et al. (2003) have recently reported a similar result. Aerial photography and questionnaires showed that farms where hunting and shooting occurred had more woodland, and had planted more new woodland and hedgerow, than did farms where these activities were absent.

Conclusions

In both the United States and the United Kingdom, attitudes toward hunting—and toward animals in general—have changed in the past several decades. Interestingly, the public's acceptance of hunting, at least in the United States, is dependent largely on hunters' abilities to justify this activity for the sake of providing food, rather than merely as a sport; simultaneously, Americans' attitudes toward wildlife have become less utilitarian. If the emphasis on the non-utilitarian values of wildlife increases, the public may also increasingly question utilitarian motivations for hunting.

Mirroring the changing perception of hunting in the United States, participation there has declined steadily over the past twenty years. Though potentially constrained by a financial dependence on this dwindling population of hunters, professionals in wildlife management appear to be placing less importance on "producing" wildlife as a "crop." Instead, broader concepts from conservation biology are increasingly prominent in the profession, with management seeking to integrate the needs of non-game wildlife species.

Management of mammalian wildlife in the United Kingdom is minimally regulated in governmental terms and lacking in any cohesive national strategy. Culling, mainly for pest control and sport, occurs largely on private land and out of public view, and public debate regarding the acceptability of hunting and shooting revolves mainly around foxhunting and hunting with dogs in general. This is perhaps unfortunate, as it has deflected attention away from other issues relating to hunting and shooting. One issue, for example, that has received little attention outside the Scottish conservation community is the very large population of red deer in the Scottish Highlands (more than 350,000, up from 150,000 at the end of the nineteenth century). For many owners of large upland estates in Scotland, red deer are a significant financial asset, bringing revenue from stalking and venison. However, the current high deer numbers pose a problem to native woodland regeneration and moorland conservation, and there have been calls for widespread reductions in deer densities across the Scottish Highlands.

The science that should, and one hopes increasingly will, underpin policies relating to wildlife has been changing rapidly. Perceptions and policies are also changing fast, within a labile cultural framework. Even between such similar nations as the United States and Great Britain, there are substantial differences in this context, and such differences become immense when the discussion is generalized across the globe. However, our short and incomplete review of this enormous topic, notwithstanding its geographical restrictions, does reveal its inescapable inter-disciplinarity and the complex entanglements of fact and perception. Ultimately, society's judgments—and policies—on wildlife issues such as this will be heavily influenced by ethical considerations. However, these judgments, and the ethics that decide them, should be based on the clearest possible understanding of what is known factually, and an equally clear appreciation of what is not known.

Notes

[1]Limitations of space preclude a full discussion of the means by which wildlife damage may be reduced through either lethal or non-lethal means. See Henderson and Spaeth (1980), Robel et al. (1981), Baker and MacDonald (1999), and Knowlton, Gese, and Jaeger (1999) for a discussion of this issue.

Figures 1 and 3 are reprinted from *The Value of Life: Biological Diversity and Human Society*, by Stephen R. Kellert. Copyright ©1996 Island Press. Reprinted by permission of Island Press/Shearwater Books, Washington, D.C., and Covelo, California. Figures 2 and 4 copyright ©1996 from "Population Change and Its Implication for Wildlife Management in the New West: A Case Study in Colorado" by M.J. Manfredo and H.C. Zinn. Reproduced by permission of Taylor and Francis, Inc., *http://www.routledge-ny.-com*.

Literature Cited

Allen, S.A. 1988. Montana bioeconomics study: Results of the elk hunter preference study. Report prepared for Montana Department of Fish, Wildlife and Parks, Helena, Mont.

Allen, G.T., D.F. Caithamer, and M. Otto. 1999. *A review of the status of greater and lesser scaup in North America*. U.S. Fish and Wildlife Service, Office of Migratory Bird Management, Washington. D.C.

Applegate, J. 1991. Patterns of early desertion among New Jersey hunters. *Wildlife Society Bulletin* 17: 476–481.

Association of Masters of Harriers and Beagles. 2000. The hunting of the hare with hound, Joint submission to the Burns Inquiry by the Association of Masters of Harriers and Beagles (AMHB) and the Masters of Basset Hounds Association (MBHA). First round evidence submission to the Committee of Inquiry into Hunting with Dogs. On the CD accompanying the Report of the Committee of Inquiry into Hunting with Dogs, CM 4763 (by T. Burns, V. Edwards, J. Marsh, L. Soulsby, and M. Winter). Norwich: The Stationary Office.

Baker, P.J., S. Harris, and C.C. Webbon. 2002. Effect of British hunting ban on fox numbers. *Nature* 419: 34.

Baker, S.E., and D.W. Macdonald. 1999. Non-lethal predator control: Exploring the options. In *Advances in vertebrate pest management*, ed. D.P. Cowan and C.J. Feare, 251—266. Furth: Filander Verlag.

———. 2000. Foxes and foxhunting on farms in Wiltshire: A case study. *Journal of Rural Studies* 16: 185–201.

Bateson, P. 1997. The behavioural and physiological effects of culling red deer. London: Report to the Council of the National Trust.

Bethke, R.W., and T.D. Nudds. 1995. Effects of climate change and land use on duck abundance in Canadian Prairie-Parklands. *Ecological Applications* 5 (3): 588–600.

Bissell, S.J. 1993. Ethical issues in state wildlife policy: A qualitative analysis. Ph.D. diss., University of Colorado.

Bissell, S.J., M.D. Duda, and K.C. Young. 1998. Recent studies on hunting and fishing participation in the United States. *Human Dimensions of Wildlife* 3(1): 75–80.

Bolen, E.G. 2000. Waterfowl management: Yesterday and tomorrow. *Journal of Wildlife Management* 64(2): 323–335.

Bradshaw, E.L., and P. Bateson. 2000. Welfare implications of culling red deer (*Cervus elaphus*). *Animal Welfare* 9: 3–24.

British Association for Shooting and Conservation. 2000. First round evidence submission to the Committee of Inquiry into Hunting with Dogs. On the CD accompanying the Report of the Committee of Inquiry into Hunting with Dogs, CM 4763 (by T. Burns, V. Edwards, J. Marsh, L. Soulsby, and M. Winter). Norwich: The Stationary Office.

British Deer Society. 2000. First round evidence submission to the Committee of Inquiry into Hunting with Dogs. On the CD accompanying the Report of the Committee of Inquiry into Hunting with Dogs, CM 4763 (by T. Burns, V. Edwards, J. Marsh, L. Soulsby, and M. Winter). Norwich: The Stationary Office.

Brown, T.L., D.J. Decker, K.G. Purdy, and G.F. Mattfield. 1987. The future of hunting in New York. *Transactions of the North American Wildlife and Natural Resources Conference* 52: 553–566.

Bryan, H. 1979. *Conflict in the great outdoors: Toward understanding and managing for diverse sportmen preferences*, Bureau of Public Administration, Sociological Studies Series 4. Tuscaloosa: University of Alabama.

Burns, T., V. Edwards, J. Marsh, L. Soulsby, and M. Winter. 2000. Report of the Committee of Inquiry into Hunting with Dogs in England and Wales. London: The Stationary Office, CM 4763.

Causey, A.S. 1989. On the morality of hunting. *Environmental Ethics* 11: 327–343.

Conover, M.R., and D.O. Conover. 1987. Wildlife management in colonial Connecticut and New Haven during their first century: 1636–1736. *Transactions of the Northeast Section of The Wildlife Society* 44: 1–7.

Côté, I.M., and W.J. Sutherland. 1997. The effectiveness of removing predators to protect bird populations. *Conservation Biology* 11 (2): 395–405.

Dasmann, R.F. 1964. *Wildlife biology.* New York: John Wiley and Sons.

Decker, D.J., R.W. Provencher, and T.L. Brown. 1984. *Antecedents to hunting participation: An exploratory study of the social-psychological determinants of initiation, continuation, and desertion in hunting.* Outdoor Recreation Research Unit Publication 84-6, Department of Natural Resources, New York State College of Agricultural and Life Sciences. Ithaca: Cornell University Press.

Decker, D.J., T.L. Brown, B.L. Driver, and P.J. Brown. 1987. Theoretical developments in assessing social values of wildlife: Toward a comprehensive understanding of wildlife recreation behavior. In *Valuing Wildlife: Economic and Social Perspectives*, ed. D.J. Decker and G.R. Goff, 76–95. Boulder: Westview Press.

Decker, D.J., T.L. Brown, N.A. Connelly, J.W. Enck, G.A. Pomerantz, K.G. Purdy, and W.F. Siemer. 1992. Toward a comprehensive paradigm of wildlife management: Integrating the human and biological dimensions. In *American fish and wildlife policy: The human dimension*, ed. W.R. Mangun, 33–54. Carbondale: Southern Illinois University Press.

Deutscher Jadgschutz Verband. 1997. *DJV Handbuch*. Verlag Deiter Hoffmann, Mainz.

Ditton, R.B., D.K. Loomis, and S. Choi. 1992. Recreation specialization: Re-conceptualization from a social world's perspective. *Journal of Leisure Research* 24(1): 33–51.

Duda, M.D. 1993. *Factors related to hunting and fishing participation in the United States. Phase I: Literature review.* Responsive Management.

Enck, J.W., D.J. Decker, and T.L. Brown. 2000. Status of hunter recruitment and retention in the United States. *Wildlife Society Bulletin* 28(4): 817–824.

Fox, N., S. Rivers, N. Blay, A.G. Greenwood, and D. Wise. 2003. *Welfare aspects of shooting foxes*. London: All Party Parliamentary Middle Way Group.

Fronczak, D. 2002. *Waterfowl harvest and population survey data.* Columbia, Mo.: U.S. Fish and Wildlife Service.

Fulton, D.C., J. Pate, and M.J. Manfredo. 1995. *Colorado residents' attitudes toward trapping in Colorado.* (Project Report No. 23). Project Report for the Colorado Division of Wildlife. Fort Collins, Colo.: Colorado State University, Human Dimensions in Natural Resources Unit.

Gill, R.M.A. 1990. *The Global Environment Monitoring System: Monitoring the status of European and North American cervids.* (Gems Information Series No. 8). Nairobi, Kenya: United Nations Environment Programme.

Grandy, J.W. 1983. The North American black duck (*Anas rubripes*): A case study of 28 years of failure in American wildlife management. *International Journal for the Study of Animal Problems, Supp.* (4): 1–35.

Harris, S. 1977. Distribution, habitat utilization and age structure of a suburban fox (*Vulpes vulpes*) population. *Mammal Review* 7: 25–39.

Harris, S., P. Morris, S. Wray, and D. Yalden. 1995. *A review of British mammals: Population estimates and conservation status of British mammals other than cetaceans.* Peterborough, England: Joint Nature Conservation Committee.

Heberlein, T.A., and E.J. Thomson. 1991. Socio-economic influences on declining hunter numbers in the United States 1977–1990. In *Transactions of the 20th Congress of the International Union Game Biologists*, ed. S. Csanyi and J. Erhnhaft, 699–705. Godollo, Hungary: University of Agricultural Sciences.

Henderson, F.R., and C.W. Spaeth. 1980. *Managing predator problems: Practices and procedures for preventing and reducing livestock losses.* Manhattan, Kan.: Cooperative Extension Service, Kansas State University.

Hewson, R. 1986. Distribution and density of fox (*Vulpes vulpes*) breeding dens and the effects of management. *Journal of Applied Ecology* 23: 531–538.

Hewson, R., and H.H. Kolb. 1973. Changes in the numbers and distribution of foxes (*Vulpes vulpes*) killed in Scotland from 1948–1970. *Journal of Zoology* 171: 345–365.

Heydon, M.J., and J.C. Reynolds. 2000a. Fox (*Vulpes vulpes*) management in three contrasting regions of Britain, in relation to agricultural and sporting interests. *Journal of Zoology, London* 251: 237–252.

———. 2000b. Demography of rural foxes (*Vulpes vulpes*) in relation to cull intensity in three contrasting regions of Britain. *Journal of Zoology, London* 251: 265–276.

Heydon, M.J., J.C. Reynolds, and M.J. Short. 2000. Variation in abundance of foxes (*Vulpes vulpes*) between three regions of rural Britain, in relation to landscape and other variables. *Journal of Zoology, London* 251: 253–264.

Holsman, R.H. 2000. Goodwill hunting? Exploring the role of hunters as ecosystem stewards. *Wildlife Society Bulletin* 28(4): 808–816.

Kellert, S.R. 1980. *Activities of the American public relating to animals.* Phase II of U.S. Fish and Wildlife Service Study. Washington, D.C.: Government Printing Office, 024-010-00-624-2.

———. 1988. Human-animal interactions: A review of American attitudes to wild and domestic animals in the twentieth century. In *Animals and People Sharing the World,* ed. A.N. Rowen, 137–175. Hanover, N.H.: Tufts University/University Press of New England.

———. 1996. *The value of life: Biological diversity and human society.* Washington, D.C.: Island Press.

Knowlton, F.F., E.M. Gese, and M.M. Jaeger. 1999. Coyote depredation control: An interface between biology and management. *Journal of Range Management* 52: 398–412.

Kohlberg, L. 1984. *The psychology of moral development.* San Francisco: Harper and Row.

Langbein, J. 1997. *The ranging behaviour, habitat-use, and impact of deer in oak woods and heather moors of Exmoor and the Quantock Hills.* Fordingbridge, England: British Deer Society.

Leopold, A. 1933. *Game management.* Madison: University of Wisconsin Press.

———. 1966. *A Sand County almanac and sketches here and there: With other essays on conservation from Round River.* New York: Oxford University Press.

Macdonald, D.W. 1980. Social factors affecting reproduction amongst red foxes (*Vulpes vulpes* L. 1758). *Biogeographica* 18: 123–175.

———. 1987. *Running with the fox.* London: Unwin Hyman.

Macdonald, D.W., and S.E. Baker. In press. Non-lethal control of fox predation: The potential of generalised aversion. *Animal Welfare.*

Macdonald, D.W., and P. Johnson. 1996. The impact of sport hunting: A case study. In *The exploitation of mammal populations,* ed. V. Taylor and N. Dunstone, 160–207. London: Chapman and Hall.

Macdonald, D.W., and P.J. Johnson. 2000. Farmers and the custody of the countryside: Trends in loss and conservation of non-productive habitats, 1981–1998. *Biological Conservation* 94(2): 221–234.

———. 2003. Farmers as conservation custodians: Links between perception and practice. In *Conservation and conflict: Mammals and farming in Britain,* ed. F.H. Tattersall and W.J. Manley. Yorkshire: Linnean Society Occasional Publication, Westbury Publishing.

Macdonald, D.W., and M.T. Newdick. 1982. The distribution and ecology of foxes, *Vulpes vulpes* (L.), in urban areas. The second European Symposium. In: *Urban Ecology,* ed.

R. Bornkamm, J.A. Lee, and M.R.D. Seaward, 123–137. New York: Halstead Press.

MacDonald, D.W., and F.H. Tattersall. 2002. *The state of Britain's mammals: 2002.* Oxford: WildCRU and Mammals Trust UK.

Macdonald, D.W., F.H. Tattersall, P.J. Johnson, C. Carbone, J. Reynolds, J. Langbein, S.P. Rushton, and M. Shirley. 2000. *Managing British mammals: Case studies from the hunting debate.* Oxford: WildCRU.

Manfredo, M.J., and H.C. Zinn. 1996. Population change and its implication for wildlife management in the New West: A case study in Colorado. *Human Dimensions of Wildlife* 1(3): 62–74.

Manfredo, M.J., D.C. Fulton, F. Ciruli, S. Cassin, J. Lipscomb, L. Skjorowski, and S. Norris. 1993. Summary of project report: Coloradoans' recreational uses of and attitudes toward wildlife. Summary of Project Report No. 6. Project Report for the Colorado Division of Wildlife. Fort Collins, Colo.: Colorado State University, Human Dimensions in Natural Resources Unit.

Mangun, J.C., D.A. Hall, and J.T. O'Leary. 1996. Desertion in the ranks: Recruitment and retention of sportsmen. *Transactions North American Wildlife and Natural Resources Conference* 61: 161–167.

Marvin, G. 2000. The problem of foxes: Legitimate and illegitimate killing in the English countryside. In *People and wildlife: Conflicts in anthropological perspective,* ed. J. Knight, London: Routledge.

Masters of Deerhounds Association. 2000. First round evidence submission to the Committee of Inquiry into Hunting with Dogs. On the CD accompanying the Report of the Committee of Inquiry into Hunting with Dogs, CM 4763 (by T. Burns, V. Edwards, J. Marsh, L. Soulsby, and M. Winter). Norwich: The Stationary Office.

Masters of Foxhounds Association. 2000. First round evidence submission to the Committee of Inquiry into Hunting with Dogs. On the CD accompanying the Report of the

Committee of Inquiry into Hunting with Dogs, CM 4763 (by T. Burns, V. Edwards, J. Marsh, L. Soulsby, and M. Winter). Norwich: The Stationary Office.

Matthews, B.E. 1993. Recruiting a new constituency for sportfishing and hunting in the 21st century. Northeast Wildlife. *Transactions of the Northeast Section of The Wildlife Society* 50: 159–166.

McFarlane, B.L., and P.C. Boxall. 1996. Participation in wildlife conservation by birdwatchers. *Human Dimensions of Wildlife* 1(3): 1–14.

McLaren, G.W., D.W. Macdonald, C. Georgiou, F. Mathews, C. Newman, and R. Mian. In press. Leukocyte coping capacity: A novel technique for measuring the stress response in vertebrates. *Journal of Experimental Physiology*.

Mighetto, L. 1991. *Wild animals and American environmental ethics.* Tucson: The University of Arizona Press.

Ministry of Agriculture, Fisheries, and Food (MAFF). 2000. First round evidence submission to the Committee of Inquiry into Hunting with Dogs. On the CD accompanying the Report of the Committee of Inquiry into Hunting with Dogs, CM 4763 (by T. Burns, V. Edwards, J. Marsh, L. Soulsby and M. Winter). Norwich: The Stationary Office.

Minnesota Department of Natural Resources. 1992. *Constituent inventory: What Minnesotans think about hunting, fishing, and native plant management.* St. Paul: Minnesota Department of Natural Resources, Division of Fish and Wildlife.

Muir, J. 1901. *Our national parks.* New York: Houghton Mifflin.

Muth, R.M., D.A. Hamilton, J.F. Organ, D.J. Witter, M.E. Mather, and J.J. Daigle. 1998. The future of wildlife and fisheries policy and management: Assessing the attitudes and values of wildlife and fisheries professionals. *Transactions of the North American Wildlife and Natural Resources Conference* 63: 604–627.

Myrberget, S. 1990. Wildlife management in Europe outside the Soviet Union. *Norsk Institut for Naturforskning Utredning* 18: 1–47.

National Coursing Club. 2000. Questions 2–17, First round evidence submission to the Committee of Inquiry into Hunting with Dogs. On the CD accompanying the Report of the Committee of Inquiry into Hunting with Dogs, CM 4763 (by T. Burns, V. Edwards, J. Marsh, L. Soulsby, and M. Winter). Norwich: The Stationary Office.

National Gamekeepers' Organisation. 2000. First round evidence submission to the Committee of Inquiry into Hunting with Dogs. On the CD accompanying the Report of the Committee of Inquiry into Hunting with Dogs, CM 4763 (by T. Burns, V. Edwards, J. Marsh, L. Soulsby, and M. Winter). Norwich: The Stationary Office.

Newman, C., D.D. Buesching, and D.W. Macdonald. 2003. Validating mammal monitoring methods and assessing the performance of volunteers in wildlife conservation: *Sed quis custodiet ipsos custodies.* *Biological Conservation* 113: 189–197.

Nichols, J.D., F.A. Johnson, and B.K. Williams. 1995. Managing North American waterfowl in the face of uncertainty. *Annual Review of Ecology and Systematics* 26: 177–199.

Oldfield, T.E.E., R.J. Smith, S.R. Harrop, and N. Leader-Williams. 2003. Field sports and conservation in the United Kingdom. *Nature* 423: 531–533.

Organ, J.F., and E.K. Fritzell. 2000. Trends in consumptive recreation and the wildlife profession. *Wildlife Society Bulletin* 28(4): 780–787.

Paquet, P., and A. Hackman. 1995. *Large carnivore conservation in the Rocky Mountains: A long-term strategy for maintaining free-ranging and self-sustaining populations of carnivores.* Toronto: World Wildlife Fund.

Parkes, C., and J. Thornley. 1994. *Fair game—The law of country sports and protection of wildlife.* London: Pelham Books.

Peyton, R.B. 2000. Wildlife management: Cropping to manage or managing to crop? *Wildlife Society Bulletin* 28(4): 774–779.

Phelps, R.W., W.R. Allen, and S. Harrop. 1997. *Report of a review of hunting with hounds.* London: Countryside Alliance.

Phillips, R.L., R.D. Andrews, G.L. Storm, and R.A. Bishop. 1972. Dispersal and mortality of red foxes. *Journal of Wildlife Management* 36: 237–248.

Posewitz, J. 1994. *Beyond fair chase: The ethic and tradition of hunting.* Helena, Mont.: Falcon Publishing, Inc.

———. 1999. *Inherit the hunt: A journey into the heart of American hunting.* Helena, Mont.: Falcon Publishing, Inc.

Produce Studies Ltd. 1995. *Farmers' attitudes to fox control.* Newbury, Berkshire, England: Produce Studies, Ltd.

Robel, R.J., A.D. Dayton, F.R. Henderson, R.L. Meduna, and C.W. Spaeth. 1981. Relationships between husbandry methods and sheep losses to canine predators. *Journal of Wildlife Management* 45(4): 894–911.

Rohlfing, A.H. 1978. Hunter conduct and public attitudes. *Transactions of the North American Wildlife and Natural Resources Conference* 43: 404–411.

Roosevelt, T. 1900. *The wilderness hunter.* New York: G.P. Putnam's Sons.

———. 1913. Our vanishing wildlife. *Outlook* 103: 161–162.

Schmidt, R.H. 1996. A modest proposal to assist in the maintenance of a hunting culture. *Wildlife Society Bulletin* 24(2): 373–375.

Storm, G.L., R.D. Andrews, R.L. Phillips, R.A. Bishop, D.B. Siniff, and J.R. Tester. 1976. Morphology, reproduction, dispersal and mortality of mid-western red fox populations. *Wildlife Monographs* 49: 1–82.

Stroud, D.A., S. Gibson, J.S. Holmes, and C.M. Harry. 1999. The legislative basis for vertebrate pest management in Europe (with examples from the UK). In *Advances in Vertebrate Pest Management*, ed. D.P. Cowan and C.J. Feare, 85–108.

Fürth: Filander Verlag.

Tapper, S.C. 1992. *Game heritage: An ecological review from shooting and gamekeeping records.* Fordingbridge, Hants, England: The Game Conservancy Trust.

Teel, T.L., R.S. Krannich, and R.H. Schmidt. 2002. Utah stakeholders' attitudes toward selected cougar and black bear management practices. *Wildlife Society Bulletin* 30(1): 2–15.

Theodori, G.L., A.E. Luloff, and F.K. Willits. 1998. The association of outdoor recreation and environmental concern: Reexamining the Dunlap-Heffernan thesis. *Rural Sociology* 63(1): 94–108.

U.S. Census Bureau. 1996. *Intercensal estimates of the total resident population of states: 1980 to 1990.* Washington, D.C.: U.S. Department of Commerce, Bureau of the Census.

———. 2001. *Ranking tables for states: 1990 and 2000.* Washington, D.C.: U.S. Department of Commerce, Bureau of the Census.

U.S. Department of the Interior, Fish and Wildlife Service, and U.S. Department of Commerce, Bureau of the Census. 1997. *1996 National Survey of Fishing, Hunting, and Wildlife-Associated Recreation.* Accessed at *http://federalaid.fws. gov/surveys/surveys.html* survey _trends.

U.S. Department of the Interior, Fish and Wildlife Service and U.S. Department of Commerce, U.S. Census Bureau. 2002. *2001 National Survey of Fishing, Hunting, and Wildlife-Associated Recreation.* Accessed at *http://federalaid.fws. gov/surveys/surveys.html* survey _trends.

U. S. Fish and Wildlife Service. 1981. 1980 hunting and fishing license revenues continue to increase. U.S. Department of the Interior, U.S. Fish and Wildlife Service. News release, June 1.

———. 2001. Number of anglers and hunters remains steady. U.S. Department of the Interior, U.S. Fish and Wildlife Service. News release, August 15.

———. 2002. *Status of ducks.* Washington, D.C.

Voight, D.R. 1987. Red fox. In *Wild Furbearer Management and Conservation in North America*, ed. M. Novak, J.A. Baker, M.E. Obbard, and B. Mallock, 379–392. Ontario: Ministry of Natural Resources.

Wandeler, A.I. 1988. Control of wildlife rabies: Europe. In *Rabies*, ed. J.B. Campbell and K.M. Charlton, 365–380. Boston: Kluwer Academic Publishers.

Wilkins, K.A., and M.C. Otto. 2002. Trends in duck breeding populations, 1955–2002. U.S. Fish and Wildlife Service Administrative Report, Division of Migratory Bird Management, Laurel, Md.

Williams, T. 1986. Who's managing the wildlife managers? *Orion* 5(4): 16–23.

Woolf, A. and J.L. Roseberry. 1998. Deer management: Our profession's symbol of success or failure? *Wildlife Society Bulletin* 26(3): 515–521.

The Impact of Highways on Wildlife and the Environment: A Review of Recent Progress in Reducing Roadkill

Susan Hagood and Marguerite Trocmé

An Internet search using the key word *roadkill* brings up about 260,000 hits. An assuredly nonscientific sample of the first few hundred reveals that only rarely is the term used in its original context—to describe animals hit and killed in the road. It is used much more commonly now as a metaphor for feckless losers, something or someone unworthy of consideration, from losing football teams to heavy metal bands and professional wrestlers. When real roadkill—wildlife killed in roadways by passing vehicles—*is* discussed, it is more often than not in even more blackly humorous terms—"flattened fauna," "windshield paste," "road pizza"—in a lame attempt to acknowledge roadkill as an unavoidable reality of modern life.

Roadkill is not a joking matter, however, particularly within the scientific community. There it is seen as a symptom of a greater problem: the fracturing of wildlife habitat into ever-smaller pieces. This fracturing forces wild animals to cross roads to get from one piece of habitat to another or maroons animals in habitat fragments to the detriment of individuals, populations, and interdependent eco-logical functions (Figure 1). As a result the construction and use of roads is one of the greatest influences on wild plant and animal populations (Ashley and Robinson 1996; Groot, Bruinderink and Hazebroek 1996; Forman 2000; Forman and Deblinger 2000).

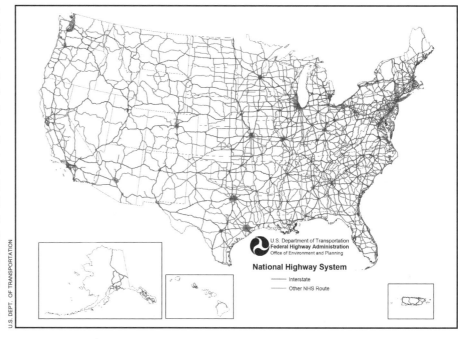

U.S. DEPT. OF TRANSPORTATION

Figure 1.
The National Highway System includes 256,000 miles of interstate and other major highways and comprises 6.5 percent of public roads in the United States.

Pave It and They Will Come

In 1954 U.S. President Dwight D. Eisenhower appointed a committee to assess the nation's highway needs. The primary recommendation of the committee, chaired by a member of the board of directors of General Motors, was construction of a federally funded interstate highway system; indeed, the committee considered no alternative (Jackson 1985). The resulting Interstate Highway Act of 1956 authorized this system, "the most ambitious public-works program undertaken in American history" (Flink 1988, 175–176). This statute obligated the federal government to pay for 90 percent of the cost of constructing 41,000 miles of toll-free express highways. At the same time, the federal government virtually ignored mass transit, sending it into a decline that continues today (Kay 1997). "The interstate system helped continue the downward spiral of public transportation and virtually guaranteed that future urban growth would perpetuate a centerless sprawl" (Jackson 1985, 249).

More than 3.9 million miles of public roads now crisscross the United States, according to the Federal Highway Administration (Table 1). The number of vehicular miles traveled in the United States increased by more than 500 percent between 1950 and 2000, and the number of vehicles registered by 360 percent. In contrast the population of the United States increased a relatively modest 86 percent during this period. In 1950 41 percent of Americans lacked "personal automobility" in the form of the family car (Flink 1988); by 1997 that number had declined to 9 percent (Kay 1997).

The increase in automobility during the past five decades has much to do with improving economic conditions, which put a car within reach of an increasing percentage of white Americans (Flink 1988; Kay 1997).[1] It is also a result of growth patterns that render residents dependent on cars. Federal policies following the end of World War II encouraged the development of relatively inexpensive single-family homes at some distance from crowded city centers (Kay 1997). The American dream became firmly centered on a house and yard of one's own. The picket fence was optional but not the garage, which

Table 1
Selected Highway Statistics, 1950, 2000
(in millions)

	1950	2000
Miles of public roads*	3.3	3.9
Miles traveled by all vehicles**	458.3	2,749.8
Number of vehicles registered**	49.2	225.8
Total U.S. population***	151.3	281.4

* Source: Federal Highway Administration Office of Infrastructure
** Source: Federal Highway Administration Highway Statistics Series
*** Source: U.S. Census Bureau

assumed a prominent position at the front of the house.

Suburban housing in the United States has changed with economic good times and two-income families; a growing population; and neglect of urban housing, schools, infrastructure, and industry. The relatively modest 1950s and 1960s ranch, Cape Cod, and split level houses on quarter-acre lots that typified the post-World War II construction boom were preferred over higher density housing (Jackson 1985). Today, bigger houses on bigger lots—many with three-car garages—gobble up even more land ever further from the urban/suburban cores (Heimlich and Anderson 2001). The loss of land, particularly land in agricultural production, has increased substantially.

In this new suburban and exurban landscape, it is perhaps surprising that only 22.5 percent of the time spent behind the wheel is for commuting to, or in the course of, work (Federal Highway Administration's Nationwide Personal Transportation Study, in Kay 1997). Most of the driving time is consumed by errands for which a car is a necessity because developers build housing on farmland miles from grocery stores, drug stores, movie theaters, and libraries. "We have deserted the compact cities and inner suburbs that offer varied housing, walkability, and public transportation" (Kay 1997, 20).

Changes in Wildlife Populations

Long before the automobile changed the American landscape, human pressure was wreaking havoc on wildlife populations. Between 1869 and 1889, for example, the number of bison (*Bison bison*) on the American plains plummeted from 60 million to 150, as armed railroad passengers laid waste to millions, augmenting federal efforts to subdue the Plains Indians by reducing an important food source (Bolen and Robinson 1995). Perhaps the most numerous bird species that ever existed, the passenger pigeon (*Ectopistes migratorius*), was slaughtered to extinction by the early 1900s, aided by the development of a telegraph and rail system that enabled market hunters to keep abreast of the location of pigeon colonies and ship large numbers of birds to waiting cities (Cobb 1987, in Bolen and Robinson 1995). This legacy of destruction includes other species as well—the Labrador duck (*Camptorhyncus labradorius*), the heath hen (*Tympanuchus cupido cupido*), and the Carolina parakeet (*Conuropsis carolinensis*). It very nearly included the elk (*Cervus elaphus*), the pronghorn (*Antilocapra americana*), and the beaver (*Castor canadensis*).

In response to the unbridled slaughter, state wildlife agencies were organized in the early 1900s to protect declining species. A principal objective of most such agencies was to restore game species to their former abundance by imposing and enforcing restrictions on hunting and trapping; protecting and improving habitat; and reintroducing species to depleted areas. There are a number of examples of the success of this effort, none better than the white-tailed deer (Odocoileus virginianus). Over-hunted and suffering the effects of habitat destruction, white-tailed deer populations were estimated at just 500,000 as the nation entered the twentieth century (Bolen and Robinson 1995), down from an estimated peak in the year 1500 of perhaps 24 to 33 million (McCabe and McCabe 1997). Eastern state wildlife agencies made the recovery of these deer a priority, restricting hunting, establishing protected game lands, relocating deer to depleted areas, and providing nutrition in the form of food plots on private and public land. Changes in land use associated with the mid- to late twentieth century (e.g., division of large blocks of habitat into smaller parcels, with agricultural fields abutting forest fragments and suburban development) encouraged the growth of deer populations. At the end of the twentieth century, an estimated 24 million white-tails roamed the United States (http://www.nature.nps.gov/facts/fdeer2.htm).

Other species, including raccoons, opossums, skunks, foxes, woodchucks, coyotes, crows, and grey squirrels, increased in population in many areas as a result of their ability to persist in human-dominated landscapes.

Contemporary roadkill levels therefore reflect a convergence of events: the recovery of a few species; the ability of others to thrive in human-dominated landscapes; the destruction of habitat, forcing animals into ever-closer contact with people; and the construction of more and more roads handling increased traffic volumes at increased speed. As a result of these factors, the sight of dead animals in the road is a part of virtually every car trip we take. Without more sympathetic policies and structures, transportation and its effects almost certainly will figure in the proximate if not ultimate calculus of future extinctions.

Ecological Impact of Highways

The broken bodies of wild animals strewn along roadsides are only the most visible evidence of the ecological effects of highways on wildlife and the environment. Roads also destroy, degrade, and fragment habitat. Thirty-eight million acres of America are covered by the asphalt of roads and parking lots, and 1.5 million acres of arable land disappear beneath an asphalt cap every year (Kay 1997).

Environmental Degradation

Removal of native vegetation; grading, filling, and paving; and the use of the heavy equipment required in each of these steps obliterate wildlife habitat and kill any organisms unable to move out of the path of destruction. Soils disturbed in the process are washed in greater or lesser amounts into local watersheds despite the presence of erosion control fencing; aquatic habitats may therefore be degraded as well. Public roads and associated rights-of-way occupy approximately 1.5 percent (53,044 square miles, or 137,384 square kilometers) of the land area in the United States (Turrentine, Heanue, and Sperling 2001), representing habitat that is completely or largely lost to most wildlife species.

Chemical Alteration of Roadside Habitats

Roadside rights-of-way are affected chemically in numerous ways. Trombulak and Frissell (2000) identify chemicals commonly found along roadsides as well as their potential effects on vegetation and ecosystems. Heavy metals from automobile exhaust, including lead, cadmium, nickel, and zinc, are deposited in roadside environments. These chemicals settle in roadside soil and vegetation (Lagerwerff and Specht 1970), unless they enter watersheds. Accumulation in roadside plants occurs in direct proportion to the intensity of traffic use (Goldsmith, Scanlon, and Pirie 1976); negative effects on plants range from decreased vigor to death (Trombulak and Frissell 2000). Organic pollutants, including dioxins, and polychlorinated biphenyls occur at higher levels in soils along highways. These pollutants can reduce plant vigor and negatively affect aquatic life at some distance from the road on which they were deposited (Maltby et al. 1995). Deicing salts alter the pH of roadside soils and can damage vegetation. These salts also attract large mammals to roadsides, increasing the likelihood of collisions with automobiles (Fraser and Thomas 1982).

Vehicles both import and create dust, which can, like chemical pollution, negatively affect aquatic systems and reduce roadside plant growth and vigor (Farmer 1993).

Roadside Wildlife Habitats

Highway rights-of-way typically are maintained as grassy clearings. Though lost as habitat to many species, these areas are used by some. Adams and Geis (1983) found that, compared with adjacent habitats, the population density of small mammals was greater in interstate rights-of-way, but lesser along country roads with reduced right-of-way habitat. Other authors have reported use of roadside habitats by small mammals (Oxley, Fenton, and Carmody 1974), as well as by ungulates (Carbaugh 1970; Bellis and Graves 1971; Feldhamer et al. 1986), and insects (Munguira and Thomas 1992). Three times as many mice were found in the highway right-of-way than outside the right-of-way fence, presumably because of increased habitat suitability in the mown right-of-way (Gibeau, unpublished 1994 data, in Gibeau and Heuer 1996). Coyotes were apparently attracted by this availability of prey and may have been subjected to increased mortality from vehicle collisions as a result (Gibeau and Heuer (1996). Bird species dependent on increasingly rare grasslands also may use roadsides for nesting (Laursen 1981; Warner 1992), although the density of birds in this habitat is reduced relative to habitats unassociated with roads (Kuitunen, Rossi, and Stenroos 1998). Gibeau and Herrero (1998) note that a dynamic tension exists between grizzly bears (*Ursus arctos*) and roads. While grizzly bears are acutely sensitive to the disturbance that road use causes in their habitats, they nonetheless may be attracted to rights-of-way, which typically have earlier snow melt and "green up" compared with adjacent forested areas, and an abundance of mast-producing shrubs in the intermediate habitat between right-of-way and forest (Gibeau and Herrero 1998). Presumably, this same tension exists for other species, whether rare or common.

Haskell (2000) found that soil macroinvertebrates are significantly less abundant and less diverse in areas close to forest roads, as compared with areas further away. Leaf litter also was reduced in proximity to roads. Reduction in leaf litter and the macroinvertebrates it harbors may affect the ground-foraging birds, salamanders, and other animals that rely heavily on these organisms.

Wildlife Behavior and Exploitation

Highways influence the behavior of wildlife in a number of ways. The noise associated with well-used roads apparently disrupts communication between individual birds, for example. As a result highway noise degrades nesting habitat for sensitive forest and grassland-nesting species for distances from the road of 650 meters to 1–3 kilometers, respectively (Forman

and Deblinger 2000). In more extensive studies of the effects of road noise on avian reproduction, European researchers concluded that the most sensitive grassland-nesting species are reduced in density within 930 meters of a main road (Reijnen et al. 1995; Reijnen, Foppen, and Meeuwsen 1996). European research also indicates that road illumination has a negative effect on the choice by the black-tailed godwit (*Limosa l. limosa*) of breeding habitat (de Molenaar, Jonkers, and Sanders 2000). Colorado mule deer (*Odocoileus hemionus*) appear to avoid otherwise suitable habitat that is adjacent to roads (Rost and Bailey 1979), as do grizzly bears (McLellan and Shackleton 1988; Mace et al. 1996), and gray wolves (*Canis lupus*) (Thiel 1985; Mech et al. 1988).

Roads provide access to lands otherwise protected from disturbance by distance and terrain. Road access is used as a measure of the suitability of an area to support large carnivores (McLellan and Shackleton 1988; Mech et al. 1988). These animals are vulnerable not only to roadkill but also to poachers and legal hunters who use roads to penetrate remote habitats (Noss et al. 1996; Trombulak and Frissell 2000). For example, hunters in Wisconsin use roads at night to locate bobcat (*Lynx rufus*) tracks after a fresh snowfall then release pursuit hounds at dawn. Eight of nine bobcat mortalities in the study area were attributed to hunting, many presumably by this road-based method (Lovallo and Anderson 1996).

Habitat Fragmentation

Roads affect wildlife not only by altering, degrading, and destroying habitats but also by isolating habitats (Mader 1984; Mader, Schell, and Kornacker 1990; Reed, Johnson-Barnard, and Baker 1996) and the wildlife populations they harbor (Reh 1989; Gerlach and Musolf 2000; Underhill and Angold 2000). All roads, whether dirt tracks or six-lane, limited-access highways, present a barrier to some

species, though the suite of affected species varies greatly (Oxley, Fenton, and Carmody 1974; Garland and Bradley 1984; Forman and Deblinger 2000; Underhill and Angold 2000). For instance, Oxley, Fenton, and Carmody (1974) found that roadways of 20 meters or more with clearances between forest edges impede the movement of small forest mammals, while those of 90 meters or more (e.g., a four-lane divided highway) are barriers to dispersal as effective as bodies of water twice as wide. Mader (1984) determined that roads effectively isolate populations of forest-dwelling mice and carabid beetles in Germany. Reed, Johnson-Barnard, and Baker (1996) found that the presence of roads (including logging roads) is a greater contributor to forest fragmentation than are clear-cut areas in Wyoming's Medicine Bow-Routt National Forest, because they dissect large forest habitats into smaller areas and increase the amount of edge habitat at the expense of interior forest habitat.

Forman et al. (1996) suggest that road densities exceeding approximately 0.6 kilometers per square kilometer (1.0 mile per square mile) are inconsistent with maintenance of healthy populations of some large carnivores. The maximum road density associated with viable populations of the gray wolf is 0.58 kilometer per square kilometer (Thiel 1985; Mech et al. 1988). Grizzly bears are most successful in habitats where humans and their developments are infrequent (Herraro 1995). The home range of male grizzly bears in interior regions of Canada's Bow River watershed averaged 1,560 square kilometers during a four-year study (Gibeau and Herrero 1997). Despite the construction of twenty-two underpasses and two overpasses, the Trans Canada Highway is a barrier to movement of female grizzly bears and alters the movements of male bears as well (Gibeau and Herrero 1997).

Mader (1984) attributes the barrier effect of roads (as well as railroads and canals) to a variety of biotic and abiotic factors. These include changes in microclimatic conditions occurring among the forest, the roadside, and the road itself; the band of physical and chemical disturbances along the road resulting from pollutants, noise, dust, vehicle lights, and increased salinity; changes in the composition of plants and animals as a function of management of roadside vegetation; and the danger of traffic mortality to animals attempting to cross the road.

Local extinctions are a common occurrence in fragmented landscapes (den Boer 1981). The persistence of a metapopulation (i.e., interconnected populations of a species) depends on the ability of individuals to move between population patches (Fahrig and Merriam 1985). The quality of habitat corridors or linkages connecting these patches is extremely important in patch and metapopulation persistence (Henein and Merriam 1990). An otherwise high quality habitat corridor that is bisected by a road in which most individuals attempting to disperse from a patch are killed is little better than no corridor at all.

Obviously, roads also affect the flow of water throughout a watershed, with effects some distance from the road (Jones et al. 2000). Hydrological changes in turn affect populations of fish, including anadromous salmonids, whose life history requires that individuals in younger age classes be able to move upstream and downstream and that adults can swim upstream to spawn. Poorly designed culverts impede or prevent this passage. Ruediger (2001) found that inadequately designed stream crossings on highways and roads have contributed significantly to the decline of salmon and steelhead trout numbers in the lower forty-eight states. At least 15,000 culverts in Washington, Oregon, and Alaska may be partial or complete barriers to anadromous species.

Road-Effect Zone

It is evident that the ecological effects of roads are not limited to the area claimed by roads and their

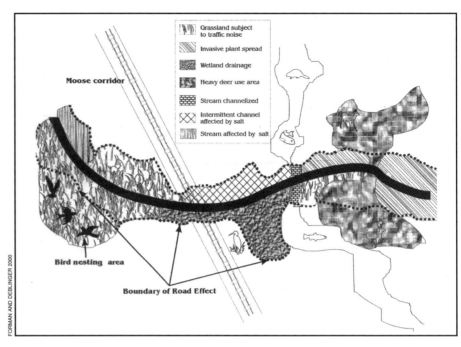

Figure 2.

Hypothetical diagram illustrating curvilinear nature of road effects for various ecological features such as high-density deer areas (road mortality), grassland bird nesting areas (noise disturbance), moose corridors (road mortality), and various wetland and waterway alterations, including exotic plant invasion, salt intrusion, and channelization.

rights-of-way. An attempt to estimate the total "road-effect zone"—that area over which significant ecological effects extend—was made by Forman and Deblinger (2000) for a 25-kilometer section of divided, four-lane highway in Massachusetts. All ecological effects believed to extend more than 100 meters from the road were mapped, including wetland drainage; stream channelization; road salt in surface waters; invasion of forests by exotic vegetation planted in the right-of-way; and alteration of habitat use in moose (*Alces alces*), deer, forest birds, grassland birds, and vernal pool amphibians. Excluded from the estimate were indirect effects, such as vehicle emissions that affect habitats at great distance from the road itself, as well as road-based wildlife habitat destruction, fragmentation, and interruption of wildlife travel corridors. The road-effect zone varied in distance based on the effect at issue, as well as the type of habitat adjacent to a particular stretch of road. For instance, road salt may affect aquatic habitats 200 to 1,500 meters from

the road. Travel corridors between blocks of suitable habitat for white-tailed deer, moose, and black bear (*Ursus americanus*) were interrupted by the road, effectively extending the road effects to the distance between the road and the habitat blocks to which access is made more difficult. Though the width was variable, the average road-effect zone extended 300 meters on both sides of the road, for a total zone of 600 meters (Figure 2). Forman (2000) estimates that 19 percent of the United States land base nationwide is affected ecologically by roads, with roads in rural areas having far greater ecological effects than those in urban areas.

Direct Wildlife Mortality

Most of the animals killed on roadways are members of relatively common species. Estimates of overall mortality are not available and in all likelihood never will be. The Humane Society of the United States (HSUS) attempted to derive an estimate several decades ago. During the 1960s a team of volunteers for The HSUS collected mortality figures along designated routes in the United States on five successive fourths of July. The figures obtained were then extrapolated to roads throughout the country, and a figure of one million animals a day was derived. Though acknowledged at the time to be only a rough estimate and entirely unreliable today, this figure continues to be used. Undoubtedly, a reliable figure will never exist. Regardless roadkill may be the single most significant human-caused source of wildlife mortality in the United States (Kline and Swann 1998).

Dozens of studies have been conducted to quantify and qualify road mortality in localized populations (see, e.g., Rosen and Lowe 1994; Drews 1995; Smith 1995; Clarke, White, and Harris 1998; Haskell 2000). Between 1985 and 1995, an average of 9 to 11 percent of the black bear population in the Bow Valley of Alberta's Banff National Park was killed by trains and cars each year (Gibeau and Heuer 1996). Huggard (1993, in van der Grift 1999) found that highway and railroad mortality resulted in a significant shift in the age structure of elk in Banff National Park and concluded that elk whose home range overlapped the road or rail were less likely to reach old age than those at some distance from the transportation corridor. The primary cause of death of moose in Alaska's Kenai National Wildlife Refuge is collision with vehicles (Bangs, Bailey, and Portner 1989). Fahrig et al. (1995) concluded that road mortality has a significant negative effect on the density of local anuran populations, many of which require different habitats for breeding, feeding, and overwintering. Aquatic breeding amphibians are more vulnerable than most other species to traffic mortality on the basis of their activity patterns, population structure, and preferred habitats (Hels and Buchwald 2001). Ashley and Robinson (1996) concluded that, of those groups of species associated with increasingly rare wetlands, amphibians as well as reptiles are particularly vulnerable to roadkill.

A number of states attempt to track kills of large animals, principally ungulates. Romin and Bissonette (1996) conservatively estimated that 500,000 deer were killed in 1991, based on state wildlife agency survey responses. Conover et al. (1995) concluded that 1.5 million deer/vehicle collisions occur annually in the United States, and estimated that 29,000 people are injured and 211 killed each year in such collisions.

Studies like these indicate that the total tally of wild animals killed by vehicles must certainly amount to millions upon millions a year in the United States alone. While roadkill rates do not limit population size in most affected species (Forman and Alexander 1998), highway mortality is further imperiling species already rare due to habitat loss and other causes. For instance, until the recent construction of a number of crossing structures under Florida highways, more than half of the known deaths of the endangered Florida panther (*Puma concolor coryi*) were due to traffic collisions (Harris and Gallagher 1989). Eleven percent of all known gray wolf mortalities in Minnesota were caused by vehicle collisions (Paquet and Callaghan 1996). Roadkill threatens the continued existence of the ocelot (*Leopardus pardalis*) in the United States (Tewes and Hughes 2001). Concern is increasingly being expressed about the effect of highway mortality on a number of reptiles, including about half of the fifty-five turtle species native to the United States (Gibbs and Shriver 2002).

The extent to which animals are struck but able to escape the roadway (to suffer for some time before dying) is unquestionably an animal welfare concern (Putnam 1997), given the scope of the problem. In addition, each situation in which motorists encounter wildlife in the roadway has the potential to result in human injury and property damage as the driver attempts to avoid the animal. The millions of incidents that occur annually thus constitute a public safety concern. Finally, constant exposure

to wildlife in the road inures roadway users to the sight of dead wildlife, potentially reducing the personal connections to wildlife that are vital to public support for its protection. It is tragic that the closest continuous association that most members of the public have with wildlife is very likely the sight of dead animals in the road.

Reducing Roadkill by Reconnecting Habitats

Research has begun to suggest ways in which the most obvious ecological effect of roads—roadkill—can be reduced. The research indicates that it may be possible to reduce the barrier effect of roads, allowing animals fully to utilize their habitats or disperse to new habitats. A number of European countries have decades of experience in such research; the United States has begun to look seriously at the issue only relatively recently but with increasing intensity. A biennial conference focusing on the topic and sponsored by federal and state transportation agencies and environmental and animal protection organizations has been held in the United States since 1994; its steady growth since 1994 is evidence of increasing concern among scientists about the ecological effects of highways.

Effectiveness of Techniques

Fencing

Fencing is commonly used to restrict access of wildlife, particularly ungulates, to roadways. To protect animals while avoiding isolating populations in small pockets of habitat, wildlife fencing must not only restrict highway access but also serve to guide wildlife to crossing structures or locations. Fencing must be constructed properly and maintained carefully to function as a deterrent to ungulate movement.

Structurally sound fences of 2.26 meters in height significantly reduced movement of white-tailed deer onto the interstate highway known as I-80 in Pennsylvania (Falk, Graves, and Bellis 1978). Feldhamer et al. (1986) found that a 2.7-meter-high fence without crossing structures reduced the number of groups of deer on an interstate highway right-of-way along I-84 in Pennsylvania compared with a fence 2.2 meters high; the higher fence did not reduce roadkill levels, however, since deer entered the right-of-way at unfenced interchanges and through large holes that were cut in the fence during hunting season to provide access for hunters to the woods beyond. Deer cross under fences that have gaps greater than 23 centimeters (Falk, Graves, and Bellis 1978). During times of food or mineral scarcity, highway rights-of-way, as currently managed, provide a strong incentive for deer to find a way over, under, or around a fence (Bellis and Graves 1971; Feldhamer et al. 1986). Clevenger, Chruszez, and Gunson (2001) found that 2.4-meter fencing associated with crossing structures significantly reduced wildlife/vehicle collisions, though there is a risk that wildlife collisions will continue at the fence ends. Ward (1982) found no reduction in collisions during the first year following construction of seven crossing structures on a Wyoming highway. Collisions occurred primarily at fence ends. Once the fence was extended to an underpass, however, collisions were reduced significantly.

Fences designed for large animals must include one-way gates in order to avoid trapping animals in the right-of-way between fences (Putnam 1997; Jackson and Griffin 1998). Alternatively, one-way ramps can be installed that permit animals to escape from the right-of-way. Indeed, ramps seem to be more effective than one-way gates in providing for escape from the roadside (Forman et al. 2003), perhaps because they appear more nat-

ural to the animal.

Many species of wildlife, including black bears, mountain lions (*Puma concolor*) and grizzly bears, can and will climb fences (Clevenger, Chruszez, and Gunson 2001); grizzly bears also will dig under (Gibeau and Heuer 1996), as will coyotes (*Canis latrans*) (Clevenger, Chruszez, and Gunson 2001). Clevenger, Chruszez, and Gunson (2001) note that carnivores gaining access to the Trans Canada Highway in Banff National Park prompted park officials to embed fences 1.5 meters underground. Fences of standard design clearly are ineffective for small animals but can be modified at the base with the addition of mesh or fine-gauge wire to prevent amphibians, reptiles, and non-climbing small mammals from squeezing through.

Researchers agree that fences must be designed and used with caution so as to avoid isolating populations in small habitat fragments (Groot Bruinderink and Hazebroek 1996; Putnam 1997; Jackson and Griffin 1998). Wildlife must be permitted to move within suitable habitat; often this requires crossing roads. Provided that fences are properly constructed and maintained, they will find their greatest utility as a means of directing wildlife to crossing structures. Highway fences large enough to restrict wildlife passage should not be used unless associated with structures or areas that provide for wildlife passage. The same caution should be extended to the omnipresent Jersey and Texas barriers, which pose an obstruction to smaller animals or trap them within the right-of-way unless constructed with an opening at the bottom that permits their escape.

Passages

Underpasses include round and oval culverts made of metal or cement, box culverts, and large spans created by elevating the road surface or spanning natural topographic depressions such as stream corridors. Bridge extensions to provide a dry crossing surface under the highway can also be

considered a type of underpass. (A full description of underpass types and dimensions is included in Forman et al. 2003).

Underpasses may be the structures most commonly used to facilitate wildlife passage across highways. Placement and design of underpasses is critical; underpasses placed in unsuitable habitat or constructed in a manner that presents animals with, for example, a long, dark tunnel through which they are unable to see and evaluate habitat on the other side will be largely ineffective. Jackson and Griffin (1998) identify several factors that must be considered when installing wildlife underpasses, including placement, size, light, moisture, temperature, noise, substrate, approaches, and fencing. Forman (1995) recommends targeting the design of each structure to at least two types of species: the largest species of interest and the species most sensitive to the road barrier. In addition, it is critical to ensure that habitat on both sides of a passage is protected for the long term and managed to encourage wildlife use.

Of the several considerations involved in passage construction, placement may be the most critical (Land and Lotz 1996); use of fencing to direct mule deer to underpasses not located along traditional wildlife trails failed to result in use of the structures (Hanna 1982). Current approaches to underpass placement rely on empirical knowledge of wildlife movements and geographic information system (GIS) analysis of regional and landscape level habitat connectivity models (Clevenger and Wierzchowski 2001).

More than twenty underpasses have been incorporated into highway conversions in Florida to accommodate movements of the highly endangered Florida panther. The location of these structures was determined by roadkill statistics, habitat characteristics, and the movements of radio-collared panthers (Land and Lotz 1996). Construction of the Florida underpasses was accompanied by placement of a 3.4-meter chain-link fence with three strands of outrigged barbed wire along the 65-kilometer section of interstate I-75 that transects panther habitat. Underpasses along I-75 are 21.2–25.8 meters wide by 48.5 meters long and include an open median. Traffic is elevated 3–4 meters off the ground. Those underpasses associated with an intersecting state road are pre-formed box culverts 2.4, 7.3, and 14.6 meters in height, width, and length, respectively (Land and Lotz 1996). According to Land and Lotz (1996), all medium-sized to large mammals found in southern Florida used underpasses of these two general designs. It is important to note that underpass use by panthers increased substantially between an earlier study (Foster and Humphrey 1995) and the 1996 study.

While placement of underpasses is critical, design also is an important factor. Summarizing ten years of observation of mule deer exiting a relatively small (3.05 by 3.05 by 30.48 meter height/width/length) concrete box culvert in Colorado, Reed (1981) found that 75 percent of deer exhibited behavior associated with wariness, reluctance, or fright. The author speculates that this reluctance may cause deer to attempt to get through or over a 2.44-meter right-of-way fence or increase the time spent at the underpass and thus their vulnerability to disturbance. Reed speculates that a larger (approximately 4 by 18 by 14 meter) open-bridge structure may better reduce the number of deer/vehicle collisions. According to Heuer (1995), lynx detoured 9 kilometers around a fence, apparently to avoid a culvert-style underpass (7 meter diameter by 50 meter length), in order to reach, in some cases, habitat immediately adjacent to the underpass on the other side of the road.

Ruediger (2001) attributes the limited effectiveness of older structures to a "least cost" approach in their construction. He stresses that future underpasses need to be planned and designed for use by multiple species, ensuring that placement, height, width, substrate, and ambient light

are considered carefully. "High, wide, and handsome" structures are more expensive to build but are likely to be more effective in saving wildlife (Ruediger 2001, 509).

Clevenger and Waltho (2000) found that human activity was consistently important in level of use of several wildlife underpasses in Canada's Banff National Park, particularly by disturbance-sensitive species (e.g., wolves, mountain lions, grizzlies, and black bears), but was less important than structural factors in determining ungulate use. These authors also found that carnivores tended to use underpasses associated with drainage systems, while ungulates avoided those travel ways. They speculate that it is likely that this difference reflects predator-avoidance on the part of ungulates rather than a direct effect of landscape characteristics on underpass use.

Jackson (1996) reports on the effectiveness of two tunnels installed in Amherst, Massachusetts, to assist spotted salamanders during breeding migrations. A 30-meter fence on both sides of the tunnel directed salamanders to it and did not seem to prevent salamanders from reaching the tunnel, no matter where along its length they encountered the fence. Successful passage was enhanced by the use of artificial light. The author speculates that increasing the size of the passage, and thus the amount of ambient light, would increase its effectiveness. Jackson notes that underpasses provided for larger animals and associated with stream crossings may deter amphibians, who do not generally migrate along stream corridors, unless appropriate substrates are provided. Underpass substrates must be moist for amphibians.

Other small wildlife tunnels, also called ecopipes or wildlife pipes, may provide passage for small and medium-sized mammals. Culverts installed not for wildlife but for hydrological purposes may nonetheless be used by wildlife and may be important in increasing the permeability of the highway or road (Forman et al. 2003).

Overpass placement is dictated by

the same factors that guide the placement of underpasses. According to Jackson and Griffin (1998), the most effective wildlife overpasses range in width from 50 meters wide on each end and narrowing to 8–35 meters in the center, to 200 meters wide. Others have found that the hourglass configuration is not necessary, and suggest that a width of 50 meters throughout the length of the underpass is more important than shape in maximizing a structure's use by wildlife (Pfister et al. 1999).

Soil on the overpasses (ranging in depth from 0.5 to 2 meters) permits the planting or growth of herbaceous vegetation, shrubs, and small trees, thereby providing temporary or permanent habitat for some species. Overpasses can also include small ponds and/or wetlands, fed by rainwater, to increase vegetative diversity and their attractiveness to a variety of wildlife species.

Jackson and Griffin (1998) note that overpasses appear to be acceptable to more species of wildlife than do underpasses. A comparison of use by species of an underpass located within 200 meters of each of two overpasses indicated that most species seemed to prefer overpasses (grizzly bears, wolves, deer, elk, moose, and bighorn sheep), while cougars preferred the underpass; black bears did not appear to have a preference (Forman et al. 2003). Compared with underpasses, overpasses are quieter, lighter, and less confining but more expensive to build.

Groot Bruinderink and Hazebroek (1996) state that both underpasses and overpasses should be reserved for the use of wildlife exclusively, with habitat at each end given the status of a refuge or sanctuary. While this is undoubtedly ideal, overpasses designed to accommodate both local traffic and wildlife are used by wildlife. Indeed, monitoring of highway bridges in Slovenia has revealed that some wild animals will utilize even structures designed only for cars if there is no other way to access needed habitat on the other side of the highway. An unobstructed view of habitat on the other side is a critical factor in structure use by wildlife, whether the structure is an overpass or underpass.

Signs

While the effectiveness of standard deer crossing signs generally has not been tested, conventional wisdom holds that the effectiveness of any warning sign diminishes as drivers habituate to them. Pojar et al. (1975) studied the effectiveness of lighted, animated, deer crossing signs in reducing deer kills and driver speed on a 1.61-kilometer stretch of highway outside Glenwood Springs, Colorado, known for relatively high deer/vehicle accidents. They found no significant difference in the rates of deer killed with the signs on and off. Mean vehicular speed slowed by 4.8 kilometers per hour with the sign on. Speeds slowed significantly when deer carcasses were placed near the signs and easily visible to drivers, whether the signs were on or off.

A new generation of lighted signs, activated only when triggered by the presence of an infrared-detected animal near the roadway, is showing promise in altering driver behavior, as evidenced by research in Finland (Taskula 1997). Tests on similar devices are currently under way in the United States. Such systems will require educational efforts to inform drivers that flashing signs are correlated directly with the presence of wildlife in or near the road, and that the systems rely on the willingness of drivers to reduce speed when signs are flashing. Confidence that drivers will do so may be misplaced (Gordon and Anderson 2001).

Reflectors

A number of reflector designs have been developed in an effort to alert roadside wildlife, particularly ungulates, to the immediate presence of traffic. The devices reflect vehicle headlights to create a temporary visual barrier to the animals. The Van de Ree reflector is a polished stainless steel mirror, 8–9 centimeters in diameter, that is mounted at a 45-degree angle to traffic to deter nocturnal deer crossings in the presence of an automobile. As noted in Waring, Griffis, and Vaughn (1991), several studies have indicated that the van de Ree roadside mirrors have not reduced kills effectively. However, Schafer and Penland (1985), while criticizing study design and sample size, noted that a few studies nonetheless evidenced some reduction in deer killed.

Mixed results have been obtained with the Swareflex roadside reflector, apparently due at least in part to inadequacies in study design. This device is a 16.5 centimeter by 5 centimeter red reflector which, when placed in series along the roadside, reflects headlights at right angles to the road and creates a temporary "optical fence." White-tailed deer kills between dusk and dawn were unchanged during periods of Swareflex use in an Illinois study (Waring, Griffis, and Vaughn 1991), even though the local deer population had declined. Schafer and Penland (1985) reported that Swareflex reflectors installed along a 3.2-kilometer section of highway in Washington State significantly reduced the number of white-tailed and mule deer killed during the test period. Methodology included covering and uncovering adjacent reflectors for periods of one to two weeks during the experimental period to compensate for changes in deer population and movement patterns during the three years of the study. Using a similar study design in Wyoming, Reeve and Anderson (1993) found that the reflectors were ineffective in reducing deer/vehicle collisions except for the first of three test periods. The authors speculate that the reduction may be based on avoidance associated with novel stimuli. During one test period, kill rates in experimental periods and sections increased.

The behavior of fallow deer was tested in Denmark using the WEGU reflector (a three-sided, 86 by 182-millimeter device with two symmetrically sloping mirrored sides) and simulated automobile headlights (Ujvári et al. 1998). The percentage of fallow deer failing to react to the light increased over the test period; the authors speculate that the animals became habituated to the reflected light and that the same result would ultimately have occurred had the 1985 Schafer and Penland study continued for a longer period of time.

The results of reflector-effectiveness studies clearly are equivocal (Sielecki 2001). A modified Swareflex reflector, the Strieter-Lite, is nonetheless in use in more than a dozen states. Anecdotal reports indicate that, in a number of locations, the reflectors are believed to be reducing collisions rates (John Strieter, personal communication, April 2000).

Road Closures

Closing roads is 100 percent effective in eliminating wildlife mortality but resistance by the public will severely restrict this option. It may be possible, however, on some roads crossed by amphibians and other animals during breeding migrations where the risk of the virtual elimination of a population is high. Roads on public lands, particularly U.S. Forest Service logging roads, occasionally are closed. In reviewing European ungulate traffic collisions, Groot Bruinderink and Hazebroek (1996), recommend road closures at night wherever possible.

Highway Speeds

Roadkills are correlated positively with vehicle speed (Pojar et al. 1975). Forman et al. (2003) report that highway speeds of 90 kilometers per hour (55 miles per hour) or higher greatly increase the likelihood of a collision. Speed limit reductions and various so-called "traffic calming devices," such as rumble strips, have been used to protect rare species in Florida (Evink 1996). In general, however, speed limit reductions have not been used extensively to reduce deer mortality (Romin and Bissonette 1996).

Characteristics of Highway Mortality

Many studies have shown that collisions with ungulates are more common at night (Case 1978; Waring, Griffis, and Vaughn 1991; Groot Bruinderink and Hazebroek 1996), with peaks at dawn and dusk as deer move to and from feeding areas (Putnam 1997), and are associated with breeding activities and dispersal (Case 1978; Feldhamer et al. 1986). Putnam (1997) speculates that most European deer species easily cross minor roads with low traffic volume throughout the year, but that crossing of major roads is associated more with seasonal movements (e.g., breeding, juvenile dispersal) than with daily activity patterns.

Many wildlife movements are predictable. In a phenomenon known as the "fall shuffle," young squirrels strike out on their own in the late summer and fall, traveling both to establish home ranges and to find and bury nuts for the coming winter. Mule deer, elk, and bighorn sheep (*Ovis canadensis*) travel from summer to winter ranges along often predictable routes. A number of salamander species undertake mass migrations in the early spring to reach ephemeral breeding pools. Roads through migratory routes can eliminate entire populations. Female snapping turtles (*Chelydra serpentine*) are driven to upland locations to lay their eggs in the spring and early summer; box turtles (*Terrapene sp.*) and other turtle species also must travel to find appropriate egg-laying sites. Indeed, any species whose breeding range is separate from foraging range offers an opportunity to predict movements and locations of animal crossings so that the need for passage structures can be analyzed.

European Leadership

Europe has in large part lost many of the habitat connections vital to healthy wildlife populations. Recognizing that, Europeans began decades ago to try to reconnect what wild habitat remained and so became international leaders in providing safe passage for wildlife. While the United States may have more time, it also has more catching up to do, particularly in attitude. In Europe thinking about the impact of roads on wildlife is second nature. In the United States, it remains the exception rather than the rule. Europe provides valuable lessons that should be followed so that the United States can move more quickly to connect and protect.

Defragmentation

The European Road Network and Its Impact

The European road network started to develop on a continental level during the Roman Empire around 63 B.C. Under the Romans the network grew to comprise 80,000 kilometers of main roads and 200,000 kilometers of secondary roads (Billard 1998). It was not until the advent of the automobile, with its need for asphalt surfaces and increasing capacity for high speeds, that roads started to have a negative effect on the natural environment. As automobile speeds rose, wildlife casualties became a cause for concern. In Switzerland a tragic accident in 1962 between a car and a red deer (*Cervas elaphus*) spurred the decision to fence all highways to keep wildlife out (Müller 2002). The main reason was to protect the automobilist. No thought was put into the fact that the fencing was going to turn the new motorway systems into impassable barriers for wildlife.

Between 1970 and 1996, the length of the European Union's trans-portation infrastructure almost doubled, covering 1.2 percent of the total available land area. Today the network is estimated at 3.5 million kilometers, with some 75,185 kilometers of motorways and 20,609 more kilometers planned (European Environmental Agency 2000).

Changes in European land use have reduced and isolated important natural and semi-natural habitats. Forests once covered 80 to 90 percent of Europe, but now cover only 33 percent. Inland wetlands such as bogs, fens, and marshes have disappeared in large numbers. (Iberia, for instance, has lost more than 60 percent of such habitats.) Many plant and animal species essential to the preservation of biodiversity are declining or threatened with extinction; 53 percent of European fish species are under threat, as are 45 percent of reptile species, 40 percent of mammals, 40 percent of birds, and 21 percent of Europe's 12,500 vascular plant species.

Roads are fragmenting remaining habitats, degrading the ecological carrying capacity, and imposing a high mortality rate on wildlife populations. There are no central statistics on fauna casualties in Europe. However, there is growing evidence that infrastructure near wetlands and ponds cause the highest wildlife mortality rates. For instance, an estimated 250,000 to 3,086,000 amphibians are run over annually in Denmark, according to three surveys (Hansen 1982; Thomsen 1992; Bruun-Schmidt 1994). In the United Kingdom, 30 million to 70 million birds are killed each year on roads (Harwood et al. 1992). In the Netherlands, approximately 17,000 hedgehogs (*Erinaceus europaeus*) are killed yearly (Huijsers and Bergers 1997). In Switzerland it was found that roads are responsible for 51.5 percent of roe deer (*Capreolus capreolus*) mortality (Bundesamt für Umwelt, Wald und Landschaft 1999). The European Review of the COST 341 Action (Trocmé et al. in press) gives a more complete overview of wildlife mortality.

Figure 3.
A fence along main road and railway in Switzerland. The mesh at bottom is for amphibians. The wider mesh is for deer and wild boar.

Mitigation Measures Limiting Mortality

Most of the mitigation measures taken in Europe concentrate on reducing wildlife casualties. Such measures include fencing which, although required along all highways in Switzerland, is not required along all European highways and is found only along rail stretches with particularly high accident rates (Figure 3). In many areas reflectors, which are supposed to make animals more aware of oncoming traffic, are installed. Studies have shown them to be rather ineffective, however (de Molenaar and Henkens 1998). The use of deterrents such as odors also has been shown to be inefficient (Trocmé et al. in press). However other changes to the habitat along roads to keep animals away from the shoulders and to increase visibility are being used successfully in different regions. Trees planted along roads have been shown to help limit bird casualties by dissuading the birds from sweeping down low above cars. Signs are used commonly but have little effect on driver behavior.

A new system has been developed that uses infrared sensors to detect larger mammals approaching the road. These sensors trigger the flashing of a wildlife-warning sign plus a speed limit sign. This has been shown to reduce accidents by 80 to 100 percent on stretches of road in Switzerland (Kistler 1998).

Reducing the Barrier Effect

Recent research has made it clear that roads are a problem for wildlife not only because of mortality, but also, and to an even greater extent, because of the fragmentation of natural habitat. One example of the negative effects of fragmentation can be seen in Switzerland, where the lynx (*Lynx lynx*) was successfully reintroduced in the 1970s, but—because the species has not been able to expand geographically—the population level remains below sustainable levels (Breitenmoser 1995). This has also been the case for the highly endangered Iberian lynx (*Lynx pardinus*) (Gaona, Ferreras, and Delibes 1998).

The first successful efforts to avoid fragmentation began in 1970 as it became clear that roads were creating barriers for wildlife. The directorate-general for Public Works and Water Management in the Netherlands started building tunnels under roads for badgers (Bekker and Canters 1997). Accompanied by fencing,

Figure 4.
Underpass for small animals, such as badgers, in Germany.

these tunnels have proven to be very effective at limiting badger mortality (Figure 4).

In 1973 France published the first technical report on how to help large wildlife cross roads (Centre Technique du Génie Rural des Eaux et Forêts 1973). But it wasn't until the late 1970s that the barrier effect began to be examined more systematically (Centre Technique du Génie Rural des Eaux et Forêts 1978).

Figure 5.
A new-generation wildlife overpass near Lipník and Becvou in the Czech Republic.

Most early wildlife passages were undersized, and only 15 percent of the first generation wildlife bridges (10 meters or less in width) actually are used. By the 1980s overpasses were being built wider; the average width now is around 50 meters, with a range of 12 to 200 meters (Trocmé et al. in press) (Figure 5). Today a wide array of wildlife passages exists (Figures 6–9).

In the 1980s the first amphibian passages under roads were built in various European countries. Amphibians are the group that probably has suffered most from mortality on roads and from the barrier effect. In Switzerland complete populations disappeared along different lakeshores when construction of roads cut off spawning ponds from wintering grounds in the hills (Oggier, Righetti, and Bonnard 2001). Today different types of amphibian passages have been tested successfully (Figure 10), but they are used only in areas where a concentrated and regular migration occurs. Where the problem is caused by a minor road with low traffic density, the road may

Figure 6.
A wildlife overpass of a different design.

Figure 7.
This badger tunnel under a railway is in the Netherlands.

M. GRAY

be closed temporarily after dusk during the spawning season. This is the cheapest and most effective solution, but it can be used only where motorists have access to other roads during the closure.

Another means of mitigating fragmentation is to adjust existing structures to facilitate their co-use by wildlife. For instance, adding a strip of soil along the edge of a highway bridge and planting with grasses encourages wildlife use, lessens the barrier effect, and demands little financial investment (Figures 11, 12).

Recently there has been growing concern about so-called wildlife traps, such as road drainage systems, into which small animals can fall but from which they cannot climb out, thus ensuring a certain and slow death. For instance, it has been found that frogs cannot jump over the sharp curbs around drains, so they slip through road drains as an escape (Ratzel 1993). This problem has been solved by slanting the curbs around the

Figure 8.
Viaducts make it possible for most animals to cross under roadways. However, it has been shown that certain insects will not cross because of the dry microclimate under the viaduct (Dumont et al. 2000).

B. RUEDIGER

drains (Figure 13). An alternate design involves a drain without a curbstone, which allows small animals to leave the danger zone (Figure 14).

Research has been conducted to determine the effectiveness of different types of passages in terms of wildlife use. Large mammals seem to prefer overpasses to underpasses. An extensive study of sixteen overpasses in Switzerland, Germany, and the Netherlands found that structures larger than 50 meters are used more by wildlife than are narrower structures (Pfister et al. 1999).

Figure 9.
Road crossings over waterways are being retrofitted in the Netherlands and elsewhere to provide a dry shelf for wildlife use. When bridges are improved, they can be lengthened to ensure that there is sufficient dry land on each side of the waterway for wildlife use.

A. LEVY

Roadside signs, fencing, and wildlife passages all are being used to reduce wildlife casualties on European roads. However it is important to note that the most efficient measures—fencing and passages—are used only on motorways. Smaller roads are responsible for higher mortality. Once traffic on a road reaches 10,000 cars a day, it has been found that many animals no longer attempt to cross the road (Müller and Berthoud 1994). At this point mortality diminishes, but the barrier effect increases. It is very difficult to solve the barrier effect of secondary roads.

B. RUEDIGER

Figure 10.
Part of an amphibian crossing under construction in Germany. The lip at the top of the metal rail prevents animals from climbing over. The grate in the bridge that handles local traffic permits light and water to enter. The rail guides animals to a large underpass that allows them to safely cross under the multi-lane highway.

Pan-European Developments

Although awareness of the problems related to wildlife and roads is widespread in Europe, the continent faces a major challenge. There are 20,609 kilometers of new motorways planned in the next decade. This will have a major impact on ecosystems, even if sensitive areas can be avoided. In order to use the wealth of existing knowledge and the synergy of experts dispersed through the European countries, a network was founded in 1996 called the Infra Eco Network Europe (or IENE, *http://www.iene.info*). In 1998 the IENE launched a five-year research program within the European Cooperation in the field of Scientific and Technical Research (COST) in which sixteen countries are participating. The main objective of the program, known as COST Action 341, is to promote a safe and sustainable pan-European transport infrastructure by recommending measures and planning procedures that will conserve biodiversity and reduce vehicular accidents and wildlife casualties.

In addition, European countries have signed the Pan-European Biological and Landscape Diversity Strategy (PEBLD) (*http://www.ecnc.nl*). The PEBLD Strategy presents an innovative and proactive approach to stop-

Figure 11.
A bridge crossing a highway has an added grass strip to encourage use by surrounding wildlife.

ping and reversing the degradation of biological and landscape diversity in Europe—innovative because it addresses all biological and landscape initiatives under one European approach and proactive because it promotes the integration of biological and landscape diversity considerations into social and economic sectors.

Between 1996 and 2016, the PEBLD Strategy seeks an integration of biological and landscape diversity considerations into transport policies and transportation infrastructure development, avoiding areas of high value as much as possible. It also seeks to prevent or mitigate the negative effects of infrastructure and transportation activities on landscapes and ecosystems.

In 2001 the Strategic Environmental Assessment Directive (SEA) was adopted by the European Parliament (SEA Directive 2001/42/EC1; *http://europa.eu.int/comm/environment/eia/eia-legalcontext.htm*). The SEA directive intends to fill the gap that currently exists between the project-level environmental impact assessment covered by the EIA Directive and the environmental integration efforts at policy level. The EIA Directive has been applied since 1985.

Going beyond integrating fragmentation concerns into road planning, many European countries are beginning to retrofit existing roads with wildlife passages where needed. In Switzerland, for example, a study has identified major wildlife corridors (Holzgang et al. 2001) and determined bottlenecks where traditional

wildlife migration patterns have been broken. These points of interruption will be retrofitted in the next fifteen years, integrating this effort into the general highway upkeep program. Similar approaches are being used in Belgium, Estonia, Hungary, and the Netherlands. Such projects are related to the PEBLD Strategy, which endeavors in a larger way to facilitate a Pan-European Ecological Network.

The Future

Roadkill can seem to be an unavoidable consequence of twenty-first century living, because of the public's feeling of helplessness to do anything to reduce roadkill; the common belief that building more roads will solve traffic congestion; the desire of many for a home in the ever-expanding exurbs; the tradition within state and federal highway agencies of building

Figure 12.
A large modified underpass in Switzerland. Wildlife use is encouraged by the addition of tree stumps and other debris.

roads as quickly and inexpensively as possible; and the failure of governments at many levels to provide adequate protection for farm and natural lands. Yet it doesn't have to be, and it certainly does not have to continue at current levels. Indeed, promising developments have been seen in making species more secure thanks to improved design and passage installation.

Much of the scientific community has recognized that roads have a pervasive influence on wildlife and the environment. That community is responding with research aimed at providing ways to reduce or mitigate negative effects. State departments of

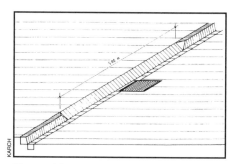

Figure 13.
Diagram of an alternate curb design for amphibian protection.

transportation have thus far limited wildlife-friendly road design, construction, and improvement projects to those benefiting threatened and endangered species, but they are beginning to think about a broader range of species. The public, while concerned about this problem, is largely unaware that measures to reduce roadkill levels are available.

The United States is fortunate in that, relative to many regions of the world, natural areas with abundant wildlife remain. Europe is well ahead of the United States, however, in building crossing structures and, most especially, in cultivating public understanding and recognition that reducing the negative effect of roads on wildlife is possible and appropriate. Educational efforts in the United States therefore are of paramount importance and must focus in large measure on the availability of alternatives to a roadside carpet of dead wildlife.

Armed with the knowledge that such alternatives exist, citizens can be urged to contact their representatives

Figure 14.
A road drain without a curbstone permits small animals to escape from the road surface.

in Congress to request legislation requiring that structures protecting wildlife be incorporated in highway construction and improvement projects whenever appropriate. An obvious legislative target includes the federal Transportation Equity Act, reauthorized every six years (the last reauthorization was in 2003—see *www.hsus.org*). Private citizens also can act as watchdogs by monitoring newspapers for announcements about proposed highway projects and demanding that the needs of wildlife be incorporated in highway construction and improvement projects. A useful guide to highway project planning is at *www.defenders.org/publications/CitizensGuide.pdf.*

Education focused on drivers also must continue. Providing drivers with (limited) information about where and when they are most likely to encounter wildlife in the road, and with the frequent admonition to reduce driving speeds in these areas, would save many animal and human lives. Much of the responsibility for reducing roadkill is placed—rightly—on motorists.

Forman and Deblinger (2000) assert that it is time to augment the traditional considerations undertaken in transportation planning and road construction—road alignment, grading, elevation, hydrologic needs, etc.—with consideration for the broad landscape processes affected by road placement and operation. Assessment of habitat wildlife movements and landscape linkages must become a part of all highway construction and expansion projects and of many maintenance activities.

Important research questions remain to be answered. While funds have been available for passage construction in many sites in Europe, research funds to monitor use of the passages have not been available. Basic studies evaluating passage use are needed in Europe as well as in North America, as are evaluations of use in conjunction with landscape features and local wildlife species and populations. Also needed are assessments of the effectiveness of passage

structures in terms of use by multiple species or multiple individuals within local populations; contribution to population genetic diversity; the influence of human activity on passage use; and placement and design of passages acceptable to a variety of amphibian and reptile species.

The impact of highways on wildlife and the environment has been called the conservation issue of the twenty-first century (B. Ruediger, U.S. Forest Service, personal communication, October 7, 2001). The United States has perhaps twenty years left before critical wildlife habitat connections are lost (M. Gray, FHWA, personal communication, March 20, 2002). Well before the end of the twenty-first century, we will have secured a place for wildlife in a landscape fractured by roads and habitat loss, or we will face "a future of soul-withering biological loneliness" (Quammen 1996, 634). Given the concern and involvement of many scientists, along with a public which proves time and again that it will act on behalf of wildlife when alternatives to its demise are at hand, there is reason for cautious optimism that roads and wildlife can coexist.

Notes

[1]Pervasive racism continued to confine African Americans to rural and inner-city poverty. Industries, freed from reliance on mass transportation for their workers by the growing number of employees with cars, relocated to areas outside the cities. Minorities who could not and remain unable to afford cars and are ill served by decaying and inadequate public transportation systems are isolated from the jobs that could lead them out of poverty (Flink 1988; Jackson 1985; Kay 1997).

Figure 2 is reproduced with the permission of Blackwell Science, Inc., Malden, Massachusetts.

Literature Cited

Adams, L.W., and A.D. Geis. 1983. Effects of roads on small mammals. *Journal of Applied Ecology* 20: 403–415.

Ashley, E.P., and J.T. Robinson. 1996. Road mortality of amphibians, reptiles, and other wildlife on the Long Point Causeway, Lake Erie, Ontario. *Canadian Field-Naturalist* 110(3): 403–412.

Bangs, E.E., T.N. Bailey, and M.F. Portner. 1989. Survival rates of adult female moose on the Kenai Peninsula. *Journal of Wildlife Management* 53: 557–563.

Bekker, G.J., and K.J. Canters. 1997. The continuing story of badgers and their tunnels. In *Habitat fragmentation and infrastructure: Proceedings, International Conference on Habitat Fragmentation, Infrastructure, and the Role of Ecological Engineering*, ed. K.J. Canters, A.A.G. Pierpers, and D. Hendriks-Heerma. Diens Weg-en Waterbouwkunde, Delft, Netherlands.

Bellis, E.D., and H.B. Graves. 1971. Deer mortality on a Pennsylvania interstate highway. *Journal of Wildlife Management* 35: 232–237.

Billard, J. 1998. *Abrégé d'histoire des routes—jean.billard@college-de-france.fr.* Accessed July 2002.

Bolen, E.G., and W.L. Robinson. 1995. *Wildlife ecology and management.* Englewood Cliffs, N.J.: Prentice Hall.

Breitenmoser, U. 1995. Lynx lynx (Linnaeus 1758)—Luchs. In *Säugetiere der Schweiz. Verbeitung, biologie, oekologie*, ed. J. Hausser, 418–423, Basel: Denkschriftenkommission der Schweizerischen Akademie der Naturwissenschaften, Birkhäuser.

Bruun-Schmidt, J. 1994. *Trafikdraebte dyr. Specialerapport*, Odense Universitet. Odense, Denmark.

Bundesamt für Umwelt, Wald und Landschaft. 1999. *Jagdstatistik 1998.* Bern, Switzerland.

Carbaugh, B.T. 1970. Activity and behavior of white-tailed deer (*Odocoileus virginianus*) along an interstate highway in a forest region of Pennsylvania. Ph.D. diss., The Pennsylvania State University.

Case, R.M. 1978. Interstate highway road-killed animals: A data source for biologists. *Wildlife Society Bulletin* 6: 8–13.

Clarke, G.P., P.C.L. White, and S. Harris. 1998. Effects of roads on badger *Meles meles* populations in south-west England. *Biological Conservation* 86: 117–124.

Clevenger, A.P. 2001. Mitigation for impacts of roads on wildlife. In *Proceedings of the International Conference on Ecology and Transportation*, 12–13. Keystone, Colo.

Clevenger, A.P., and N. Waltho. 2000. Factors influencing the effectiveness of wildlife underpasses in Banff National Park, Alberta, Canada. *Conservation Biology* 14(1): 47–56.

Clevenger, A.P., and J. Wierzchowski. 2001. GIS-based modeling approaches to identify mitigation placement along roads. In *Proceedings of the International Conference on Ecology and Transportation*, 134–142. Keystone, Colo.

Clevenger, A.P., B. Chruszez, and K.E. Gunson. 2001. Highway mitigation fencing reduces wildlife-vehicle collisions. *Wildlife Society Bulletin* 29(2): 646–653.

Cobb, E. 1987. Notes from the field: Victim of technology. *American Heritage, Invention and Technology* 2: 6–7.

Conover, M.R., W.C. Pitt, K.K. Kessler, T.J. DuBow, and W.A. Sanborn. 1995. Review of human injuries, illnesses, and economic losses caused by wildlife in the United States. *Wildlife Society Bulletin* 23: 407–414.

Centre Technique du Génie Rural des Eaux et Forêts. 1973. *Le problème de franchissement des autoroutes et route à grande circulation par les grands animaux gibiers*. Paris: Ministère de l'Agriculture.

———. 1978. Autoroute et grand gibier. Note technique 42. *Groupement technique forestier*. Paris: Ministère de l'Agriculture.

de Molenaar, J.G., and R.J.H.G. Henkens. 1998. *Effektiviteit van wildspiegels: Een literatuurstudie*. Instituut voor Bos-en natuuronderzoek, Wageningen, Netherlands.

de Molenaar, J.G., D.A. Jonkers, and M.E. Sanders. 2000. *Road illumination and nature III: Local influence of road lights on a black-tailed godwit (Limosa l. limosa) population*. DWW-Ontsnipperingreeks, part 38A. Wageningen, Netherlands: Alterra, Green World Research.

den Boer, P.J. 1981. On the survival of populations in a heterogeneous and variable environment. *Oecologia* 50: 39–53.

Drews, C. 1995. Road kills of animals by public traffic in Mikumi National Park, Tanzania, with notes on baboon mortality. *African Journal of Ecology* 33: 89–100.

Dumont, A-G., G. Berthoud, M. Tripet, S. Schneider, G. Dändliker, P. Durand, A. Ducommun, S. Müller, and M. Tille. 2000. *Interactions entre les réseaux de la faune et des voies de circulation. Mandat de recherche 8/97 sur proposition de l'Union des professionnels suisses de la route (VSS)*. Bern, Switzerland.

European Environment Agency (EEA). 2000. *Are we moving in the right direction? Indicators on transport and environment integraton in the EU*. Environmental Issues Series No 12. Copenhagen: EEA.

Evink, G.L. 1996. Florida Department of Transportation initiatives related to wildlife mortality. In *Proceedings of the Transportation-Related Wildlife Mortality Seminar*, ed. G.L. Evink, P. Garrett, D. Zeigler, J. Berry, n.p. FL-ER-58-96. Tallahassee: Florida Department of Transportation.

Fahrig, L., and G. Merriam. 1985. Habitat patch connectivity and population survival. *Ecology* 66(6): 1762–1768.

Fahrig, L., J.H. Pedlar, S.E. Pope, P.D. Taylor, and J.F. Wegner. 1995. Effect of road traffic on amphibian density. *Biological Conservation* 74: 177–182.

Falk, N.W., H.B. Graves, and E.D. Bellis. 1978. Highway right-of-way fences as deer deterrents. *Journal of Wildlife Management* 42: 646–650.

Farmer, A.M. 1993. The effects of dust on vegetation—A review. *Environmental Pollution* 79: 63–75.

Federal Highway Administration Critter Crossings. 2002. *http://www.fhwa.dot.gov/environment/wildlife-crossings/photo03.htm*. Accessed October.

Federal Highway Administration

Highway Statistics Series. 2002. *http://www.fhwa.dot.gov/ohim/hs00*. Accessed November.

Feldhamer, G.A., J.E. Gates, D.M. Harman, A.J. Loranger, and K.R. Dixon. 1986. Effects of interstate highway fencing on white-tailed deer activity. *Journal of Wildlife Management* 50: 497–503.

Flink, J.J. 1988. *The automobile age*. Cambridge, Mass.: The MIT Press.

Forman, R.T.T. 1995. *Land mosaics: The ecology of landscapes and regions*. New York: Cambridge University Press.

———. 2000. Estimate of the area affected ecologically by the road system in the United States. *Conservation Biology* 14(1): 31–35.

Forman, R.T.T., and L.E. Alexander. 1998. Roads and their major ecological effects. *Annual Review of Ecology and Systematics* 29: 207–231.

Forman, R.T.T., and R.D. Deblinger. 2000. The ecological road-effect zone of a Massachusetts (U.S.A.) suburban highway. *Conservation Biology* 14(1): 36–46.

Forman, R.T.T., D.S. Friedman, D. Fitzhenry, J.D. Martin, A.S. Chen, and L.E. Alexander. 1996. Ecological effects of roads: Towards three summary indices and an overview for North America. In *Habitat fragmentation and infrastructure*, ed. K. Canters, 40–54. Delft, Netherlands: Ministry of Transport, Public Works, and Water Management.

Forman, R.T.T., D. Sperling, J.A. Bissonette, A.P. Clevenger, C.D. Cutshall, V.H. Dale, L. Fahrig, R. France, C.R. Goldman, K. Heanue, J.A. Jones, F.J. Swanson, T. Turrentine, and T.C. Winter. 2003. *Road ecology: Science and solutions*. Washington, D.C.: Island Press.

Foster, M.L., and S.R. Humphrey. 1992. *Effectiveness of wildlife crossings in reducing animal/auto collisions on Interstate 75, Big Cypress Swamp, Florida*. Florida Game and Fresh Water Fish Commission, Tallahassee, Fla. FL-ER-50-92.

Fraser, D., and E.R. Thomas. 1982. Moose-vehicle accidents in Ontario: Relation to highway salt. *Wildlife*

Society Bulletin 10: 261–265.

Gaona, P., P. Ferreras, and M. Delibes. 1998. Dynamics and viability of a metapopulation of the endangered Iberian lynx (*Lynx pardinus*). *Ecological Monographs* 68: 349–370.

Garland, T., and W.G. Bradley. 1984. Effects of a highway on Mojave Desert rodent populations. *American Midland Naturalist* 111(1): 47–56.

Gerlach, G., and K. Musolf. 2000. Fragmentation of landscape as a cause for genetic subdivision in bank voles. *Conservation Biology* 14(4): 1066–1074.

Gibbs, J., and G. Shriver. 2002. Estimating the effects of road mortality on turtle populations. *Conservation Biology* (16)6: 1647–1652.

Gibeau, M.L., and S. Herrero. 1997. *Eastern Slopes grizzly bear project: 1996 progress report.* Alberta: University of Calgary.

Gibeau, M.L., and S. Herrero. 1998. Roads, rails, and grizzly bears in the Bow River Valley, Alberta. In *Proceedings of the International Conference on Wildlife Ecology and Transportation*, ed. G.L. Evink, P. Garrett, D. Zeigler, and J. Berry, n.p. FL-ER-69-98: 104–108. Tallahassee: Florida Department of Transportation.

Gibeau, M.L., and K. Heuer. 1996. Effects of transportation corridors on large carnivores in the Bow River Valley, Alberta. In *Proceedings of the Transportation Related Wildlife Mortality Seminar*, ed., G.L. Evink, P. Garrett, D. Zeigler, and J. Berry, n.p. FL-ER-58-96. Tallahassee: Florida Department of Transportation.

Goldsmith, C.D., P.F. Scanlon, and W.R. Pirie. 1976. Lead concentrations in soil and vegetation associated with highways of different traffic densities. *Bulletin of Environmental Contamination and Toxicology* 16: 66–70.

Gordon, K.M., and S.H. Anderson. 2001. Motorist response to a deer-sensing warning system in western Wyoming. In *Proceedings of the International Conference on Ecology and Transportation*, 549–558.

Keystone, Colo.

Groot Bruinderink, G.W.T.A., and E. Hazebroek. 1996. Ungulate traffic collisions in Europe. *Conservation Biology* 10: 1059–1067.

Hanna, P. 1982. *The impact of Interstate Highway 84 on the Sublette-Black Pine migratory deer population: A twelve-year summary, with recommendations for the mitigation of identifiable adverse impacts.* Idaho Department of Fish and Game, Project W-160.

Hansen, L. 1982. Trafikdraebte dyr i Danmark. *Dansk Ornithologisk forenings tidsskrift* 76: 97–110.

Harris, L.D., and P.B. Gallagher. 1989. New initiatives for wildlife conservation: The need for movement corridors. In *In defense of wildlife: Preserving corridors and communities*, ed. G. Mackintosh, 117–134. Washington, D.C.: Defenders of Wildlife.

Harwood, R., and S. Hilbourne. 1992. *Ever increasing circles: The impact and the effectiveness of the M25 plan.* RSNC, The Wildlife Trusts Partnership.

Haskell, D.G. 2000. Effects of forest roads on macroinvertebrate soil fauna of the Southern Appalachian Mountains. *Conservation Biology* 14(1): 57–63.

Heimlich, R., and W. Anderson. 2001. *Development at the urban fringe and beyond: Impacts on agriculture and rural land.* Economic Research Service Agricultural Economic Report No. 803. U.S. Department of Agriculture, Washington, D.C.

Hels, T., and E. Buchwald. 2001. The effect of road kills on amphibian populations. *Biological Conservation* 99: 331–340.

Henein, K., and G. Merriam. 1990. The elements of connectivity where corridor quality is variable. *Landscape Ecology* 4(2/3): 157–170.

Henke, R.J., P. Cawood-Hellmund, and T. Sprunk. 2001. Habitat connectivity study of the I-25 and U.S.-85 corridors, Colorado. In *Proceedings of the International Conference on Ecology and Transportation*, 499–508. Keystone, Colo.

Herrero, S. 1995. The Canadian National Parks and grizzly bear

ecosystems: The need for interagency management. *International Conference on Bear Research and Management* 9: 7–21.

Heuer, K. 1995. Wildlife corridors around developed areas of Banff National Park. *Progress Report for Parks Canada.* Banff, Alberta.

Holzgang, O., H.P. Pfister, D. Heynen, M. Blant, A. Righetti, G. Berthoud, P. Marchesi, T. Maddalena, H. Müri, M. Wendelspiess, G. Dändliker, P. Mollet, and U. Bornhauser-Sieber. 2001. *Les corridors faunistiques en Suisse. Cahier de l'environnement No 326.* Bern: Office fédéral de l'environnement, des forêts et du paysage.

Huggard, D.J. 1993. Prey selectivity of wolves in Banff National Park. II. Age, sex, and condition of elk. *Canadian Journal of Zoology* 71: 140–147.

Huijsers, M., and P.J.M. Bergers. 1997. *Egels en verkeer: Effecten van wegen en verkeer op egelpopulaties.* Dienst Weg-en Waterbouwkunde, Delft.

Jackson, K.T. 1985. *Crabgrass frontier: The suburbanization of the United States.* New York: Oxford University Press.

Jackson, S. 1996. Underpass systems for amphibians. In *Proceedings of the International Conference on Wildlife Ecology and Transportation*, ed. G.L. Evink, P. Garrett, D. Zeigler, and J. Berry, n.p. FL-ER-69-98. Tallahassee: Florida Department of Transportation.

Jackson, S.D., and C.R. Griffin. 1998. Toward a practical strategy for mitigating highway impacts on wildlife. In *Proceedings of the International Conference on Wildlife Ecology and Transportation*, ed. G.L. Evink, P., Garrett, D. Zeigler, and J. Berry, 17–22. FL-ER-69-98. Tallahassee: Florida Department of Transportation.

Jones, J.A., F.J. Swanson, B.C. Wemple, and K.U. Snyder. 2000. Effects of roads on hydrology, geomorphology, and disturbance patches in stream networks. *Conservation Biology* 14(1): 76–85.

Kay, J.H. 1997. *Asphalt nation: How*

the automobile took over America and how we can take it back. Berkeley: University of California Press.

Kistler, R. 1998. *Wissentschaftliche begleitung der wild anlage calstrom.* WWA-12-S. July 1995–November 1997; Schlussbericht. Zürich: Infodiesnt Wildbiologie.

Kline, N.C., and D.E. Swann. 1998. Quantifying wildlife road mortality in Saguaro National Park. In *Proceedings of the International Conference on Wildlife Ecology and Transportation,* ed. G.L. Evink, P., Garrett, D. Zeigler, and J. Berry, 23–31. FL-ER-69-98. Tallahassee: Florida Department of Transportation.

Kuitunen, M., E. Rossi, and A. Stenroos. 1998. Do highways influence density of land birds? *Environmental Management* 22(2): 297–302.

Lagerwerff, J.V., and A.N. Specht. 1970. Contamination of roadside soil and vegetation with cadmium, nickel, lead, and zinc. *Environmental Science Technology* 4: 583–586.

Land, D., and M. Lotz. 1996. Wildlife crossing designs and use by Florida panthers and other wildlife in southwest Florida. In *Proceedings of the International Conference on Wildlife Ecology and Transportation,* ed. G.L. Evink, P. Garrett, D. Zeigler, and J. Berry, n.p. FL-ER-69-98. Tallahassee: Florida Department of Transportation.

Laursen, K. 1981. Birds on roadside verges and the effect of mowing on frequency and distribution. *Biological Conservation* 20: 59–68.

Lovallo, M.J., and E.M. Anderson. 1996. Bobcat movements and home ranges relative to roads in Wisconsin. *Wildlife Society Bulletin* 24(1): 71–76.

Mace, R.D., J.S. Waller, T.L. Manley, L.J. Lyon, and H. Zuuring. 1996. Relationships among grizzly bears, roads, and habitat in the Swan Mountains Montana. *Journal of Applied Ecology* 33: 1395–1404.

Mader, H.J. 1984. Animal habitat isolation by roads and agricultural fields. *Biological Conservation* 29: 81–96.

Mader, H.J., C. Schell, and P. Kornacker. 1990. Linear barriers to arthropod movements in the landscape. *Biological Conservation* 54: 209–222.

Maltby, L., B.A. Boxall, D.M. Farrow, P. Calow, and C.I. Betton. 1995. The effects of motorway runoff on freshwater ecosystems. 2. Identifying major toxicants. *Environmental Toxicology and Chemistry* 14: 1093–1101.

McCabe, T.R., and R.E. McCabe. 1997. Recounting whitetails past. In *The science of overabundance: Deer ecology and population management,* ed. W.J. McShea, H.B. Underwood, and J.H. Rappole, 11–26. Washington, D.C.: Smithsonian Institution Press.

McLellan, B.N., and D.M. Shackleton. 1988. Grizzly bears and resource extraction industries: Effects of roads on behavior, habitat use, and demography. *Journal of Applied Ecology* 25: 451–460.

Mech, L.D., S.H. Fritts, G.L. Radde, and W.J. Paul. 1988. Wolf distribution and road density in Minnesota. *Wildlife Society Bulletin* 16: 85–87.

Müller, S. 2002. Aide-mémoire à l'usage des écologistes de toute nature et de ceux qui leur sont apprentés. In *Route et trafic, l'Union des professionnnels suisses de la route.* VSS 3/02. Zürich, Switzerland.

Müller, S., and G. Berthoud. 1994. *Sécurité faune/trafics; Manuel protque à l'usage des ingénieurs civils.* Laussane: Ecole polytechnique de Lausanne, Département de génie civil.

Munguira, M.L., and J.A. Thomas. 1992. Use of road verges by butterfly and burnet populations, and the effect of roads on adult dispersal and mortality. *Journal of Applied Ecology* 29: 316–329.

National Park Service. 2003. Natural Resource Information Division Fact Sheet: White-tailed deer in National Parks. *http://www.nature.nps-gov/facts/fdeer2.htm.* Accessed February.

Noss, R.F., H.B. Quigley, M.G. Hornocker, T. Merrill, and P. C. Paquet. 1996. Conservation biology and carnivore conservation in the Rocky Mountains. *Conservation Biology* 10(4): 949–963.

Oggier, P., A. Righetti, and L. Bonnard, eds. 2001. *Zerschneidung von Lebensräumen durch Verkehrsinfrastrukturen COST 341.* Schriftenreihe Umwelt No 332. Bundesamt für Umwelt, Wald und Landschaft; Bundesamt für Raumentwicklung; Bundesamt für Verkehr; Bundesamt für Strassen. Bern, Switzerland.

Oxley, D.J., M.B. Fenton, and G.R. Carmody. 1974. The effects of roads on populations of small mammals. *Journal of Applied Ecology* 11: 51–59.

Paquet, P., and C. Callaghan. 1996. Effects of linear developments on winter movements of gray wolves in the Bow River valley of Banff National Park, Alberta. In *Proceedings of the International Conference on Wildlife Ecology and Transportation,* ed. G.L. Evink, P. Garrett, D. Zeigler, and J. Berry, n.p. FL-ER-69-98. Tallahassee: Florida Department of Transportation.

Pfister, H.P., D. Heynen, B. Georgii, V. Keller, and F. Von Lerber. 1999. *Häufigkeit und Verhalten ausgewälter Wildsäuger auf unterschiedlichen breiten (Grünbrücken).* Schwiezerische Vogelwarte, 6204 Semapch, Germany.

Pojar, T.M., R.A. Prosence, D.F. Reed, and T.N. Woodward. 1975. Effectiveness of a lighted, animated deer crossing sign. *Journal of Wildlife Management* 39: 87–91.

Putnam, R.J. 1997. Deer and road traffic accidents—Options for management. *Journal of Environmental Management* 51: 43–57.

Quammen, D. 1996. *The song of the dodo: Island biogeography in an age of extinction.* New York: Simon and Schuster.

Ratzel M. 1993. *Strassenentwässerung—Fallenwirkung und entschärfung unter besonderer berücksichtigung der amphibien.* BNL, Karlsruhe, Germany.

Reed, D.F. 1981. Mule deer behavior at a highway underpass exit. *Journal of Wildlife Management* 45:

542–543.

Reed, R.A., J. Johnson-Barnard, and W.L. Baker. 1996. Contribution of roads to forest fragmentation in the Rocky Mountains. *Conservation Biology* 10(4): 1098–1106.

Reeve, A.F., and S.H. Anderson. 1993. Ineffectiveness of Swareflex reflectors at reducing deer-vehicle collisions. *Wildlife Society Bulletin* 21: 349–354.

Reh, W. 1989. Investigations into the influence of roads on the genetic structure of populations of the common frog *Rana temporaria*. In *Amphibians and roads: Proceedings of the Toad Tunnel Conference*, ed. T.E.S. Langton, 101–103. Rendsburg, Federal Republic of Germany, Bedfordshire, England.

Reijnen, R., R. Foppen, and H. Meeuwsen. 1996. The effects of car traffic on the density of breeding birds in Dutch agricultural grasslands. *Biological Conservation* 75: 255–260.

Reijnen, R., R. Foppen, C. ter Braak, and J. Thissen. 1995. The effects of car traffic on breeding bird populations in woodland. III. Reduction of density in relation to the proximity of main roads. *Journal of Applied Ecology* 32: 187–202.

Romin, L.A., and J.A. Bissonette. 1996. Deer-vehicle collisions: Status of state monitoring activities and mitigation efforts. *Wildlife Society Bulletin* 24: 276–283.

Rosen, P.C., and C.H. Lowe. 1994. Highway mortality of snakes in the Sonoran Desert of southern Arizona. *Biological Conservation* 60: 143–148.

Rost, G.R., and J.A. Bailey. 1979. Distribution of mule deer and elk in relation to roads. *Journal of Wildlife Management* 43: 634–641.

Ruediger, B. 2001. High, wide, and handsome: Designing more effective wildlife and fish crossings for roads and highways. In *Proceedings of the International Conference on Ecology and Transportation*, 509–516. Keystone, Colo.

Schafer, J.A., and S.T. Penland. 1985. Effectiveness of Swareflex reflec-tors in reducing deer-vehicle accidents. *Journal of Wildlife Management* 49: 774–776.

Sielecki, L.E. 2001. Evaluating the effectiveness of wildlife accident mitigation installations with the wildlife accident reporting system (WARS) in British Columbia. In *Proceedings of the International Conference on Ecology and Transportation*, 473–489. Keystone, Colo.

Smith, D.J. 1995. *The direct and indirect impacts of highways on the vertebrates of Payne's Prairie State Preserve*. Gainesville: University of Florida, Department of Wildlife Ecology and Conservation. FL-ER-62-96.

Taskula, T. 1997. The moose ahead. *Traffic Technology International* 42: 170–173.

Tewes, M.E., and R.W. Hughes. 2001. Ocelot management and conservation along transportation corridors in southern Texas. In *Proceedings of the International Conference on Ecology and Transportation*, 559–564. Keystone, Colo.

Thiel, R.P. 1985. The relationship between road densities and wolf habitat suitability in Wisconsin. *American Midland Naturalist* 113: 404–407.

Thomsen, K. 1992. *Projekt vildtregistrering*. Rapport udarbejdet for Falck Danmark. Lyngby, Denmark: COWI A/S.

Trocmé, M., S. Cahill, J.G. De Vries, H. Farrall, L. Folkeson, G. Fry, C. Hicks, and J. Peymen, eds. In press. *COST 341—Habitat fragmentation due to transportation infrastructure: The European review*. Brussels: Office for Official Publications of the European Communities.

Trombulak, S.C., and C.A. Frissell. 2000. Review of ecological effects of roads on terrestrial and aquatic communities. *Conservation Biology* 14: 18–30.

Turrentine, T., K. Heanue, and D. Sperling. 2001. Road and vehicle system. In *Proceedings of the International Conference on Ecology and Transportation*, 5–6. Keystone, Colo.

Ujvári, M., H.J. Baagøe, and A. B. Madsen. 1998. Effectiveness of wildlife warning reflectors in reducing deer-vehicle collisions; a behavioral study. *Journal of Wildlife Management* 62: 1094–1099.

Underhill, J.E., and P.G. Angold. 2000. Effects of roads on wildlife in an intensively modified landscape. *Environmental Review* 8: 21–39.

U.S. Census Bureau. 2002. *http://www.census.gov*. Accessed November.

U.S. Forest Service. 2000. Map of U.S. roads.*http://www.fhwa.dot.gov/environment/wildlifecrossings/overview.htm*. Accessed November.

van der Grift, E.A. 1999. Mammals and railroads: Impacts and management implications. *Lutra* 42: 77–98.

Ward, A.L. 1982. Mule deer behavior in relation to fencing and underpasses on Interstate 80 in Wyoming. *Transportation Research Record* 859: 8–13.

Waring, G.H., J.L. Griffis, and M.E. Vaughn. 1991. White-tailed deer roadside behavior, wildlife warning reflectors, and highway mortality. *Applied Animal Behavior Science* 29: 215–223.

Warner, R.E. 1992. Nest ecology of grassland passerines on road rights-of-way in central Illinois. *Biological Conservation* 59:1–7.

Farm Disease Crises in the United Kingdom: Lessons to Be Learned

10

CHAPTER

Michael C. Appleby

Introduction

Over the last fifteen years, a diverse succession of disease-related crises has befallen farm animal and food industries in the United Kingdom. Some have involved animal health, with little risk to humans. Some have involved human health, with animals acting as a reservoir for infection but little affected themselves. Some, however—including the most alarming—have involved both animal and human health through zoonoses, diseases transmittable from animal to human. All of these crises are linked in the public mind and in many commentaries, and indeed there are issues that many of them share. The most common of these is concern for food safety, but concern for animal welfare is also a recurrent theme. These concerns play out against a backdrop of:

- Prevalent attitudes, including complacency, about issues of biosecurity, from animal health to food safety;
- Relevant legislation, law enforcement, and law breaking;
- The practices of transporting animal feed, animals, and animal products; and

- An emphasis on the economics of animal production to the exclusion of all other considerations.

Few of these crises have been limited to the United Kingdom, but the problems do seem to have been worse and more frequent there.

Salmonella in Eggs

In 1988 a government minister's statement that "most egg production in the United Kingdom is infected by salmonella" received wide publicity (BBC 1999). The statement proved to be true, and it was confirmed that salmonella bacteria from eggs cause food poisoning. Egg sales fell by about half. To some extent this was a "non-story," since salmonella had not recently increased, the number of eggs affected was small, and the health risk for consumers was relatively minor. (Healthy adults are unlikely to suffer more than a stomach upset even from raw, infected eggs, although children and old people may be more seriously affected. Cooking infected eggs kills the bacteria.) However, the scare

demonstrated clearly that public expectations of food safety had increased, and understandably so, since an earlier time when occasional food poisoning was routine.

Fifteen years later, the food industry is only beginning to grapple with this heightened expectation. The industry's complacency has been hard to shake off and, although perhaps ill-founded, this could be justified at least partially by the fact that the poultry sector has led other agricultural sectors in health care for its animals. Because of the susceptibility of chickens and other poultry to disease, in the years following World War II the industry developed a positive approach to health control, including farm design, hygiene, preventative vaccination, and general management (Julian 1995). Perhaps the most important element of general management has been the "all in, all out" approach in which houses are emptied completely between one flock's departure and the next's arrival. The ability to clean facilities thoroughly between flocks and to reduce transmission of disease vectors from old to young animals, has made a paramount contribution to poultry health. It also underscores the irony of the 1988 scare's relationship to poultry products rather than to others more vulnerable. (The approach is only now, many years later, being adopted by other agricultural sectors such as pig farming.)

Despite all this, the industry has not eliminated salmonella in eggs, in part, perhaps, because there are many different types of bacteria involved. The consequences for poultry are variable (Curtis 1990); mortality ranges from 1 to 75 percent (Sainsbury 2000) but is usually low. By contrast, "a few areas of the world, notably Scandinavia, have been able to virtually rid themselves of salmonella infections in animals" (113).

The furor in the United Kingdom provoked an extensive response from the government, including three orders introduced in 1989. The Zoonoses Order required registration of flocks, regular testing for salmonella, and stringent measures if it was detected. The Processed Animal Protein Order and the Importation of Processed Animal Protein Order required salmonella testing of such protein, intended for feeding animals—although it is notable that these orders did not identify the sort of problem that was even then exacerbating Bovine Spongiform Encephalopathy, or BSE (see the next section). The promise of such measures, and their implementation, reassured the public. Egg sales slowly recovered. However, salmonella in eggs still has not been eliminated in the United Kingdom and in most of the European Union (EU). Sainsbury (2000, 116) suggests that even if it were, this status would be difficult to maintain. He comments as follows about the lack of effective government policy to reduce salmonellosis and other zoonoses:

Our poultry...will always be vulnerable to the introduction and re-infection from other sources, such as wildlife, over which we have no control, the whole environment around them and above all from man himself....Also, animal products, including poultry, enter the United Kingdom from European Union sources in an almost unrestricted way, and several EU countries have no salmonella control programmes. Poultry products are currently entering the United Kingdom from other parts of the world where salmonella control programmes are absent. Thus, with people and animal products constantly putting our birds at risk, the United Kingdom government's policy is, at the least, worrying.

By contrast, Pennington (BBC 1999)—professor of bacteriology at the University of Aberdeen and well known due to the *E. coli* inquiry (see page 153)—suggests that salmonella should not still be a problem:

I don't know why we have a problem with salmonella still, probably because we have not worked hard enough to try to get rid of it. We shouldn't have a problem with salmonella. We know how to sort it out. Other people have sorted it out, we should have had it sorted out long ago.

In 2001 the EU Commission announced that it would target salmonella poisoning as a number one priority in a food safety crackdown, bringing in new controls affecting producers of breeding poultry, laying hens, broilers, turkeys, and pigs over the next eight years (Meade 2001).

In the United States, about 40,000 cases of salmonellosis are reported annually (more probably go unreported), and about 1,000 deaths (Marler Clark, L.L.P., P.S. 2001). Evidence that a significant number of these cases derives from animal products is circumstantial, but convincing, given the extent of infection in poultry and other units (Altekruse, Cohen, and Swerdlow 1997):

The doubling of salmonellosis incidence in the last two decades has accompanied modern food industries' centralized production and large-scale distribution. ...The trend toward larger markets and consolidation of industry has exacerbated the *Salmonella*

enteritidis problem in another way. Changes in egg production have adversely affected infection control in poultry flocks. In 1945, a typical hen house contained 500 birds. By 1995, many houses contained 100,000 hens, and multiple houses were often linked by common machinery, resulting in large flocks with common risk profiles. Large-scale distribution of shell eggs from infected flocks has caused outbreaks in which contaminated eggs were distributed in many states over a period of months.

Bovine Spongiform Encephalopathy

As its name indicates, BSE—a disease discovered in 1986—causes the brains of cattle to become spongy. The resulting behavior, such as staggering, has given rise to BSE's common name, "mad cow disease." After 1986 the incidence of BSE increased gradually and then rapidly, peaking in 1992 at more than 3,000 cases per month in the United Kingdom. Early on, there was concern that BSE might be transmittable to humans, and in March 1996 it was confirmed that such is probably the case. Eating infected animal material is the likely cause of a new variant of Creutzfeldt-Jakob disease (vCJD), which has similar physical symptoms in humans to those of BSE in cattle. As of 2000 about 115 people had died from vCJD, mostly in the United Kingdom, according to an official inquiry set up in 1997 and chaired by Lord Phillips (Phillips, Bridgeman, and Ferguson-Smith 2000).

BSE must have become established in U.K. cattle in the 1970s. Its origin is not known, but a major possibility is that it arose from a similar disease in sheep called scrapie (Horn et al. 2001). Other sources suggested include a mutation in a single cow, zoo antelopes (Phillips, Bridgeman, and Ferguson-Smith 2000), and U.S.

cattle (H.W. Reid, Moredun Research Institute, personal communication, June 27, 2001). The latter idea stems from the fact that U.S. mink have had outbreaks of a similar disease since the 1940s, of which beef is a likely source (Phillips, Bridgeman, and Ferguson-Smith 2000).

It quickly became clear that the disease was spread by feeding cattle meat and bone meal (MBM) from animal carcasses. The biological agent that causes scrapie may have changed to make it infective in cattle. Alternatively or in addition, new management practices introduced in the 1970s and 1980s probably increased infectivity; these included changes in how MBM was produced, and increased feeding of MBM to young calves (Horn et al. 2001).

In 1988 the Ministry of Agriculture, Fisheries, and Food (MAFF) introduced a ban on feeding ruminant protein to ruminants. This was followed in 1990 by a ban on using material from cattle tissue most likely to be infective (brain, spinal cord, and intestines) for human food, and another in 1991 on using such material for feeding pigs and poultry. Unfortunately, implementation of these bans was made less effective by two mistaken assumptions. First, it was thought that the infection was coming directly from sheep. In fact, whatever its original source, the infection now was being spread by MBM from infected cattle being fed to other cattle. This had a self-amplifying effect that was not understood for several more years: as more animals were infected, so the rate of infection accelerated. The assumption that scrapie was responsible also inappropriately lessened the urgency of measures to protect human health, as scrapie is not transmittable to humans. Second, it was thought that infection was possible only if a large amount of infective material was eaten, whereas it proved that as little as one gram was needed. Perhaps because of this assumption, farmers and feed suppliers were relaxed about continuing, illegally, to use existing stocks of MBM for their cattle and to export MBM around the world. There also was contamination of cattle feed from that prepared for pigs and poultry (Phillips, Bridgeman, and Ferguson-Smith 2000).

The result of the mistaken assumptions was that the disease became much more widespread than it otherwise might have. As of 2002 there had been more than 180,000 cases of BSE in the United Kingdom. In the rest of Europe, more than 3,000 cases had been reported; presumably these started from MBM from the United Kingdom, but recycling of infected MBM also is likely to have been a problem within those European countries. There also had been a small number of cases in non-European countries; these involved imported animals.

One reason it was difficult to understand—and therefore control—BSE more quickly is that the disease has a long incubation period; it takes four to six years before infected cattle show symptoms. Most have been slaughtered before then. For a long time, it was mistakenly believed that animals not showing symptoms could not infect others. Indeed, confidence that beef was safe to eat meant that for some time even animals slaughtered because they were showing symptoms were used for human food. The incubation period in humans may be ten or more years.

With increased knowledge of BSE, including its probable transmission to humans, a complete ban was imposed in the United Kingdom in March 1996 on use of all mammalian MBM in farm animal feed. Even this ban could be described as conservative, and indeed there is a lack of clarity on exactly what has been banned. Phillips, Bridgeman, and Ferguson-Smith (2000) get it wrong in their summary (vol. 1, 66):

> [Previous measures] were replaced after 20 March 1996 by the radical step of banning the incorporation of all animal protein in animal feed.

Phillips, Bridgeman, and Ferguson-Smith are suggesting that, despite all that had happened up to that point, the ban still seemed radical. That certainly is not true now, especially since the ban includes not "all animal protein" but only mammalian MBM. They make this clear elsewhere, but this still leaves room for confusion. It remains legal, for example, to feed poultry protein to animals, including poultry. Even as of 2002 a complete ban on intra-species recycling was only being considered, not pressed.

Whether or not the ban was radical when it was introduced, MAFF resisted it for a long time. It seems bizarre now, but this resistance came in the face of proposals from feed manufacturers, as represented by the U.K. Agricultural Supply Trade Association (UKASTA) (Phillips, Bridgeman, and Ferguson-Smith 2000):

> MAFF was concerned not to do anything that would lead UKASTA members to cease using animal protein as an ingredient of feed for non-ruminant animals. UKASTA, for its part, was anxious that its members should be able to continue to do this without incurring risk of prosecution should it result, on occasion, in cross-contamination of ruminant feed. UKASTA was to threaten repeatedly that it might have to advise its members to cease using animal protein, while MAFF officials sought to allay UKASTA's anxieties. (vol. 1, 63)

No cases of BSE had been diagnosed in the United States as of mid-2003. Importation of ruminants and ruminant by-products from countries with BSE have been banned for some years, and in 1997 the U.S. Food and Drug Administration banned the use of mammalian carcasses in the production of feed for ruminants. A study commissioned by the U.S. Department of Agriculture concluded that risk of BSE in the United States is low (Harvard Center for Risk Analysis 2001), but some commentators argue that there is much too little surveillance, especially as compliance with feed rules is known to be weak (Newman 2001).

At the height of the BSE epidemic there were at least four serious public concerns in addition to the obvious worries about possible effects on human health and the farming industry. First was a view that MAFF was divided in its loyalties on the BSE issue and could not be trusted to defend consumers' interests as well as those of farmers. Second, there was a perception that the government had concealed the truth about the risk to humans. Phillips, Bridgeman, and Ferguson-Smith (2000) reject both of these charges. Nevertheless, they acknowledge (vol. 1, xviii) that "confidence in government pronouncements about risk was a further casualty of BSE." One consequence of this (in combination with other crises, particularly the outbreak of *E. coli* discussed next) was the establishment in 2000 of an independent Food Standards Agency. Another was redistribution of MAFF's responsibilities after the 2001 general election and its replacement with a Department of Environment, Food, and Rural Affairs.

The third public concern had to do with the effects of the disease on the cattle themselves. There has been surprisingly little discussion of the actual impact of BSE on cattle welfare. However, Phillips, Bridgeman, and Ferguson-Smith (2000) make it clear that vCJD is very unpleasant for humans (Table 1), and it may be presumed that BSE in cows has at least some similar mental as well as physical effects. Furthermore, media coverage suggested that concern for the animals involved was not limited to considerations of suffering. It also expressed that it is wrong for animals to have a disease, especially one seen as avoidable, irrespective of its mental effects, and that killing of animals (including healthy herd mates of cows with BSE) is of serious ethical concern. The concern about killing may be based in part on the fact that the animals are not being used for meat or other purposes. It also is possible that the concern simply came to the fore because the killing was brought to public attention. These ideas will be discussed again below, in the context of foot and mouth disease.

The fourth and most fundamental concern was that the whole process of

Table 1
Symptoms of vCJD in Humans

An early age of onset or death (average 27.6 years, range 18–41 years).

A prolonged duration of illness (average 13.1 months, range 7.5–24 months).

A predominantly psychiatric presentation including anxiety, depression, withdrawal, and progressive behavioral changes.

First evidence of neurological involvement in four patients was dysaesthesiae (unpleasant abnormal sensations) in the limbs and/or face.

Development of a cerebellar syndrome, with problems with gait and limb muscle coordination after a period of weeks or months.

Development of forgetfulness and memory disturbance, often late in the clinical course, which progressed to severe cognitive impairment and a state of akinetic mutism (paralysis and inability to speak) in the majority of cases.

Development of muscle twitching or spasms in the majority of patients (myoclonus), preceded by purposeless involuntary movements in some (chorea), with EEG appearances typical of sporadic CJD absent.

Source: Phillips, Bridgeman, and Ferguson-Smith 2000, 8:2

forcing herbivores to eat animal protein, of making cows into cannibals, was an unnatural practice. This may be partly a concern for the cows, partly a feeling that treating animals unnaturally is wrong in itself, and partly an opinion that it should have been obvious that such a practice would lead to disaster. Phillips, Bridgeman, and Ferguson-Smith (2000) reject this last point:

> The practice of feeding MBM to animals in the United Kingdom dates back at least to 1926....It is a practice which has also been followed in many other countries. It was recognised that it was important that the rendering process should inactivate conventional pathogens. Experience had not suggested that the practice involved any other risks. In these circumstances we can understand why no one foresaw that the practice of feeding ruminant protein to ruminants might give rise to a disaster such as the BSE epidemic. (vol. 1, 20)

If producers were going to give cattle supplementary protein to boost their productivity, then perhaps it was not unreasonable for them to use animal protein that was readily available

and had the right mix of nutrients. However, the practice now can be seen to be part of a general approach to animal agriculture, common particularly in the second half of the twentieth century, that pushed for increased production at decreased cost with scant regard for the animals concerned. It now is well recognized that dairy cows are under huge metabolic stress to maintain their greatly increased milk production, with many effects on welfare such as negative energy balance and lameness (Webster 1994). In developed countries most people do not need milk to be as cheap as it currently is, so that less economy-oriented dairy systems—those that do not use protein supplementation—could be adopted.

The most important question now is not whether the practice of feeding cattle protein to cattle was culpable, but how to adapt agriculture to reduce the chance of similar disasters in future—disasters that are perhaps intrinsically unforeseeable. An important part of the answer must be to reduce the emphasis on cheap production and to take into account the evolutionary history and biology of the animals involved—in other words, to treat the animals more naturally.

Escherischia coli O157

Many strains of the bacterium *Escherischia coli* (*E. coli*) live harmlessly in the guts of humans and animals. One of the exceptions is *E. coli* O157, a virulent, toxin-producing strain first identified as causing human illness in 1982. Infection is frequent; for example, there are an estimated 73,000 cases of infection and 61 associated deaths in the United States each year (Centers for Disease Control and Prevention 2001). The main reservoir is in cattle and sheep, for whom it causes no illness. The main route of human infection probably is contamination of meat by animal feces. Heating of meat kills *E. coli*, but only if it is thorough. People also can be infected directly by live animals and each other—for example, in nursing homes where hygiene is poor.

An outbreak of *E. coli* food poisoning in central Scotland in 1996 affected about 500 people, 18 of whom died (Pennington Group 1997; most of this account depends on this report, supplemented by Pennington 1999). This was the world's second highest number of deaths from such an outbreak.

Events moved with impressive speed (Table 2). A likely outbreak was identified on Friday, November 22, 1996, with fifteen confirmed or suspected cases. By that evening it was known that at least eight had eaten food from John Barr's butcher shop in Wishaw (although that did not prove it was the source) and health officials visited the premises. On Saturday, November 23, an outbreak-control team was formed, chaired by a local health board consultant. On Wednesday, November 27, Barr's closed. On Thursday an inquiry was announced in Parliament, chaired by Professor Hugh Pennington of Aberdeen University.

Barr's shop was indeed the source. He had supplied contaminated food to many private customers and several institutions and groups. These included the three clusters worst affected. Eight people who died had been at a church lunch in Wishaw on Sunday, November 17; six who died were at a nursing home in Bonnybridge (all whom were aged 69 or older); and a number of non-fatal cases had followed a birthday party on Saturday, November 23. Some cases resulted from sales Barr made from the back door of the shop after it was shut on November 27.

The main problem was that Barr and his staff did not keep raw and cooked meat properly separated. This was exacerbated by a general lack of proper hygiene in the handling and preparation of food. When contaminated raw meat came in, the contamination spread to cooked meat, which customers did not heat enough to make safe. Thus the contamination got progressively worse rather than being eliminated. In January 1998 Barr's company was fined for breaching food hygiene regulations.

Because failure to follow regulations contributed to this outbreak, the Pennington Group (1997) emphasized the need to educate people on the importance of such regulations, and to improve enforcement of compliance. But it also stressed the importance of events all along the way from cattle to table—on the farm, during animal transport, at the slaughterhouse, during meat transport, in premises processing and selling food, and in the home. The report recommended new regulations, better education, and a general change in attitude to improve hygiene. Involvement of farms, slaughterhouses, and food distributors will be mentioned here.

Farmers have a responsibility to send animals to slaughter in clean condition. This is affected by a number of factors, such as whether they are given clean, dry bedding and whether they are crowded in holding yards (which increases the likelihood that they will soil each other (C.B. Tucker, University of British Columbia, personal communication, June 30, 1999). The Pennington Report also criticizes a practice of "feeding up" cows before slaughter to increase live weight and hence the price obtained; feeding up increases the chance of intestines bursting during removal, and hence contaminating carcasses. By contrast, in instances where the same company both owns and slaughters animals, it is common for food to be withheld before slaughter.

Slaughterhouses also must avoid slaughtering dirty cattle, and must

Table 2
Events in the 1996 Outbreak of *E. coli* Food Poisoning in Central Scotland

Sunday, November 17	Wishaw Parish Church lunch
Friday, November 22	Likely outbreak identified Barr's butcher shop visited by health officials
Saturday, November 23	Outbreak Control Team formed Birthday party at Cascade Public House, Wishaw
Wednesday, November 27	Barr's closed
Thursday, November 28	Expert Group set up under Professor Pennington
Thursday, December 5	Fatal Accident Inquiry announced
Tuesday, December 31	Pennington Group submitted interim report
March 1997	Report commissioned on setting up a Food Standards Agency
April 1997	Pennington Group submitted final report
2000	Food Standards Agency established

improve various practices to safeguard hygiene. The Pennington Group comments that:

> There clearly has to be a cultural change amongst slaughterhouse operators and their staff.... Notwithstanding commercial considerations and the implications of, for example, piece rates of payment for workers [in which they get paid for work done rather than time worked], the speed of the production process within abattoirs needs to be controlled so as to permit the achievement of adequate food safety standards. (1997, 19)

The report includes this statement concerning food distributors:

> The distribution chain of meat and meat products from Barr's was diverse and complex and it took some days for the details on that to be unravelled from a painstaking investigation of the company's records. That caused delays in relation to the identification, publicly, of some of the outlets involved or potentially involved in the outbreak. Some 85 outlets...were eventually identified as being supplied by the company, making the task of outbreak management and control extremely difficult. (5)

So, while response to the Barr's outbreak was rapid, it could have been more rapid—and prevented many cases—if it had not been for this complexity of food distribution.

Around the time of this outbreak, other food safety problems also were publicized, including the danger of Listeria in unpasteurized cheeses. As a response to the accumulating list of such problems, the United Kingdom's Labor Party commissioned a report in March 1997 on the possibility of setting up a food standards agency. Labor won the general election that May, formed the new government, and, shortly thereafter, accepted the report's proposals. The Food Standards Agency was established in 2000.

Classical Swine Fever

Classical swine fever (CSF), or hog cholera, is one of the most important virus diseases of pigs. It is a fast-spreading disease, limited to pigs, with high mortality. Outbreaks are intermittent in Europe. There was a major outbreak in the Netherlands in 1997, for example, and many, smaller outbreaks in Germany (where it is endemic in wild boar) from 1998 to 2000. North America is free of CSF.

A CSF outbreak in southeast England started on August 8, 2000. On August 14 movement restrictions were imposed, which, over the next four months, would affect 264 farms suspected of disease and 907 more in the infected areas. CSF was confirmed on sixteen farms; 41,000 pigs were slaughtered on those and neighboring farms as a direct result of the outbreak and 34,000 more as "dangerous contacts."

On December 30 (Anonymous 2001) the outbreak was confirmed to be over, and movement restrictions were lifted. While the outbreak was confined and eliminated relatively rapidly, it had a severe financial effect on a pig industry that already was in difficulties; many pig farmers left the business. It is also noteworthy that the outbreak was at its height when the Phillips report on BSE was published in October 2000.

The most likely source of disease is thought to have been an infected pork product, illegally imported, perhaps dropped on the farm by a member of the public or a wild animal (Gibbens et al. 2000). Initial detection was slow, perhaps in part because CSF's symptoms are similar to those of other, prevalent diseases. The disease probably was present in June, so that movements of pigs to other farms already had occurred before CSF was identified (Sharpe et al. 2001). Subsequently there was some spread between neighboring farms, but no evidence of irresponsible movements. By contrast, one of the ways in which disease spread in the

Netherlands in 1997 was via trucks moving between farms (Elbers et al. 1999). Another major problem in the Netherlands was the concentration of its industry, enabling the virus to spread readily from house to house and farm to farm.

In many ways, control of the U.K. outbreak was a success story, and one that must have influenced decisions on handling foot and mouth disease, which followed hot on its heels. However, it renewed concerns about vigilance and effective surveillance for diseases, and about general attitudes regarding the importance of disease control. (The United Kingdom's state veterinary service has been reduced in size, and the number of veterinarians working in large animal practices has been declining (Anonymous 2000).) It also renewed concerns about the killing of animals, many of whom were found to have been healthy. There is an effective vaccine for CSF, but EU and U.K. policy is not to use it on animals who have the disease, who are suspected of having it, or who might become infected. This is because vaccinated animals cannot be distinguished from infected animals, so vaccination hinders eradication. An EU directive adopted in 2001 continued this policy but placed increased emphasis on development of "marker vaccines" that would allow vaccinated and infected pigs to be distinguished.

Foot and Mouth Disease

Foot and mouth disease (FMD) appeared in northern England in February 2001 and rapidly became an epidemic. It broke out on a pig farm and spread to neighboring sheep farms. Sheep from this farm were moved around the country before the disease was diagnosed. Three days after the diagnosis, the U.K. minister for agriculture imposed a complete ban on animal movements. By then, however, the disease had been established for several weeks; the Department of Environment, Food, and

Rural Affairs (DEFRA)—which replaced MAFF in June 2001—estimated that there had probably been over 2 million movements of sheep in that period. Many of these movements were not recorded, as they should have been. Furthermore, farmers continued to move animals illegally during the crisis (Lashmar 2001). Some of these movements were for the animals' sake—for example, because they were in fields with insufficient food—and the government soon issued guidance and help for such cases. However, some movements must have been for commercial reasons. Some animals were moved abroad both before and after the ban, and the disease spread to the Netherlands, France, and Ireland. It reached Ireland by an illegal movement of animals across the border from Northern Ireland.

This was the first outbreak in the United Kingdom since 1967, apart from a small outbreak on the Isle of Wight, off the south coast, which rapidly was controlled. The latter demonstrated, though, just how infective the disease is, as it was caused by the virus blowing across from France. DEFRA attributed the decades-long period without infection, in a world with widespread FMD, to tightened control of imports from countries with the disease after 1967 and improved hygiene and animal health standards. However, illegal importation of meat is common, with more than 200 consignments intercepted on their way into the United Kingdom every month and unknown numbers missed. Some of these go to restaurants, and waste food from a restaurant was found at the pig farm in question. Use of waste food for pigs has been common, and although it is supposed to be heated at 100°C for an hour—which would kill the FMD virus—this often does not happen (Lashmar 2001). (Feeding of waste food to pigs now is banned.) While exactly what happened on this farm has yet to be established, it seems that the farmer failed to notice symptoms of FMD, although his pigs were infected for several weeks before offi-

cials traced the source of the outbreak to his farm.

So far, Australia, New Zealand, and the United States have managed to keep FMD out, presumably by more rigorous import controls than are achieved in Europe.

As with CSF, during the 2001 epidemic, the policy of the United Kingdom and the rest of the EU was to slaughter animals with FMD, those who might have it, and those who risked spreading it. The main reason was commercial: a country with infected or vaccinated animals may not export animals or meat to countries free of the disease. At the peak of the epidemic, about fifty farms where the disease was present were identified daily. After about two months, the number had dropped to fewer than ten per day. The outbreak had a long "tail," with three or four farms being infected per day before the disease finally was eliminated late in the year. More than 1,900 farms were affected directly, and 7,000 neighboring farms also were cleared of animals. About 4 million animals were slaughtered.

The slaughter policy was hugely controversial. This was largely a result of the issue's high profile, as television broadcasts showed thousands of farm animals being killed, many of them healthy, and their carcasses burned. Individual stories of pet animals and prime breeding herds received considerable publicity. As with BSE, even though the farm animals would eventually have been killed anyway, the fact that they were being prematurely and very visibly killed was morally repugnant to many people. The outrage probably was exacerbated by the fact that, for many, the killing was seen not to have a useful purpose—such as meat production—but to be done for defense of a meat export trade that they regarded as unnecessary. Indeed, losses to the tourism industry, caused by people being unable to move around in the countryside, heavily outweighed the value of the meat exports. Furthermore, suggestions that the disease is not very severe if

left untreated gave rise to discussion of whether it should be allowed to continue rather than eradicated by draconian measures. (In fact, symptoms of the disease vary in severity; it sometimes causes considerable suffering and in particular causes major problems in breeding animals, such as abortion and loss of milk production, and mortality in the young.) On balance, it seems appropriate to eradicate an eradicable disease. However, even though FMD was eventually eradicated, it might break out again sooner or later. If that were to happen, the U.K. government says it would employ vaccination rather than extermination as its strategy in dealing with the disease. (Countries in which FMD is endemic use regular vaccination and, as is the case for CSF, development of marker vaccines has been proposed.)

To re-emphasize the commercial basis of the policy not to vaccinate, the decision to end vaccination in the EU in 1991 was taken on the basis that a major outbreak every ten years would be less costly than annual vaccination (Nettleton and Reid 2001).

There were reasons other than the slaughter policy for controversy. It was apparent that the United Kingdom was ill-prepared for the crisis. The early slaughter and carcass disposal were relatively slow, delaying containment of the epidemic. In addition, the methods used for handling and slaughtering animals evidently were not as humane as they might have been. Accusations also were made against farmers. Some were seen to be profiteering by pushing claims for compensation higher than reasonable, with the direct cost of FMD reaching £1 billion by August. There were suspicions that some deliberately spread the infection to their own animals to claim compensation above market values (Hetherington and Lomax 2001). On the other hand, many farmers were hurt both emotionally and financially by the crisis; a number even committed suicide.

Apart from inquiries into the epidemic and its handling, the FMD crisis finally precipitated wide-ranging discussion of the future of farm animal production in the United Kingdom. One result was establishment by the government of a Policy Commission on the Future of Farming and Food, which produced a report (2002) emphasizing the importance of sustainability.

Is the United Kingdom Exceptional?

One obvious question that arises from this succession of crises is whether the United Kingdom is doing something different from other countries, something culpable. It is true that agriculture is more industrialized in the United Kingdom than in many other European countries, with larger farms and a smaller proportion of the population involved. It also is true that the drive for greater and cheaper food production after World War II was stronger in the United Kingdom than elsewhere, arguably because the United Kingdom is an island nation. It is possible that these factors led to widespread laxity in food handling, which magnified the disease crises. However, it also is apparent that the United Kingdom is not the only country with such problems. Reprehensible actions occur elsewhere; for example, in 1999 it became known that human and animal feces were being incorporated illegally into feed for farm animals in France (Meade 1999). This practice was both repellent and as risky as those that gave rise to BSE. While the United Kingdom has been hit particularly hard by farm animal diseases in recent years, this must at least partly have been bad luck. The lessons to be learned are relevant to all countries.

Biosecurity

When international travellers enter the United States or New Zealand they are asked whether they are bringing in food and whether they have visited farms or plan to do so. While this is done with varying stringency, it is strikingly different from the lax approach used in other countries. Indeed, New Zealand is the only country with a minister for agriculture and biosecurity, and its Biosecurity Authority produces a regular magazine intended for the general public as well as specialists. By contrast, although DEFRA launched a biosecurity campaign in the United Kingdom in June 2001, it was aimed solely at farmers.

Obviously, other countries should adopt policies on biosecurity similar to those of New Zealand. Given that classical swine fever and FMD probably were introduced into the United Kingdom by illegal imports, the fact that the United States and New Zealand have remained free of FMD must partly be luck. However, stringent regulations and stringent enforcement of those regulations must reduce the chance of disease transmission.

The United States and New Zealand are not blame-free: they are guilty of double standards in restricting imports while aggressively exporting agricultural products. So long as these export policies continue, the two countries risk exporting any disease that does get into their animals or animal products in the future. They also reinforce the tendency to regard such exportation as routine, acceptable, and inevitable. In fact, on the contrary, it is evident that international movement of animal feed, animals, and food from animals is dangerous, largely unnecessary and damaging to animal welfare and the environment (Lucas 2001). Ways must be found of reducing such movement.

Similarly, movement of animal feed, animals, and food from animals within countries must be reduced. A major factor in the foot and mouth epidemic was the enormous scale of sheep movements. Animals often are driven very long distances to slaughterhouses, for instance, frequently passing by nearer slaughterhouses on the way. For biosecurity and animal welfare, animals should be slaughtered at facilities as close as possible to the farm where they are produced; yet the number of slaughterhouses in the United Kingdom has declined considerably over recent years. Local food production and consumption clearly are desirable for animal health—and many other reasons (Valen 2001). Traceability—the principle that it should be possible to track any product "from farm to fork" or vice versa—also is gaining importance, with obvious relevance to animal health and food safety.

Biosecurity frequently has been regarded with complacency. It is imperative that vigilance become the norm, with systems in place in the food industry that lead to containment or prevention of disease.

In the United States, such vigilance has been discussed much more since the events of September 2001 raised the possibility that disease outbreaks might be introduced purposefully. It is striking that little of that discussion has addressed the fundamental structure of the U.S. agricultural industry, despite the prominent role such structure was seen to have had in causing the crises in the United Kingdom—and the fact that the agricultural industry in the United States is much more concentrated and more intensive than that of the United Kingdom, and that there is much more movement in the United States of animal feed, animals, and food from animals. The future is difficult to predict, but it does seem extremely likely that if there is a serious outbreak of a disease such as FMD in the United States—whether accidental or deliberate—it could rapidly become very serious, indeed. These issues would then be given the attention they deserve. What seems surprising, especially as salmonellosis and *E. coli* infection already are widespread, is that such attention isn't already forthcoming. It would obviously be better to address these issues properly before such an outbreak—reducing the chance of it occurring—than after.

Economics of Animal Production

Biosecurity will not come cheap. However, it is increasingly apparent that pressure for cheap food has incurred many external costs, that "cheap food at any price" is not a sustainable policy, and that cost-cutting elsewhere (such as in veterinary surveillance) also has been damaging. As the Pennington Group (1997) emphasized in relation to *E. coli*, disease control includes events on the farm, during animal transport, at the slaughterhouse, during transport of meat, in premises processing and selling food, and in the home—and supply of animal feed should be added to the beginning of that sequence. Improvement of disease control at all those stages will require expenditure. How is it to be paid for? One mechanism might be a levy on food from animals, to be spent on improving animal health and welfare. As the cost of animal products in a meal usually accounts for only a small proportion of its selling price, most consumers would hardly notice such a change.

Cheap food production has not generally increased profits of farmers, because profits constantly are pared away by price competition. Income for many farmers is low and unreliable, which must affect their attitude to and limit their spending on animal health and welfare. A decent, reliable income for farmers—not huge wealth, but a reasonable living—must be part of a sustainable future for farming.

On the farm, relevant issues include:

- Group size: Maintaining smaller groups of animals restricts disease transmission.
- Housing conditions: Giving animals sufficient space and clean, dry conditions, including bedding, increases their health and cleanliness. Hygiene is not increased by barren conditions.
- Feeding methods: These are critical and have many effects on health and welfare. Consideration must be given to the biology of the animals involved, that is, to treating the animals as naturally as possible.
- Concentration of animals: Large, closely spaced units increase disease transmission. Small, well-spaced houses and farms should be favored.

Consideration also should be given to licensing farms or farmers. Most farmers are not criminal or irresponsible, but it should be possible to exclude the minority who are.

Minor increases in expenditure on food and on other aspects of biosecurity related to food production could produce major improvements in farm animal health and welfare. Mechanisms should be explored to achieve these changes.

Literature Cited

Altekruse, S.F., M.L. Cohen, and D.L. Swerdlow. 1997. Emerging food-borne diseases. *Emerging Infectious Diseases* 3: 285–93.

Anonymous. 2000. Editorial: Developing a strategy for surveillance. *Veterinary Record* 147: 429.

———. 2001. Classical swine fever: Movement restrictions lifted. *Veterinary Record* 148: 3.

British Broadcasting Corporation (BBC). 1999. Salmonella remains a threat. *http://news.bbc.co.uk*. Accessed June 2001.

Centers for Disease Control and Prevention (CBC). 2001. *Escherischia coli O157: H7*. *http://www.cdc.gov*. Accessed June.

Curtis, P. 1990. *A handbook of poultry and game bird diseases*. Third edition. Liverpool, England: Liverpool University Press.

Elbers, A.R.W., A. Stegeman, H. Moser, H.M. Ekker, J.A. Smak, and F.H. Pluimers. 1999. The classical swine fever epidemic 1997–1998 in the Netherlands: Descriptive epidemiology. *Preventive Veterinary Medicine* 42: 157–184.

Gibbens, J., S. Mansley, G. Thomas, H. Morris, D. Paton, T. Drew, T. Sandvik, and J. Wilesmith. 2000. Origins of the CSF outbreak. *Veterinary Record* 147: 310.

Harvard Center for Risk Analysis. 2001. *Risk analysis of Transmissible Spongiform Encephalopathies in cattle and the potential for entry of the etiologic agent(s) into the U.S. food supply*. Cambridge: Harvard Center for Risk Analysis.

Hetherington, P., and S. Lomax. 2001. Farmers accused of infecting livestock. *Guardian Weekly*, August 2–8: 9.

Horn, G., M. Bobrow, M. Bruce, M. Goedert, A. McLean, and J. Webster. 2001. Review of the origin of BSE. *http://www.maff.gov.uk*. Accessed June.

Julian, R.J. 1995. Population dynamics and diseases of poultry. In *Poultry Production*, ed. P. Hunton, 525–560, Amsterdam: Elsevier.

Lashmar, P. 2001. Pig keepers with links to centre of the outbreak fined over untreated swill. *Independent*, March 15.

Lucas, C. 2001. *Stopping the great food swap*. European Parliament: The Greens.

Marler Clark, L.L.P., P.S. 2001. About Salmonella. *http://www.about-sal-monella.com*. Accessed June 2001.

Meade, G. 1999. Cows fed human sewage. *http://www.mad-cow.org*. Accessed June 2001.

———. 2001. EU food safety crack-down targets salmonella cases. *Irish Independent*, August 2.

Nettleton, P., and H. Reid. 2001. Foot and mouth disease. *The Moredun Foundation News Sheet* 3: 11.

Newman, L. 2001. Risk of BSE in U.S.A. is low, say U.S. investigators. *Lancet* 358: 9298.

Pennington Group. 1997. *Report on the circumstances leading to the 1996 outbreak of infection with E. coli O157 in central Scotland, the implications for food safety and the lessons to be learned*. Edinburgh: The Stationery Office.

Pennington, T.H. 1999. Food scares: Science, politics, and the media. Public lecture, University of Edinburgh, Scotland, April 28.

Phillips, Lord, J. Bridgeman, and M. Ferguson-Smith. 2000. Report, evidence and supporting papers of the inquiry into the emergence and identification of Bovine Spongiform Encephalopathy (BSE) and variant Creutzfeldt-Jakob disease (vCJD) and the action taken in response to it up to 20 March 1996. Norwich: The Stationery Office.

Policy Commission on the Future of Farming and Food. 2002. *Farming and food: A sustainable future*. London: The Cabinet Office.

Sainsbury, D.W.B. 2000. *Poultry health and management: Chickens, ducks, turkeys, geese, quail*. Fourth edition. Oxford, England: Blackwell.

Sharpe, K., J. Gibbens, H. Morris, and T. Drew. 2001. Epidemiology of the 2000 CSF outbreak in East Anglia: preliminary findings. *Veterinary Record* 148: 91.

Valen, G. 2001. *Local food project: A how-to manual*. Washington, D.C.: The Humane Society of the United States.

Webster, A.J.F. 1994. *Animal welfare: A cool eye towards Eden*. Oxford, England: Blackwell.

The EU Ban on Battery Cages: History and Prospects

CHAPTER

Michael C. Appleby

Introduction

On June 15, 1999, the European Union (EU) passed a directive on the welfare of laying hens, requiring that battery cages (so called because they are arranged in batteries of rows and tiers) be phased out by 2012. Enriched laying cages (which may also be arranged in batteries but which provide increased area and height, when compared with conventional cages, and a perch, nest box, and litter area) will still be allowed. This chapter outlines how this directive came about, and the social, economic, and political issues involved. It considers prospects for the future, both within and outside the EU, and implications for welfare of laying hens in the United States.

The Council of Europe and the European Union

First it is necessary to explain the institutions involved. One influential grouping—little known, even in Europe—is the Council of Europe. The Council was established in 1949 to increase cooperation among nations; it represents most of the countries of Europe (the number was

forty four in 2002). Perhaps its most important activity is the preparation of conventions. The only one widely known is the European Convention on Human Rights, and most people assume that the EU produced it. One area in which the council has been active is animal welfare. Indeed it has stated that "the humane treatment of animals is one of the hallmarks of Western civilisation" (Appleby, Hughes, and Elson 1992). In 1976 it produced the Convention on the Protection of Animals kept for Farming Purposes. Though not legally binding on member countries until they ratified it, member countries accepted the responsibility to include the convention's provisions in their national legislation. This convention will be considered later.

The EU, which has existed under a number of names, such as the European Community and the European Economic Community, started as a subset of the Council of Europe and now includes fifteen countries (Table 1). It has three key bodies. The European Commission is appointed by member countries to run the show, including drafting legislation. The European Parliament consists of members elected by constituents in each country; it shares with the

Council of Ministers the power to legislate. The Council of Ministers (sometimes called the Council of the EU but not to be confused with the Council of Europe) is the main decision-making body. It includes one representative from each country; a confusing feature, however, is that these representatives vary. For agricultural matters, the Council of Ministers consists of the ministers of agriculture from fifteen countries. A vital aspect of the Council is that its presidency is held for six months by each country in turn, and the presiding country takes most of the initiative for that period, often attempting to impose its own agenda. The United Kingdom presided for the first half of 1998. Germany presided for the first half of 1999. Both periods were critical in the course of the battery cage issue, as shall be seen.

The EU can enact regulations and directives, among other legislation. Regulations are binding throughout the EU and overrule any contradictory national legislation. Directives, by contrast, are not operative in the member countries. They direct each country to pass national legislation to put them into effect. This requirement is binding, so that countries will have at least the same minimum stan-

Table 1
Countries of the European Union and the System of Qualified Majority Voting Used by the Council of Ministers*

Country	Votes	Country	Votes
Austria	4	Italy	10
Belgium	5	Luxembourg	2
Denmark	3	Netherlands	5
Finland	3	Portugal	5
France	10	Spain	8
Germany	10	Sweden	4
Greece	5	United Kingdom	10
Ireland	3		
Total		**87**	
Required for Directive to be adopted		**62**	
Blocking minority		**26**	

*Number of votes is determined primarily by population.

Source: Council of the European Union 2003

---

dards (for example, the same minimum space allowance for hens in cages). It has to be said, though, that when countries are unenthusiastic about directives they may delay passing legislation as long as possible and skimp on the details. If they wish, countries may legislate for higher standards within their own borders—for example, a greater space allowance in cages—but they cannot generally restrict imports of related products from other member countries—such as eggs produced more cheaply. (For one exception, see the section on page 164 on Sweden.) For regulations and directives, the mechanism is as follows: The Commission drafts legislation, either on its own initiative or when requested to do so by the Council. The Parliament may amend the draft. The Council amends it further and passes or rejects the final version, with joint authority from the Parliament. On matters such as those of concern here, this decision is made by "qualified majority," with votes weighted by countries' populations (Table 1).

The emergence of these complex structures is in large part accounted for by the diversity of the countries of Europe, and all that this has meant historically and politically. That diversity is further reflected in attitudes about animals.

Attitudes about Animal Welfare

It is well recognized that concern for animal welfare varies across Europe, being generally stronger in the north—particularly the United Kingdom, the Netherlands, Germany, and Scandinavia—and weaker in the south. Reasons are complex. A number of factors correlate with this variation, including temperature (it is hotter in the south, which affects how animals are kept) and religion (Catholicism is commoner in the south, Protestantism in the north, and this affects attitudes). The most persuasive explanation, though, is that concern has developed largely in people who were less involved with animals than were others. The United Kingdom and the Netherlands, for example, are more industrialized than many other countries, and pressure for animal protection has come mostly from city dwellers rather than those involved in farming. A revealing snapshot was provided in 1981 by a review of which countries had then ratified the Council of Europe's 1976 Convention on the Protection of Animals kept for Farming Purposes (Table 2). Of the twenty-one member countries, most of the eleven that ratified first were from the north and had an average of only 6 percent of the population involved in agriculture. Switzerland is relatively southern but also relatively industrialized and ratified early, along with northern nations. Countries that ratified later had a population average of 21 percent involved in agriculture. Most of these countries were southern. Though a northern country, Ireland was in this group, too, and 23 percent of its population was involved in agriculture. The north-south dichotomy may have reflected not only differences in attitude but also the fact that, where many people are engaged in agriculture, governments are unwilling to impose restrictions that may affect their livelihood. Indeed, the agricultural industry has always been particularly vociferous and effective in lobbying for its interests.

It is relevant to note that priorities other than animal welfare may also influence welfare, and that such priorities also vary among countries. Norway, for example, has legislation to limit farm size because it regards rural employment as important, and this limitation probably has some benefits for animal welfare. France puts emphasis on food quality, which also has some positive effects: many people believe that non-cage eggs taste better, and some of these eggs are probably bought in France for this reason.

In recent years concern for animal

---

welfare has grown in southern Europe, as indicated by public opinion polls. There is public sympathy for high-profile campaigns by celebrities such as Brigitte Bardot, and scientists and scientific bodies have increased their interest in, and support for, animal welfare research. The story that follows is, therefore, not simply one of the north outvoting the south or browbeating it into agreement. However, southern governments do continue to be less positive than northern governments about animal welfare (Sansolini 1999a).

Publication of Ruth Harrison's *Animal Machines* in the United Kingdom in 1964 had a huge, international impact. It greatly increased awareness of factory farming methods, including battery cages, and concern for farm animal welfare. The U.K. government set up the Brambell Committee (which issued a report in 1965), passed the Agriculture (Miscellaneous Provisions) Act in 1968, and established an independent Farm Animal Welfare Council (FAWC). Both the Brambell Report and FAWC have had an international influence, too, including their development of the concept of Five Freedoms (Table 3).

Table 2
Ratification of the Council of Europe's 1976 Convention on the Protection of Animals Kept for Farming Purposes by 1981, and the Proportion of Each Country's Population Involved in Agriculture

Ratified	Agricultural Labor (percent)	Not Yet Ratified	Agricultural Labor (percent)
Belgium/Luxembourg	4	Austria	9
Cyprus	—	Greece	30
Denmark	8	Iceland	9
France	9	Ireland	23
Netherlands	5	Italy	12
Norway	8	Liechtenstein	—
Sweden	5	Malta	5
Switzerland	5	Portugal	26
United Kingdom	2	Spain	17
West Germany	4	Turkey	54
Average	**6**		**21**

Source: Ludvigsen et al. 1982

Table 3
The Five Freedoms*

Animals should have:

Freedom from hunger and thirst	by ready access to fresh water and a diet to maintain full health and vigour
Freedom from discomfort	by providing an appropriate environment, including shelter and a comfortable resting area
Freedom from pain, injury and disease	by prevention or rapid diagnosis and treatment
Freedom to express normal behaviour	by providing sufficient space, proper facilities, and company of the animal's own kind
Freedom from fear and distress	by ensuring conditions and treatment which avoid mental suffering

*The concept originated from a phrase in the Brambell Report (Brambell 1965) and was developed by the U.K. Farm Animal Welfare Council (1997)

Brambell Report: Farm animals should have freedom "to stand up, lie down, turn around, groom themselves and stretch their limbs."

Source: FAWC

Housing Systems for Laying Hens

Another important development in the United Kingdom and elsewhere, beginning in the mid-1970s, was work on alternatives to battery cages. In the developed world, by about 1970 most hens kept for egg production (called laying hens or layers) were housed in conventional laying cages or battery cages. It is widely acknowledged that battery cages cause many welfare problems. They compromise most or all of FAWC's Five Freedoms, and indeed contravene the very limited "freedoms" listed in the Brambell Report (Table 3). Work on alternative housing systems, primarily aimed at reducing welfare problems, was most active in the 1970s and 1980s.

Much of this work was funded by national governments in northern Europe. The main emphasis was on use of non-cage systems such as deep litter, straw yards, and free range in the United Kingdom (Appleby et al. 1988; Gibson, Dun, and Hughes 1988; Keeling, Hughes, and Dun 1988); slatted floors in Denmark (Nørgaard-Nielsen 1986); and tiered wire floors in the Netherlands (Ehlhardt and Koolstra 1984). There also was work in the United Kingdom and Germany on a modified cage called the Get-away cage (Elson 1981; Wegner 1990). However, all these systems have one major welfare problem that battery cages do not. Birds in these facilities have to be beak-trimmed—a mutilation that has become increasingly controversial—otherwise cannibalism is likely, often affecting a high percentage of birds. The cannibalism apparently is related to group size, which in all these systems is larger than in battery cages.

Therefore, work began in the mid-1980s, in Edinburgh and elsewhere, on modifying cages for small groups. What have come to be called enriched or furnished cages provide increased area and height compared with conventional cages, and also a perch, a nest box, and a litter area. The term *furnished cages* probably is best, because it is descriptive rather than judgmental (Appleby et al. 2002), but the EU 1999 directive refers to *enriched cages*, so that term will be used here. The author suggests that welfare is improved in enriched cages, and more reliably so than in alternative approaches such as percheries and free range systems (Appleby 1993). This argument is still controversial and unfamiliar to the public. The public tends to think that "free range" means small, farmyard flocks, whereas commercial free range systems house hundreds or thousands of hens. Such conditions have numerous problems, including—to emphasize the point—the fact that unless part of the birds' beaks is amputated, the birds often peck each other to death.

Other important work on improving cages included that of scientist Ragnar Tauson in Sweden. He surveyed the incidence of trapping and injury of caged hens (Tauson 1985). This led to design of improved cages, use of which resulted in reduction in incidence (Tauson 1988). Tauson also developed an abrasive strip which, when attached to the egg guard behind the food trough, prevents overgrowth of claws (Tauson 1986).

Beginning in 1979 the EU financed background scientific work on poultry welfare in a "farm animal welfare co-ordination program." The author was employed under this program starting in 1981 (Appleby 1983). Another important effort has been the series of European symposia on poultry welfare held by the World Poultry Science Association every four years; the first symposium took place in 1981 (following a predecessor in Denmark in 1977), and the sixth was in Switzerland in September 2001.

Two problems arose in general understanding of the production methods used. First, systems were given a bewildering variety of names—those already listed as well as aviaries, percheries, and others—and, second, systems had no official specifications. Eggs sold as free range, for instance, might come from hens allowed to "range" only inside a house or only if they could find one small exit from a huge building. The EU addressed these problems in 1985 by imposing a regulation defining four labels that can be put on eggs and the corresponding conditions in which hens must be kept (Table 4). In the absence of one of those labels, eggs are presumed to come from cages. This regulation immediately slowed the name-changing and had a

---

Table 4
Criteria Defined by the EU for Labeling of Eggs

Label	Criteria
Free range	Continuous daytime access to ground mainly covered with vegetation Maximum stocking density 1,000 hens/hectare
Semi-intensive	Continuous daytime access to ground mainly covered with vegetation Maximum stocking density 4,000 hens/hectare
Deep litter	Maximum stocking density 7 hens/m² A third of floor covered with litter Part floor for droppings' collection
Perchery or barn	Maximum stocking density 25 hens/m² Perches, 15 cm for each hen

Source: Commission of the European Communities 1985

big impact on how non-cage hens are kept. For example, there are no laws in any EU country on maximum floor stocking rates but to get a premium for deep litter eggs a producer must not exceed seven hens per square meter. Exceeding the limit means selling the eggs unlabeled, at a loss.

The battery cage system is the least costly approach in use for egg production (Table 5). However, over the same period, in the 1970s and 1980s, a market for non-cage eggs was developing. Some people, again particularly in the north of Europe, will pay more for such eggs either because they are concerned about the welfare of hens or because they perceive the eggs to be more nutritious, tasty, or healthful. Thus some producers continued to keep hens in non-cage systems, covering the higher cost with a higher selling price for the eggs. No full economic analysis of enriched cages has been published, but egg production probably costs around 10 percent more from these than from battery cages (Appleby 1998). This is cheaper than using most non-cage systems, but since eggs from enriched cages cannot be given any of the labels in Table 4, shoppers cannot distinguish them from battery eggs. As a result farmers will not use enriched cages unless required to do so by law.

Egg labels often confuse customers. Many people think (or perhaps hope) that eggs sold under names that sound appealingly rural or wholesome do not come from cages, but such brand names actually have no official status. About 20 percent of eggs sold in the United Kingdom do come from non-cage systems, either free range or barn. In the Netherlands, Germany, and Denmark, deep litter eggs (which are called "scratching eggs" in their languages) are more popular. In recent years, some supermarkets in northern Europe have responded to customer concerns by labelling eggs from caged hens as such. The EU as of 2002 was moving toward making this labelling mandatory.

Table 5
Cost of Egg Production in Different Systems, Relative to Laying Cages with 450 Square Centimetres Per Bird

System	Space	Relative Cost (%)
Laying cage	450 cm²/bird	100
Laying cage	560 cm²/bird	105
Laying cage	750 cm²/bird	115
Laying cage	450 cm²/bird + nest	102
Shallow laying cage	450 cm²/bird	102
Get-away cage	10–12 birds/m²	115
Two-tier aviary	10–12 birds/m²	115
Multi-tier housing	20 birds/m²	105–108
Deep litter	7–10 birds/m²	118
Strawyard	3 birds/m²	130
Semi-intensive	1,000 birds/ha	135 (140 including land rental)
Free range	400 birds/ha	150 (170 including land rental)

Source: Elson 1985

Space refers in cages to cage floor area, in houses to house floor area, and in extensive systems to land area

Developments in Individual Countries

Animal welfare legislation in individual European countries shows a dichotomy that reflects differing attitudes. Northern countries have detailed laws, with codified lists of actions that are prohibited. Southern countries tend simply to state that animals must not be ill-treated. Legislation also is enforced more strictly in some countries than in others.

Several northern countries have passed legislation or made other changes over the last half century that have affected the welfare of caged hens both within and outside their borders. This section considers Denmark and the United Kingdom (both of which joined the EU in 1973), Sweden (which joined in 1995), and Switzerland (which is not a member).

Denmark

In 1950 Denmark passed a comprehensive Protection of Animals Act, which stated (T. Ambrosen, University of Copenhagen, personal communication, May 16, 2001) that:

Animals must be properly treated and must not by neglect, overstrain or in any other way be subject to unnecessary suffering; Anyone keeping animals should see that they have sufficient and suitable food and drink, and that they are properly cared for in suitable accommodation.

This language was interpreted as prohibiting battery cages, so there were no cages in Denmark for many years. However, Danish companies started building farms over the border in Germany and bringing the eggs to Denmark. By the 1970s the law was being flouted with impunity: battery cages were being installed in Denmark and even supported by government grants. A compromise was reached in 1979, when a new law was passed that allowed cages, but with a minimum area of 600 square centimeters per bird. In a typical cage of 2,500 square centimeters, this meant housing four instead of five birds. Denmark became a net importer of eggs rather than a net exporter, but the Danish egg industry survives, even if smaller than before.

United Kingdom

The U.K. Agriculture (Miscellaneous Provisions) Act of 1968 had important provisions in addition to those already mentioned, particularly a requirement to produce Codes of Recommendation for the Welfare of Livestock. Contravention of these is not a legal offense in itself but can be used as evidence in prosecution for cruelty. (In the same way, breaking the better-known Highway Code by driving on the wrong side of the road is not illegal but would be evidence in a prosecution for dangerous driving.) The 1969 Code for domestic fowls stated:

> In cages holding three or more lightweight birds, the floor area should normally allow not less than 1 sq m per 39.1 kg liveweight. For heavier birds the allowance should not normally be less than 1 sq m per 44 kg liveweight. (Ministry of Agriculture, Fisheries, and Food 1969, 5)

Strains of heavier brown hens were becoming common in the United Kingdom by 1969, and they soon became ubiquitous. This was an interesting result of consumer preference: people bought brown eggs (which come from brown birds) even though they cost more, because the eggs were perceived to be tastier or more natural than white ones (which come from white hens). Brown birds weighed about 2.5 kilograms by the end of the laying year, so they ought to have been given more than 550 square centimeters of living space. They probably had about 500 square centimeters, corresponding to a body weight of 2.2 kilograms.

In the late 1970s, the U.K. Parliament set up a Select Committee on Agriculture, whose members chose to consider animal welfare before anything else. They produced a report in July 1981 concluding that:

> Agreement should be sought in the European Community to a statement of intention that after, say, five years egg production will be limited to approved methods which will not include battery cages in their present form. . . . This should be pursued during the UK Presidency. . . . Meanwhile the Minister should seek Community agreement to a minimum standard for adult laying birds in battery cages of not less than 750 sq cm per bird. He should refuse to agree to anything less than 550 sq cm. (House of Commons 1981, 53)

The proposal for a ban on battery cages received widespread publicity, but the timing was poor. The United Kingdom had just started a six-month term as president of the Council of the EU, and it was too late for the detailed preparation that the battery cage action would have needed. Perhaps partly for this reason, the proposal was not taken up by the U.K. government.

The U.K. Farm Animal Welfare Council (FAWC) also arose from the 1968 Act, and it has produced a succession of influential reports. These include an assessment of egg production systems (1986), a report on the welfare of laying hens in colony systems (1991), and a report on the welfare of laying hens (1997).

Sweden

In 1988, at a time when Sweden perhaps did not expect to join the EU, the country passed a new Animal Welfare Act. This required that, starting in 1989, all new cages should provide 600 square centimeters per hen. The country also took account of Tauson's work (mentioned above), mandating, for example, that by 1994 all cages should be fitted with a claw-shortening system and a perch. More radical change was to follow (R. Tauson, Swedish Agricultural University, personal communication, August 20, 2000):

> Animals should be able to perform natural behaviours and be protected against disease and unnecessary suffering;
> Hens for egg production should not be kept in cages from 1999,
> But alternatives must not mean
> Impaired animal health,
> Increased medication,
> Introduction of beak trimming or
> Impaired working environment.

Despite the ban on cages, remarkably little was done on alternative systems in the next few years, by either the government or the industry, and the industry suggested that the required conditions would be "difficult, if not downright impossible to meet" (Fredell 1994, 1). More than 40 percent of producers said they would leave egg production and predicted that imports would rise to more than 60 percent (Sörensen 1994).

Tauson agreed that the required conditions were inconsistent with a cage ban, and started work on enriched cages in collaboration with this author (Abrahamsson, Tauson, and Appleby 1995). In 1997 Sweden accepted the industry's arguments and deferred implementation of the ban, requiring instead that all cages be enriched. (By then Sweden was in the EU.) A ban on cages remains on the statutes but in abeyance; enriched cages were introduced in Sweden on a large scale beginning in 1998 (Tauson 2000; Tauson and Holm 2001).

The actual threat from imports was not as great as the industry claimed. Restrictions on imports are not generally allowed within the EU. However, the Swedish egg industry is almost free of salmonella, so that Sweden can refuse imports from countries with salmonella—including the rest of the EU, apart from Finland.

Switzerland

Switzerland is the only country in the world to have banned laying cages. The ban was imposed in 1992, after a 1978 referendum in which citizens were informed of the economic consequences of the proposed action. Not being in the EU, Switzerland can restrict imports of cheaper eggs. Some imports are permitted, though, despite the fact that they come from systems that are illegal in Switzerland, because the country's egg production is insufficient to meet demand.

The Swiss law is framed as a ban on any enclosure for fewer than forty birds. Various designs based on the Dutch tiered-wire floor systems are used (Matter and Oester 1989). Performance of these, and the welfare of the birds, were relatively poor at first but have improved with experience (Fröhlich and Oester 2001).

The 1976 Convention and the 1986 Directive

From the late 1970s on, an underlying influence on poultry welfare was the Council of Europe's 1976 Convention on the Protection of Animals kept for Farming Purposes. As mentioned above, once members ratified the convention they were obliged to take it into account in their countries—and that included all the countries in Table 2, except Turkey (which still has not ratified). It also includes other countries that subsequently joined the council. The convention was concerned with the care, husbandry, and housing of farm animals, especially those in intensive systems (Table 6). Its recommendations are couched in general terms, but the drafting committee commented that it tried to lay down principles precise enough to avoid a completely free interpretation, yet wide enough to allow for different requirements. Because the convention itself is very broad, the Council of Europe has a standing committee with a responsibility for elaborating more specific requirements. One of the first areas in which it became active was that of poultry welfare.

In addition to individual countries, the EU became a party to the convention in 1978. Not surprisingly, the EU decided it should act on the welfare of laying hens. After several years of negotiation, an EU directive was adopted in 1986 which establishes minimum standards for the protection of hens in battery cages (Commission of the European Communities 1986). By January 1988 all newly built cages had to provide 450 square centimeters of space per hen and meet other requirements (Table 7); these standards were to apply to all cages by January 1995.

In hindsight the directive seems minimalist to many in Europe. However, it was one of the first Europe-wide statutes that actually specified how animals were to be kept. Prior to this approximately half the hens in Europe were given less than 450 square centimeters each, and probably few cages in Europe met all the

Table 6
Extracts from the Convention on the Protection of Animals Kept for Farming Purposes

Article 3 states:	Animals shall be housed and provided with food, water and care which—having regard for their species and to their degree of development, adaptation and domestication—is appropriate to their physiological and ethological needs, in accordance with established experience and scientific knowledge.	**Article 5**	deals with lighting, temperature, humidity, air circulation, ventilation and other environmental conditions such as gas concentration and noise intensity.
		Article 6	deals with the provision of food and water.
Article 4 states:	The freedom of movement appropriate to an animal, having regard to its species and in accordance with established experience and scientific knowledge, shall not be restricted in such a manner as to cause it unnecessary suffering or injury. Where an animal is continuously tethered or confined it shall be given the space appropriate to its physiological and ethological needs.	**Article 7**	deals with inspection, both of the condition and state of the animal and of the technical equipment and systems.

Source: Council of Europe 1976

Table 7
Extracts from the EU 1986 Directive Laying Down Minimum Standards for the Protection of Laying Hens Kept in Battery Cages

A minimum area of 450 cm² per bird and 10 cm of feeding trough per bird	Cage height of at least 40 cm over 65 percent of the cage area and nowhere less than 35 cm
A continuous length of drinking trough providing at least 10 cm per bird or if nipple drinkers or drinking cups are used, at least two shall be within reach of each cage	Cage floors capable of supporting adequately each forward-facing claw and not sloping more than 8 degrees, unless constructed of other than rectangular wire mesh

Source: CEC 1986

criteria specified for area, feeding space, height, and floor slope. The governments of southern Europe resisted inclusion of a space allowance as high as 450 square centimeters, agreed to this provision reluctantly, and subsequently implemented it slowly. However, all members of the EU did have to translate the directive into national legislation. In the United Kingdom, for example, this was done in 1987. The United Kingdom also amended its Welfare Code to recommend only the legal minimum of 450 square centimeters (Ministry Of Agriculture, Fisheries, and Food 1987). Denmark and Sweden, by contrast, continue to provide more than the minimum.

Developments Leading to the 1999 Directive

One further provision of the directive raised the possibility of future changes, for example a ban on cages, by saying that:

> Before 1 January 1993 the Commission shall submit a report on scientific developments regarding the welfare of hens under various systems of rearing. (Commission of the European Communities 1986, 3)

The Scientific Veterinary Committee (Animal Welfare Section) of the commission did produce a report in 1992 (de Wit 1992), but it did not receive widespread circulation or pub-

licity and the commission took no direct action on it. In that same year, however, the commission issued a draft for a new directive (Commission of the European Communities 1992) which surprised everyone by recommending that cages should provide 800 square centimeters of area and 20 centimeters of perch per hen. A minimum height of 50 centimeters was included, with a height of at least 60 centimeters over 65 percent of the area. This was generally interpreted as "testing the water" rather than a serious proposal, and no mention of 20 centimeters of perch or 60 centimeters of height was ever seen again—although requirements for 800 square centimeters of area and 50 centimeters minimum height were retained to the next stage.

Meanwhile much relevant research continued. For example, in 1989 Dawkins and Hardie reported that brown hens take up 475 square centimeters just standing still and 1,272 square centimeters simply turning around.

By 1995 the commission had decided that it had to take further action, and asked the Scientific Veterinary Committee to update its report. The updated report, issued in 1996, listed welfare benefits and deficiencies of cages and non-cage systems. It concluded that:

> Because of its small size and its barrenness, the battery cage as used at present has inherent severe disadvantages for the welfare of hens. . . .To retain the advantages of cages and over-

come most of the behavioural deficiencies, modified enriched cages are showing good potential in relation to both welfare and production. . . . Mainly because of the risk of feather pecking and cannibalism, [non-cage] systems have severe disadvantages for the welfare of laying hens. (109)

In the first half of 1998, the United Kingdom held presidency of the council and was pressing for change. That March the commission brought out another proposal for a new directive. The proposal was oddly framed, however, requiring hens to be provided with nests and litter but stating that:

> Member states may authorise derogation from [those requirements] in order to permit the use of battery cages if the following conditions are met:
> (a) At least 800 cm² of cage area . . . shall be provided for each hen;
> (b) Cages shall be at least 50 cm high at any point. (Commission of the European Communities 1998, 5)

Enriched cages, "equipped with litter, perches, and a nestbox," were mentioned as a possible housing system; they were required to be 50 centimeters high but no more than that.

Then a critical coincidence occurred: Sweden started introducing enriched cages on a commercial basis. In late 1998 a number of key players in the Council of Ministers and the Commission's Directorate-General for Agriculture were able to visit Sweden and see the cages for themselves. They doubtless took note of the fact that egg production from enriched cages is cheaper than from most non-cage systems.

Meanwhile Germany, hungry for substantial progress on animal welfare during its forthcoming presidency of the council in the first half of 1999, was gearing up to ensure adoption of the directive in that period. The German presidency—that is, the German ministry of agriculture, with support from the rest of the German government—recognized that the proposed directive did not give enough details of enriched cages for these to be properly regulated. They put forward an amended version in early January. This avoided the words *battery* and *enriched* altogether, and said that:

All cage systems [must] comply at least with the following requirements:
(a) Where the cage contains eight hens or more, at least 550 cm² of cage area... must be provided for each hen;
(b) Where the cage contains fewer than eight hens, at least 800 cm² of cage area must be provided for each hen. . . .
(f) Cages must also provide: a nest and an area with or without litter enabling hens to peck and scratch. (Commission of the European Communities 1999a, 7)

In other words, they proposed to ban battery cages, but not enriched cages.

The European Parliament—which, it will be remembered, is the directly elected, democratic body representing the public throughout the EU—debated the proposed directive in late January 1999. In the convoluted political process that constitutes the EU, the version it debated was that first proposed, not the version amended by Germany. However, the members of Parliament were aware of the German initiative and most of them

agreed with it. The Parliament amended the first version of the directive, voting heavily to replace the derogation for battery cages with a provision that "the use of battery cages shall be prohibited": the vote was 58 percent for, 38 percent against, 4 percent abstaining. The increasing concern for animal welfare among southern Europeans may be illustrated by the fact that the amendment was presented by an Italian member of the Parliament and signed by Italian and Greek members, among others (Sansolini 1999b). The Parliament did not delete the mention of enriched cages as a permissible system, though. Thus it, too, voted to ban battery cages but not enriched cages.

This was the first stage of the debate to hit the headlines, making the front page at least in the poultry and animal welfare press, if not in the popular media. The coverage emphasized that the European Parliament had voted to ban batteries. But the most important stage was still to come. The final decision would be taken by the Council of Ministers. Strictly speaking, the decision might not be completely final. If the Council did not act as the Parliament wanted, the Parliament could then require it to think again—as it did recently when the Parliament voted to ban sales of cosmetics tested on animals and the Council demurred. However, the Parliament might well not have persisted, so the Council decision would be momentous.

The 1999 Directive

The next months were busy. Governments put the proposals out for consultation—for example, the author was on the list of those consulted by the U.K. government. Lobbying intensified because the Council would be using qualified majority voting (Table 1) so that, if several countries voted against the directive, it would fall. Indeed, the directive probably would not even reach a vote because,

although the Council does not need unanimity, it attempts to achieve it, rather than forcing minority countries to accept change against their will. If several countries were known to be planning to vote against the directive, the Council probably would have deferred the vote and considered further amendments.

Those thought most likely to vote against were France, Greece, Italy, Portugal, and Spain; these countries have a total of 38 votes, more than the 26 needed for a blocking minority. Portugal, for example, stated publicly that it planned to vote against (Aguirre y Mendes 1999). Groups supporting the ban, such as Eurogroup for Animal Welfare and Compassion in World Farming (CIWF), were particularly active in lobbying those five countries but also lobbied countries thought to be in favor—to ensure their continued support and to persuade them to put pressure on the possible dissenters. The action that received most publicity was a hunger strike by Adolfo Sansolini, the Italian head of Compassion in World Farming's campaign in Mediterranean countries. On May 20, 1999, Italy announced that it would support the ban (Sansolini 1999b).

Details of the negotiations among the EU ministers of agriculture are, of course, not public. It is possible that some who opposed the ban finally agreed to support it in return for some other political favor. Stories have circulated that they were warned that, if the directive failed, there would be increased pressure for more radical change, such as a complete ban on cages. It also happened that the final vote came just after a discussion on the dioxin scandal (Commission of the European Communities 1999b), which is rumored to have diminished any trust that the agricultural industry could be left to regulate itself. (Not long before, there had been a widespread problem in Belgium of dioxin contamination of animal feed, leaving toxic residues in the carcasses after slaughter.) Serendipity may well have played some part in the vote. However, it can also be said that this was a vote whose time had come.

On June 15, 1999, thirteen of the fifteen countries voted for the directive (Compassion in World Farming 1999). Only Austria voted against, and it did so because it did not believe the directive went far enough. Spain abstained.

The key provisions of the directive are shown in Table 8. It will phase out barren battery cages by 2012, with an interim measure requiring 550 square centimeters per hen by 2003. All new cages starting in 2003 and all cages starting in 2012 must provide 750 square centimeters per hen, as well as a nest box, a perch, and a litter area for scratching and pecking. Requirements for non-cage alternatives also change. Litter is not currently required in percheries (Table 5), but as of 2007 it will be needed in all houses. (The situation will be reviewed before the end of 2004.)

Not surprisingly, given the complex process leading up to the directive and the various forms it went through, there was confusion for some time about exactly what had been decided. Headlines were along the lines of "Battery Cages Banned." As many people, even within industry and welfare groups, were unaware of the existence of enriched cages or gave them little thought, they believed that cages had been prohibited altogether. The situation was clarified to some extent by articles such as that by Elson (1999), entitled "Laying Cages to be Enriched, Not Banned," but it still is not clear what actually will happen on most commercial farms, as shall be seen below.

Commentary

Welfare groups enthusiastically welcomed the directive. Compassion In World Farming (1999), for example, called it a "huge victory for animal welfare." However, the groups are unenthusiastic about enriched cages. Peter Stevenson (2001a) of Compassion In World Farming calls on the industry not to install these, but instead to move to non-cage systems.

The Royal Society for the Prevention of Cruelty to Animals (RSPCA) (undated [a], 9) says that "as more producers become familiar with the design and management of alternative systems, enriched cages offer few benefits." The RSPCA's Freedom Foods standards do not allow cages. The group does not mention the problems of beak trimming, cannibalism, and occupational safety in alternative systems. In this context, the EU Scientific Veterinary Committee report may be recalled; it described both battery cages and non-cage systems as having severe welfare disadvantages but said that modified enriched cages had good potential for both welfare and production (Scientific Veterinary Committee 1996).

Perhaps the most important point is that it seems extremely unlikely that a complete ban on cages would have been possible in the EU in 1999 or the foreseeable future. Such a ban would have faced the arguments that caused Sweden to defer its own ban in 1997—arguments that there would be problems in both practical and welfare terms. It also would have been much more difficult for the countries of southern Europe to accept a change that would have had even more economic impact; some of the northern countries might also have rejected such a change. Finally, the Council of Ministers may believe that the EU can protect an industry shouldering 10 percent cost increases against competition from the rest of the world, but it probably would have balked at a higher cost increase.

There is, therefore, a strong case that it was the availability of enriched cages as a viable system that enabled the ban on battery cages to be accepted. Some commentators suggest that enriched cages will not be economically competitive with non-cage alternatives (Compassion in World Farming 1999) and thus will never be common commercially outside Sweden. Even if that is true, however, the cages have moved the issue forward. Germany decided in 2001 that, in the context of a Europe-wide phasing out of battery

cages, it will disallow enriched cages within its own borders, producing a situation similar to that in Switzerland. This is despite Germany's part in promoting the directive, including its provision for enriched cages. The Netherlands and the United Kingdom are considering similar moves (Department for Environment, Food and Rural Affairs 2002).

What was the egg industry's response to passage of the directive? It was horrified. In the United Kingdom, egg producers met on June 15, the very day of the decision, and "as details of the directive were revealed, they were received with a stunned silence" (Cruickshank 1999). A September meeting of the International Egg Commission, representing thirty-three countries, including all of the major producing countries except China, resolved to raise $1 million for action to overturn the ban. The resolution was supported by countries worldwide, including the United States. One reason must have been solidarity in face of what was perceived as a direct attack on the European members; in addition, "a domino effect is feared by the United States, Canada, and Australia" (Farrant 1999).

The industry may have been encouraged in the hope that it could overturn the ban by the complex circumstances leading up to the vote. Ben Gill, president of the U.K. National Farmer's Union, wrote to the U.K. Minister of Agriculture describing the changes as "ill thought through" (Cruickshank 1999). However, the complexities should not be taken as indicating that Europe was half-hearted on this measure. Such a negative conclusion is denied by the strength of the vote in Parliament and by the fact that fourteen of fifteen ministers voted for or wanted the ban.

At least since publication of *Animal Machines* in 1964, "Ban the Battery Cage" has been one of the most common protest calls. In the twentieth century, it probably was surpassed as a popular cause by very few others, such as "Votes for Women" and "Ban the Bomb." Ruth Harrison lived to see

Table 8
Extracts from the EU 1999 Directive Laying Down Minimum Standards for the Protection of Laying Hens

Un-enriched (conventional) Cages

From 1st January 2003 no new conventional cages may be brought into service and existing cages will have to provide 550 cm² per bird and a claw shortener

From 1st January 2012 conventional cages are prohibited

Enriched Cages

From 1st January 2002 enriched cages must provide:

- 750 cm² per bird, of which at least 600 cm² is at least 45 cm high
- A minimum total cage area of 2,000 cm²
- A nest
- Litter such that pecking and scratching are possible
- 15 cm perch per hen
- 12 cm of food trough per hen
- A claw shortener

Alternative Systems

From 1st January 2002 new non-cage systems must have:

- A maximum of 9 hens per m² of usable area
- Litter occupying at least one third of the floor
- 15 cm perch per hen

From 1st January 2007 all non-cage systems must comply with these conditions

Review

By 1st January 2005 "the Commission shall submit to the Council a report, drawn up on the basis of an opinion from the Scientific Veterinary Committee, on the various systems of rearing laying hens, and in particular on those covered by this Directive, taking account both of pathological, zootechnical, physiological, and ethological aspects of the various systems and of their health and environmental impact.

"That report shall also be drawn up on the basis of a study of the socio-economic implications of the various systems and their effects on the Community's economic partners.

"In addition, it shall be accompanied by appropriate proposals taking into account the conclusions of the report and the outcome of the World Trade Organisation negotiations."

Source: Commission of the European Communities 1999c

---

the directive passed (and, characteristically, immediately started considering how it could be improved), but died in 2000. If full implementation of the directive is achieved by 2012, as planned, it will be forty-eight years after *Animal Machines* fired the indignation of the European public. Taking half a century to achieve just one of the changes called for in that book, and arguably only partially at that, is hardly rushing things.

Immediate Developments

What happens next obviously will be affected by the timing and content of the EU Scientific Veterinary Committee's review and the subsequent Commission report (Table 8).

Installation of non-cage systems probably will increase slowly in the short term. Those who are ahead of the game will get premiums for their egg sales for the next few years.

Various manufacturers are offering models of enriched cages, and research on design details is in progress. The U.K. Ministry of Agriculture, for example, commissioned research on cage height, group size, and space allowances with the intention of making the results available to the Scientific Veterinary Committee's review in 2003 or 2004. However, few enriched cages will be installed outside Sweden before the Commission report is out.

No doubt producers continued to install conventional cages right up to December 2002. Some used models that are convertible to enriched cages; for example, a model of this kind is sold by Big Dutchman, the largest European cage manufacturer. Others used standard models, taking the risk that they will be usable only until 2011 (J. Campbell, Glenrath Eggs, personal communication, March 15, 2001), or perhaps a while longer if the directive's deadline is not strictly enforced.

The review will consider performance of different systems (including enriched cages in Sweden) and their "socio-economic implications," together with "the outcome of the World Trade Organization negotiations" (Table 8). So the latter must be considered next.

World Trade Organization Rules

Negotiations are under way to extend the rules for free trade established by the World Trade Organization (WTO) to agricultural products, preventing individual countries and trade zones such as the EU from limiting imports, subsidizing exports, or applying any other process that favors domestic versus foreign producers. The EU proposes that animal welfare be taken into account in trade, by allowing labelling; agreements between trading partners that safeguard welfare; or payment of subsidies to producers who maintain high welfare (European Communities 2000). This will meet resistance from other countries, including the United States. However, it is possible that welfare can be taken into account even under existing WTO rules. Article XX of the WTO's General Agreement on Tariffs and Trade says (Stevenson 2001b, 13):

> Nothing in this agreement shall be construed to prevent the adoption or enforcement by any contracting party of measures:
> a) necessary to protect public morals,
> b) necessary to protect human, animal or plant health.

The possibility of using this article to justify measures within the EU to protect animal welfare has not yet been fully explored. This possibility is strengthened by the fact that the United States recently used similar arguments to justify a ban on trade of dog and cat fur (United States Congress 2000). The act's preamble states (Stevenson 2001b) that:

> The trade of dog and cat fur products is ethically and aesthetically abhorrent to U.S. citizens;
> [The] ban is also consistent with provisions of international agreements to which the United States is a party that expressly allow for measures designed to protect the health and welfare of animals:
> [U.S. consumers have a right to] ensure that they are not unwitting participants in this gruesome trade.

Thus the United States cannot consistently argue against attempts by the EU to prevent import of battery eggs, on the grounds that banning of batteries in Europe is a matter of public morality and protection of animal health.

Perhaps some countries will suggest that such attempts by the EU to prevent import of battery eggs are protectionist rather than concerned with welfare. However, under no possible construction could it be argued that the ban on use of batteries within Europe—with all its fantastical history—is itself motivated by protectionism. One additional piece of evidence against such an interpretation is that any tightening of legislation on housing of laying hens always has been resisted by the industry (cf Jorêt 1998). Examples in the United Kingdom and Sweden have been mentioned above, and the horror provoked in egg producers by the 1999 directive has been described. Clearly, egg producers did not regard the legislation as a potential defense against imports from the rest of the world. Nevertheless, not unexpectedly they did ask for protection; indeed, they believe that the Commission and the agriculture ministers have promised it (Farrant 1999). In fact, most reports, from varied sources, recommending tighter legislation on housing of laying hens in Europe have recommended such protection (House of Commons 1981; Scientific Veterinary Committee 1996; Farm Animal Welfare Council 1997; Royal Society for the Prevention of Cruelty to Animals undated [b]). Still this cannot be described as protectionism. Certainly protection of European egg producers is envisaged, but on the two grounds of fairness and animal protection. It would be unfair to require producers to adopt more costly, humane systems and then suffer competition from cheaper, inhumane imports. And this would not protect animals if sales of eggs from cages outside Europe displace egg production from more humane systems in Europe; the common phrase is that "we would be exporting our welfare problems." Clearly, if the main effect of the directive is a great reduction in European egg production and substitution by battery egg production elsewhere in the world, it will have failed in its intentions. The Scientific Veterinary Committee suggested that "high standards of laying hen welfare can only be implemented and sustained if the EU market is protected against imports of eggs from third countries with lower standards" (Scientific Veterinary Committee 1996, 111).

If the EU succeeds in restricting import of battery eggs, or in other measures such as being allowed to label eggs from different systems or subsidize farmers required to renounce batteries, the Commission surely will recommend few, if any, changes to the directive. In that case, changes to existing battery cage systems will accelerate in 2010 or so. Indications are that most producers will choose to use enriched cages rather than other alternatives, particularly in the colder northern countries.

However, success for the EU in the WTO negotiations is not assured.

Prospects Under Free Trade

What will the socio-economic implications be if such protection cannot be achieved? Could the directive still be implemented? Yes, it could. The chance of a great reduction in European egg production is small. The suggestion of the Scientific Veterinary Committee (1996), just quoted, probably is an overstatement. So is the following statement by Jorêt (1998) in responding for the U.K. egg industry to proposals for the directive: "There is no point in legislating our own industry out of existence only to turn round and import that product from those very same systems, but operated to much lower standards than were in use at home." The phrase, "legislating our own industry out of existence," is an exaggeration. For years, as mentioned, Denmark has had more stringent legislation on cages than the rest of Europe. Its egg industry survives, albeit perhaps smaller than it might otherwise have been. If this applies to trade within Europe, it applies even more to the threat of longer-distance imports to European countries from outside Europe, at least with regard to whole eggs (which the industry calls "shell eggs"). The industry acknowledges this. Mary Ann Sörensen of the Federation of Swedish Egg Farmers considers that the importance of freshness in shell eggs should enable countries to retain this market for local production (Farrant 1999). Similarly, Mike Ring, director general of the International Egg Commission, says that "the EU shell egg market will be largely protected by the freshness needs of that market" (Farrant 1999).

There is a possibility, though, that imports of processed eggs, which make up 25 percent of European egg production, would rise. In fact, as these would be from battery cages, the result would be to continue a trend that already is present. References to people's willingness to buy non-cage eggs apply mainly to fresh eggs; few people consider where the eggs come from in processed food. If other countries increase exports of processed eggs to Europe, it is likely that European egg production would shrink under the proposed changes, but it would not disappear.

Precisely how the European Commission, Parliament, and Council would act in response to such a likelihood is hard to predict, but it is difficult to believe that they would backtrack completely and rescind the ban on battery cages. Given the manifold circumstances leading to the ban, such a move would be seen as a betrayal and would lead to a huge outcry. It seems more likely that, if anything, compromise proposals would be made, lengthening the phase-out period for batteries, for example, or reducing the space requirements in other systems. One additional argument for Europe "putting its own house in order" in this matter, despite world-wide pressures, is that there is reason to believe that the rest of the world will eventually follow. Canada, Australia, and New Zealand—and McDonalds and other chain restaurants in the United States—already have moved toward matching European space allowances

in battery cages. The egg industry also believes that the European battery ban may in due course lead to a "domino effect" in the United States, Canada, and Australia (Farrant 1999).

If Europe cannot protect its egg producers under WTO rules, there will be considerable discussion and lobbying. One additional complicating factor is the potential accession of up to twelve new countries as EU members; these countries are likely to argue that they need more time for implementation than those with a head start. Nevertheless, it is almost certain that there will be major changes to the housing of many or most laying hens in Europe in 2010 and 2011.

Long-term Prospects

Obviously, longer-term prospects depend on many factors, including the WTO negotiations, but one point needs to be made. It has been emphasized that non-cage systems have two major, alternative welfare problems: cannibalism, and the beak trimming required to prevent it. If strains of birds can be developed that do not show cannibalism, then eventually cages probably will be phased out altogether. Such genetic selection is possible (Muir 1996). However, it is not in the economic interests of the poultry breeders, for two reasons: adding any such criterion would reduce breeders' ability to breed for other, more profitable characteristics, and success would favor the move from cages to other systems, which the industry sees as unfavorable. Thus one of the most important requirements for long-term improvement of laying hen welfare is legislation requiring such selection against cannibalism. If that legislation is passed, enriched cages will perhaps have been a medium-term development, although certainly one that facilitated further change. However, non-cage systems do have other prob-

lems that remain to be solved, such as parasite infestation and poor working conditions for operatives.

Implications for the United States

What are the lessons from such a labyrinthine history for a single country such as the United States?

1. Don't expect too much too soon. The First (and so far only) North American Symposium on Poultry Welfare was held in 1995 (in Edmonton, Canada)—compared with the European Symposia that effectively started in 1977—and related changes of attitude still have not gathered pace.

2. Change is possible. One of the most important agents for that change is public opinion. Politicians in every European country and related institution comment that they receive more letters on animal welfare than on any other subject, and that this influences and strengthens them in countering industrial muscle. American politicians make similar comments. Furthermore, it seems that expectations of American citizens are being affected by developments in Europe. Differences between the American political system and that in Europe probably will mean, however, that even more public pressure will be needed to effect similar change in the United States.

3. The United States is a single country, but as a union of semi-autonomous states it has much in common with the EU. Individual European countries were successful acting alone, and these actions finally led to communal action. Similarly, single American states could take the lead, and persuade others to follow, on hen housing as on hog factories.

4. In fact, most of the above history shows that piecemeal change is worthwhile in itself, and finally leads to wholesale change. This obviously applies to labelling. Much of the dis-

cussion about labelling refers to giving consumers a choice. In regard to welfare, choice is not actually what is desired; it is desirable to improve the welfare of all hens, not just a small, labelled proportion of them. Yet the fact that some people buy Free Range eggs—and Freedom Foods demonstrates that a significant proportion will "put their money where their mouth is"—has led the way for more widespread change. Labelling schemes in the United States—such as the Farm Free label of the American Humane Association—could receive much more emphasis, to useful effect.

5. Similarly, the initiative by McDonalds in 2000 to require its egg suppliers to increase their cage size parallels the actions by some European supermarkets and has influenced other commercial companies to make similar moves. It is possible that nongovernmental action to influence market structure is a more promising route than regulation in the United States (Thompson 2001).

6. The EU ban on battery cages is the cumulative result (and even now only a partial result) of activity on many different fronts. Some of these have not even been discussed in this account, such as the pressure on the EU to agree—which it finally did (Commission of the European Communities 1997)—that animals are "sentient beings," not just products. Any campaign in the United States must be similarly multifaceted, bringing pressure to bear on all relevant groups, including producers, retailers, consumers, legislators, and the media.

Note
Another version of this article is cited as Appleby 2003.

Literature Cited

Aguirre y Mendes, A. 1999. Portugal—Press campaign and political lobbying. *Agscene* 135: 9.

Abrahamsson, P., R. Tauson, and M.C. Appleby. 1995. Performance of four hybrids of laying hens in modified and conventional cages. *Acta Agriculturae Scandinavica* 45: 286–296.

Appleby, M.C. 1983. Nest-site selection by domestic hens. *CEC Farm Animal Welfare Programme Evaluation Report, 1979–1983*: 34–38.

———. 1993. Should cages for laying hens be banned or modified? *Animal Welfare* 2: 67–80.

———. 1998. The Edinburgh Modified Cage: Effects of group size and space allowance on brown laying hens. *Journal of Applied Poultry Research* 7: 152–161.

———. 2003. The European Union ban on conventional laying cages: History and prospects. *Journal of Applied Animal Welfare Science* 6 (2): 103–121.

Appleby, M.C., G.S. Hogarth, J.A. Anderson, B.O. Hughes, and C.T. Whittemore. 1988. Performance of a deep litter system for egg production. *British Poultry Science* 29: 735–751.

Appleby, M.C., B.O. Hughes, and H.A. Elson. 1992. *Poultry production systems: Behaviour, management and welfare*. Wallingford, England: CAB International.

Appleby, M.C., A.W. Walker, C.J. Nicol, A.C. Lindberg, R. Freire, B.O. Hughes, and H.A. Elson. 2002. Development of furnished cages for laying hens. *British Poultry Science* 43.

Brambell, R. 1965. *Command Paper 2836*. London: Her Majesty's Stationery Office.

Commission of the European Communities (CEC). 1985. Amendment 1943/85 to Regulation 95/69, also amended by 927/69 and 2502171. *Official Journal of the European Communities* (July 13).

———. 1986. Council Directive 86/113/EEC: Welfare of battery hens. *Official Journal of the European Communities* (L 95) 29: 45–49.

———. 1992. *European Communities draft recommendations No. VI/2327/92*. Brussels: CEC.

———. 1997 *Protocol on the welfare and protection of animals*. Brussels: CEC.

———. 1998. *Proposal for a Council Directive laying down minimum standards for the protection of laying hens kept in various systems of rearing*. Brussels: CEC.

———. 1999a. *Proposal for a Council Directive laying down minimum standards for the protection of laying hens [Amendment from the German Presidency]*. Brussels: CEC.

———. 1999b. Press release. *http://ue.eu.int/newsroom/main.cfm?LANG=1*.

———. 1999c. Council Directive 1999/74/EC laying down minimum standards for the protection of laying hens. *Official Journal of the European Communities* August 3, L 203: 53–57.

Compassion in World Farming (CIWF). 1999. Europe agrees ban on battery cages: Huge victory for animal welfare. *Agscene* 135: 10.

Council of Europe. 1976. *Convention on the Protection of Animals Kept for Farming Purposes*. http://conventions.coe.int/Treaty/EN/Treaties.

Council of the European Union. 2003. Qualified majority. *http://ue.eu.int/en/Info*.

Cruickshank, G. 1999. Egg producers call for unity to fight cage ban. *Poultry World* (August): 1–3.

Dawkins, M.S., and S. Hardie. 1989. Space needs of laying hens. *British Poultry Science* 30: 413–416.

Department for Environment, Food and Rural Affairs. 2002. Consultation on a possible ban on the use of enriched cages for laying hens in England. *http://www.defra.gov.uk/corporate/consult/enrichedcages/letter.htm*.

de Wit, W. 1992. The welfare of laying hens kept under various housing systems: Report to the EC. *Proceedings, World's Poultry Congress, Amsterdam*: 320–323.

Ehlhardt, D.A., and C.L.M. Koolstra. 1984. Multi-tier system for housing laying hens. *Pluimveehouderij* (December 21): 44–47.

Elson, H.A. 1981. Modified cages for layers. In *Alternatives to intensive husbandry systems*, 47–50. Potters Bar, England: Universities Federation for Animal Welfare.

———. 1985. The economics of poultry welfare. In *Proceedings, Second European Symposium on Poultry Welfare*, ed. R.M. Wegner, 244–253. Celle, Germany: World's Poultry Science Association.

———. 1999. Laying cages to be enriched, not banned. *Poultry World* (August): 16.

European Communities. 2000. *European Communities proposal: Animal welfare and trade in agriculture*. WTO Committee on Agriculture, Special Session, Paper G/AG/NG/W/19: *www.wto.org*, Trade Topics, Agriculture, Negotiations.

Farm Animal Welfare Council (FAWC). 1986. *An assessment of egg production systems*. Tolworth, England: FAWC.

———. 1991. *Report on the welfare of laying hens in colony systems*. Tolworth, England: FAWC.

———. 1997. *Report on the welfare of laying hens*. Tolworth, England: FAWC.

Farrant, J. 1999. IEC's world action to keep cages. *Poultry World* (November): 1–4.

Fredell, R. 1994. Welcoming remarks. In *Future egg production in Sweden: Prospects for alternatives to conventional cage keeping of laying hens in a larger scale in Sweden*, ed. M.A. Sörensen, 1. Kunsängen, Sweden: Kronägg.

Fröhlich, E.K.F., and H. Oester. 2001. From battery cages to aviaries: 20 years of Swiss experience. In *Proceedings, 6th European Symposium on Poultry Welfare*, ed. H. Oester and C. Wyss, 51–59, Zollikofen,

Switzerland: World's Poultry Science Association.

Gibson, S.W., P. Dun, and B.O. Hughes. 1988. The performance and behaviour of laying fowls in a covered strawyard system. *Research and Development in Agriculture* 5: 153–163.

Harrison, R. 1964. *Animal machines*. London: Stuart.

House of Commons. 1981. *First report from the Agriculture Committee, Session 1980–81: Animal welfare in poultry, pig and veal calf production*. London: Her Majesty's Stationery Office.

Jorêt, A.D. 1998. Walking the animal welfare tight-rope—An egg industry view. In *Farm animal welfare: Who writes the rules? Programme & summaries*, ed. British Society for Animal Science, 2. Edinburgh: British Society for Animal Science.

Keeling, L.J., B.O. Hughes, and P. Dun. 1988. Performance of free range laying hens in a Polythene house and their behaviour on range. *Farm Buildings Progress* 94: 21–28.

Ludvigsen, J.B., J. Empel, F. Kovacs, M. Manfredini, J. Unshelm, and M. Viso. 1982. Animal health and welfare. *Livestock production science* 9: 65–87.

Ministry of Agriculture, Fisheries and Food (MAFF). 1969. *Codes of recommendations for the welfare of livestock: Domestic fowls*. London: MAFF Publications Office.

———. 1987. *Codes of recommendations for the welfare of livestock: Domestic fowls*. London: MAFF Publications Office.

Matter, F., and H. Oester. 1989. Hygiene and welfare implications of alternative husbandry systems for laying hens. In *Proceedings, Third European Symposium on Poultry Welfare*, ed. J.M. Faure, and A.D. Mills, 201–212. Tours, France: World's Poultry Science Association.

Muir, W.M. 1996. Group selection for adaptation to multi-hen cages: Selection program and direct

responses. *Poultry Science* 75: 447–458.

Nørgaard-Nielsen, G. 1986. *Behaviour, health and production of egg-laying hens in the Hans Kier system compared to hens on litter and in battery cages*. Rapport til Hans Kier Fond, Forseningen tel Dyrenes Beskyttelsei Danmark, 1–198.

Royal Society for Prevention of Cruelty to Animals (RSPCA). Undated (a). *Home to roost: The future for laying hens*. Horsham, England: RSPCA.

———. Undated (b). *Conflict or concord? Animal welfare and the World Trade Organization*. Horsham, England: RSPCA.

Sansolini, A. 1999a. Europe in brief. *Agscene* 134: 13.

———. 1999b. Italian turning point. *Agscene* 135: 7.

Scientific Veterinary Committee (Animal Welfare Section). 1996. *Report on the welfare of laying hens*. Commission of the European Communities Directorate-General for Agriculture VI/B/II.2.

Sörensen, M.A. 1994. Economical and political considerations of keeping laying hens in Europe and in the EU: The Swedish case. In *Future egg production in Sweden: Prospects for alternatives to conventional cage keeping of laying hens in a larger scale in Sweden*, ed. M.A. Sörensen, 85–96. Kunsängen, Sweden: Kronägg.

Stevenson, P. 2001a. An ethical approach to farm animal husbandry. In *Proceedings, Ethics and Animal Welfare 2001: Relationships between Humans and Animals*. Conference, Stockholm, May. (Comment cited is not in the printed abstract.)

———. 2001b. *The WTO rules: Their adverse impact on animal welfare*. Petersfield, England: Compassion in World Farming Trust.

Tauson, R. 1985. Mortality in laying hens caused by differences in cage design. *Acta Agriculturae Scandinavica* 35: 165–174.

———. 1986. Avoiding excessive

growth of claws in caged laying hens. *Acta Agriculturae Scandinavica* 36: 95–106.

———. 1988. Effects of redesign. In *Cages for the future*, Cambridge Poultry Conference, 42–69. Nottingham, England: Agricultural Development and Advisory Service.

———. 2000. Furnished cages and aviaries: Production and health. *Proceedings, 21st World Poultry Congress, Montreal*: 8–17.

Tauson, R., and K.E. Holm. 2001. First furnished small group cages for laying hens in evaluation program on commercial farms in Sweden. In *Proceedings, 6th European Symposium on Poultry Welfare*, ed. H. Oester, and C. Wyss. 26–32. Zollikofen, Switzerland: World's Poultry Science Association.

Thompson, P.B. 2001. Book review: What should we do about animal welfare? *Applied Animal Behaviour Science* 73: 81–82.

U.S. Congress. 2000. Dog and Cat Protection Act. *U.S. Congress Proceedings PL 106/476* Chapter 3: sections 1441–1443.

Wegner, R.M. 1990. Experience with the get-away cage system. *World's Poultry Science Journal* 46: 41–47.

The State of Meat Production in Developing Countries: 2002

Neil Trent, Peter Ormel, Jose Luis Garcia de Siles, Gunter Heinz, and Morgane James

Introduction

Billions of animals are killed for food annually in developing countries, more than half of them without the benefit of stunning (a procedure that induces an unconscious state through administration of a severe blow to the skull or the application of an electrical charge).

The slaughter process begins most often with food animals crowded into inadequate vehicles with little protection from the elements and transported long distances without water over harsh roads. In a typical developing country, few slaughter facilities have any government oversight of sanitation or veterinary care. Animals may be stunned by repeated hammer blows to the head. They may be stabbed with sharp knives until they collapse. While the animals are still conscious, their throats are cut, and they die from excessive blood loss after minutes of struggling.

These brutal methods cause immense animal suffering. They also have significant economic impact: bruising of the meat renders it unfit for human consumption; damage to the hides causes loss of product; and worker injuries result in decreased productivity. At the same time, unsanitary methods spread such diseases as salmonellosis, cholera, *E.coli* poisoning, and Listeria and cause contamination of the meat, a serious public health concern.

More humane transport, handling, and slaughter practices and the introduction of modern systems and equipment in the slaughter process not only decrease animal suffering but also provide economic benefits for the human population, as the amount of meat and hide wasted is reduced. At the same time, worker and meat safety is greatly increased.

Two organizations—one dedicated to the elimination of animal suffering and the other to encouraging sustainable agriculture and rural development—have joined forces to address animal welfare issues in the global livestock industry. The mission of The Humane Society of the United States (HSUS) and its international arm, Humane Society International (HSI), is to create a humane and sustainable world for all animals, including people, through education, advocacy, and the promotion of respect and compassion. The Food and Agriculture Organization (FAO) of the United Nations has as a specific priority to increase food production and food security while conserving and managing natural resources. The aim is to meet the needs of both present and future generations by promoting development that does not degrade the environment and is technically appropriate, economically viable, and socially acceptable.

Since 1994 HSI has worked with the FAO to introduce techniques and equipment for humane transport, handling, and slaughter of food animals in developing areas. The most important of these techniques is the use of the captive bolt stunner (see sidebar on page 181).

HSI has underwritten the cost of FAO slaughter-training workshops, providing equipment, and/or participating in presentations in Asia and the Caribbean. HSI also has produced a laminated poster for FAO use in its training workshops, cosponsored the publication of a booklet (*Guidelines for Humane Handling, Transport, and Slaughter of Livestock*), and begun development of a training video for distribution worldwide.

As part of this collaboration with the FAO, HSI has solicited overviews on the various aspects of animal welfare and the livestock industry in Latin America (contributed by FAO representatives Jose Luis Garcia de Siles and Peter W. Ormel); the Asia-Pacific region (contributed by FAO consultant Gunter Heinz); and South Africa (through a case study of the status of livestock contributed by Morgane James of the National Council of SPCAs).

Table 1
World Livestock Population, 1961–2001 (in million heads)

Species	1961	1971	1981	1991	2001	Percent Overall Growth	Percent Annual Growth
Cattle and Buffaloes	954	1,106	1,236	1,331	1,516	59	1.5
Pigs	348	551	707	791	923	166	4.1
Poultry	4,082	5,729	8,158	12,319	18,734	359	9.0
Sheep and Goats	1,203	1,301	1,435	1,635	1,743	45	1.1

Overview/ Latin America

Introduction

Food security has been defined as access by all people at all times to adequate quantities of safe food required for a healthy and active life. Although food availability has increased noticeably during the last thirty years in developing countries, there currently are more than 800 million people without adequate access to food, and more than 24,000 people die each day because of lack of adequate food supply.

In developing countries, where diets are composed of a few staple foods, meat and meat products are especially important in preventing malnutrition and contributing to food security.

In developing countries some traditional methods of handling, processing, and marketing of meat under-mine quality, and poor sanitation leads to considerable loss of product as well as to the risk of food-borne diseases (Garcia de Siles et al. 1997).

The safety of meat calls for control from the farm until the time the meat is consumed. It is recognized that stock handling, slaughtering conditions, carcass dressing, and meat handling as well as the hygienic and environmental surroundings, contribute to the nutritional properties and commercial value of the finished products.

Evolution of Meat Production

As shown in Table 1, the world livestock population[1] has grown steadily for all major species involved[2] over the last forty years.

In terms of slaughter, the global view is very similar, with moderate increases in the number of ruminants slaughtered and larger increases in the total numbers of pigs and poultry slaughtered (see Table 2).

The increase in the number of animals slaughtered per year led to a 280 percent increase in the production of meat at the world level over the last forty years.

Regional Comparison

The number of animals slaughtered worldwide per region[3] is presented in Table 3. For each species involved, Asia leads the world in terms of number of animals slaughtered per year.

Livestock Evolution in Latin America and the Caribbean

In Latin America and the Caribbean, the cattle and buffalo population more than doubled from 1961 to 2001 (see Table 4).

During this same period, the total meat production in Latin America and the Caribbean increased from 7.9 million metric tons to more than

Table 2
Animals Slaughtered Worldwide, 1961–2001 (in million heads)

Species	1961	1971	1981	1991	2001	Percent Overall Growth	Percent Annual Growth
Beef and Buffaloes	155	181	212	236	299	93	2.3
Pigs	313	533	680	861	1,172	274	6.9
Poultry	6,367	11,122	18,528	27,367	45,926	621	15.5
Sheep and Goats	364	432	507	646	788	117	2.9

Table 3
Animals Slaughtered Worldwide
Per Region: 2001 (in million heads)

Region	Cattle and Buffaloes	Pigs	Poultry	Sheep and Goats
Africa	29	12	2,539	151
Asia	98	678	17,396	439
Europe	53	294	7,440	98
Latin America and the Caribbean	65	62	8,581	31
North America	41	119	9,525	4
Oceania	12	8	510	66
World	**298**	**1,173**	**45,991**	**789**

31.7 million metric tons. This increase was caused mainly by the increase in the production of poultry meat, and to a much lesser extent, by the increase in beef and pork production (see Figure 1).

Subregional Comparison in Latin America and the Caribbean

The number of animals slaughtered in the Latin American/Caribbean[4] subregion is presented in Table 5. Brazil leads the region in terms of number of animals slaughtered for cattle and buffaloes, pigs, and poultry, whereas the most sheep and goats are slaughtered in the Merco Sur and the Andean countries.

Livestock Revolution

Over the past decade, the International Food Policy Research Institute, the FAO, and the International Livestock Research Institute have combined their efforts to produce a global view of the developments in the livestock sector to 2020 against the background of world globalization.

A revolution is taking place in livestock production that could have vast implications for people and the environment in both developed and developing countries. This livestock revolution is being caused by population growth, urbanization, and income growth in developing countries, which have led to a massive increase in the demand for products of animal origin, such as meat, milk, and eggs. However, unlike the so-called green (or environmentally-conscious) revolution, which was supply driven, the livestock revolution is demand driven.

The increased demand for meat and meat products has come from a growing urban population with changing diets and sufficient income to increase animal products in their diets.

A major change of this revolution is a shift in the balance of meat consumption from developed countries to developing countries. The developed countries showed an annual growth in meat consumption of only 1.0 percent from 1982 to 1994. At the same time, the developing countries increased their meat consumption by 5.4 percent annually. In 2020 people in developing countries are expected to consume a total of 188 million metric tons of meat, whereas people in developed countries are expected to consume 115 million metric tons.

These expected consumption increases will lead to equivalent increases in production, with production of livestock products growing most rapidly in areas where consumption grows (Table 6).

Total meat production for developing countries in 2020 is expected to reach 183 million metric tons; for developed countries the projected

Table 4
Livestock Population in Latin America and the Caribbean, 1961–2001 (in million heads)

Species	1961	1971	1981	1991	2001	Percent Overall Growth	Percent Annual Growth
Cattle and Buffaloes	176	224	294	330	360	105	2.6
Pigs	50	65	74	76	81	61	1.5
Poultry	359	577	1,071	1,461	2,513	601	15.0
Sheep and Goats	155	148	143	146	117	(25)	(0.6)

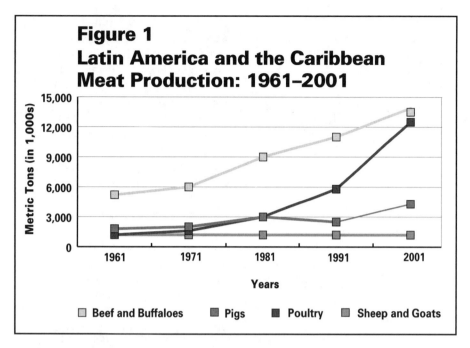

Figure 1
Latin America and the Caribbean Meat Production: 1961–2001

Metric Tons (in 1,000s) vs. Years

☐ Beef and Buffaloes ■ Pigs ■ Poultry ■ Sheep and Goats

total production in the same year is 121 million metric tons. However, the rapid growth in products of animal origin has not been, nor is it expected to be, evenly distributed across or within countries.

The livestock revolution will produce a drastic increase in the capacity of existing production and distribution systems and have possible effects in such key areas as environmental pollution, public health, food safety, and animal welfare. The changes that are inherent to the livestock revolution can be seen both as threats and as opportunities for the sustainable development of developed and developing countries.

When not managed well, these changes could give rise to various problematic situations, with negative effects for animal welfare, public health, and the environment. Animal welfare is a growing ethical concern, especially in developed countries. There, public awareness of environmental contamination of natural resources (air, water, and land) by intensive livestock production systems is high. Many countries have established rules and regulations to mitigate and compensate for the effect these production systems have on the environment. However, developing countries generally have much less experience with the negative

environmental and public health effects of these systems. This might explain a general absence of policies and regulations in many developing countries with regard to monogastric production systems. Given the drastic increase these systems will suffer in the near future and their general proximity to urban centers, this regulatory vacuum easily could lead to substantial environmental problems and important increased dangers for public health.

Several basic aspects of the livestock revolution offer threats as well as opportunities to the sustainable development of countries and regions (Delgado et al. 1999):

(1) the revolution implies a substantial increase in livestock production in the near future;
(2) the majority of this increase will be in developing countries;
(3) the function of livestock will change from non-tradable, multipurpose to more market-oriented functions;
(4) people will continue to substitute grains for meat and milk in their diets;
(5) the rapid increase in monogastric production systems will lead to a rapid increase in the use of cereal feeds;
(6) the stress on grazing systems and expansion of monogastric production systems close to urban centers will increase;
(7) rapidly changing technologies will be incorporated into intensive production systems.

The livestock revolution is a demand-driven process that cannot be stopped. The final overall effects (positive and negative) for the rural poor, the environment, public health, and

Table 5
Number of Animals Slaughtered in Latin America and the Caribbean, 2001
(in million heads)

Region	Cattle and Buffaloes	Pigs	Poultry	Sheep and Goats
Brazil	30	25	4,641	7
Mexico	7	14	1,107	5
Andean Countries	8	9	1,204	8
Caribbean	0	1	157	0
Central America	3	5	604	1
Merco Sur	17	9	868	10
Latin America and the Caribbean	**65**	**63**	**8,581**	**31**

animal welfare depend on the willingness of developing countries to regulate the projected changes.

Slaughtering Meat Animals in Developing Countries

Both meat quality and quantity are very much affected by pre-slaughter conditions. In developing countries meat animals are transported from the farm to the slaughterhouse on foot, by road, or by rail. Frequently livestock must travel on foot for several days to reach the abattoir. Since the distances involved often are quite substantial and the management of the animals during this process is poor, transportation has deleterious effects that result in significant food losses.

Livestock who have traveled long distances on foot or in transport frequently are insufficiently rested before slaughter, negatively affecting the quality of the meat. Often holding pens are overcrowded, causing unnecessary stress to the animals.

The quality and condition of the carcass and its storage depend greatly on the care taken prior to slaughter. Nervous, tired, and excited animals may have a raised body temperature, causing imperfect bleeding. Muscular fatigue reduces glycogen content in the blood, which after slaughter changes into lactic acid, thus causing favorable conditions for spoilage and the growth of food-borne bacteria. Fatigue and excitement also cause penetration of bacteria from the intestinal tract to the meat.

Holding animals in vehicles or lairages without adequate litter and/or drainage frequently results in fecal soiling of the skin. Cattle entering slaughterhouses often are very dirty, their legs covered with manure. In these cases, the knife used for bleeding and de-hiding will have to cut through manure and fecal residues, resulting in a great possibility for meat contamination.

Slaughter methods vary widely and include, among others, simple decapitation (in India), severing the medulla (in some Latin American countries), and severing of the major blood vessels with or without previous stunning.

Animals going to slaughter should be rendered unconscious in order to make death as stress-free and painless as possible. Nevertheless, in the Jewish (kosher) and the Muslim (halal) slaughter of livestock, stunning generally is not allowed, and the animal is bled directly, using a sharp knife to cut the throat and sever the main blood vessels. This results in sudden and massive loss of blood, with loss of

Table 6
Projected Trends in Production of Various Livestock Products, 1993–2020

Region/Product	Projected Annual Growth of Total Production 1993–2020 (percent)	Total Production 1993 2020 (million metric tons)		Per Capita Production 1993 2020 (million metric tons)	
Developed Countries					
Beef	0.6	35	38	26	28
Pork	0.4	37	41	29	29
Poultry	1.2	27	36	21	26
Meat	0.7	100	121	78	87
Developing Countries					
Beef	2.6	22	44	5	7
Pork	2.7	39	81	9	13
Poultry	3.0	21	47	5	7
Meat	2.7	88	183	21	29

Source: Delgado et al. 1999

Notes: Total and per capita production for 1993 are calculated from FAO (1998). Projections are updated figures, following the same format as that reported in Rosegrant et al. 1997. Meat includes beef, pork, mutton, goat, and poultry. Milk is cow and buffalo milk and milk products in liquid milk equivalents. Metric tons and kilograms are three-year moving averages centered on the two years shown.

consciousness and death. These types of slaughtering can be very unsatisfactory since the animal may not be rendered unconscious and may suffer considerable discomfort and pain in the slaughter process. Many Muslim authorities permit some form of preslaughter stunning such as electric stunning of cattle, sheep, and poultry (see sidebar on page 181) (Chambers and Grandin 2001).

The use of humane methods in the handling of livestock prevents needless suffering, results in safer working conditions, reduces meat losses, and improves meat quality. However, cruelty to animals exists in developing countries because of unsatisfactory slaughtering procedures and infrastructures. Animals may be pulled, beaten, or dragged on their way to slaughter and are allowed to see other animals being slaughtered. Animals frequently are slaughtered without being stunned. These practices need to be examined, since people in many developing countries take cruelty to animals for granted and its prevention is often an acquired concept (Mann 1984).

Dressing the carcass, which is defined by the Codex Alimentarius (a collection of international food standards adopted by the Codex Alimentarius Commission, responsible for execution of the FAO/WHO Food Standards Program) as the progressive separation of an animal into a carcass (or sides of a carcass), other edible parts, and inedible parts, is the next step in the slaughter process.

The essential problem in many developing countries is the failure to provide for hoists or hooks, hardware which permits the dressing of carcasses to take place off the floor. The contamination resulting from floor dressing of carcasses is considerable, especially where the removal of hides and the cleaning of stomachs are carried out in the same location as the dressing of the carcass itself.

Rural Slaughter

In developing countries, a high percentage of animal slaughter takes place in rural areas under very primitive conditions that do not meet even minimal technical and hygienic requirements. Animals are slaughtered in all kinds of places, such as converted buildings or rooms, under the shade of trees, and on open, bare ground.

Because of the level of bacterial contamination, meat produced under such conditions can deteriorate easily and lead to food poisoning. Since there is no meat inspection, meat from sick or parasite-infested animals may well be a vector in spreading disease, affecting human beings as well as animals. In addition, unsatisfactory slaughtering techniques can cause unnecessary losses of meat and valuable by-products. Such losses constitute a major constraint in increasing animal production.

The simplest structure used in slaughtering and dressing livestock is the gantry hoist. Animals who have been slaughtered on the ground are then hoisted via the gantry so that the carcass can be dressed. One step better than the gantry method is utilization of a slaughter slab, an area of concrete on which the animal is slaughtered and dressed. When rural slaughtering takes place on relatively small premises, very simple equipment, such as hooks or ropes for hanging animals and chopping blocks for breaking down carcasses, may be available. However, it remains a common practice to dress carcasses on the building floor.

Under these conditions, the utilization of animal by-products generally is low or nonexistent, since the by-products are considered a nuisance. Improved slaughter methods can result in edible by-products which, properly utilized, may be a source of animal protein for human consumption. They can assist in increasing living standards in rural communities by improving the nutritional level, and at the same time increasing employment possibilities.

Urban Slaughter

Many of the large-scale slaughterhouses in developing countries are in poor condition. These usually are located in or around large cities and may be categorized as follows:

(a) Old and dilapidated slaughterhouses established originally on the outskirts of cities but now found within the city limits due to rapid expansion of the urban area. These slaughterhouses present a serious environmental hazard, in addition to using unsanitary slaughtering and meat handling practices;

(b) Slaughterhouses built in the last two decades, with an excessively high level of technical equipment. Problems with ongoing maintenance, inadequate staff training, and high energy consumption have resulted in much of the specialized equipment being shut down. Consequently, many of these plants now resemble the ones mentioned under category (a); and

(c) Slaughterhouses for export, which are technically and hygienically of a very high standard, since they have to comply with export requirements. The local population usually does not benefit from these quality meat-producing plants because their products are too expensive and are directed to external markets.

Even in larger towns, abattoirs that have been designed specifically to supply meat to the expanding centers of urban population all too often are unsatisfactory from a hygienic viewpoint.

Once the meat leaves the abattoir, its hygienic quality also is influenced by careless and poor handling. Carcasses, quarters, unwashed offal, and other items are placed together on the floor of the market or on dirty concrete or wooden tables in meat shops, increasing the microbiological contamination of the meat.

Humane Stunning: Two Techniques

Captive Bolt Stunning

The captive bolt stunner is used commonly in stockyards, slaughterhouses, and packing plants where animals are slaughtered for food. The primary objective of the captive bolt stunner is immediately to induce an unconscious state by administering a severe blow to the skull. The captive bolt is a humane stunner—not a humane killer—and stunning must always be followed immediately by bleeding out.

Captive bolt stunners are comprised of a steel bolt with a flange and a piston at one end that is held in the barrel. The piston fits tightly into the breech and the bolt is free to move forward and backward in the barrel. Upon firing, the expansion of gases, produced by the explosion of the charge, propels the piston forward, and the bolt projects through an aperture in the front of the barrel. The bolt remains captive in the barrel, however, because the flange at the rear prevents it from passing through the hole. The impact of the flange at the front of the barrel is absorbed by either cellular buffers (also known as recuperator sleeves) or a grease collar, depending on the type of stunner.

There are two types of captive bolt stunners: penetrating and non-penetrating. Penetrating stunners cause unconsciousness as a result of a concussive blow to the skull and the physical damage caused by the entry of the bolt into the brain. They are generally preferred, as they result in more rapid unconsciousness and death. Non-penetrative stunners have a "mushroom-headed" bolt which comes in contact with the skull but does not enter the brain. They cause unconsciousness due to concussive force alone and should only be used on cattle.

Both types of stunner are powered by blank cartridges. Cartridges vary in strength and are classified according to the amount of propellant they contain, as measured in grains. It is most important that the correct cartridges be used for each model of stunner.

It also is essential that the correct cartridge be used for the size and species of animal being stunned. In emergency situations, it is acceptable to use a cartridge designed for a larger species, but never one designed for a smaller species. To obtain maximum effect, the muzzle of the captive bolt stunner must be held firmly against the head of the animal.

Electrical Stunning

Electrical stunning involves passing (by means of voltage, or electrical pressure) an electric current (the rate of flow of electricity) through the brain, severely disrupting the brain's normal electrical activity and causing an immediate state of unconsciousness and insensibility to pain.

Electrodes must be placed on the animal in a manner to ensure good electrical contact, and they must span the brain, enabling the current to pass through it. The animal remains unconscious while his or her throat is cut and dies from loss of blood. It is important to note that an animal may recover from a stun if his or her throat is not cut quickly.

Physiological Effects of Stunning

The initial effect on the animal is immediate unconsciousness, accompanied by what is known as "tonic" activity. The animal collapses, stops breathing, and becomes rigid. This period of rigidity normally lasts for ten to twenty seconds following stunning. The forelegs may be flexed initially and then gradually straighten out, but this depends on the species and the severity of the blow. Tonic activity is followed by a period of involuntary kicking, which gradually subsides.

If an animal is stunned properly, he or she collapses immediately. There is no rhythmic breathing, no blinking, no corneal reflex, and no vocalizing. The animal has a fixed, glazed expression and relaxed jaw, and the tongue is hanging out.

Bleeding Out

To prevent the risk of recovery, animals must be bled out (sometimes referred to as "sticking" or exsanguination) as soon as possible after stunning, ideally while the animal is still in the tonic (rigid) phase. Bleeding out involves severing the carotid arteries and jugular veins of the ventral neck and thorax region. The animal then dies from loss of blood. It is important that all major blood vessels are severed. If only one carotid artery is cut, the animal may take over a minute to die.

Whenever an animal is stunned using a captive bolt stunner, he or she must be bled out within fifteen seconds to ensure a rapid and painless death. A maximum stun-to-stick interval of fifteen seconds is essential for all species in the field.

The most practical method of bleeding out is to make a deep transverse cut with a six-inch knife across the animal's throat at the angle of the jaw (i.e., a cut across the throat). The cut should be deep, severing the blood vessels, trachea and esophagus, and continue until the blade of the knife touches the spine. The intention is to severe the carotid arteries and the jugular veins.

—Neil Trent

When meat is sold on one or two market days, meat stalls often are crowded, and customers lean on the stall; the meat becomes contaminated through contact with their hands, bank notes, baskets, clothes, and other objects. The behavior of butchers is not always the most appropriate from a hygienic point of view and may contribute to the problem.

In urban areas the traditional marketing of meat begins with early morning slaughter and delivery of the unchilled meat to the marketplace a few hours later. The FAO recommends that in the long term this be improved to a complete "cold chain" system, with the meat being cooled down at the slaughterhouse and then transported in refrigerated trucks to controlled butcher outlets. The development of the meat sector, in particular in the rapidly expanding population centers, will have to move in this direction for both public health and environmental reasons (Garcia de Siles et al. 1997).

The availability of shelf-stable meat products is very important for a continuous supply of animal protein and essential minerals during periods when there is no fresh meat available. Shelf life ranging from a few days to a number of months can be achieved, depending on the processing methods. Meat processing therefore is essential to enhance food security and cope with periodic deficits in meat supply.

However, in many developing countries the hygienic conditions of the manufacturing process are generally very poor. Machinery is obsolete, places are dirty, and meat is handled carelessly.

The FAO Contribution

Dramatic changes in the current situation of the meat sector are difficult to achieve in the short to medium term, as they would require considerable investment in facilities and infrastructure. Developing countries cannot afford this capital investment.

The FAO addresses this issue through technical strategies and technology packages that include *inter alia* assistance for improved hygiene, handling, and preservation of livestock products; development of appropriate processing technologies, including development of low-cost and shelf-stable meat products; and establishment of small-scale meat processing plants.

1. Slaughter Facilities

It is evident that unsatisfactory slaughtering techniques and lack of appropriate slaughtering facilities may cause unnecessary losses in meat as well as in valuable by-products. Under these circumstances, commonly found in developing countries, the establishment of slaughter facilities of a sufficiently high standard but still simple and inexpensive would improve the above conditions. For these reasons the FAO has developed a model project in which the main component is a small-scale, modular slaughterhouse. In addition, designs have been prepared for the construction of a meat market in order to facilitate the integration of production, processing, and marketing. Further details of this slaughterhouse design and operation can be found in FAO publications (FAO 1988, 1994).

2. Processing

Taking into consideration that an uninterrupted cold chain for meat cannot be expected in many developing countries in the near future, the FAO is assisting developing countries in the use of existing national and alternative regional meat preservation.

3. Training

The lack of adequately trained personnel in the meat and dairy industry has been recognized as one of the main constraints limiting the improvement of the hygienic and technical quality of meat. Training is therefore a prioritized integral component of FAO projects for meat and dairy sector development. For strategic delivery of training, FAO focuses on regional training of trainers courses to stimulate the multiplier and catalytic effect at member country level.

Animal Welfare in the Livestock Sector in Asia-Pacific

Asia, which is home to almost half of the world's human population, traditionally has also been a region with a large livestock population. Year 2000 statistics reveal that, of the global livestock population, Asia—including the Pacific countries—rears 35 percent of cattle, 97 percent of buffaloes, 59 percent of pigs, 42 percent of sheep, 59 percent of goats, 46 percent of chickens, and 88 percent of ducks.

Over the last decades, Asia had average annual growth rates in livestock production of up to 7 percent. In the medium term, Asia will continue to display the world's highest growth rates for livestock, approximately 3 percent, compared with 1.7 percent annual global growth.

The Asia-Pacific region comprises three developed countries—Japan, Australia, and New Zealand—and twenty-seven developing countries. Animal welfare issues usually are higher on the agenda in the developed Asian-Pacific countries than in the developing countries. In particular, New Zealand and Australia have stringent animal welfare laws and detailed rules and regulations.

However, even in well-organized animal welfare environments, unprecedented animal suffering may occur. Australia exports not only meat from cattle and sheep but also live animals. Although the numbers of livestock sent to not-too-distant Southeast Asian countries such as Indonesia and the Philippines are high, no major animal suffering has been reported, as transport distances are relatively short.

The situation is different when

lucrative Near East markets are supplied with sheep and cattle for slaughtering upon arrival according to the Moslem halal method—cutting the throat without pre-stunning. In the past many animals did not survive the long voyage. To shorten transport distances, it is now required that these shipments disembark exclusively from Western Australian seaports. (As a consequence of loss of life due to extreme high temperatures in the summer of 2002, Australia announced it would ban cattle transport until cooler weather returned.) New Zealand banned all live animal shipments to overseas markets some years ago.

In Japan animal welfare is governed by economic and public health factors. *Guidelines for Industrial Livestock Rearing* (Cabinet Office of Japan 1987) and *Slaughter Methods for Livestock* (Cabinet Office of Japan 1995) have been introduced. Due to the emergence of food poisoning from enterotoxins produced by microorganisms in meat, slaughter guidelines were strengthened in 2000, and more stringent requirements for livestock transports and holding pens at slaughterhouses must be followed.

In developing Asia the countries with the largest human population also account for the largest livestock numbers. Livestock is used for food (meat, milk), industrial products (mainly leather), and draft power for agriculture and transport. In rural areas manure from livestock still plays an important role as a fertilizer. In the pig and poultry sector of developing Asia, there is a strong trend toward industrial production.

China is by far the largest producer of pigs in Asia, due to the enormous demand created by more than one billion people. China also accounts for 55 percent of Asian chicken production and 78 percent of duck production.

Large and small ruminants in Asia are kept primarily under traditional rearing on pastureland. Around some large population centers, dairy cows may be kept under semi-industrial conditions, and there are also a few feedlots for cattle fattening.

Cattle prevail in India (46 percent of Asia-Pacific's total), where they are used only for milk production. India also has the highest buffalo population in Asia, followed by Pakistan and China. Buffaloes in India, Pakistan, Nepal, and Bangladesh are of the riverine type kept predominantly for milk. Buffaloes in Southeast Asia are of the swamp type; they are not suitable for milk production but serve for draft power and are slaughtered for meat at the end of their working lives.

Regrettably, swamp buffalo populations in Southeast Asia have been declining rapidly over the last ten to fifteen years, being replaced by motorized vehicles. It is feared that this development will work against small farmers and deprive many of their livelihood, as buffaloes may be more cost-effective than motorized vehicles, and buffalo manure is the much-needed fertilizer for agriculture.

Small ruminants (sheep and goats) in developing Asia are kept for meat only.

Industrial livestock production of so-called short-cycle animals (pigs and chicken) for meat and eggs is increasing greatly in and around the population centers, as per-capita meat consumption in urban areas is increasing. The impact on livestock production is best illustrated by the example of China. Over the last two decades, the annual per-capita meat consumption in China has gone up from 5 kilograms to more than 30 kilograms. Egg production accounts for comparable increases. Growth rates in most other Asian countries also are high, and one can imagine the challenges faced by industrial livestock producers regarding procurement of feed, environmental problems with animal waste, and proper organizing of livestock marketing and slaughtering.

From the animal welfare point of view, the arguments against industrial livestock production in Asia are the same as those voiced worldwide: sows confined for piglet production in narrow boxes and layer hens confined in small cages. In Asia, where duck eggs are very popular, layer ducks may also be kept this way.

Traditional livestock production systems generally create reasonable conditions for animal well-being. However, there are problem areas. For example, millions of cows in India, who have their role in socio-cultural tradition, are otherwise little used for agricultural production, and are not adequately cared for, fed, and watered. Buffaloes play an important role in India as milk-producing livestock, but there is little interest in young male buffaloes, who are unused for meat production. Consequently, the rural practice is to separate male buffalo calves from their mothers shortly after birth and abandon them to die.

In Asian countries with cold winters, the traditional livestock sector suffers from very different problems. In Mongolia, for example, during the course of two consecutive winters, millions of livestock died of starvation during snowstorms. It is clear that action must be taken to provide better shelters and basic feed reserves for the animals during the winter.

The above are a few examples of livestock suffering on traditional farms. More pronounced and widespread suffering—and not infrequent cruelty—occurs in Asian countries, as elsewhere in the developing world, from the moment when livestock is selected for slaughtering. This stressful and often torturous period lasts from the farm gate to the slaughterhouse. The poorer the infrastructure in the livestock marketing and slaughterhouse sector, the more animal suffering occurs.

The vast majority of Asian livestock is kept in China. China has made enormous progress in the abattoir sector, in particular through provision of large-scale and rather efficient slaughterhouses in the population centers. During the past two decades, transport of livestock by road, rail, and boat also has been improved. The Ministry of Agriculture is the central authority responsible for the supervision and control of abattoirs and provides recommended best practices for hygiene, transport, and animal welfare. While such guidelines are very helpful, training of meat sector personnel in techniques and humane treatment of animals still is lacking, nor is the subject of animal welfare adequately covered at veterinary and agricultural universities. Nevertheless, all large abattoirs have been equipped with tools, such as captive bolt pistols and electrical tongs, for stunning of livestock. In some cases, technically advanced boxes for electrical cattle stunning have been introduced. In China's vast rural areas, there remains scope for modernization of the meat sector and improvements in humane treatment of livestock.

Indonesia also has a reasonable infrastructure in the slaughterhouse sector. Although Indonesia is a predominantly Moslem country, a rather liberal approach is taken toward prestunning of animals; efficient electrical stunning equipment (for cattle) and captive bolt pistols are widely used.

The situation for slaughter animals in the other two large countries in the region, India and Pakistan, is very different. India has a number of slaughterhouses producing buffalo meat for export. These abattoirs must comply with export requirements by using adequate livestock transport by rail or truck, good holding pens, and prestunning with captive bolt pistols prior to bleeding. However, for the rest of the slaughter animals, centuries-old conditions prevail, the only difference being that, because of the high demand for meat, all facilities for transport, holding, and slaughtering are hopelessly over their capacity.

Small animals, such as pigs, and large and small ruminants generally are transported in trucks, most loaded well over capacity. Over shorter distances, these animals may be made to walk. For millions of large ruminants (mostly buffalo) in India, the typical range for the journey to the slaughterhouse can be as far as 300–400 kilometers, during the course of which they lose as much as 5 percent or more of their weight.

Some years ago there was a report from India describing how the legs of young buffaloes were broken deliberately by livestock handlers in order to immobilize the animals in waiting pens or transport facilities.

One special aspect of large slaughter animals on the Indian subcontinent is the cross-border transport of cattle and buffalo from India to Pakistan. India has the world's largest cattle population. The cow is a sacred animal to Hindus and cannot be slaughtered. Due to lack of resources in India, however, the cow cannot be fed adequately either. Up to 50 percent of Pakistan's large slaughter animals come from India during certain periods of the year. Some of the animals entering Pakistan illegally travel up to 1,000 kilometers further, into Afghanistan, many dying en route as they traverse this desert region without adequate food and water.

Most slaughterhouses in the subcontinent are obsolete. Stunning equipment is not used. Ritual Moslem slaughter in Pakistan does not permit pre-stunning. In other areas, due to overcapacity and poor infrastructure, slaughtering is carried out very inhumanely and in full view of other live animals. Furthermore, as slaughterhouse waste disposal systems also are obsolete, animals often are kept waiting for slaughter amidst mountains of waste—such as intestinal content, manure, and inedible carcass parts—dumped around the slaughterhouses.

In the other countries of the subregion, Bangladesh and Nepal, there is almost no abattoir infrastructure, and animals are slaughtered along roadsides and rivers under the most primitive conditions. In Nepal overcrowded road transports of buffaloes across several mountain passes in one long journey, with the animals hardly able to stand and in many cases lying virtually on top of each other, pose an additional animal welfare problem.

The slaughterhouse sector in Southeast Asian countries (Myanmar, Thailand, Vietnam, Malaysia, Philippines) is better organized. Malaysia, in particular, has a good slaughterhouse infrastructure with efficient

sanitary inspection and proper transport and handling of livestock. Prestunning is acceptable in this predominantly Moslem country. Thailand and Vietnam have completed new slaughterhouse projects where prestunning using proper equipment is carried out. Thailand has a thriving poultry export industry which complies with international standards for animal welfare. In Thailand's domestic slaughter sector, special government entities have been set up that deal with guidelines for humane treatment of slaughter animals; however, binding laws have not yet been published.

Regarding animal welfare laws and legislation, the Philippines is one of the most advanced countries of the region. An animal welfare act, as well as several codes and regulations, are in place. In each major slaughterhouse, one member of the veterinary staff is responsible for animal welfare issues. The Philippine government's commitment is evidenced by the fact that the international Manila Conference on Animal Welfare, an initiative of the Department of Agriculture, was to be held in 2003. The conference goal was to produce a Manila Declaration on Animal Welfare, recognizing animal welfare as a common objective for all people and all nations.

Many are of the opinion that standards for animal welfare are perceived differently in Asia than in the West. Consequently, there is fear that it may be difficult to make a major impact in the Asian animal welfare sector. It is true that laws and regulation on animal welfare, which have been established in almost all countries of the region, are not strongly enforced at present by the authorities.

On the other hand, there are encouraging developments—and considerable progress—in a number of Asian countries toward the humane treatment of slaughter animals. It must be acknowledged that much of the progress was triggered by economic factors and considerations for easier animal handling. The desirable side effect, however, is less suffering for the animals.

In Southeast Asia some peculiar methods are used to transport live small animals to market. Chickens and ducks are tied head-down to bicycles, rickshaws, and motorbikes. Fortunately, such methods will disappear automatically with the change of marketing systems, away from the traditional markets, where chicken are slaughtered in front of the customer, toward the newly emerging supermarkets. The increasing popularity of supermarkets will have other indirect positive repercussions for animal welfare. Meat will have to meet certain hygienic standards when a longer shelf life must be guaranteed, thus requiring that supplies come from properly controlled slaughter plants.

Pigs in Southeast Asia are squeezed into baskets and transported on bicycles, etc., to market and slaughter facilities. In the absence of any alternative transport means, this method probably is acceptable, since the pigs are released upon arrival and the transport distances usually are short.

However, another method for individual transport of pigs, practiced in the small to medium slaughterhouse sector in Thailand, inflicts great suffering on the animals. Pigs being moved to slaughterhouses are forced into crates made of steel bars. These crates are so small as to allow almost no movement. Pigs are kept waiting inside the crates, sometimes from morning to night, without water and ventilation. They will be killed, still confined to the crate, by sticking a long knife into their necks. Fortunately, this method of transport and killing, which is very labor-intensive, will disappear gradually with the introduction of industrialized pig slaughtering. It is more economical to transport pigs collectively on trucks and keep the whole group together in a holding pen before slaughtering.

In large-animal slaughtering, efficient immobilization must be coupled with immediate unconsciousness of the animal. Most industrial cattle slaughterhouses in Asia use captive bolt pistols for this purpose; a few even use electrical stunning in spe-

cially designed boxes. Both methods are recommended from the technical and animal welfare point of view.

The adequate electric stunning of cattle using electrodes to heart and nose is absolutely painless and of particular interest to Moslem countries. However, the equipment is costly and hence only warranted for larger slaughter operations.

All cattle/buffalo slaughterhouses in Asia outside the Moslem sphere of influence, and even occasionally there, have no objections to using captive bolt pistols, since their use results in the immediate collapse and unconsciousness of the animal, so that slaughtering can start without risk for the slaughter men. However, most medium and small slaughterhouses cannot cover the costs of captive bolt pistols or, more importantly, do not have access to cartridges and spare parts. Instead, they must resort to the inhumane methods of using a sharp-pointed knife to sever the spinal cord or bringing the animal down with a hammer blow.

In camel slaughtering, also daily practice in some parts of Asia, a very inhumane method is the severing of the Achilles' tendons, which leads to the collapse of the animal in full consciousness. The animals may also be immobilized by bending the joints of the fore and hind legs. This forces the animal into a painful position, where he or she may remain for many hours before the Halal throat cut is carried out.

In Moslem ritual slaughtering, cattle and buffaloes are thrown on the ground with a sudden pull, their necks stretched, and the large blood vessels cut with a big, sharp knife. In many Moslem communities, electrical stunning or use of non-penetrative captive bolt stunners is acceptable; others, however, are adamant in refusing any kind of pre-stunning. Time is ripe for Moslem authorities to discuss the issue and to study and evaluate available new technical methods for stunning.

Jhatka is a ritual slaughter method practiced by Sikhs in northern India on sheep and goats only. The head is

chopped off the animal with one stroke. In traditional Indian pig slaughtering without pre-stunning, the pig is thrown on his or her back. A short rope is tied round the muzzle to prevent biting and to help press the head of the animal to the ground. A straight, clean cut is made anterior to the sternum, which severs the jugular vein, and with another cut the heart is punctured. In the rest of Asia, where no proper method for pig stunning is available, pigs are knocked down with the blow of a pole, hammer, or axe.

In the course of industrial Asian livestock production and slaughtering, prospects are good that efficient, scientifically developed stunning methods will be employed on a larger scale in Asia. At present the main constraints affecting the widespread introduction of stunning equipment are the cost and the challenge of importing the equipment and spare parts from overseas. Efforts in some Asian countries to manufacture stunning equipment locally and at cheaper prices have not been successful. Currently new approaches are being taken by veterinary authorities in some countries. The assistance of development projects and NGOs is envisaged.

In the Philippines national veterinary authorities, in cooperation with engineering departments, developed a program to manufacture electrical tongs for pigs, captive bolt pistols for bovines, and the ammunition necessary for captive bolt pistols. The FAO, in cooperation with some other donor organizations and HSI, is committed to cooperate in the project.

It would be most beneficial if inexpensive electrical stunning equipment for pigs could be made available. The economic benefits of import versus in-country development of captive bolt pistols need to be analyzed, and, whether the pistols are imported or not, a supply of suitable ammunition for them must be assured. Responsible veterinary authorities in the individual countries should become involved in the distribution of the ammunition to the slaughterhouses.

Table 7
Livestock Population in South Africa, 1961–2001 (in million heads)

Species	1961	1971	1981	1991	2001	Percent Overall Growth
Cattle	12.527	11.234	13.2	13.5	13.74	9.68
Pigs	1.492	1.205	1.348	1.539	1.540	3.22
Poultry	.0187	.0263	.0313	.0883	.1193	537.97
Sheep and Goats	37.9	33.1	31.6	32.6	28.8	(24.01)
Goats	5.13	5.36	5.79	6.2	6.55	27.68

If such a system could be brought into function, a great step forward toward humane treatment of slaughter animals in Asia would be made.

Humane Slaughter in South Africa

Introduction

South Africa is a vast and diverse country; however, only 12 percent is arable. Lack of water is one of the most severe constraints faced by the farming community. Because of this, crop production is not a viable activity over large parts of the country, and extensive livestock (especially sheep) production is undertaken in the drier areas, particularly in the western and central parts of the country (Table 7).

Species Utilized for Slaughter

Poultry, pigs, cattle, and sheep represent the largest numbers of animals slaughtered for commercial production in abattoirs. The number of goats slaughtered is difficult to determine because in rural areas many are kept and slaughtered for home consumption (Table 8).

Although not bred for this purpose, equines also are slaughtered. Surplus, unwanted, and non-viable equines are purchased and slaughtered for export to Europe, for provision to local niche markets or for feeding to captive predators, such as lions.

There is a variety of farming systems in South Africa, from very traditional and extensive to intensive and modern (Table 9). The diverse cultures influence how many animals are farmed.

The vast majority of poultry are farmed under intensive systems for both egg and meat production. In recent years there has been an increase in the production of free-range products; although this still is a relatively small niche market, consumers are becoming more aware and opting to purchase these products despite their higher cost.

The majority of pigs also are farmed under intensive systems. The tethering of sows in not permitted. Phase-out of existing tethering systems has been nearly completed, with only two producers still using a limited number of tethers.

Although some sheep are fattened in feedlots, the majority are farmed under extensive grazing systems. The vast majority of goats are farmed under extensive grazing systems, many in communal grazing areas.

While high numbers of cattle are fattened in feedlots, a large number also are kept in extensive grazing systems.

Legislation

In 1962 South Africa's first animal welfare legislation, the Animals Protection Act No. 71, was promulgated. This act covers all animal species and does not exclude any sector of animal utilization (Table 10).

Other acts relating to animals, such as the Livestock Brands Acts 1962 (Act No. 87 of 1962), do not necessarily incorporate welfare requirements. The SPCA (society for the prevention of cruelty to animals) movement enforces specific welfare legislation, with qualified and authorized inspectors trained through a national course to perform these functions. Investigations are undertaken and, where appropriate, offenders are charged and prosecuted. Under certain sections of the Animals Protection Act and regulations pertaining to the act, authorized inspec-

Table 8
Number of Animals Slaughtered in South Africa, 2001 (in million heads)

Cattle and Buffaloes	Pigs	Poultry	Sheep and Goats
2.79	2	.3689	10.71

tors have the power to arrest, seize relevant evidence, and seize animals in need of immediate care.

Codes of Practice

A number of codes of practice exist and, while they are not legally enforceable, they are accepted as the norm as underwritten by the different sectors of the livestock industry. The Animals Protection Act is enforceable in all situations where animals are utilized, kept, or slaughtered. Although specific requirements are set down in the relevant abattoir legislation, charges can be made against perpetrators of cruelty as defined by the Animals Protection Act. Conviction on charges of animal cruelty can result in fines, imprisonment, and confiscation of animals.

The Department of Agriculture has appointed inspectors who monitor the conditions at abattoirs, but the focus is on hygiene, of both the facility and the carcasses. These inspectors also are in a position to ensure that the abattoir regulations are adhered to in terms of facilities, handling, and slaughter methods. Failure to comply with the legislation can result in fines and either temporary or permanent closure of the abattoir (Table 10).

Table 9
Commercially Utilized Species/ Products in South Africa

Species	Main Product Farmed for (excluding by-products)
Cattle	Meat Milk Hides and other by-products
Sheep	Meat Wool/pelts
Goats	Meat Mohair
Calves	Veal/calf meat
Poultry	Eggs Meat
Ostriches	Feathers Skin Meat
Pigs	Meat
Rabbits	Meat Pelts
Game	Meat Trophies/tourism

Slaughter Requirements

South Africa has a wide range of cultures and beliefs; eleven official language groups represent this diversity.

The manner in which animals are slaughtered is as diverse as these groups, and the slaughtering of animals for ritual as well as food purposes is very important to many (Table 11).

However, in order to ensure meat

Table 10
South African Legislation Incorporating Animal Welfare

Name of Legislation	Purpose of Legislation
The Animals Protection Act No. 71 of 1962	Protect animals Define offenses Define responsibilities of animal owners
The Meat Safety Act, 2000 (Act No. 40 of 2000) and regulations	Define acceptable practices associated with the slaughtering of animals
The Performing Animals Protection Act No. 25 of 1935	Protection of animals Relating to animals used for safe-guarding and entertainment
Standing Regulations under the Animal Slaughter, Meat, and Animal Products Hygiene Act, 1967 (Act No. 87 of 1967)	To define the manner in which animals are handled, held, and slaughtered To ensure standards set out are adhered to in the production of animal products
The Societies for the Prevention of Cruelty to Animals Act, 1993 (Act No. 169 of 1993)	To provide controls over societies for the prevention of cruelty to animals. To define specific standards that must be adhered to

sold to the public conforms to recognized standards, products offered for sale must be derived from animals slaughtered in approved abattoirs and in compliance with specific conditions set down in legislation. Abattoirs operate according to a grading system, with A grade being the highest. The system dictates the number and type of animals that may be slaughtered on a daily basis, and the facilities required. The manner in which animals may be handled, offloaded, and held-over prior to slaughter are specified in the regulations, which currently are being revised. Pre-stunning of animals (including poultry) in abattoirs is a legal requirement, although exemption from pre-stunning may be granted in cases of animals slaughtered for religious purposes, i.e., kosher and halal.

In order to accommodate the formerly disadvantaged sectors of the community, much smaller grade abattoirs, which slaughter only a few animals per week, have been approved. These small abattoirs are not required to have the same infrastructure as the larger abattoirs. They supply meat directly to their local communities, "warm" off the hook. Cold rooms, etc., are not required; however, pre-stunning is required (Table 12).

Slaughtering of animals outside abattoirs is permitted only for home consumption and not for commercial use or gain. In such cases the abattoir legislation does not apply, but the Animals Protection Act remains enforceable. Illegal slaughter does occur—individuals may set up "bush" abattoirs, where animals are slaughtered and the carcasses filtered into the commercial market.

Stock theft is rife in South Africa. In an attempt to curb this, the Livestock Brands Act has been revised to make marking of stock mandatory.

The majority of halal slaughter in abattoirs is undertaken in the same manner as slaughter for commercial purposes, and animals are pre-stunned.

Kosher Slaughter

The pre-stunning of animals is unacceptable for meat to be considered kosher. Through negotiations with the Jewish community, advances have been made concerning the manner in which animals are restrained prior to slaughter and in achieving post-stunning of cattle and calves in twenty seconds.

As much as slaughter without pre-stunning is of concern, the manner in which animals are handled and presented for cutting of the throat is in many cases of equal or greater concern. Shackling and hoisting of live animals is totally unacceptable in South Africa and is a prosecutable offense.

Table 11
Slaughter Methods Used by Different Cultural Groups and Others in South Africa

Type	Most Commonly Used Species	Brief Description of Slaughter Methods
Kosher (Jews)	Cattle, calves, sheep, poultry	Animals are restrained using specific equipment and have their throats cut without pre-stunning. Post-stunning is undertaken in most instances. Slaughter normally takes place in an abattoir.
Halal (Moslems)	Cattle, sheep, poultry, goats	Most halal slaughter is undertaken in the same manner as for commercial slaughter, and pre-stunning is undertaken. In some instances no pre-stunning is undertaken and the throats are cut. Slaughter normally takes place in an abattoir, however for certain occasions animals are slaughtered at communal site or at private homes, without pre-stunning.
Traditional (African)	Cattle, goats, sheep	Animals may sometimes be shot or pre-stunned. In most instances pre-stunning does not occur and cattle are poll stuck, then cast and their throats cut. Sheep and goats are cast and their throats cut. Other methods include stabbing, neck-breaking, etc. Slaughter takes place outside of abattoirs.
Home Consumption	All species	Animals, especially large stock, may be shot prior to bleeding. The majority of animals, such as sheep, have their throats cut without pre-stunning. Slaughter takes place outside of abattoirs.
Commercial	All species	Animals are pre-stunned and then bled. Slaughter takes place in a registered and approved abattoir.

Table 12
Stunning Methods in Abattoirs in South Africa

Species	Stunning Methods
Large stock—Cattle, horses, donkeys, large boars/sows	Captive bolt pistol Use of firearm in some circumstances
Small stock—Sheep, goats, pigs	Electrical stunning with the use of stunning tongs applied to the head Captive bolt in some circumstances/where there is no electricity
Poultry	Electrical stunning by positioning the head in a fixed head-stunning unit Electrical stunning via current in water bath
Rabbits	Electrical stunning by positioning the head in a fixed head-stunning unit
Ostriches	Electrical stunning with the use of stunning tongs Electrical stunning by positioning the head in a fixed head-stunning unit

The restraint method currently used for cattle is a rotating stun box, with feet clamps. The cattle are individually moved into a stun box and their feet are clamped together with hydraulically operated metal clamps. The box is then rotated, and the animal, lying on his or her side and prevented from moving by the restraint of the feet, is suspended by the feet. The head is pulled back with the aid of a "devil's fork," a semicircular metal frame which gives the operator leverage to hold the head and neck in an upside down, still position. This allows the *shochet* (a Jewish slaughterman) free access to the arched throat, providing relative safety for personnel but at great expense to the animal.

Attempts currently are being made to install an upright slaughter box, which will eliminate the need to rotate cattle for the cutting of the throat.

Traditional Slaughter

The slaughtering of animals plays an important role in traditional African culture. It is undertaken at various events, such as marriages, births, deaths, and initiation rites, and for numerous reasons, such as celebration and cleansing rites and communication with ancestors. Methods of traditional slaughter of farm animals vary according to the tribal group undertaking the slaughtering, and the reason for the slaughter. Slaughter generally takes place on private property. In most cases the animals are restrained and cast, and the throat is cut. Restraint and casting of cattle often is attempted by stabbing the animal behind the poll to sever the spinal cord and render the animal immobile. Although still conscious, the animal has limited movement, and the cutting of the throat can be performed in relative safety.

Pre-stunning of animals is recommended and encouraged. In some cases participants have allowed the SPCA to pre-stun the animal by means of a captive bolt pistol. There remains, however, a great deal of resistance to pre-stunning.

In some cases the animal is required to vocalize prior to death to indicate that the ancestors have accepted it. While some animals, particularly goats, will vocalize readily, others are inhumanely treated until they do so.

Traditional festivals and occasions also may dictate the manner in which the animal is treated and killed. This is a very sensitive issue and, unfortunately, intervention by animal welfare in these ceremonies often is perceived (erroneously) as racially motivated and in conflict with constitutional rights of individuals and organizations.

Ostrich Slaughter

In 1993 South Africa was supplying approximately 90 percent of the world demand for ostrich products and the export of fertile eggs or live birds was not permitted. The single-channel marketing of ostrich and ostrich products ceased with deregulation in 1993, and the market consequently opened, although the export of breeding material still was strictly controlled. As a result, and with an increase in the demand for ostrich products, an increase in the number of producers and abattoirs was seen.

Eventually breeding stock was permitted to leave the country. Shipments of live birds have been investigated and monitored as far afield as Malaysia and the United Arab Emirates. This created concern in the international welfare community, as attempts were made to establish ostrich farming in various countries where climate, management, and specialist knowledge was not available.

While ostriches are valued for their skins, feathers, and meat, the manner in which some producers were harvesting the feathers was found to be unacceptable. Eventually a code of practice was drawn up with the industry, detailing the requirements for feather harvesting and making it illegal to pluck "green" feathers. Only certain "ripe" feathers may be plucked, and clipping of other feathers is permitted. The process is monitored and controlled.

Ostriches' physiological and behavioral requirements are different from those of other farm animals; consequently the manner in which they are held, handled, and slaughtered is more problematic. Due to the positioning and small size of the brain, stunning with a captive bolt pistol is not reliable; therefore ostriches are electrically stunned.

Ostriches are potentially very dangerous and can inflict life-threatening injuries with their powerful legs. This influences the manner in which they are restrained both before and after slaughter. The head of the bird must be held manually for correct placement of the stunning tongs or placed in a small stunning box and restrained prior to electrical current being switched on. Following stunning the ostrich collapses into a sitting position and the legs and feet thrash wildly. In most abattoirs the stunning area is partitioned with steel sheets to protect workers from the powerful, spontaneous kicking of the unconscious bird. Immediately following stunning, after the bird has dropped, a hinged, heavy metal bar is placed over the legs and secured in position. This is to minimize kicking and allow the workers the opportunity to place the shackle over the legs so that the ostrich can be hoisted and bled. Investigation into improved restraint and stunning methods is ongoing.

Slaughter of Game

Game—animals such as impala, springbok, blesbok, kudu, and warthogs—are presented at the abattoir in carcass form for dressing and processing. The stress (and costs) of live capture, the danger in handling, and the inability to restrain the animals humanely for slaughter dictate that these animals be shot on site and field dressed.

Shooting of game for commercial use generally is undertaken as a culling operation. The numbers involved and the fact that the animals are not going to be used for trophy purposes means that shots to the brain are favored. Head shots also limit the damage to the carcass and the resultant loss in edible meat.

Crocodiles are farmed primarily for their valuable skin, which is used in the fashion industry. They are reared communally and, when they reach the desirable size, they are slaughtered. They are presented for slaughter by isolating an individual from the other animals, sometimes placing a sack loosely over the snout to calm the animal. Then the animal is shot in the brain with a firearm, at close range.

Exportation of Animals

Due, in part, to the vastness of the country and also for economic reasons, animals are moved great distances to central sale points or abattoirs. Transportation of livestock by rail is no longer permissible, so that ground transport is now undertaken by road. Large numbers of animals (predominantly sheep, goats, and cattle) are imported into South Africa from neighboring Namibia. Often these animals are in transit for up to three or four days, resulting in exhaustion, dehydration, bruising, injuries, and even death.

Domestic, wild, and farm animals routinely have been transported by air to various destinations and for various reasons. International Air Transport Association regulations specify the manner in which these animals can be handled, contained, and moved. Due to the high cost, moving animals by air generally is not undertaken for animals who are to be slaughtered, since they have a lower financial value than those destined for breeding.

In recent years, with the opening up of international trade, there has been a marked increase in the exportation of slaughter animals by sea, although this is undertaken on a relatively small scale compared with the numbers of animals exported from such countries as Australia. Task teams have been formed to investigate this issue, and attempts have been made to encourage the government either to legislate against this practice or at the very least to regulate it. At the present time, the only controls exerted by the government are those relating to animal health and conditions imposed by the country of destination. Animal welfare is not a criterion. As a result a code of practice was drawn up by the NSPCA and other members of a subcommittee of the Livestock Welfare Coordinating Committee in 2000 to detail minimum requirements for live export.

Acknowledgements

Gunter Heinz expresses his sincere gratitude to Hamid Ahmed (Pakistan); Kohei Amamoto (Japan); Ho Hon Fatt (Singapore); and D. Narasimha Rao (India) for their valuable contributions and advice to the Asia Pacific section of this essay.

Notes

[1] All data presented on the evolution of meat production have been obtained from FAOSTAT Statistics Database (FAO 2002).

[2] Cattle and buffaloes, pigs, poultry, and sheep and goats.

[3] Six world regions were defined: Africa, Asia, Europe, Latin America and the Caribbean, North America, and Oceania.

[4] Six subregions have been defined: Andean Countries, Brazil, Caribbean, Central America, Merco sur, and Mexico.

Literature Cited

Cabinet Office of Japan. 1987. *Guidelines for industrial livestock rearing.* Tokyo.

———. 1995. *Slaughter methods for livestock.* Tokyo.

Chambers, P.G., and T. Grandin. 2001. Guidelines for humane handling, transport and slaughter of livestock. Rome: FAO.

Delgado, C., M. Rosegrant, H. Steinfeld, S. Ehui, and C. Courbois. 1999. *Brief: Livestock to 2020: The next food revolution.* Washington, D.C.: International Food Policy Research Institute. At *http://*

www.ifpri.org/pubs/catalog.htm.

Food and Agricultural Organization (FAO). 1988. Standard design for small-scale modular slaughterhouses. FAO Animal Production and Health Paper 73. Rome: FAO.

———. 1994. Manual para la instalación del pequeño matadero modular de la FAO. FAO Animal Production and Health Paper 85. Rome: FAO.

———. 2002. FAOSTAT Statistics Database. Rome: FAO. *http://apps.fao.org.*

Garcia de Siles, J.L., G. Heinz, J.C. Lambert, and A. Bennett. 1997. Livestock Products and Food Security. World Congress on Food Hygiene, August 1997.

Mann, I. 1984. Guidelines on small slaughterhouses and meat hygiene for developing countries. Geneva: World Health Organization.

Rosegrant, M.W., M. Agcaoili-Sombilla, R.V. Gerpacio, and C. Ringler. 1997. Global food markets and U.S. exports in the twenty-first century. Paper presented at the Illinois World Food and Sustainable Agriculture Program conference "Meeting the Demand for Food in the 21st Century: Challenges and Opportunities for Illinois Agriculture," Urbana-Champaign, May 28.

The State of Wild Animals in the Minds and Households of a Neotropical Society: The Costa Rican Case Study

Carlos Drews

Introduction

Our daily choices and behaviors determine to a large extent the impact of our lives on the environment and on our fellow creatures. The sharing of our living quarters with native wildlife is one dimension of such choices and conduct. Currently, there are two obvious manifestations of living with wildlife: the highly questionable acquisition and keeping of wild animals as pets (for example, parrots) and the colonization of our living quarters by animals (for example, bats). The ways in which each person manages these situations are the result of tradition, education, and the scheme of values that governs one's beliefs, perceptions, and actions. Opposition to keeping wild animals as pets based on ethical considerations and tolerance of the presence of bats in the attic are manifestations of an amicable, compassionate, and respectful attitude toward wild animals. As a working hypothesis, an analysis of the relationship between how people think

about wild animals—whether they keep them and how they care for them in their homes—may serve as a lens through which to better observe the relationship between attitudes and behavior in the field of animal protection.

The study of attitudes in a society provides insight into variables that may be pertinent to people's everyday decisions and practices involving animals. This essay addresses the relationship between attitudes, knowledge, and behavior in the context of the protection of wild animals in the Neotropics and ventures to draw some conclusions about the state of wild animals from this perspective. The Neotropics, a biogeographical region that extends from the Yucatan peninsula to the southern tip of South America, includes some of the most biodiverse countries of the world. Its nations share a common history of Iberian colonization but are nonetheless comparatively heterogeneous in their cultures and social

arrangements. Contrary to the number of sources available with information about social attitudes toward animals in the United States (see Herzog, Rowan, and Kossow 2001), surveys based on extensive samples are scant for the Neotropics.

Nassar-Montoya and Crane (2000) reviewed some of the information about attitudes toward animals in Latin America in a series of essays written by experts expressing their perceptions of such attitudes. An additional source of information for this analysis is the national survey about the relationship between Costa Ricans and wild animals carried out in 1999. The survey includes a formal analysis of attitudes, perceptions, knowledge, and practices involving wildlife, with an emphasis on pet keeping. A professional surveying organization administered personal interviews to 1,024 adults and 177 minors, aged nine to seventeen, from a representative, nationwide sample of 1,024 households (for methodological details see

Drews 2001, 2002a).[1] The instrument for the study of attitudes, a battery of questions subject to factorial analyses, was based on Stephen Kellert's conceptual and methodological framework (e.g., Kellert and Berry 1980; Kellert 1996). In an attempt to provide a robust picture of the relationship between Costa Rican society and wildlife protection, attitudes toward hunting are included in the analysis. Consequently, the analysis sets Costa Rica as a case study and discusses the possible implications of the findings for the rest of the region. Data for Costa Rica shown below come from that survey, unless otherwise indicated. In 2000 a similar, nation-wide survey was carried out in 1,012 Nicaraguan households. Some preliminary results of that study are also included in this chapter (Zegarra and Drews 2002).

Animals Involved in Wildlife Trade

An estimated 30,000 primates, 2–5 million birds, 2–3 million reptiles, and 500–600 million ornamental fishes are traded globally each year to satisfy the demand for live animals for the pet trade, zoos, and laboratories (Nilsson 1977; Hemley 1994). Most of these animals are native to tropical countries and wild caught (that is, taken from wild populations rather than produced in captivity) (e.g., Clapp and Banks 1973; Clapp 1975). These estimates do not include the great proportion of animals who die prior to entering international trade, which, in the case of birds, could result in some 100 million individuals being extracted yearly from the wild (e.g., Inskipp 1975). The Neotropics supplies a great volume of wild animals, both legally and illegally, to North America, Europe, and Asia (e.g., Poten 1991; Cedeño and Drews 2000). Green iguanas (3.4 million animals) from South and Central America, for example, ranked first among the non-native reptile species

imported into the United States between 1989 and 1997 (Franke and Telecky 2001).

In Latin America there is a constant, and by-and-large illegal, demand for wildlife, especially for psittacids and other birds to keep as pets (e.g., Bolivia: Martínez 2000; Colombia: Nassar-Montoya 2000; Chile: Muñóz-López and Ortiz-Latorre 2000; Ecuador: Touzet and Yépez 2000; Mexico: Benítez-García and Durán-Fernández 2000; Panama: Rodríguez 2000; Salvador: Ramos and Ricord de Mendoza 2000; Venezuela: De Alió 2000). Such demand has been inferred mainly from the detection of a large volume of illegal trade, confiscations, and donations of unwanted pets to rescue centers and zoos (contributions in Nassar-Montoya and Crane 2000).

End consumers are rarely aware of the animal welfare and species conservation implications of such trade in live animals. Injury and death during capture, transport, and quarantine are common. The number of animals lost in the process greatly exceeds the numbers that reach the end consumers (Redford 1992). The survival of wild populations can be compromised from overexploitation. These same concerns apply to the trade of animals for the pet market within tropical countries, but the lack of data has obscured thus far the magnitude of the phenomenon. Beissinger (1994), for example, pointed out the lack of information on—and the urgent need to quantify the demand for—parrots in Latin America as one of the challenges facing those working for their conservation. Local use, consumption, and trade of wild animals (Carrillo and Vaughan 1994), including felids and parrots for pets, have been recognized as having a stronger impact on wild populations in Central America than international trade (Barborak et al. 1983).

Recently, however, a colossal effort by the Brazilian organization Rede Nacional De Combate Ao Trafico De Animais Silvestres has generated a wealth of information about wildlife trade in the largest Neotropical coun-

try (Rede Nacional De Combate Ao Trafico De Animais Silvestres 2001).[2] An estimated 38 million animals in Brazil are taken yearly from the wild for the wildlife trade. Of that number a considerable proportion escape injured, die during capture, or are discarded because of their poor condition, and about 4 million individuals are illegally traded in the country. Birds make up the great majority of these animals, accounting for 82 percent of confiscations between 1999 and 2000. The Internet emerges as a new and powerful medium for a clandestine wildlife market. In 1999 Rede Nacional De Combate Ao Trafico De Animais Silvestres found 4,892 advertisements involving Brazilian fauna in illegal transactions. By virtue of the sheer numbers of animals involved in the chain of extraction, trade, and captivity, this issue stands out as probably the most important determinant of the state of the wild animals in the Neotropics.

Reasons for Concern

Pets have been commonly and affectionately kept in Middle America since pre-Columbian times (e.g., Mexico: Benítez-García and Durán-Fernández 2000). Animals at home are part of Costa Rican culture and routine: 71 percent of households keep at least one animal (Drews 2001). Overall 68 percent of Costa Rican adults report keeping a pet (domestic, wild, or both). These values are high by international standards, exceeding the incidence of pets in Germany, Netherlands, the United States, Australia, and Japan (Drews 2001, Kellert 1993a). The proportion of households in Costa Rica keeping dogs (53 percent) is 3.6 higher than the proportion of households keeping cats (15 percent). Cats are much less popular than dogs as companion animals in Costa Rica than they are in the United States or Australia.[3] In Nicaragua the proportion of households keeping dogs and cats, 56 percent and 17 percent respectively, is similar to Costa Rica.

The proportion of households that keep livestock is higher in Costa Rica than in the United States or Germany. While 6.4 percent of U.S. respondents and 10 percent of German respondents raised livestock in the preceding two years (Kellert 1980; Schulz 1985, respectively), in Costa Rica 25 percent of households kept livestock at the time of the survey. The proportion of households that keep horses in Costa Rica (4.5 percent) and Nicaragua (4.4 percent) is three times higher than the 1.5 percent recorded in the United States (American Veterinary Medical Association 1997).

There are few studies of the incidence of wild animals kept as pets in tropical households. Wild, native species are found in 24 percent of Costa Rican households (Drews 2001). This incidence is similar in Nicaragua (22 percent) (Zegarra and Drews 2002) and higher than the incidence in a sample suburb in Panama (14 percent, Medina and Montero 2001). Although parrots are the majority of the wild animals kept as pets, there are at least 45 animal species commonly kept in Costa Rica, including other birds, reptiles, mammals, amphibians, fishes, and invertebrates. These are typically taken from their natural habitat to satisfy the pet market. The extraction from the wild and the keeping of such animals is by-and-large illegal and often involves endangered species. Over half of the respondents have kept a parrot at some point in their lives. A conservative estimate suggests that about 151,288 parrots are kept currently as illegal pets in Costa Rica (Drews 2001). The preference for parrots as pet birds in Costa Rica and Nicaragua is in line with such preference in other societies.[4] In the United States, for example, parrots correspond to 65 percent of species of pet birds kept (Kellert 1980).

The initiative to obtain a wild animal comes mainly from adults. The presence of minors in the household, however, increases the likelihood that an animal will be kept as a pet. In a quarter of all cases, the idea to acquire a wild animal came from a minor. The widespread belief among Costa Rican (Drews 1999a, 2000a) and Nicaraguan adults that keeping a wild animal fosters love and respect for nature in children probably also helps trigger the purchase.

Conditions in captivity suggest that the welfare of wild animals in people's households is severely compromised (Drews 2000a). The pet is kept in an enclosure smaller than a large television set in 77 percent of the cases, and without the company of any conspecifics in 75 percent of cases. Diets are by-and-large inadequate, and only 16 percent of keepers of wild animals have ever given veterinary care to their animals. An average survivorship of four years for captive parrots (Drews 2000b), animals with a lifespan of several decades, testifies to the inadequacy of the typical husbandry situation. In spite of this, however, a great majority of pet keepers in Costa Rica and Nicaragua state that their animals fare well. There is an evident need to disseminate information about what determines the well being of an animal.

The majority of wild animal purchases were spontaneous: 82 percent in the case of parrots, 61 percent in the case of turtles, and 63 percent of the fish (Drews 1999a). Eight percent of adults who kept a wild animal at home at some point reported cases of venomous stings or bites that caused bleeding; half of these cases involved minors. This fact, in addition to the burden of work associated with the care of the animal (which typically falls onto a female member of the family), probably led 39 percent of the pet keepers to express reservations about keeping wild animals as pets (Drews 2000a). Some 23 percent asserted that they would rather not keep the animal they already had. Only half of the captive animals were replaced after they died or escaped.

All parrot species, primates, and felids documented as pets in Costa Rica are endangered or vulnerable under IUCN (formerly International Union for the Conservation of Nature, now the World Conservation Union) criteria and/or national legislation (Solís et al. 1999). With the exception of white-faced capuchin monkeys, these species are all listed under the Convention on International Trade in Endangered Species of Wild Fauna And Flora (CITES), indicating global concern about the potential harm to their wild populations from international trade. Local trade of these species to satisfy the illegal pet market poses an additional burden on the viability of their wild populations, in addition to other pressures such as habitat destruction. In Costa Rica the yearly extraction rate of parrots from the wild to satisfy the national demand for pets is in the range of 25,000–40,000 chicks (Drews 2000b). This figure does not take into account mortality during capture and transport, which would at least double the estimate (Pérez and Zúñiga 1998). This Costa Rican figure alone exceeds the volumes exported from Central America for the international pet market (Drews in preparation), just as Beissinger (1994) had anticipated. The yearly, mostly illegal, extraction of parrots in Venezuela for international trade is on the order of some 5,000–75,000 individuals (Boher-Bentti and Smith 1994; Desenne and Strahl 1991, 1994). If the thus far unknown incidence of parrots in Venezuelan households is similar to those in Costa Rican households, it is quite likely that the national demand there also exceeds the volumes exported.[5] These calculations show that the internal pet market is a stronger threat to wild populations and compromises the well being of more individuals, than does international trade. The importance of studying and quantifying pet-keeping practices and the associated market in Neotropical countries is evident, therefore, both in the context of species conservation strategies (also Beissinger 1994; Morales and Desenne 1994) and in the context of animal protection considerations associated with the capture, handling, care, and captive fate of these numerous individuals.

Attitudes toward Animals in Costa Rica

A nationwide survey in Costa Rica, based on Stephen Kellert's conceptual framework for the study of attitudes, revealed in 1999 a society with an "animal friendly profile," based on five attitude dimensions toward animals (Drews 2002a). Overall Costa Rican adults have a strong *sentimental* attitude, that is, an expression of feelings of affection, toward animals. In contrast, the *materialistic* attitude, which regards animals as resources (Kellert's utilitarian attitude) and praises acts of control over them (Kellert's dominionistic attitude), is weak. This reflects a prevailing opposition to the act of hunting per se: because of harm inflicted on individual animals rather than because of its potentially detrimental effect on natural populations. There is a strong *inquisitive* attitude, corresponding to a widespread interest in learning about the biology of animals and their habitats. High scores on the ethical attitude indicate concern for the ethical treatment of animals and nature. The *schematic* attitude emphasizes the role of aesthetic appearance in the preferences for certain animals and acknowledges feelings of aversion, dislike, or fear of some animals. Scores for this attitude were weakly positive. That said, the attitude profile of Costa Ricans is probably incomplete, given the relatively small battery of questions used in this study.

Kellert (1993a) compared the attitudes toward wildlife in the United States, Germany, and Japan using a standardized methodology. Direct comparisons of attitude score levels between these countries and Costa Rica are not possible due to differences in the composition of question clusters for each attitude and in the scoring method. The relative importance of certain attitudes, however, is amenable to comparisons with Costa Rica. Feelings of affection toward animals scored high among other attitudes in these four countries.[6] The relatively high importance of moralistic traits was similar in the United States (from Kellert 1993a) and in Costa Rica. Germany stands out in the dimension of concern for the ethical treatment of animals, however, by virtue of a score much higher than on any other attitude. In fact, most Europeans are more negative toward the use of animals in research and testing, as well as toward factory farming practices, and are more supportive of organic farming than are Americans (Herzog, Rowan, and Kossow 2001). In contrast, the moralistic attitude garnered one of the lowest attitude scores in Japan. The utilitarian and dominionistic attitude scores were particularly low in relation to other attitudes in Germany and Costa Rica (low materialistic attitude), and relatively high in Japan. The schematic attitude, which includes aesthetic and negativistic elements, was of intermediate importance in Costa Rica. The negativistic attitude was relatively strong in Japan and in the United States, whereas in Germany it scored relatively low.

The profile of Costa Rican attitudes toward animals contrasts greatly with that of another tropical country, Botswana, where the prevailing attitude of the public was utilitarian (Mordi 1991). The next most pronounced attitude in Botswana was the *theistic*, an attitude introduced by Mordi in his study design, in which the population dynamics of wildlife was believed to be controlled by the supernatural. Other attitudes with high scores in Botswana were the *scientistic*, the *neutralistic*, and the *negativistic*. *Humanistic* feelings toward animals were rare in Botswana, probably because wild animals cannot be friends of the public and meat at the same time (Mordi 1991).

Costa Ricans feel protective toward animals, as reflected in their attitudes and law. They relate to wildlife through strong affection, aesthetic appreciation, ethical concern, and a strong desire to learn. Overall, the general public condemns expressions of mastery over wildlife and the hunting of animals for recreation or even sustainable use (see below). Such a relatively consistent trait is probably the product of the cultural homogeneity of Costa Rican society. In 1924 a series of legal measures were taken to safeguard the well being of animals, including, among several regulations for the husbandry and care of livestock, a ban on bullfighting involving physical injury and death of the bull, cockfighting, dogfighting, cat fighting, and the use of slingshots against birds. A common theme of these protective attitudes and measures is that the suffering and cause of death of the animals involved are visible: bleeding injuries result from fights, bad handling, or the use of a weapon. In contrast, the suffering of caged animals, for example, is subtle and not easily visible to an uninformed person. A cognitively more demanding process is required to appreciate the animal's suffering, one that combines common sense with additional information. The use of wild animals in circuses and other public performances was banned in Costa Rica in July 2002. The average audience for such performances is not directly confronted with a visible suffering of the animals involved. This ban and a recent series of publicity campaigns against the keeping of wild animals as pets in Costa Rica by government agencies and non-governmental organizations (compiled by Trama and Ramírez 2002) are signs of an increasing awareness of animal protection issues in this society.

Attitudes toward Animals in the Neotropics

Current attitudes toward animals in Latin America are shaped by a multicultural heritage. Attitudes toward wildlife in the Caribbean coast of Costa Rica, for example, can be related to the history of colonization by various ethnic groups, e.g., African,

Caribbean, Hispanic, and their resulting blends in modern culture. Therefore, marine turtles, for example, may have a different significance in different cultures: as deity, merchandise, food, medicine, aphrodisiac, subject of scientific research, protected animal, managed animal, tourist attraction, or art (Vargas-Mena 2000). These categories are not necessarily mutually exclusive for any given person. With the addition of two categories—the animal as subject of superstition and as pet—they inspired an analysis of attitudes toward wildlife in Colombia that illustrated the influence of indigenous and colonizing cultural traits (Nassar-Montoya 2000). Ramos and Ricord de Mendoza (2000) offer a description of current views on wildlife in El Salvador citing these attitudes: utilitarian or consumptive, cruel or contemptuous, dominionistic, compassionate, and naturalistic or scientific. Elements of Kellert's typology can be associated with most of the above-mentioned cultural meanings and views on animals.

In general, a utilitarian attitude, devoid of awareness about the threats to wildlife and the importance of its protection, seems common among Latin Americans (contributions in Nassar-Montoya and Crane 2000). Not just commercial exploitation but also subsistence hunting for food can lead to population declines of various Neotropical wild animals (Bedoya-Gaitán 2000). Ignorance about the finiteness of wildlife as a resource can be high among societies that commonly utilize animals (e.g., Botswana: Mordi 1991). Previous studies in Colombia and El Salvador and on the Caribbean coast of Costa Rica suggested that the utilitarian, materialistic view of wild animals as food and as a source of income is possibly the most prevalent in the region. However, according the recent national survey, in Costa Rican society, the prevailing attitudes toward animals are the sentimental and inquisitive, whereas utilitarian views on wildlife are not popular (see also public opinion about hunting, below). Direct

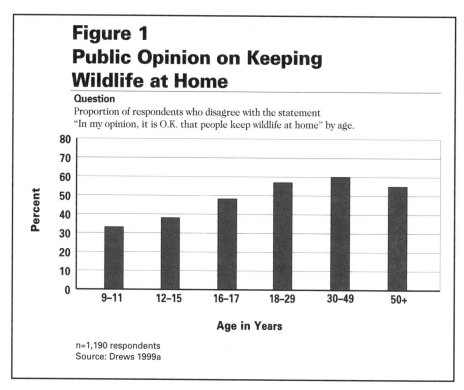

Figure 1
Public Opinion on Keeping Wildlife at Home

Question
Proportion of respondents who disagree with the statement "In my opinion, it is O.K. that people keep wildlife at home" by age.

Age in Years

n=1,190 respondents
Source: Drews 1999a

comparisons of attitudes among Latin American societies are hampered by the different methodologies used to characterize them. Nevertheless, the results of this Costa Rican study suggest that the Neotropical region may be more heterogeneous in its attitudes toward animals than previously thought. The Costa Rican profile is probably not representative of Latin America. For instance, while 59 percent of Costa Rican adults disapprove of keeping wild animals as pets (Figure 1), in Nicaragua only 39 percent of adults share that disapproval.

Hunting

The proportion of the population that participates in hunting is smaller in Costa Rica than in the United States. Only 2.4 percent of Costa Rican respondents said to have hunted or captured a wild animal, excluding fish, during the year previous to the survey.[7] Kellert (1993a) reported that 14 percent of Americans, 4 percent of Germans, and 1 percent of Japanese hunted during the two years previous to the corresponding studies. Every fifth Costa Rican adult fished in a river and every tenth adult fished in the sea during the year previous to the study.[8]

Although overall participation in hunting was small in Costa Rica, 13 percent of the adults ate meat of a wild animal during that year. This result is surprisingly high given that, with few exceptions, there is no legal access to wild animal meat in public establishments in that country.

Social attitudes and public opinion toward hunting have been studied mostly in developed nations (e.g., the United States: references in Herzog, Rowan, and Kossow 2001; Germany: Schulz 1985; Japan: Kellert 1993a). Although figures from such surveys need to be interpreted and compared with caution, in the light of differences in the phrasing of questions and their impact on the outcome of the study (Herzog, Rowan, and Kossow 2001), there are some recognizable trends. The general public in these nations disapproves of recreational hunting per se, with some allowances for subsistence hunting and meat consumption.[9] This pattern is found in Costa Rica, too.

Neither hunting nor hunters enjoy a generalized acceptance in Costa Rica. The majority (89 percent) of respondents consider recreational hunting an act of cruelty (Table 1). This is a well-established stance in

Table 1
Adults' Acceptance of Hunting in Costa Rica

Question	Definitely Yes (percent)	In General Yes (percent)	In General No (percent)	Definitely No (percent)	Sample Size
Do you agree with the use of venison as long as deer are not endangered?	18.5	26.2	19.2	36.1	1,006
Do you admire the skill and courage of a person who hunts successfully in the wild?	11.9	15.3	19.3	53.5	1,017
If there are enough crocodiles in Costa Rica, do you approve of the hunting of some to sell their hides?	7.4	9.6	21.2	61.8	1,016
Do you consider any kind of hunting for entertainment or sport an act of cruelty to the animals?	71.3	17.5	4.5	6.8	1,020
Do you think that the main reason to protect deer is to safeguard the supply of venison?	28.5	24.8	15.5	31.2	1,010

Note: These questions were part of a large battery of items in a nationwide survey carried out in 1999 about the relationship between society and wildlife. They did not appear clustered in the questionnaire. The difference between the total sample of 1,021 adults interviewed and the sample size reported for each question correspond to missing or "I don't know" answers.

Costa Rican society, with no significant differences related to gender, urban or rural setting, socioeconomic level, or education. The proportion of respondents sharing strongly this opinion increases significantly with age (Figure 2).[10] Two thirds of the adults interviewed do not admire the skill and courage of hunters (Table 1). This Costa Rican stance is similar to that of Japanese and German respondents, who expressed considerable opposition to hunting per se (Kellert 1993a). In the United States, 56 percent of respondents felt that hunting was morally wrong (Princeton Survey Research Associates 1991, cited in Herzog, Rowan, and Kossow 2001). A majority of Americans objected to the activity if it was justified only on the basis of its sporting or trophy values (Kellert 1989, 1993a; Rutberg 1997). In contrast, a majority of Americans supported hunting if the meat was utilized. In Costa Rica there is less disapproval of hunting for deer meat (55 percent) than of hunting for crocodile hides (83 percent). Female respondents disapprove of hunting for the use of venison and hides significantly more strongly than do males.[11] The more likely acceptance of hunting for meat than for hides or for recreational purposes in general mirrors a similar trend in the United States and Japan (Kellert 1993a). The opposition to hunting for venison and hides in Costa Rica is probably a matter of ethical principle, irrespective of species conservation considerations (see phrasing of questions in Table 1).

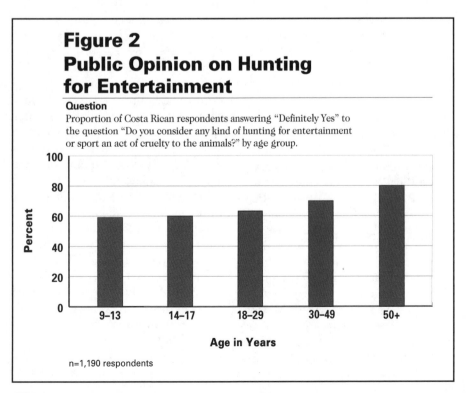

Figure 2
Public Opinion on Hunting for Entertainment

Question

Proportion of Costa Rican respondents answering "Definitely Yes" to the question "Do you consider any kind of hunting for entertainment or sport an act of cruelty to the animals?" by age group.

n=1,190 respondents

A slight majority of respondents justified protection measures for deer on the grounds of safeguarding the supply of venison, a utilitarian reason (Table 1). Most of the opponents of this utilitarian motive were well-educated, urban adults of high socioeconomic status. A higher education level was associated with a stronger rejection of hunting for venison or hides, less admiration of the skill and courage of hunters, and a stronger disapproval of utilitarian reasons for the protection of wildlife.

The overall disapproval of hunting by the Costa Rican public shown above reduces the viability of projects such as commercial utilization of animals taken from the wild for their meat or hides, the establishment of hunting grounds, and the conceivable promotion of Costa Rica as an international destination for trophy and sport hunters. This country maintains a "green" profile in the eyes of the international community and benefits from this image through the income generated from ecotourism. Currently, therefore, Costa Rica values its live animals more highly than it does carcasses or products thereof. There are no legal exports of wild animals for the international pet market from Costa Rica (Gómez and Drews 2000). In the context of a non-consumptive use policy, the use of native wildlife for pets within the country is contradictory. Taking live parrot chicks from nests may not be generally regarded as hunting and keeping them alive in captivity may not be seen as consumptive.

Living with Bats

In the tropics people commonly share their homes with bats, albeit often unknowingly. Modifications of the landscape through logging and through urban and agricultural development have reduced the number of natural roosts for these nocturnal mammals. Several species, however, find adequate shelter in buildings. In Costa Rica at least every tenth adult is aware of the presence of bats in his or her home (Drews 2002b). The incidence of

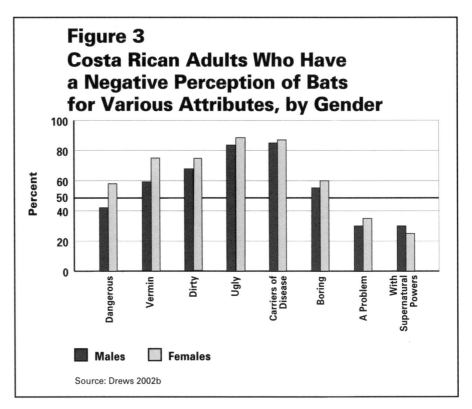

Figure 3
Costa Rican Adults Who Have a Negative Perception of Bats for Various Attributes, by Gender

Source: Drews 2002b

bats in people's homes is three times higher in rural than in urban areas. At least 87,020 household countrywide share their shelter with bats, a very conservative estimate given that their presence is often unnoticed.[12] A fifth of interviewees knew of bats inhabiting a nearby school and one quarter reported their presence in a nearby church. The species of bats living in buildings feed on insects, nectar of flowers, or fruit. They are harmless and free of diseases that could be transmitted to humans. The vampire bat is not commonly found in people's quarters. Perceptions of bats worldwide are loaded with prejudices and superstition, which have turned these animals into victims of dislike and unjustified eradication, and Costa Rica is no exception.

Changing attitudes toward bats is a challenging goal. Understanding the nature of the relationship between the society concerned and these animals is a prerequisite for such an endeavor. Costa Rican adults were asked to select one of four choices along a semantic gradient for various attributes.[13] The percentage of answers inclined toward a negative perception of the bats is shown in Figure

3. Most respondents perceive the bats as vermin, dirty, ugly, carriers of disease, and boring. About half consider them dangerous. A fifth of the interviewees attribute supernatural powers to these animals. Female adults have a more negative perception of the bats than do males.

Although in some cases a colony of bats under the roof may cause bad odors and stains on the ceiling, the majority of respondents did not perceive the presence of these animals as problematic (Figure 4). Interviewees who reportedly had bats in their homes, however, considered these a problem in 44 percent of the cases, in contrast to only 28 percent of those who did not notice bats at home.[14] There were no significant differences between these two groups with regard to any of the remaining attributes shown in Figure 3.

Perceptions of bats are closely linked to the level of education (Figure 4). Extremes on the negative side of the attributes studied are found mainly among the less educated. Superstition and fears seem to fade along with increased education. The tolerance of bats at home reflects knowledge about their biology, responsibility in attending to the needs of other species, and success in challenging the negative myths about bats that still prevail in Costa Rica. This exercise suggests that environmental education efforts are a promising avenue toward a more animal friendly society. It is illustrative of similar processes that govern the perception that the bush is hostile, the urge for biological sterility in urban settings, and the simplistic dichotomy between good and bad organisms. The readiness to share the living space with live members of the national biodiversity without resorting to their control in captivity is a firm step toward a harmonious co-existence with nature.

Linking Attitudes and Knowledge to Practices

The decision to obtain a wild animal to keep at home is conceivably the product of highly heterogeneous influences, including cultural upbringing and surrounding, attitudes, social condition, education, knowledge of natural history, tradition, gender, and family composition, as well as logistical and legal considerations (Drews 1999b). Aesthetic appeal of the animals, compassion, affection, and a desire to please and stimulate children are important motives for the acquisition of wild animals as pets in Costa Rica. The sentimental attitude was stronger in those who decided to keep a wild animal at home than in those adults who did not initiate the acquisition. Thus, keepers provide wild pets inadequate care despite their strong affection for animals. The result supports the hypothesis that a marked sympathy for and false empathy for the pets perpetuates this practice in Costa Rica (Drews 1999b).

There are further contradictions between attitudes and people's behavior, showing that the relationship

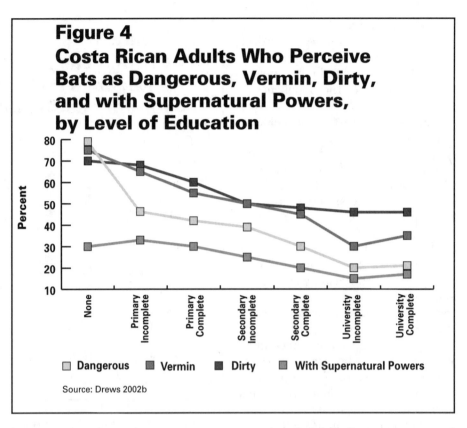

Figure 4

Costa Rican Adults Who Perceive Bats as Dangerous, Vermin, Dirty, and with Supernatural Powers, by Level of Education

□ Dangerous   ■ Vermin   ■ Dirty   ■ With Supernatural Powers

Source: Drews 2002b

between thought and action is not usually straightforward and can be quite complex. Biophilia, the innately emotional affiliation of human beings to other living organisms (Wilson 1984), can be conceptually linked to values and attitudes toward animals (Kellert 1993b). Biophilia probably contributes to the positive feelings of Costa Ricans toward wild animals, then backfires as it encourages the keeping of wild animals, condemning them to an alien environment and permanent captivity. The contradiction between attitudes and practices is further illustrated by the fact that, despite a stronger affinity with animal protection among households of high socioeconomic status, the percentage of households with wildlife did not differ among the socioeconomic strata (Drews 2000a).[15] At the root of such contradictions may be the invisibility of the animal's suffering. Rather than changing the attitudes of Costa Ricans toward animals, the challenge is to increase the awareness about the animals' needs and thereby trigger the ethical concern for their well being.

The underlying assumptions of any such environmental education efforts

are that individual attitudes toward wild animals influence people's behavior, and that attitudes are influenced by culture, and as such are amenable to changes over time. These assumptions, if true, should enable the fostering of respect and compassion through example, guided experiences, and relevant information, conveyed emotionally and intellectually, about the role of the living environment in people's lives. (Values education constitutes a synthesis of cognitive and affective learning, pertinent in this context [c.f. Kellert 1996]). The teaching of values needs to accompany any education effort oriented toward encouraging animal protection and biodiversity conservation.

Understanding the link between attitudes and practices poses an acute challenge to the design of awareness campaigns. Herzog, Rowan, and Kossow (2001) analyzed social attitudes in the United States toward the use of animals in research, the wearing of fur, hunting, farm animal issues, diet choice, and public support of animal protection philosophy. The study illustrates the existence of contradictory results, both from methodological constraints and flaws and from a "real" lack of correspondence between attitudes and action. For example, in general, public opinion in the United States has become more supportive of animal protection issues in the past fifty years. However, although the majority of Americans have favorable views of the animal rights movement (Roper Center for Public Opinion 1994), their daily behaviors, including meat-eating, are not necessarily compatible with such perception. Positive feelings toward animals do not necessarily lead to kind treatment, respect, and consideration of the animal's needs (e.g., Herzog, Rowan, and Kossow 2001). The strength of an attitude, and its associated beliefs and emotions, may be decisive to its likelihood of being translated into corresponding behaviors (Herzog, Rowan, and Kossow 2001). Some individuals may have attitudes toward animals that are peripheral or superficial. Such a collection of preferences and isolated opinions has been referred to as "non-attitudes" or "vacuous attitudes" (Eagly and Chaiken 1993). These may have little real salience in a person's life but can affect responses on opinion polls. The treatment of animals is not an issue of high priority to most people.

Adults who keep wildlife have better biological knowledge than those who never kept wildlife as pets (Drews 2002a). Costa Ricans ranked highest in the percentage of correct answers to five questions about animals, in comparison to U.S. and Japanese citizens (calculated from Kellert 1993a, Figure 5).[16] Such knowledge of natural history per se, however, does not translate into more animal friendly practices, as seen by the widespread keeping of wildlife as pets under conditions of concern. Specific key aspects seem to be dimly represented in biological curricula, such as the social needs of wild animals, their drive for dispersal, exploration, and coverage of wide areas in search of resources and mates, the effects of stress generated by constrained freedom of movement, among others.

Previous research suggested that most Costa Ricans have a fairly superficial understanding and awareness of environmental problems (Holl, Daily, and Ehrlich 1995).

A slight majority of Costa Rican adults do not consider acceptable the keeping of wild animals as pets. This tendency, however, is not mirrored among minors aged nine to seventeen (Figure 1). Nature-related values seem to develop later in children than other moral values. Young children typically view nature in highly instrumental, egocentric, and exploitative ways (Kellert 1996). In the course of further development, however, these values change in emphasis toward less utilitarian, negativistic, and dominionistic ones. American children between thirteen and seventeen years of age begin to comprehend relationships among creatures and habitats, as well as people's ethical responsibilities for exercising stewardship toward the natural world. This is reflected in a sharp increase in moralistic, ecologistic, and naturalistic values of nature (Kellert 1996). Costa Rican children seem to follow this pattern, with regard to their increasing disagreement with people keeping wildlife at home with age (Figure

1). The proportion of respondents who disagree with that practice among nine to eleven year olds, the youngest of the sample, is nearly half that of the adults. This proportion increases steadily with age towards adulthood, reaching 59.5 percent of the Costa Rican adults interviewed (Drews 1999a, 2000a). This suggests a progressively increasing awareness about ethical arguments against the keeping of wildlife at home.[17] Given the central role that children can play in the family initiative to obtain a wild animal, this age group becomes a key target for awareness education—in the hopes of speeding up their acquisition of moralistic values of nature, which may prevent or hinder the acquisition of a wild animal.

The belief that a wild animal kept as a pet stimulates in children love and respect for nature is probably erroneous. Being able to observe a wild animal at close range is a thrilling and stimulating experience. If that animal is in a cage, however, detached from its habitat and natural behavior and deprived of the freedom to come and go as it pleases, the experience is much less rewarding and perpetuates the idea that people can control and subdue nature at will. It is plausible

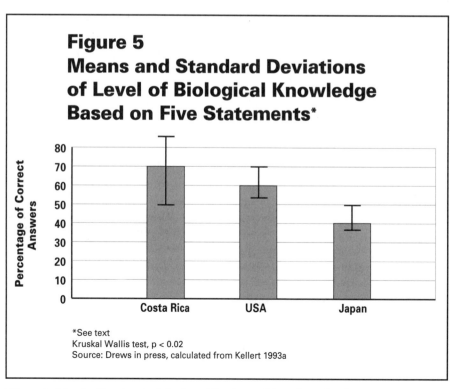

Figure 5
Means and Standard Deviations of Level of Biological Knowledge Based on Five Statements*

*See text
Kruskal Wallis test, p < 0.02
Source: Drews in press, calculated from Kellert 1993a

that outdoor activities—a guided confrontation with the habitat of these species, their ecological role, and their individual needs—stimulates the interest in and reverence for nature more strongly than does the caged animal in the backyard. Such has been the approach taken by the biological education program of the Guanacaste Conservation Area in Costa Rica, which hopes to produce better citizens by increasing their biological literacy (Valverde 2000).[18]

Lessons from and for the Neotropics

Any progress toward reducing the levels of trade and the incidence of wild animals kept as pets will have a significant and strong positive impact on the state of wild animals in the Neotropics. Progress in such a reduction of numbers seems distant. Nonetheless the information platform about trade, pet keeping habits, and attitudes toward animals has improved considerably in the past five years. Similarly awareness campaigns and more efficient networking between similarly minded organizations in the region are contributing to progress in this direction. The human resources and organizational apparatus dedicated to wildlife protection, both at a government and private level, are growing toward their consolidation. There are indications of an increasing public awareness and concern about wildlife protection in Costa Rica and other countries of the Neotropics: the use of wild animals in circuses has been banned in Costa Rica, the state of Rio de Janeiro (Brazil), and some municipalities of Colombia since 2001.

Confiscated animals from the illegal trade are the tip of an iceberg. Their proper attention in rescue centers is one of the many tasks that a society needs to accommodate in its animal protection agenda. There has been slow progress in the field of wildlife rescue in the Neotropics

(Drews 1999c). At the turn of the century, however, various countries have well-established rescue centers, and information about the peculiarities of rescue techniques for Neotropical animals is becoming available.

Academics from the fields of biology, ethology, and veterinary medicine have a key challenge ahead: the production of material that visualizes the suffering of wild, Neotropical animals kept as pets, in relation to their social and ecological needs in the wild. An efficient integration of such material in a society with an affectionate and inquisitive attitude toward animals should trigger ethical concern about the habit of keeping wild animals as pets. A look at perceptions of bats has shown that education is a promising avenue for the improvement of social attitudes toward wild animals. Ultimately, animal-friendly attitudes should translate into animal-friendly actions. The absence of parrots in Neotropical households and the tolerance of bats in the attics will show the success in the endeavor to move toward a more compassionate, biologically literate society, respectful of wild animals.

Acknowledgements

I am grateful to Humane Society International (HSUS/HSI, Washington, D.C.) for funding the Costa Rican and Nicaraguan surveys and the preparation of this manuscript. Stephen Kellert provided advice and documents during the early stages of the survey. The Regional Wildlife Management Program of the National University of Costa Rica and personnel from Unimer Research International (San José, Costa Rica) provided logistical support. My sincere thanks to the people of Costa Rica who were interviewed and shared their practices, attitudes, and knowledge about wildlife in a most forthcoming manner.

Notes

[1] With four million inhabitants and 51,100 km², Costa Rica is a small country.

[2] Rede Nacional de Combate ao Tráfico de Animais Silvestres (National Network for the Fight against Illegal Wild Animal Trade, *www.renctas.org.br*).

[3] Dogs are kept 1.2 to 1.3 times more often than cats in U.S. households (AVMA 1997 and American Pet Products Manufacturers Association 2000, respectively), and 1.5 times more often than cats in Australian households (*www.petnet.com.au/statistics.html*, accessed March 17, 2000).

[4] Some species of parrot is kept in 91 percent of households that keep wildlife in Nicaragua.

[5] Venezuela has a population of about 23 million inhabitants, nearly six times more than Costa Rica. If extraction rates for the national pet market are similar in these countries, Venezuela would need about 150,000–240,000 parrot chicks to satisfy this demand.

[6] The humanistic attitude, which is similar to the sentimental dimension identified in Costa Rica, was the most common perspective of animals in a U.S. sample of adult citizens (Kellert 1989).

[7] Males represented 80 percent of the 24 people who reportedly hunted the previous year. Among these 24 people, 46 percent reported having hunted more than once in that year.

[8] 30 percent of male and 13 percent of female adults fished in a river, 16 percent of male and 4 percent of female adults fished in the sea.

[9] The percentage of people participating in hunting has decreased in the United States in the past thirty years (Herzog, Rowan, and Kossow 2001).

[10] Spearman's correlation coefficient r=1.0, n=5, p<0.05.

[11] Chi-square=18.7, df=3, p<0.001, chi-square=14.9, df=3, p<0.01, respectively.

[12] According to the national census of 2000, there are 937,210 homes in Costa Rica.

[13] E.g., rated from dangerous to harmless, with four other options between them. Frequencies of the two options showing an inclination toward a negative perception were pooled to calculate percentages shown in Figure 4. Significant differences between males and females are indicated in Figure 3 by asterisks (chi-square tests, NS= not significant, * = p<0.05, *** = p<0.001).

[14] Chi-square=10.7, df=3, p<0.02.

[15] In Nicaragua the incidence of wildlife kept as pets was significantly higher among middle and high strata households than among households of low socioeconomic level.

[16] Respondents were asked in Costa Rica, the United States, and Japan to state for each of the following five statements whether it was true or false: (1) spiders have ten legs, (2) most insects have backbones, (3) a seahorse is a kind of fish, (4) snakes have a layer of slime to move more easily, and (4) all adult birds have feathers.

[17] In line with this view, both ethical principles and logistical considerations account, in about equal proportions, for 74 percent of reasons put forward for not having ever had a wild animal at home. A further 5 percent indicated dislike for wild animals, and only 4 percent noted that keeping wild animals as pets is illegal.

[18] *www.acguanacaste.ac.cr*.

Literature Cited

American Pet Products Manufacturers Association (APPMA). 2000. *National pet owners survey 1999–2000*. Greenwich, Conn.: APPMA.

American Veterinary Medical Association (AVMA). 1997. *U.S. pet ownership and demographics sourcebook*. Schaumburg, Ill.: Center for Information Management, AVMA.

Barborak, J., R. Morales, C. MacFarland, and B. Swift. 1983. *Status and trends in international trade and local utilization of wildlife in Central America*. Turrialba, Costa Rica: Wildlands and watershed program, CATIE.

Bedoya-Gaitán, M. 2000. Cacería y conservación de fauna en la comunidad indígena Ticuna de Buenos Aires. In: *Actitudes hacia la fauna en Latinoamérica*, ed. F. Nassar-Montoya and R. Crane, 177–188. Washington D.C.: Humane Society Press.

Beissinger, S.R. 1994. La conservación de los psitácidos del neotrópico: Retos para los biólogos, gerentes, y gobierno. In: *Biología y conservación de los psitácidos de Venezuela*, ed. G. Morales, I. Novo, D. Bigio, A. Luy, and F. Rojas-Suárez, 141–147. ISBN 980-07-1717-X, Caracas: privately published.

Benítez-García, M.A., and L. Durán-Fernández. 2000. Aspectos socio-culturales y políticos en las actuales actitudes hacia la fauna silvestre en México. In *Actitudes hacia la fauna en Latinoamérica*, ed. F. Nassar-Montoya and R. Crane, 98–117. Washington D.C.: Humane Society Press.

Boher-Bentti, S., and R. Smith 1994. Comercio ilegal de guacamayas y loros. In: *Biología y conservación de los psitácidos de Venezuela*, ed. G. Morales, I. Novo, D. Bigio, A. Luy, and F. Rojas-Suárez, 277. ISBN 980-07-1717-X. Caracas: privately published.

Carrillo, E., and C. Vaughan, eds. 1994. *La vida silvestre de mesoamérica: Diagnóstico actual y estrategia para su conservación*. Heredia, Costa Rica: Editorial de la Universidad Nacional EUNA.

Cedeño, Y., and C. Drews. 2000. Comercio internacional de fauna silvestre en Centroamérica entre 1992 y 1996. Technical report. Programa Regional en Manejo de Vida Silvestre, Universidad Nacional, Heredia, Costa Rica.

Clapp, R.B. 1975. *Birds imported into the United States in 1972*. Washington, D.C.: U.S. Department of Interior, Fish and Wildlife Service, Special Scientific Report—Wildlife No. 193.

Clapp, R.B., and R.C. Banks. 1973. *Birds imported into the United States in 1971*. Washington, D.C.: U.S. Department of Interior, Bureau of Sport Fisheries and Wildlife, Special Scientific Report—Wildlife No. 170.

De Alió, L.W. 2000. El uso de la fauna silvestre como mascota en Venezuela. In *Actitudes hacia la fauna en Latinoamérica*, ed. F. Nassar-Montoya and R. Crane, 129–136. Washington, D.C.: Humane Society Press.

Desenne, P., and S. Strahl. 1991. Trade and the conservation status of the family Psittacidae in Venezuela. *Bird Conservation International* 1: 153–169.

———. 1994. Situación poblacional y jerarquización de especies para la conservación de la familia Psittacidae en Venezuela. In: *Biología y conservación de los psitácidos de Venezuela*, ed. G. Morales, I. Novo, D. Bigio, A. Luy, and F. Rojas-Suárez, 231–272. ISBN 980-07-1717-X. Caracas: privately published.

Drews, C. 1999a. Wildlife in Costa Rican households—A nationwide survey. Technical report, Washington, D.C.: Humane Society International.

———. 1999b. Simpatía y empatía hacia la fauna: Las raíces de tenencia de mascotas silvestres. In *Rescate de fauna en el neotrópico*, ed. C. Drews, 31–52. Heredia, Costa Rica: Editorial Universidad Nacional.

———. 1999c. Rescate de fauna en el Neotrópico: cerrando el milenio. In *Rescate de fauna en el neotrópico*, ed. C. Drews, 495–520. Heredia, Costa Rica: Editorial Universidad Nacional.

———. 2000a. Caracterización general de la tenencia de animales silvestres como mascotas en Costa Rica. In *Actitudes hacia la fauna en Latinoamérica*, ed. F. Nassar-Montoya and R. Crane, 45–55. Washington, D.C.: Humane Society Press.

———. 2000b. Aspectos del mercado en torno a la tenencia de animales silvestres como mascotas en Costa Rica. In *Actitudes hacia la fauna en Latinoamérica*, ed. F. Nassar-Montoya and R. Crane, 147–160. Washington D.C.: Humane Society Press.

———. 2001. Wild animals and other pets kept in Costa Rican households: Incidence, species, and numbers. *Society and Animals* 9(2): 107–126.

———. 2002a. Attitudes, knowledge and wild animals as pets in Costa Rica. *Anthrozoös* 15(2): 119–138.

———. 2002b. Convivencia con murciélagos en Costa Rica. *Ambientico* 103: 12–13. *http://www.ambientico.una.ac.cr/drewsmurc.htm*.

Eagly A.H., and S. Chaiken. 1993. *The psychology of attitudes*. Orlando, Fla.: Harcourt Brace Jovanovich College Publishers.

Franke, J., and T.M. Telecky. 2001. *Reptiles as pets*. Washington, D.C.: The Humane Society of the United States.

Gómez, J.R., and C. Drews. 2000. Movimientos internacionales de flora y fauna de los apéndices CITES en Costa Rica entre 1992 y 1998. Technical report. Heredia, Costa Rica: Programa Regional en Manejo de Vida Silvestre, Universidad Nacional.

Hemley, G., ed. 1994. *International wildlife trade: A CITES sourcebook*. Island Press, Washington, D.C.

Herzog, H., A. Rowan, and D. Kossow. 2001. Social attitudes and animals. In: *The state of the animals: 2001*, ed. D. Salem and A. Rowan, 55–69. Washington, D.C.: Humane Society Press.

Holl, K.D., G.C. Daily, and P.R. Ehrlich. 1995. Knowledge and perceptions in Costa Rica regarding environment, population, and biodiversity issues. *Conservation Biology* 9: 1548–1558.

Inskipp, T.P. 1975. *All heaven in a rage: A study of the importation of birds into the United Kingdom*. London: Royal Society for the Protection of Birds, published in cooperation with the Royal Society for the Prevention of Cruelty to Animals.

Kellert, S.R. 1980. Phase II: Activities of the American public relating to animals. Technical report, Washington, D.C.: U.S. Fish and Wildlife Service.

———. 1989. Human-animal interactions: A review of American attitudes to wild and domestic animals in the twentieth century. In *Animals and people sharing the world*, ed. A.N. Rowan, 137–175. Hanover and London: University Press of New England.

———. 1993a. Attitudes, knowledge, and behavior toward wildlife among the industrial superpowers: United States, Japan, and Germany. *Journal of Social Issues* 49: 53–69.

———. 1993b. The biological basis for human values of nature. In *The biophilia hypothesis*, ed. S.R. Kellert and E.O. Wilson, 42–69. Washington, D.C.: Island Press.

———. 1996. The value of life. Washington, D.C.: Island Press.

Kellert, S.R., and J.K. Berry. 1980. *Phase III: Knowledge, affection and basic attitudes toward animals in American society*. Washington, D.C.: U.S. Department of the Interior, Fish and Wildlife Service.

Martínez, N. 2000. Situación actual del manejo de la fauna silvestre en Bolivia. In *Actitudes hacia la fauna en Latinoamérica*, ed. F. Nassar-Montoya and R. Crane, 3–11. Washington D.C.: Humane Society Press.

Medina, C., and A. Montero. 2001. Censo de la fauna silvestre en cautiverio en la comunidad de Nueve de Enero, Corregimiento de Amelia D. de Icaza, Distrito de San Miguelito, Panamá. Honors diss., Panama City, Panama: Escuela de Biología,

Universidad de Panamá.

Morales, G., and P. Desenne. 1994. Plan de acción y conservación de los psitácidos venezolanos. In *Biología y conservación de los psitácidos de Venezuela*, ed. G. Morales, I. Novo, D. Bigio, A. Luy, and F. Rojas-Suárez, 299–307. ISBN 980-07-1717-X. Caracas: privately published.

Mordi, A.R. 1991. *Attitudes toward wildlife in Botswana*. New York: Garland Publishing Inc.

Muñóz-López, E., and A. Ortíz-Latorre. 2000. Rehabilitación y actitudes hacia la fauna silvestre en Chile. In *Actitudes hacia la fauna en Latinoamérica*, ed. F. Nassar-Montoya and R. Crane, 71–84. Washington, D.C.: Humane Society Press.

Nassar-Montoya, F. 2000. Actitud y pensamiento sobre la fauna silvestre en Colombia. In *Actitudes hacia la fauna en Latinoamérica*, ed. F. Nassar-Montoya and R. Crane, 27–43. Washington, D.C.: Humane Society Press.

Nassar-Montoya, F., and R. Crane, eds. 2000. *Actitudes hacia la fauna en Latinoamérica*. Washington, D.C.: Humane Society Press.

Nilsson, G. 1977. *The bird business: A study of the importation of birds into the United States*. Washington, D.C.: Animal Welfare Institute.

Pérez, R., and T. Zúñiga. 1998. *Análisis del comercio de psitácidos en Nicaragua*. Managua, Nicaragua: WCS/WWF.

Poten, C.J. 1991. A shameful harvest: America's illegal wildlife trade. *National Geographic* 180 (9): 106–132.

Princeton Survey Research Associates. 1991. Great American TV Poll #2—USPSRA. 91TV02.R30. Sponsored by Troika Productions and Lifetime Television.

Ramos, L.A., and Z. Ricord de Mendoza. 2000. Tenencia de fauna silvestre en El Salvador. In *Actitudes hacia la fauna en Latinoamérica*, ed. F. Nassar-Montoya and R. Crane, 85–95. Washington, D.C.: Humane Society Press.

Redford, K.H. 1992. The empty forest.

BioScience 42(6): 412–422.

Rede Nacional de Combate ao Tráfico de Animais Silvestres. 2001. *1° relatório nacional sobre o tráfico de fauna silvestre*. Brasilia: Rede Nacional De Combate ao Trafico De Animais Silvestres.

Rodríguez, J. 2000. Situación de la vida silvestre en Panamá. In *Actitudes hacia la fauna en Latinoamérica*, ed. F. Nassar-Montoya and R. Crane, 119–128. Washington, D.C.: Humane Society Press.

Roper Center for Public Opinion. 1994. Question US–PSRA. 092194, R24S. Times Mirror. July 12.

Rutberg, A.T. 1997. The science of deer management: An animal welfare perspective. In *The science of overabundance: Deer ecology and population management*, ed. W. J. McShea, H.B. Underwood, and J.H. Rappole. Washington, D.C.: Smithsonian Institution Press.

Schulz, W. 1985. Einstellung zur natur. Ph.D. diss., Ludwig-Maximilians-Universität.

Solís, V., A. Jiménez, O. Brenes, and L.V. Strusberg. 1999. *Listas de fauna de importancia para la conservación en Centroamérica y México*. San José, Costa Rica: IUCN-ORMA, WWF-Centroamérica.

Touzet, J.M., and I. Yépez. 2000. Problemática del tráfico de la fauna silvestre en el Ecuador. In *Actitudes hacia la fauna en Latinoamérica*, ed. F. Nassar-Montoya and R. Crane, 57–69. Washington, D.C.: Humane Society Press.

Trama, F., and O. Ramírez. 2002. Decomisos de fauna silvestre en carreteras: Un indicador del éxito de campañas de concientización? Technical report. Heredia, Costa Rica: Programa Regional en Manejo de Vida Silvestre, Universidad Nacional.

Valverde, J.F. 2000. Programa de educación biológica en el área de Guanacaste, Costa Rica. In *Actitudes hacia la fauna en Latinoamérica*, ed. F. Nassar-Montoya and R. Crane, 214–219. Washington, D.C.: Humane Society Press.

Vargas-Mena, E. 2000. Significados

culturales de la tortuga verde (*Chelonia mydas*) en el Caribe costarricense. In *Actitudes hacia la fauna en Latinoamérica*, ed. F. Nassar-Montoya and R. Crane, 161–176. Washington, D.C.: Humane Society Press.

Wilson, E.O. 1984. *Biophilia*. Cambridge: Harvard University Press.

Horse Welfare Since 1950

14

CHAPTER

Katherine A. Houpt and Natalie Waran

Introduction

There are approximately 6.9 million horses in the United States, more than in any other country in the world (American Horse Council 2000) (Table 1). That fact alone should inspire Americans to improve equine welfare, although it must be said that the state of domesticated horses is better now than it was fifty years ago.

The advances that have been made in veterinary medicine, including surgical technique and, especially, anesthesia, mean that diagnosis of an intestinal torsion or displacement is no longer an automatic death sentence. Improvements in surgery for lameness and in anti-inflammatory drugs have eliminated such painful practices as blistering or pin-firing a lame horse's lower limbs, ostensibly to expedite the healing process. Improvements in nutrition and in control of infectious disease have allowed many horses to live into their twenties, thirties, or beyond.

Horse husbandry has improved in one respect: unlike in days past, few horses are kept tied with halter and lead rope in narrow "tie" stalls in dark and dirty stables. But horse husbandry has worsened in another: more horses live in box stalls or isolated in small, grassless corrals than in natural herds on pasture now that fewer horse owners live in rural areas. Box stalls (typically 10–12 feet square) allow the horse to turn around, walk several paces, and lie

down in lateral recumbency, but they do not provide a natural social environment that even tie stalls—where horses are stabled closely one to another—provide. Typically a stalled horse seldom has access to a natural, high roughage diet and is fed limited amounts of high-concentrate feed and/or hay that are quickly consumed. Such management leaves a horse in a virtual wooden box with long periods of physical inactivity. This unnatural state leads to the development of stall aggression, stall walking, weaving, wood chewing, or cribbing, or to difficulty in handling. Controlling these "vices" often is done using inhumane methods.

A situation unchanged since the

days of Anna Sewell's *Black Beauty* (2001), published originally in 1877, is that a horse seldom is kept by one owner for his or her entire adult life. Often a horse changes hands—and careers—a number of times over his or her lifetime. After leaving the breeding farm, an animal may start out as a race horse, then be sold and retrained as a hunter, jumper, event horse, or equitation horse when his or her racing career is over. He or she may then be sold several times when outgrown by one owner, found to be unsuitable for another's level of experience, or not competitive enough for a third. In mid-life or later, he or she may then be used as a lesson, rental, or camp horse, and finally, when

Table 1
Number of Horses and Participants by Industry, 1999

Activity	No. of Horses	No. of Participants
Racing	725,000	941,400
Showing	1,974,000	3,607,900
Recreation	2,970,000	4,346,100
Other*	1,262,000	1,607,900
Total	**6,931,000**	**7,062,500****

*Includes farm and ranch work, police work, rodeo, and polo.

**The sum of participants by activity does not equal the total number of participants because individuals could be counted in more than one activity.

Source: American Horse Council

infirm, unrideable, or simply too old to be useful, be sold at auction and sent to slaughter. Relatively few horses die of old age, although some fortunate retirees may be euthanized due to age-related ailments.

At the turn of the millennium, the most pressing welfare issues of the domestic horse surround conditions found in slaughter and transport to slaughter; pari-mutuel racing; the pregnant mare urine (PMU) industry; the competitive and show industry; and in the development of husbandry-related stereotypes. (Urban carriage horses are a highly visible problem in some localities, since they usually are part of a local tourist industry, but they often generate concern out of proportion to their relatively small numbers.)

Slaughter and Transport to Slaughter

Sound, well-behaved, well-trained horses are relatively scarce and can be expensive as a result. There is, however, an oversupply of horses who are lame, suffer from chronic obstructive pulmonary disease or are otherwise infirm, or are unmanageable, unwanted, untrained, or past their useful life.

The fate of most of these "problem" horses is to be slaughtered. Most horses are sold for slaughter for human consumption (primarily outside the United States) rather than for pet food, or are rendered, as they were fifty years ago. They are slaughtered at one of two slaughter plants in the United States, both in Texas. The number of horses being slaughtered is decreasing, as fear of zoonotic diseases and competition from other countries increase (Table 2).

Horses at slaughter are stunned with a captive bolt pistol, then exsanguinated, which should result in a painless death. As with all slaughter procedures, however, much depends upon the competence of the personnel using the equipment provided.

Cruelty can occur if the horse is injured in the handling process, badly frightened, whipped to be persuaded to move, or not properly stunned (Reece, Friend, and Stull 2000). The greater equine suffering occurs not at slaughter but during transport and in the pens used to confine the horses before and after transport. Many slaughter-bound horses begin their journey far from Texas and obviously must be transported long distances as a result. Heat stress is an additional factor in the summer months.

There have been several studies of transport to slaughter under simulated or actual transport conditions. Horses transported for twenty-eight hours in summer can lose 10 percent of their body weight, which results in considerable dehydration (Friend et al. 1998). After transportation for twenty-four hours, 15 percent of the horses (three of twenty) in the Friend et al. study were judged unsuitable for further transport on the basis of weakness or high body temperature. The more crowded the horses, the more likely they are to fall and, once down, to be trampled. In another study horses transported in more crowded (less than 1.3 square meters per horse) conditions had fewer injuries but were more dehydrated and had greater changes in white blood cell counts (Stull 1999). Provision of water in the trailers during rest stops would help the horses compensate for the water they are losing as sweat, but not all horses in the trailers would be willing to move to water since that would involve entering another horse's personal space (Gibbs and Friend 2000). Double-decker (or possum belly) trucks cause more injuries to horses in the upper levels than do single-deck trucks because the entrances are narrow (Stull and Rodick 2000). The percentage of injured horses was 29 percent for double-decker trailers and 8 percent for single deck trailers. Cortisol, body temperature, and white blood cells were found to be affected by transport. The greatest cause of injury to transported horses, however, was fighting, caused by mixing unfa-

Table 2
Horses Slaughtered and Processed at Packing Plants in the United States

Year	Number
1990	345,900
1991	276,700
1992	243,500
1993	169,900
1994	107,000
1995	109,900
1996	105,900
1997	87,200
1998	72,100
1999	62,813
2000	47,134
2001	56,332

The number has dropped substantially in the past ten years.

Source: U.S. Department of Agriculture National Agricultural Statistics Service

miliar horses, who normally establish dominance through physical intimidation in corrals prior to loading (Grandin, McGee, and Lanier 1999). The Grandin, McGee and Lanier study found that 8 percent of horses arriving at a slaughter plant exhibited serious welfare problems. In addition 30 percent had visible bite wounds. Examination of the carcasses revealed bruises on 25 percent of all the slaughtered horses, more than 50 percent of which were kick or bite wounds. Other problems included foot and limb injuries such as fractures, wounds (including infected wounds), and thinness to the point of emaciation. Owner neglect must have been the major cause of the poor body condition of the latter horses.

The federal Commercial Transport of Equines for Slaughter Act, passed in 1996, stipulates that double-decker trailers can no longer be used to transport equines, the ceilings of equine transport trailers must be six feet (three meters) high, and horses must be rested and watered every twenty-eight hours. In 2002 Representative Connie Morella of Maryland introduced H.R. 3781 in Congress; the bill would ban slaughtering of horses for meat. Such a ban could actually increase equine suffering if horses were transported for slaughter to Mexico, where there are fewer animal care laws, or if horses were allowed to starve to death because they could no longer bring a few hundred dollars from slaughter buyers at auction.

Local health codes and lack of land leave those owners who euthanize old or ill horses at home (probably the most humane ending for a horse) few options for body disposal other than commercial renderers. More retirement homes for elderly horses are needed. Care must be taken that horses at these facilities live in compatible groups and have adequate feed available. All too often good intentions may lead to welfare problems when inadequate funds are available and/or the managers of retirement homes are not experienced in equine management.

Racing

Although Standardbreds, Arabians, Quarter horses, and other breeds are raced in the United States, Thoroughbred racing is the best known. More than 54,000 Thoroughbred races were held in 38 states in 2002 (Jockey Club 2003). Racing raises several important welfare issues, including the rate of injury among horses racing or in training; the use of medication (both legal and illegal); the racing of two-year-old horses; insurance claims on ill or suffering horses; and the fate of the overwhelming majority of racehorses who have no monetary value to the breeding industry. The rate of injury during an actual race is relatively low (3.3 per thousand race starts). The rate of fatal injury is 1.4 per thousand starts (Mundy 2000).

Horses may race only seven to twelve times a year but may typically stay in training almost year-round. One way to reduce the number of musculoskeletal injuries in racehorses is to determine the factors associated with injuries. Length of pre-race conditioning is an example. A humeral fracture was found to be most likely to occur when the horse returns to training after a two-month period out of training. Apparently lack of high-speed workouts can lead to disuse osteoporosis (Carrier et al. 1998). Musculoskeletal injuries of all types were found to be more likely to occur when horses are exercized less (Cohen et al. 2000). Nonfatal injuries were most likely to be sesamoid, metacarpal, or carpal fractures (Estberg et al. 1998). Track design is another important potential cause of injury during racing. Increasing the radius of corners, the degree of banking, and the placement of inclines on straight sections will reduce strain on the outside leg and consequently reduce low-grade injuries.

Training methods that reduce the load the horse carries may also reduce injury. Using a treadmill or a swimming pool allows the horse to exercise without carrying a rider, whose weight increases the load on the horse's bones (Evans 2002). There are no statistics concerning injuries during training, but because it is estimated that only 50 percent of Thoroughbred foals actually race, the injury rate must be high. The catastrophic injuries, particularly those in televised races, are most likely to be highly publicized. For example Landseer, a Thoroughbred, sustained a fracture during a Breeders Cup race in October 2002 and was euthanized immediately.

Thoroughbreds "off the track," who are no longer usable or profitable for racing, can usually be sold for riding, either as hunters, three-day eventing prospects, or trail/companion horses. Such animals may excel at the very top of competition. Of the seventy horses identified as starters in the 2002 Rolex Kentucky CCI**** (the highest level of internation competi-tion) three-day event, for example, forty-four were identified as Thoroughbreds, including five of the eventual top ten finishers, although not all necessarily ever had raced (Sorge 2002). Nevertheless many Thoroughbreds do eventually end up at slaughter. McGee, Lanier, and Grandin observed 1,473 horses at auction and 1,348 horses at slaughter plants (2001). They found that Thoroughbred or Thoroughbred type horses constituted about 7 percent of all auction horses and 16 percent of all slaughter horses.

Another problem in racing is age-related. Centuries ago the Jockey Club in Britain declared that all Thoroughbred horses would be given a birth date of January 1 to avoid having to print updated programs during the racing season reflecting the changing ages of horses born through the late spring and summer. This tradition is also followed in the United States. Because horses typically begin race training and competition as two and three year olds—far before they mature physically—this tradition has led to breeding mares to give birth earlier and earlier in the calendar year so that the foal will be as old as possible when he or she races. The motivation in turn has led to great advances in the study of equine reproduction, aimed at bringing mares into breeding condition months before the natural spring season. Mares can be "tricked" into spring-like seasonal readiness by the use of artificial light in their barns, but such interference with the natural cycle can cause problems. Some mares are very dangerous during the transition from the non-breeding to the breeding season, when they come into heat but do not ovulate and, hence, are exposed to high levels of estrogen for long periods. Stallions, although less seasonal than mares, can have problems: they are more apt to exhibit poor libido or to "savage" (aggressively attack) mares bred in the winter than those bred in the spring.

The horses that suffer the most from this unnatural breeding season, however, are the foals. Foals born in

January or February in the northern half of the United States are subjected to cold barn temperatures, which may slow the development of standing and teat seeking. Horses born in New York are more likely than those in Florida to acquire insufficient maternal antibodies (Leblanc et al. 1992). The primary cause of this failure of passive immunity is probably climatic; the foal is slower to move in the cold. Failure of passive immunity allows the foal to fall victim to infections of the umbilical cord, respiratory tract, etc., because he or she has not yet acquired immunological protection. Inclement weather may keep the mare and foal indoors so that the young horse does not learn to recognize his or her mother in a group and does not get the exercise needed for optimum muscle development. A change in the Thoroughbred industry to "true" birthdays would wreak havoc for a year or two but would be in the best interests of the horse.

Standardbred horses, who raced in harness pulling a lightweight two-wheeled cart called a sulky, are not so easy as Thoroughbreds to retrain for other uses because they trot or pace rather than canter, and their gaits are not comfortable for a rider (although some are bought by those who eschew modern technology, such as the Amish and Mennonites, as driving animals). McGee, Lanier, and Grandin (2001) found that 4 percent of the horses at both auctions and slaughter plants were Standardbreds.

An unpublicized welfare issue involves those horses who are successful at racing and/or breeding and therefore are insured for a large amount of money. Insurance companies may insist that an insured horse who suffers from a permanently painful condition be kept alive to avoid paying the horse's value. Conversely an unsuccessful horse may be worth more dead than alive: a 1994 federal investigation of a scheme to kill horses for insurance money resulted in 23 indictments of riders, trainers, and owners (Englade 1996; *Chronicle of the Horse* 1998).

The Pregnant Mare Urine Industry

The use of horses for production of estrogen came to the attention of the public approximately ten years ago. The resulting criticism of the PMU industry and the industry's response are a good example of humane problem solving.

Equine estrogens were, until recently, almost the only substances available for treatment of the symptoms of menopause and the prevention of osteoporosis in women. Other benefits of this so-called hormone replacement therapy were a reduction in the risks of heart disease and age-related cognitive decline. Pregnant mares produce the most estrogens and produce the most between the third and ninth months of their pregnancies. They are, therefore, the mares used in the PMU industry. They foal and are rebred on pasture during the spring and summer. During the fall and winter, the mares are housed in barns in tie stalls while straddling rubber harnesses suspended from the ceiling that are used to collect urine.

Public criticism of the PMU industry focused on the mares' restricted access to water, their lack of exercise during the long months of housing, and the fate of the foals born but not utilized by the PMU industry.

Producers limited the mares' access to water for economic reasons. Because the volume of urine collected from each farm was limited and producers were paid on the basis of grams of estrogen produced, it was in their best economic interest to concentrate the urine. They did so by providing small amounts of water periodically from automatic waterers. Water intake was reduced gradually in the fall, to 3–4 1/100 kg body weight, as compared to 5–6 l/100kg of intake when water is freely available. This degree of water restriction increases osmotic pressure of the plasma and produces clinical signs of dehydration and behavioral signs of increased

motivation for water, but it is not life threatening (Houpt et al. 2001). In response to the negative publicity in the media, however, and criticism by an expert committee invited to tour the farms, the limit on volume of urine collected per farm was eased in 1999. Automatic waterers still are used and controlled, ostensibly to keep the stalls drier and to prevent the mares from dunking their hay into the water. (Hay dunking and playing with an automatic waterer so that the water spills on the floor are annoying behaviors that are tolerated by non-PMU horse owners, but the problem is exacerbated in PMU horses by the close proximity of the hay and water sources.)

In the PMU industry, mares remain in their stalls for days to months at a time because of the inclement weather in north central America during the winter and because of the labor and dangers to the horses involved in removing the harnesses and releasing the horses outside. The issue of lack of exercise has been addressed experimentally by two groups. When released after confinement for two weeks, the industry median time between opportunities for the horse to exercise, mares showed compensatory increases in locomotion in comparison to mares exercised daily. The behaviors in the stalls of exercised and confined mares were similar (Houpt et al. 2001). Physiologically the confined mares were not stressed (Freeman et al. 1999), but in late pregnancy they tended to be more edematous in the legs and abdomen (Houpt et al. 2001). Stereotypic behaviors did not develop in the mares chronically confined in tie stalls, probably because in both studies the horses were provided with free choice hay, which will most closely simulate the natural grazing pattern. Flanngian and Stookey (2002) observed 110 horses on ten PMU farms and found a prevalence of stereotypic behavior of 5 percent, less than that observed by McGreevey et al. (1995a) in box-stalled Thoroughbreds. Although the mares could not lie in lateral recumbency, they could lie in sternal recumbency (McDonnell et al. 1999). Horses unaccustomed to tie stalls may be reluctant to lie down, but this reluctance is unrelated to the size of the horse: draft horses laid down, but some Thoroughbreds did not (Houpt et al. 2001). Recent studies have shown that horses will work harder for a grain reward than for release from a tie stall and will work as hard for access to another horse as for release from confinement. When tested repeatedly at fifteen-minute intervals after release, horses chose to spend thirty minutes in a paddock with other horses but elected to spend more time if they were confined for more than twenty-four hours (Lee 2000).

The issue that has not been studied is the fate of PMU foals. Originally most of the foals were of draft-breed type, for which there was less of a market, rather than of lighter-build, riding type; they were sold as weanlings and eventually slaughtered for meat after a period in a feedlot. The welfare problems of transport to and handling at slaughterhouses in general have been dealt with, above, but conditions in the feed lots have not been studied. The young horses are not stalled and presumably have plenty of food, but issues of their environment (mud, manure, disease, aggression among the horses, crowding, etc.) have not been addressed. In response to criticism of the PMU industry for producing horses virtually for the meat market, more "light" (as opposed to draft-type) horses now are used for breeding, and some of the resulting foals are being sold as sport or pleasure horses (Freeman 2000). The main problem in selling them is one of timing and location—a large number of foals are available all at one time, which makes them difficult for the existing market to absorb, and they are in North Dakota, Alberta, or Saskatchewan, far from the populous U.S. east and west coasts, where demand would be greater.

Managing the Performance Horse

Horses kept for performance or competition, as well as many companion horses, generally spend a great deal of time intensively housed and managed. The stabled/stalled horse experiences different pressures from those kept less intensively. Although food, water, veterinary care, grooming, and shelter are provided, such conditions deviate considerably from the behavioral patterns of the wild or free-ranging horse. Stereotypic patterns of behavior, such as weaving; cribbing and its associated behavior, wind-sucking; wood-chewing; head-nodding; and stall-walking, are particularly associated with stabling. These sorts of behaviors have been estimated to affect 10 to 40 percent of stabled horses in the United Kingdom (Nicol 1999) and, in general, more of these behaviors are seen in racing Thoroughbreds. Stereotypic behaviors such as these are considered to be abnormal since they represent qualitative and quantitative differences in behavior when compared with the behavior seen among free-living horses. Stereotypes are rarely observed in free-ranging horses, difficult to explain in functional terms, undesirable to horse owners, and considered to be indicative of welfare problems the horse has had or is currently experiencing (Cooper and Mason 1998). The behaviors generally are considered to be "stable vices," and are viewed as unsoundness, leading to a reduction in a horse's desirability and value (Houpt 1982; Luescher, McKeown, and Dean 1998).

As more research into the causes of these behaviors is completed, it is becoming clear that the traditional views held about these behaviors are incorrect. When viewed by the layperson, cribbing apparently involves the grasping of a surface (usually horizontal) in the teeth (McGreevy and Nicol 1998a) and the swallowing of air. Cribbing surfaces include hori-

zontal edges of feed and water buckets and wood surfaces such as stall boards and fences (e.g., Winskill et al. 1996). Wind-sucking involves the same contraction of neck muscles and apparent engulfing of air, but without grasping, and often is accompanied by an audible "grunt" (Karlander, Mansson, and Tufvesson 1965; Baker and Kear-Colwell 1974; Kusaari 1983). Traditionally horse owners have believed the horses who crib do so because they are bored and/or hungry. The traditional view is that the horse who is hungry will swallow air while cribbing that will fill his or her stomach. However recent work has demonstrated that horses do not gulp in and swallow air while performing this behavior, as previously believed. When the air movements in the respiratory tracts of wind sucking horses were traced, it became apparent that little or no air is swallowed (McGreevy et al. 1995b).

Recent survey studies have investigated the causes and effects of some commonly observed equine stereotypes (e.g., McGreevy, French, and Nicol 1995; McGreevy et al. 1995a; Luescher et al. 1998; and Redbo et al. 1998). These consistently relate the incidence of stereotypes to a number of management factors, including social isolation and the feeding of concentrates with little access to fiber. Despite the problems inherent in conducting longitudinal studies of the development of stereotypic behavior, the results of work on weaning and on feeding practices following weaning (Nicol 1999) show the importance of feeding fiber and of avoiding high grain diets during early development. Horses have evolved to digest a high fiber diet and to spend up to sixteen hours foraging each day. Intensively managed horses are expected to perform energy-consuming tasks, and they require a controlled diet rich in the nutrients that enable them to do so. Being stabled (stalled) also presents problems in that horses have no control over the timing of their feeding, the type of food, the amount of contact they have with conspecifics or even the amount of exercise they have. All of these factors lead to problems. The stabled (stalled) horse may be highly motivated to seek social contact or to have access to food, and this can lead to behavioral frustration. Undesirable behavior such as stall-walking and weaving may be the result of the animal attempting to deal with his or her frustration. Providing horses with a high grain diet may ensure that they have enough energy for performance, but a high grain diet has been shown to cause changes in the digestive system (etc.), leading to cribbing (Nicol et al. 2001).

Various studies have been carried out to determine the effectiveness of the current and new methods for dealing with stereotypic behavior. Many stables used for housing racehorses are fitted with weaving bars, or grills, that are supposed to stop (or block) a horse from being able to perform the behavior. Weaving grills (McBride and Cuddeford 2001), anti-cribbing devices (such as collars) (McGreevy and Nicol 1998a), and pharmacological intervention (Dodman et al. 1987) all have been shown to be of little value in permanently stopping the behaviors. Recent studies also have measured the horses' physiological distress responses, such as heart rate and adreno-cortical activity (Broom and Johnson 1983), to test if there are any underlying effects on horse welfare of treatment for stereotypic behavior (Lebelt, Zanella, and Unshelm 1998; McGreevy and Nicol 1998b; McBride and Cuddeford 2001). Generally these studies have found that preventative measures alone cause more problems for the horses, probably because they treat the symptoms rather than the underlying cause of the behavior. The horses appear to be more stressed when prevented from performing the behavior, indicating a compromise of horse welfare. A number of alternative, less invasive approaches have been studied. These include foraging devices designed to allow the horse to "trickle-feed" and "work" for food (e.g., Winskill et al. 1996; Henderson and Waran 2001); feed additives such as fiber and anti-acids (Johnson et al.

1998; Nicol et al. 2001); increased social contact (Cooper, McDonald, and Mills 2000); and even mirrors in the stable (Mills and Davenport in press; McAfee, Mills, and Cooper 2002). Initial results from such studies are encouraging, and further work is required in this area.

Restriction of normal social behavior and the feeding of a low fiber, high grain diet are the two main factors consistently related to the performance of stereotypic behavior in horses. Horses used for performance purposes should be prevented from developing such undesirable behaviors by ensuring that management and housing are considered from the horse's perspective. Horses are social grazing animals. They have physical and behavioral needs (see Cooper and McGreevy 2002) that can be met under conditions of domestication through such measures as feeding high fiber diets, allowing social contact, changing early weaning and feeding practices, giving the animals greater control of their environment, removing restrictions on highly motivated behavior, and understanding the degree to which the horses have had to adapt in order to serve human needs.

Performance-enhancing and Conformation-enhancing Techniques

There are three types of horses: those who labor symbiotically with farmers or ranchers to plow, to handle livestock, or to pull loads; those who live as companion animals and who may or may not have to carry a rider for a few hours a week; and performance horses. Performance horses have a very different relationship with their owners from that of pleasure or companion horses. Although the owner of a performance horse may like or even love the horse, his or her main goal is to

win in competitions. The competition may be conformation, high jumping, barrel racing, or dressage, but in all cases if the horse does not win, an effort will be made to improve performance. Sometimes these efforts involve more training, but at other times the welfare of the horse can be compromised. This is probably more likely to happen when the person who owns the horse and who expects the horse to win is not the same as the trainer or manager whose livelihood depends on satisfying the goals of the owner.

Hoof and Pastern Manipulation

Allowing the horse's hooves to grow to a length incompatible with normal gait in order to obtain an exaggerated gait in the show ring, myectomy (cutting the muscles of the tail), and tail setting harnesses on "gaited" horses such as American Saddlebreds are examples of the at least mildly uncomfortable methods used to improve a horse's performance. If despite these interventions the horse's performance does not improve, he or she is sold as the first step in the descent to auction and perhaps the slaughterhouse.

More invasive are such practices as "soring," in which a caustic compound is applied to the pasterns (above the hooves) of Tennessee Walking horses, then chains linked around the pasterns so that resulting wounds will be abraded as the animal moves. The pain encourages the animals to lift their forelegs high and carry their weight back on their hind quarters in an exaggerated gait, or "lick," an action admired by judges. The Horse Protection Act passed in 1970 prohibits soring, but there is insufficient funding to allow veterinary inspectors to ensure compliance. Lay inspectors are used, but they usually are affiliated with the industry in some way (DeHaven 2000). One suggestion to improve compliance has been to hire veterinarians who are not equine practitioners but who could, after a training course, examine horses at shows in their immediate area. This would eliminate the need for—and possible conflict of interest by—lay examiners.

Other issues of horse welfare seem to be purely cosmetic but are rooted in competitive advantage. These are exemplified by the treatment of the tails of show horses.

Tail Docking

The original purpose of tail docking, or amputation, may have been to prevent tangling of the tail of a driving horse with the reins, especially if the driver was standing on the ground rather than high above the wagon or carriage. Long tails would interfere with the driver's ability to control the horse while plowing. Another reason for tail docking is convenience of harnessing, since a docked tail does not have to be threaded through the crupper or breeching. Because very few horses are used for plowing in the United States, the only reason for docking today is cosmetic. It is practiced with Hackneys and draft horses. In addition to the immediate pain of docking, horses with shortened tails suffer because they cannot defend themselves from flies. Docked horses also cannot effectively signal aggressiveness by lashing their tails from side to side, or signal exuberance by raising the tail.

Other Tail Manipulations

The tail also is important in showing two different types of performance horses—Arabians and Western pleasure horses (the latter of whom typically are Quarter horses or color-breed horses).

Arabians are judged for their alertness and spirit. An aroused horse, especially a playful one, will carry his or her tail high. Exhibitors may try to mimic that natural high tail carriage by gingering their horses. Gingering involves placing ointment with a high concentration of ginger into the horse's rectum and anus. The horse raises his or her tail in response to the irritation of the chemical. The

process is not only uncomfortable for the horse but also unethical from a competitive standpoint. Although evidence of gingering can be detected by thermograph, the testing technique is too sensitive to use in the field (Turner and Scoggins 1985).

The optimal tail carriage for Western pleasure horses is just the opposite of that of Arabians. The ideal Western pleasure horse is relaxed and submissive to the rider's riding aids (legs, seat, hands, and voice), a state expressed through a flaccid tail. Such a look has been so well rewarded by judges of Western pleasure classes that to achieve it, if not the reality of voluntary submission, unethical exhibitors have enervated the tail by cutting the nerves or have used local anesthesia to temporarily prevent tail lashing. (The latter is often a sign of resistance to the rider's aids and thus a disobedience to be penalized.) Evidence of these practices can be detected electromyographically (Coulter and Luttgen 1994). Other practices to induce calmness are working the horse to near-exhaustion before an event or administering a small dose of a tranquilizer such as acepromazine to chemically calm the animal.

Pleasure Horses

Pleasure horse owners have the closest bonds with their horses. They are most likely to affect their horses' welfare negatively through ignorance of basic horsemanship or an inability to support the horses financially.

An ignorant owner may overfeed a horse, let a horse eat poisonous lawn clippings, or overwork a horse who is out of condition—just a few of the myriad mistakes that can have disasterous consequences to a horse's well-being.

Many young horse owners can barely afford to feed a horse, so that any veterinary care, even preventative, is out of the question. (They may be unaware of the true cost of horse ownership over and above that of the animal's feed. A joint survey by the American Veterinary Medical Associa-

tion, American Animal Hospital Association, and Association of American Veterinary Medical Colleges [Brown and Silverman 1999] found that horse owners reported they would pay an average of $1,827 for a 75 percent chance of curing their horse of an ailment and $828 for a 10 percent chance. They further reported that they would pay an average of $165 per month to keep their horse healthy.)

Other horse owners may experience a reversal of fortune or circumstance yet be reluctant to part with a horse due to personal attachment or unwillingness to sell at a loss. The horse's care may suffer as a result.

Carriage Horses

Approximately one thousand to two thousand horses are used to pull carriages in various North American cities (Merriam 2000). The most urgent problem for these horses is heat stress: carriage rides typically are purchased by tourists, and tourists travel during the summer months when temperatures are high. In southern regions, hours of operation should be limited to cooler times of the day and evening. Horses should have access to water every two hours. Walking or, worse yet, trotting on a paved surface, possibly up and down hills, increases the chance of horses developing lameness. Carriage drivers may be ignorant of basic horse health and therefore may not notice lameness, dehydration, signs of colic, or other health or welfare issues. Carriage horses should be examined every few weeks by a veterinarian.

Some horses may suffer from long-term exposure to air pollution, particularly if they are driven in high traffic areas. Use in high traffic areas also can increase the number of horse-automobile collisions. Carriage horses should have their work hours regulated and their living quarters kept clean, well bedded, and ventilated.

Literature Cited

American Horse Council. 2000. The economic impact of the horse industry in the United States. Washington, D.C.: American Horse Council.

Baker, G.J., and J. Kear-Colwell. 1974. Aerophagia (wind-sucking) and aversion therapy in the horse. *Proceedings of the American Association of Equine Practitioners* 20: 127–130.

Broom, D.M., and K.G. Johnson. 1983. *Stress and animal welfare*. London: Chapman and Hall.

Brown, J.P., and J.D. Silverman. 1999. The current and future market for veterinarians and veterinary medical services in the United States (executive summary). *Journal of the American Veterinary Medical Association* 215(2): 161–183.

Carrier, T.K., L. Estberg, S.M. Stover, I.A. Gardner, B.J. Johnson, D.H. Read, and A.A. Ardans. 1998. Association between long periods without high-speed workouts and risk of complete humeral or pelvic fracture in Thoroughbred racehorses: 54 cases (1991–1994). *Journal of American Veterinary Medical Association* 212(10): 1582–1587.

Chronicle of the Horse. 1998. "Final Insurance Fraud Defendants Have their Day in Court," *Chronicle of the Horse*, May 29.

Cohen, N.D., S.M. Berry, J.G. Peloso, G.D. Mundy, and I.C. Howard. 2000. Association of highspeed exercise with racing injury in Thoroughbreds. *Journal of the American Veterinary Medical Association* 216(8): 1273–1278.

Cooper, J., and G.J. Mason. 1998. The identification of abnormal behavior and behavioral problems in stabled horses and their relationship to horse welfare: A comparative review. *Equine Veterinary Journal Supplement* 27: 5–9.

Cooper, J., and P. McGreevy. 2002. Stereotypic behavior in stabled horses: Causes, effects, and prevention without compromising horse welfare. In *The welfare of horses*, ed. N. Waran, 99–124. Dordrecht: Kluwer Academic Publishers.

Cooper, J.J., L. McDonald, and D.S. Mills. 2000. The effect of increasing visual horizons on stereotypic weaving: Implications for the social housing of stabled horses. *Applied Animal Behavior Science* 69: 67–83.

Coulter, S.B., and P.J. Luttgen. 1994. Electromyographic examination of tail altered horses. *Equine Practitioner* 16(4): 14–17.

DeHaven, W.R. 2000. The Horse Protection Act—A case study in industry self-regulation. *Journal of the American Veterinary Medical Association* 216(8): 1250–1253.

Dodman, N.H., L. Shuster, M.H. Court, and R. Dixon. 1987. Investigation into the use of narcotic antagonists in the treatment of a stereotypic behavior pattern (crib-biting) in the horse. *American Journal of Veterinary Research* 48: 311–319.

Englade, K. *Hot blood*. 1996. New York: St. Martin's Press.

Estberg, L., S.M. Stover, I.A. Gardner, B.J. Johnson, R.A. Jack, J.T. Case, A. Ardans, D.H. Read, M.L. Anderson, B.C. Barr, B.M. Daft, H. Kinde, J. Moore, J. Stoltz, and L. Woods. 1998. Relationship between race start characteristics and risk of catastrophic injury in Thoroughbreds: 78 cases (1992). *Journal of the American Veterinary Medical Association* 212(4): 544–549.

Evans, D.L. 2002. Welfare of the racehorse during exercise training and racing. In *The welfare of horses*, ed. N. Waran, 181–201. Dordrecht: Kluwer AcademicPublishers.

Flanigan, G., and J.M. Stookey. 2002. Day-time time budgets of pregnant mares housed in tie stalls: A comparison of light versus draft mares. *Applied Animal Behavior Science* 78: 125–144.

Freeman, D.A. 2000. The pregnant mares' urine industry—Management and research. *Journal of the American Veterinary Medical Association* 216: 1239–1242.

Freeman, D.A., N.F. Cymbaluk, H.C. Schott II, K. Hinchcliff, and S.M. McDonnell. 1999. Clinical, bio-chemical and hygiene assessment of stabled horses provided continuous or intermittent access to drinking water. *American Journal of Veterinary Research* 60: 1445–1450.

Friend, T.H., M.T. Martin, D.D. Householder, and D.M. Bushong. 1998. Stress responses of horses during a long period of transport in a commercial truck. *Journal of the American Veterinary Medical Association* 212(6): 838–844.

Gibbs, A.E., and T.R. Friend. 2000. Effect of animal density and trough placement on drinking behavior and dehydration in slaughter horses. *Journal of Equine Veterinary Science* 20(10): 643–650.

Grandin, T., K. McGee, and J.I. Lanier. 1999. Prevalence of severe welfare problems in horses that arrive at slaughter plants. *Journal of the American Veterinary Medical Association* 214: 1531–1533.

Henderson, J.V., and N.K. Waran. 2001. Reducing equine stereotypes using the Equiball™. *Animal Welfare* 10: 73–80.

Houpt, K.A. 1982. Oral vices of horses. *Equine Practice* 4: 16–25.

Houpt, K., T.R. Houpt, J.L. Johnson, H.N. Erb, and S.C. Yeon. 2001. The effect of exercise deprivation on the behavior and physiology of straight stall confined pregnant mares. *Animal Welfare*: 10: 257–267.

Jockey Club, The. 2003. *http/home.jockeyclub.com/factbook*. Accessed March.

Johnson, K.G., J. Tyrrell, J.B. Rowe, and D.W. Petherick. 1998. Behavioral changes in stabled horses given non-therapeutic levels of virginiamycin. *Equine Veterinary Journal* 30: 139–142.

Karlander, S., J. Mansson, and G. Tufvesson. 1965. Buccostomy as a method of treatment for aerophagia (wind-sucking) in the horse. *Nordisk Veterinar Medicin* 17: 445–458.

Kusaari, J. 1983. Acupuncture treatment of aerophagia in horses. *American Journal of Acupuncture* 11: 363–370.

Lebelt, D., A.J. Zanella, and J. Unshelm. 1998. Physiological correlates associated with cribbing behavior in horses: Changes in thermal threshold, heart rate, plasma B-endorphin, and serotonin. *Equine Veterinary Journal Supplement* 27: 21–27.

Leblanc, M.M., T. Tran, J.L. Baldwin, and E.L. Pritchard. 1992. Factors that influence passive transfer of immunoglobulins in foals. *Journal of the American Veterinary Medical Association* 200(2): 179–183

Lee, J.Y. 2000. Motivation of horses for release from straight stall confinement and for exercise. Masters thesis, Cornell University.

Luescher, V.A., D.B. McKeown, and H. Dean. 1998. A cross-sectional study on compulsive behavior (stable vices) in horses. *Equine Veterinary Journal Supplement* 27: 14–18.

McAfee, L.M., D.S. Mills, and J.J. Cooper. 2002. The use of mirrors for the control of stereotypic weaving behavior in the stabled horse. *Applied Animal Behavior Science* 78: 159–174.

McBride, S.D., and D. Cuffeford. 2001. The putative welfare-reducing effects of preventing equine stereotypic behavior. *Animal Welfare* 10: 173–189.

McDonnell, S.M., D.A. Freeman, N.J. Cymbaluk, H.C. Schott, II, K.W. Hinchcliff, and B. Kyle. 1999. Behavior of stabled horses provided continuous or intermittent access to drinking water. *American Journal of Veterinary Research* 60: 1451–1456.

McGee, K., J.L. Lanier, and T. Grandin. 2001. Characterizations of horses at auctions and in slaughter plants. *Animal sciences research reports: 2001.* Fort Collins, Colo.: Colorado State University Department of Animal Sciences.

McGreevy, P.D., and C.J. Nicol. 1998a. Prevention of crib-biting: A review. *Equine Veterinary Journal Supplement* 27: 35–38.

———. 1998b. Physiological and behavioral consequences associated with short-term prevention of crib-biting in horses. *Physiology and Behavior* 6: 15–23.

McGreevy, P.D., N.P. French, and C.J. Nicol. 1995. The prevalence of abnormal behaviors in dressage, eventing, and endurance horses in relation to stabling. *Veterinary Record* 137: 36–37.

McGreevy, P.D., P.J. Cripps, N.P. French, L.E. Green, and C.J. Nicol. 1995a. Management factors associated with stereotypic and redirected behavior in the Thoroughbred horse. *Equine Veterinary Journal* 27: 86–91.

McGreevy, P.D., J.D. Richardson, C.J. Nicol, and J.G. Lane. 1995b. A radiographic and endoscopic study of horses performing an oral stereotypy. *Equine Veterinary Journal* 27: 92–95.

Merriam, J.G. 2000. Urban carriage horses, 1999—Status and concerns. *Journal of the American Veterinary Medical Association* 216(8): 1261–1262.

Mills, D.S., and K. Davenport. In press. The effect of a neighbouring conspecific versus the use of a mirror for the control of stereotypic weaving behavior in the stabled horse. *Animal Science.*

Mundy, G.D. 2000. Racing. *Journal of the American Veterinary Medical Association* 216(8): 1243–1246.

Nicol, C.J. 1999. Stereotypes and their relation to management. In *Proceedings of the British Equine Veterinary Association Specialist Days on Behavior and Nutrition,* ed. P.A. Harris, G.M. Gomarsall, H.P.S. Davidson, and R.E. Green, 11–14. Harrowgate, England: BEVA.

Nicol, C.I., A.D. Wilson, A.I. Waters, P.A. Haris, and H.P.B. Davidson. 2001. Crib-biting in foals is associated with gastric ulceration and mucosal inflammation. In *Proceedings 35th International Society for Applied Ethology Congress,* ed. J.P. Garner, J.A. Mench, and S.P. Heekin, 40. Davis, Calif.: Center for Animal Welfare.

Redbo, I., P. Redbo-Torstensson, F.O. Odberg, A. Hedendahl, and J. Holm. 1998. Factors affecting behavioral disturbances in racehorses. *Animal Science* 66: 475–481.

Reece, V.P., T.R. Friend, and C.R. Stull. 2000. Equine slaughter transport—Update on research and regulations. *Journal of the American Veterinary Medical Association* 216(8): 1253–1258.

Sewell, A., I. Andrew (Illus.), N. Lewis (foreword). 2001. *Black Beauty: His grooms and companions: The autobiography of a horse.* London: Kingfisher Press.

Sorge, M. 2002. James C. Wofford handicaps the Rolex Kentucky CCI**** field. *The Chronicle of the Horse.* April 19.

Stull, C.L. 1999. Responses of horses to trailer design, duration, and floor area during commercial transportation to slaughter. *Journal of Animal Science* 77: 2925–2933.

Stull, C.L., and A.V. Rodiek. 2000. Physiological responses of horses to 24 hours of transportation using a commercial van during summer conditions. *Journal of Animal Science* 78: 1458–1466.

Turner, T.A., and R.D. Scoggins. 1985. Thermographic detection of gingering in horses. *Equine Veterinary Science* 5(1): 8–10.

U.S. Department of Agriculture National Agricultural Statistics Service (USDA NASS). 1990–2001. Annual slaughter release.

Winskill, L.C., R.J. Young, C.E. Channing, J. Hurley, and N.K. Waran. 1996. The effect of a foraging device (a modified Edinburgh foodball) on the behavior of the stabled horse. *Applied Animal Behavior Science* 48: 25–35.

Wild Horses and Burros in the United States

15
CHAPTER

Allen Rutberg

Treatment of wild horses and burros has improved remarkably over the last fifty years. In the mid-twentieth century, free-ranging horses and burros suffered horribly at the hands of "mustangers" who captured them at will and whim, sometimes using the most brutal of techniques, including aerial pursuit and shooting or crippling key herd members. The horses were packed into livestock trucks hurt, bleeding, and exhausted, and shipped to slaughter without stopping for rest or watering (Ryden 1999). Unprotected by law, only the good will of a few ranchers protected these abused animals. Public awareness of the plight of the wild horses began to grow in the late 1950s, in large part because of the efforts of Velma Johnston, better known as "Wild Horse Annie," a Nevada-born rancher who witnessed, documented, and publicized the cruelties of the mustangers. First shocked to action after following a blood trail from a truck transporting mustangs to slaughter, Johnston roused the American public, and especially schoolchildren, to demand action from Congress (Ryden 1999). Congress first responded with the "Wild Horse Annie" Act of 1959 (P.L. 86-234), which banned pursuit of unbranded horses on federal land by aircraft or motor vehicle. Later Congress enacted the Wild Free-Roaming Horse and Burro Act of 1971 (P.L. 92-195). One of the great success stories of animal protection, the 1971 act declared it to be federal policy that "wild free-roaming horses and burros shall be protected from capture, branding, harassment or death; and to accomplish this they are to be considered in the area where presently found, as an integral part of the natural system of the public lands" (16 U.S.C. §1331). (The "public lands" are defined as federal land managed by the Bureau of Land Management [BLM] and the U.S. Forest Service, which therefore excludes national parks and national wildlife refuges.) The act charged the BLM with locating, inventorying, and managing these animals. Regrettably, the BLM—which truly is a land management agency—was unprepared and ill-equipped to undertake this charge.

Passage of the act was the clearest possible statement that the American public would not and will not tolerate any kind of cruelty or abuse of wild horses. This message has been reinforced repeatedly in the form of public outrage, widespread media coverage, and a generous influx of reward money that occurs whenever wild horses are reported to have been shot, maimed, or otherwise abused. In December 1998, for example, thirty-three unbranded, free-roaming horses were found dead of gunshot wounds near Reno, Nevada. (Because these horses were shot on state rather than federal lands, they were not protected by the 1971 act.) The international outrage generated by this senseless killing stimulated the formation of an unusual coalition of wild horse advocates, animal welfare groups, ranchers, and prosecutors to lobby for new state legislation making the malicious killing of unbranded livestock a felony. In June 1999, less than seven months after the shooting, Nevada S.B. 396 was signed by the governor after having been passed unanimously by both houses of the legislature (Nevada Legislature, 70th Session Bill Information, *http://www.leg.state.nv.us/70th/Reports/*). According to the *Reno Gazette Journal* (Associated Press 2002), the judge presiding over the trial of the three men accused of killing the horses reportedly received tens of thousands of letters from people upset about the case.

What is a Wild Horse?

The dramatic shift in the treatment of wild horses reflects a deeper shift in American public attitudes towards horses and other animals. Most clearly Americans have come to view wildlife more from a moralistic and humanistic perspective and less from a dominionistic perspective, although utilitarian views still are strong regionally (Kellert 1996). And wild horses and burros are wildlife, aren't they?

The answer to that question depends on whom you ask and when you ask, which is one reason why it often is so difficult to resolve issues concerning wild horse management. Many (but not all) ranchers whose livestock share the public lands with wild horses and burros continue to view them as misplaced livestock. These ranchers see the wild horses and burros as, at best, useless and, at worst, pests who destroy the range on the meager productivity of which they depend. Many wildlife managers view the wild horses and burros as undesirable because they cannot be hunted or because they are exotics who divert resources from native species or interfere with natural processes.

But there also are deep differences among those who consider themselves advocates for horses. For example many wild horse advocates ride, show, breed, and buy and sell horses, and their attitudes toward wild horses are strongly shaped by that experience. Some with this background hold fundamentally utilitarian attitudes and see wild horses as little more than domestic horses with certain exciting breed characteristics or developmental potential. Horse advocates with a strong utilitarian perspective tend to support aggressive management of wild horses, including removal of selected animals from the herds to attain certain color, conformation, behavioral, or breed standards (e.g., "Spanish") in the wild population; breeding of adopted wild horses; and formation of "shadow" herds of domestic horses that match certain attributes of the wild population. Often they consider some herds to be intrinsically more valuable than others because of their genetic or phenotypic attributes. Other wild horse protectionists may take a position based on traditional humane philosophies, in which all wild horses—regardless of appearance, genetics, or behavior—are considered equally valuable, and breeding of

adopted horses is discouraged, just as breeding of animals adopted from an animal shelter is discouraged. Under the humane perspective, wild horses are wild, but only up to a point: when necessary managers should intervene by providing feed and water, controlling the population, or carrying out euthanasia of hopelessly sick or injured animals to assure the health and well-being of individual animals and prevent mass starvation. Yet another group of wild horse advocates takes the position that wild horses and burros are and should be treated as truly wild animals who are part of and subject to natural ecological processes. From this perspective flows a non-intervention philosophy and a strong hands-off approach to management, including an acceptance of suffering and death as a result of "natural" processes. When these diverse positions are applied to specific issues, controversy follows.

Can Wild Horses Survive on Public Lands?

The BLM has made a number of improvements in its range management practices over the last five years. It has strengthened the scientific foundation of its horse and burro management by introducing population modeling into its herd management plans and directly monitoring genetic diversity in a number of populations (e.g., Singer and Schoenecker 2000). The BLM also is standardizing its range inventory methods and its processes for making land use decisions, both of which have varied widely from state to state and district to district, and have furnished ample opportunities for abuse (General Accounting Office [GAO] 1990; BLM 1997).

In addition the BLM has been funding research on wild horse contraception since the 1980s. The first trials were disastrous; scores of wild horses died and more suffered terribly, not

because of the contraceptive agents under test (steroid hormone implants, some of which were effective), but because some subjects were misfitted with collars, while others were separated from their home ranges and died of dehydration (National Research Council 1991). In 1992 however the BLM began working with The Humane Society of the United States (HSUS) to support field trials using the porcine zona pellucida (PZP) vaccine; this work followed up on the initial successes of trials on Assateague Island National Seashore (ASIS), Maryland, carried out by Kirkpatrick, Turner, and Liu (Kirkpatrick, Liu, and Turner 1990; Kirkpatrick 1995; Turner et al. 1997). A decade of research since then has produced a one-year, one-shot PZP immunocontraceptive vaccine. While work continues to develop a longer-acting vaccine, the BLM also is carrying out extensive field testing and developing the policies and infrastructure necessary to begin widespread field application of the PZP vaccine (Turner et al. 2001, 2002). But public pressure will be required to assure that improved process and improved science lead to healthy herds of wild horses and burros.

After passage of the 1971 act, the BLM located and delineated 304 public lands "herd areas" which were known to support wild horses. Because they were "snapshots" of herd locations, it is unlikely that these herd areas fully circumscribed the areas used by the horses and burros. For a variety of reasons—some sensible, some dubious—the BLM chose to manage horses and burros on only 215 of these designated "herd management areas," or HMAs; from the remainder, horses were removed permanently. As of 1998 the number of HMAs had dropped to 211, with 204 being the target goal for 2005 (BLM 2002, n.d.). Moreover fourteen HMAs did not support any wild horses or burros in 1998 (BLM n.d.). (Part of the reduction was caused by the transfer of land, including several burro HMAs, from the BLM to the National Park Service by the California Desert Protection Act of 1994.) Thus there has been a gradual ratcheting down of habitat available to wild horses and burros.

Whether wild horse and burro numbers have increased or declined historically is debatable. According to BLM figures, the number of wild horses reported in the year 2000 (43,629) closely matches the 42,666 wild horses reported in 1974; burro numbers have clearly declined, from 14,374 reported in 1974 to 4,995 reported in the year 2000 (BLM 1996, BLM 2000). However the reliability of BLM numbers has often been questioned. In fiscal year 2001, the BLM began implementing a five-year plan ("The Strategy to Achieve Healthy Rangelands and Viable Herds") to reduce the number of wild horses and burros on the range to approximately 27,000, on 204 HMAs. This is a cause for concern, not just because of the total reduction in numbers, but also because the reduction would set average herd size at just over 130, which suggests that many HMAs will contain herds that are too small to be genetically and demographically viable in the long term (Singer and Schoenecker 2000). In 1996 there were almost sixty HMAs with target populations at fifty or below (BLM 1996).

Ultimately however what will determine whether wild horses and burros survive is the condition of the range on which they depend. A century and a half of overgrazing public lands by livestock means that horses and burros compete with livestock and wildlife for a very slender resource base (GAO 1988, 1990). Deterioration of the public lands is reflected not only in the impetus to further reduce horse numbers, but also in the decline in BLM-licensed grazing allocations for livestock. In Nevada, for example, where about half of all federally protected wild horses live, BLM grazing allotments for livestock declined from 3.13 million AUMs (animal-unit-months, roughly the amount of forage a cow eats in a month) in 1960 to 2.10 million AUMs at the time the act was passed in 1971, then to a mere 1.7 million

AUMs in 2001, a decline of 63 percent over 40 years (BLM 2001 and previous). Horses are not principally to blame for the deterioration of public lands. Over the 270 million acres of federal land grazed by livestock, livestock outnumber horses on the range by approximately a hundred to one, and most public lands do not contain wild horses (GAO 1990). But regardless of where the blame lies, the land is poor, and the margin of subsistence vanishes rapidly when it is stressed further by fire or drought. Year after year the BLM carries out unplanned "emergency gathers" of horses and burros to head off catastrophic mortality due to dehydration or starvation. In many areas horses and cattle alike will need to be removed to allow the land to recover its productivity and resilience.

The Adopt-a-Horse Program

Since the mid-1970s, the BLM has relied principally on the Adopt-a-Horse and Adopt-a-Burro programs to dispose of surplus animals removed from the public lands. Roughly every three to five years in a given herd management area, horses or burros are rounded up (often with the use of helicopters) and sent through a system of corrals in the field, after which some are returned to the range and others designated for adoption. Some adoptions occur on site, but most animals enter an "adoption pipeline" in which they may be held in corrals or pastures for varying lengths of time before being sent out to satellite locations for adoption. The horses remain government property for at least one year, after which title may pass to the adopter (16 U.S.C. §1333 (c)). This program, which adopted out 185,326 horses and burros between 1972 and 2001 (BLM 2001), is the BLM's best showpiece—and a destructive and unshakeable addiction. Scores of favorable articles tell heartwarming stories about adoption successes, humanizing what usually is perceived as an impersonal and uncaring feder-

al colossus. But the good news has often been shadowed by frustration and horror. Throughout its existence the adoption program has been plagued by accounts of failed adoptions (many wild horses require extra patience and training), and of wild horses diverted for exploitation and sale-for-slaughter by duplicitous "adopters."

Again the BLM has taken great strides in improving the efficiency and humaneness of the adoption program. Roundups have been increasingly professionalized, making them safer for horse and wrangler alike. Tracking of animals within the adoption pipeline has been improved dramatically, with systems in place to identify animals who have been shipped to multiple adoptions without success. Gelding of stallions is strongly encouraged, and horses in increasing numbers receive some training prior to adoption. Through a series of cooperative agreements, the BLM has vastly expanded its ability to monitor adopted horses and provide mentors to new adopters. The BLM has even established cooperative agreements with U.S. slaughterhouses so that the BLM can be notified when horses bearing the distinctive BLM freeze marks are identified on site. Nevertheless the BLM's adoption pipeline typically adds 5,000–8,000 horses and burros each year to an already overcrowded domestic population. The result is that some horses, wild or otherwise, will be neglected or sold to slaughter.

To a large extent, the adoption program drives the whole wild horse and burro program. In fiscal year 2000 the operations budget for off-the-range management—capturing, housing, caring for, feeding, transporting, and adopting "surplus" horses and burros—was twelve times the size of the budget for monitoring the range and inventorying horses (BLM 1999). Under the 2001–2005 "Strategy" plan, the BLM expanded its capacity so as to hold approximately 20,000 horses and burros in short-term and long-term holding facilities; recent accounts suggest that capacity has been filled (BLM 2002, Smith 2002). At this writing approximately half of the program budget is being spent maintaining these horses (J. Fend, BLM, personal communication, July 2002).

The adoption habit leaves precious few resources for monitoring or improving the condition of the horses' rangelands or observing the wild horses themselves—which is, after all, what the whole program is supposed to be about. The adoption program also warps management goals in other ways: it probably is not a coincidence that national wild horse population targets historically have been set at levels that would produce surpluses matching the number that the BLM believes it can adopt out (e.g., BLM 1992).

The survival of wild horses and burros in the western United States requires a commitment from the BLM and the public to restore the condition of the land and to assure wild horses and burros their fair share of that land. The BLM remains plagued by its multiple use mandate, a legal requirement to balance the needs of livestock, recreational users, resource extractors, wildlife, and wild horses and burros. That balance ultimately depends on who weighs in most heavily in the land use planning process. In the past livestock growers have brought the most weight to bear, as they have the advantage of local access to government and also are suffering deeply, along with their animals, from the deterioration of the land. By legal action and public pressure, horse advocates must assure that the land is restored, and that there are enough horses and burros, in enough places, to guarantee their survival in perpetuity.

To ensure the welfare of its adoptees (as well as strengthen its on-the-range management), the BLM must reduce the number of surplus horses and burros coming off the range. If adoption demand determines population levels on the range, then the BLM will always be under pressure to reduce wild horse and burro populations to levels that threaten their long-term survival—unless population and reproduction can be disconnected. At Assateague Island National Seashore, Maryland, the National Park Service (working with The HSUS) has led the way in humane and sensitive management of wild horses. Since 1995 ASIS has been balancing the needs of horses with the needs of their fragile barrier island environment through an innovative horse immunocontraception program (National Park Service 1995). This program has stabilized the resident wild horse population without the need for euthanasia, roundups, adoptions, or direct handling of the animals. A contraception program, designed to minimize effects on social structure, behavior, and genetics, probably is the BLM's best chance to sustain adequate numbers on the range while reducing the number of animals entering the adoption program. After more than fifteen years of research into horse contraception, the BLM is close to having and using that tool, and it should not falter now.

Literature Cited

Associated Press. 2002. Fines, brief jail terms handed down in Nevada horse shooting. *http://www.rgj. com/news/printstory.php?id+776 5.* Accessed September 18.

Bureau of Land Management (BLM). 1992. Strategic plan for management of wild horses and burros on public lands. Washington, D.C.: U.S. Department of the Interior, BLM.

——. 1996. Tenth and eleventh report to Congress on the administration of the Free-roaming Wild Horse and Burro Act for fiscal years 1992–1995. Washington, D.C.: U.S. Department of the Interior/U.S. Department of Agriculture.

——. 1997. Report of the Wild Horse and Burro Emergency Evaluation Team. Washington, D.C.: U.S. Department of the Interior, Bureau of Land Management (available at *http: //www.blm.gov:80/ nhp-pubs/97whb_eval/*).

——. 1999. Final FY2000 statistics. Data table. October 25.

——. 2000. Public land statistics. Washington, D.C.: U.S. Department of the Interior, BLM (available at *http:// www.blm.gov: 80/ natacq/ plsOO/*).

——. 2001. Public land statistics. Washington, D.C.: U.S. Department of the Interior, BLM (available at *http: // www.blm.gov: 80/ natacq/ plsOl/*).

——. 2002. Wild horse and burro management: Fiscal year 2003. BLM Budget Justifications (available at *http://www.blm.gov/ bud-get/2003just.html*).

——. n.d. Wild horse information. Taken from EOY statistics 9/30/98. Data table.

General Accounting Office (GAO). 1988. Rangeland management: More emphasis needed on declining and overstocked grazing allotments. GAO/RCED 88–80, Washington, D.C.

——. 1990. Rangeland management: Improvements needed in federal wild horse program. GAO/RCED 90–110, Washington, D.C.

Kellert, S.R. 1996. *The value of life.* Washington, D.C.: Island Press.

Kirkpatrick, J.F. 1995. Management of wild horses by fertility control: The Assateague experience. Sci. Monogr. NPS/NRASIS/NRSM-95/26, Washington, D.C.: National Park Service.

Kirkpatrick, J.F., I.K.M. Liu, and J.W. Turner, Jr. 1990. Remotely delivered immunocontraception in feral horses. *Wildlife Society Bulletin* 18: 326–330.

National Park Service. 1995. Environmental assessment: Alternatives for managing the size of the feral horse population of Assateague Island National Seashore (ASIS). Berlin, Md.: ASIS.

National Research Council. 1991. *Wild horse populations: Field studies in genetics and fertility.* Washington, D.C.: National Academy of Science Press.

Ryden, H. 1999. *America's last wild horses*. Guilford, Conn.: Lyons Press.

Singer, F.J., and K.A. Schoenecker, comps. 2000. *Managers' summary—Ecological studies of the Pryor Mountain Wild Horse Range, 1992–1997*. Fort Collins, Colo.: U.S. Geological Survey.

Smith, C. 2002. BLM struggles to save wild horses suffering from the drought. *http://www.sltrib.com/2002/Aug/08182002/utah/utah.htm*. Accessed April 7, 2003.

Turner, J.W., Jr., I.K.M. Liu, D.R. Flanagan, K.S. Bynum, and A.T. Rutberg. 2002. Porcine zona pellucida (PZP) immunocontraception of wild horses (*Equus caballus*) in Nevada: A 10 year study. *Reproduction Supplement* 60: 177–186.

Turner, J.W. Jr., I.K.M. Liu, D.R. Flanagan, A.T. Rutberg, and J.F. Kirkpatrick. 2001. Immunocontraception in feral horses: A single inoculation vaccine provides one year of infertility. *Journal of Wildlife Management* 65: 235–241.

Turner, J.W., Jr., I.K.M. Liu, A.T. Rutberg, and J.F. Kirkpatrick. 1997. Immunocontraception limits foal production in free-roaming feral horses in Nevada. *Journal of Wildlife Management* 61: 873–880.

About the Contributors

Michael C. Appleby is vice president, Farm Animals and Sustainable Agriculture, of The HSUS. He received a Ph.D. in animal behavior from the University of Cambridge. For twenty years he carried out research on behavior, husbandry, and welfare of farm animals at the Poultry Research Centre (now Roslin Institute) outside Edinburgh, Scotland, and at the University of Edinburgh, contributing to European legislation phasing out battery cages for hens and gestation crates for sows. He is the author of *What Should We Do About Animal Welfare?* and editor of *Animal Welfare*.

Arnold Arluke is professor of sociology and anthropology at Northeastern University and senior research fellow at the Tufts Center for Animals and Public Policy, both in Massachusetts. His research explores contradictions in human-animal relationships and how people manage these conflicts. He is co-author, with Clinton Sanders, of *Regarding Animals*, which provides an in-depth investigation of this subject.

Elizabeth A. Clancy is director of Education and Outreach at Bide-A-Wee Home Association, a humane society in the metropolitan New York area. She previously was a research associate at Tufts University School of Veterinary Medicine and adjunct instructor of veterinary ethics at Becker College (Leicester, Massachusetts). She received the degree of Master of Science in Animals and Public Policy at Tufts in 1996.

Marion W. Copeland is a tutor and lecturer in the masters program at the Center for Animals and Public Policy, Tufts University Veterinary School. Her interest is in literature that features more-than-human-animals as protagonists, narrators, and major symbols.

Bill DeRosa is executive director of the National Association for Humane and Environmental Education (NAHEE), a division of The HSUS, in East Haddam, Connecticut.

Carlos Drews received his Ph.D. from Cambridge University and has been on the staff at the National University in Costa Rica since 1995, teaching behavioral ecology and conservation biology. He organized the First Neotropical Workshop on Wildlife Rehabilitation and Release in 1997 and is editor of *Wildlife Rescue in the Neotropics* (in Spanish). He has been a member of the Council of CITES Scientific Authorities of Costa Rica since 1999 and was a delegate at the CITES Conferences of the Parties in 2000 and 2002. He is also a guest professor at the universities of Erlangen and Hannover, teaching conservation of neotropical biodiversity.

José Luis García de Siles is senior animal production officer and agricultural department group leader for the Regional Office of the FAO (Food and Agricultural Organization of the United Nations) for Latin America and the Caribbean in Santiago de Chile. He holds a Ph.D. in animal industries from The Pennsylvania State University. He specialized in meat technology and has worked extensively in Latin America, Asia, and Africa.

John W. Grandy is senior vice president, wildlife and habitat protection, of The HSUS. He is the former executive vice president of Defenders of Wildlife, in Washington, D.C. He received his Ph.D. in wildlife ecology from the University of Massachusetts and has served on advisory committees to the Secretary of the Interior and the Director of the U.S. Fish and Wildlife Service.

Susan Hagood is wildlife issues specialist, Wildlife and Habitat Protection, for The HSUS. Her primary responsibilities include the humane resolution of conflicts between humans and wildlife. She is a Ph.D. candidate in the marine, estuarine, and environmental sciences program at the University of Maryland, where her research focus is the interaction of wildlife with roads.

Gunter Heinz is former animal production officer, FAO Regional Office for Asia and the Pacific, Bangkok, Thailand.

Katherine A. Houpt is a veterinarian and holds a Ph.D. in behavioral biology. She is a diplomate of the American College of Veterinary Behaviorists and is certified as an applied behaviorist by the Animal Behavior Society. She is a professor in clinical sciences at Cornell University, College of Veterinary Medicine, in New York State, where she directs the Animal Behavior Clinic and undertakes research on equine behavior and welfare. She is the author of *Domestic Animal Behavior*.

Paul G. Irwin is president and chief executive officer of The HSUS, the nation's largest animal protection organization, and president of Humane Society International. He has served as president of the World Society for the Protection of Animals (WSPA). An ordained United Methodist minister, he is also the author of *Losing Paradise: The Growing Threat to Our Animals, Our Environment, and Ourselves*.

Morgane James is field inspector, farm animal unit, National Council of Societies for the Protection of Animals, South Africa. She began her animal welfare career at the SPCA Boksburg in 1983 and qualified as a senior inspector in 1987. She joined what was then known as the National Livestock Unit, her main focus and responsibility being education at the grassroots level.

David W. Macdonald is director of Oxford University's Wildlife Conservation Research Unit and A.D. White Professor at Cornell University. He is a vice president of the Royal Society for the Prevention of Cruelty to Animals (RSPCA) and chairman of the IUCN/SSC Canid Specialist Group and was scientific advisor to Lord Burns's report to the U.K. government on hunting with dogs. One of the most recent of his award-winning television documentaries and books is the *New Encyclopaedia of Mammals*.

Heidi O'Brien is communications coordinator at NAHEE. She received her master's degree in animals and public policy at Tufts University School of Veterinary Medicine and has worked on farm animal welfare and animal sheltering issues.

Peter Ormel is associate professional officer in animal production for the regional office of the FAO for Latin America and the Caribbean in Santiago de Chile. He has a master's degree in Tropical Animal Production and Health from the University of Edinburgh. He specialized in sustainable rural development.

Andrew N. Rowan is senior vice president for research, education, and international issues and chief of staff of The HSUS. He is author of *Of Mice, Models, and Men*; coauthor of *The Animal Research Controversy: Protest, Process, and Public Policy*; and coeditor of *The State of the Animals: 2001*.

Allen Rutberg is senior scientist for wildlife and habitat protection for The HSUS and a clinical assistant professor at the Tufts University School of Veterinary Medicine. He is coauthor of "Fertility Control in Animals," which appeared in *The State of the Animals: 2001*.

Elizabeth Stallman is wildlife scientist for wildlife and habitat protection for The HSUS, where she works on issues related to the management of wildlife on public lands, conservation of threatened and endangered species, and the protection of predators and "nuisance" species subjected to lethal control. She received her Ph.D. in biopsychology from the University of Michigan in 2001, having completed her dissertation on the behavioral ecology of yellow-bellied marmots.

Neil Trent is executive director of Humane Society International. A graduate of the law enforcement division of the RSPCA, he gained broad practical animal protection experience in different capacities for the RSPCA in England, the Bahamas, and Australia and as field officer, and later field services director, for WSPA. He is an expert in all aspects of humane handling, transport, and slaughter of livestock.

Marguerite Trocmé is a scientific officer at the Swiss Agency for the Environment, Forest and Landscape. She is the main editor of the *European Review of Habitat Fragmentation due to Linear Transportation Infrastructure*, to be published by the COST 341 action. She is part of a European network of experts and institutions involved in the phenomena of fragmentation caused by transport infrastructure. She received her master's degree in environmental science from the Federal Polytechnicum in Lausanne, Switzerland.

Bernard Unti received his Ph.D. from American University in 2002. His essay "A Social History of Postwar Animal Protection" appeared in *The State of the Animals: 2001*.

Paul Waldau holds a Ph.D. in ethics from Oxford University, a law degree from UCLA, and a master's degree from Stanford University. He is clinical assistant professor at Tufts University School of Veterinary Medicine, a faculty member at the Center for Animals and Public Policy, and an adjunct faculty member at Boston College Law School and Yale Law School. He is the author of *The Specter of Speciesism: Buddhist and Christian Views of Animals* and co-editor of *A Communion of Subjects: Animals in Religion, Science, and Ethics*, the papers of the 1999 conference "Religion and Animals." He is vice president of The Great Ape Project-International and director of The Great Ape Legal Project.

Natalie Waran is senior lecturer/ MSc course director, Applied Animal Behaviour and Animal Welfare, at the University of Edinburgh. She is the editor of *The Welfare of Horses*.

Steven M. Wise, Esq., has taught animal rights law at the Harvard, Vermont, and John Marshall law schools and has practiced animal protection law for twenty years. He is the author of *Rattling the Cage: Toward Legal Rights for Animals* and *Drawing the Line: Science and the Case for Animal Rights*.

Index

Page numbers appearing in italics refer to tables or figures

A

Abe, Masao
  pluralism and, 92
Adams, C.J.
  moral significance of nonhuman animals, 94–95, 96
Adams, L.W.
  population density of small mammals
    and highway rights-of-way, 133
Adams, Richard
  animal stories, 57
Administrative Procedures Act
  standing and, 100–101
Adopt-a-Horse and Adopt-a-Burro programs, 219–220
The Adventures of a Donkey, 55
Aesop's fables, 52–53
AHA. *See* American Humane Association
AHES. *See* American Humane Education Society
ALDF. *See* Animal Legal Defense Fund
All Party Parliamentary Middle Way Group
  humaneness of shooting foxes and, 120–121
American Academy of Religion
  "Caucus on Religion, Animals, and Ethics," 87
American Animal Hospital Association
  survey of horse owners on what they would pay
    for treating their horses, 213
American Fondouk
  activities, 2
American Humane Association
  Angell's address on the subject of humane
    education, 28–29
  Black Beauty and support for, 55
  compulsory humane education and, 30
  euthanization estimates, 16
  Farm Free label, 172
  name change from International Humane Society, 1
  promotion of the publication of textbooks
    on humane education, 30

youth education resources source, 34
American Humane Education Society
  Bands of Mercy and, 30
  children's literature series, 29
  field representatives, 31
  humane education resources, 28
  Rowley's leadership, 30–31
American Pet Products Manufacturers Association
  calculating the number of dogs in a community, 12–13
  National Pet Owners Survey, 13
  national surveys on pet populations, 10
American Society for the Prevention of Cruelty to Animals
  Black Beauty and support for, 55
  essay contests, 30
  establishment of, 1
  humane education department, 30
  *Kids, Animals & Literature: Annotated Bibliography of
    Children's Books with a Positive, Humane Theme*, 58
  youth education resources source, 34
American Veterinary Medical Association
  national surveys on pet populations, 10
  number of Americans owning dogs and cats, 10–11
  regional differences in pet care-giving, 11–12
  survey of horse owners on what they would
    pay for treating their horses, 213
Andersen, Hans Christian
  children's fairy tales, 56
Anderson, S.H.
  reflectors and roadkill, 139
Angell, George T.
  address to the American Humane Association, 28–29
  Bands of Mercy and, 29, 30
  children's literature and, 29
  comments on *Black Beauty*, 55
  compulsory humane education movement and, 29
  education of children as a long-term response
    to the spread of animal cruelty, 28
  humane education and public order, 28

Massachusetts Society for the Prevention
of Cruelty to Animals founder, 1
Animal Defense and Anti-Vivisection Society
International Humanitarian Bureau, 2
Animal Family, 59
Animal Intelligence, 86
Animal Law
animal rights and, 104–105
Animal law since 1950. *See also specific legislation*
anti-cruelty statutes, 99–100
biomedical research and, 100
common law *versus* legislation for changes in, 103
criminal statutes, 103
exemptions of many humans from anti-cruelty
statutes, 100
food animals and, 100
law reviews and, 104
law school courses and, 93, 104–105
legal conferences and, 104
legal education and, 104–105
legal protection for great apes, 101–102
penalties for violating laws, 99–100
Roman law and, 102–103
"standing" doctrine, 100–101
term "anti-cruelty," 99
Animal Legal Defense Fund
conferences, 104
legal cases in defense of nonhuman animals, 101
Animal Machines, 161, 168–169
Animal People
reports on shelter animal handling, 23
Animal Rescue League of Boston
humane education research, 38
Animal Rights: Current Debates in New Directions, 104
Animal rights movement, 92, 95
Animal Sheltering magazine, 23
Animal shelters. *See also* No-kill controversy
adoption predictors, 24
adoption rates for cats and dogs, 19
age, breed, and sterilization status study, 20
animal intake/disposition experience of one large
California shelter, *17*
behavior programs, 23–24
budgets for, 16, 23, 35, 36
children participating in animal shelter humane
education programs annually, *34*
collaboration trend, 23
content of animal shelter humane education
programs, *35*
credentials of animal shelter member most directly
involved in humane education, *37*
data collection and analysis and, 22–24
data collection and storage problems, 16
decisions leading to adoption and euthanasia,
24–25, 80
educational events attendance, 23
euthanasia and, 15–18, 19, 20–21, 24–25, 67–83, 93

focus of, 22–23
historical perspective of shelter demographics
in the United States, 14–16
humane education budget, *36*
job title of animal shelter staff member most directly
involved in humane education, *37*
Legislation, Education, and Sterilization policy, 14–15
marketing strategies, 24
number of animals handled, 16
number of humane education staff per animal
shelter, *36*
Odds Ratio for relinquishment, 21
Olin's survey of, 33–37
partnerships with college and university academic
departments, 41
range of entities, 16
relinquishment study, 19–20
returned-to-care-givers data, 15, 20
risk factors for relinquishment, 21–22
shelter tours, 34, 43
software packages for, 23
staffing issues, 35, 36, 37
total annual budgets, *35*
total number of, 16
types of humane education programs
offered by, *34*
"virtual shelters," 24
Animal Welfare Act
amendments to, 101
definition of "animal" 101
minimal provisions, 100
Animorph series of children's books, 59
Anno, M.
children's books, 61
Anno's Aesop, 61
"The Ant and the Grasshopper," 52
Anthropocentrism, 88, 91, 93, 94
APPMA. *See* American Pet Products Manufacturers
Association
Argus, Arabella
children's books, 55
The Arkansaw Bear, 57
Armstrong, Karen
pluralism and, 92
Ascione, F. R.
assessment of changes in children's attitudes, 40
People and Animals follow-up study, 40
transference theory and humane education, 38
Ashley, E. P.
amphibian and reptile vulnerability to roadkill, 136
Asia/Pacific countries. *See also specific countries*
animal suffering and, 183–184
cold winters and livestock production, 183
developed and developing countries comprising
the region, 182
growth rate in livestock production, 182

industrial livestock production of short-cycle animals for meat and eggs, 183
livestock population, 182
livestock uses, 183
perception of standards for animal welfare, 184
progress toward humane treatment of slaughter animals, 184
supermarket increase, 185
swamp buffalo uses, 183
ASPCA. *See* American Society for the Prevention of Cruelty to Animals
Assateague Island National Seashore, Maryland
wild horse contraception research, 218, 220
wild horse management example, 220
Association of American Veterinary Medical Colleges
survey of horse owners on what they would pay for treating their horses, 213
Australia
battery cages and, 171
foot and mouth disease and, 155
incidence of pets in the home, 194
livestock exports, 182–183
Austria
animal law courses, 104
AVMA. *See* American Veterinary Medical Association

B

Babe, 57–58
Babe the Gallant Pig, 57, 62
Bahamas
street dog control programs, 7
Baker, S.E.
Wiltshire farmers' attitudes toward hunting, 121–122
Baker, W.L.
roads and habitat fragmentation, 134
Bands of Hope, 29
Bands of Mercy
enrollment, 30
formation of, 29
longevity and impact of, 30–31
number formed, 30
Bangladesh
buffalo production and, 183, 184
slaughterhouse infrastructure, 184
Barbauld, Anna Letitia
children's books, 53, 54, 55
The Bat Poet, 59
Bateson, P.
attacks by dogs in deer kills, 120
Bats
Costa Rican adults who have a negative perception of bats for various attributes, by gender, *199*
Costa Rican adults who perceive bats as dangerous, vermin, dirty, and with supernatural powers, by level of education, *200*
perception link to education level, 199–200

worldwide perceptions of, 199, 202
Battery cages. *See* EU ban on battery cages
Baym, N.
animal stories and humane education, 54
Be Kind to Animals Week, 31
Bean, Michael
"wildlife law" definition, 104
Bears
"Libearty" bear protection initiative, 8
Beautiful Joe, 29, 55–56
Behaviorism, 86
Beissinger, S.R.
lack of information on parrots as one of the challenges facing conservationists, 194
Bergh, Henry
American Society for the Prevention of Cruelty to Animals founder, 1
Berry, Thomas
environmental themes, 96
Biomedical research. *See* Laboratory animals
Biophilia
definition, 51
hypothesis of, 53
link to values and attitudes toward animals, 200
role of children's literature in, 51–65
Biosecurity
farm animal diseases and, 156–157
Birds
demand for in Latin America to keep as pets, 194
Birkholz, E.
dog and cat adoption, euthanasia, and returned-to-care-giver statistics, 20
Bishop, Amy Bend
American Fondouk founder, 2
Bison
reduction in number of, 132
Bissonette, J.A.
estimates of deer killed along roads, 136
highway speeds and roadkill, 139
road densities and populations of carnivores, 134
Black Beauty
humane education and, 29, 31, 53, 55, 56, 207
BLM. *See* Bureau of Land Management
Blount, M.
animal stories and humane education, 55
Blueberries for Sal, 54, 58
Botswana
attitude towards animals, 196
Bovine spongiform encephalopathy
effects on cattle, 152
forcing herbivores to eat animal protein and, 152
incidence, 150
incubation period, 151
meat and bone meal feed and, 151–152
Ministry of Agriculture, Fisheries, and Food feeding regulations, 151–152
mistaken assumptions and, 151

number of cases in the United Kingdom
and Europe, 151
public concerns about, 151–152
scrapie and, 150–151
transmissibility to humans, 150
Bowling Green University
euthanasia study, 25
Bradshaw, E.L.
attacks by dogs in deer kills, 120
Brazil
ban of the use of animals in circuses, 202
wildlife trade and, 194
Brestrup, C.
pet population policy views, 24
Bridgeman, J.
bovine spongiform encephalopathy, 151, 152, 154
British Association for Shooting and Conservation
hunting in the United Kingdom and, 120
Brown, T.L.
decrease in the amount of time spent hunting
in the United States, 111
BSE. See Bovine spongiform encephalopathy
Buddha
parables, 52, 53
Buffalo
India and, 183, 184
Latin America/Caribbean and, 176–177
Nepal and Bangladesh and, 183, 184
Bureau of Land Management
Adopt-a-Horse and Adopt-a-Burro programs, 219–220
ensuring the welfare of adoptees, 220
estimates of the number of wild horses
and burros, 219
herd management areas, 218–219
multiple use mandate, 220
operations budget for off-the-range
management, 219–220
range management practices, 218
standardization of range inventory methods
and land use decisions, 218
"The Strategy to Achieve Healthy Rangelands
and Viable Herds," 219
Wild Free-Roaming Horse and Burro Act provisions
and, 217
wild horse contraception research, 218
Burros. See Wild horses and burros in the United States
Bushmeat
International Fund for Animal Welfare and, 3
Bushong, D.M.
horse transport study, 208
Butler, Nicholas Murray
Columbia University's humane education
donation and, 31

C

Caldecott, Randolph
drawings for "Bye, Baby Bunting," 61
California
animal intake/disposition experience of one
large California shelter, 17
dog and cat population surveys, 15
Humane Education Evaluation Project, 39
Camels
slaughtering methods, 185
Cameron, L.
effects of intensive classroom-based interventions
on the attitudes of eighth-graders, 38
Campbell, Colin
trends in New Jersey shelter intakes and
euthanasia, 18–20
Canada
battery cages and, 171
Cannon, Janelle
children's books, 59
Captive bolt stunners, 181, 185, 208
Carbone, C.
estimates of deer killed by shooting, 125
estimates of fox culls, 124
farmers' judgments about the humaneness
of different methods of killing foxes, 123
Caribbean. See Latin America/Caribbean
Carmody, G.R.
roads and habitat fragmentation, 134
Carolina parakeets
extinction of, 132
Carpenter, C.R.
study of the great apes, 87
Carriage horses, 207, 213
Carroll, Lewis
children's books, 56
Cats. See also No-kill controversy
acquisition sources, 13, 14
adoption predictors, 24
adoption rates, 19
euthanasia data, 15–18, 19, 20–21, 24–25
feral/stray populations in the United States, 13–14
number of Americans owning, 10–11
risk factors for relinquishment: Indiana
(Odds Ratio), 22
sterilization rates, 11
trends in New Jersey shelter intakes and
euthanasia, 19
United States demographic data, 9–22
Cattle
bovine spongiform encephalopathy and, 150–152
Escherischia coli 0157 and, 153–154
India and, 183, 184
Latin America/Caribbean and, 176–177
South Africa and, 186
"Caucus on Religion, Animals, and Ethics," 87

Center for the Expansion of Fundamental Rights
animal rights issues, 104
Center for the Respect of Life and the Environment
Humane Society International and, 3
international conference sponsor, 87
Chameleon software, 23
Character education
"core" or "consensus" values and, 42
federal grants to state departments of education
for, 42
humane education and, 29, 42, 44
post-Civil War period, 29
public and legislative support for, 42
Charlotte's Web, 57, 58, 62
Chicago
humane education, 30
Chicken Run, 58
Chickens. *See also* EU ban on battery cages;
Salmonella in eggs
China and production of, 183
Children and adolescents
attitudes toward hunting, 113
belief that keeping a wild animal fosters love
and respect for nature in children, 195, 201
development of nature-related values, 201
humane education, 27–50
Children's literature
adult readers/interpreters and, 61–62
anthropomorphism and fantasy, 58–59
biophilia and, 51–65
books that inspire benevolence toward the
coyote, 60–61
children's confusion about themes of, 61–62
current trends, 58
depiction of boys in, 54
effects of pictures in, 59, 61
folktales, parables, and fables, 52–53
humane themes of children's books, 52–58
kindness to animals and, 27–29, 32
maligned animals, 59
nineteenth century, 54–56
as a part of lifelong humane education, 62
seventeenth and eighteenth centuries, 53–54
teaching of values, 51–52
twentieth century, 56–58
China
annual per capita meat consumption, 183
pig production, 183
slaughterhouses and, 183–184
Chruszez, B.
fencing and roadkill, 137
CITES. *See* Convention on International Trade
in Endangered Species of Wild Fauna and Flora
CIWF. *See* Compassion in World Farming
CJD. *See* Creutzfeldt-Jakob disease

Clancy, E.A.
dog and cat adoption, euthanasia, and
returned-to-care-giver statistics, 20
Clark, Stephen
believers' ethical abilities, 88
Classical swine fever
source of disease, 154
Cleo and the Coyote, 60
Clevenger, A.P.
fencing and roadkill, 137
highway speeds and roadkill, 139
road densities and populations of carnivores, 134
wildlife use of underpasses, 138
Click, Clack, Moo: Cows That Type, 58
Cobb, John
pluralism and, 92
Codex Alimentarius Commission
carcass dressing definition, 180
"Cognitive ethology," 95
"Cognitive Revolution," 87
Cohen, Jeremy
dominion charge of Genesis, 91–92
Cohn-Sherbok, D.
pluralism and, 92
theological work, 87, 95
Coleridge, Samuel Taylor
comments on Barbauld's contributions, 55
"willing suspension of disbelief," 53
Colleges. *See* Higher education
Colombia
attitudes toward wildlife, 197
ban of the use of animals in circuses, 202
Colorado
box culverts, 138
hunting attitudes, 113–114
Jefferson County students and the Fireman Tests, 38
State Teachers College humane education course
of study, 30
Columbia University
humane education donation, 31
Commercial Transport of Equines for Slaughter Act
provisions for horse welfare, 208–209
Committee on Legal Issues of the Association
of the Bar of New York City
educational seminars, 104
Community and stray dog populations
control programs, 7
Companion animals in the United States. *See also*
Cats; Dogs
acquisition sources, 13
attachment levels, 11–12
base-line population data, 9–11
characteristics of animal care-giving households
and their pets, *11*
data collection organizations, 10
data gathering approaches, 10
data uses, 9

future directions, 24–25
historical perspective of animal shelter
   demographics, 14–16
household surveys, 10
humane education and, 34
life stage differences in pet care-giving, 13
National Council on Pet Population Study
   and Policy and, 19–21
national dog and cat demographic data, 9–22
new research directions, 24–25
percent of households with animals, *11*
pet care-giving by species, *13*
pet population estimates, *10*
population dynamics model, 18–19
regional data reliability, 16
regional differences in pet care-giving, 11–13, 25
risk factors for relinquishment, 21–22
shelters and data collection and analysis, 22–24
telephone random digit dial technology for surveys, 10
Compassion in World Farming
   comments on EU's 1999 directive, 168
   lobbying efforts, 167
Conference of Educational Associations
   humane education and, 31
"Conference on Homeless Animal Management
   and Policy," 81–82
Connecticut
   closed season for deer hunting, 108
   Humane Education Evaluation Project, 39
Conover, M. R.
   deer/vehicle collisions, 136
Convention for the Protection of Great Apes, 102
   Convention on International Trade in
      Endangered Species
species included, 195
Convention on International Trade in Endangered
   Species of Wild Fauna and Flora
   International Fund for Animal Welfare and, 3
   pressure to adopt more animal-friendly policies, 6
Convention on the Protection of Animals kept
   for Farming Purposes, 159, 160, 165
Costa Rica. *See also* Wild animals in Costa Rica
   Guanacaste Conservation Area biological
      education program, 202
   means and standard deviations of level of biological
      knowledge based on five statements, *201*
   percentage who participate in hunting, 197
   survey of attitudes toward animals, 193–194
Cott, J.
   animal stories and humane education, 54
Council of Europe
   animal welfare activities, 159
   Convention on the Protection of Animals kept
      for Farming Purposes, 159, 160, 165
   representation, 159

Crane, R.
   survey of attitudes toward animals in
      Latin America, 193
Creutzfeldt-Jakob disease
   bovine spongiform encephalopathy and, 150–152
   symptoms in humans, *152*
Crickwing, 59
Cripps, P.J.
   stereotypic behavior of box-stalled horses, 210–211
Crocodiles
   Costa Rican attitudes toward hunting for hides, 198
   slaughtering methods, 190
Cronin, Doreen
   children's books, 58
"Cropping" of game species, 109
CSF. *See* Classical swine fever
Currie, Quinn
   Black Beauty retelling, 56
Cutshall, C.D.
   road densities and populations of carnivores, 134
   highway speeds and roadkill, 139

D

Daigle, J.J.
   attitudes of professional associations of wildlife
      biologists and wildlife managers toward hunting,
      114–115
Dalai Lama
   theological writings, 96
Dale, V.H.
   highway speeds and roadkill, 139
   road densities and populations of carnivores, 134
D'Amato, Anthony
   animal law articles, 104
Darwin, Charles, 86
Davies, Brian
   International Fund for Animal Welfare founder, 3
Dawkins, M.S.
   space used by brown hens, 166
Deblinger, R.D.
   road-effect zone, 135
   road placement and operation planning, 144
Decker, D.J.
   decrease in the amount of time spent hunting
      in the United States, 111
Declaration for the Protection of Great Apes, 102
Deen, Mawil Y. Izzi
   environmental themes, 96
Deer hunting. *See* Hunting in the United Kingdom;
   Hunting in the United States
Deer Management Groups
   hunting in the United Kingdom and, 120
Denmark
   ban on hunting with dogs, 108
   battery cages and, 163–164, 170
   deep litter system for housing laying hens, 163

Protection of Animals Act, 163–164
slatted floor systems for housing laying hens, 162
WEGU reflectors and roadkill, 139
Denver Dumb Friends League
Pets for Life National Training Center, 24
Developed countries. See also Developing countries;
specific countries
meat consumption, 177
projected trends in production of various livestock
products, 1993–2020, *179*
total meat production, 177–178
trends in approval of recreational hunting, 197
Developing countries. *See also* Meat production
in developing countries; *specific countries*
animal protection issues, 1
community and stray dog populations, 7
diets, 176
meat consumption, 177
projected trends in production of various livestock
products, 1993–2020, *179*
total meat production, 177
wildlife protection issues, 8
Dewey, Ariane
children's books, 61
Dixon, K.R.
fencing and roadkill, 137
Djerassi, C.
dog and cat contraceptive pill, 15
lack of data as a roadblock to efficient and effective
program development, 16
Doctor Doolittle, 56
Dogs. *See also* No-kill controversy
acquisition sources, 13, 14
adoption predictors, 24
adoption rates, 19
community and stray dog populations in
developing countries, 7
euthanization data, 15–18, 19, 20–21, 24–25
feral/stray populations in the United States, 13–14
number of Americans owning, 10–11
risk factors for relinquishment: Indiana
(odds ratio) (table), 21
sterilization rates, 11
trends in New Jersey shelter intakes and
euthanasia (table), 18
United States demographic data, 9–22
Dowidchuk, A.
shelter budgets, 16
*Drawing the Line: Science and the Case for
Animal Rights*, 101
DuBow, T.J.
deer/vehicle collisions, 136
Duck hunting in the United States
black duck population, *117*
breeding-ground surveys, 116–118
canvasback breeding populations, *118*
carrying capacity and, 118–119

mallard breeding populations, *119*
North American duck breeding populations, *116*
North American scaup populations, *117*
pintail breeding populations, *116*
population dynamics of various species, 116–119
predators and, 119
refuges and, 116
"total duck" argument, 117
treaties, 116
Ducks
China and production of, 183
Duffield Family Foundation
Maddie's Fund and, 67

E

Early Lessons, 54
EarthVoice
Humane Society International and, 3
land preservation activities, 8
Eck, Diana
pluralism and, 92
Eckert, Allan W.
children's books, 59
Education. See Higher education; Humane education
Eggs. *See* EU ban on battery cages; Salmonella in eggs
Egoff, S.
comments on *Charlotte's Web*, 57
fantasy in children's literature, 59
Eisenhower, Pres. Dwight D.
national highway system in the United States, 131–132
El Salvador
current views of wildlife in, 197
Electrical stunning, 181, 185, 190
Elephants
immunocontraceptive vaccine to manage
populations, 8
International Fund for Animal Welfare and, 3
Enck, J. W.
decrease in the amount of time spent hunting
in the United States, 111
England. *See* Hunting in the United Kingdom;
United Kingdom
Enriched or furnished cages. *See* EU ban
on battery cages
Environmental Law
law review devoted to environmental law, 104
Equine estrogen industry. See Pregnant mare
urine industry
Equine therapy, 55. *See also* Horses
Escherischia coli 0157
description of the bacterium, 153
number of cases in the United States, 153
outbreak in Scotland, 153
route of human infection, 153
slaughtering methods and, 153–154
EU ban on battery cages

beak trimming and, 162, 171

cannibalism and, 162, 171

Convention on the Protection of Animals kept for Farming Purposes and, 165

converting battery cages to enriched cages, 169

cost of egg production in different systems, relative to laying cages with 450 square centimetres per bird, *163*

developments in individual countries, 163–165

egg industry's response, 168, 170

enriched or furnished cages and, 162, 164, 166–167, 168, 169

extracts from the EU 1986 directive laying down minimum standards for the protection of laying hens kept in battery cages, *166*

"free range" definition, 162

genetic selection and, 171

housing systems for laying hens, 162–163

immediate developments, 169

implications for the United States, 171–172

labeling regulations, 162–163, 172

long-term prospects, 171

1986 directive establishing minimum standards for the protection of hens in battery cages, 165–166

1999 directive on battery cages, 166–168

problems in understanding of the production methods, 162–163

prospects under free trade, 170–171

Scientific Veterinary Committee's report on the welfare benefits and deficiencies of cages and non-cage systems for laying hens, 166, 168, 169

welfare problems of battery cages, 162

World Trade Organization rules and, 169–170

EU Commission

salmonella poisoning as a number one priority in food safety, 150

Eurogroup for Animal Welfare

lobbying efforts, 167

programs and activities, 3–4

Europe. *See also specific countries*

bovine spongiform encephalopathy and, 151

changes in land use and wildlife habitat, 140

historical background of road construction, 140

mitigation measures limiting wildlife mortality, 141

pan-European developments in roadkill reduction, 142–143

reducing the barrier effect of roads, 141

roadkill reduction and, 140–143

wildlife traps in roads, 142

European Community

rights of nonhuman animals, 103

European Cooperation in the field of Scientific and Technical Research, 140, 142

European Review of the COST 341 Action roadkill and, 140, 142

European Union. *See also* EU ban on battery cages

attitudes about animal welfare, 160–161

classical swine fever vaccine and, 154

Convention on the Protection of Animals kept for Farming Purposes, 159, 160, 165

Council of Ministers, 159

countries of the European Union and the system of qualified majority voting used by the Council of Ministers, *160*

criteria for labeling of eggs, *162*

directive requirements, 159–160

European Parliament, 159, 167

foot and mouth disease vaccine and, 155

mechanism for directives and regulations, 160

members, 159

1999 directive on battery cages, 166–168

Scientific Veterinary Committee's report on the welfare benefits and deficiencies of cages and non-cage systems for laying hens, 166, 168, 169

slaughtering of animals with foot and mouth disease, 155

Euthanasia

animal shelters and, 15–18, 19, 20–21, 24–25, 67–83, 93

no-kill controversy, 67–83

reasons for requesting, 20

Evangelium Vitae, 94

F

Fables. *See* Folktales, parables, and fables

Fahrig, L.

effect of road mortality on the density of anuran populations, 136

highway speeds and roadkill, 139

road densities and populations of carnivores, 134

"Fair chase" concept of hunting, 107, 109, 112

FAO. *See* Food and Agriculture Organization

Farm and draft animals

children's books and, 58

humane education and, 34

humane slaughter initiatives, 7

Farm disease crises in the United Kingdom

biosecurity, 156–157

bovine spongiform encephalopathy, 150–152

classical swine fever, 154

confidence in the government and, 152

Department of Environment, Food, and Rural Affairs and, 152, 154–155

economics of animal production and, 157

Escherischia coli 0157, 153–154

factors in, 156

Food Standards Agency and, 152, 154

foot and mouth disease, 154–156

licensing of farms and farmers and, 157

Ministry of Agriculture, Fisheries, and Food and, 151–152

Policy Commission on the Future of Farming and Food, 156

salmonella in eggs, 149–150
using levies on food to improve animal health
and welfare and, 157
Farm Sanctuary
animal shelter operated by, 58
Fauna and Flora International
land preservation activities, 8
Favre, David
anti-cruelty laws, 99
Federal Highway Administration
highway statistics, 132
Feldhamer, G.A.
fencing and roadkill, 137
Fennell, L.A.
marketing strategies for shelters, 24
Fenton, M.B.
roads and habitat fragmentation, 134
Ferguson-Smith, M.
bovine spongiform encephalopathy, 151, 152, 154
Ferrier, David
relationship of humans to other primates, 86
Finland
lighted signs to reduce roadkill, 139
Fireman Tests
humane education and, 38
First North American Symposium on Poultry Welfare, 171
Flannigan, G.
stereotypic behavior of PMU horses, 210–211
Florida
panther/vehicle collisions, 136
"traffic calming devices," 139
underpasses to accommodate panthers, 137–138
Fly By Night, 59
FMD. *See* Foot and mouth disease
Folktales, parables, and fables
humane themes, 52–53
Food and Agriculture Organization
cold chain system for meat marketing, 182
collaboration with the Humane Society
International, 175
global view of the developments in the livestock
sector, 177
humane slaughter initiatives, 7
meat processing and, 182
mission, 175
pressure to adopt more animal-friendly policies, 6
slaughter facilities and, 182
training of personnel in the meat and dairy
industry and, 182
Foot and mouth disease
animal movements and, 154–155, 156
profiteering by farmers, 155
slaughter policy controversy, 155
tourism industry losses and, 155
use of waste food for pigs and, 155
vaccine for, 155
For Pity's Sake, 29

Forman, R.T.T.
highway speeds and roadkill, 139
road densities and populations of carnivores, 134
road-effect zone, 135
road placement and operation planning, 144
underpass design, 137
Forum on Religion and Ecology
Web site, 93
Four Months in New Hampshire, 29
Foxhunting. *See* Hunting in the United Kingdom
France
emphasis on food quality, 160
foot and mouth disease outbreak, 155
report on helping wildlife cross roads, 141
France, R.
highway speeds and roadkill, 139
road densities and populations of carnivores, 134
French, N.P.
stereotypic behavior of box-stalled horses, 210–211
Friend, T.H.
horse transport study, 208
Frissell, C.A.
chemicals commonly found along roadsides, 133
Fritzell, E.K.
attitudes of professional associations of wildlife
biologists and wildlife managers toward
hunting, 115
changes in student interest and attitudes and
curriculum and course content in university
fisheries and wildlife programs, 114
Further Adventures of Jemmy Donkey, 55
The Further Adventures of Nils, 59

G

Game Conservancy Trust
trends in pest and quarry species on large estates, 125
Garner, R.L.
study of chimpanzees, 86
Gates, J.E.
fencing and roadkill, 137
Geis, A.D.
population density of small mammals and highway
rights-of-way, 133
Genetic engineering of animals
human disease modeling, 91, 93
George Washington University
animal law courses, 104
Georgetown University
animal law courses, 104
Germany
attitudes about animal welfare, 160
ban on enriched cages, 168
ban on hunting with dogs, 108
cage systems for laying hens, 167
classical swine fever outbreak, 154
deep litter eggs, 163

EU Council of Ministers and, 159
Get-away cages, 162
incidence of pets in the home, 194
Kellert's comparison of attitudes toward
  wildlife in, 196
opposition to hunting, 198
percentage who participate in hunting, 197
proportion of households keeping livestock, 195
rights of nonhuman animals, 103
roads and habitat fragmentation, 134
Gibeau, M.L.
  grizzly bears and roads, 134
Gilkey, Langdon
  pluralism and, 92
Gill, Ben
  comments on the battery cage ban, 168
Goats
  slaughtering methods, 185
God in Creation: An Ecological Doctrine of Creation, 94
Goldman, C.R.
  highway speeds and roadkill, 139
  road densities and populations of carnivores, 134
Goodall, Jane
  influence of Doctor Doolittle and Tarzan on, 56
  studies of chimpanzees, 87, 92
Goosebumps series, 57
Gould, Jay
  comments on Goodall's work, 87
Graham, Bob
  children's books, 58
Grandin, T.
  percentage of Standardbred horses at auctions
    and slaughter plants, 210
  Thoroughbred horses who end up being
    slaughtered, 209
welfare of horses arriving at slaughter plants, 208
The Great Ape Project: Equality Beyond Humanity, 102
Great apes
  cost of maintaining a chimpanzee over his
    natural lifespan, 102
  legal protection for, 101–102
  studies of, 86–87
The Great Apes, 86–87
Great Britain. See Hunting in the United Kingdom;
  United Kingdom
Great Depression
  humane education and, 32
Green, L.E.
  stereotypic behavior of box-stalled horses, 210–211
Green iguanas
  exportation of, 194
Griffin, C.R.
  factors to consider when installing underpasses, 137
  overpasses and wildlife, 138

Griffin, D.
  "Cognitive Revolution" and, 87
Griffis, J.L.
  van de Ree roadside mirrors and roadkill, 139
Grim, John
  international conference organization, 87
Groot Bruinderink, G.W.T.A.
  road closures and roadkill, 139
  underpasses and overpasses and wildlife habitats,
    138–139
The Guardian of Education, 54
Guidelines for Industrial Livestock Rearing, 183
Gunson, K.E.
  fencing and roadkill, 137

H

Hamilton, D.A.
  attitudes of professional associations of wildlife
    biologists and wildlife managers toward hunting,
    114–115
Hanne, M.
  animal stories and humane education, 55
Hardie, S.
  space used by brown hens, 166
Hare hunting. See Hunting in the United Kingdom
Harman, D.M.
  fencing and roadkill, 137
Harrison, Rex
  film version of Doctor Doolittle and, 56
Harrison, Ruth, 161, 168–169
Harrop, S.R.
  patterns in habitat management, 125
Harvard University
  animal law courses, 104
Haskell, D.G.
  abundance and diversity of macroinvertebrates
    in areas close to forest roads, 134
Hastings University
  animal law courses, 104
Hazebroek, E.
  road closures and roadkill, 139
  underpasses and overpasses and wildlife
    habitats, 138–139
Heanue, K.
  highway speeds and roadkill, 139
  road densities and populations of carnivores, 134
Heath hens
  extinction of, 132
Heberlein, T.A.
  rural populations and hunting, 112
Hens. See Chickens; EU ban on battery cages;
  Salmonella in eggs
Herrero, S.
  grizzly bears and roads, 134

Herzog, H.
  social attitudes in the United States toward the use
    of animals in research, the wearing of fur, hunting,
    farm animal issues, diet choice and public support
    of animal protection philosophy, 200–201
Hessel, Dieter
  environmental themes, 96
Heuer, K.
  lynx avoidance of underpasses, 138
Hick, John
  pluralism and, 92
Higher education
  "animal law" courses in law schools, 93
  changes in student interest and attitudes and
    curriculum and course content in university
    fisheries and wildlife programs, 114
Highways. See Roadkill reduction
Hillman, James
  animal stories and humane education, 53
Historical background
  advocacy of major international organizations, 7
  animal protection around the world, 5–6
  animal protection congresses, 1–2
  beginnings of organized animal protection, 1–2
  community and stray dog control, 7
  companion animal demographics in the United
    States, 9–25
  current state of animal protection, 4, 6
  duck hunting in the United States, 116
  economic development and animal protection, 1
  EU ban on battery cages, 159–172
  farm and draft animal initiatives, 7
  highway construction, 132
  humane education, 27–50
  hunting in the United States and the United
    Kingdom, 107–109, 126
  international treaties dealing with animal
    protection issues, 7
  neotropics, 193, 196–197
  post-World War II animal protection activities, 2–3
  regions of the world and their animal protection
    programs, 4–6
  religion and animals, 1, 85–96
  road construction in Europe, 140
  types of international activities, 6
  wildlife protection issues, 8
The History of Robins, 54
Hog cholera. See Classical swine fever
Hohfield, Wesley
  classification of legal rights, 103
Holsman, R.H.
  criticisms of hunters, 118–119
Hong Kong SPCA
  conference, 4
Hope, 58
Horse Protection Act
  protection against "soring," 212–213

Horses. See also Wild horses and burros in the
    United States
  advances in veterinary medicine and, 207
  box stalls and, 207
  captive bolt stunning, 208
  carriage horses, 207, 213
  diet for, 211–212
  double-decker trailers for transport of, 208
  euthanizing horses at home, 209
  hoof and pastern manipulation, 212–213
  horse husbandry improvements, 207
  horses slaughtered and processed at packing
    plants in the United States, 208
  managing the performance horse, 211–212
  number of horses and participants by industry, 1999,
    207
  number of horses in the United States, 207
  performance-enhancing and conformation-enhancing
    techniques, 212–213
  pleasure horses, 213
  pregnant mare urine industry, 210–211
  proportion of households keeping horses in Costa
    Rica, Nicaragua, and the United States, 195
  racing horses, 209–210
  slaughter and transport to slaughter, 208–209
  social contact and, 211–212
  "soring" of Tennessee Walkers, 212–213
  stereotypic behavior problems, 210–212
  tail carriage and show horses, 213
  tail docking, 213
Houk, Randy
  children's books, 58
Housholder, D.D.
  horse transport study, 208
HSI. See Humane Society International
Huggard, D.J.
  highway and railroad mortality in Banff National
    Park, 136
Humane education
  alternative methodologies, 43
  Angell's influence, 28–29
  back-to-basics movement and, 42
  Bands of Mercy and, 29, 30–31
  Be Kind to Animals Week, 31
  character education and, 29, 41, 42, 44
  children's literature role, 27–29, 32, 51–65
  classroom access issues, 43
  classroom visits and shelter tours, 34, 43
  common school movement, 28
  compulsory humane education movement, 29–30, 32
  credentials of educators, 35
  current era and, 33–36
  "curriculum blended" lessons and materials, 42
  decline in the number of activists and, 32
  effects of outreach efforts, 44
  empirical evidence to support, 37–38
  era of organized animal protection, 28–29, 43–44

failure of the institutionalization of, 31–32, 44
Fireman Tests and, 38
future of, 41
goal of, 51
Humane Education Evaluation Project, 38–39, 40
immigration and, 28
implications for the process of class formation, 27–28
kindness-to-animals ethic, 27–28, 33
lack of immediate results and, 36, 37
Mann's universal schooling concept and, 28
manuals and textbooks with systematic lesson
    plans, 30
mid-twentieth century and, 32–33
milestones in humane education: a pre-World
    War II chronology, 45–48
"nature study," 32–33
non-school options, 43
Olin's animal shelter survey and, 33–37
partnerships with colleges and universities, 41, 43
*People and Animals: A Humane Education
    Curriculum Guide*, 38–39
post-Civil War period, 29
post-World War II period, 32
Potter League for Animals humane education
    program, 40–41, 42
professional development workshops and instructional
    materials for teachers, 43
professional humane educator emergence, 30
recent research, 39–41
role-playing and empathy-building techniques, 38
as a "special interest" topic, 34, 42, 43
state curriculum standards and, 42
subsidizing the hiring and placement of humane edu-
    cation specialists within humane societies, 44
technology-based methodologies, 43
Web resources, 42
World War I and, 31
Humane Education Evaluation Project, 38–39, 40
Humane Society International
    collaboration with the Food and Agriculture
        Organization, 175
    mission, 175
    programs and activities, 3
    wildlife rehabilitation programs, 8
Humane Society of the United States
    animal shelter survey, 15
    "Compassion Workshops," 25
    estimates of wildlife mortality along roads, 135–136
    euthanasia study, 25
    list of shelters, 16
    mission, 175
    national conferences to address the pet population
        crisis, 14–15
    Pets for Life National Training Center, 24
    resources for humane education, 32
    shelter survey, 16
    "Statement on Free-Roaming Cats," 13–14

stray-cat feeding survey, 14
wild horse contraception research, 218
Wildlife Land Trust, 119
youth education resources source, 34
Hunting in the United Kingdom. *See also* Wild
    animals in Costa Rica
    attitudes toward, 121–123
    ban on hunting with dogs in Scotland, 108
    damage reduction and, 124
    deer in Scotland and, 126
    effect of fox damage and hunting participation
        on the perceived humaneness of different
        control methods, *124*
    ethical considerations, 107
    farmers and fox control, 122–123
    farmers' attitudes toward hunting on their
        land, *122*
    foxhunting, 107
    habitat preservation, 125
    historical background, 107–108, 126
    hunting and shooting as monitoring tools, 125
    "hunting" versus "shooting," 119–121
    "lamping" and, 120
    number of deer killed per year, 124–125
    percentage of English farmers replying "yes" when
        asked whether they believed a method was effective
        or humane in controlling foxes, *123*
    privately owned land and, 108, 126
    public attitudes toward wildlife management, 108
    public opinion poll regarding fox hunting, 121
    reasons why people hunt or shoot, 124
    responses of urban dwellers and farmers regarding the
        acceptance and need for fox control, *121*
    shooting at earths, 120
    subsistence hunting, 107
    urban and rural residents and, 121
    use of dogs and, 108
    voluntary regulation by the Independent Supervisory
        Authority for Hunting, 108
    wildlife management, 108
    wildlife reduction and, 123–125
Hunting in the United States. *See also* Wild animals
    in Costa Rica
    age group differences in the wildlife value orientations
        of Coloradans, *114*
    age variations in attitudes toward, 113–114
    average number of days hunted per year, 111
    bird watchers and, 115, 119
    bounties on wolves and cougars, 108
    changes in "utilitarian value" over time, *113*
    criticisms of hunters by their peers, 118–119
    "cropping" of game species, 109
    data and observations on duck hunting, 116–119
    decrease in the number of hunters, 110
    demographic changes and, 107
    divisions among hunters, 115, 118–119
    duck stamps, 107–108

effects of hunters' influence on management
    decisions, 108
ethical considerations, 107
excise taxes and, 108
"fair chase" concept, 107, 109, 112
"harvestable surpluses," 107
historical background, 107–109, 126
hunter recruitment efforts, 111
hunters' "right to hunt" legislation, 109
hunting and fishing licenses, 107–108, 115
Lacey Act and, 109
meat hunters, 115
Migratory Bird Hunting Stamp Act and, 109
Migratory Bird Treaty Act and, 109
nature hunters, 115
percentage of survey respondents who felt that
    hunting was morally wrong, 198
percentage of the United States population holding
    a hunting license, 110
Pittman-Robertson Federal Aid in Wildlife Restoration
    Act and, 109
popularity of hunting, 110
problems associated with hunting and hunters, 114
public acceptance of, 112–114
refuges and parks and, 109, 116
regional differences in wildlife value orientations
    of Coloradans, 113
road-based methods of hunting bobcat
    in Wisconsin, 134
rural populations and, 112–113
specialization and, 115, 118
sport hunters, 115
state wildlife agencies and, 133
states showing an increase or decrease of 2 percent or
    more in hunting popularity, 1980, 2000, 111
states that currently have a constitutional amendment
    guaranteeing the right to hunt for all citizens, 110
subsistence hunting, 107, 108, 112
suffering of animals and, 114
types of hunters, 115
urbanization and, 112–113
wildlife management professionals and, 107–108,
    114–115
Hurry!, 58
Hymn in Prose, 54

I

IFAW. See International Fund for Animal Welfare
IHS. See International Humane Society
Illinois
    compulsory humane education movement, 29–30
    reflectors and roadkill, 139
Importation of Processed Animal Protein Order
    salmonella in eggs and, 150

Independent Supervisory Authority for Hunting
    fox cull data, 125
India
    animal protection activities, 1, 4
    buffalo and cattle production, 183, 184
    pig slaughtering methods, 185
    sheep and goat slaughtering methods, 185
    slaughterhouse infrastructure, 184
    street dog control programs, 7
Indiana
    pet population estimates, 10
    risk factors for relinquishment: Indiana (Odds Ratio),
        21, 22
Indonesia
    slaughterhouse infrastructure, 184
Infra Eco Network
    research program, 142
International Air Transport Association
    animal transportation regulations, 190
International Convention for the Regulation of Whaling
    International Whaling Commission formation, 87
International Directory of World Animal Protection
    source for information, 4
International Egg Commission
    battery cage ban and, 168
International Food Policy Research Institute
    global view of the developments in the livestock
        sector, 177
International Fund for Animal Welfare
    programs and activities, 3
International Humane Congress
    activities, 1–2
International Humane Society
    establishment of, 1
International Livestock Research Institute
    global view of the developments in the livestock
        sector, 177
International Society for the Protection of Animals
    disaster and emergency relief work, 3
International Whaling Commission
    formation of, 87
    pressure to adopt more animal-friendly policies, 6
Internet
    wildlife trade and, 194
Interstate Highway Act
    national highway system construction, 132
Ireland
    foot and mouth disease outbreak, 155
Isaacs, Susan
    humane education and, 31–32
ISPA. See International Society for the Protection
    of Animals
Israel, A.
    dog and cat contraceptive pill, 15
    lack of data as a roadblock to efficient and effective
        program development, 16
IWC. See International Whaling Commission

J

Jackson, S.D.
   effectiveness of underpasses to assist spotted
      salamanders, 138
   factors to consider when installing underpasses, 137
   overpasses and wildlife, 138
Jacques, Brian
   children's books, 57
James, Mary
   children's books, 59
Japan
   animal protection activities, 1, 4
   animal welfare laws, 183
   incidence of pets in the home, 194
   Kellert's comparison of attitudes toward wildlife
      in, 196
   means and standard deviations of level of biological
      knowledge based on five statements, *201*
   opposition to hunting, 198
   percentage who participate in hunting, 197
Jarrell, Randall
   children's books, 59
Jeffries, Richard
   children's books, 56
Jochle, W.
   dog and cat contraceptive pill, 15
   lack of data as a roadblock to efficient and effective
      program development, 16
Johnson, P.J.
   estimates of deer killed by shooting, 125
   estimates of fox culls, 124, 125
   farmers' judgments about the humaneness of different
      methods of killing foxes, 123
   patterns in habitat management, 125
Johnson-Barnard, J.
   roads and habitat fragmentation, 134
Johnston, Velma
   plight of wild horses and, 217
Jones, J.A.
   highway speeds and roadkill, 139
   road densities and populations of carnivores, 134
Jorêt, A.D.
   egg industry response to the EU's directive, 170
The Jungle Books, 56, 57
Jurnove, Marc
   Animal Legal Defense Fund legal cases and, 101

K

Kellert, S.R.
   age group differences in attitudes toward hunting, 114
   conceptual and methodological framework for the
      study of attitudes toward animals, 194, 196, 197
   hunting and the changing values of children, 113
   percentage of Americans who participate
      in hunting, 197
   surveys of hunting in the United States, 112–113
   three types of hunters, 115
   "utilitarian" attitude toward hunting, 113
Kennedy, L.
   effects of pictures in children's literature, 61
Kessler, K.K.
   deer/vehicle collisions, 136
*Kids, Animals & Literature: Annotated Bibliography of
   Children's Books with a Positive, Humane Theme*, 58
Kilner, Dorothy
   children's books, 53–54
KIND News newspaper, 34
King-Smith, Dick
   children's books, 57
Kingsley, Charles
   children's books, 56
Kipling, Rudyard
   children's books, 56, 57
Kirkpatrick, J.F.
   wild horse contraception research, 218
Kohl, Judith and Herbert
   observing animals in nature, 52, 59
Kossow, D.
   social attitudes in the United States toward the use
      of animals in research, the wearing of fur, hunting,
      farm animal issues, diet choice and public support
      of animal protection philosophy, 200–201
Krannich, R.S.
   Utah residents' opposition to bear and cougar
      hunting, 114, 118

L

Laboratory animals
   anti-cruelty laws and, 100
   cost of maintaining a chimpanzee over his natural
      lifespan, 102
   federal protection of, 92
   legal protection for great apes, 101–102
   religion and, 86, 91, 93, 96
   retirement sanctuaries, 102
Labrador ducks
   extinction of, 132
Lacey Act
   hunting regulations, 109
Lagerlof, Selma
   children's books, 59
Land, D.
   underpass use in Florida, 138
Langbein, J.
   estimates of deer killed by shooting, 125
   estimates of fox culls, 124
   farmers' judgments about the humaneness of different
      methods of killing foxes, 123
Lanier, J.
   percentage of Standardbred horses at auctions and
      slaughter plants, 210

Thoroughbred horses who end up being
    slaughtered, 209
welfare of horses arriving at slaughter plants, 208
LAPS. *See* Lexington Attachment to Pets Scale
Latent tensions in the no-kill controversy
    dangerous animals and, 78
    differing approaches to the problem of
        overpopulation, 74–77
    differing perceptions of what constitutes
        suffering, 77–79, 80
    ethical and emotional drawbacks of bonding
        closely with the animals, 76
    evangelical quality of no-kill advocates, 73
    "fighting the good fight" and, 74–75
    formal guidelines to euthanasia decisionmaking, 75,
        76–77, 81
    grief of workers, 75–76
    humane identities and, 72–73
    isolation of workers from the realities
        of shelters unlike their own, 74
    lifestyle issues, 73–74
    "Maria" case, 75–76
    perception of workers as humane, 77–79
    perceptions of humane, 77–79
    presumptions and accustomed ways of working, 74
    pro-life movement and, 73
    problem animal rehabilitation, 74–75
    quality of life issues, 77–78, 80
    relating to animals with one's head rather
        than one's heart, 76
    "rescue instinct" of workers, 74–75, 76
    "spoiling period" for animals who are going
        to be euthanized, 75, 76–77
    vested interests, 72–74
    "warehousing" animals, 77–78
Latin America/Caribbean. See also specific countries
    animals involved in wildlife trade, 194
    demand for wildlife to keep as pets, 194
    livestock evolution, 176–177
    livestock revolution, 177–179
    meat production, *178*
    number of animals slaughtered, *178*
    number of people without adequate access
        to food, 176
    subregional comparison, 177
Law schools. *See* Higher education
Leader-Williams, N.
    patterns in habitat management, 125
"The Legal Status of Non-Human Animals"
    conference, 104
Legislation. *See* Animal law since 1950; *specific
    pieces of legislation*
Legislation, Education, and Sterilization
    animal shelter population reduction policy, 14–15
Leopold, Aldo
    "cropping" of game species, 109
    hunters' dependence on gadgets, 115, 118

LES. *See* Legislation, Education, and Sterilization
"Let's Get a Pup!" Said Kate, 58
Levy, Elizabeth
    children's books, 60
Lewin, Betsy
    children's books, 58
Lewis, C.S.
    anti-vivisection essay, 88–91, 95
Lexington Attachment to Pets Scale
    attachment levels, 11–12
"Libearty" bear protection initiative, 8
The Life and Perambulations of a Mouse, 53–54
Linzey, Andrew
    theological work, 87, 95
Listeria
    unpasteurized cheese and, 154
Little Coyote Runs Away, 60–61
Little Downy, 54
Liu, I.K.M.
    wild horse contraception research, 218
Livestock. *See specific types of livestock*
Locke, John
    educational theories, 53
    value of cultivating kindness to animals in children, 27
Lofting, Hugh
    children's books, 56
Loranger, A.J.
    fencing and roadkill, 137
Los Angeles
    municipal spay-neuter clinic and differential
        licensing system, 15
Lotz, M.
    underpass use in Florida, 138
Luke, C.J.
    dog and cat adoption, euthanization, and
        returned-to-care-giver statistics, 20

M

Macdonald, D.W.
    estimates of deer killed by shooting, 125
    estimates of fox culls, 124, 125
    farmers' judgments about the humaneness of different
        methods of killing foxes, 123
    patterns in habitat management, 125
    urban and rural residents' differences in opinion
        regarding hunting, 121
    Wiltshire farmers' attitudes toward hunting, 121–122
MacDonald, George
    children's books, 56
Mad cow disease. *See* Bovine spongiform encephalopathy
Maddie's Fund
    goals of, 67
    shelter collaboration, 23
Mader, H.J.
    barrier effect of roads, 134–135
    roads and habitat fragmentation, 134

Magee, W.H.
    animal stories and humane education, 56
Malaysia
    slaughterhouse infrastructure, 184
Malcarne, V.
    role-playing and empathy-building techniques, 38
Manfredo, M.J.
    attitudes of Colorado residents toward
        hunting, 113–114
Manifest tensions in the no-kill controversy
    behavior problem misrepresentation, 71
    classification of animals and, 71
    criticism of open admissionists, 70
    dishonesty, 70–72
    misrepresentation of euthanasia, 72
    "no-kill" concept, 71–72
    provocative language and, 69, 78, 79
    sharing the burden of euthanasia and, 69, 71
    view of euthanasia as "dirty work," 68–70
    view of no-kill shelters as "picky," 72
    view of open admissionists as "baddies," 69, 76
Manila Conference on Animal Welfare, 184
Manila Declaration on Animal Welfare, 184
Mann, Horace
    universal schooling concept, 28
Manning, A.M.
    state pet population estimates, 10
Marcus, L.S.
    anthropomorphism and fantasy, 58
    effects of pictures in children's literature, 59, 61
Marion, Jolene
    animal law course, 104
Martin, M.T.
    horse transport study, 208
Mary Poppins, 57
Masri, B.A.
    theological work, 87, 96
Massachusetts
    acquisition sources of dogs and cats in, 13
    closed season for deer hunting, 108–109
    compulsory humane education movement, 29
    effectiveness of underpasses to assist spotted
        salamanders, 138
    road-effect zone study, 135
    stray and surrendered dog and cat populations
        in shelters, 20
    telephone surveys, 10
Massachusetts Society for the Prevention of Cruelty
    to Animals
    Black Beauty and support for, 55
    establishment of, 1
    international activities, 4
    investigation to measure the impact of its statewide
        humane education project, 39–40
    telephone survey, 10
Master of Foxhounds Association
    fox cull data, 125

foxhunting rules, 120
Mather, M.E.
    attitudes of professional associations of wildlife
        biologists and wildlife managers toward hunting,
        114–115
McCloskey, Robert
    children's books, 54, 58
McCully, Emily Arnold
    children's books, 58
McDaniel, Jay
    environmental themes, 96
    pluralism and, 92
McDonald's Corporation
    battery cages and, 171, 172
    suit against, 100
McFague, Sallie
    pluralism and, 92
McGee, K.
    percentage of Standardbred horses at auctions
        and slaughter plants, 210
    Thoroughbred horses who end up being
        slaughtered, 209
    welfare of horses arriving at slaughter plants, 208
McGreevey, P.D.
    stereotypic behavior of box-stalled horses, 210–211
Meat production in developing countries
    animal suffering and, 175, 183–184
    animals slaughtered worldwide, 1961–2001, 176
    animals slaughtered worldwide per region: 2001, 177
    Asia/Pacific countries, 182–186
    availability of shelf-stable meat products, 182
    bleeding out after stunning, 181
    dressing the carcass and, 180
    evolution of meat production, 176
    gantry hoists and, 180
    hygienic conditions and, 180, 182
    Jhatka ritual slaughtering method, 185
    kosher slaughter method, 179–180, 288
    Latin America, 176–177
    livestock revolution, 177–179
    Muslim halal slaughter methods, 179–180, 183, 184,
        185, 188
    physiological effects of stunning, 181
    projected trends in production of various livestock
        products, 1993–2020, 179
    rural slaughter, 180
    slaughter slabs and, 180
    slaughtering process, 175, 179–182
    South Africa, 186–190
    spread of disease and, 175, 180
    stunning methods, 179, 180, 181, 184, 185, 188, 190
    transportation of animals, 179, 182, 184, 185, 190
    urban slaughter, 180, 182
    world livestock population, 1961–2001, 176

Melson, G.F.
  animal characters in children's literature, 58
  biocentricity of human development, 53
  reading levels and available resources, 62
  Society of Friends and animal and nature contact, 55
Mental Evolution in Animals, 86
Mighetto, L.
  Darwin's theory of natural selection as a catalyst
    for the concern of humanitarians for animal
    welfare, 109
  interpersonal differences among hunters, 115
Migratory Bird Hunting Stamp Act
  hunting regulations, 109
Migratory Bird Treaty Act
  hunting regulations, 109
Miller-Rada "commitment to pets" scale, 11
Minnesota
  gray wolf/vehicle collisions, 136
Moltmann, J.
  Gifford Lectures on religion, 94
Montminy-Danna, M.
  Potter League for Animals humane education
    program evaluation, 40–41, 42
  transference theory and humane education, 38
Morella, Rep. Connie
  bill to ban the slaughter of horses for meat, 209
Morocco
  animal protection activities, 2
Mosier, J.E.
  acquisition sources of dogs and cats in Las Vegas, 13
Moss, Cynthia
  studies of elephants, 92
MSPCA. *See* Massachusetts Society for the Prevention
  of Cruelty to Animals
Muir, John
  urbanization and the appreciation of nature, 112
Murphy, Eddie
film version of *Doctor Doolittle* and, 56
Muth, R.M.
  attitudes of professional associations of wildlife
    biologists and wildlife managers toward hunting,
    114–115

N

NAHEE. *See* National Association for Humane and
  Environmental Education
Nassar-Montoya, F.
  detection of a large volume of illegal trade
    in wild animals, 194
  survey of attitudes toward animals in Latin
    America, 193
Nasser, R.
  acquisition sources of dogs and cats in Las Vegas, 13
National Association for Humane and Environmental
  Education
  Character Education Partnership, 41

foundation of, 32
Humane Education Evaluation Project, 38–39, 40
KIND Children's Book Award, 58
KIND News newspaper, 34
*People and Animals: A Humane Education Curriculum
  Guide*, 38–39
National Canine Defense League
  conferences in Eastern Europe, 4
National Council on Pet Population Study and Policy
  age, breed, and sterilization status study, 20
  mission, 19
  Regional Shelter Survey of reasons for relinquishment
    of animals to shelters, 21–22
  shelter relinquishment study, 19–20
  shelter role in euthanization, 20–21
  shelter surveys, 19
  Web site, 23
National Education Association
  endorsement of humane education, 30
National Park Service
  wild horse management example, 220
Nature Conservancy
  land preservation activities, 8
"Nature study," 32–33
NCPPSP. *See* National Council on Pet Population
  Study and Policy
NEA. *See* National Education Association
Neotropics. *See also specific countries in Latin
  America and South America*
  attitudes toward animals, 196–197
  description of the geographic region, 193
  historical background, 193, 196–197
  public awareness campaigns about wild animals
    kept as pets, 202
  rescue centers for wild animals, 202
  supply of wild animals for export, 194
Nepal
  buffalo production and, 183, 184
  slaughterhouse infrastructure, 184
Netherlands
  animal law courses, 104
  attitudes about animal welfare, 160
  badger tunnels under roads, 141
  classical swine fever outbreak, 154
  deep litter eggs, 163
  foot and mouth disease outbreak, 155
  incidence of pets in the home, 194
  number of hedgehogs killed on roads, 140
  tiered floor systems for housing laying
    hens, 162, 165
Nevada
  acquisition sources of dogs and cats in Las Vegas, 13
  grazing allotments for livestock, 219
  malicious killing of unbranded livestock law, 217
New England Anti-Vivisection Society
  publication of C.S. Lewis's anti-vivisection essay, 89

New Jersey
    trends in shelter intakes and euthanasia, *18–20*
New York
    compulsory humane education movement, 29, 30
    Normal School at Oswego's humane education, 28
New York City
    ASPCA animal intake, *15*
    measurement of the effectiveness of humane
        education, 30
New York Times
    ASPCA and the no-kill controversy article, 74
New Zealand
    agricultural export policies, 156
    banning of all live animal shipments, 183
    battery cages and, 171
    biosecurity, 156
    foot and mouth disease and, 155
    legal protection for great apes, 102
Newbery, John
    children's literature and, 53
Newdick, M.T.
    urban and rural residents' differences
        in opinion regarding hunting, 121
Nicaragua
    approval of keeping wild animals as pets, 197
    belief that keeping a wild animal fosters love and
        respect for nature in children, 195
    incidence of pets in the home, 194–195
    incidence of wild animals kept as pets, 195
    proportion of households keeping horses, 195
Nicol, C.J.
    stereotypic behavior of box-stalled horses, 210–211
Nissen
    study of the great apes, 86
No-kill controversy
    adoptability of animals and, 71–72, 74–77
    ambiguity of terms, 82
    common ground for, 79–82
    core professional identity of shelter workers, 67
    identification with those in the opposing camp, 80–81
    internal dissent within the two camps, 79
    latent tensions, 68, 72–79
    manifest tensions, 68–72, 79
    maturation of the issue, 81–82
    notion of welfare, 82
    organizational changes and, 81–82
    provocative language and, 69, 78, 79, 81–82
    research methods, 67–68
    shared values of the two camps, 79–80
North American Migratory Bird Treaty
    duck hunting and, 116
North Shore Animal League
    conferences in Eastern Europe, 4
Norway
    legislation limiting farm size, 160

Nussbaum, Martha
    animal law articles, 104

O

Odds Ratio for relinquishment of animals to shelters, 21
O'Hare, T.
    Potter League for Animals humane education program
        evaluation, 40–41, 42
    transference theory and humane education, 38
Oklahoma
    compulsory humane education movement, 29, 30
Oldfield, T.E.E.
    patterns in habitat management, 125
Olin, Jaime
    animal shelter survey, 33–37
On the Origin of Species, 86
Open-admissions animal shelters. See No-kill controversy
Operation Outreach USA, 56
Organ, J.F.
    attitudes of professional associations of wildlife
        biologists and wildlife managers toward hunting,
        114–115
    changes in student interest and attitudes and
        curriculum and course content in university
        fisheries and wildlife programs, 114
Original Stories, 54
Ostriches
    electrical stunning of, 190
    feather harvesting methods, 189–190
    slaughter methods, 190
    world demand for, 189
Our Dumb Animals
    Bands of Mercy and, 30
    circulation figures, 31
Our Goldmine at Hollyhurst, 29
Oxley, D.J.
    roads and habitat fragmentation, 134

P

Pace University School of Law
    animal law course, 104
Paine, Albert Bigelow
    children's books, 57
Pakistan
    buffalo and, 183
    Muslim halal slaughter method, 184
Pan-European Biological and Landscape Diversity
    Strategy
    roadkill reduction and, 142–143
Panama
    incidence of wild animals kept as pets, 195
Pannenberg, Wolfhart
    theology and nature, 94
Parables. *See* Folktales, parables, and fables
Parliament of the World's Religion
    inclusive features of the document, 94

Parrots
  average year of survival as pets, 195
  extraction rate from the wild in Costa Rica, 195
  number kept as illegal pets, 195
Passenger pigeons
  extinction of, 132
Patronek, G.J.
  household panel survey approach, 10
  Indiana pet population estimates, 10
  relinquishment risk factors, 21
  trends in New Jersey shelter intakes and
    euthanasia, *18–20*
Paul, E.S.
  transference theory and humane education, 38
Payne, Katy
  studies of elephants and whales, 92
Payne, Roger
  studies of whales, 92
PEBLD. *See* Pan-European Biological and Landscape
  Diversity Strategy
Pecos Bill, 61
Pedlar, J.H.
  effect of road mortality on the density of anuran
    populations, 136
Penland, S.T.
  reflectors and roadkill, 139
Pennington, T.H.
  salmonella in eggs, 150
Pennington Group
  Escherischia coli 0157 and, 153, 157
Pennsylvania
  compulsory humane education movement, 29
  euthanasia at animal shelters, 20
*People and Animals: A Humane Education
  Curriculum Guide*
  assessment of changes in children's attitudes, 40
  Attitude Transfer Scale, 39
  components, 38–39
  follow-up study, 40
  Revised Aggression Scale, 39
People for the Ethical Treatment of Animals
  international activities, 4
  support for open-admissions shelters, 73
Performance horses
  "cribbing" behavior, 211, 212
  feeding fiber and avoiding high grain diets during
    early development, 211
  social contact and, 211–212
  stall-walking, 212
  stereotypic patterns of behavior, 211
  weaving behavior, 212
  wind-sucking behavior, 211
PETA. *See* People for the Ethical Treatment of Animals
Petfinder.com, 24
PetWhere software, 23
Peyton, R.B.
  criticisms of hunters, 118

Philippines
  animal welfare and, 184
  stunning equipment manufacture, 185
Phillips, Lord
  bovine spongiform encephalopathy, 151, 152, 154
Pigs
  China and production of, 183
  classical swine fever, 154
  electrical stunning for, 185
  foot and mouth disease, 154, 155
  South Africa and, 186–187
Pitt, W.C.
  deer/vehicle collisions, 136
Pittman-Robertson Federal Aid in Wildlife
  Restoration Act
  hunting regulations, 109
PMU. *See* Pregnant mare urine industry
Pojar, T.M.
  road sign effectiveness, 139
Poole, Joyce
  studies of whales, 92
Pope, S.E.
  effect of road mortality on the density of anuran
    populations, 136
Pope Pius IX
  views on nonhuman animals, 88
Population dynamics model for pets, 18–19
Porcine zona pellucida
  wild horse contraception and, 218
Poresky, R.H.
  transference theory and humane education, 38
Porter, Gene Stratton
  children's books, 29, 55–56
Potter, Beatrix
  animal stories, 53, 56, 57
Potter League for Animals
  humane education program, 40–41, 42
Poultry. *See also* Chickens; EU ban on battery cages;
  Salmonella in eggs
  South Africa and, 186
Pregnant mare urine industry
  equine estrogen uses for menopause symptoms
    and osteoporosis, 210
  fate of PMU foals, 211
  lack of exercise issue, 210
  public criticism of, 210
  stereotypic behavior and, 210–211
  water restriction and, 210
Preston, Stella H.
  New York Humane Education Committee and, 29, 30
Processed Animal Protein Order
  salmonella in eggs and, 150
Prosence, R.A.
  road sign effectiveness, 139
Purchasing Power Parity
  source for information, 4

Putnam, R.J.
    seasonal movements of deer, 140
Pyle, Robert Michael
    anthropomorphism in children's books, 58–59

R

Rabbit Hill, 57
Racing horses
    age-related problems, 209
    insurance scams, 210
    musculoskeletal injuries, 209
    retraining for other uses, 210
    sale of "off the track" horses for riding, 209
    training methods that reduce the load the
        horse carries, 209
    types of horses raced, 209
    unnatural breeding season and, 209–210
    welfare issues, 209
Radford, Mike
    anti-cruelty laws, 99
    term "anti-cruelty," 99
Radner, D. and M.
    differences between humans and other species, 91
Rahner, Karl
    pluralism and, 92
Ramos, L.A.
    current views of wildlife in El Salvador, 197
The Rational Brutes: or, Talking Animals, 54
Rattling the Cage: Toward Legal Rights for Animals, 101
Rawls, Wilson
    children's books, 59
Ray, J.J.
    transference theory and humane education, 38
Rede Nacional De Combate Ao Trafico De Animais
    Silvestres
        information about wildlife trade in Brazil, 194
Redwall series, 57
Reed, D.F.
    box culverts in Colorado, 138
    road sign effectiveness, 139
Reed, R.A.
    roads and habitat fragmentation, 134
Reeve, A.F.
    reflectors and roadkill, 139
Regan, Tom
    film on the use of nonhuman animals for
        experimentation, 86
Religion and animals
    Abrahamic traditions, 88, 90–91, 94, 95, 96
    academic study of religion and, 87–88, 93
    "animal law" courses in law schools, 93
    animal protection activities and, 1
    animal rights movement, 92, 95
    anthropocentrism, 88, 91, 93, 94
    behaviorism and, 86
    believers' ethical abilities, 88

Catholic Church and, 94–96
    "cognitive ethology," 95
    "Cognitive Revolution" and, 87
    companion animals and, 92–93
    competing tensions, 90–91
    continuing role for traditions, 96
    culturally significant stereotypes, 89
    end of the twentieth century, 93
    environmental concerns, 93, 96
    "evolutionary synthesis" and, 87
    fundamental questions for religions, 96
    genetic engineering of animals to model human
        diseases, 91, 93
    Hindu, Jain and Buddhist traditions, 90, 94, 95, 96
    human diseases and nonhuman animals, 85
    ignorance of nonhuman animals and, 87–88
    image of God and dominion, 91–92
    indigenous traditions and, 90–91, 94, 95, 96
    instrumentalist view, 88
    Lewis's anti-vivisection essay, 88–91
    life sciences and, 87, 92
    mid-century winds of change, 88–89
    moral status of nonhuman animals, 88
    negative and positive factors pushing change, 92
    negative views, 85
    new century and, 93–95
    1900–1950: the dismissal of nonhuman lives, 85–87
    pluralism, 92
    positive views, 85
    pre-1950 era, 88
    prevailing context and reality, 92–93
    prospects in the twenty-first century, 95–96
    realities of change, 92
    religion's role in the transmission of basic images
        and values regarding living beings, 85
    traditional and compassionate views, 89–90
    use of nonhuman animals for experimentation, 86, 91
    use of parables, 52
"Religion and Animals" conference, 93
Reuther, Rosemary Radford
    pluralism and, 92
Reynolds, J.
    estimates of deer killed by shooting, 125
    estimates of fox culls, 124
    farmers' judgments about the humaneness of different
        methods of killing foxes, 123
Rickaby, Joseph
    moral status of nonhuman animals, 88
Ricord de Mendoza, Z.
    current views of wildlife in El Salvador, 197
Ring, Mike
    EU shell egg market, 171
Roadkill reduction
    barrier effect of roads, 134–135, 136, 141
    changes in wildlife populations, 132–133
    characteristics of highway mortality, 140
    chemical alteration of roadside habitats and, 133

deer/vehicle collisions, 136, 139
deterrent odors and, 141
direct wildlife mortality, 135–136
ecological impact of highways, 133–136
ecopipes and, 138
education focused on drivers and, 144
effectiveness of techniques, 136–139
effects of noise on avian reproduction, 134
environmental degradation and, 133
factors in, 133
"fall shuffle" and, 140
fencing and, 136–137, 141
flow of water throughout a watershed and, 135
future directions, 143–144
growth patterns that render residents dependent
    on cars and, 132
habitat fragmentation, 134–135, 141
highway speeds and, 139
infrared sensors and, 141
local extinctions and, 135
national highway system in the United States,
    131–132
negative effects of road illumination, 134
pan-European developments, 142–143
public safety and, 136
reconnecting habitats and, 136
reflectors and, 139, 141
research questions to be answered, 144
road closures and, 139
road-effect zone, 135
road signs and, 139
"roadkill" definitions, 131
roadside wildlife habitats, 133–134
state wildlife agencies and, 133
suburban housing and, 132
underpasses and overpasses and, 137–139, 141–142
wildlife behavior and exploitation, 134
wildlife pipes, 138
wildlife traps and, 142
Roberts, Charles G.D.
    naturalistic romances, 57
Robinson, J.T.
    amphibian and reptile vulnerability to roadkill, 136
Rohlfing, A.H.
    problems associated with hunting and hunters, 114
Rollin, Bernard
    society's changing view of animals, 96
Romanes, George
    animal studies, 86
Romin, L.A.
    estimates of deer killed along roads, 136
Roosevelt, Theodore
    hunting comments, 112
    identification of three groups of people concerned
        with wildlife conservation, 115
Rowan, A.N.
    euthanasia estimates, 16

household panel survey approach, 10
number of animals handled in shelters, 16
social attitudes in the United States toward the use of
    animals in research, the wearing of fur, hunting,
    farm animal issues, diet choice and public support
    of animal protection philosophy, 200–201
state pet population estimates, 10
Rowley, Francis
    Bands of Mercy and, 30–31
    humane education editorial, 31
    promise of immediate results from humane education
        and advocate involvement, 36
Royal Society for the Prevention of Cruelty to Animals
    comments on enriched cages, 168
    Freedom Foods standards, 168, 172
    International Department, 3
    programs and activities, 3
    role model for animal protection societies, 1, 3
RSPCA. See Royal Society for the Prevention of Cruelty
    to Animals
Ruediger, B.
    decline of salmon and steelhead trout due to stream
        crossings on highways, 135
    effectiveness of underpasses, 138
Rushton, S.P.
    estimates of deer killed by shooting, 125
    estimates of fox culls, 124
    farmers' judgments about the humaneness of different
        methods of killing foxes, 123
Ryan, Donna
    Black Beauty illustrations, 56
Ryden, Hope
    children's books, 60

S

Sahn, Jennifer
    morality and literature, 51
Sainsbury, D.W.B.
    lack of effective government policy to reduce
        salmonellosis, 150
Sale, Roger
    anthropomorphized animals in stories, 52, 58
Salmonella in eggs
    cleaning facilities between flocks and, 149–150
    mortality in poultry, 150
    susceptibility of chickens and other poultry
        to disease, 149
San Francisco SPCA
    humane identity and, 72–73
Sanborn, W. A.
    deer/vehicle collisions, 136
Sansolini, Adolfo
    hunger strike, 167
Saudi Arabia
    animal protection activities, 1
Saunders, Margaret Marshall, 29, 55–56

Savesky, K.
    obstacles to classroom access, 43
Scandinavia. *See also specific countries*
attitudes about animal welfare, 160
Schafer, J.A.
    reflectors and roadkill, 139
Schmidt, R.H.
    Utah residents' opposition to bear and cougar
        hunting, 114, 118
Schneider, R.
    California dog and cat population surveys, 15
School programs. See Humane education
SEA. *See* Strategic Environomental Assessment Directive
Seals
    International Fund for Animal Welfare and, 3
Sendak, Maurice
    children's books, 57, 59, 61
Seton, Ernest Thompson
    anthropomorphic portrayal of animals, 115
    naturalistic romances, 57
Sewell, Anna, 29, 31, 55, 56, 207
    Black Beauty and, 53
Sharma, Arvind
    pluralism and, 92
Shaw, Lemuel
    common law definition, 103
Sheep
    Escherischia coli 0157 and, 153
    foot and mouth disease and, 154–155, 156
    scrapie and, 150–151
    slaughtering methods, 185
    South Africa and, 187
Sheldon, Edward A.
    humane education and, 28
Sheperd, Paul
    animal stories and humane education, 53
Shirley, M.
    estimates of deer killed by shooting, 125
    estimates of fox culls, 124
    farmers' judgments about the humaneness of different
        methods of killing foxes, 123
Shoebag Returns, 59
Shultz, William
    Bands of Mercy and, 30
Sivaraksa, Sulak
    pluralism and, 92
    environmental themes, 96
Slaughter Methods for Livestock, 183
Smart, Ninian
    pluralism and, 92
Smith, Huston
    pluralism and, 92
Smith, Jonathan
    pluralism and, 92
Smith, R. J.
    patterns in habitat management, 125
Smith, Wilfred Cantwell

    pluralism and, 92
Society for the Protection of Animals in North Africa
    animal protection example, 4
Society of Friends
    therapeutic environment using animal and nature
        contact, 55
Software
    for animal shelters, 23
Song of the Wild, 59
Sörensen, Mary Ann
    importance of freshness in shell eggs, 171
South Africa
    Animals Protection Act, 187, 188
    codes of practice, 187
    commercially utilized species/products, *187*
    exportation of animals, 190
    farming systems, 186
    free-range products, 186
    grading system for meat, 188
    kosher slaughter, 188
    legislation incorporating animal welfare, *187*
    Livestock Brands Acts, 186, 188
    livestock population in South Africa, 1961–2001, *186*
    Livestock Welfare Coordinating Committee, 190
    Muslim halal slaughter method, 188
    number of animals slaughtered in South Africa, 2001,
        186
    ostrich slaughter, 189–190
    pre-stunning of animals, 188, 189
    slaughter methods used by different cultural groups
        and others in South Africa, *188*
    slaughter of game, 190
    slaughter requirements, 187–188
    SPCA movement, 186
    species utilized for slaughter, 186–188
    stunning methods in abattoirs in South
        Africa, *189*
    traditional slaughter of farm animals, 188–189
SPANA. *See* Society for the Protection of Animals
    in North Africa
Sperling, D.
    highway speeds and roadkill, 139
    road densities and populations of carnivores, 134
St. Francis of Assisi
    compassionate views on nonhuman animals, 88, 94
"Standing" doctrine
    constitutional requirements, 100
    prudential requirements, 100–101
Stellaluna, 59
Stevenson, Peter
    comments on enriched cages, 168
Stewart, Potter
    comments on pornography, 103
Stillman, William
    Bands of Mercy and, 30
    New York Humane Education Committee and, 29, 30

Stine, R.L.
  children's books, 57
Stookey, J.M.
  stereotypic behavior of PMU horses, 210–211
Stowe, Harriet Beecher
  children's books, 54–55
Strategic Environmental Assessment Directive
  roadkill reduction and, 143
Strauss, Susan
  morality and literature, 51
  narrative reasoning, 51–52
  stories and gaining the perspective of other
    animals, 52, 59
  storytelling workshops, 62
Strete, Craig Kee
  children's books, 60–61
Strieter-Lite reflectors
  roadkill reduction and, 139
The Strike at Shane's, 29, 55–56
Summer of the Monkeys, 59
Sunstein, Cass
  animal law articles, 104
Swanson, F.J.
  highway speeds and roadkill, 139
  road densities and populations of carnivores, 134
Swareflex reflectors
  roadkill reduction and, 139
Sweden
  Animal Welfare Act, 164
  ban on hunting with dogs, 108
  battery cages and, 164–165, 166–167, 169
  import restrictions, 165
Switzerland
  amphibian passages under roads, 141–142
  battery cages and, 165
  fencing of highways, 140
  infrared sensors to reduce roadkill, 141
  negative effects of fragmentation on lynx, 141
  number of roe deer killed on roads, 140
  study to identify wildlife corridors along roads, 143

T

Tattersall, F.H.
  estimates of deer killed by shooting, 125
  estimates of fox culls, 124
  farmers' judgments about the humaneness of different
    methods of killing foxes, 123
Taub, Edward
  conviction for failing to provide veterinary care
    to a monkey, 100
Tauson, Ragnar
  laying hen cage design, 162, 164
Taylor, P.D.
  effect of road mortality on the density of anuran
    populations, 136
Teel, T.L.

Utah residents' opposition to bear and cougar
    hunting, 114, 118
Tennessee Walker horses
  "soring" and, 212–213
Thailand
  slaughterhouse infrastructure, 184, 185
Thomas, Keith
  mental life of animals and, 86
Thompson, Caroline
  film version of *Black Beauty*, 56
Thomson, E.J.
  rural populations and hunting, 112
Timmins, Thomas
  Bands of Mercy and, 29
Tinykin's Transformations, 56
*Toward a Theology of Nature: Essays on Science
    and Faith*, 94
Tracy, David
  pluralism and, 92
Traill, Catharine Parr
  children's books, 53, 54
Transportation Equity Act
  wildlife needs and, 144
Travers, P.L.
  children's books, 57
Treaty of Amsterdam
  rights of nonhuman animals, 103
Trimmer, Sarah
  children's books, 53, 54
Trombulak, S.C.
  chemicals commonly found along roadsides, 133
Tucker, Mary Evelyn
  international conference organization, 87
  pluralism and, 92
Turner, J.W.
  wild horse contraception research, 218
Turrentine, T.
  highway speeds and roadkill, 139
  road densities and populations of carnivores, 134

U

The Ugly Duckling, 56
UKASTA. *See* United Kingdom Agricultural Supply
  Trade Association
Uncle Tom's Cabin, 54–55
United Kingdom. *See also* Farm disease crises in the
  United Kingdom; Hunting in the United Kingdom
  Agriculture (Miscellaneous Provisions) Act, 164
  alternatives to battery cages, 162
  animal law courses, 104
  attitudes about animal welfare, 160
  battery cages and, 161–162, 164, 169
  Brambell Committee, 161, 162
  Codes of Recommendation for the Welfare
    of Livestock, 164
  EU Council of Ministers and, 159, 166

Farm Animal Welfare Council, 161–162
Get-away cages, 162
legal protection for great apes, 101–102
"McLibel" case, 100
non-cage systems for housing laying hens, 162
number of birds killed on roads, 140
percentage of eggs coming from non-cage
   systems, 163
Select Committee on Agriculture, 164
Welfare Code amendment, 166
United Kingdom Agricultural Supply Trade Association
   bovine spongiform encephalopathy and, 151
United States. *See also* Companion animals in the
   United States; Hunting in the United States; *specific
   states and cities*
agricultural export policies, 156
anti-cruelty laws, 99–100
ban on dog and cat fur trade, 170
ban on importation of ruminants and ruminant
   by-products from countries with bovine spongiform
   encephalopathy, 151
battery cages and, 171–172
biosecurity, 156–157
common law changes to benefit nonhuman
   animals, 103
foot and mouth disease and, 155
green iguanas imported to, 194
incidence of pets in the home, 194
Kellert's comparison of attitudes toward wildlife
   in, 196
means and standard deviations of level of biological
   knowledge based on five statements, *201*
number of cases of *Escherischia coli* 0157, 153
number of horses in, 207
parrots kept as pets, 195
percent of households with animals, *11*
percentage who participate in hunting, 197
pet population estimates, *10*
proportion of households keeping horses, 195
proportion of households keeping livestock, 195
salmonellosis mortality, 150
social attitudes toward the use of animals in research,
   the wearing of fur, hunting, farm animal issues,
   diet choice and public support of animal protection
   philosophy, 200–201
"standing" doctrine, 100–101
state bar association animal law sections, 104
Universities. *See* Higher education
University of California-Los Angeles
   animal law courses, 104
U.S. Census Bureau
   inclusion of pet data questions, 9–10

U.S. Department of Agriculture
   Animal Legal Defense Fund legal cases and, 101
   number of nonhuman animals killed for food, 100
   risk of bovine spongiform encephalopathy
      estimate, 151
U.S. Food and Drug Administration
   ban on the use of mammalian carcasses in the
      production of feed for ruminants, 151
U.S. Sportsmen's Alliance
   criticisms of hunters, 119
Utah
   residents' opposition to bear and cougar hunting, 114

V

Vaida, M.L.
   California dog and cat population surveys, 15
Valentine's Gift, 53, 62
Van de, Ree reflectors
   roadkill reduction and, 139
Vaughn, M.E.
   van de Ree roadside mirrors and roadkill, 139
Venezuela
   extraction rate of parrots from the wild, 195
   incidence of parrots in households, 195
Verdi, 59
Vermont Law School
   animal law course, 104
Vietnam
   slaughterhouse infrastructure, 184
"Virtual shelters," 24
Vitz, Paul
   morality and literature, 51

W

Wallace, A.R.
   studies of orangutans, 86
Walsh, John C.
   rescue operations, 3
Waltho, N.
   wildlife use of underpasses, 138
Ward, Keith
   pluralism and, 92
Waring, G.H.
   van de Ree roadside mirrors and roadkill, 139
Washington State
   reflectors and roadkill, 139
The Water-Babies, A Fairy Tale for a Land-Baby, 56
Waterfowl hunting
   Migratory Bird Treaty Act and, 109
Watership Down, 57
Watson, John
   essay on the mental life of animals, 86
WBTA. *See* Migratory Bird Treaty Act
We Are All Noah, 86
Weber, C.V.
   People and Animals follow-up study, 40

Wegner, J.F.
  effect of road mortality on the density of anuran
    populations, 136
WEGU reflectors
  roadkill reduction and, 139
Wenstrup, J.
  shelter budgets, 16
Western Institute for Research and Evaluation
  Humane Education Evaluation Project and, 39
WFPA. *See* World Federation for the Protection
  of Animals
Whales
  animal advocacy and, 7
White, E.B.
  children's books, 57
White, L., Jr.
  Christian doctrine of creation, 91
  refocusing of Christianity, 94
White, T.H.
  children's books, 56
Wild Animals I Have Known, 115
Wild animals in Costa Rica
  absence of legal exports of wild animals for the
    international pet market, 199
  adults' acceptance of hunting, *198*
  attitude towards animals, 196, 197
  ban of the use of animals in circuses, 196, 202
  belief that keeping a wild animal fosters love and
    respect for nature in children, 195, 201
  biophilia and, 200
  Costa Rican adults who have a negative perception
    of bats for various attributes, by gender, *199*
  Costa Rican adults who perceive bats as dangerous,
    vermin, dirty, and with supernatural powers,
    by level of education, *200*
  education level effect on attitudes toward
    hunting, 199
  extraction rate of parrots from the wild, 195
  hunting, 197–199
  incidence of pets in the home, 194
  incidence of wild animals kept as pets, 195
  knowledge of natural history and care of, 201
  legal measures to safeguard the well being
    of animals, 196
  linking attitudes and knowledge to practice, 200–202
  living with bats, 199–200
  motives for the acquisition of wild animals as pets, 200
  parrots kept as illegal pets, 195
  pets classified as endangered or vulnerable, 195
  presence of minors in the household and pet
    animals, 195
  proportion of households keeping horses, 195
  proportion of households keeping livestock, 195
  public opinion on hunting for entertainment, *198*
  public opinion on keeping wildlife at home, *197*
  reasons for concern, 194–195
  recreational hunting and, 197

  socioeconomic factors and, 200
  survey of attitudes toward animals, 193–194
  values education, 200–201
  welfare of wild animals in people's households, 195
Wild Free-Roaming Horse and Burro Act, 217
"Wild Horse Annie" Act, 217
Wild horses and burros in the United States
  Adopt-a-Horse and Adopt-a-Burro programs, 219–220
  breeding standards for, 218
  contraception issues, 218, 220
  definition of a wild horse, 217–218
  growth of the awareness of the plight of, 217
  herd management areas, 218–219
  "mustangers" and, 217
  non-intervention philosophy, 218
  overgrazing of public lands and, 219
  ranchers' view of, 218
  survival issues on public land, 218–219
  wild horse advocates view of, 218
The Wild Pups: The True Story of a Coyote Family, 60
WildAid
  education programs, 8
Wildlife. See also Wild animals in Costa Rica; *specific
    animals*
  animals involved in wildlife trade, 194
  in back yards, 93
  end consumers of illegal trade and needs of, 194
  humane education and, 34
  international protection programs, 8
  number of animals lost in the illegal trade
    process, 194
Wildlife Conservation Society
  veterinary programs, 8
Wilkes, Steve
  legal protection for great apes, 102
Willard, Frances
  Women's Christian Temperance Union leadership, 29
Williams, L.W.
  acquisition sources of dogs and cats in Las Vegas, 13
Williams, T.
  criticisms of hunters, 118, 119
Winter, T.C.
  highway speeds and roadkill, 139
  road densities and populations of carnivores, 134
Wisconsin
  road-based methods of hunting bobcat, 134
Witter, D.J.
  attitudes of professional associations of wildlife
    biologists and wildlife managers toward hunting,
    114–115
"The Wolf in Sheep's Clothing," 52
Wolfson, David
  food animals and anti-cruelty laws, 100
Wollstonecraft, Mary
  children's books, 53, 54
Women's Christian Temperance Union
  Department of Mercy, 29

The Wonderful Adventures of Nils, 59
Wood Magic, 56
Woodward, T.N.
  road sign effectiveness, 139
World Conservation Union
  pets classified as endangered or vulnerable
    kept in households, 195
World Council of Churches
  pluralism and, 92
World Federation for the Protection of Animals
  programs and activities, 3
World Health Organization
  community and stray dog control, 7
World Poultry Science Association
  symposia on poultry welfare, 162
World Society for the Protection of Animals
  "Libearty" bear protection initiative, 8
  programs and activities, 3
World Trade Organization
  battery cages and, 169–170
  extending the rules for free trade to agricultural
    products, 169–170
  pressure to adopt more animal-friendly policies, 6
Wright, Phyllis
  Legislation, Education, and Sterilization population
    reduction policy and, 14
WSPA. *See* World Society for the Protection of Animals
WTO. *See* World Trade Organization
Wyoming
  reflectors and roadkill, 139

Y

Yerkes, R.M.
  study of the great apes, 86–87

Z

Zinn, H.C.
  attitudes of Colorado residents toward hunting, 113
Zoonoses Order
  salmonella in eggs and, 150

The first volume in the *State of the Animals* series is available for $29.50 (plus $3.00 shipping and handling) from Humane Society Press, 2100 L Street, N.W., Washington, D.C. 20037.

The State of the Animals: 2001
edited by Deborah J. Salem and Andrew N. Rowan

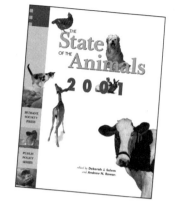

Overview
Paul G. Irwin

A Social History of Postwar Animal Protection
Bernard Unti and Andrew N. Rowan

Cruelty to Animals: Changing Psychological, Social and Legislative Perspectives
Frank R. Ascione and Randall Lockwood

Social Attitudes and Animals
Harold Herzog, Andrew N. Rowan, and Daniel Kossow

From Pets to Companion Animals
Researched by Martha C. Armstrong, Susan Tomasello, and Christyna Hunter

Farm Animals and Their Welfare in 2000
David Fraser, Joy Mench, and Suzanne Millman

Progress in Livestock Handling and Slaughter Techniques in the United States, 1970–2000
Temple Grandin

Animal Research: A Review of Developments, 1950–2000
Andrew N. Rowan and Franklin M. Loew

The First Forty Years of the Alternatives Approach: Refining, Reducing and Replacing the Use of Laboratory Animals
Martin L. Stephens, Alan M. Goldberg, and Andrew N. Rowan

Is There a Place in the World for Zoos?
David Hancocks

Another View of Zoos
Richard Farinato

Animal Protection in a World Dominated by the World Trade Organization
Leesteffy Jenkins and Bob Stumberg

Urban Wildlife
John Hadidian and Sydney Smith

Fertility Control in Animals
Jay F. Kirkpatrick and Allen T. Rutberg